Retail Marketing in the Modern Age

Retail Marketing in the Modern Age

Prashant Chaudhary

Assistant Professor, Sinhgad Institute of Management &
Computer Application (SIMCA), Pune

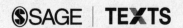

Los Angeles | London | New Delhi
Singapore | Washington DC | Melbourne

First published in 2016 by

⑤SAGE | TE✕TS

SAGE Publications India Pvt Ltd
B1/I-1 Mohan Cooperative Industrial Area
Mathura Road, New Delhi 110 044, India
www.sagepub.in

SAGE Publications Inc
2455 Teller Road
Thousand Oaks, California 91320, USA

SAGE Publications Ltd
1 Oliver's Yard, 55 City Road
London EC1Y 1SP, United Kingdom

SAGE Publications Asia-Pacific Pte Ltd
3 Church Street
#10-04 Samsung Hub
Singapore 049483

Published by Vivek Mehra for SAGE Publications India Pvt Ltd, typeset in Stone Serif 9.5/11.5 pts by Diligent Typesetter India Pvt Ltd, Delhi and printed at Saurabh Printers Pvt Ltd, Greater Noida.

Library of Congress Cataloging-in-Publication Data

Name: Chaudhary, Prashant Vilas, author.
Title: Retail marketing in the modern age / Prashant Vilas Chaudhary.
Description: Thousand Oaks, Calif. : SAGE, 2016. | Includes bibliographical
   references and index.
Identifiers: LCCN 2016014130 | ISBN 9789351508694 (pbk. : alk. paper)
Subjects: LCSH: Marketing. | Retail trade.
Classification: LCC HF5415 .C4838 2016 | DDC 658.8/7—dc23 LC record available at https://lccn.loc.gov/2016014130

ISBN: 978-93-515-0869-4 (PB)

The SAGE Team: Amit Kumar, Indrani Dutta, Sudeshna Nandy and Rajinder Kaur

To my greatest source of inspiration
My mother,
Nanda Chaudhary

To my partner in life,
Jyoti Chaudhary

To my loving sister,
Preeti Garibe

and

To my moral support
My brother,
Amit Chaudhary

Thank you for choosing a SAGE product!
If you have any comment, observation or feedback,
I would like to personally hear from you.
Please write to me at **contactceo@sagepub.in**

Vivek Mehra, Managing Director and CEO, SAGE India.

Bulk Sales

SAGE India offers special discounts
for bulk institutional purchases.

For queries/orders/inspection copy requests
write to **textbooksales@sagepub.in**

Publishing

Would you like to publish a textbook with SAGE?

Please send your proposal to **publishtextbook@sagepub.in**

Get to know more about SAGE

Be invited to SAGE events, get on our mailing list.

Write today to **marketing@sagepub.in**

Contents

List of Abbreviations

APEC	Asia-Pacific Economic Cooperation
ASEAN	Association of Southeast Asian Nations
ATES	Amazon Trained Ecommerce Specialist
ATL	above the line
AWS	Amazon web services
BATNA	Best Alternative to Negotiated Agreement
BIT	bilateral investment treaty
BTL	below the line
CAIT	Confederation of All India Traders
CECA	Comprehensive Economic Cooperation Agreement
CFO	chief financial officials
CII	Confederation of Indian Industry
COD	cash on delivery
CoS	committee of secretaries
CRM	customer relationship management
CSC	Common Service Center
CSR	corporate social responsibility
DGE&T	Directorate General of Employment & Training
DIPP	Department of Industrial Policy & Promotion
DIY	do it yourself
DOM	distribution order management
EBO	exclusive brand outlet
ED	Enforcement Directorate
EDLP	everyday low price
EOSS	end of season sale
ERP	enterprise resource planning
EU	European Union
FBA	fulfillment by Amazon
FDI	foreign direct investment
FIPB	Foreign Investment Promotion Board
FISME	Federation of Indian Micro, Small, and Medium Enterprise
FMCG	fast-moving consumer goods
FoB	freight on board
FTA	free trade agreement
FTP	foreign trade policy
GATT	General Agreement on Tariffs and Trade
GDP	gross domestic product
GMROI	gross margin return on investment
GMV	gross merchandise value
GST	goods and services tax
HNWI	high-net-worth individual
HR	human resources
HRM	human resource management
ICT	information and communication technology
IT	information technology
JIT	just in time

JV	joint venture
KPI	key performing indicator
MBO	multi-brand outlet
MBRT	multi-brand retail trading
MCCIA	Mahratta Chamber of Commerce Industries & Agriculture
MEIS	Merchandise Exports from India Scheme
MFN	most favored nation
MNC	multinational company
MoU	memorandum of understanding
MSME	micro, small, and medium enterprise
NAFTA	North American Free Trade Agreement
NBFC	new age nonbanking finance company
NCDPD	National Centre for Design & Product Development
NGO	nongovernmental organization
NRI	nonresident Indian
OFC	optical fiber cable
OTB	open to buy
OVAOI	Online Vendor Association of India
PMS	performance management system
POD	point of difference
PR	public relation
RAI	Retailers Association of India
RBI	Reserve Bank of India
RCEP	Regional Comprehensive Economic Partnership
RFID	radio frequency identification
ROI	return on investment
SBRT	single-brand retail trading
SBU	strategic business unit
SCA	sustainable competitive advantage
SCM	supply chain management
SEIS	Services Exports from India Scheme
SEO	search engine optimization
SKU	stock-keeping unit
SME	small and medium enterprise
SOA	selling on Amazon
SSS	same stores sales
TMR	target market relation
UPC	Universal Product Code
USITC	US International Trade Commission
VAT	value-added tax
VC	venture capitalist
VM	visual merchandising
VMS	vertical marketing system
WMS	warehouse management system
WOS	wholly owned subsidiary
WTO	World Trade Organization

Foreword

Sam Walton, the founder of Walmart, had famously declared, "There is only one boss—the customer. And he can fire everybody in the company from the chairman on down, simply by spending his money somewhere else." Amazon has a mission statement that begins with the goal of being "the earth's most customer-centric company." Similarly, Tony Hsieh, the CEO of Zappos, refers to their aim of being "maniacal about customer service" in a *Harvard Business Review* article. According to Michael Dell, the founder and CEO of Dell Inc., the three words that essentially distinguish the winners from the losers in today's business scenario are: "the customer experience"! A great customer experience is the outcome of a symphonic and harmonizing interplay of a number of factors. The three key dimensions of customer-centric growth in companies include (a) the creation of total customer experience across the touch points, rather than just providing functional products and services to customers, (b) a shared purpose and passion across the organization toward serving customers, and (c) a strong customer insights treasure within the organization developed by unleashing the power of big data. This book precisely captures these factors and vividly describes all of them with the help of various concepts, appropriate examples, and case studies from national and international players in the industry.

Here, the author presents a refreshingly new paradigm for the management students and professionals by explaining how the emerging markets offer a unique growth opportunity in the 21st century. Energized by demographics and geopolitics, the global economic axis is shifting inevitably eastward. From changing geopolitical equations to world economic forces, demographics and enabling technologies such as mobility, social media, cloud computing, and big data has created a fertile basis for innovation in these markets. I have been in the business of retailing for almost two decades and found it very true. Many standard business functions in retailing have been undergoing radical transformations, and the biggest one has been brought about by digital technology.

Today, ensuring your customers stay loyal to you is tough, more so in the digital world. Today's retailers, both brick-and-mortar and online are facing new challenges. Consumers are increasingly becoming time-poor and information-rich. Their aspirations are touching new heights and they demand better service and quality with lower prices and more value for their efforts and money. Digitization in retailing has become a win–win situation for customers and businesses. For customers, digitization and e-commerce has brought convenience, transparency, and better deals and price points. On the other hand, businesses have benefited from a huge expansion in market size, an easier reach to the customers, reduction in transaction costs, and improved efficiency in business. Digitization and mobile devices have delivered the power of technology in the hands of shoppers where they compare prices, place orders, and post reviews—anywhere and anytime. In effect, the power balance between retailers and buyers is shifting. Hence, one of the challenges brought about by the digital world to retailers has been to keep innovating- through its offerings and across its functions, operations, and customer touch-points. Through the comprehensive set of case studies and examples, the author demonstrates that creativity, design thinking, frugal innovation, and overall shopping experience is essential for value creation for businesses, especially brick-and-mortar retailers and the customers they serve.

From product to quality to price points to customer experience and service quality, every parameter that affects the buyer or buyer's decisions is easily measured and compared. Every touch point with the customer is duly scrutinized by the digital world. So, the most crucial element that differentiates companies is perceived brand image and the resultant strong customer loyalty. Customer loyalty comes as a result of consistent emotional experiences, perceived economic value and brand image, level of customer engagement with the brand, and functional aspects of the products and services. Here, engaging effectively with the customer plays a major role right from customer acquisition to customer retention. This book moves this further and faster forward.

Today, the next big thing on the agenda of the retailers is personalization that adds emotional experience. We have seen that, today, content, campaigns, marketing, promotions, customer service, and even loyalty programs are being personalized. Retailers are increasingly integrating social media not just to discover the entire universe of buyers, but for personalization as well. This book, by virtue of its contents, provides an essential blueprint for how retailers across the world are approaching this business imperative in the right manner. The practical roadmap and many contemporary concepts elaborated in this book catch the beat of the new customer-led world order where sensuality, empathy, synergy, omni-channel approach, velocity, deep customer engagement, and great shopping experience come as standard. Here, through this book, Professor Prashant Chaudhary has succeeded admirably in opening up a new chapter in the theory and practice of retailing and retail marketing in the modern age!

Shamsunder S. Kamat
Regional Controller
Shoppers Stop Ltd

Preface

I have been associated with the world of marketing (through my work experience in institutional project, business, research, and academics) for over a decade through my tenure with several multinational companies (MNCs) in different roles and capacities and also through my teaching experience in one of the leading business management institutes in Pune. Here in the backdrop of subject domain of this text, I would like to highlight my work experience with Lifestyle International, which provided me a platform to sharpen my skills and enhance the knowledge base regarding the intricacies of business of retailing.

The rationale behind writing this book is to highlight the facts and new realities that have emerged in the business world and also to present some fresh perspective toward the conceptual knowledge base, in the context of retail marketing management. Today, we can see that the half-life of knowledge is getting shorter and shorter with new breakthrough technologies, innovations, and evolving business models. In his book titled *Paradigm Shift*, the philosopher Thomas Kuhn opines that every discipline goes through a cycle where the existing perspective goes through a transformation and only after that will we be in a position to add value to the prevailing wisdom, that eventually makes it more relevant. This has happened historically with science, literature, philosophy, and the arts. A similar shift is happening in marketing management as well. Today, we are in that twilight zone, especially in the context of the business of retailing. In retail marketing management, most knowledge is contextual for the times, ecosystem, and circumstances. As times change, we need to discover, synthesize, and churn out new text and theories that are contemporary and which give full justice to the changed context, ecosystem, and the circumstances.

There have been three major transformations in contexts in recent times on which I have tried to highlight and focus on to the best of my knowledge, experience, and expertise. The first is the digital revolution, which has been very disruptive in the way retailers manage and organize the "marketing and branding" component of their business in the direction to enhance customer loyalty behavior. The e- and m-commerce world has now turned all that on its head, and brand loyalties in the retail space have taken a huge beating, giving retailers and marketers sleepless nights. Many thinkers believe that in this digital age, no sustainable emotional connect will be possible with any single brand. We cannot deny the fact that e-commerce is generally characterized by lack of brand loyalty, and all traditional notions of branding will get challenged in this space. So the pertinent question all business heads and brand managers in retailing space are now facing is: How should they contest this new buying phenomenon and what specifically are the actions that are needed in this new world of e-commerce?

The second factor is globalization and its implications on both the macro- and micro-level of environmental factors. Globalization has brought dynamism, especially in Indian business environment, during the first decade of this century. This prompted unprecedented transformations for most of the organizations, especially in the retail sector. In this scenario, an organization's competitiveness would depend not only on its ability to adapt to these changes with agility but also on being proactive in invigorating itself for the demand of the future.

The third is the tectonic shift in consumer expectations, buying behavior, and consumer psychology. Consumers today are increasingly living a mobile routine, progressively getting tech savvy, and proactively getting brand-conscious. They are deeply inclined toward associating with the brand that is an imprint of their personality. Keeping all these things at the back of the mind, mindful of the brick-and-mortar players have turned their strategies—principally communications, branding, and consumer engagement—to offer the finest shopping experience across the touch points. They are increasingly emphasizing on hiring and managing "right talent" who understand design sense, ethnography, technology, and relationship building to create a collaborative organization. They are also focusing on developing the domain-specific skills and enhancing the service culture. This eventually helps them to occupy the most prominent mind-space, which they can leverage to enhance customer patronage loyalty toward their brand and garner affinity.

All the three major transformations are playing a crucial role in catalyzing the evolution of new models and ecosystems in the retailing landscape. This has also forced many successful retailers and brands to undergo an elemental change in how they like to operate. They need to develop and deliver a "consistently branded experience" for their customers. The essence of the brand should be apparent in every interaction a customer has with the retailer, enabling customers to form an emotional attachment with the brand.

Here I have designed the flow of the concepts in such a way that the reader first understands the gravity of "need for change" through a detailed discussion on e-commerce and its overall impact on the business of retailing, which is followed by influence of globalization. Then the text drives the reader through several other new strategies and initiatives that the brick-and-mortar retailers are adapting, besides sufficient consideration for traditional ones, to face the new challenges and to grab new opportunities. The detailed coverage, with fresh perspectives—to positioning and brand management, visual merchandising (pervasive creativity), the pyramid of performance, private-label brands (PLBs), human resource management (HRM), customer relationship management (CRM) and social media strategy, among others—ensures the holistic approach of the book toward the subject. Meanwhile, the reader also gets exposure to the evolving models and emerging ecosystems of retailing that have created opportunity for the coexistence of the off-line and online retailing.

Here I have adopted the strategy of integrating the fundamental concepts of marketing (branding) with contemporary retail concepts and then complementing this blend with appropriate contemporary examples from international and Indian retail scenario. The content and flow of this book is an expression of the style that I have developed with the assistance and cooperation of many professionals in the field. I owe them a debt of gratitude. I would like to acknowledge my sincere thanks to many other individuals, including my students, who were the constant source of energy for me during the evolution of this manuscript.

Acknowledgments

I would like to express gratitude toward many individuals and institutions, all of who have made significant contributions to enhance the "content" of this book, because it is ultimately the measure of "quality" of any work of this kind. They provided a wealth of the contemporary knowledge/information and also the inputs/insights regarding the innovations and new developments that are happening in the world of retailing. Many of them were inspirations for illustrative examples, diagrams, and sources of photographs/images that were very crucial to make the text contemporary, up-to-date, and visually exciting and interesting.

I am very thankful to Shamsunder Kamat for his willingness to write the foreword for this book. A graduate from engineering stream, Kamat has done his masters in management studies from Mumbai University. He has an extensive experience in retail industry spanning over around two decades, with Shoppers Stop Ltd, which is one of the leading brands in the department store category. Kamat is currently working at the position of Regional Controller (West). It is extraordinary that despite his extremely busy schedule and the tight publication deadline imposed on him, he generously accepted the invitation to write the foreword and helped me to convey the "value proposition" of this book to the audience.

Meanwhile, it has been a matter of great delight to work with various members of SAGE's editorial and production teams. While I have been directly exposed to only a few of them, I express my sincere thanks to everyone who diligently worked on my dream project and extended their unflinching support to bring it to the reality. In addition, I want to acknowledge the reviewers of this text for their valuable suggestions and inputs. The "value" of these suggestions was not less than the "value" of guidelines typically given by a mentor.

I would like to extend my special thanks to Amit Kumar, Indrani Dutta, Sudeshna Nandy, and the entire SAGE team who worked determinedly and acted as a catalyst in accelerating the entire process that eventually resulted in timely and successful publication of this textbook project.

Finally, I would like to take special pride in expressing my deepest gratitude to all my beloved family members. I would like to take this opportunity to convey my sincere thanks to all of them for their unwavering support, dedication, commitment, encouragement, and sacrifices they extended to me. They have been a constant source of motivation for me, without which I could not have achieved this success and would not have succeeded in making my dream come true.

Prashant Chaudhary

About the Author

 **Prashant Chaudhary** is currently working with Sinhgad Institute of Management & Computer Application (SIMCA), Pune as Assistant Professor, imparting quality education in the field of business and management. Prior to this stint, he has worked with several MNCs at different positions and capacities. The companies are Vedanta Group's Sterlite Copper (I) Ltd, Kansai Nerolac Paints Ltd, Dubai-based Landmark Group's Lifestyle International Pvt. Ltd, and Häfele India Pvt. Ltd. He comes with a good experience in retail industry through his work experience with one of the leading department store chain, Lifestyle International. Lifestyle International is the retail wing of Dubai-based conglomerate, Landmark Group. With this, he brings a rich experience with the retail sector and has leveraged that experience for enhancement and enrichment of the content of this text, with a pragmatic approach.

As mentioned earlier, author has a good experience in academics as well, which he has leveraged to strengthen the "conceptual" component of the text and used the tried-and-class-tested pedagogy and teaching material to bring clarity to the subject matter. He has published several research papers in national and international journals based on various critical aspect of retail marketing. He also has registered for his PhD program at one of the leading universities of India and is pursuing his research work in the same subject domain. Prior to this book, he has also coauthored a book titled *Selling and Negotiation Skills*, which is one of the very successful texts in the subject area and one of the famous titles, specifically in Pune and Mumbai universities.

Prashant spends his "free" time visiting business leaders to understand the emerging trends and changing consumer behavior and identify challenging problems to solve. As far as hobbies are concerned, he loves traveling to exotic places and has passion for reading, writing, acting, theater, and watching movies.

About the Author

Chapter 1

Fundamentals of Retailing

Introduction

The word retailing has its origins in the French verb *retaillier*, which means to cut a piece or to break a bulk. This refers to one of the fundamental retailing activities: to buy in larger quantities and sell in smaller quantities. For example, a convenience store would buy dozens of boxes of soaps but would sell in single units. However, a retailer is not the only type of business entity to "break bulk." Wholesalers also buy in larger quantities and sell to their customers in smaller quantities. Hence, it is basically the type of customer that actually distinguishes a retailer from other distributive traders and not the activity. The distinction here is that a retailer sells to final consumers, unlike a wholesaler who sells to a retailer or other business organizations. Thus, the definition of a retailer is "any establishment that is engaged in selling merchandise for personal or household consumption and rendering services incidental to the sale of such goods."

The retailing business we see today is not the same as it was in the past. It has gone through the several stages of evolution in the way retailing is done. Retail business is still undergoing a rapid transformation in its marketing practices. Until a few years ago, we bought most items of daily use from small shops in our neighborhood (mom-and-pop store) or a market close by.

These shops such as *Kirana* stores or general stores or clothing and apparel shops are owned by individuals, who usually run the shop themselves and sell their goods with the help of a few assistants. Gradually, the department stores came into being due to the growing sophistication of this sector. This was the beginning of the organized sector. In the last few years, however, the concept of large departmental stores and shopping malls changed the face of retailing. Today, the traditional formats like grocers, hawkers, and other mom-and-pop stores coexist with modern formats like departmental stores, supermarkets, hypermarkets, shopping malls, and non-store retailing units such as teleshopping and multilevel marketing. On the other hand, with the advancement of information technology (IT) and communication, electronic retailing, which is also called as e-retailing or e-tailing, is a burgeoning phenomenon and has drastically changed the way the business of retailing is done. The growth of e-commerce has radically changed the way world does business in every conceivable aspect. Today, the consumers can buy the products online from their electronic devices such as computers and laptops from the virtual marketplace from anywhere and at any time. The products are displayed on the shopping portal of the e-retailer and payments can be made through online payment systems like e-banking or by payment in cash on delivery (COD) of the merchandise at the place where the delivery is required. In addition, there exist many businesses that carry out retailing activity and are not in themselves classified as retailers. For example, a factory may engage in retailing activity by selling its products in their own shop located in their manufacturing premises. The term "retailing" applies not only to the selling of tangible products, such as apparel, electronic goods, or pairs of shoes, but also to the selling of services. The consumption of the service offered coincides with the retailing activity itself. Companies that provide food items, traveling services and aromatherapy sessions are all essentially retailers, as they sell to the final consumer, and yet customers do not receive goods from these retailers in a shopping bag.

Thus, this chapter will mainly focus on introduction to the business of retailing, its significance, and the emergence of various formats in retailing. Hence, this chapter mainly deals with the understanding of the concept of retail business and functions performed by a retailer. It will also cover the analysis of retail sector industry in India and implications of the recent foreign direct investment (FDI) policy in retail sector of India. We will also try to understand the legal framework and provisions, regulatory environment, and strengths, weaknesses, opportunities, and threats (SWOT) in the context of changing dynamics of Indian retail landscape.

Primary Classification of Retailers

The retail sector can be primarily classified as unorganized and organized retailing. Let us discuss each of these concepts briefly.

Unorganized Retail

As discussed earlier, the Indian retail industry was traditionally dominated by small family-run *kirana* stores or neighborhood mom-and-pop store. These shops are characterized by very small area and limited assortment and varieties stacked in a small place, inefficient upstream processes, poor infrastructure and lack of modern technology, inadequate funding, and absence of skilled manpower. This traditional way of retailing is known as unorganized retailing. In India, unorganized retailing includes units whose activity is not registered by any statute or legal provision, and/or those that do not maintain regular accounts. Hence, this sector is characterized by small and scattered units that sell products or services out of a fixed or mobile location. It consists of unauthorized small shops—conventional *kirana* shops, general stores, corner shops, among various other small retail outlets—but these small shops remain as the radiating force of Indian retail industry. These traditional units generally include *haats*, *mandis*, melas, and the local baniyas/kiranas, *paanwalas*, and others like cobblers and vegetable/fruit vendors and are termed as the unorganized retailers.

Organized Retail

Organized retailers are those who are licensed for trading activities and registered to pay taxes to the government. Organized retail is nothing but a retail place where all the items are classified and segregated according to their utility, form, and nature and brought under one roof. They are placed in different departments and displayed very systematically with their price points. These items are then selected by the customer and billed at point of sale (POS) with a computerized receipt of payment. Meanwhile, the customer is assisted by the sales staff with a professional approach. Organized retailing thus provides merchandise with wide variety and deep assortment with a large number of stock-keeping units (SKUs). An SKU is a single item of merchandise for which separate stock and records of sales are maintained.

Organized retail deals with multiple formats, which is typically a multi-owner chain of stores or distribution centers run by professional management. Today, organized retailing has become an experience characterized by comfort, service assistance, convenience, style, and speed. It is something that offers a customer more pleasure, brand association, variety and choice for selection, loyalty benefits, entertainment, and, hence, a complete shopping experience.

The Retailer Within the Distribution Channel

From a traditional marketing point of view, the retailer is one of many possible organizations through which goods produced by the manufacturer flow on their way to their final consumers. These organizations/firms perform various roles by being a member of a distribution channel. For example, a soft drink producer will use a number of distribution channels for its confectionery, which involve members such as agents, wholesalers, convenience stores, supermarkets and vending machine operators. Hence, these channel members, or marketing intermediaries as they are sometimes referred to, typically perform the functions that a manufacturer does not have the resources to perform.

As shown in Figure 1.1, a distribution channel is a set of chain of firms/intermediaries that facilitate the movement of products from the point of production (POP) to the POS to the end consumer, and retailers are the final contact to business transaction in a distribution channel that links manufacturers to consumers. In this flow or chain, wholesalers come before the retailers, and it is also essential to understand the term "wholesaler" as both wholesalers and retailers are intermediaries in distribution channels. Wholesalers are typically involved in selling to individuals or organizations for their business use or for resale purpose. In other words, wholesalers buy and resell merchandise to retailers and other merchants and not to the end consumers. Generally, wholesalers sell in large quantities/volumes. They take the title of the goods and also provide credit facility to the retailers. Hence, a wholesaler acts as an intermediary between the manufacturer and the retailer.

Retailing thus may be understood as the final step in the distribution of merchandise, for consumption by the end users. In easy terms, any individual or firm or organization that sells products to the final consumers is performing the function of retailing. They endeavor to satisfy customer needs by having the right merchandise, at the right price, at the right place,

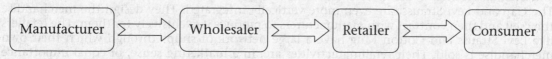

Figure 1.1: *The Distribution Channel*

in a convenient way when the customer wants it. This creates real added value or utility value for the end consumers. This comes from four perspectives, and they are as follows:

1. The form utility of the merchandise that is acceptable to the customer.
2. The time utility by keeping the store open when the consumers prefer to shop.
3. The place utility being available at a convenient location.
4. The ownership utility when the merchandise is sold.

In this way, retailers provide a platform for manufactures to sell their merchandise. This also includes activities/functions such as displaying the merchandise in the most attractive way, alongside related or alternative items at a geographic location and at a place that is convenient for a consumer to access during shopping. These intermediaries facilitate the distribution process by providing points where deliveries of merchandise are altered in their physical state (such as being broken down into smaller quantities, or being repackaged) and are made available to customers in convenient and/or cost-effective locations. Over the period of time, using price as a competitive weapon—by introducing ranges of own branded goods (private labels, PLs) and developing attractive persuasive shopping environments and experience— retailer brands have been successful in achieving the consumer loyalty toward their retail stores/outlets. This shift of power to the retailer has been further enhanced by IT that has enabled them to gain a deep understanding of their customers' purchasing behavior, patterns, and preferences.

For instance, Amazon.com maintains a data warehouse with information about what each customer has bought. By using this pool of data and information, customers returning to its portal are immediately recognized and suggestions based on their past purchases are made. Also, e-mails are sent to the customers when new books in the subject area of their interest are published. Hence to gain loyalty, retailers focus on customer service, which is defined as the summation of acts, elements, and value that enables and allows consumers to receive/gain what they desire or need from the respective retail establishment. The brick-and-mortar stores leverage their customer base by making it convenient and engaging to buy at stores, over the Internet. To take on the non-store retailers, these physical retailers are becoming more than just stores to buy products by offering entertaining and educational experiences to their target customers. These features improve customers' visual experiences, provide them with a unique shopping experience, and enhance the loyalty behavior and hence sales potential by enabling them to "touch, feel, and try before they buy." Although in some distribution channels, the manufacturing, wholesaling, and retailing activities are performed by independent firms, most distribution channels have some vertical integration.

The Vertical Marketing System

Currently, vertical integration means that a firm/company performs more than one set of activities in the distribution channel, for instance, a retailer invests in wholesaling or manufacturing. For example, many large retailers—such as Walmart, Reliance Retail, and Future Group—are involved in both wholesaling and retailing activities. They procure/buy directly from manufacturers; the merchandise are then shipped to their warehouses for storage, and then distributed to their stores, and finally sold to end consumers. Other retailers, such as The Gap and Levi Strauss, are even more vertically integrated. They design the merchandise they sell and then contract with manufacturers to produce it exclusively for them. The retailers like Levi Strauss and Cotton King have a large network of shops through which their own merchandise is sold. Their retailing activities are, in a marketing sense, of equal importance to their manufacturing activities (irrespective of the financial contributions of each activity), and the two facets of the business are highly integrated. So in order to describe this type of situation, the concept of vertical marketing system (VMS) has emerged.

Meaning

A VMS consists of all levels of independently owned businesses across a distribution channel. Goods and services are distributed through one of these types of VMSs, which are independent, partially integrated, and fully integrated, as given in Table 1.1.

The independent firm VMS typically consists of levels of independently owned firms like manufacturers, wholesalers, and retailers. This type of system and arrangement is often used and desirable when:

- The manufacturers have to reach a wider market or retailers are small.
- Company resources are low and channel members want to share costs and risks.

Independent retailers strive to capitalize on their targeted consumer base and gain customer loyalty by playing the role of a customer-friendly retailer brand and build a strong brand image.

In a partially integrated VMS, two independently owned businesses across the channel perform/ deliver all production and distribution functions without the interference of the third. In the most common form of this system, a manufacturer and retailer complete all transactions, including shipping, storing, and other functions of distribution without the involvement of independent wholesalers. A partially integrated system is most appropriate in the following situations:

- Manufacturers and retailers are big.
- Selective or exclusive distribution is required.
- Unit sales are moderate (not very high).
- Company is rich in resources.
- Better channel control is desired.
- Available wholesalers are very expensive or they are not available.

Table 1.1: *Vertical Marketing System: Key Functions and Ownership*

Type of Channel	Channel Functions	Ownership
Independent systems	Manufacturing	All the functions are performed independently by different firms
	Wholesaling	
	Retailing	
Partially integrated systems	Manufacturing	All the functions are performed by two-channel members having all resources, facilities, and control
	Wholesaling	
	Retailing	
Fully integrated systems	Manufacturing	All functions are performed by a single-channel member
	Wholesaling	
	Retailing	

As the name itself suggests, a fully integrated VMS is a single enterprise that performs all production and distribution functions and eliminates the other possible channel members. Advantages of this system to a firm are: total control on strategic planning and decisions, direct contact with end consumers, room for higher retail markups without raising prices, exclusivity over the merchandise or service offered, self-sufficiency, and retention of profits within the enterprise. Previously, this system was often employed only by the manufacturers, but today retailers have moved upward in the value chain. Some wholesalers have concerns either way to deliver better value to their customers.

Hence, the VMS usually gives a more pragmatic view of the retail industry in developed economies. Many large multiple retailers in India like Big Bazaar, Reliance Megamart, More, and Spencer's are actively involved in core marketing functions that were at one time left to the producers. These functions are product development, branding, promotion, public relations (PR), and advertising. Conversely, many producers are also involved in retailing activities, either by running their own retail outlets, exclusively for their own products/merchandise, or by performing functions that at one time were limited to the retailers, like visual merchandising (VM), display and shelf space management.

So here a tricky question arises: "What is the relevance or importance of the retailer" if it is easier and cheaper to buy the products directly from those who produce them? The answer to this question is generally "No." There may be situations where it is cheaper and convenient to buy directly from manufacturers; retailers perform significant functions that increase the value of the products and services they sell to consumers and facilitate the distribution of those products and services for those who produce them.

These functions are:

- Providing varieties and assortments of products and services
- Breaking the bulk
- Holding the inventory
- Providing the services

So by providing varieties and assortments, breaking the bulk, holding the inventory, and providing the services, retailers ultimately increase the value consumers receive from their products and services.

For example, a conveniently located home-improvement center, for instance, Home Centre by Lifestyle, sells one dining set that is available when the customer wants to see and buy it. The retailer helps the customer by displaying various designs and combinations under one roof and its sales staff help the customer to the select the appropriate dining set by providing information regarding its dimensions, material, price, design options available, offers, and so on. This helps the customer to understand the product and select the right one as per its requirement and space available/planned for it. The home-improvement center has varieties and assortment like four-chair, six-chairs, or eight-chair dining sets available in different colors, textures, designs, and materials.

Strategic Retail Management

Strategic retail management involves key strategic decision areas that incorporate determining a market strategy, merchandising management, organizational structure, financial strategy, pricing strategy, location strategy, human resource (HR) strategy, information systems, supply chain strategies, and CRM strategies. The formulation of a retail market strategy is primarily based on analyzing the environment and the firm's strengths and weaknesses. When major environmental changes or technological disruptions occur, the existing strategy and the rationale behind it are reviewed and modified accordingly. At this stage, the retailer decides what, if any, strategic changes are required to take advantage of new opportunities or to counter new threats that emerge in the existing business environment. Hence, formulating and implementing a retail strategy are fundamentally based on an understanding of the macro- and microenvironments. This is categorically described in detail in the following chapters of this book with appropriate examples.

In this process, the retailer firm plans to focus its resources to accomplish its organizational objectives. It identifies:

- The target market, or markets, toward which the retailer is planning to direct its efforts.
- The type/nature of the merchandise and services the retailer needs to offer to serve the needs and expectations of the target audience.
- The right image and positioning strategy.
- The way to build a sustainable competitive advantage (SCA).

Besides this, the retailers have to perform at the key strategic decision areas that involve positioning strategy, determining a market strategy, financial strategy and financial merchandise management, location strategy, organizational structure and HRM strategy, technology and information systems and supply chain management (SCM), CRM, and loyalty program strategies.

The positioning strategy involves the decisions on how the retailer brand can be positioned successfully so that the target customer can associate and relate themselves with the brand. The selection of a retail market strategy hinges on analyzing the environment and the firm's strengths and weaknesses vis-à-vis opportunities and threats. When major environmental changes occur, the current strategy and the notion behind it are reviewed and revised accordingly. The decision makers then decide what, if any, strategy modifications or innovations are required to take advantage of new opportunities or avoid new threats in the environment at both macro- and microlevel.

The trend of developing private-label brands (PLBs) is fast catching up in the current retail environment among the Indian retailers as it presents the retailers and consumers with a win–win solution. With the changing consumer habits, preferences, and improved perceptions toward the PLBs, most of the retailers are focusing on developing and building strong in-house brands across various price points to attract the customers and increase the loyalty. Chapter 6 explains the strategic importance of PLBs in the contemporary retailing scenario.

Financial variables such as sales, costs, expenses, profits, assets, liabilities, manpower productivity, cost of inventory, and owner's equity are used to evaluate the market strategy and its implementation. Today, we can see that there is increasing focus on profitable growth in the sector. Most retailers seem to be focusing on transformation of existing operations rather than introducing new formats. In a nutshell, leading retailers seem to be driving the dual themes of expansion and internal improvement for sustainable growth. Furthermore, retailers expect that customer sentiments will improve, which will provide further impetus to the growth of the organized sector. So, it is a constant challenge and a requirement for organizations in retail industry to periodically reinvent their business models. Also, while choosing investors too, retailers need to develop relationships with those who hold a long-term view and provide strategic support to the business along with financial infusion.

In addition, the decisions regarding location strategy are vital for both consumer and competitive reasons. Generally, location is consumers' one of the topmost considerations while selecting or patronizing a store. Consumers typically buy grocery items at the closest superstore and patronize the shopping mall that is most convenient to reach from their home or office. Second, location offers an opportunity to gain a sustainable and long-term advantage over competition because it cannot be duplicated or imitated. When a retailer grabs the best location, a competing retailer in the same format is left with the second-best location. Today, consumers are also divided between value-based purchases and aspiration-based shopping. Thus, retailers need to cater the dual desires of the consumer, which could be enabled by installing multichannels.

In the case of HRM, the retailer's market and people (HR) strategy must be consistent with the organization's financial objectives, positioning, and image. The leaders in retail industry need to focus on developing and handling people, creating self-disruptions and constant reinvention, learning to deal with the complexities of the industry, and, finally, being there for the long haul while handling the intermittent failures along the way. The leaders need to manage business complexities and maker volatilities for which they have to understand art, science, and mathematics of retailing. A retailer's organization structure and HRM strategy are closely linked to its market strategy because service is the integral part of retail business. Retailing is majorly a labor-intensive function. Therefore, retailers are constantly challenged to reorganize and improve the human part of their structures to become more efficient. The HR strategy is quintessentially the reflection of the business strategy of the retail firm. The HR executives in charge need to act as business partners for management and are expected to deliver strategic and practical operational solutions in the form of HR functions based on comprehensive knowledge of the business. The retailers that target customer segments seeking high-quality customer service need to impart proper training to the sales staff. One of the arts needed most critically by the leaders, irrespective of any industry or sector, is of handling people and coordinating with them. They also need to develop and groom people by mentoring and coaching them so that the "purpose" can be passed on. This approach motivates the people and drives them to inculcate the "culture of service" and enables them to deliver the expected levels of service. This ensures there is a very capable and cohesive team in place that is able to support the long-term vision of the company.

The next important component is financial merchandising management, which is also one of the most important functions that retailers have to perform efficiently and effectively in order to achieve the operational excellence. For instance, retailers that attempt to serve national or regional markets must make trade-offs between the efficiency of centralized buying and the need to tailor merchandise and services to local needs. The IT and SCM systems are the backbones and offer a significant opportunity for retailers to gain strategic advantage in the contemporary retailing environment. Retailers are continually and continuously developing sophisticated and hi-tech computer and distribution systems to monitor flows of information and merchandise from vendors to retail distribution centers to retail stores. The POS terminals read product and price information that is encoded into Universal Product Codes (UPCs) or radio frequency identification (RFID) devices affixed to the merchandise. This information is then transmitted to the distribution hub or directly to vendors on real-time basis. These technologies are integral part of an overall inventory management system that enables retailers to offer a wider selection of merchandise to the customers, and it also decreases their investment in inventory that ultimately reduces the cost. The basic idea is, understanding the customer's expectations and their buying behavior in order to provide them with the goods and services they want. And even more important is to understand and cater to the wants of the retailer's most valued and loyal customers. These loyal customers majorly contribute to retailer's total sales and profits; here the CRM plays a very important role. CRM is not just a program but a business philosophy consisting of set of strategies, loyalty programs, and systems that are designed to build, maintain, and increase loyalty behavior of most valued customers toward that retailer.

Today, customers have a plethora of options that provide them the luxury of deciding what, how, and when they want something. Hence, this makes imperative for retailers to listen to their target audience, understand their expectations, and deliver it with the highest possible level of service standards. In today's era of web, Internet, and mobile retailing, retailers are extensively using data analytics to identify their most valued customers and analyze their buying behavior and preferences. Using advanced and predictive analytics techniques, they can better understand customer preferences, track behavioral changes, closely observe the trends, and determine customers' likely future purchases. It can further help anticipate demand for specific merchandise to tailor store-level assortment, optimize inventory, and personalize store-level experiences to suit the need of target audience. All these inputs are eventually used for strategy formulation and also designing special programs to achieve their patronage loyalty.

Consider the classic example of international brand LVMH Moët Hennessy Louis Vuitton SE, usually shortened to LVMH. It is one of the leading luxury goods groups in the world and based in France. LVMH was formed as a conglomerate in 1987 when Louis Vuitton merged with Moët Hennessy in a whopping US$4 billion deal. LVMH's famous brand names such as Christian Dior, Dom Pérignon, Givenchy, and Moët & Chandon are recognized all over the world. Though the parent company LVMH may be relatively new, many of their luxury brands have a long-dated history. While Moët & Chandon came to existence in 1743, Hennessy started its journey in 1765. The group operates over 3,000 stores, present in over 50 countries, and employs over 1,10,000 people. LVMH has consistently acted as a pioneer in new and emerging markets, and is perhaps the most international luxury conglomerate.

It currently holds around 15% of the world market for luxury goods. This market grows by about 10% annually, and so it attracts very strong competition. LVMH has achieved and sustained its market position by developing the LVMH galaxy of brands as a big talent academy for recruiting, cultivating, and deploying industry-leading personnel. Internationally known and famous brands such as Gucci, owned by PPR; Richemont, the Cartier's owner; or Bvlgari are in the brand portfolio of this group. LVMH's organizational structure is very effective and strategically differentiated to that of a typical conglomerate. The group strategically comprises 70 exceptional houses that make products of high quality. LVMH manages some of the most prestigious fashion labels in the business that include Louis Vuitton, Marc Jacobs, Kenzo, Céline, and Givenchy in its portfolio of 70 of the world's most celebrated luxury brands.

LVMH is the only conglomerate that has developed strategic presence in all five key sectors and verticals of the luxury market: fashion and leather goods, wines and spirits, perfumes and cosmetics, watches and chronographs and jewelry, and selective retailing. This is along with other activities and holding companies. The entire organization focuses on shared costs and synergies, both backward and forward, of its value chain and the groups, which act as strategic business units (SBUs). Now these SBUs are operated in such a way that they can sell nationally known, high-quality products in a fashion that cater local cultural tastes, flavors, and preferences and take into consideration the local rules and regulations.

These five SBUs are as follows:

1. The LVMH fashion and leather goods SBU operates world-famous labels such as Louis Vuitton, Fendi, Céline, Donna Karan, Marc Jacobs, Loewe, Les Tanneries Roux, Kenzo, Emilio Pucci, Thomas Pink, Berluti, and Rossimoda.

2. The activities of the wines and spirits SBU include the champagne and wines branch, and the cognac and spirits branch.
3. The perfumes and cosmetics SBU operates through the French houses Christian Dior, Kenzo, Guerlain, Acqua di Parma, Givenchy, and other brands.
4. The watches, chronographs, and jewelry SBU markets the brands such as TAG Heuer, Dior watches, Hublot, Zenith, De Beers, Chaumet, and Fred, among others.
5. The selective retailing SBU operates in two segments: travel retail and the selective retail concepts represented by Sephora and Le Bon Marché.

Additionally, LVMH operates travel and beauty products retail stores and also retail stores for luxury products on cruise ship. It also operates the department stores under the brands of Sephora, DFS, Starboard Cruise Services, and Le Bon Marché Rive Gauche. LVMH also operates yachts and attraction parks, as well as offers media services through an editorial website.

The profit margin in the luxury segment is typically high, and control over production, distribution, and advertising is imperative for profitability. LVMH ensures that production standards are the highest and its "Made in France" label is used appropriately so as to appeal to its market niches. The country-specific advantage is obvious, and it materializes globally and necessitates so little adaptation in the group's forward strategy. Because it only sources in France, Italy, and Switzerland, LVMH keeps the dream alive for its worldwide customers.

Photo 1.1: *Louis Vuitton Store in Miami*

Source: us.louisvuitton.com (accessed on 12 May 2016)

The company also markets its brand names internationally so that buyers everywhere are familiar with them. One way it does this is by setting aside 11% of all sales to be used exclusively for advertising. On a centralized basis, LVMH also uses a common laboratory for cosmetics research, employs bulk media buys so that it gets the most value from its promotion expenses, and integrates the operations for all of the branch offices in each group to ensure maximum efficiency. By carefully overseeing major operations from the top while allowing the individual SBUs to make those decisions that directly affect their own local markets, LVMH employs a combination of "tight and loose" control that it uses to maximize its international presence to the extent it has become the most global retail company. The organization also performs well on the corporate social responsibility (CSR) front, which has helped them to further strengthen their brand image. For over two decades, the environment department at LVMH has contributed to reducing the environmental impact of the group and its houses. This initiative enabled the group to make considerable progress in environmental protection. The development has been initiated and achieved as part of LIFE—short form for "LVMH Indicators for the Environment"—an action program that is integrated in the strategic plan of the group's 70 houses. The action program incorporated the consideration for environment-friendly designs, responsible sourcing of raw materials, social and environmental responsibility of vendors, and sustainability of production process activities, among others.

Let us consider the example of Future Lifestyle Fashions that has successfully set the styles, trends, and expression for Indian lifestyle fashion business. It was formed in January 2013 through the consolidation of the lifestyle fashion businesses of Future Group. Today, it acts as an integrated fashion company with presence across key segments and formats within the fashion industry—from design and manufacturing to distribution and retailing. They strategically integrated some of their most popular lifestyle retail destinations like Central, Planet Sports, and Brand Factory, along with over 20 national and international fashion brands with business and management professionals, entrepreneurs, and fashion designers. The company has set a vision to create an Indian expression of fashion and develop a fashion business that is globally benchmarked. The company houses some of leading fashion labels and PLBs such as John Miller, Scullers, Indigo Nation, Urbana, Lombard, Urban Yoga, RIG, Bare, Jealous 21, Holii, and Spunk, among others. They also have the exclusive licenses of a number

Photo 1.2: *The Visual Embodies the Styles, Trends, and Expression for Indian Lifestyle Fashion*

Source: http://www.futuregroup.in/businesses/lifestyle_fashion.html (accessed on 12 May 2016)

of leading international brands that are marketed and distributed by the organization. These include Converse, Lee Cooper, UMM, Manchester United, and Daniel Hechter. The Future Lifestyle Fashions also operates joint ventures (JVs) with high-end French brand Celio, leading handbag maker Hidesign, and global footwear major Clarks. It holds stakes in companies that operate brands such as Mother Earth, Mineral, Trésmode, and Turtle.

Most of these brands have their independent distribution network and are retailed through around 150 exclusive brand outlets (EBO) and over 250 multi-brand outlets (MBOs) and department stores across the nation. Its flagship format, Central, is among the country's leading department store chain with 23 stores in major cities in India and offers over 400 brands to customers. A little larger "aLL" flagship offers a unique retail experience for consumers looking for plus-size fashion merchandise. The company's outlet store chain, Brand Factory, targets and caters to the aspirational youth, and the specialty chain, Planet Sports, offers sportswear and sports goods.

If we talk about online retailers, they bring in a diverse range of products by forging tie-ups with several other off-line retailers across categories, which is helping them offer an array of products on a single online platform, making it a one-stop destination for every shopper.

For instance, Flipkart has signed a strategic partnership with three of the country's largest home retail brands: HomeTown (Future Group), HomeStop (Shoppers Stop), and @home. These strategic tie-ups with top-notch furniture and home-improvement brands introduced a new range of products to Flipkart's existing portfolio of 1,000-plus brands. The associations bring together products from these home retailers backed by Flipkart's e-commerce platform and expertise to the end customer. Despite the fact that these retailers have off-line presence in key markets and a few online channels too, the association helps them tap Flipkart's consumer base across geographies. By virtue of this, customers can now access and explore an exhaustive range of products (furnishing to do-it-yourself (DIY) tools and home care to décor) from these brands and also their PLs. This offers customers more variety to choose from and convenient reach to some of the leading brands. Hence, this marriage of the best of off-line brands with the online retailer's distribution and technology expertise bring more varieties and a comprehensive shopping experience for the customers, across the geographies.

Elements of Retail Marketing Mix

To implement a retail marketing strategy, management of a brick-and-mortar retailer develops a retail mix that satisfies the needs of its target audience with the right shopping experience. The retail mix is the perfect blend of factors retailers use to satisfy customer needs, influence their purchase decisions, and connect with them not only on transactional level but also on emotional level. Elements in the retail mix include the brand positioning, merchandise mix and level of services offered, right pricing, PLBs, advertising and promotional programs, physical environment, store design, layout and ambience, VM and display, PR and social media strategy, location strategy, philanthropic and CSR activities, CRM, and loyalty programs. The merchandisers in the retail organization decide on how much and what types of merchandise to buy, the variety and assortments, from where to procure the merchandise and the purchase terms, the retail prices to set, and how to advertise and promote merchandise. The visual merchandisers work on how the visual effects are created by using various elements like color, lighting and display themes and the fashion in which the merchandise shall be displayed. Store managers in association with HR executives determine how to recruit, select, and motivate sales associates. They also work on where and how merchandise will be displayed, complying with maintaining the planograms, day-to-day store operations, and inventory management. All these components of marketing mix of modern retailing are discussed in detail in the successive chapters of this book (Figure 1.2).

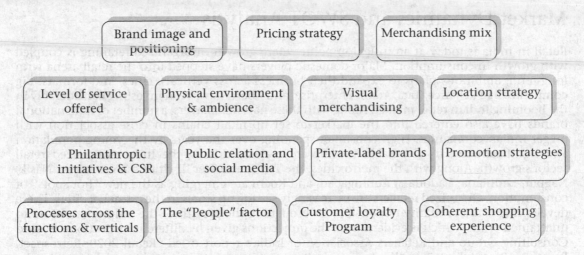

Figure 1.2: *Components of Marketing Mix of Modern Retailing*

The Retail Industry and Its Contribution to the Economy

The Indian retail industry has presently emerged as one of the most dynamic and fast-paced industries as several players have started to enter the market. It accounts for over 10% of the country's gross domestic product (GDP) and around 8% of the employment in India. The country is today the fifth largest global destination in the world for retail. Ever since the opening of the Indian economy in 1992, the service sector is taking a lead in driving the economy. Retailing has become an important wheel of India's growth engine. The retail landscape in India has undergone a marvelous change. Traditionally, a major part of retail was in the unorganized sector. But over the years, there has been a distinct movement toward the organized way of retailing (as evinced in most dynamic and emerging sectors worldwide) with several players having entered the terrain. As this is an industry that requires heavy initial investments in infrastructure, supply chain, technologies, and inventories, and breakeven has a longer gestation period, many players are still striving for desired profitability. But the future does seem to be promising. Further, with the online medium of retail gaining more and more acceptance, there is a tremendous growth opportunity for retail companies, both domestic and international.

With its significant young population, the urban areas of India house increasing number of nuclear families with double income attributed to the growing percentage of working women. Furthermore, economic and regulatory policies are becoming more favorable for the retail industry. India's booming IT sector is also creating technological innovation for facilitating operations in this sector. Modern retail has captured the imagination of Indians as cable/satellite television, through their lifestyle channels, have ignited the passion for modern retail. With the growth in the retail industry, the corresponding demand for real estate is also being created. This has further been fueled by real estate companies developing huge malls, large sprawling shopping centers, and huge shopping complexes/destinations that offer almost all kinds of entertainment and shopping and dining experiences under one roof. In fact, customer buying behavior of the new generation of Indians has altered the complexion of shopping in terms of formats and experience.

Market Dynamics and SWOT Analysis

Retail in India is today at an inflexion point where growth of organized retailing is coupled with growth in consumption. Major domestic players have stepped into the retail arena with long-term, ambitious plans to expand their business across verticals, cities, and formats. Big companies like Reliance, Tata, Adani Enterprise, and Bharti have been investing considerably in the booming Indian retail market. Along with these national players, a number of transnational brands have also entered into the market to set up retail chains in close association with bigger Indian companies. High consumer spending over the years by the young population and significant rise in disposable income are majorly driving the Indian organized retail sector's growth. Along with the metro cities, the Tier II and Tier III cities such as Jaipur, Nasik, Nagpur, Ludhiana, Vadodara, Aurangabad, and Kochi are emerging as the new "hot spots" of consumption. Organized retailers are increasingly setting up stores in these smaller cities. These developments are primarily responsible for propelling the growth of the industry to hitherto unattained orbits, which is evident from the projections given by different institutions. Boston Consulting Group and Retailers Association of India's report titled "Retail 2020: Retrospect, Reinvent, Rewrite" projects that India's retail market is expected to double to US$1 trillion by 2020 from US$600 billion in 2015, driven by income growth, urbanization, and attitudinal shifts. In this report, they also have forecasted that while the overall retail market will grow at 12% per annum, modern trade will grow twice as fast at 20% per annum, and traditional trade at 10%. Even Tier I and Tier II cities and towns have experienced a major shift in consumer preferences and lifestyles, the result of which they have emerged as attractive markets for retailers to expand their presence. The key drivers of the Indian retail industry are:

- An increase in the double-income household trend.
- Growing liberalization of the FDI policy in the past decade.
- Conducive regulatory environment due to expected reforms.
- Emergence of nuclear families.
- Demography dynamics (approximately 60% of Indian population is below 30 years of age).
- Large working population.
- Still a reasonable real estate prices in many of the big cities of India.
- Increase in disposable income and customer aspiration.
- Rising affluence amid consumers and increasing number of high-net-worth individuals (HNWIs).
- Demand as well as increase in expenditure for luxury items.
- Higher brand consciousness and growing preference for branded products and higher aspirations.
- Increasing urbanization.
- Increased efficiency due to development in supply chain.
- Plastic revolution (increasing use of credit cards for categories relating to apparel, consumer durable goods, food and grocery, and so on).

The New Affluent Consumers of India: Drivers of Retail Hope

A survey was conducted by the Visa Affluent Study 2015 across affluent consumers in China, Australia, Hong Kong, Japan, Indonesia, South Korea, Singapore, and India. The study incorporated male and female cardholders between the age group of 18 and 55 years with a defined minimum income.

India ranked third in the study, when the respondents were asked about their plan to increase or decrease their discretionary spending. The list was topped by Indonesia, followed by China.

The survey highlighted that majority of India's affluent consumers are optimistic about the country's economic situation, believing that it will improve further. The study also sensed the positive sentiment in their outlook about their personal and household incomes, which they were expecting to rise, in the years to come. It is also observed that these sentiments drive them to spend more on discretionary item. According to the reports, the average annual household income of India's affluent consumers is ₹15 lakh, while the average age is 34 years. They are younger than most Asia Pacific markets.

For a nation like India that is hungry for growth, affluent consumers are evolving by leaps. Outward manifestations of affluence continue to be ownership of multiple real estate properties, jewelry, luxury cars, branded cloths, and other lifestyle indulgences.

Limitations

Although the growth potential in the sector is immense, there are obstacles, too, that could slow the pace of growth for new entrants. Lack of basic infrastructure, rigid regulations and high personnel costs, real estate costs, and highly competitive domestic retailer groups are some such challenges. In terms of global comparison of the organized retail sector penetration, other developing countries such as China, Thailand, Malaysia, and Indonesia are significantly ahead of India. So at this crucial stage, it is necessary to learn from the experience of developed markets like the USA and other G8 countries and relook at structural issues such as:

- A long way to meet international standards.
- Lack of efficient supply chain management.
- Lack of retail space of required size and quality.
- No fixed consumption pattern.
- Shortage of trained manpower.
- Lack of proper infrastructure and distribution channel.
- The scarcity of premium retail space, coupled with the high cost of retail space, creates an economic disparity in terms of buying power for the consumer.

The Indian consumer is highly mass based; they are aspirational, but also keen on value for money. The Indian consumer needs high-quality products at competitive prices. Spending on indulgence goods is not as low as it appears, but it is definitely done with great precaution. The Indian mind-set is still beset by the desire to save for three generations, and so this reduces the overall consumption in the market. Hence, aspiration and desirability are key factors in the Indian market. The consumption is low and per consumer buying power is lower. Careful calibration of these parameters can help guide to formulate the future strategies of retail in India.

Because of these factors, e-commerce is rapidly becoming the future growth opportunity as it negates the high costs of real estate and allows for a farther reach than a traditional shop. It is expected that the online retail will be at par with the physical stores in five years. India is expected to become the world's fastest-growing e-commerce market on the back of robust investment activity in the sector and the rapid increase in Internet users. Online retail business is the next-gen format that has high potential for growth in the near future. It is expected that India's e-commerce market will grow from US$2.9 billion in 2013 to over

US$100 billion by 2020. This growth is driven by demand-side factors such as substantial rise in the Internet penetration, increasing speed of broadband connections, and increasing use of smartphones not only in urban area but also in rural, and by supply-side factors such as increased proliferation of venture capitalists (VCs)/private equity-funded e-commerce start-ups.

In a Nutshell

- Regulatory factors: Liberalization of FDI policies in retail coupled with the expected roll-out of the Goods and Service Tax (GST).
- Supply-side factors: Rapid real estate and infrastructural development, easy availability of credit, innovative physical and online channels, and increased service orientation.
- Demand-side factors: Rising disposable income, increasing urbanization, highly aware and affluent young population, growing number of working women, and changing consumer preferences led by increased discretionary spends.

After conquering physical stores, retailers are now foraying into the domain of e-retailing. The retail industry is all set to test waters over the online medium, by selling products through websites. An emerging trend in this segment is the brick-and-mortar retailers are coming up with their online portals: the virtual formats where customer orders are taken online through these web portals. These orders are then delivered at their physical stores or delivered at the doorstep the very same day or the following day. This trend is called as the omni-channel strategy and catching up with most of the poster boys of the physical retailing in the segments like apparel, home improvement, electronics, fashion, and lifestyle. Here the strategy is, off-line would feed the online demand. The inclusion of high-tech devices in the organized retail segment has been something to reckon with in the past few years. Use of computerized systems and processes for merchandise planning and management, control of inventory costs and supplies and real-time replenishment of goods, internal store billing, and so on have changed the face of product retailing. Convergence of technology, e-commerce, and physical shops in the future is bound to occur. Macy's, for instance, has managed to create a consistent and standard shopping experience and product portfolio across the online and physical models.

Let us consider the example of Pantaloons, India's leading fashion retailer; it has entered into a strategic tie-up with online fashion retailer Jabong.com to retail its exclusive brands. This partnership has many synergistic effects on the business of the retailers both by virtue of their respective strengths and by the expertise. Let us have a look on the same then.

The tie-up combines the strengths of the two companies and eventually boosts turnover by leveraging the huge potential of online retail. On the other hand, Pantaloons leadership mettle in the fashion retail space attributed to its vast portfolio of well-established exclusive brands strategically complements Jabong's vast reach to millions of online consumers across the geographies of market. While Pantaloons is India's biggest women's apparel player, Jabong is a leader in women's fashion in online space. Hence, this strategically outlined association makes Jabong.com a home to ethnic wear brands such as Rangmanch, Akkriti, and Trishaa, along with casual wear brands like SF Jeans and Candies, New York.

As far as the market presence and reach is concerned, Pantaloons is expanding in both metros and Tier II cities and has always strived to enhance the accessibility of its products by developing new channels for reaching the target audience. This objective channelized Pantaloons to make its online debut through Jabong to reach out to millions of online consumers. This alliance allows Pantaloons to reach out to not only metro and the Tier II cities but also tier III markets where Jabong has consolidated a strong position today. In a nutshell, with this association with Jabong, Pantaloons can further enhance the outreach and penetration of the brand into pin codes where the brand does not have physical presence.

SWOT Analysis of Retail Industry in India

The Indian retail sector is a growing phenomenon, and relaxation in FDI norms has generated even more interest in the Indian retail market. As per retailers' point of view, infrastructure, economic growth and changing demographics, and the inherent strength of the Indian economy are the most important drivers of retail followed by increase in FDIs and growth of real estate.

In the growing markets, retailing has become one of the major emerging trends in the entire economic cycle. The retail price index is frequently referred to economic indicator. It is a measure that is based on a "basket" of products across all retail sectors and compares prices over time in order to reveal the changes in the cost to households of typical purchase needs. An increasing number of Indian consumers are ascending the economic pyramid to form an emerging and aspiring middle class, and many business groups are attracted in the past few years, including some renowned business groups like Bharti, Future, Raheja, Reliance, and Aditya Birla to establish hold, showing the future growth in times to come.

In addition, the penetration of organized retail in India is still very low, hovering somewhere around 8%, especially when compared to developed nations such as the UK and the USA, which have retail penetration of around 80% and 85%, respectively. In addition to that increasing purchasing power, disposable income, new policy reforms (refer to Figure 1.3), and

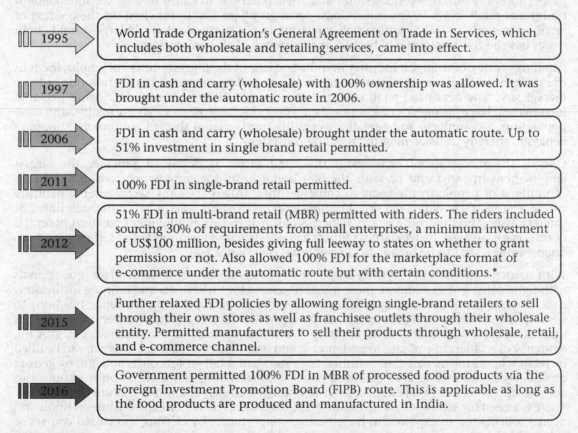

1995 — World Trade Organization's General Agreement on Trade in Services, which includes both wholesale and retailing services, came into effect.

1997 — FDI in cash and carry (wholesale) with 100% ownership was allowed. It was brought under the automatic route in 2006.

2006 — FDI in cash and carry (wholesale) brought under the automatic route. Up to 51% investment in single brand retail permitted.

2011 — 100% FDI in single-brand retail permitted.

2012 — 51% FDI in multi-brand retail (MBR) permitted with riders. The riders included sourcing 30% of requirements from small enterprises, a minimum investment of US$100 million, besides giving full leeway to states on whether to grant permission or not. Also allowed 100% FDI for the marketplace format of e-commerce under the automatic route but with certain conditions.*

2015 — Further relaxed FDI policies by allowing foreign single-brand retailers to sell through their own stores as well as franchisee outlets through their wholesale entity. Permitted manufacturers to sell their products through wholesale, retail, and e-commerce channel.

2016 — Government permitted 100% FDI in MBR of processed food products via the Foreign Investment Promotion Board (FIPB) route. This is applicable as long as the food products are produced and manufactured in India.

Figure 1.3: *Implementation of FDI Policies in Chronological Order*

* For more details on this, please refer web resources of this book

changing spending pattern have essentially captured the attention of foreign companies that are showing their interest to enter India.

However, though the organized retailers in India have experienced fast growth over the last decade, this growth has been achieved at a significant cost. In spite of substantial investment of time and capital during this gestation period, the difference between actual and expected returns is a concern. One cannot deny the fact that India's existing retailing ecosystem is not efficient. There is an undesirable loss of value in both the manufacturer and consumer prices, which eventually results in depriving the manufacturers of a fair value for their effort, while compelling millions of inflation-affected, low- or middle-income people to pay much more at the retail than what they should be paying. This ecosystem is also not fully efficient for the state governments in particular when it comes to getting their fair share of local taxes, and not fully favorable for the central government when it comes to getting its share of indirect taxes, because many small- and medium-scale manufacturers can lucratively evade the taxation net by using the loopholes of current distribution channels containing a profusion of middlemen.

Besides regulatory, supply chain, and infrastructural support, one of the most crucial enablers of the sector is the availability of legal, low-cost, rightly located space to establish new outlets. Hence, suitable amendments need be made in urban planning norms that will provide sufficient space at strategic locations that are close to the residential catchment areas. The next step is to bring an equitable "zoning" policy that effectively addresses both the issues pertaining to proper location for large-format stores and their potential to cause trouble for independent traditional retail stores in select locations. An appropriate and improvised (in the context of retailing scenario in India) zoning policy relating to big-box and relatively large-format chain stores has the right potential to balance the existence of all retail formats.

Retailing is one of the largest industry in India and one of the biggest sources of employment in the country. India is becoming an emerging, exciting, dynamic retail destination due to large market size, low organized retail penetration, strong GDP growth rate, increasing personal income, and large number of inspirational customers like middle class, young people, and rural population. E-commerce and e-retail are creating fundamental shift in consumers' shopping behavior, thereby transforming the retailing ecosystem.

One of the most crucial facts about the retail sector is, today, it provides the largest employment in India and presents the best opportunity for employment creation for tens of millions of people in the years to come. Further, this is the only sector after agriculture where relatively less skilled or even unskilled workers can also make a living through direct or indirect association with the sector. Hence, any threat to this employment creation potential of this sector—especially when India suffers a major deficit in creating jobs or self-employment opportunities—has to be pragmatically analyzed (see Figure 1.4).

With an increase in flow of FDI, there is a possibility of significant rise in demand for professionals with right skills, and in addition, there would be a need for the trainers and training institutions also. Though there are training institutions in India for retail, the big challenge has been to develop the expected level of learning initiative as there are not enough teachers with practical understanding of changing retail landscape with the upsurge of e-commerce and growing tendency of retailers to embrace hybrid models and omni-channel strategy. This gap can be filled by retail schools hiring part-time (visiting) high-standard retail professionals and also by getting professors and trainers to get exposed to practical aspects of retailing. Retail organizations can also set up centers of excellence to build relevant HR strategies and for training the trainers. There is a need for setting up niche training institutes focused on retail and business schools and degree colleges too to explore this huge business opportunity by offering specialized courses or value-added programs in the subject area. Strategic collaborations between academia and retail industry can also be carved out to bridge the talent gap by providing low-cost access to skill development for retail with employers' need at the heart of the curriculum.

Strengths

- Emerging retail formats like malls, hyper-/supermarkets, and specialty stores that provide product, service and entertainment at one place.
- Indian consumers have high disposable incomes, which translate into high consumption levels.
- Large number of earning young population.
- Growth of real estate and Improvement in infrastructure.
- Huge agricultural sector offering an abundance of raw materials.

Weaknesses

- Demographic differences between the regions require a regionally adjusted approach to business.
- Presence of a significant number of strong and well-established players in the sector limits market entry potential.
- Deficiency of skilled workforce
- Relatively small domestic market limits growth opportunities.
- High real estate and distribution cost are the obstacles for growth of retail in India.

SWOT Analysis

Opportunities

- Increasing awareness of consumers about products and services.
- Changing consumers' requirements and lifestyles.
- Emerging and aspiring middle class.
- Increasing purchasing power: disposable income, new policy reforms, and changing spending pattern.
- Private label sector has been boosted by economic downturn.
- R&D and innovation capacity.
- Technology investments.
- Digital revolution and analytical insights.

Threats

- Economic slowdown is having an adverse effect on consumer spending.
- Rigid government policies and regulations restrict the entry of new players.
- Price competition among retailers puts downwards pressure on margins.
- Entry of international players in Indian markets consumes the share of Indian retailers.
- Shopping culture has not fully developed yet and the conversion rate is still low.

Figure 1.4: *SWOT Analysis of Retail Industry*

Holistic Overview of Foreign Direct Investment in Indian Retail Industry

Introduction

FDI is a measure of foreign ownership of domestic productive assets such as land, factories, and organizations. FDIs have become the key economic driver of globalization, accounting for over half of all cross-border investments. It is cross-border investment where foreign assets are invested into the organizations of the domestic market, excluding the investment in stock.

It brings private funds from overseas (foreign countries) into products or services. The domestic company in which foreign money is invested is usually being controlled by the investing foreign organization. For instance, a German company taking major stake in a company in India. Their return on investment (ROI) is based on the performance of the project.

Definition

FDI or foreign investment can refer to the net inflow of funds to acquire a long-term management interest in an enterprise operating in a foreign economy. It is the accumulation of equity, reinvestment of retained earnings, other long-term sources of capital, and short-term funds as presented in the balance of payments.

Over the latter half of the first decade of this century, India, along with some other developing nations, has been one of the most wanted and desired destinations for investors across the world and is being considered as one of the world's most lucrative retailing destinations.

This is because of the following reasons:

- Availability of cheap labor
- Uninterrupted availability of raw material
- Less production cost compared with other developed countries
- Quick and easy market penetration

The retail sector in particular has witnessed a constant buzz and excitement surrounding government policy to reframe and revisit the policy framework. With the upsurge of organized retailing and e-retailing, India's retail sector is on its way to modernization. Traditional markets are making way for new formats such as departmental stores, supermarkets and specialty stores, and e-tailers (see Figure 1.5). Westernized malls providing with world-class products, international brands, elegant ambience and professional sales associates, and value-added services can be seen coming up in metros and Tier II cities, introducing the Indian consumer to an implausible shopping experience.

The Government of India, through its reforms in FDI for retailing, seems to be repositioning the Indian retail sector on the global map to attract investments. India categorizes retail trading into single-brand retail trading (SBRT) and multi-brand retail trading (MBRT). Currently, FDI under SBRT is permitted to the extent of 100% and FDI under MBRT is permitted to the extent of 51% with some conditions applied and subject to government approval. While the FDI policy for SBRT has received encouraging and positive response, the FDI policy for MBRT has been sluggish to gain the traction among international retailers. According to the Department of Industrial Policy & Promotion (DIPP), the Indian retail industry in the single-brand segment received FDI equity inflows to the tune of US$275.38 million in the period April 2000–January 2015.

The government recently reiterated the present position that nonresident entities can undertake SBRT business in India, but clarified that such entities can do so through one or more wholly owned subsidiaries (WOSs) or JVs. Also, in the financial budget of 2016–17, the Government of India expanded the FDI policy by opening up the door for the food sector (processed food) to 100% FDI for multi-brand retailers via the Foreign Investment Promotion Board (FIPB) route, provided food products are produced and manufactured in India. The existing rule on FDI in multi-brand retailing of any product mandates that, at least 30% of raw materials have to be sourced from the domestic market. However, in the case of food processing, a foreign retailer is mandated to procure 100% of raw materials from domestic sources to be eligible to bring in

Single-brand retail trading (SBRT) and exclusive brand outlets (EBOs)	Multi-brand retail trading (MBRT)
Exclusive showrooms either owned or franchised out by the manufacturer.	Focus on particular product categories and carry most of the brands available
A complete range of all the products/brands manufactured by the said manufacturer under one brand name.	Almost all brands are available for a single product type and the focus is on the diverse nature of product.
For example, exclusive showroom/franchise outlets of Louis Phillipe, Van Heusen, Allen Solly, Cotton King, Levi's, Peter England, and GAP	Customers have more choice as many brands are available in the store
	For example, Shoppers Stop, Lifestyle, Central, and Pantaloon

RETAIL FORMATS

Convergence retail outlet	E-retailers
Display most of the categories ranging from grocery, vegetables, and fruits as well as consumer goods, FMCG products, electronics, and white goods, etc.	It is online shopping facility for buying and selling products and services.
The focus is on the diverse nature of consumer needs.	Near about all types of product categories and all brands are available with e-retailers. Some e-retailers deals in specialized products or services.
One-stop shop for many customers; many product lines of different brands are available in store.	For example, Flipkart, Snapdeal, Amazon, and Myntra
For example, Big Bazaar, Easy Day, D-Mart etc.	

Figure 1.5: *Different Formats in Business of Retailing*

100% FDI. If a foreign retailer doesn't wish to source the entire raw material from the domestic market for multi-brand retailing in processed food products, it can still set up a retail outlet. However, in such a case, the FDI will be restricted to 51% only. Hence, this policy is formulated in order to address the concerns of stakeholders by obligating the foreign players to buy the entire produce from Indian farmers.

This essentially means that foreign (or say, global) retailers (such as Walmart, Marks and Spencer (M&S), Tesco, and so on) who are in the business of multi-brand processed food retailing can set up retail outlets in the country, but they will have to sell food products manufactured by Indian producers. Previously, with the FDI in MBRT being permitted to the extent of 51% only; foreign retailers had to partner (by forging JVs) with local companies to launch their operations in India or their operations have so far been limited to the business-to-business (B2B) segment in India, selling products to organizations, businesses, and institutions.

The chief financial officials (CFOs) in the Indian retail sector trust that the below mentioned moves can be some of the changes which could bring desired momentum to FDI in retailing:

- Allowing FDI in B2C online retail and increasing FDI cap in the MBRT
- Clarity on provisions of sourcing
- Revisiting and clarity on investment in back end
- Limiting the role of the state

There is a major division on the opinion on the impact on the growth of organized retail in the country. But there is no doubt on the role that FDI—has played and can play—in supplementing domestic resources and in ensuring employment generation, which eventually acts toward the development of an economy. However, still there is an extended way to go before FDI in Indian retail can be realized in its totality.

However, if we think from a different angle, we find that we need to brush up our domestic staffing in retail stores, especially considering the fact that international retailers bring more refined global experience to our country in order to lure and satisfy the end consumers in a better way. So here the major concern is whether the industry is ready to deal with the demands and challenges that retail would bring with global expansion. This means that the demand for the experienced professionals having exposure to international way of retailing is high. One thing we must mention here is that the Indian professionals have good knowledge about Indian consumers and their consumption patterns. Thus, the clause of only 51% for FDI in MBRT (with the exception of multi-brand retailing of processed food products that are produced and manufactured in India for which 100% FDI is allowed through FIPB) makes it essential to forge alliance between international and domestic retail companies. This combination creates the amalgamation of know-how of international retail operations with the knowledge of Indian consumer behavior and consumption pattern, brought in by Indian professionals.

Foreign Direct Investment in India

FDI comes to India in two ways.

To tap the unprecedented growth of retail sector, major players like large industrial houses and MNCs have entered this area, and they have expansion and collaboration plans with big Indian partners, owing to the nature of Indian retail market.

1. Direct route/automatic route: It does not require prior approval either of Reserve Bank of India (RBI) or the government.
2. Government route: Government route means that investment in the capital of resident entities by nonresident entities can be made only with the prior approval from FIPB.

Regarding the FDI policy on SBRT, the DIPP has clarified that FDI policy on SBRT equally applies to Indian brands (and foreign brands) seeking foreign investment. Under the policy, 100% foreign investment is allowed in SBRT, of which 49% is through the automatic route, and proposals above that ceiling require government (FIPB) approval. (This simply means, while 100% FDI is allowed in SBRT, proposals beyond 49% require prior approval from the government.)

The DIPP statement also reiterate that a nonresident entity or entities, whether or not the brand owner, can undertake "SBRT" for the specific brand, directly or through a legal agreement with the brand owner. This allows single-brand retailers to operate in multiple formats, such as their own outlets, franchise stores, and wholesale.

Nevertheless, the clarification is without injustice to other conditions, which include the condition that in proposals involving FDI beyond 51%, sourcing of 30% of the value of goods purchased need to be from India, "preferably" from micro, small, and medium enterprises (MSMEs), village and cottage industries, and artisans and craftsmen, in all sectors. Here, government has eased the norms by asking foreign single-brand firms to source 30% from India, while replacing the word "mandatory" by more generous "preferably." However, retail trading by means of e-commerce would not be permissible for companies with FDI engaged in SBRT.

These policy measures have sorted out many issues (owing to the stiff riders in the policy) of single-brand retailers by fulfilling their demand to relax the "mandatory" 30% sourcing norms and allowing their own outlet and franchising, as they wanted to run company-owned direct retail outlets as well as franchise outlets, which happened after government has clarified that the nonresident entity/entities will now be allowed to undertake SBRT business through "one or more WOSs or JVs." So with these policy relaxations, there are huge chances of many single-brand retailers—such as Tommy Hilfiger, Hennes & Mauritz (H&M), Swarovski, Skechers, Adidas, and Nike, among other marquee international brands—to enter the Indian market, as government is allowing them to operate across multiple platforms.

Hence, there exists a huge untapped opportunity in the retail sector, thus having vast scope for new entrants, driving large investments into the country. A good talent pool, huge markets, and availability of raw materials at comparatively cheaper costs are expected to make India lead as one of the world's best retail economies. Nevertheless, retailers need to take cognizance of the fact that both back-end and front-end operations require investment and hence requires to be developed in a way appropriate to their overall business operations. Allowing the FDI in retail sector brings greater challenges also, for both existing and potential market players alike. To address these challenges, retailers have to adapt to the new market realities, galvanize its supply chains, leverage the core competencies, and tactically counter its competitors in a competitive and sustainable way.

SWOT Analysis of Foreign Direct Investment in Retailing Sector

There are relation and linkages among critical parameters like growing consumerism, economic development, proliferation of branded products, rise in per capita income, and retail modernization. The high economic growth leads to the rise in per capita income, which in turn influences and alters the consumption pattern. With the proliferation and persistence of liberalization and globalization, various international retailer brands enter the different regional and national economies. This eventually results in the augmentation of awareness level of consumers, as they incline to experiment with different products and brands. This proliferation of brands leads to increase in demand, thereby raising the demand of the retail space. Thus, retail modernization is a crucial part of the economic development process. So this requires a strategic approach toward the formulation the FDI policies and deep consideration to whole lot of environmental factors, both internal and external. Hence in any strategic planning process, two factors, namely internal and external environmental factors, play an important role. A comprehensive and pragmatic inspection of these factors is imperative for arriving at the final structure of the planning process.

The internal environmental factors can be classified as strengths and weaknesses. While the factors that are external to the sector can be classified as opportunities and threats. Hence, the strategic analysis of environmental factors is referred as SWOT analysis. This analysis provides the strategic inputs and vital information that is very useful in understanding the retail sector resource mobilization and capabilities to the competitive environment in which it operates. Finally, this analysis will be instrumental in formulation of strategies for future growth and development of the sector.

Strengths

- Boost up competition: Inviting and welcoming the FDI in retail industry can prove advantageous for India as it will increase the competition in retail players in domestic market. It is one of the striking characteristics of competition; it demands efficiency, effectiveness, differentiation, and innovation, which eventually results in reduction of cost, price, and continuous improvement in quality of products. So as the competition increases, the competitors are compelled to serve the quality of products at competitive and reasonable price points with better shopping experience in the case of business of retailing.
- JVs with deep-pocketed multinational players act as a rich financial resource for the existing domestic organized retailers.
- Benefits to consumers: Consumer will get more varieties and assortments of products at competitive prices as compared to the regular market prices. They will have more choices and options and can get many international brands under one roof. This will ultimately increase the purchasing power of the consumers and will improve their standard of living.
- Benefits to farmers: In most of the cases, in the business of retailing, the intermediaries have dominated the interface between the manufacturers or producers and the end consumers. Hence, the farmers and manufacturers lose their margins as the major share is eaten up by these intermediaries. This issue can be resolved by FDI, as farmers can sell their produce directly to the retailers or might get contract farming where they might supply to a retailer based upon demand and can reap good margins.
- Generate employment opportunities: Retail industry is a workforce-intensive sector. The domestic retail sector is increasing providing vast job opportunities. A brick-and-mortar retailer requires huge manpower to perform different jobs and operations like in-store jobs, customer service, jobs in back-end warehousing, and logistics.
- Large-scale investments: It has also contributed to large-scale investments in the real estate sector with major national and global players investing in devolving the infrastructure and construction of the retailing spaces.

Weaknesses

- Lack of infrastructure: Lack of efficient infrastructure has been one of the major issues of concern that has led the process to an incompetent market mechanism. For example, though India is one of the largest producers of vegetables and fruits, lack of efficient logistics infrastructure and insufficient penetration of resources like cold storage has considerably affected the retailing of these perishable items. Higher FDI in such sectors can help India address such issues by channelizing the resources in the right manner.
- High retail real estate rentals: Though we can see that the Indian economy is growing at a fast rate compared to that of other developing nations, and the urbanization is also growing phenomenon, it is also true that this development is not inclusive. While the urban area is developing with a fast rate, the growth of small town and rural areas is very sluggish. This has resulted in the concentration of population in urban areas and has resulted in phenomenal rise in property prices, and retail real estate rentals have escalated significantly. This has substantially increased the investment required in the business, which eventually affects the profitability of the business.

- Also there is scarcity of right retail sites that are desired by high-end retailers. For such retailers, it is imperative to be very cautious while selection of the site and location for their store as it is closely related to the image of their brand. While for the big-box retail formats such as supermarkets and hypermarkets, a big store size is required and also should be at the location that is convenient to the target audience. In the congested cities, it becomes very challenging for these retailers to identify and acquire such sites and operate the store with desired profitability.

- Threat for retailers: Though the permission of 51% FDI is MBRT, implementation of any business format will be potentially troublesome for the retailers. The biggest challenge is restrictions posed by unwillingness of the state governments in order to get political mileage. One cannot deny the possibility of states going against the policy with the shift in ruling party that opposes FDI. Such volatile political situations cannot bring positive sentiments among the international players.

- FDI policy expansion of 2016 that allows 100% FDI in multi-brand retailing of processed food products with given riders may prove beneficial to Indian retail chains (such as Reliance, D-Mart, Future Group, and so on) by operating food-only stores. However, there exists a possibility that it may not benefit the foreign supermarket majors (such as Walmart, M&S, Tesco, and so on) to the same extent, as they might not opt to change their international format to sell processed food products only. Hence, this may act as a discouraging factor for these foreign players to set up shops in India. But, at the same time, we cannot deny the possibility that these multinational retailing chains could set up food-only outlets.

Opportunities

- Improving merchandising, inventory management and warehousing, and distribution ecosystem: The operational expertise and technological know-how from global retailing firms in the functions such as merchandising management, inventory management, warehousing, and distribution lend itself to continuous improvement in the merchandising and integrated SCM, which are the crucial components of business of retailing. For example, we can see that the proportion of wastage of food items is very high in India, which is only because of lack of efficient distribution and logistics infrastructure. This eventually results in rise in inflation (increase prices of food items) due to the shortage of supply through abundance in availability. Here both the farmers who produce it and the consumers who consume have to suffer the losses.

- So allowing for 100% FDI in the MBRT of domestically processed food (in the financial budget of 2016–17) is expected to give farmers greater access to the market and will also encourage food processing firms to innovate.

  The objectives of this FDI policy expansion are to:

  1. Encourage big multi-national retail chains in the food and food processing sectors to set up outlets in India, enable them to create back-end infrastructure (like cold chains), and bring in the latest technology to the farm sector.
  2. Reduce wastage, improve efficiency of farming, provide an assured market to farmers, help farmers realize better prices, increase income of farmers, and control food inflation.
  3. Enable farm diversification and encourage global giants to produce locally rather than importing items, which is in line with the government's Make in India initiative.

- This far-reaching reform is not only expected to give impetus to the food processing industry but also benefit farmers, and create new employment opportunities.

- Indian multi-brand retail chains are in a better position to attract foreign capital in the food segment. Hence, 100% FDI in food processing retail can give some kind of a level-playing field to brick-and-mortar players vis-à-vis their online competition.

- As multinational players are expanding their operation, domestic players are also building a robust supply chain, devising strategies to differentiate, and improving their operations to counter the international players. All these efforts will encourage the investment and generate higher employment in logistics and SCM.

- The inflow of FDI in retail sector will provide the financial resources for development of the delivery and supply chain ecosystem, infuse technological advancements, enhancing production and manufacturing possibilities and influx of capital flows, which in turn assist in maintaining general macroeconomic stability.

- The entry of new players and investors increases the healthy competition, which eventually results in the improved quality standards and also the cost-competitiveness. With this, consumers get better quality, shopping experience, service, and selection of products at competitive prices.

- However, the industry lacks the talent pool with required skill sets to leverage this huge potential of retail industry for generating employment, and this presents good opportunity for employment in training and development. The training and development personnel in retail organizations, or associated with other institutions, can play a crucial role to cross-train and build a retail-ready workforce.

- The growth of retail industry with the influx of FDI leads to creation of more job opportunities. This also opens new avenues and new markets for the small and medium enterprises (SMEs), village and cottage industries, artisans and craftsmen, in all sectors, and other budding entrepreneurs in way of greater market reach, professional marketing, and SCM support.

Threats

- Loss in employment: There is another school of thought that debate on the issue of employment and job losses. The retailing sector of India is still controlled by unorganized players as over 90% of the retail industry is still unorganized. So the entry of big giants of retail industry like Walmart may put an adverse impact on the business of these independent, unorganized stores or may even compel them to close their business, which will directly lead to massive job losses as there number is very high in India.

- Sustaining of loss strategy: Another threat and challenge Indian companies and some business experts perceive is the sustaining of the loss by initially reducing the price to penetrate and capture the market, a usual strategy and tactic adopted by big players. With their scale and financial capacity, they can easily afford to reduce the prices in initial stages in order to triumph over the competition and wash them out to become a monopoly power. Once they capture the market, they may raise the prices and drive the market on their own terms. It would lead to very inequitable or unbalanced competition and eventually result in large-scale exit of small and medium-sized domestic retailers, especially the small family-managed outlets, resulting in large-scale displacement of people employed in and dependent on the retail sector.

- Such kind of monopolistic powers are harmful not only to the consumers but also for their suppliers. Because such situations will give a very strong bargaining power to these big players, and they can put a huge pressure on the suppliers/vendors, compressing their margins.

- As these players are foreign players, this kind of situation will result in the repatriation of profits outside India, affecting the economy adversely.

- It would lead to asymmetrical growth, which is always harmful to the inclusive development and will cause social discontent and economic inequality. Such kind of market volatility, imbalance, and instability is very corrosive for the culturally and socially diverse country like India.
- One another viewpoint on this issue is that the Indian retail sector, particularly organized retail, is still not fully matured; it is still undersized and in a nascent stage. So it is essential that the domestic retail sector is to be allowed to nurture and strengthen first, before fully opening this sector to foreign investors.
- The frequently expressed fear of those against FDI in retail is that international retailers will dump cheap and substandard merchandise produced in China and elsewhere. However, one cannot deny the fact that such cheap and poor-quality merchandise is indeed being imported or smuggled into India. Such substandard and spurious merchandise is then retailed through the unorganized retail ecosystem, which is causing a significant loss to the exchequer of customs duties while making the unwary consumers buy poor-quality merchandise.

Importance of Indian Retail Market for the International Players

The Indian retail sector has come off age and has gone through major transformation over the last decade with a considerable shift toward organized retailing. With over 92% business coming from the fragmented unorganized sector, such as traditional family-run mom-and-pop stores and corner stores, the Indian retail sector offers huge potential for growth and consolidation. In India, the consumer market has hit a tipping point, and when we try to position at scale, India is the biggest market next to China. We have 100 million-plus consumers with a single-law ecosystem, a single currency, and while also relatively low on technology adoption. This is driving the investor ecosystem, and those who missed the boat in China are looking to capture the market in India.

A.T. Kearney, a US-based global management consulting firm, has ranked India as the fourth most attractive nation for retail investment among 30 flourishing markets. Favorable demographics, increasing urbanization, increasing number of nuclear families, rising affluence amid consumers, growing preference for branded products, and higher aspirations are other factors that will drive retail consumption in India. Union Minister of Commerce and Industry, Government of India, has stressed on India building a culture of branding and marketing its products to the rest of the world. The ministry is also willing to take steps to start a free trade agreement (FTA) with the European Union (EU).

Opportunities

- 100% FDI in single-brand retail
- 51% FDI in multi-brand retail (with the exception of multi-brand retailing of processed food products that are produced and manufactured in India)
- Liberalization policy of allowing 100% overseas capital in multi-brand processed food retailing through approval from the FIPB

Key Drivers

- In the case of single-brand retailing, proposals involving FDI beyond 51% stipulate mandatory 30% of sourcing from India, "preferably" from MSMEs, village and cottage industries, artisans, and craftsmen.

- Out of the first US$100 billion investment—50% should be utilized for back-end infrastructure.
- In the case of multi-brand retailing of processed food products, a foreign retailer is mandated to procure 100% of raw materials from domestic sources to be eligible to bring in 100% FDI. Hence, this is applicable as long as the food products are sourced and manufactured within India and subject to the approval from the FIPB.

Expected High Growth Rate Categories

- Apparel retailing
- Luxury retailing
- Food and grocery retailing

The Government of India has taken various initiatives to improve the retail industry in India. Some of these initiatives are:

- The FIPB has cleared five retail proposals from companies such as Bestseller, Puma SE, and Flemingo. Additionally, the board cleared three 100% single-brand retail proposals worth US$35.77 million, suggesting renewed interest in India's growing retail market.
- IKEA has entered into a memorandum of understanding (MoU) with the Government of Telangana to set up its first store in India at Hyderabad. The Swedish home furnishing retailer has announced the purchase of its first land parcel to build retail stores in Hyderabad. The IKEA Group is the first major single-brand retailer to get FDI approval in India and plans to open several stores in Delhi NCR, Hyderabad, Karnataka, and Maharashtra. IKEA retail outlets have a standard design, and each location entails an investment of over ₹500 crore.
- The Government of India is also in the final phase of talks with the states for the GST Bill to be implemented. This bill is seen as a key to facilitating industrial growth and improving the business climate in the country.
  (Government of India has proposed GST under which taxes on interstate supply of goods and services would go to the consuming state. Once implemented, it will simplify the supply chain and bring down cost/price. The GST was originally proposed to be introduced with effect from April 2010 but yet to be rolled out. Difference in opinion among states, insistence of states on commitment of the federal government to compensate for possible revenue losses, coverage of specific products, and procedural delays together with consensus on the Constitutional Amendment Bill are the major impediments that are delaying the introduction of GST in the country.)

IKEA Group is looking toward India as a promising market. The Swedish retailer is exploring opportunity to source, retail, conduct CSR initiatives through IKEA Foundation and empower social entrepreneurs through next-generation projects. IKEA has been sourcing from India for the last 28 years and planning to double its sourcing volumes by 2020. By all these initiatives, IKEA is essentially in the process to bring a unique shopping experience through their inspiring stores offering affordable home furnishing products.

Following IKEA, another Swedish chain, H&M, has made a big-bang entry and opened its first store in the country at Select Citywalk Mall, Delhi, in October 2015. Its traditional rival, Zara, which is another European (Spain-based) fast fashion brand, entered Indian retail landscape through the JV with Tata Group's Trent. Globally, H&M and Zara are competing for the first position. While H&M has moved into Zara's domain of fast fashion by churning out new styles and bringing them to the stores in record time, Zara has responded by creating an affordable line to match H&M's price points.

Gap, one of the world largest fashion brand by sales, entered India in May 2015. Zara has become the first brand in India to cross US$100 million sales mark. In North America, both H&M and Inditex's Zara are giving tough fight to the US-based Gap. Along with India, the H&M is also expanding its presence in China and USA. Once a top fashion retailer for teenagers and young adults, Gap's position and popularity has been challenged by Zara and H&M, which offer fast fashion and trendy cloths for less.

In its international expansion spree, H&M is also focused on e-tailing and has gone online in Romania, Poland, Portugal, the Czech Republic, Hungary, Slovakia, Belgium, and Bulgaria, among others.

Besides this, the Indian luxury consumer landscape is witnessing strong evolutionary undercurrents that are reshaping the consumer profile and the way luxury players operate in the space. Several luxury brands such as Gucci, LVMH, Jimmy Choo, and Gap are increasing their presence in the luxury malls, high streets, and airports. Though these players continue to expand their presence cautiously, this is attributed to the growing sense of buoyancy and optimism about the future potential of the Indian luxury market supported by favorable regulatory environment and FDI rules. Liberalization of FDI policy in retail sector could further provide impetus to the entry of large international retailers. The first movers are expected to be international retailers in the single-brand retail across the categories such as fashion/apparel, luxury watches and shoes, followed by international multi-brand retailers in categories across food, grocery, and home furnishing, where there are the large domestic counterparts who are keen to look at JVs and tie-ups.

Summary

1. Organized retail is emerging as the new phenomenon in India, and despite the slump, the market is growing exponentially.
2. As economic growth brings more of India's people into the consuming classes, organized retail lures more and more existing shoppers.
3. Consumer markets in emerging market economies like India are growing rapidly owing to the healthy economic growth.
4. The growing middle class is an important factor contributing to the growth of retail in India.
5. Hence, with this huge potential and large population, India is set for high growth in consumer expenditure.
6. With India's large "young" population and high domestic consumption, the macro trends for the sector look favorable.
7. Both organized and unorganized retail players should work together to improve the overall retail industry, while generating new benefits for their own customers and for better prospects of this industry, as a whole.
8. The share of e-commerce is growing steadily and has presented the customers with an ever-increasing choice of products at the lowest rates.

9. E-commerce is probably creating the biggest disruption in the retail industry, and this trend will continue in the years to come as almost everything is sold on the Internet at present.

10. This means that pretty much all of the retail industry faces the challenge of either being a part of e-commerce or taking it head-on.

11. Opportunities and ways are available for brick-and-mortar retailers to take advantage of the digital retail channels (e-commerce), which would enable them to spend less money on real estate while reaching more customers in Tier II and Tier III cities.

12. Nevertheless, the long-term outlook for the industry remains to be positive on the back of rising incomes, favorable demographics, entry of foreign players, and increasing urbanization.

Review Questions

1. Analyze the nature and importance of retailing in India with a critical approach.
2. Explain VMS in detail with appropriate example and practical illustrations.
3. "The phenomenal upsurge of e-commerce has changed the face of retail industry." Explain this statement in the context of strategic retail marketing management with appropriate examples.
4. Explain how the demographic factors of India are creating huge opportunity for retail players.
5. How the demography of India presents huge opportunities for retail industry and which are those factors that are acting as limitations. Explain in detail.
6. How will you look toward the retail industry in the context of its employment generation potential from various viewpoints?
7. How will you analyze the Indian retail industry by using the tool of SWOT analysis? Suggest some innovations that you think should be implemented in order to fill the gaps in the regulatory policies.
8. What is FDI? What can be the impact of FDI in retail industry on the retailing ecosystem of India?
9. How will you do a critical analysis of FDI policies for single-brand (with riders) and multi-brand policies with their implications?
10. Explain the significance of Indian retail market for international retail players with appropriate examples.
11. Write short notes on:

    • Vertical marketing system
    • Retailer in distribution channel
    • New trends in retailing
    • Significance of Indian retail market for international players
    • Current FDI policies for SBRT and MBRT
    • SWOT analysis of Indian retail industry

Topics for Group Discussion

- Is FDI in retail sector good for India?
- FDI in retail sector will increase employment or it will leave the small retailers unemployed?
- FDI in retailing a bane or a boon.
- The condition of 30% sourcing preferably from the SMEs regarding the FDI in single-brand retailing. Discuss with multidimensional viewpoints.

Chapter 2

Retail Formats and Classification of Retailers

Introduction

In the business of retailing, organizations adopt several varieties of channels, shapes, and sizes. We have discussed the meaning and process of retailing in the very first chapter. The objective of this chapter is to capture the diversity of the retail industry in terms of the variety of store formats that are followed in the business of retailing. In Indian scenario, formats have been found to be influencing the choice of store as well as orientation of the shoppers. Also, retailers are experimenting with alternate format with differing success rates. Retail outlets essentially differ in terms of the:

- Ownership of the retail business itself, the characteristics of the premises.
- Infrastructure, ambience, and so on (the format).
- The orientation of the merchandise portfolio and range.
- Service-level and pricing considerations.

While some types and formats of retailing are centuries old; the new kinds of retail outlets have emerged and are developing with technological advancement, proliferation of globalization, changing consumer behavior, and their increased expectations. These new formats are constantly evolving to offer a better shopping experience to the consumers.

Retail Formats

Hence, retail format is basically the store "package" that the retailer offers to the target audience. Retail players are categorized on the basis of different retail formats that are essentially based on the retail operation. These formats are mainly defined on the basis of the size of the store, the type of merchandise sold, the pricing strategy followed, and also the location. Thus, a format is defined as a type of retail mix that is followed or used by a set of retailers that offers some unique benefit that helps in attracting shoppers. It is the mix of variables that retailers use to develop their business strategies and constitute the mix as merchandise assortment, pricing, transactional convenience, preferential approach, channel, experience, and the overall business model. Hence, a format is essentially the retailing model for delivering the value promised to the customers so as to create an SCA. It is generally observed that customers prefer different formats for their different needs, but sometimes they also do the cross-buying. While books are increasingly being bought through online portals, grocery and food items are purchased at store-based formats. Many times, shoppers buy similar kind of merchandise through separate formats. For instance, for buying apparels and fashion merchandise, consumers not only prefer brick-and-mortar department stores but also online fashion retailers. This happens because while off-line department stores allow them to feel, touch, and try the merchandise, online fashion retailers higher selection and convenience of shopping. Hence, it can be observed that, with availability of more and more choices, customers try to optimize the value derived and hence split their shopping across different formats. However, it is also true that some shoppers patronize one of the formats and prefer to do most of their shopping from that format. It is, therefore, essential that a retailer should select the value and then choose the "format or formats" that deliver the value to the fullest.

Thus, before finalizing on the format selection, retailers evaluate the enablers and deterrents in the retail marketplace. Deterrents consist of variables that would hamper the smooth operation and growth of the format in a specific marketplace. This primarily involves identifying the key drivers of growth, the shoppers' profile, and shoppers' expectations and preferences. It also means evaluating the nature of competition and challenges in the marketplace. Here the retailer decides the elements of the retail mix to satisfy the target markets' needs more effectively and efficiently than its competitors.

The choice of retail mix elements enables the retailer to:

- Decide the type, design, and structure of selected format or combination of formats.
- Select the retail value proposition that the store would like to offer to shoppers (unique value the format is offering) (Figure 2.1).

Retailers develop a mix by using the following elements, essentially based on the value identified and the environmental factors.

Variety and Assortment of Merchandise

- Variety is the number of different merchandise categories a retailer offers.
- Assortment is the number of different items a retailer offers in a specific merchandise category.
- SKU is nothing but a single unit of each different kind of merchandise.

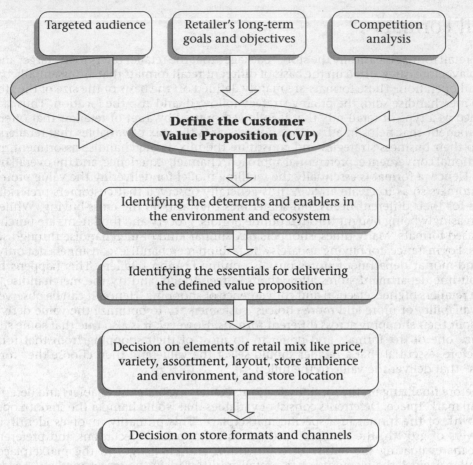

Figure 2.1: *Retail Format Selection Process*

For example, department stores, a category killer, and online stores all sell apparels. However, department stores sell many other categories of merchandise in addition to apparels, so here they have a greater variety. The category killer (or say specialty store) sells only one or very few category (say denim jeans), necessarily stocks more assortments of this category, and hence more SKUs. They carry more designs, almost all brands, sizes, colors, patterns, and so on, and hence deeper assortments than general retailers such as department or discount stores, while online retailers can offer a huge selection across the categories at various price points.

Other elements are store ambience—atmosphere and amenities provided, pricing considerations, customer service level, and location preferences. Besides all these factors, the major transformation the retail industry has witnessed is growing tendency of off-line retailers embracing the online retailing channels, and vice versa is also true. The reason for going the hybrid or omni-channel way is the huge growth of e-commerce and changing consumer behavior and shopping preference. Brick-and-mortar retailers have taken cognizance of the online model's ability to reach wider customer base across the geographies with comparatively very less investment. This would never have been achievable in a pure off-line retailing model. On the other hand, online retailing model also want to offer coherent shopping experience to their targeted audience by adding certain feature to the shopping experience that are otherwise not possible with pure-play online model. The major macroeconomic driver of this phenomenon is a young demographic supported by Internet penetration, rising income levels, growing adoption of smartphones/mobile devices, and growing aspirations. In addition, at an individual level, greater access to a wide range of merchandise (especially beyond the major cities) and convenience (access at the click of a button), which is supported by the options like COD payment model, have been the key online (both through desktop and mobile) shopping adoption trigger. This synergy has prompted many brick-and-mortar retailers to tie up with online players to widen their reach. The off-line retailers can leverage their "physical" assets to develop and build strong "clicks and bricks" retailing models that are able to deliver flawless shopping experience across multiple channels (omni-channel strategy) that eventually build and strengthen the customer loyalty.

For example, department store chain Shoppers Stop entered into an exclusive strategic partnership with e-retailer Snapdeal to expedite its omni-channel strategy. Though Shoppers Stop already has its own e-commerce shopping portal, they would have reached out to a small segment. However, this strategic association with well-established marketplace model of Snapdeal helps Shoppers Stop to reach a wider audience by adding newer markets across geographies. This tie-up gives not only a pan-Indian reach to Shoppers Stop but also an opportunity to design and develop omni-channel shopping experience. Customers can buy the merchandise on Shoppers Stop's online store on Snapdeal and pick up the merchandise at Shoppers Stop's off-line store or can get it delivered at their home from the nearest Shoppers Stop brick-and-mortar outlet. This synergistic partnership brings Snapdeal's market reach and technology together with the power of Shoppers Stop as a brand on its marketplace. Snapdeal also hosts online retailing model of Tata-owned Croma. Similarly, Future Group as part of their omni-channel strategy has an exclusive partnership with Amazon, intended to leverage multiple channels such as web, mobile, or brick-and-mortar stores.

However, this kind of off-line and online retail collaboration requires meticulous consideration for pricing and merchandising management for prevention of any kind of cannibalization. This may happen because the company is now operating through multiple retailing formats such as off-line stores, own online portal, and presence on the marketplace model of other retailer. So the brands that the retailer sells through its online and off-line model generally have separate listing on the marketplace model also. Here, there is a possibility of duplication of brands, perhaps with different price tags. These kinds of situations may confuse the customer or the customer may end up shopping at the lowest price, which may eventually lead to loss of business in the form of cannibalization (gain of one model of the retailer at the cost of its other model).

Classification of Retailers

The term "retail institution" refers to the basic format design or structure of a business. Classification for retail institutions is necessary to enable firms to better understand and enact upon their own strategies: selecting an organizational mission, choosing an ownership alternative, defining the goods/service category, marketing/branding strategies, and setting objectives and goals.

Table 2.1 shows a breakdown of each category. The classification is not mutually exclusive; that is, an institution may be correctly placed in more than one category. For example, a department store unit may be part of a fashion retailer chain, have a store-based strategy, and also have online presence or a hybrid channel.

Table 2.1: *Classification and Type of Retail Formats*

Classification of Retailers	Types of Retailers	
Ownership based	Independent	
	Retail chains	
	Franchise	
	Leased department	
	Vertical marketing system	
	Consumer cooperative	
Store based	Convenience stores	Food-based retailers
	Conventional supermarket	
	Food-based superstores	
	Combination stores	
	Box stores (limited-line stores)	
	Warehouse stores	
	Specialty stores	General merchandising
	Variety stores	
	Department store	
	Full-line discount store	
	Off-price chain	
	Factory outlet	
	Membership club	
	Flea market	
Non-store based	Direct selling	
	Telephonic selling	
	Vending machine	
	Television retailing	
	E-retailing	
	Mobile retailing	

Ownership Based

Retailing is one of the few sectors in our economy where entrepreneurial activity is extensive and increasing. Although retailers are primarily small (approximately 80% of all stores are operated by firms with one outlet and over one-half of all firms have two or fewer paid employees), there are also very large retailers.

Retail firms may be independently owned, chain owned, franchisee operated, leased departments, owned by manufacturers or wholesalers, or consumer owned. From the positioning and operating perspective, each ownership format delivers unique value. Retail executives need to work on the strengths and weaknesses inherent in each of these formats to be successful.

Independents

Independents typically are individual (sole) traders, or family-run business operation that owns a single retail unit or may be few times a network of less than 10 branch outlets. Most of the independents are run entirely by the owners and/or their families and may not have paid staff. The high number of independent retailers is associated with the ease of entry into the marketplace, owing to low capital requirement and no or relatively simple licensing procedures. These stores may offer a specialized product range with very narrow variety such as unbranded garments or may be a wide variety of miscellaneous product items, for instance, a grocery and general merchandise shop in a village. The ease of entry into retailing is reflected in the low market shares of the leading firms in many goods/service categories as a percentage of total category sales. However, most of these outlets are basic mom-and-pop stores with very basic offerings, fixed prices, and no ambience. These are highly competitive stores due to cheap land prices and labor.

Due to relative ease of entry into retailing, there is a great deal of competition, resulting in the high rate of retail business failures among new firms.

These stores have a great deal of flexibility in choosing retail formats and locations. They target smaller consumer segments rather than the mass markets. At first, as only one store location is involved, detailed specifications can be set for determining best location, product assortments, prices, store running hours, and other factors consistent and relevant with their target segment. Second, they have low investments in terms of lease, fixtures, workers, and merchandise. Third, independents often act as specialists and acquire skills and expertise in a niche for a particular goods/service category. Decision-making in these stores is usually centralized as the owner operator is typically at the premises, having a full decision-making authority, a strong entrepreneurial drive, and commitment as they have personal investment in the business. Hence, success or failure has huge implications, and there is a lot of ego involvement. They are consistent in their efforts as they generally adopt just a single strategy.

There are some disadvantages and challenges the independent retailers have to face.

1. They have limited bargaining power with suppliers as they often buy in small quantities.
2. Reordering may be tough, if minimum order requirements are too high for them to qualify.

To overcome this problem, a number of independents form buying groups to increase the bargaining power. Due to low economies in buying and maintaining inventory, the transportation, ordering, and handling costs are higher. These stores often have operations that are labor intensive, sometimes with little or no automation or computerization (typically observed in the markets of developing countries). Ordering, taking inventory, marking items, ringing up sales, and bookkeeping may be done manually as most independents tend to find investment in technology and training not feasible. Compared to other formats, independents incur high costs of advertising due to limited access to advertising media and may pay higher amounts compared to regular users. There is often disruption when the owner is ill, on vacation, on a work break, or retires. They can allocate limited amount of time and resources toward long-term planning. To offset these disadvantages of economies, they offer complementary merchandise and services. Often while all stores in the chain offer the same merchandise, independents can provide merchandise compatible with and preferred by the local market needs.

Retail Chains

A chain retailer operates multiple outlets (store units) under a common brand name or banner. Most "high street" retailers fall into the category of the retail chains that are also called as multiple retailers. This terminology is applied to retail organizations that have a centralized operations and presence at multiple locations across a nation, region, or continents through branch outlets. These outlets are essentially operated under a common brand and ownership. Retail chains can range from two stores to the retailers having over 1,000 outlets. Some retail chains are divisions or under the SBUs of larger corporations or holding companies. Private chain retailers are often family-owned and family-run businesses, and allow for a higher degree of personal operational control than in a publicly owned business.

Chain retailers have several advantages. They enjoy strong bargaining power with suppliers due to the volumes of purchases. They generally bypass wholesalers and directly negotiate with the manufactures. Most of the items are directly procured from the manufacturers. Suppliers service the orders from chains promptly and extend a higher level of service and after-sales support. New brands/designs/categories reach these stores faster. Most of these chains sell PLBs. Chains achieve efficiency due to the centralization of purchasing and warehousing and atomization of the systems and processes. Wider geographic coverage of markets allows chains to utilize all forms of media right from television to social media. These retail chains invest considerable time and resources in long-term planning and monitoring opportunities, countering emerging challenges and threats.

Chain retailers many times face the challenges of limited flexibility, as they need to be consistent and uniform throughout in terms of formats, ambient factors, prices, promotions, product assortments, and VM principles and practices. Chain retailers are bound to have high investments in multiple leases, strategic prime locations, fixtures, product assortments, and employees. Due to their widespread availability, these retailers need to implement effective and efficient systems and processes to ensure control, better communication, and timely deliveries. Hence, such retailers focus on managing a specific retail format for a better strategic advantage and increased profitability. Some chain retailers capitalize on their widely known brand image and adopt flexibility to current market scenario.

Franchising

Franchising is basically a business format that is widely used in retailing. Large retail corporations often use this format or channel to scale their geographical presence and penetration through partner organizations that are offered franchise rights to run the organization's business with their brand name and business style. Hence, franchising is essentially a contractual agreement between a franchiser and a franchisee that allows the franchisee to operate a retail outlet using a trade or brand name and format developed and supported by the franchiser. In a franchise contract, the franchisee pays a lump-sum price plus a royalty on all sales for the right to operate a store in a specific location. There are mainly two beneficial aspects:

- For franchisee, it reduces the risk factor as the business is operated with tried-and-tested and proven business process know-how and the brand image of the franchiser.
- For the franchiser, it is in terms of utilizing franchisee's physical and financial resources to expand the business in new markets and geographies.

The International Franchise Association defines franchising as a "continuing relationship in which the franchisor provides a licensed privilege to do business, plus assistance in organizing, training, merchandising, and management" in exchange for fees and royalties from the franchisee. Hence, franchising is the process of expanding a business whereby a company (franchiser) offers or grants a license to an independent business owner (franchisee) to sell its products or render its services. A franchise, therefore, is a legal agreement that permits a business to furnish a product, name, trademark, or idea to an independent business owner.

Hence, it is a method of doing business that practice:

- The use of a firm—"franchisee"—pursuant to a license of another firm's—"franchiser"— brand name, business model, brand or corporate image, and business identity.
- Along with its (franchiser) secret business know-how.
- To utilize its intangible assets in particular market/geographic area for a specified period.
- With predecided financial returns (in the form of royalty or fee) to the franchiser.

The franchisee also agrees to operate the outlet in accordance with standard operating procedures, practices, and processes prescribed by the franchisers. The franchiser provides assistance in locating, building and designing the store, and developing the products and/or services sold. It also extends its support and shares its expertise in training, advertising, and promotional activities. These standardized practices, procedures, and operations significantly enhance the franchisee's chances of success and help them eliminate the inefficient, trial-and-error type of learning.

Another important competitive advantage that a franchisee can have, over the independent small business owner, is leveraging the franchiser's centralized and large-volume buying power. The franchisers often pass on—the cost savings from quantity discounts—to the franchisee. For instance, it is unlikely that a small, independent ice-cream parlor can match the huge buying and bargaining power of Baskin-Robbins with its thousands of retail ice-cream stores.

Many international players have already entered India and have adopted the franchise route to grow and expand. It is the market demand, coupled with the growing spirit of entrepreneurship among Indians that is driving the growth of franchising in India. The global brands such as KFC (Kentucky Fried Chicken), Subway, Domino's, and Baskin-Robbins, among others, have adopted variations of the franchise models, and other international brands are contemplating entry plans into India. For instance, franchisees are the backbone of Subway's network because all the Subway outlets are individually owned and operated by independent franchisees.

Types of Franchise

There are four major types of franchises: business format franchises, product franchises, manufacturing franchises, and business opportunity ventures.

Business Format Franchises. This is the most common type of franchise. Here a company expands by supplying an established business concept/format, including its brand name, symbol, and/or trademark to independent business owners. In this arrangement, the franchisee acquires the right to use or follow a business format and also the best practices and processes associated with it. The franchiser company generally assists the independent owners significantly in launching and operating their businesses. In return, the business owners pay fees and royalties to franchiser. Hence, the franchisee acquires the right to use all the elements of a fully integrated business operation.

Some of the examples are fast-food restaurants such as McDonald's, Domino's Pizza, and KFC. Such franchisees maintain the design and styling aspects determined by the franchiser in their retail environments, ranging from the product offered to store design, ambience, atmospherics, and internal infrastructure to service standards to deliveries.

Product Franchises. In these franchise agreements, the franchisee gets the right to use the brand/trade names, trademark, and/or products from the franchiser. Through this kind of agreement, manufacturers allow retailers to distribute their products and use their brand names and trademarks. They also monitor and control on the way retail stores distribute their products. In return of these rights, store owners pay royalties/fees or buy a minimum quantity of products.

Some of the examples are Tommy Hilfiger, Arrow, Scullers, Cotton King Stores, Reebok stores and Bata stores who operate under this kind of franchise agreement.

Manufacturing Franchises. In this case, franchiser offers the right to produce and sell goods to a manufacturer under its brand name and trademark. This type of franchise is generally popular among food and beverage companies.

For example, soft drink bottlers and canners often obtain franchise rights from soft drink companies to produce, bottle, and distribute soft drinks. The major soft drink companies supply the concentrate to them, which are further processed, packed, and distributed by the regional manufacturing franchises.

One example is Gemini Distilleries Pvt Ltd, Goa, a manufacturing franchise of Bacardi Ltd for manufacturing of winery products.

Business Opportunity Ventures. This concept works on the format in which an independent business owner buys and distributes the products from one company. The company supplies the business owner with clients or accounts, in return of which the business owner pays the company a predecided fee.

For example, the business owners may obtain vending machine routes and distribution rights, through this type of franchise arrangement (e.g., coffee vending machine).

Retailer brands and companies often look toward franchising as a key operating model for expansion from scale, geographical coverage, and time perspectives.

For example, Gap is looking forward to script a new story in India as it struggles to maintain customer loyalty in markets across the world. The company was set up in 1969 by Doris and Donald Fisher and has presence in around in 90 countries through around 3,300 company-operated stores and 400 franchise stores. In India, its franchisee is Arvind Lifestyle Brands and opened its first store in Delhi, five years after its rival Zara did and a few weeks before H&M announced its plans. Zara, Gap's Spanish rival, has JV with Tata's Trent. Gap, Zara, and H&M are the brands that are popular even before they entered India. So Gap hopes to leverage the increasing fashion consciousness and latent awareness the Indian consumer has about its brands. Under the franchise arrangement that the two have drawn up, Arvind has invested in infrastructure and Gap is providing support in terms of brand name, merchandise, layouts, fixtures, and so on. Arvind sources the merchandise from Gap's global sourcing to which they have a direct access. Gap has manufacturing facilities in and around India, which is another strategic advantage.

Advantages of Franchising

Franchising offers a number of advantages to both franchisers and franchisees, which help to understand why franchising has been so successful. Overall, franchising worldwide has had the effect of offering consumers lower prices through efficient distribution of products, and consistent quality through standardization. This has been particularly true with the expansion of retail franchising. It is debatable that without retail franchising if these two areas, higher quality and lower prices (i.e., consumer value), would have improved at the rate that they have throughout the world market. Also the brand-name recognition and customer loyalty

Brand awareness and brand desirability are the key factors for a premium brand to be successful. GAP is retaining its premium positioning in India and sells the same merchandise here that they sell in a New York or London store.

Photo 2.1: *Convening Brand Message through Merchandise Display and Visuals*

Source: www.benettongroup.com (accessed on 12 May 2016)

are greatly enhanced through standardized offering that leads to shared long-term success. Franchising is undoubtedly a fast-growing model for business expansion in the retail sector and is also going to be an increasingly significant part of the growing services sector of the Indian economy in the years to come.

Both demand- and supply-side factors are expected to contribute to the growth of franchising.

The demand-side factors:

- Growing purchasing power of the middle class: burgeoning consumer class with increased disposable income and an increasing appetite for consumption are the growth drivers for both franchisers and franchisees.
- Growing consumption and willingness to spend.
- Increasing preference for branded and quality products among consumers.
- More global exposure and increasing aspirations to adopt.
- Growing inclination toward the international brands.

The supply-side factors:

- Growing awareness of franchising as a business opportunity and its relative low-risk profile.
- Growing number of passionate and opportunity-driven entrepreneurs.

- A surge in entrepreneurial force, complemented with risk-taking tendencies and abilities, has prompted many, especially those who do not have any business background, to prefer franchising-based business models.
- Favorable government policies, such as the liberalization of FDI in retail, motivate foreign brands to enter Indian market.
  (However, recent clarifications issued by DIPP on FDI regulations in multi-brand retail allowing foreign retailers to open only—company-owned company-operated (CoCo model)—outlets could be a limitation to be addressed to grow in retail franchising in India. This change is expected to have a major impact on the foreign multi-brand retailers such as 7-Eleven and Carrefour, which primarily operate on a franchise model for global expansion.)

Franchising has played a vital role in job creation, direct and indirect, particularly for the young and educated workforce, besides providing vast entrepreneurial opportunities for those who are less experienced but passionate to start their own business.

However, any form of business ownership has specific advantages and challenges or limitations. So one should carefully analyze and evaluate the agreement in the context of its own strengths—weakness and available opportunities and possible threats—before getting into the business. It is the value of the brand and uniqueness of the business concept of the franchiser that essentially attract franchisees to invest in. Although the assurance on investment returns given by franchisers is another aspect and rationale that tempts the franchisee, it is the ability of franchisee to understand and operate the business that leads the decision-making process. Besides that, India is not a "uniform" market, and it becomes more complicated in the case of India where consumers belong to diverse cultural backgrounds. Several languages, traditions, behavioral patterns, cultures, and socioeconomic diversities make it a set of multiple markets. So it becomes imperative for an international franchiser to understand all diversified tastes and preferences to establish and expand business in India.

Let us discuss the example of branded jewelers who are looking at the franchisee route to expand their retail footprints, a strategic turn prompted by the volatility in gold prices and resultant erosion of margins. The retailers in these segments like Rajesh Exports, Gitanjali Group, TBZ (the Original), PN Gadgil (PNG) Jewelers, and others have opted for this route to grow their businesses to manage the shrinking margins. Higher property rentals that push up the operational cost also figure among the reasons for choosing the franchise route.

Other reasons for opting franchise route are as follows:

- In today's world, the brands have to make an effort to reach to customers, and franchising model is a global tactic to achieve deep penetration and explore newer markets.
- Brands do not want to limit themselves with constraints of high investment costs and grab the expansion opportunity whenever they find like-minded partners who share the values, ethos, and commitment to the brand.
- Sometimes, retailers do not get a property at prime locations at a suitable price, which leads them to go for franchisee route.

Gold is the capital-intensive business and therefore franchise route is the most acceptable model among the retailers. Bengaluru-based Rajesh Exports, which retails jewelry under the brand name Shubh, and Gitanjali Group opted for franchisee route for expanding their business. PNG has also decided to take up the franchisee route for marketing its newly launched silver line of jewelry, Silvostyle. PNG has launched a subsidiary, Style Quotient, for silver jewelry business.

Benefits to Franchiser

- Franchisers benefit from these formats because they allow companies to expand much more quickly than they could otherwise. Franchising offers a relatively fast way to expand with comparatively less capital as the majority of the capital for expansion is provided by franchisee enterprise. Hence, franchiser can capture a share of a national or regional market without having to invest huge amounts of money with relatively short span of time.

- Local franchisee ownership not only promotes political and cultural acceptability but also lessens some of the negativity surrounding the buying products not produced in the home country. In addition, it reduces much of the political risk surrounding foreign investment policies.

- It is mainly a good developmental tool in the countries where financial resources are not adequate and where there exists a need to stimulate individual initiative.

- The lack of funds and skilled professionals can cause a company to grow slowly. However, through franchising, a company has to invest a very little on both the factors, because the franchisee supplies both.

- A company also can ensure it has competent, skillful, and highly motivated owner/managers at each outlet through franchising. It provides the franchiser with the ability to grow, without the cost and inconvenience of locating and developing key managers.

- As the owners are largely responsible for the success of their outlets, they will take the ownership with responsibility and put a sincere, strong, constant efforts to make sure their businesses run smoothly and prosper. For example, 7-Eleven leverage technology to enable profitable operations of the franchise store, which include payroll processing invoice payments, taxes, store audits, monthly financial statements, and inventory management.

- In addition, companies have a choice to provide franchising rights to only qualified people. The franchiser has the opportunity to acquire a broad base of knowledge concerning local customs–consumer behavior and market conditions, political affiliations, economic networks, and industry experience of the franchise partner. This in turn substantially enhances the probability of success for both the franchiser and franchisee(s).

- If we look at earning part, franchisers can earn a steady income from franchises through franchise royalties and fees. Convenience retailer 7-Eleven has a unique royalty system, which is based on gross profit and not on sales turnover. This system essentially links franchiser's growth to the profit-making ability of its franchisees.

- Many franchisers believe that franchising not only help to keep the brand relevant to their target consumers but also garner higher profitability for the system—the franchiser and franchisee ecosystem—as a whole.

Let us discuss the example of Siyaram Silk Mills. Siyaram's deals in blended high-fashion shirting and suiting fabrics. Siyaram's Fashion Avenue is a franchise model and presents an attractive business opportunity for entrepreneurs. The styles and designs of their blended fashion apparels have had a rich and vibrant journey of creating fashion trends with a strong brand portfolio, which includes some famous brands like Siyaram's, J. Hampstead, Mistair, MSD, and Oxemberg. Today, it is one of the largest Indian manufacturers of blended fabrics having presence through a network of thousands of outlets and over hundred franchise stores across India. Siyaram's has extensive presence in larger cities (metros and Tier I cities) and is continuously expanding in smaller cities (Tier II and Tier III cities). Siyaram's has effectively used the franchising model as a cost-effective avenue to expand its presence across India, especially beyond the metros and large cities. The apparel retailing requires a good knowledge of local tastes and preferences, which varies extensively across the diverse country like India. Siyaram's assists the franchisee in setting up operations and supports them to run various functions like marketing, advertising and promotions, store layout, IT, inventory management and POS, and billing management. It often helps franchisees to raise funds.

While the franchise model has strategically helped Siyaram's to leverage the local expertise that franchisees bring, the franchisees leverage Siyaram's strong brand awareness to connect with consumers. This creates a win–win situation for both the partners, and the resultant synergy enables them to grow fast.

Benefits to Franchisee

- The franchisee needs to bear much less risk through franchising a company or brand than through starting a new venture from the starting point.
- The lower risk is related to other advantages of franchising that stem from being part-nered or affiliated with an established and experienced organization with proven abilities and capabilities.
  For example, Archies, a retailer of gift card and gift articles, invests a lot of time and effort to support and set up the franchisees during the incubation period and imparts the franchisee with its knowledge, expertise, and experience in this niche segment of retailing. This primarily includes providing assistance for developing store layout, facility planning and architectural design of the store, interiors, VM, fixtures, and store ambience, among others. The experienced and expert employees of Archies help streamlining the operations of franchisee during initial days. Also visits to best Archies stores are organized to make the franchisees understand and learn best and innovative practices in gift retailing.
- Because of its identification and association with an established brand-name, it often reaches the breakeven point faster.
- The franchiser generally has international, national, or regional name and recognition. Thus, the franchisee has the advantage of identifying his business with a widely recognized brand name, which usually provide good brand awareness and trust factor. Archies has exclusive tie-ups with global brands, such as Keel Toys, Cow Parade, Carte Blanche, Russ Berrie, and Paper Island, which provide its franchisees with a unique product range for growing the business.
- Operational support is an apparent area of collaboration between franchisers and franchisees. Franchisers provide franchisees with a proven and efficient method of operation through their experience in the business, with management assistance and training. The franchiser offers managerial training programs, start-up trainings, SCM and procurement management, operating guidelines, troubleshooting methods, and so on to franchisees to reduce the number of franchise casualties.
- The "people" factor is one of the most important components in retail franchising as frontline employees are the face of the brand, interacting directly with the customers. Hence, the franchisees are often supported with well-defined training and development program. It encompasses the framework for recruitment and selection, well outlined and continuous upgradation of skills of operational, technical, and sales staff.
- Franchisers also provide franchisees with marketing assistance and advantages in terms of brand equity because they realize that their ultimate success hinges on the success of the franchisees.
- Franchisers usually conduct national or regional marketing campaigns developed and designed by professional advertising agencies.

- They also help franchisees to run local ad campaigns and promotions. Franchisers often help franchisees to design promotional programs, press releases, and advertisements at different occasions. Such activities help in building the brand, increase the credibility of the offering, and ensure increased brand awareness and recall among the target clientele.

- All of these traits and aspects of franchise agreements can significantly increase the chances of an outlet's success.

- Moreover, franchisers sometimes help franchisees to raise funds to establish their business. However, once a franchiser identifies a suitable prospective franchisee, it may offer direct financial assistance in specific areas, such as inventory, purchasing equipment, or even sometimes the franchise fee. Many franchisers are offering direct financial assistance, as the start-up costs of some franchises are increasing.

- Financial institutions may be more willing to lend if a well-known franchiser is backing the applicant—especially if the franchiser is well established, rather than based on a new concept.

- Franchisers often assist the franchisee for market research, demographic analysis, new product innovations, extensive location analysis and so on, and also for developing business and marketing plan as per the requirement and behavior of local market. Location is one of the most important and decisive aspect for success of any retail or franchise venture. In fact, industry experts consider the three most significant factors in retailing and franchising to be location, location, and location.

  For example, Archies supports its franchisees in all possible areas relevant to setting up of a store. It mainly includes location assessment, store launch, advertising, IT support, training, setting up supply chain, and so on and so forth. Location becomes more crucial for retailers operating in niche segments like gifting, and acquiring right property at right location is imperative for success in this segment. Similarly, McDonald's is also known for its expertise to acquire prime locations in high traffic areas having a good visibility and covering the targeted catchment area.

- Many times, franchisers offer territorial protection to a franchisee. This essentially gives franchisee the right to exclusive distribution of a brand, within a particular geographic area.

Possible Drawbacks of Franchise Arrangement

- In return for the benefits franchisees receive, they have to pay fees and royalties to the franchisers, or the franchiser may demand a share of the franchisees' sales revenues, which can be a major expenditure and need to be checked thoroughly because it may reduce the economic benefits of the investment.

- Other additional start-up costs may include purchase and preparation of site, signs, fixtures, equipment, other infrastructure, management assistance, and training.

- Franchisers may impose continuing royalty fees as profit-sharing devices. This is a percentage of gross sales with a required minimum, or a flat-level fee levied on the franchise. The variable royalty fee, which increases as sales increase, is popular among some franchises.

- Franchisers may impose some other types of continuing fees, for instance, continuing fees for advisory services, sharing management expertise, advertising, rent, and technical assistance. So a franchisee needs to find out which type of support is required and determine what benefits and services the fees cover. To determine this, franchisees itemize what they are getting for their investment and then find out whether the cost corresponds to the benefits provided.

- In addition to the payment of fees and royalties, franchisees are expected to give up some control over their own businesses and lose their own identity.
- Franchisees are often subjected to tight supervision by the franchiser. Although the franchisee owns the business, he or she does not have the complete autonomy of an independent owner.
- Franchisees usually need to follow guidelines given by franchiser and conform to the standard operating procedures recommended by the franchiser. The compliance with standards is usually determined by periodic inspections, which sometimes become a burden to the franchisee.
- Moreover, franchisees usually cannot implement changes without franchisers' approval. In most of the cases, the franchise agreements specify that the franchise can sell only those products that are approved by the franchiser. For instance, if a coffee-house franchise that sells only beverages and pastries cannot serve customer demand for sandwiches. Hence, it cannot offer them anything extra without the consent of the franchiser. In few other instances, the franchisee may be required to implement specific rules even though it believes they are inappropriate or unfair in specific conditions or market scenarios.
- One cannot deny the possibility of franchisee falling victim to the franchiser company's circumstantial problems. So while a particular business owner may be doing well, the franchiser itself may encounter business problems, perhaps because of operational issues, management inefficiency, financial issues, and problems in business environment, or any other reason that affects the business.
- In such cases, the turnaround becomes very difficult because of the complete reliance on the franchiser.

Franchising and Entrepreneurship

With a wide range of rewarding business prospects in the country, the business fraternity has experienced a boom over the past few years. The concept of franchising has created a stir in the business sector, offering many business opportunities to young entrepreneurs to climb up the ladder of success. This has prompted entrepreneurs and other investors to leap forward to spend time, efforts, skills, expertise, and money to establish their own business. Entrepreneurship involves several kinds of risks—strategic, financial, and operational—associated with it. An entrepreneur undertakes the risk ranging right from the inception of the business idea until the time the business is established and operational in the current scenario of cutthroat competition. Hence, it is obvious to state that choosing an option that is not only rewarding but also less risky is a wise man's decision that has less financial tolerance to the uncertainty.

It requires a great deal of efforts to start a business in any sector. But a budding concept for any entrepreneur is to tread on the franchise route. Hence in today's global economic scenario, the growth of franchising is inevitable because it offers aspiring new business owners the best possible chance of succeeding.

1. Good deal for beginners: By presenting a proven business model, coupled with hands-on training, franchising is capable of transmuting novices into accomplished entrepreneurs.
2. Sense of independence: Franchising means you are the owner. Hence, it gives you a satisfaction of establishing something on your own. This is the route that leads you to become a professional entrepreneur.
3. Proven blueprint: After venturing into franchising, an entrepreneur is legally entitled to adopt the tried-and-tested business model and format, procedures, processes, practices,

and overall code of conduct developed by the franchiser. Thus, an entrepreneur will reap the benefits of a proven track record of the franchiser.

4. Reduction in risk: The risk of failure is comparatively lower than starting a new business. This is so because when entrepreneur buys a franchise, he or she buys the system that works.

5. Easier finance: An entrepreneur receives financial assistance from the franchiser, as they make arrangements with the banks and other financial institutions to lend money.

6. Low cost and high on returns: The primary benefit that a franchisee reaps is the low cost of investment. This is due to the reduction costs and the savings made in administrating, promoting, and advertising the franchise brand/outlet. In addition, association with an established brand-name ensures assured profits and ROIs.

7. Mentor and peer support: With this professional support from the franchiser, which acts as a mentor, an entrepreneur becomes competent to operate its set of business activities and operations, in a relatively comfortable atmosphere of shared risk factor.

8. Platform for business development: Once the entrepreneur gets associated with an established brand-name, it becomes easy to win and earn the targeted customers. This can be achieved with the help of the brand strength/image and consumer loyalty toward that brand.

9. Exclusive territorial rights: By venturing into a franchise, the franchiser guarantees predetermined territory to the franchisee that assists in succeeding within that region.

Hence, franchise investment is one of the safest business heavens that demands less cost and risk. Besides these characteristics, indulging in business franchising is a win–win situation for the three parties involved: franchiser, franchisee, and the end user of the product/service.

Leased Department

A leased department is a section or department in a retail store that is generally rented by a manufacturer. As the name itself suggests, the lessee pays rent to the store and is responsible for all aspects of business. However, to ensure the overall consistency, the store may impose operating restrictions for the leased department. The leased departments choose to operate in categories that are generally on the periphery of the store's major product lines such as in-store bookshop/kiosk, SIM card kiosk of a telecom company, beauty salons, photographic studios, and food courts.

In this kind of arrangement, the leased department operators get benefited as the main store generates immediate sales for leased departments. This eventually reduces the total expenses through economics of scale in shared facilities (such as display windows and security equipment) and through pooled advertising. Also lessees' image is reinforced by their association with these branded stores. However, sometimes, there may be inflexibility due to the restrictions and limitations entailed by the operations of the main store. There is always the possibility of revision of the rent to the higher side by the stores or there is uncertainty in renewal of leases when they expire.

Leased departments help the stores in generating greater walk-ins by acting as supplementary in providing complete shopping experience under one roof. The stores get benefited from expertise of lessees in the areas such as personal merchandise displays management and inventory management as store staff might lack the merchandising ability to handle and sell certain products. This is also a regular source of revenue and hence reduces costs as leased departments pay for inventory and personal expenses.

But occasionally, this may also be a source of conflict with lessees as leased departments may follow operating practices and procedures that do not fall in line with those of the stores or if the lessees adversely affect store's brand image and customers are facing issues for which host stores is getting blamed, which in turn tarnishes the image of the store.

Vertical Marketing System (refer Chapter 1)

Consumer Cooperatives

A consumer cooperative is the retail firm in which a group of consumers invest in the enterprise and the executives are elected. A cooperative is fundamentally managed on the notion that the customers of a business are also the owners of the business. There is an inbuilt arrangement and system of sharing of the profits or savings that accrue—among the consumer—members. Such retailers are typically small in size but many in number and are most popular with retailing food items and eatables.

They started mainly with the objective to guard against the malpractice that many retailers indulge in either by charging higher prices or by offering inconsistent quality of merchandise. There are some limitations to the performance of consumer cooperatives because consumers may not have the professional expertise in buying, handling, and selling products, and the cost savings and reduction in selling prices have not been as expected in many cases. The cooperative retail movement has literally been left behind in the face of strong competition from the multinational players after the proliferation of globalization and expansion of e-retailing. The fragmented nature of organizational structure prevented timely upgradations and transformations in reaction to the changes in the retail environment.

Store-based Retailers

Most of the large retail organizations have grown using a particular retail format. Using a particular format to a certain extent is often considered to be a crucial component of a successful strategy for that retailer. So adopting a winning format that is designed in the context of SWOT analysis of that organization and effectively implementing that format throughout the geographical expansion eventually enable the retailer to obtain economies of scale, efficiency, and a strong brand image and brand recall. Therefore, an understanding of the different retail formats used is imperative for gaining an understanding of a winning retail strategy.

Retail institutions may be classified by store-based strategy mix and divided into food oriented and general merchandise.

Food-oriented Retailers

Six major strategic formats are used by food-oriented retailers: convenience store, conventional supermarket, food-based superstore, combination store, box (limited-line store), and warehouse store. These are discussed in the following sections.

Convenience Stores

A convenience store is a well-located store and very convenient to reach. It is often called as the "mom-and-pop" stores. The major reasons for its patronage are the overall ease of shopping, credit facility, and personalized services. Because of these reasons, consumers frequently shop at these stores even when it charges average to above-average prices, and carries a moderate number of categories and items. It stays open at convenient hours and also for long hours of the day. It typically provides an average shopping ambience, atmosphere, and customer services. It is increasingly becoming difficult to find big spaces to open large stores at right locations and the rentals are not either affordable or justifiable. For instance, retailers like

Kishore Biyani's Future Group (such as KB's Fair Price, Nilgiris, and KB's Conveniently Yours), Mukesh Ambani's Reliance Retail (Reliance Fresh), and Tata's Trent (Star Daily) are coming with smaller ones after big-box stores. The convenience stores tend to offer a limited line of convenience merchandise and have a smaller assortment and smaller pack sizes.

- The Future Group's convenience stores are generally spread over the area of 1,500–1,800 sq. ft and keep 700–1,500 SKUs.
- The Star Daily stores offer dairy, bakery, meat, and other products and open at 7:00 am, two to three hours before the large stores of the chain. The area of these stores range from 2,000 to 5,000 sq. ft.

Hence, they are very convenient to buy, for emergency requirements, sundry household grocery items, and fill-in merchandise. These neighborhood stores cater to people who want to buy groceries very quickly and can afford to come midweek. In the urban areas where traveling takes longer, retailers are thinking to go to customers rather than customers coming to them.

However, these format stores are facing stiff competition from supermarkets and hypermarkets that have started running for longer hours and comparatively huge stocks of both food and nonfood items and also from the online grocery shops.

Conventional Supermarket

A conventional supermarket is a self-service food store offering grocery and other food items, bakery items, milk products, meat, and so on, with limited sales of nonfood items, such as beauty and health products and general merchandise, at discounted or lower prices. They are large in size and carry 10,000–11,000 items. They are chosen due to self-service, volume sales, low prices, and easy parking. The self-service factor allows supermarkets to reduce the costs, as well as increase volume. It was once the most common format; today, they are facing intense competition not only from other types of food stores but also from online grocery retailers.

For instance, discount store chains are able to challenge supermarket prices because of their effective and efficient distribution systems and focus on reduction of inventory investments by aggressively selling fast-moving items. On the other hand, convenience stores offer greater customer convenience; food-based superstores and combination stores have more product lines to offer with greater variety, as well as better gross margins; and box and warehouse stores have lower operating costs and prices. Membership clubs are also competing with their discount prices and promotional offers.

Food-based Superstores

Food-based superstores cater to consumers' grocery needs and offer them a place where they can buy fill-in general merchandise. Superstores are large supermarkets ranging from 25,000 to 50,000 sq. ft. Management expertise is better focused in food-based superstores. Food-based superstores efficiently offer a destination for one-stop shopping, stimulate impulse purchases, and also feature high-profit general merchandise. Some of the major advantages of this format are it is less costly and comparatively easier to redesign and convert supermarkets into food-based superstores than combination stores. Many consumers feel more comfortable shopping in specialized food stores than combination stores. Most of the supermarket chains have also started offering food items to compete with these formats.

Combination Stores/Supercenters/Supermarkets/Hypermarkets

A supercenter is basically a combination or blending of a discount department store with an economy supermarket. Hypermarkets are big-box formats with an average store size that

Photo 2.2: *A Food-based Superstore*

Photo credit: Amit Kumar

ranges between 50,000 and 1,20,000 sq. ft. Supermarkets are smaller version of hypermarkets, and the store size varies from around 10,000–25,000 sq. ft. They typically are food-based retailers that essentially carry supermarket and general merchandise retailing into one facility with the latter typically accounting for around 25–40% of total sales. The supercenters have a size of around 1,50,000 sq. ft in which about 40% of their space is generally devoted to grocery items and the rest to the discounted general merchandise. Usually, they are set up on one level (single story) and often follow more functional, "grid pattern layout" of aisles and shelving (e.g., Big Bazaar, Easyday, Walmart, HyperCity, RPG Spencer's, and Shoprite Hyper, among others). HyperCity has identified two formats for the stores going ahead: about 45,000–50,000 sq. ft for the large stores and 25,000–30,000 sq. ft (compact format) for smaller stores.

A hypermarket is essentially a very large retail store offering low prices that brings discount store together with a superstore food retailer in single warehouse-like building. Hypermarkets are characteristically unique in terms of the store size; everyday low prices (EDLP), low operating margins, and the size of general merchandise assortment. Hence, they are operated on the basis on four main concepts:

- Everything available under one roof, essentially a one-stop shopping experience
- EDLP strategy
- Ample space for parking
- Service level is low

The major limitation of this format is browsing and walking around different departments inside the big store is time consuming and sometimes very tiring. Sometimes, it becomes hard to find a merchandise as the service level is low and checkout lines can be very long on weekends and during festive seasons or special promotional offers.

Whereas the actual advantage that the supermarket offered the customer was self-service and a much faster process of shopping the general day-to-day or everyday items, the consumers who prefer the one-stop shopping experience tend to travel all the way to visit these destinations. They achieve cost savings and operational efficiencies through their scale of operation, which is typically large. Here the impulse buying is also high. These formats offer a wider choice of merchandise items at lower prices.

Advantages of Large-format Retail Stores. Large-format retail stores often give the opportunity and create conducive environment that compel the shoppers to add more merchandise items to their shopping cart. Shoppers generally visit a large-format store in order to have a better shopping experience and spend much more time. These consumer aspirations make it a predecided shopping destination wherein the format provides the shopper with a huge selection of merchandise items across the categories that otherwise would be possible across three or four stores. Hence, it helps in a planned purchase by offering almost everything under one roof. Large-format stores have the advantage of being spacious and are well stocked, being rich in merchandise SKUs on display and sale. However, one cannot deny the possibility that large formats due to their sheer size and scale may become less personal and less customized.

Therefore, to create a shopping destination experience and to cater to the consumer expectations effectively, large-format stores majorly focus on:

- Selecting right store location, right store size, and competitive pricing strategy.
- Wider merchandise assortment.
- Assortment that is relevant to the catchment area.
- Customer-oriented VM that infuse a sense of privacy.
- VM that is more strategic and engaging, besides being aesthetic, to ensure that the customer can handle the space without being lost or losing interest.
- Eye-catching focal points, window display, and cross-merchandising strategies to hold the interest level.
- Well-planned demarcation of different zones and departments.
- Offering customer convenience and amenities like children play area, big parking areas, leisure areas, food courts, and so on.

In the case of large formats, the display is more organized and less intrusive with sufficient space to appreciate the huge collections. This creates relaxed atmosphere to browse through with a feeling of comfort and sense of privacy while shopping, which in turn helps to build emotional connection between customer and the merchandise. This is further enhanced by effectively deploying the VM practices and tools.

Warehouse Store or Membership Clubs

A warehouse club or store is a retailer that offers a limited range and assortment of general merchandise and food items with limited services, at low prices, to ultimate consumers and small businesses. It appeals to price-conscious consumers and to those who can shop there, who are members of that enterprise. Its inventory turnover rate is several times higher than that of a department store. These stores are generally large in size and located in low-rent areas. They have simple store interiors, and very basic things are done regarding store atmosphere and ambience. Aisles are sufficiently wide to facilitate pickup pallets of merchandise. Specific brands and items differ from time to time as the stores buy merchandise available with special promotional offers directly from manufacturers. The clubs pass on these savings to shoppers through lower prices. Most warehouse clubs have two types of members. First are wholesale members who typically are small business people and second are individual members who purchase for their own use. Most of the warehouse or membership clubs operate in similar way as a cash-and-carry outlets do as the consumers have to buy a minimum volume of merchandise or maybe of value specified by the cash-and-carry retailer.

The key challenge faced by membership clubs is the limited size of their final customer market segment, and the major limiting factor is the lack of brand continuity. As merchandise is usually bought only when special deals are available, brands may be temporarily or permanently out of stock. In addition, many consumers do not like shopping in warehouse settings.

General Merchandising Retailers

Department Stores

A department store is a large retail outlet with an extensive assortment (width and depth) of merchandise and services that are organized into separate departments for the purpose of buying, promotion, customer service, and so on. They typically are lifestyle stores where the merchandise constitutes apparels, lifestyle products, and the merchandise other than food and grocery. They offer high-quality service to consumers in a very attractive and aspirational store atmosphere. A department store is often a multilevel store (generally two to three stories) that is divided into clearly defined areas or departments according to merchandise categories. While many department stores offer width and depth of merchandise across segments so that almost every shopping need can be catered, for instance, Shoppers Stop, Lifestyle, Harrods, Westside, Trent, and Globus, among others. Many department stores concentrate on fewer categories in order to offer a wide selection within those categories (e.g., fashion brands such as Ralph Lauren and Max, and Crossword Bookstores). Department stores are unique in terms of the store ambience and atmospherics, merchandise and services offered, and hence the overall shopping experience they create.

They offer a full range of services from altering clothing to loyalty programs. The department store has been responsible for many innovations, including advertising prices, implementing the one-price policy (whereby all shoppers pay same price for the same merchandise or service), developing computerized billing and checkouts, and adding branch outlets and decentralized or matrix structure of management where there are operational and functional executives managing various functions and verticals. However, they are increasingly facing competition

Photo 2.3: *A Department Store*

Photo credits: Amit Kumar

from the sophisticated retail offerings from a growing number of specialty stores and e-retailers (and online marketplaces), particularly in the categories like fashion, which essentially is the most important product classification for them. Department stores no longer have brand exclusivity for a lot of items they sell, as the manufacturer brands are available at specialty stores, discount outlets, and on e-retailer's portal also. So the department stores have focused on creating their own brands (PLBs). They have also signed exclusive licensing agreements with fashion designers and other brands in order to build a unique selling proposition (USP) and develop exclusivity proposition. Department stores run very effective loyalty programs to increase the customer patronage behavior.

Full-line Discount Store

A full-line discount store targets the middle-class and lower-middle-class shoppers who prefer value in terms of heavy discounts and lucrative offers. So they have the image of a low-cost, high-volume, and fast turnover outlet. It sells a wide merchandise assortment for less than the regular price points. It is likely to carry some selected range of product lines that is available at department stores.

Discount stores can be very minimal in terms of store environment and service. Billing and checkout point (POS) is centralized. Buildings, equipment, and fixtures are comparatively less expensive, and operating costs are lower than that of traditional department stores. However with increasing competition from other formats, full-line discount retailers are increasingly focusing on creating attractive shopping environments, developing PL merchandise, focusing on apparel and clothing segment and improving store footfalls by offering easily accessible convenience store merchandise (e.g., Big Bazaar and D-Mart).

Off-price Stores

The off-price retail chains offer brand names and designer labels at a low price in a limited but efficient service environment. The off-price retailers basically buy canceled orders of other retailers, irregular stocks and overruns of manufacturers, and end-of-season merchandise items for a fraction of their original wholesale prices. The most critical aspect of off-price retailing is buying merchandise and establishing profitable relationships with suppliers in the long term. Because of this pattern of opportunistic buying, it often happens that the same type of merchandise may not be available in stock at every point of time and usually different bargains will be available on next visit. The inventory turnover of off-price stores is considerably higher than that of departmental stores. There are mainly three types of off-price retail stores:

1. Factory outlet stores: Factory outlet stores are the off-price retailers that are generally owned by manufacturers or by specialty store or department chains. A manufacturer-owned off-price retail store typically offers discontinued merchandise, manufacturer closeouts and unsold stock of previous seasons, canceled orders, irregulars, and, quite a few times, seasonally the first-quality merchandise. It provides an opportunity to manufacturers and retailers to sell off the unwanted merchandise without hampering the image of the brand. These formats make the products and brands accessible and affordable to customers who might not normally be able to afford them, or who are attracted to heavy discounts on big brands.
2. Closeout retail stores: These are off-price retail stores that offer a broad but still consistent assortment of general merchandise, apparels, and soft home-improvement items, among others.
3. Single-price retail stores: These are basically the closeout stores that offer all the merchandise at a single price point.

However, the sales growth of off-price retailers has slowed over last few years because of the following factors:

- Significant rise in sales and promotion by department stores.
- Heavy discounts offered by e-retailers on branded merchandise with services like home delivery and payment options such as COD and so on.
- Consumers are increasingly becoming fashion conscious, following new trends and preferring fresh stocks with vibrant designs and colors.
- Improved and more sophisticated inventory management systems have reduced the amount and incidents of excess production that can be purchased by off-price retailers.

Category Killers or Category Specialists

A category killer or specialist is basically a discount store that offers a narrow variety with deep assortment and SKUs of merchandise. They essentially offer a comprehensive assortment of a specific category at low or discounted prices with usually a self-service approach. Hence, they virtually "kill" a category of merchandise for other retailers. This model of retailing the complete assortment with all possible SKUs endow them with high bargaining power, which in turn acts as a Best Alternative to Negotiated Agreement (BATNA). With this competitive advantage, the category killers can negotiate low prices, excellent terms, and assured supply when items are scarce. These benefits are eventually passed on to the customers in the form of low or discounted prices. For example, Croma by Tata and Next by Vijay Sales are some of the players in this category.

However, there are some challenges, which are as follows:

- All competitors in a category offer similar assortments (merchandise) at almost same price points and with the same level of service.
- Hence, there is less scope for creating differentiation on the basis of elements of retail mix.
- Because of aggressive price competition, the category killers often face difficulties to achieve targeted bottom line (profit margins).

Therefore, to address these challenges, category killers constantly focus on reducing costs by improving operational efficiency continuously and continually. They are acquiring smaller chains to obtain economies of scale and expanding into relatively less competitive markets in the world.

For instance, many home-improvement centers operate as the category specialist.

- The merchandise in these stores is displayed like that of in a warehouse atmosphere.
- However in this case, the merchandise varies significantly across the country or region, and there are opportunities to create differentiation on the basis of customer service.
- Sales associates are available to assist customers in selecting merchandise through demonstrations and workshops.
- They offer equipment and material used by DIY stores and artisans for home improvement.
- They essentially provide material and information that enable consumers to improve and maintain their homes.

With all these characteristics, the DIY stores do not face the same level of intensity of competition as other category specialists do. Many online retailers are also adopting this format in their unique way of doing the business of retailing.

For example, The Children's Place (TCP) is the largest pure-play children specialty apparel retailer in North America. It offers fashionable, high-quality, and head-to-toe children outfits at various price points. The specialty retailer of children's apparel and accessories has entered Indian market through a franchise agreement with Arvind Lifestyle Brands Ltd. TCP is the country's first head-to-toe fashion destination for children aged 0–14 years, offering the merchandise across the categories from clothing accessories like party wear, everyday casuals, outdoor wear, beachwear, innerwear, nightwear, and winter wear to fashion accessories like fashion jewelry, sunglasses, footwear, ties, scarves, belts, hair accessories, bags, and purses for boys and girls. Hence, they offer branded fashion wear from apparel to accessories for kids—available in all fits and sizing across various price points—all available under one roof.

Variety Store

Variety stores are named so because they offer a large variety of merchandise under one roof, including both food and nonfood items. A variety store handles a very wide assortment of inexpensive and popularly priced merchandise and services. They typically offer items like stationary and other items required for school goers, health and beauty aids, inexpensive gift articles, lady's accessories, light hardware, decorative lighting solutions, toys, confectionery items, general housewares, and other miscellaneous items. Unlike other formats, variety stores typically do not carry full product lines, do not deliver the products, and may not be departmentalized. However in case of large organized variety stores, the boundaries of definition are becoming increasingly hazy. This blending combines the merchandise and brand choice of the department store with the low price orientation of the variety store, with service level and store environment lying somewhere in between. For instance, some variety stores like Marks & Spencer have transformed virtually into department stores. The increased space enables them to offer merchandise items across the width and depth of the product range.

Flea Market

Flea markets are basically rooted in the centuries-old tradition of street retailing in unorganized way; often, shoppers touch, feel, and, if possible, try the product. The buyers and sellers often get into street-bargaining over the prices of the merchandise. A flea market consists of many retail vendors offering a wide range of items in plain surroundings and can easily evade taxes. Their operating costs are very low. The merchandise is not necessarily discounted every time, but prices are generally open for negotiation. While the flea markets are typically located in the traditional old crowed bazaars and across the narrow lanes, many are located in nontraditional locations as well, which are not usually associated with retailing, such as stadiums and arenas, temporary or seasonal shopping festival sites, among others. Many other flea markets are located at sites that are abandoned by other mainstream organized retail formats like department stores and superstores. In a flea market, individual retailers own the shop space or acquire it on rental, which may be on a monthly, yearly, or, may be, seasonal basis, and it may be indoor or outdoor. Shopping in the flea markets has been reduced significantly with the increased tendency of consumers to shop at organized online and off-line retail stores. With growing awareness among the consumers, the flea markets are increasingly perceived and believed by some to overstate or misrepresent the quality of merchandise.

Non-store-based Retailers

Non-store retailing is the form and format of retailing in which the business of retailing is operated without using brick-and-mortar stores. The non-store retailers are classified on the basis of the medium they use to communicate and transact with their customers, such as direct selling, telephonic selling, vending machines, teleshopping (television retailing), and e-retailing (online retailing). Today, we can see that non-store retailing, especially e-retailing, is increasingly preferred and patronized by those:

- Who face time constraints,
- Who do not have easy access to stores,
- Millennial who are always connected to Internet, and
- Who prefer the convenience of buying 24/7 and seek delivery at location and time of their choice.

E-retailing

E-retailing or online retailing refers to a wide range of online retailing activities for products and services. After globalization, the world now is termed as the "global village" and has gone about bringing both business and customer closer than before. India is a very young country, and aspirations are extremely high among the youth of today, who is always connected to the Internet. E-retailing (or simply e-tailing) is basically a retail format in which the retailer and customer interact with each other through an interactive web portal (digital network). After this virtual interaction, the customer orders the merchandise directly through the interactive network only. Payments are done by the customer through online banking services (e.g., using the debit or credit card) or through COD option. E-retailer then arranges the last-mile delivery to the location preferred by the customer. Hence, the parties involved in transaction essentially interact electronically (digital or virtual) rather than by physical exchanges or direct physical contact.

Though this process is quite popular, this definition is not comprehensive enough to capture recent developments in this new and revolutionary business phenomenon that is hybrid retailing or omni-channel retailing. Various unique elements differentiate online shopping from the traditional brick-and-mortar retailing model. Besides offering expanded product variety with convenience of shopping, the online model also makes it comparatively very easy for customers to access and compare information about product features and prices available from multiple sources at a click of a button. For instance, visiting the sites of four e-retailers would take few minutes, which is just a fraction of time needed for driving up to one physical store. The search and navigation systems within online stores replace physical browsing through endless aisles at a traditional brick-and-mortar retailer. Thus, a more comprehensive definition of online retailing is: E-retailing is the integrative use of online interface through web-based communications and digital information processing technology in transactions of retail business to develop, create, transform, and redefine relationships for value creation between or among the business organizations, and between business organizations and end customers.

Types of E-commerce

There are different types of e-retailers and many different ways to characterize these types. These e-retailers are mainly distinguished on the basis of market relationship they exist on, that is, who is selling to whom. So this way of distinction brings different types of e-retailers such as B2C (business to consumer), B2B (business to business), and C2C (consumer to consumer). The other way of distinction is based on the model they are following, that is, marketplace or inventory based.

Business to Consumer: B2C e-retailing is the e-commerce transaction between retailer and consumers. Some of the examples are online retailers such as Myntra, Flipkart, Jabong, and Snapdeal, who sell directly to the end consumers.

Business to Business: B2B e-retailing is nothing but the e-commerce transaction between or among the companies. Hence, as the terminology itself suggest, this is essentially e-commerce that deals with relationships between and among businesses.

For example, Bengaluru-based StoreRoom.in is specialized in household goods. Walmart launched its e-commerce portal Best Price. Besides that Industrybuying.com and BazarA2Z. com are among other players in the B2B e-commerce space. Foxconn has piloted an electronics goods marketplace flnet.com in China, which sells components it produces for Apple, Huawei, Samsung, and Xiaomi. Amazon's Indian subsidiary Amazon Wholesale India has launched its wholesale e-commerce site, AmazonBusiness.in.

Consumer to Consumer: C2C e-retailing is the e-commerce transaction between two consumers that is taking place on the online portal of online player. That is, C2C is simply a transaction between private individuals or consumers. Such transactions can happen in the form of online auction also.

For example, auctions facilitated through an online portal (marketplace), such as eBay, which allows online real-time bidding for the merchandise items being sold. Other players in this segment are OLX, Quikr, and so on.

Peer-to-peer: Peer-to-peer e-retailing is the e-commerce where both the transacting parties install particular software/application through which they can exchange the files or money or payment in computer without the intervention or assistance of a market maker.

For example, Gnutella is a software application that allows consumers to share music tracks with each other directly, typically without any charge and without the intervention of a market maker as in case of C2C e-commerce. Other players in this category are Napster, Freenet, and so on.

Distinction on the Basis of a Business Model

As mentioned earlier, there is one more way of distinguishing the e-retailers, which is based on retailing models: inventory or non-inventory (marketplace) adopted by them. In a pure marketplace model, the online retailer does not hold any merchandise inventory. Once order is placed online, the supplier or seller of that merchandise directly delivers it to the shopper. The online retailer just gets its predecided commission on the sale. Most of these marketplace stores follow the "managed marketplace" model wherein they ensure high quality for their merchandise by suitable quality checks, maintaining uniform packaging standards (standard packaging format across geographies for merchandise purchased on their portal) through fulfillment centers and rapid last-mile delivery via their own logistic arms or through third-party logistics (3PL) support but does not hold any inventory (e.g., eBay, Snapdeal, Flipkart, and Pepperfry). While in the case of inventory-based model, the online retailer holds the inventory by purchasing the merchandising from sellers/vendors (e.g., Jabong, Myntra, FirstCry, and 99labels).

With the growing competition and increasing pressure on profitability margins, the focus of online players is on reducing and streamlining operational costs without hampering the quality of service offered to the customers. Marketplace model helps to cut cost by eliminating investment in holding inventory, but issues related to uniformity in quality of merchandise and overall delivery experience remains as a challenge (Table 2.2). While in the case of inventory-based model, it ensures the uniform customer experience, but the retailer needs to bear the cost of carrying the inventory. With many advantages and disadvantages associated with both the inventory-based and marketplace model, e-retailers need to evaluate the most viable strategy. The selection of an appropriate business model depends upon the nature of merchandise mix and service offered by online retailer, which is coupled with intended customer service standards.

Table 2.2: *Marketplace Model*

Marketplace Model	
Strength	**Weakness**
Ease of widening the merchandise portfolio	Merchandise quality and packaging are often nonuniform
No cost of inventory	Dependence on third-party suppliers
Ease of expansion	Lack of uniformity in overall customer experience
Opportunity	**Threats**
Acts as a platform for entrepreneurs and SMEs for growth and expansion	Quality of Merchandise and delivery experience may not be uniform
Higher profit margins	Possibility of entry of counterfeits or substandard merchandise into the supply chain
Ease of scaling up operations with quick expansion	The nonuniformity in shopping experience may hamper brand image
Inventory-based Model	
Strength	**Weakness**
Ease of offing a consistent delivery experience	Requires substantial investment in maintaining the inventory
Greater control on quality of merchandise and also packaging	Growth is dependent on the performance of the brands
Greater control on discounts and promotional offers	Higher cost of operations
Opportunity	**Threats**
Huge scope for growth in a given category—category leadership	Low stock turnover
Opportunity to utilize the physical store for delivery	Strong competition from other online retailers operating in same category
Opportunity for creating omni-channel shopping experience	Possibility of losses due to damage, defects, shrinkage, etc.

Other models are PL and white label. PL reflects a business where an e-retailer sets up its in-house brand merchandise, which it sells through its own website. This model offers a wide-ranging products and pricing to its customers and competes with branded labels. Here, margins are typically higher than third-party branded goods.

White label involves the setting up of a branded online store managed by the e-retailer or a third party. The brand takes the responsibility of generating website traffic and providing services by partnering with payment gateways. It helps build trust, customer affinity, and loyalty and provides better control of brand and product experience.

SWOT Analysis

For instance, in the case of merchandise that is not standardized in terms of design and available in large variety (say furniture and home-improvement items), the marketplace model is more suitable. Because here, the marketplace model helps the online player to scale his operation more quickly without adding high working capital costs. Online marketplace is often an attractive proposition for entrepreneurs and other sellers as it provides a platform for faster growth and higher reach across geographies at lower distribution cost. It also extends marketing and payment support, and the supplier can better focus on other critical functions related to its business. However, in the marketplace model, there are often issues related to uniformity in product quality, shipping cost, and discounts offered that can lead to friction with either supplier or consumer.

On the other hand, inventory-based model is viable for the online players that offer specialized categories with a limited range and can be stored with ease. This model by virtue of its nature broadly helps to ensure more uniform customer service standards through suitable quality checks and uniform packaging, and maintain optimum delivery experience. However in inventory-based model, the online retailer needs to manage its inventory cost. Besides, it needs to invest in developing expertise in demand forecasting and seamlessly supply chain to achieve desired customer service standards.

Hence, the online layers operating in either of the two business models often pick up best practices from the other model and suitably incorporate into their respective operational strategy in order to improve the overall shopping experience and profitability. For example, Pepperfry operate fulfillment centers where it receives the merchandise ordered online. The merchandise then passes through suitable quality checks and uniform packaging before getting delivered for last-mile delivery. These kinds of operations require a high level of consistency and efficiency coupled with continuous coordination with sellers.

However, some online players follow a hybrid model, which is essentially a combination of both managed marketplace and inventory-based model, in a suitable proportion (ratio) to ensure the perfect blend, in terms of service levels and profitability. For example, Yebhi.com operates on the combination of both the models.

Advantages and Disadvantages of Off-line Stores

Pros

- Established brand-name/image
- Better impact due to physical visibility
- Consumer can touch, feel, and try the product; this aids trust and brand visibility
- Established quality
- Merchandising skills
- Consumer acceptance of current proposition
- Human interaction makes the service and shopping experience more "lively"

Cons

- The brick-and-mortar (physical) nature restricts the store in a specific catchment area
- Inertia of static model
- Limited physical space allows display of limited merchandise
- The process of change, transformation, innovate, and so on is tedious and also involves a higher cost
- Lack of execution speed because of sturdy operating procedures and processes

- High operating cost specifically because of expenses on rentals
- Technology competence
- There is paucity of better or prime retail avenues
- Physical setup limits the footprint to selected geographies
- Traditional retail "mind-set"
- Human errors in service can be sometimes harmful to the brand image

Advantages and Disadvantages of Online Stores

Pros

- Convenience of shopping and also selling
- Features like last-mile home delivery and payment options like COD are unique competitive advantages
- There are no time restrictions for shopping and selling on online store
- Online store can easily be accessed through many devices, which gives a huge reach to online retail players
- Enables the customers to access the product description or product knowledge very easily
- Unlimited merchandise can be featured, and there is almost no limitation of scale and reach
- Low operating cost and overheads because of virtual nature
- Online model provides higher ease of implementing changes, transformations, innovations, and so on, in relatively lesser time and with relatively lesser cost implications
- More structured real-time inventory control is easily possible
- Enables the retailer to understanding consumer behavior effectively with the use of data and information obtained from data analytics and trend analysis
- Effective IT and communication infrastructure enables fast execution and better customer interface
- Networked commerce model gives convenience and transparency of transactions

Cons

- No touch, feel, and try experience: For a certain product categories and certain set of customers, touch, feel, and try experience while buying remains a constraint in the online model
- High advertising costs
- It can lead to a quick obsolescence if the online retailer brand does not keep pace with changing technology and consumer expectations
- As the e-commerce industry is still not evolved completely, sometimes the online retail transaction through online transactions face challenges such as trust-deficit and security concerns due to lack of human interface

Many advantages of online retailers eventually resulted in a trend called as "showrooming" where customers browse and "touch-feel-try out" the merchandise in a brick-and-mortar store and then go on to purchase it through online retail portals. This has been seen potentially as a huge threat to the brick-and-mortar store formats. While shopping has and will always be preferred with a tactile experience where all the senses have to be entertained, the constraint of online retailing with its regular (traditional) form is that it only depends on the sensation of sight. While retailing through off-line store format can involve the sense of ambience, environment, visual displays, smell, and, most importantly, the touch-feel-try experience, which is invincible, for instance, for many categories like apparel and jewelry, customers still like to "touch and feel" a fabric, try on outfits, and enjoy the VM done in the store. This gives them a better idea and inputs regarding design and styles most suitable for them and also regarding "adds on" something, perhaps some accessories, to make it more interesting. Many times, customers also seek personalized consultation by store sales associates, and such human interface adds value to the overall shopping experience. Hence, such unique advantages of off-line retailers eventually resulted in the trend called as "webrooming" wherein customers browse online but buy in brick-and-mortar stores. This trend of "webrooming" is prevailing in the situations like customer is buying the product for the first time or when it is necessary to touch-feel-try the product or when customer interaction is needed or when some level of customization is required.

The success of any retail format is quintessentially measured in terms of increased reach and accessibility of a retailer brand. In today's retailing scenario, consumers are increasingly connected and spend much of their time on mobile and web application. As customers today are switching between channels (showrooming and webrooming) in completing their purchase, it is increasingly becoming crucial for the retailers to be accessible to the full set of their target segment and to be present across all possible channels. So the need is definitely a fusion of off-line and online presence to reach out to shoppers—who are tech savvy, short of time, and still prefer the tactile aspects of shopping experience of a brick-and-mortar store.

Hybrid Format and Omni-channel or Multiple-channel Retailing

Retailing today is not just about off-line (brick-and-mortar) model or online (e-retailing). Even in the brick-and-mortar model, retailers are using cutting-age technologies like tablets as registers, store maps and merchandise identification in aisles provided by GPS trackers, and information regarding promotions, offers, new arrivals, and so on popping up on customer's mobile devices while they are shopping in the store. But still there is a wide gap between the two models, and both the models have their own advantages and limitations. Besides, the process of going off-line way for an online player essentially involves maintaining a well-stocked brick-and-mortar store with rental overhead costs, inventory, and other legal and commercial procedures. So we can see that both off-line and online retailers are trying to overcome these challenges and limitations by going the omni-channel way and by creating omni-channel shopping experience that embraces a growing list of customer touch points. Consumer journeys today have become shorter and complicated. Impulse buying is on the rise, and consumers now end up having different experiences online and off-line. So here there is a need for creating a seamless shopping experience across online and off-line channels by leveraging the power of omni-channel marketing. The omni-channel marketing puts the consumer at the center and offers her/him the choice and convenience to decide when, where, and how to shop. This enables the retailers to convey same message across mediums as both online and on-ground touch points become interlinked.

The economics of retail—both off-line and online—are equally sustainable if done strategically, which involve well-thought-out fusion of these two models. The omni-channel retail model is a further economical evolution in this fusion, as it enhances the ROI of both the physical store and the online portal. Retailer's ROI increases as the customer walking into the store can now buy from a much larger selection that may be available online. Hence, a retailer can operate smaller stores (reduced rentals) with less inventory (reduced cost of inventory), and e-retailing model can improve economics by using stores as points for delivery, returns, exchange, and so on (reduced cost of delivery logistics and also reverse logistics). Such kinds of models are popularly known as clicks-and-bricks. Some of the world's largest retailers are using their brick-and-mortar store setups as mini distribution hubs. Retailers, including Walmart, Gap, and Best Buy, are routing online orders to nearest stores as this path significantly reduces the cost and time for fulfilling these orders, because delivering the merchandise from warehouses that are generally located far away from customer's home is comparatively a costly affair. For example,

61

Amazon has tied up with Bharat Petroleum's retail store brand In & Out for a store pickup service in Delhi and Mumbai.

Besides, merchandise and product portfolio management, pricing and promotions are virtually independent of a channel. Thus, e-tailers are adopting the strategy of keeping off-line ventures capital-light. For instance, some online players have also adopted the *franchise model* to go off-line, thereby off-loading a lot of the economics onto the franchisees. Franchising has become an attractive proposition for the online retailers in the categories such as furniture and home improvement and white goods, which have a component of last-mile delivery, installation, and servicing as well.

In a nut shell, it is a real value-creating business model that eventually enables the retailer to:

- Create a coherent shopping experience for their target customers.
- Make decision-making as easy as possible for the consumers.
- Create awareness about the brand proposition.
- Increase their chances of interacting with the brand at several touch points.
- Increase the sales revenues through multi-channel approach and eventually gives economies of merchandise sourcing.
- Increase customer loyalty and add new customers in their fold. Retailer that follow an integrated approach and offer customized solutions based on real-time information, interests, and consumer data are bound to command greater loyalty.
- Leverage same brand lineage, inventory, and many other common assets.
- build the brand, thereby reinforcing the trust and credibility factor among the customers.
- Improve brand presence and experiment with customer experience.
- Reduce the operating cost and hence enhance the bottom line.
- Develop more effective and conducive environment for running CRM and loyalty programs.

Hence to be relevant, it is imperative for retailer brands to be consistent in their approach, and omni-channel model offers this flexibility and consistency.

For example, there are some basic needs like "touch-feel-try" experience that customers have while shopping certain categories like apparels and fashion accessories. Hence, it is essentially a "journey" of trying on something and thinking about it, and then putting it on again. So to connect and engage with the customers, it becomes imperative for fashion retailers to enable them to go on to that journey. This is possible only when they have physical presence. But at the same time, they need a wider reach also with huge selections available, and this is possible only with the online presence. These online retailers are also using these brick-and-mortar outlets to promote their PLBs.

For example, after successfully operating through around 20 EBOs and around 350 MBOs, Agwani Fashions launched online shopping website (successonline.co.in). Being an independent men's premium fashion brand, it also acts as an extension of service the retailer tends to offer in their off-line stores. Here the online platform is an extension of the off-line model. It adds to the convenience of the buyer who can shop from home or office easily on the run through a smartphone. They have standardized sizes and fit, and customer can get the look and feel of the merchandise from images and detailed descriptions on the website. Similarly, Arvind Mills, which operated the brands such as Lee, Arrow, Tommy Hilfiger, and Wrangler in India, has come up with its online venture Creyate. This online shopping portal also lets the users to customize shirts and jeans online. This is in line with the notion that just going online is not sufficient and there has to be some differentiation.

This trend of going online is witnessed not only in fashion category but also in the categories such as consumer electronics and white goods as increasing number of people are buying big-ticket items such as washing machine, TV, and fridge online. The Tata-led Croma operates its online store CromaRetail.com and earns handsome revenues.

It is also a great idea and opportunity to build brands the online way first, especially in categories like furniture, where the unit economics of off-line is very poor as it essentially requires large spaces and high rentals.

For instance, online furniture store mobelhomestore.com primarily offers furniture, home–improvement, and home décor products. Furniture and home-improvement category is typically a high-value purchase for a customer, and they generally want to see and feel the merchandise physically, before buying it. This makes e-commerce platform a little tough selling proposition, due to the nature of the product category. But it is certainly complementing to their brick-and-mortar store. While the brick-and-mortar model gives them maximum revenue, the e-commerce model gives a chance to reach out to a wider audience. FabFurnish, another furniture retailer, operates through off-line stores that are basically presented as the concept stores having area of around 5,000–10,000 sq. ft. These concept stores are much smaller than the traditional off-line furniture stores, which are typically spread in the area of around 30,000–50,000 sq. ft. In this small area, they display limited designs, but this helps them to make their consumers confident about brand value and merchandise quality. Similarly, many online furniture retailers are in the process of off-line concept stores across cities. These are basically large-format kiosks equipped with iPads and touch screens that allow customers to browse through various designs and assortments and experience the merchandise. These concept stores act as a brand-building platform rather than as sale points.

Lenskart, the eyewear e-retailer, has opened off-line stores through franchise model where people can get their eyes checked. They found out the major factors that prevent people from buying spectacles online. They observed that customers wanted to get their eyes checked before they buy spectacles, they wanted to be very sure about the technical specifications, and also wanted see how the pair of eyeglasses would look on their face. So being physical in nature, the off-line stores enable Lenskart to cater all these needs of its customers with the physical advantages of buying an eyewear along with wide selection available online. Lenskart is strategically focusing on Tier II and Tier III markets where there is dearth of affordable and good eye checkup facilities and wide range of eyewear selection to choose from.

Even in the mature market like USA, many e-retailers such as One Kings Lane in home décor, Bonobos in apparel, and Warby Parker in eyewear segments have opened physical stores to engage the customers, to connect with them, and to offer them a complete shopping experience. Hence, perfect synergies can be achieved by combining some of the core retailer strengths with an online business channel. Many synergies are possible out of the fusion and traditional perspective of looking at off-line or online as silos is being trashed. Because either off-line or online can remain isolated as increased synergy between different channels, including online, off-line and m-retailing (mobile retailing), is the way forward for retail growth. Hence, a new opportunity is being created, which is not just an incremental benefit but could also prove to be decisive because shoppers too are increasingly becoming "hybrid" in their shopping behaviors.

Mobile Retailing (M-Retailing)

Today, the world is driven by technology, and the age of machines has taken over and has ensured a comfortable life for the humankind. We are living in the digital smart age where we have access to web and Internet technologies at our fingertips. One of the most significant features of the evolution of communications technology has been the consistent augmentation of mobile phones. It has redefined the way how we communicate and also how we transact, which can be attributed to the mobility and convenience of transaction that a smartphone today provides. Today, it is not only a need or necessity but also the reflection of elevated prosperity. With the growing mobile penetration, people are using it as a means to resolve many of infrastructural impediments in their day-to-day activities and transactions as this behavior is increasing; retailers are connecting with their target audience through the mobile devices. Besides business, this growth has transformed mobile devices into a social object, nurturing social and behavioral changes.

If we look at the things in the context of Indian e-commerce market, unlike many global markets, India is evolving into a "mobile first" market. It is evident from the fact that:

- A significant proportion of (around 65%) e-commerce traffic for many players (like Flipkart and Amazon India) comes through mobiles (combining the traffic through mobile browsers and apps), and this proportion is increasing with exponential rate.
- A majority of sales of leading e-retailers are coming from mobile devices.

This is making India one of the largest m-retailing markets in the world, and e-retailers are increasingly investing on mobile-related promotions. Retailers are continuously updating the way they use search engine optimization (SEO) and exploring multiple touch points to connect to consumers.

One of the major e-commerce drivers has been the high online purchasing behavior in the Tier II and Tier III cities, and even in rural areas, due to easy access to merchandise and services, which were otherwise not accessible to these consumers. However, limited per capita availability of personal computer across the country and limited broadband penetration have essentially necessitated the use of mobile devices as the preferred media to access Internet and do online shopping for many customers located beyond the major cities of India. On the other hand, the growing adoption of smartphones with significant reduction in prices has supported this evolution.

Hence, the following factors make mobile transactions convenient and mobiles as the preferred channel for commerce:

- The freedom of shopping at any place, at any point of time, and without the hassle of turning on another computer device and connecting it to the Internet.
- Availability of cheaper and affordable smartphones.
- Increased use of larger-screen mobile phones (tablets).
- Bigger memory of mobile phones.
- Continuous evolution of higher-generation mobile Internet networks (2G, 3G, 4G, etc.), which is continuously improving the ease of Internet browsing in terms of speed and capacity.
- Telecom operators are coming up with attractive promotional offers to motivate the customers to get converted (upgraded) into higher-generation mobile Internet networks (i.e., from 2G to 3G, etc.).
- Better browsing capabilities.
- The telecom operators are coming up with affordable and competitive data plans. Also the ease of mobile number portability and free roaming are other factors that are favorable to the development.
- Evolution of the mobile app-driven m-commerce ecosystem.

- The features like COD are attracting more and more customers. This has enabled the retailers to overcome the trust deficit in online payments and lack of credit card/debit card penetration.
- Evolution of mobile-based payment models and mobile wallet ecosystem. E-retailers are focusing on providing payment options such as mobile wallet, net (mobile) banking, and EMI (easy monthly installments) facilities to make the transaction faster, safer, and more convenient.

Hence, all the aspects running in tandem with each other are set to lead a true revolution in the field of online retailing. According to the survey reports, when it comes to consumer time spent; the mobile apps have already outshined the web, and are second only to time spent on watching television. To capture this opportunity, e-retailers appear to be investing heavily on primary objective of improving the mobile user experience.

They are looking forward to capture mobile customer's mindshare through providing exclusive discounts on app usage, special promotions in order to push the desktop/laptop customers toward app usage, and motivate them to install their apps on mobile phones.

- A mobile app is nothing but a software application that is specifically developed for use on small mobile computing devices like tablet and smartphones and not for laptop or desktop or computers.
- While the search engines on the Internet can easily browse a retail store site and index, apps are closed systems that act as a more engaging platform for retailers to target smartphone user customers by offering a great shopping experience through their apps.
- Apps also allow them to engage with users (customers) more, as they are "connected" (logged in on their devices) throughout the day so the integration of apps in the marketing strategy has become inevitable. Today, apps are integral component of mobile marketing strategy of almost every retailer, as they (apps) perform throughout the life cycle of engagement of the consumer and across the buying process.

This phenomenon has potential to create more loyal customers than those created through landing on the portal through online search engines. Retailers are also looking to enable their staff to provide better customer service through mobile. For instance, an app can be used for the order management process of retail organization. Hence, apps quintessentially offer value-added functionalities, and growing number of users prefer this convenience and experience, which eventually has changed the way shopping is done.

For example, for improving the customer experience, Flipkart has used cutting-edge technologies like visual search, while designing its app. This technology enables the customer to just simply point the app at any merchandise, say a shirt, to get similar options on the portal. Other fashion online retailers are also coming with similar technology solutions to enhance the user experience as the app enables the consumers to access their collection in time of few seconds.

Online women fashion retailer LimeRoad has come up with the app that posts new styles, trends, and merchandise updates from customers and vendors almost every 30 seconds. This is to ensure that the user will have something new and fresh to see every time she logs in. The merchandise and "looks" created by users are streamed along with new arrivals—new designs and trends.

Online personal stylist platform Voonik has come up with the app wherein the app's swipe-to-like interface allows the user swipe to the right if they find some attractive/interesting apparel or accessory. Similarly, it allows the user swipe to the left if they are not interested in

Photo 2.4: *LimeRoad Shopping App*

Source: http://www.limeroad.com/mobile-apps/ (accessed on 12 May 2016)

the merchandise. Once swiped right, it will keep the user posted on the promotional offers/discounts and availability for that item over time.

Online furniture retailer Urban Ladder has come up with new augmented reality versions app features that assists the users to visualize and build their own wardrobes by using the app. They can explore different dimensions, colors, and also compare the prices.

Retailers are also coming up with attractive promotional offers exclusively for their app users; for example, Amazon's "Appiness Day" sale and Flipkart's "Big App Shopping Days" to motivate the customers download their mobile application and use it for shopping.

Hence, as the mobile traffic is growing, online players are prioritizing their platforms for enhancing user engagement by creating consumer-centric apps equipped with specialized tools, which eventually decreases pressure on costs. Designing and building apps is a scientific art, and even after the initial investment, it needs continuous investment in enhancement, modification, and nurturing the customer network that the app is intended to bring together. It is equally essential to develop propositions that would lead to shopping convenience and consumer delight. This essentially involves a constant emphasis on designing smart app with various interactive features, reviews by various forums, thorough testing, leveraging inputs from user experience and feedbacks, and building dynamic apps that is adaptive to version modifications and technologies used in the mobile devices. For instance, an app equipped with bar-code scanning function helps the consumers to instantly search merchandise specifications online and also compare the prices. A growing number of retailers are equipping their employees with smartphones and tablets and also continuously improving their in-store integration with mobile devices.

App structures are being designed and/or redesigned on the basis of customer usage patterns and preferences, which enable the e-retailer to move beyond the constraints of mobile screen space and also leverage on certain features of the mobile ecosystem such as camera, contacts, sensors, gyroscope, integration with GPS, and social media. Online retailers are also focusing on developing the lighter apps, which require low bandwidth, to address the issues like space constraints (referring to phone memory consumed by the app) and user connectivity problems. They are also trying to offer limited off-line functionality. Hence, with all these efforts, retailers are ensuring that their app should work smoothly even when networks are highly unreliable and the content and usage pattern are well synchronized. Also, the technology glitches and security threats that negatively affect customer sentiment during online transaction are taken care by payment options like COD facility.

Promotion of the apps is equally essential because it ensures high adoption rate and consistently growing user base. Detailed analytics of several aspects such as the engagement time, types of mobile devices being used, frequency of access, preferred content, recommendations of the app, and other customer behavior patterns are crucial in order to garner the maximum returns from the investment made in designing, developing, and maintenance of the app.

Mobile is fundamentally transforming the dynamics of shopping, which has been driven by the strategic focus toward developing and investing in technology that eventually enable the retailers to create a holistic shopping experience. They are gaining foothold in the value chain by addressing a number of customer touch points with the help of mobile technology. It is creating huge opportunity not only for retail companies but also for entrepreneurs and mobile-first start-ups to optimize the customer experience at multiple touch points.

For instance, online fashion retailer Myntra adopted "app only" model in May 2015. However, one thing that should also be mentioned here is that there is a large proportion of consumers who still prefer a bigger screen of desktop/laptop to view the merchandise before buying and also compare prices online. Thus, most of the leading players such as Flipkart, Amazon, Snapdeal, Paytm, and others are cautious of going the "app only" way. Though the leading players like Snapdeal and Flipkart have seen robust traffic through the mobile platform, there are still a huge number of customers using desktops and laptops to shop online. This has convinced these retailers to be present where their customers are and to offer them choice as to how they want to shop by adopting the inclusive strategy rather than app-only strategy.

Mobile Wallet: A Gateway to Mobile Payment Ecosystem. With the number of smartphone users increasing by leaps and bounds and the growing popularity of e-commerce, it was obvious that the digital payments industry will take off. Mobile-based cardless and cashless mode of payment (also referred as m-wallets) has emerged as one of the biggest beneficiaries of a fast maturing digital payment industry in the country. India, traditionally, has always been a cash economy with low financial inclusion and limited penetration of banking services. However, with the evolution of the mobile digital wallet, the paradigm has shifted very rapidly. With this change, the leading players like Paytm, MobiKwik, Citrus Pay, Airtel Money, Oxigen, mRupee, and M-Pesa, among others, then tied up with e-commerce players, enabling payments on their sites through mobile wallets at a convenience of single touch or tap.

Putting the things in simple words, the digital mobile wallet is a virtual account created through a service provider where the user loads a certain amount of money. This amount can then be used to make quick payments and purchases without the hassle of carrying cash around, remembering multiple passwords, or worrying about debit/credit card frauds, and so on. The money credited in a digital wallet is stored in an escrow account and is completely secure as per strict RBI norms. Also, because the consumer decides how much money to store in a digital wallet, the risk of losing one's entire savings due to a fraud is not there, an exposure which is there in cards and net banking.

With this convenience and safety, consumers began to make a behavioral switch in favor of digital wallets as a quick, safe, and hassle-free means of transacting online. The use of mobile wallets for range of payments grew manifolds with the increasing awareness about its benefits and resultant adoption of digital wallets. As the use of these digital wallets is becoming widespread, the consumer stands to gain even more. One of the most obvious advantages is the increase in the number of brick-and-mortar stores where one will be able to pay through digital wallets. For a majority of these players providing digital mobile wallet services, the key to scaling up lies in creating more "use cases" (more range of payments) for these services. The key success factor is creating trust factor and cultivating a highly engaged digital customer base by offering the ease of use and security. Looking at things through the customer loyalty perspective and differentiation of services, the key considerations for mobile digital wallet players are to enhance customer experience and engagement, product stickiness, and increase use cases for these services. Mobile wallet service providers also have to think in terms of long-term incentives to encourage consumers to spend more time on their platform. They also need to ensure that their loyalty programs provide consumers ease of earning as well as redeeming these earned points.

Television Retailing (T-Retailing or T-Commerce)

India's retail landscape has witnessed rapid changes in recent years that are primarily attributed to the increasing disposable incomes and a growing number of nuclear families with evolving lifestyles, the inclination of consumers toward best deals, and overall convenience of shopping. These changes in consumer behavior are the major driving forces for making television retailing a growing phenomenon today. Many consumers prefer shopping from home as it is more comfortable, time-saving, and convenient. The television shopping allows one to relax on a comfortable recliner chair, drink a hot coffee, watch the favorite TV show or movie, and simultaneously order the merchandise that is being displayed for sale on the television by a retailer. Developing and building a brick-and-mortar model is a costly affair as it essentially requires huge capital investment. Besides, the infrastructural hassles with limited Internet penetration in several areas of the country have prompted some retailers to explore newer avenues to reach out to wider audience without the dependency on Internet network, especially in areas where modern retail penetration continues to be low. The growth of leading television home-shopping companies such as HomeShop18 and Star CJ has been reasonably good, if not exceptional, because of the widespread nature of television and the limited penetration of the Internet. According to the reports, there are still millions of households in the country that receive content through television and do not have access to the Internet. In such situations, the option of television retailing acts as an attractive proposition for these retailers.

Though the television home-shopping industry made its foray in India almost a decade earlier, the segment is witnessing a phase of resurgence by effectively leveraging the reach of cable and satellite (direct-to-home platforms) in India. There has been a turnaround after the arrival of 24-hour dedicated TV home-shopping channels. Over these years, the credibility factor has greatly improved for the Indian television home-shopping business. The success of two major channels of this industry, HomeShop18 and Star CJ, launched in 2008 and 2009, respectively, prompted more players to enter the market. For instance, started as an e-commerce platform, Naaptol launched Blue, a 24-hour dedicated TV channel. In addition, it has also launched Hathway Shoppe in a strategic collaboration with leading multisystem operator (MSO) Hathway, which is exclusively available on the MSO's digital platform. Other key players in this segment are Best Deal TV, Bagittoday, DEN-Snapdeal TV Shop, HBN Telebrands, Planet M Shopping, and TVC Retail.

There are many synergies that exist here as that of in online–off-line collaborations. For example, the television channel DEN-Snapdeal TV Shop is a JV between Snapdeal and cable distribution platform DEN Networks. Hence, through this JV, Snapdeal is leveraging its distribution network and DEN's reach to enable customers to access a wide assortment of merchandise across fashion, lifestyle, home, and electronics categories with attractive value deals. Similarly, HomeShop18 has expanded into the digital space with the launch of HomeShop18.com. The central idea behind such ventures is, while the online model (through Internet and mobile) will attract the more astute digital customer, the home-shopping is intended to play the role of mass reach and high-volume sales that eventually results in improved profitability.

According to various market research reports, women are the key driving force behind sales of home-shopping channels in India. The significant contribution by women comes in the backdrop of housewives patronizing the convenience of shopping from home while watching TV. The purchase decisions regarding women-centric products like home and kitchen appliances are majorly influenced by women, and these are the categories that are generally sold through these channels. They also offer other women-centric fashion and lifestyle products such as saris, dress materials, home furnishings, and accessories, with the ease of shopping from home and quick access to merchandise information through television content.

The television home-shopping channels also promote and offer merchandise with a high majority being PLBs and small- to mid-scale brands. While the online retailers offer millions of items and are focused on driving valuations through exponential top-line growth, television home-shopping companies have delivered balanced growth with profitability by offering limited number of items. The primary target market of TV home-shopping channels is the Tier II and Tier III cities, small towns, and rural areas, which are basically a try-and-feel market. Above all, around 80–95% of TV home-shopping sales are driven by COD. Here the logistical hassles often lead to delayed deliveries and consumers refusing to accept the delivery. This eventually translates into higher return rate, that is, added cost of reverse logistics. This in turn adversely affects the business economics of TV home-shopping players. Thus to maintain the profitability, the television retailers are consistently focusing on quality of merchandise, improving on the trust-deficit factor and building effective and efficient SCM ecosystem.

For example, Star CJ's foray into the mass market of television shopping has been deliberate. It gradually entered with premium brands having credibility, such as Dell, Samsung, BlackBerry, Satya Paul, and Tanishq, and eventually expanded into categories such as small kitchenwares, appliances and home furnishing, and home-improvement items. Like e-retailers, the TV home-shopping players such as Naaptol and TVC are also using the extraordinary penetration of delivery services of India Post to counter the last-mile delivery challenges, especially in the case of small town and rural area. Homeshop18 operates a "virtual shopping wall" at the Delhi international airport's domestic terminal to bring a different user experience to the off-line model. Also, with the proliferation of smartphones, most of the TV home-shopping players have streamlined their m-retailing operations to maximize traffic, revenue, and profitability.

Summary

In a nutshell, we can conclude here that the retail industry works on several formats. These formats are generally classified into store and non-store formats and also on the basis of their ownership. Each format has its own structure and operational attributes that distinguishes it from others. This distinction gives a format its unique "retail value proposition"—the basic reason why customer should shop there. This proposition is a combination of the variables of the retail mix that consists of merchandise, display, pricing, accessibility, and service. A retailer needs to identify one aspect that would provide SCA. The selection is dependent on the target customers, competition, and the objectives of the retailers. Shoppers have broadened their shopping across formats, and this is why, even after the proliferation of several formats, each one of them is still surviving and thriving with certain modifications and improvisations.

The rationale for e-retailer companies to consider brick-and-mortar store compellingly lies in the fact that the majority of retail sales still happening off-line. This scenario is prompting retailers to understand, adopt, and enable omni-channel presence to enable shoppers a range of platforms to shop at (i.e., brick-and-mortar, computers, mobile Internet devices, etc.). Hence, the click-and-mortar model of modern retailing looks beyond the traditional way of retailing as it is done. A hybrid model essentially maintains a healthy balance between off-line and online presence and provides a holistic experience to consumers. This eventually reinforces the trust factor with the physical feel of products along with the convenience of access to a larger inventory online. Typography is about how the online and brick-and-mortar retailers are merging together in this new evolving landscape.

As far as the m-commerce is concerned, it is imminently becoming evident that power of mobiles is evolving with the development of communication media and IT. Although the trade-off between platforms may depend on the customer base, business model, and future strategy, it is more likely that, going forward, m-commerce could be the prevailing online commerce model in India. It is rapidly becoming the need of the hour to be mobile (app) focused to have a bigger footprint in the business of retailing. Hence, the strategic moves like designing new customer applications, development of functionalities for leveraging data and analytics, and the integration of app with existing legacy systems enable an app model to create a new platform of engagement between retailers and their target audience. Retailers are putting all their strength into technology acquisition as it will be vital for increasing customer loyalty and also for ensuring profitability. All of their innovation and development is app first, and it will keep on being their flagship experience.

Review Questions

1. What do you mean by retail formats? Explain in detail the process of format selection.
2. How are the retailers classified on the basis of ownership? Explain with appropriate examples.
3. How are the retailers classified? Explain all the formats of retailing briefly with appropriate examples.
4. What do you mean by franchising? Analyze the importance of franchising for franchiser and franchisee with appropriate examples.
5. "Franchising is a boon for entrepreneurs." Explain the statement in detail with appropriate examples.
6. Critically analyze franchising in the context of its possible limitations and disadvantages.
7. Explain e-retailing with appropriate examples.
8. How will you analyze the marketplace and inventory-based model of e-retailing?

9. Explain the significance of omni-channel retailing model in the context of advantages and disadvantages of both online and off-line retailing.
10. "Omni-channel model of retailing is a burgeoning phenomenon." Analyze this statement in the context of current retailing scenario.
11. Explain the significance of m-retailing with appropriate examples.
12. Critically analyze the television retailing (t-retailing) scenario with appropriate examples.
13. Write short notes on:

   - Franchising
   - E-retailing
   - M-retailing
   - T-retailing
   - Hybrid retailing and omni-channel shopping experience
   - App retailing: a tool for enhancing consumer engagement

Chapter 3

E-retailing

- **E-retailing and e-commerce**
- **Important features of e-commerce**
- **E-retailing ecosystem and its importance**
- **Role of e-retailing in employment generation, propagation of entrepreneurship in all of its forms, and creation of entrepreneurship opportunities for women**
- **Advantages, limitations, and major challenges**
- **Logistics and supply chain management in e-retailing**

Introduction

With rapid growth and penetration of the Internet and globalization of market, the retail sector has become an increasingly competitive and dynamic business environment. Business and marketing activities have undergone a paradigm shift after the invention and proliferation of Internet technologies, and the Internet/web technology started revolutionizing commerce, marketing, retailing, shopping, and advertising/promotional activities. There are two key infrastructure elements that enabled the growth of e-tailing:

1. Penetration of devices through which to access the Internet
2. Proliferation of technology enabling Internet access

This proliferation of Internet access and usage has changed the manner in which such Internet-habituated consumers pick up trends, form opinions, learn about new things, and consume merchandise. In the context of Indian e-tailing scenario, one of the key reasons why such trends emerged is India's demographic features. India is predominantly young with a median age of 26 years. This will continue to be the case for the next 10 years. With the projected median age of 29 years in 2020, by 2020, 40% of India would have been born after the launch of the Internet and mobile phones in the country. Thus, for a sizeable population of Indians, access to the Internet and the use of mobile phones will be a norm to which they will not have to make transition to, unlike previous generations. Thus for these young consumers, spending time on the Internet will be as normal as watching television is for today's consumers.

In today's era of globalization, companies are using the Internet technology to reach out to their valued customers and providing them with a point of contact 24/7. E-commerce and e-marketing are the two important terms in the new Internet-based business domain. E-commerce can be defined as a way of conducting business by companies and customers performing electronic transactions through the Internet. E-marketing (also known as Internet marketing, web marketing, and online marketing, etc.) can be defined as the promotion of products or services through the Internet, whereas e-tailing can be defined as selling products and services by a retailer using the Internet. E-tailing is also defined as retailing conducted online.

E-commerce

E-commerce means using the Internet and the web for business transactions and/or commercial transactions, which typically involve the exchange of value (e.g., money) across organizational or individual boundaries in return for products and services. Here we focus on digitally enabled commercial transactions among organizations and individuals. E-business applications turn into e-commerce precisely, when an exchange of value occurs. Digitally enabled transactions include all transactions mediated by digital technology and platform; that is, transactions that occur over the Internet and the web.

Hence, e-tailing is a subset of e-commerce, which encapsulates all "commerce" conducted via the Internet. It refers to that part of e-commerce that entails the sale of product merchandise and does not include sale of services, namely railway tickets, airlines tickets and job portals.

There are three types of destinations that cater to retail sales:

- Traditional retail: brick-and-mortar
- Corporatized retail: brick-and-mortar
- Corporatized retail: e-tailing

Importance of E-commerce

Today, we can see e-commerce is becoming a part of study of almost all the courses in management and commerce. It is an integral part of any book or manuscript that is written on retailing, and it claims a significant share in this text also. The reason behind this lies in the fact that e-commerce technology is different and more powerful than any of the other technologies we have seen in the past century. While these other technologies transformed economic life in the 20th century, the evolving Internet and other ITs will shape the 21st century in many ways. The foremost of these is the rise of a sizeable class of Internet-habituated consumers, and then is the creation of an ecosystem essential for e-tailing's growth. In India's case, both these factors are poised to fall into place rapidly.

Prior to the development of e-tailing, the process of marketing and selling goods was a mass-marketing and/or sales force-driven process. Consumers were considered as passive targets of advertising (promotional) "campaigns," and branding blitzes were intended to influence their long-term product perceptions (brand positioning) and immediate purchasing behavior. Selling was conducted in typical well-insulated "channels." Consumers were viewed to be trapped by geographical and social boundaries, unable to search widely for the alternatives with best price and quality. Information about prices, costs, and tariffs could be hidden from the customers to get the resultant profitable "information asymmetries" for the selling firm. Here, information asymmetry means any disparity in relevant market information among parties in a transaction. E-commerce has challenged much of these traditional retail business norms, assumptions, and behavior.

Features of E-commerce

From the business point of view, there are two models of e-commerce. The first model is known as "marketplace" model, which works like exchange for buyers and sellers. This model provides a platform for business transactions between buyers and sellers to take place, and in return for the services provided, the "market place" provider earns commission from sellers of goods/services. Ownership of the inventory in this model vests with the number of enterprises that advertise and promote their products on the website and are ultimate sellers of goods or services. The "marketplace," thus, works as a facilitator of e-commerce. Different from the "marketplace" model is the second model of business known as "inventory-based" model. In this model, ownership of goods and services and marketplace vests with the same entity. This model does not work as a facilitator of e-commerce, but is engaged in e-commerce directly.

Convenience of Shopping and Selling

India's leading online fashion marketplaces, Jabong and Myntra, in their three years of operations (2012–2014), probably at the threshold of a revolution, garnered impressive top-line numbers and, more importantly, a gigantic three-digit and four-digit growth figures that signal a tipping point in how urban Indians will dress themselves—they are likely to move most of their clothes shopping to fashion e-tailers. In addition, online retail has passed the inflection point as customers have stopped questioning its viability and authenticity. In these three years, Jabong's and Myntra's top lines have outperformed those of established and leading brick-and-mortar fashion retailers, Zara, Levi's, and Marks & Spencer, which have been in business in India for between 5 and 10 years, while the growth of the big brick-and-mortar chains, Shoppers Stop and Future Lifestyle Fashion, which have been in operations for two decades or more, has really slowed down in comparison over the same period. All this has happened because consumers can get international brands such as Dorothy Perkins, Mango, River Island, FCUK, Guess, Desigual, Scotch & Soda, and not-so-high-priced Harpa and Femella under one roof and on one click. Jabong and Myntra also attribute their growth to an increase in its product portfolio and exclusive tie-ups, especially with international brands. Consumers will neither get to browse thousands of designs at physical stores nor will they be able to visit them every day. But they could visit a virtual store every single day, shop at their own convenience, and even return products they don't like, and all these can be done from the comfort of their home.

The phenomenal urbanization and an exponential growth of urban population all over the world have forced urban consumers to look for convenience in all modes of living, including shopping. Each day is increasingly packed with an ever greater range of activities, leaving ever lesser time for such discretionary activities as shopping. These consumers are therefore seeking alternatives that can free up more time in their crunched and packed schedules. This trend is accentuated by the increasing participation of women in the workforce. Most of these consumers, being from the working population, spend significant amount of time at workplaces having access to the Internet-enabled devices and steady Internet connection. Therefore, there is a disruptive growth in the adoption of Internet and mobile shopping, online travel bookings, and other such activities. Fashion e-tailers attribute their success to multiplier effect from good customer experience and some serious brand-building efforts.

Another start-up called SafetyKart.com is symptomatic of the unpredictable times that we live in. This e-tailer stocks up on more than 3,000 safety products from across 200 categories. The range of products covers everything from pepper sprays and antipollution masks to mosquito killers and surveillance equipment. SafetyKart.com was started by SRV Damage Preventions, exclusive partners of ShockWatch Inc., based out of Texas. In September 2014, a separate company was formed under the name of SafetyKart Retail Pvt. Ltd.

The portal's objective is to protect users from any kind of calamity or disease and to build a platform where unique and innovative safety products and services are made easily available to consumers. The central idea is to start something in the space of safety and, at the same time, increase awareness about the importance of safety. The online retailer caters to various consumer segments and work profiles—senior citizens to adventure sports enthusiasts, travel, home and office, and so on. The products are sourced from across the world and allow customers to compare before arriving on a purchase decision. Moving forward with the intention to be remembered as the incubator of a safety ecosystem in India, the portal is adding many more safety-specific services to create this ecosystem.

From the selling perspective, one of the most important features of e-commerce technology is that the technical standards of the Internet, web-based technologies and the platforms on which they are operated, and therefore the technical standards for conducting e-commerce are universally uniform—they are shared and followed by all nations and national political economies around the world.

Online merchandising brings many advantages because of its virtual nature. Some of these advantages are as follows:

1. As it is only visual or pictorial representation, a large number of SKUs can be displayed.
2. Because of the virtual nature, there is no physical merchandise; hence, issues of perishable goods and obsolescence of products do not arise.
3. As the product offerings are multitude in nature, a wider customer base can be addressed.

The new ways to rope in vendors are:

- Evangelists
- YouTube channels
- Tie-ups with state handicraft centers and institutes
- Exploring manufacturing hubs

E-commerce has become a preferred channel for retailers as it allows seller to connect with customers who cannot buy off-line due to distance or lack of time. The technical uniformity of the Internet and e-commerce substantially brings market entry cost down. It is the cost retailers/sellers need to bear just to bring their products to market and display the merchandise in the physical store. This in turn increases the overall ease of doing the business of retailing. At the same time, to the delight of consumers, it significantly reduces the cost of shopping—by curtailing the efforts required to find suitable products at appropriate/expected price points. Hence, e-tailing enables the sellers to develop and design a marketspace, where numerous products tagged with their technical and price point descriptions can be inexpensively displayed for all to view from anywhere and at any point of time. With this virtual nature of e-tailing, it is possible for the first time in history of retailing to easily maintain the display of merchandise across wide categories, assortments, and SKUs at a relatively low cost. This feature makes the product and price comparison simpler, faster, more accurate, and, at the same time, more convenient. In addition, the risk of physical storage space and inventory costs is minimal.

Let us consider the example of lingerie retailer Zivame.com. Lingerie, by definition, is extremely intimate, and customers want to feel comfortable literally and metaphorically with their purchases. But customers were having to compromise between aspiration and accessibility.

Previously, most of the other national and international brands and both off-line and online retailers had overlooked the value proposition in this segment. This prompted an enthusiastic women entrepreneur, Richa Kar, founder and chief executive of Zivame ("radiant me" in Hebrew), to fill the glaring gap in the assortment. And she started the online portal. Zivame was born from yet another insight that Indian women are uncomfortable buying lingerie from shops where the sales staff are men. But it was also not so easy because they faced a big hurdle of consumer behavior when they started—lingerie buying online was unheard-of. So their challenge was to find out how long it will take to get woman users online, same-day delivery, reverse logistics, and how to keep merchandise fresh in a category where there is very less opportunity for innovation. But as off-line buying was also an uncomfortable experience, consumers were waiting for a better experience, and they are now finding it online. So they wanted to be the go-to destination for women when it came to lingerie. It is part of building their confidence.

Today, the online portal has been evolved as India's largest online lingerie-only store with numerous offerings. As a niche player, their product strategy is to offer every possible product in the category. As the international brands' price points are difficult to match in the price-conscious Indian market, the online retailer decided to provide PLs in that category. In November 2013, Zivame launched its first PLB Penny Goddess and targeted the fuller women segment. In January 2014, Zivame introduced Coucou, an in-house brand offering reasonably priced lingerie for younger customers with special attention to their needs. Today, Zivame offers over 2,000 lingerie styles from 45 national and international brands such as Enamor, Triumph, Wonderbra, Jockey and alike. However, Coucou and Penny Goddess comprise almost 40% of the e-retailer's revenue. This example categorically shows that how e-tailing can increase the ease of product portfolio management and effectiveness of merchandising.

Other leading online retailers like Flipkart, Snapdeal, and Amazon have initially been facing the challenge of relatively low number of vendors, resulting in fewer categories available on the portal. To address this issue, they have come up with a slew of programs to get millions of sellers from across the country to their marketplaces. The initiatives range from launching dedicated YouTube channels and tying up with state handicraft centers to scouting and exploring for manufacturing hubs across cities. This movement of online retailers is prompted and motivated from the fact that there are millions and millions of small and medium businesses (SMBs) in India that present a lucrative opportunity to increase their merchandise/product base. Hence to tap this source, these leading players of e-tailing business have devised multiple programs to grow their seller portfolio. On the other hand, there are thousands of examples of sellers/manufactures in small towns who were earlier selling through their own arrangements and had limited market reach. But, now suddenly the entire country opened up to them through these platforms of online retailers.

Vendor Management

Today, we can see the emergence of many online players like ShopClues, Paytm, and others that are posing challenging competition to the established order of Flipkart, Snapdeal, and Amazon. This scenario has started a race among them for not only acquiring customers but also chasing sellers to board on their platforms. The behavior of sellers on these online platforms is not very different from the customers of these platforms. Both are demanding in their own ways and expect a high value. While the customers expect better discount and services and browse various platforms to compare or search better deals, the sellers on these portals expect higher revenues and hence may list on multiple platforms at once. The sellers would always like and want to be present on a marketplace that provides them the right opportunities to grow, has a high likelihood of surviving, and potential for succeeding in the long term. In this way, the sellers look at incentive to stay on and build their reputation.

To achieve the loyalty behavior of these stakeholders, the online players increasingly focus on creating a clear brand proposition and promise to get new sellers on board. And hence the game is evolving from just acquiring sellers and merchants to staying continuously and continually meaningful and relevant for them. To attract the sellers and merchants, online marketplaces are running a variety of initiatives and programs, such as exclusive fulfillment and warehousing facilities, among others.

For instance, Flipkart, Amazon, and Snapdeal are also offering lucrative promotional rates for commissions per order and also competitive delivery charges they levy on sellers, as well as temporarily waiving fees pertaining to subscription, packaging, and inventory storage. Amazon's "Chai Cart" program is designed to create awareness among local small entrepreneurs and sellers in small cities and towns. Flipkart launched a promotional program named "Seller Advantage Week" to assist new sellers across the country to bring their business online. Sellers who registered during the promotion period were eligible for special offers like free cataloging, zero-percentage commission, and other related support services. The objective of the "Seller Advantage Week" was to ensure a flawless on-boarding and registration experience for new sellers and spruce up their business to match the requirements of online marketplace. The promotion is a part of Flipkart's national seller campaign, "Apne Sapne Jee Kar Dekho" (Live Your Dreams), that was essentially initiated to offer guidance and support to new sellers to kick-start a hassle-free online foray.

Simultaneously, these online marketplaces are providing in-depth assistance to onboard merchants who have only known the off-line world because a lower commission is not sufficient for winning their trust and loyalty. If we think from sellers' perspective, they would obviously like to board the platform that will provide them the highest traction. So the online marketplaces tend to provide all the support to them, which shows that they want different types of sellers to sign in and succeed on their portals. Merchants tend to prefer seamless, cost-efficient options for delivery of products as logistics is one of the crucial factors in the business of online retailing. If the delivery is late, customers may tend to cancel orders and try out from somewhere else. Most of the times, sellers prefer 3PL partners that are tied up with the online players as it makes the process more simple, convenient, integrated, predictable, and cost-effective as well. The e-tailers offer multiple delivery logistics options to sellers, including the choice to ship on their own. Generally, the sellers opt for their own courier and delivery system when they are operating through their own online platform.

As e-commerce has become a common phenomenon, e-tailers are encouraging sellers and entrepreneurs to set up businesses online and providing perks and benefits such as:

- Warehousing services
- Marketing support like cataloging and packaging
- Seller workshops, training programs, and merchant summits
- Working capital assistance and capital financing
- Infrastructure like Seller University and seller app
- Payment services and swift payment cycle
- Support for overseas sales

We have discussed about the market reach and logistics support provided by online players to the sellers. Nevertheless, the third most important support they offer to sellers to encourage them to join their online channels is the financial assistance. In order to woo them, online players such as Flipkart, Snapdeal, eBay, and Amazon are tying up with nonbanking lenders for extending loans to those interested to sell products through their online marketplaces. Many times, small businesses face the capital crunch and strive to get loans. So to extend a financial support to them, online retailers are teaming up with several New Age nonbanking finance companies (NBFCs) such as NeoGrowth, Capital Float, and Capital First, and also with online finance firms such as Lendingkart and loan facilitators like SMEcorner to provide the sellers with fast and hassle-free loans.

For instance, State Bank of India, the nation's largest lender, has tied up with Amazon India to assist e-commerce sellers to access loans. SMEcorner has simultaneously partnered with many e-commerce players and several leading NBFCs. With the help of these alliances, SMEcorner plays the role of a catalyst in securing easier and hassle-free loans for sellers from the organized lenders.

Similarly, the Alibaba-backed digital payments company Paytm is providing tech tools such as web marketers, content writers, and photographers and has also created a directory of service providers that extend loans to SMEs along with finance and accounting firms, all through its GoBig platform. It is a fact that many of the SMEs do not know from where and how to get their merchandise items photographed or even from where and how to get soft loans for their ventures. In such situations, the directory helps them to find out the right partners. This is in line with the Paytm's objective to become a true marketplace by connecting buyers and sellers through its platform. Its e-commerce foray is a reflection of Alibaba-owned Taobao, an e-commerce site in China.

So in a nutshell, the e-tailers have to strive for winning the trust and loyalty of not only consumers but also sellers to be a winner in this business of online retailing. It is all about building the trust and credibility of the platform. Hence, they are increasingly focusing on creating a robust ecosystem for aspiring entrepreneurs and existing business owners with a highly scalable platform to grow their business.

The Ubiquity Feature

In off-line commerce, a marketplace is a physical place or store we visit for the transactions. For example, the advertisements through the media like television, print ads, and radio typically motivate and direct the consumer to visit some specific place *physically* and make a purchase. E-commerce, in contrast, is characterized by its feature of ubiquity: it is *virtually* available just about everywhere, at all times. It liberates the market from the confinement of physical space and makes the shopping possible from your desktop, at home, at work, or even from your car, using gadgets like tabs, laptops, and smartphones. This result in the creation of an ecosystem, which is called *marketspace*—it is a marketplace which extends beyond traditional boundaries and which is free from a temporal and geographic location. In any country where e-tailing has achieved reasonable success, consumers have shown signs of evolution on two dimensions that has enabled e-tailing market's growth—access to the Internet and Internet usage beyond browsing. In countries like India, consumers are displaying positive traction on both of these. The Internet browsing behavior of Indians has dramatically changed and this change has been almost disruptive—Indian consumers today are not only spending longer hours on the Internet but also conducting myriad activities that were nonexistent a few years ago.

Another trend that emerged recently and which is expected to grow further is the collaboration between established off-line brands and online platforms leveraging and complementing each other's competencies and consequently establishing a symbiotic relationship. Brands across segments have started realizing the importance of e-tailing by virtue of its ubiquity and are partnering with online marketplaces for launching products, exclusively online. Brands such as Croma, HomeTown, Micromax, Puma, John Players, Biba, Wills Lifestyle, Jack & Jones, Satyug Gold, Wonderchef, and Godrej Nature's Basket, which have a strong presence in the off-line segment, are now present on Snapdeal.com to widen their reach to the larger customer base across different parts of the country.

The pragmatic explanation to this phenomenon explicitly lies in the fact that the ubiquity of e-commerce lowers the cognitive energy requirement for transaction in a marketspace. Cognitive energy is nothing but the mental effort required to complete a task. It is a natural human behavior in which they generally seek to reduce cognitive energy outlays and outlets. When given a choice, humans choose the most convenient path. Hence to the delight of consumers, ubiquity not only reduces the transaction cost—the cost of participating in a market—but also increases the convenience of shopping and purchasing—as in this case, it is no longer necessary that you spend time and money traveling all the way to a market. Though e-commerce business in India is still a nascent industry, with increasing digital connectivity and affordable mobile devices, more and more people are buying and selling online. The m-commerce has already emerged as a key trend and is enabling e-tailing to develop as an even more inclusive phenomenon. The other trend that is acting as a catalyst in the propagation of this phenomenon is evolving ability of e-commerce companies to undertake complex data analytics for business decisions, and enabling consumers to purchase far more categories of products than they have bought online in the past.

Interactivity and Richness

Unlike any of the commercial technologies of the 20th century, with possible exception of the telephone, e-commerce technology allows for interactive conversation and communication, that is, they enable two-way communication between seller/retailer and consumer. On the other hand, the Internet is rapidly becoming an inseparable part of lives of people all over the world across the spectrum of "online" activities, and the Internet users are rapidly graduating to complex and interactive Internet usage, from merely accessing e-mails and casual browsing in the past. Television or print media, for instance, cannot ask viewers for any feedback or cannot enter into two-way conversations with them. Also it cannot obtain the information about customer behavior and preferences. In contrast, all of these interactive activities are possible on an e-tailer's web portal. Interactivity allows an online retailer to engage a consumer in ways similar to how a brick-and-mortar retailer provides face-to-face experience. But here in the case of online retailers, it is on a massive, global scale, unlike the physical retailers. However, in the case of brick-and-mortar retailers, by virtue of its physical nature, the salespeople have opportunity to provide personal, face-to-face service using aural and visual cues while selling and/or interacting with customers. This empowers the interaction with *richness of information*, which is nothing but the effectiveness of the content of the message and its power to engage the customer by virtue of the customization of the information. Prior to the development of web-based technologies, there was a trade-off between richness and reach: the larger the audience reached, the less rich the message. E-commerce technology has changed the scenario and the traditional trade-off between richness and reach. The online retailers can deliver "rich" marketing messages to the target audience with the help of visuals, text, video, audio, social media, and so on, in a way not possible with traditional advertising media such as radio, print ads, television, or magazines.

For example, today, online retailers are using content marketing and interactive information to connect with the target audience. Most of the start-ups working in the online space find content-based marketing or content marketing as a medium to connect with customers and prefer it over the traditional direct marketing. This focuses on generating relevant content that educates and creates awareness among customers instead of pitching brands directly. Content marketing allows the e-commerce players to engage the customers effectively by sharing information that is useful for them. BuildMyEvent, a Mumbai-based platform, connects its customers to venues for their events. It also provides a platform for its vendors to connect with customers via their blog instead of individual marketing. As new start-ups cannot afford big-budget advertising and promotional campaigns, unlike heavyweight brands, they have to do things in a different way, either around the product/brand or around the content. The latter option is more feasible, and content marketing helps them to do that. Today, we can see that people are getting sick of the bombardment of advertisements, so here is the diversity of content-based marketing on the more engaging platform of social media. These firms need to start spinning stories to which the customers can connect to and through which the brand can be successfully promoted.

Companies are also realizing that for building a strong brand they need to provide the customers with relevant content that they are more likely to share, spread, and recall, and that is the way viral marketing happens. Let us consider the example of Mumbai-based Planet SuperHeroes, an online retailer of superhero merchandise. Now this portal runs a blog that provides information regarding superhero stuff and trivia and engages its customers via its Twitter and Instagram handles. Trying to explore and tap the customer's creativity, Planet SuperHeroes organized a photo contest in which they relied on user-generated content. It was in the form that if the customers had a superhero-themed party, they wanted to observe how well they used and carried the props, how they have used the original superhero merchandise, and how well they displayed and performed the character. The portal helped them to upload those pictures and organized a contest that helped Planet SuperHeroes to go viral.

Ease of Obtaining Information and Promoter of "Culture of Uniformity"

The web and the Internet vastly increase information density—the total amount and quality of information available to all market participants, consumers, sellers, and retailers alike. The marketplace model of e-commerce brings the sellers and buyers on the same platform that eventually increases the transparency of the entire ecosystem. E-commerce technology and portals are reducing information collection, storage, processing, and communication costs significantly. At the same time, they are increasing the accuracy, perceived value, and timeliness of the information—making information more useful, precise, effective, and productive than ever. Hence, the enhanced price transparency has the significant effect of pulling down price differentials in the market. In this context, buyers are provided much more time to compare prices and make better buying decisions. This context essentially provides the buyers with valuable inputs and sufficient time to compare prices and enables them to make better buying decisions.

E-commerce is advantageous for retailers as well. Online retailers can research and discover much more about consumers; this allows retailers to segment the market and/or the catchment area more precisely and accurately. The online retailers also have enhanced their abilities to differentiate their offerings in terms of price points, brand, and quality. Search ranking, which is crucial to attract prospective customers, requires frequent generation of unique content. Unlike the scenario a few years back, the search engines like Google are now giving extra emphasis on creation and designing original content and frequent updating to rank the portal. Hence, it becomes imperative for the firms to invest sufficient time and efforts in doing research before developing content.

Internet technology and mobiles have dismantled traditional information hierarchies by touching million lives at once with the spread of "anywhere, anytime" communication infrastructures. This has a ripple effect in terms of social empowerment and inclusive growth. The "culture of uniformity" is growing further with increasing adaptation of smartphones.

All these essentially hold the key to redefining India as a connected knowledge economy. For instance, in India, purchasing practice of local distributors and wholesalers is old-fashioned and unorganized, with high information asymmetry. There is a fair level of inefficiency in the ecosystem, and there is wide room for improvements and innovation, so it is ripe for tech-based platforms and models to make big business. Moreover, B2B online markets enlarge boundaries for dynamic and negotiated pricing wherein multiple buyers and sellers collectively participate in price-setting and two-way auctions. In China, the leading online retailer Alibaba came to prominence by providing a platform to China's unorganized B2B sector.

Taking cue from this scenario, many e-tailing start-ups and online retailers have joined India's B2B ecommerce industry, mostly into the wholesaling, distribution, and industrial products business. Industrybuying.com, BazarA2Z, and StoreRoom.in are among new players in the B2B segment, trying to ride on the remarkable growth of the industry in the near future with older players such as IndiaMART and Walmart's BestPrice.in. The newcomers have strategically tended to focus on specific vertical categories, such as industrial or safety products and electronics. Industrial products in India are generally not cataloged in one place and are very fragmented. One has to contact many vendors to negotiate and buy each product. So, developing a single Internet platform/portal and gathering all this information under one single virtual roof would be of great value. With these characteristics, these B2B e-tailers receive positive feedback in terms of convenience of their virtual stores, coupled with a variety of payment options and efficient delivery solutions from mom-and-pop stores, offices and institutions, hotels, restaurants, caterers, and other institutional customers.

Personalization/Customization

Chennai- and Gurgaon-based eShakti makes custom-designed clothing for women in the USA. Founded in 2001 as a lifestyle products firm for Indians living in the USA, eShakti is into the business of producing and retailing customized apparel for women. Given the height and size differences across the population (in the USA), there is a big need in women's fashion for apparels that fit and fall well. eShakti has customers across 10,000 cities in the USA with design teams based in both the USA and India. What really differentiates and gives an edge to eShakti over others is the use of advanced technology to customize apparel at a lower cost. A customized garment is designed using software tools based on the measurement provided. It also shows the different shapes of fabrics that will assemble together to go to make the garment. The virtual dress is then draped digitally on the three-dimensional image to see how the garment fits with desired fall. Hence before scissor is laid to fabric, the entire garment is virtually made. eShakti makes the clothing in its own manufacturing units and local factories. It neither stocks products nor does it have to warehouse its merchandise. The products are shipped directly to the customers.

Another Chennai-based portal Cherrytin.com, an online gift store, offers personalized gifts. Cherrytin.com came up with a content-based advertisement based on "Bad Gift Syndrome," and has been producing content via its blog for the past few years and has been updating it twice a week.

Customization at scale is becoming a powerful trend, having the potential to disrupt otherwise established business models. The traces of personalization have been existent in some sectors of business, but not in as big a way as it is in today's digital era. Personalized recommendations today are becoming the part and parcel of e-commerce. The leading players such as Flipkart, Amazon, and Snapdeal are at it persistently. By leveraging the big data, which is available at the fingertips, e-retailing is about to get even more personalized. E-commerce technology provides opportunity for personalization: retailers can target their marketing messages to specific individuals by formulating and designing the message to a consumer's name, according to her/his interests, and past purchases. Hence, marketing is also being changed from mass-value messaging to personalized-value messaging.

The interactive nature of e-commerce technology makes it easy to obtain appropriate information about the consumer at the moment of purchase, and later it is leveraged for personalization and customization of the product, designing targeted messages/campaigns,

Photo 3.1: *Customized Fashion by eShakti.com*

Source: http://www.eshakti.com/HowItWorks.aspx (accessed on 12 May 2016)

and also for designing the CRM and loyalty programs. Investors are evaluating a number of online companies, especially in niche retailer segments such as web-only fashion, baby care, gifting, and eyewear. This results in achievement of desired level of personalization and customization, which otherwise is unthinkable with existing commerce technologies.

Let us consider the example of some online fashion start-ups. We can see that personalized fashion is fast growing and is a niche space but with immense growth potential. In today's style-conscious but time-pressed world, choosing the right outfit through online is becoming far easy. Though there are numerous choices and discounts offers available on regular fashion websites, somewhere they still lack when it comes to personalized fashion advice by stylists. However, the start-ups such as Voonik, StyleCracker and 20Dresses are changing the online fashion landscape. These portals offer consumers more sophisticated personalized product selection and style advice by building an expert curation algorithm into their platform; in this way, they are bridging the gap between a fashionista and a common man and make a trajectory to offer handpicked outfits for style preferences from across the web. It helps the consumer to think out of the box and understand what exactly would look good on them and also to play and experiment with different styles and designs. Currently, this portal showcases women's outfits from online retailers, including Zovi, Fashionara, Jabong, and Myntra; in return, they earn a commission for each product they direct to the website. Hence, Voonik helps mimic a real-life shopping experience online and helps people find things that look good on them. This is a service that unfolds to offer a personalized shopping experience.

Similarly, Mumbai-based StyleCracker started by investment banker Dhimaan Shah and former Vogue stylist Archana Walavalkar offers a personalized styling platform where people can make fashion-related queries and receive tailor-made advice. The idea emerged when the founders realized consumers were not asking for more products but were emphasizing the need for personal advice. Hence, they made a strategic blend of styling with intelligent technology from which they obtained a hugely scalable business model. The portal shows women how to wear what they already own in several different ways and also picks merchandise from online retailers like Myntra, Jabong, and Koovs as well as off-line retailers like Shoppers Stop to make a stylish outfit.

There is a feeling that styling is only for the upmarket few and comes at a huge cost; at 20Dresses.com, they want to democratize fashion styling and bring it to every common woman. In persuasion of this change in consumer behavior toward fashion and styling, 20Dresses.com styles customers with its own PL collection.

Enabler for Filling the Gaps: Churning Out Value Proposition

It has been seen that the young brigade of online fashion retailers have retained the brand names of those they acquire, which clearly indicate that it is not just scale that is important for them but also the acquired brand's loyal base and value proposition. It is evident from Flipkart's acquisition of Myntra to Snapdeal's buyout of Exclusively.com, where the buyers have preferred to let the acquired entity exist and operate separately. One of the key reasons for these companies to retain the brand identity of the new company under their aegis is to keep the brand positioning intact, as the brand image is integral part of any brand. This allows them to harvest dividends of the hard work, resources, and the fortune of millions already spent on them.

There are three major reasons that come forward behind this strategy:

1. The acquisitions have two parts: first is the consumer servicing and then there is the back end or supply chain. The latter is more complex, while keeping the acquired entity separate helps in retaining the brands' loyalty at the front end.
2. An added benefit of maintaining two separate profit and loss (P&L) accounts could be that the acquiring company can keep a tab on how its acquisition is doing.
3. Making an acquisition is easier than integration, which is a greater challenge. There are cultural challenges and differences in ethos and even in go-to-market strategies. So, it is not easy to merge two young organizations.

Hence in totality, all these features, facets, and trends suggest many new possibilities for marketing and selling. The need is to better understand your target segment and present your value proposition. The entire e-commerce segment is based on heavy marketing for brand creation and promotion. So, the valuation of a company when it gets acquired is not only for the business it does but also for the brand's value. E-commerce technology makes it possible for online retailers to know much more about consumer preferences, emerging high-growth prospect categories, upcoming fashion trends, consumer buying behavior, and so on, and to be able to use this information more effectively to find the gaps and niches. For instance, *Flipkart's acquisition of Myntra*; while Flipkart is known as a horizontal marketplace focused on books and consumer electronics, Myntra is among the leading names in the online fashion space. The characteristics of online retailing also make it possible for retailers to know more about other retailers in the same segment or category than was ever true in the past, and this presents the opportunity that retailers might collude with prices rather than collide and compete, and drive the overall average prices up.

In February 2015, e-commerce major Snapdeal acquired Exclusively.com (formerly Exclusively.in), the definitive online destination for premium and luxury fashion. The acquisition of Exclusively is similar to that of domestic e-commerce firm, and Snapdeal's rival, Flipkart acquiring online fashion retailer Myntra in May 2014, making it the biggest consolidation in the e-commerce space in India.

The motivation behind this strategic acquisition was to complement Snapdeal's existing ecosystem and provide a consolidated offering for the luxury and lifestyle shopper, making it India's first online luxury mall, further strengthening its fashion business and reaching US$2 billion in gross merchandise value (GMV is the total value of goods sold) in the fashion category that year. This acquisition strategically put Snapdeal in a better position to compete with Flipkart, which acquired Myntra and Rocket Internet-backed fashion portal Jabong.

> **Gross Merchandise Value (GMV):** GMV is the key e-commerce industry metric that measures a firm's growth based on the maximum price of goods and services sold on its platform and not by actual revenue.

Importantly, Exclusively.com continues to function as an independent site, and all aspects of Exclusively.com's online shopping experience have remained intact, with new collections and service augmentations in the pipeline. With its nationwide reach, robust technology platform, and deep consumer insights, Snapdeal supports Exclusively.com to scale up and expand its current business and reach. Exclusively.com was the first company to offer Indian designer wear online. Exclusively has built and grown a cache of leading premium Indian designers, brands, and boutiques. It retails products of hundreds of leading Indian designers on its site, including leading designers like Manish Malhotra, Tarun Tahiliani, Manish Arora, Anita Dongre, and Rohit Bal, among others. Commenting on the announcement, Snapdeal's cofounder and CEO Kunal Bahl said that Snapdeal has always operated ahead of the curve in the e-commerce space, especially when it comes to category leadership, and Exclusively.com complements their existing line of products; it does not compete or collude but fits well into their overall strategy of focusing on fashion as a category. He also added that though Exclusively.com is fully owned by Snapdeal, he and his team have taken a conscious decision to retain the brand, sell its products as part of an independent line, and have looked after by its founders.

India continues to witness a surge in demand from consumers across the country for premium and luxury products; however, the access to luxury brands is severely limited. With increased awareness and growing disposable incomes, premium and luxury consumption in India is seeing a significant upward trend. With the geographical limitations of the brick-and-mortar model, luxury and premium segments can only be grown by sharing access with the consumer. This prompted Snapdeal to bring exclusively.com into their family, for offering access and availability to the widest range of aspirational, high-end products and services, at the doorsteps on a single click, to their customers and users. The idea is also to make luxury products available to smaller cities, Tier I and beyond, where luxury is difficult to access and also to provide a platform for young and independent designers who may otherwise not have the resources to buy physical retail space to showcase their talent. The company, which is competing head-on with Flipkart and Amazon India, is looking at customization and perfect packaging so that the consumer gets a sense of luxury while receiving the product.

Another classic example of this *fixing the gap strategy* is a Mumbai-based entrepreneur whose Seniorshelf.com caters exclusively to senior citizens with mobility aids, toilet safety products, and items meant for arthritis patients. The venture was inspired by a personal experience when he went to visit his parents and then spent three hours searching for a blood pressure machine that was just not available. With this experience, he realized that there is virtually

Photo 3.2: *Exclusively.com Was the First Company to Offer Indian Designer Wear Online*

Source: http://www.exclusively.com/ (accessed on 12 May 2016)

no retail—online or off-line—that is catering to the elderly, while they are the most vulnerable ones and the market has ignored them as a consuming class with needs of their own. A similar situation faced by the promoters of oldisgoldstore.com led to the opening of this south India-based online and off-line retailer, which sells health-care products exclusively for senior citizens.

In India, there are more than a 100 million people who are over the age of 60. This figure is higher than the entire population of many of the countries in the world. With improved health care, the average age has been increased and this is increasing the need for home health care. This means that there is a significant growing market for e-commerce players in this sector. Adding to it better life expectancy and we can see the market size increasing and gaining a substantial traction in the years to come. This has prompted some e-tailers in India to come up with products and offerings exclusively for senior citizens, turning their attention to a category of consumers that they had previously ignored in their race to reach and serve the growing young population in the country.

Hence, there is an enormous potential to *leverage this gap* and enable elderly access products and services easily regardless of which part of the country they live in. To explore this opportunity and provide a flawless experience for the elderly, some e-commerce players have tied up with various medical services companies that provide doctors, nursing physiotherapy, diagnostics, and equipment at home. One such company, Portea, whose customer base is predominantly the elderly population, is also associated with e-commerce players catering to senior citizens. Lenskart, which sell lens online, provides at-home eye care and checkup service from certified eye specialists for the elderly. They provide not only power test but also cataract care.

Not only the leading e-commerce players but also the big conglomerates have acquired start-ups, and it is proving to be a win–win deal for all. While the cash-crunched start-ups offer technology, the giant enterprises bring in scale and funds. For example, Godrej Group's retail chain Nature's Basket acquired EkStop.com. Mahindra Group has acquired Babyoye when the start-up was at the threshold of closing its operations. The objective of Mahindra Group was to spruce up its troubled retail venture, Mom & Me stores with the addition of Babyoye. With these strategic acquisitions, Mahindra and Godrej are now better positioned in their respective retail businesses as they got infused with new technologies brought by the acquired start-ups.

The E-retailing Ecosystem and Its Importance to Economy

The formalization and growth of e-tailing is playing a pivotal role in bringing sustainability and economic viability to many facets of the economy. It not only provides direct and indirect employment but also supports such infrastructure industries such as logistics and telecom by acting as a catalyst for demand creation. It has given impetus to entrepreneurship development by providing business opportunities to merchandise vendors and service providers, and reduce transaction costs (tax leakages, distribution costs, etc.), by providing accessibility to quality products/solutions in an effective and efficient manner (Figure 3.1).

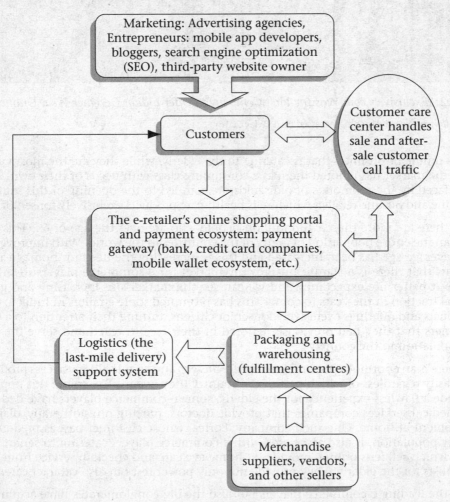

Figure 3.1: *The E-commerce Ecosystem to Ensure Great Customer Experience*

The growth of e-tailing has positive effects on the economy because of following reasons:

- It generates employment.
- It facilitates the growth of allied industries.
- It promotes entrepreneurship in many of its forms and avatar.
- It reduces transaction cost.
- It has promoted the growth of SMEs.

In China, Alibaba Group run multiple companies and affiliated entities in e-commerce and allied segments. Besides the B2B trading platform, Alibaba.com, the group has entities such as online payment escrow service Alipay; C2C online shopping platform Taobao Marketplace; tmall.com, an online retail platform to complement Taobao; group shopping website juhuasuan.com; comparison shopping website eTao.com; third-party online payment platform Alipay; e-commerce data mining and processing platform Alibaba Cloud Computing; and AliExpress, an online retail service for small Chinese businesses.

Employment Generation

E-tailing's employment potential is rarely discussed because of its current size and scale. However, it has two dimensions, the absolute volume of employment and the attractiveness of e-tailing as a destination for high-quality talent. Flipkart has launched an exclusive online store for Banarasi saris in association with the Development Commissioner (DC) Handlooms, Ministry of Textiles. The company had announced an initiative to bring the work of local Varanasi weavers online, as a part of its "Flipkart Kaarigar Ke Dwaar" (Flipkart at the door of artisan) program. The exclusive online Banarasi handloom sari store will offer a wide range of weaves created by the weavers in Varanasi and other parts of India. The portal has also signed an MoU with the Federation of Indian Micro, Small, and Medium Enterprise (FISME), the Directorate General of Employment & Training (DGE&T), and with Ministry of Labour and Employment to help Indian MSMEs retail their range to the customers across the globe.

Employment in logistics is presently generated by 3PL providers who are engaged in order deliveries, and also, in some cases, with e-tailers who have in-house last-mile delivery expertise. However, e-tailing being in its nascent stage, these are severely limited in terms of capability and scale. With the further growth of e-tailing to the projected size of US$76 billion by 2021, the logistics industry will witness the emergence of players with scale. To tap this opportunity, some of the existing players may grow in size, while other established logistics solution providers may tweak their business models. Many new players may also emerge.

Warehousing jobs demand the recruitment of people for order processing centers that are engaged in the function of integrating orders from various vendors with orders received from the customers. Orders are received from a large base of customers in small units, in typical basket size of two to three. On another front, orders are placed with a large number of vendors in high volumes. In some cases, orders are channelized directly to the vendors who ship the products directly to the customer. This process demands high precision and expects order picking and processing capabilities with minimal room for error. In mature e-tailing markets, this function is carried out by fulfillment centers. Fulfillment centers are the places and points in the supply chain where parcels are received, picked, packaged, and readied for delivery to the customer. If e-tailing in India has to grow to the projected size, it will require massive warehousing and order-processing capabilities, and this has prompted the established and start-up e-commerce logistic players to invest heavily in setting up more and more fulfillment centers to expand their delivery footprints across larger geographies. These functions thus present huge potential for employment generation.

Today in e-tailing markets, technology-related functions have evolved to such high levels of complexity that many e-tailing companies view themselves as specialists in web technology and analytics. Thus, the industry has managed to attract the best engineering and management brains.

Besides the above functions, e-tailing also requires workforce in several other roles like customer care, online merchandising, creative and technical web design and development, vendor management, content development and photography, and experts in SEO and social media optimization. Besides these novel jobs, people are required for the regular functions like HR, finance and accounts, and administration.

Facilitate Growth of Allied Industries

The leading e-tailers like Amazon, Flipkart, and Snapdeal are exploring the country's millions of SMEs to host a unique assortment of products on their online stores. In turn, such tie-ups are helping SMEs gain access to an otherwise elusive market, and an association with the established marketplaces of Amazon, Flipkart, and Snapdeal leading to building of prominence and confidence among their targeted consumers. SMEs have limited resources when it comes to reaching out to an audience and building a brand. These e-tailers are also providing them with specialized training, logistics, infrastructure, and technology support to these SMEs to enrich their product selection in categories like handicrafts, apparel, jewelry, fashion accessories, and leather goods. An exposure to the online channel also helps SMEs cut through intermediaries like wholesalers and retailers, thus streamlining payment processes.

In addition, logistics and warehousing industry is witnessing a healthy growth with the exponential growth of e-commerce and e-tailing. Several large logistics players such as FedEx, DTDC, Blue Dart, and DHL and also the new brigade of start-ups such as Ecom Express and Delhivery are enjoying increased business turnover. Over these years, demand for warehousing also has increased due to increased leasing by these e-tailers. This has led to the rise of 3PL. 3PL is the outsourcing of a company's warehousing requirements to a third-party company. Instead of leasing a building, hiring the staff and investing in a warehouse management system (WMS), and negotiating rates for various functions and activities, letting the experts and dedicated players to take care of logistics is the fast emerging trend. Hence by adopting 3PL for warehousing and shipping needs, these retailers can focus on their core functions. Other benefits are reduced total delivery cost for their customer, entry of local expertise in new markets, and reduced inventory cost. For instance, Amazon offers services like Fulfillment and Easy Ship to enhance a seller's logistics capabilities. They do all the heavy lifting on behalf of the sellers so that they can focus on pricing and selection. Amazon has also tied up with the Federation of Indian Export Organization, Manufacturers Association of Information Technology, Trade India, and Export Promotion Council of Handicrafts to identify SME clusters and to promote the benefits of selling online. Snapdeal has introduced services like Payship and Snapdeal Plus to enhance logistics capabilities of SMEs, besides launching an exclusive mobile app. The e-tailer also helps the SMEs secure loans from banks and NBFCs. Flipkart, on its part, has tied up with the FISME and the National Centre for Design & Product Development (NCDPD) to help small manufacturers and artisans. The e-tailer is also working with the center to train people in semi-urban and rural areas to prepare and enable them for employment at Flipkart or its business partners. The online marketplace has also inked a pact with the textile ministry to provide an online marketing platform to handloom weavers across the country. Additionally, the growth in e-tailing has boosted the growth in organized real estate as well, particularly in logistics infrastructure and large office spaces.

With all these SMEs, entrepreneurial start-ups, technology start-ups, and logistics players, the legendary 240-year-old India Post has also jumped on to the bandwagon and is experiencing the growth by providing logistics services. India Post, founded as an arm of the East India Company, was a vital strategic institution for decades, but its relevance declined dramatically with the rise of landline phones, mobile communication devices/gadgets, and Internet technology. Use of e-mails for communication made its postcards and inland letters significantly obsolete and redundant. Despite its mainstay business struggling for relevance, the institution continued to have several advantages over its competitors, most notably its vast network of around 1.5 lakh offices and a trained and skilled workforce of about 5.5 lakh employees across the country. With these strategic competitive advantages, India Post has begun leveraging their strength. The online retailers may have been the bane of the brick-and-mortar retail trade, but for this relic from the past, they are proving to be a boon. For India Post, which is fighting a long battle for relevance in a digital economy, the explosive growth in the New Age business has offered it a fresh lease of life and given an opportunity to dream big. The boost has been catalyzed by the e-tailers such as Flipkart and Amazon signing up for its services, and with the theater of activity for the e-commerce sector moving to the country's remote corners. With this new focus, the India Post is targeting a 50-fold increase in e-commerce revenue, and to justify its achievability, they point out that India Post has managed to expand e-commerce delivery revenues from ₹20 crore to ₹100 crore in just one year, and due to the explosive growth of the sector, an exponential increase in revenue is only expected. India Post started COD pilots with Amazon in 2013 but the service captured momentum only in 2014, when it signed up players such as Flipkart, Snapdeal, and ShopClues.

Promote Entrepreneurship

For a long time, small businesses in the developing nations like India have struggled to expand because of geographical constraints and distribution challenges. They manufacture great products but have to struggle not only for marketing and branding their products but also to build a nationwide distribution network to reach the targeted consumer. This consumes all their energy and resources and put barriers in their path toward the growth. In addition, it is extremely difficult for them to ensure that their products are stocked by distributors across the country, given their limited working capital. At the same time, because of the limited financial strength, they cannot afford to set up a chain of stores. This result in a small business that consumes most of their energy and resources, and leaves these small firms with less room to focus on their core competence to manufacture a great product based on consumer feedback.

Here, e-commerce has emerged as the solution, by changing the way the business is done, whether in the B2C or in the B2B segment, locally or globally. One of the most successful and convincing arguments in favor of e-tailing's business model is its ability to motivate, promote, and boost entrepreneurship. Online marketplaces are enablers for small as well as large sellers, retailers, and brands, giving them the access to an online platform where they are able to extend their reach nationally while supplying locally. The synthesis of this latent desire of small businesses to expand nationally has been the driving force to e-commerce success. Even as e-commerce is seen as a consumer-centric industry, small entrepreneurs are its backbone. Today, we can see that many of today's leading e-tailing businesses was the start-ups a few years ago. The trend continues as more and more names are joining the club. However, it is a less talked about the fact that the growth of e-tailing creates enabling and favorable conditions and opportunities for entrepreneurship across the entire e-tailing value chain and ecosystem. It has truly democratized the expansion of a small business, and to achieve this, the e-commerce industry has had to transcend physical boundaries to create a highly empowered network of related industries, entrepreneurs, and people-driven enterprises, which resulted in the emergence of the synergistic scenario referred as "we-commerce." This is positively influencing the development of entrepreneurship in three ways:

1. It is providing easy access to consumer markets (new and existing), having potential to enable the growth of merchandise vendors.
2. It is opening up opportunities for entrepreneurs to become service providers to the e-tailing business.
3. It has also created opportunity and platform for practicing and boosting the social entrepreneurship.

Easy Access to Consumer Markets

Flyer's Bay, a toy product line (remote-controlled helicopters) started in Delhi, exemplifies the easy access part of consumer market. Initially, the young entrepreneurs, who founded this start-up, posted their products on Facebook, gathering likes from everywhere where they started selling one or two products every day. The game changer for them was logging on to Snapdeal.com and listing their products on the portal. As a consequence, Flyer's Bay has grown multifold with an established presence nationally. This is the collaborative power of e-commerce.

The growth of e-tailing is resulting in the emergence of tremendous opportunities for merchandise vendors to explore and expedite new consumer markets, both domestic and international, helping them achieve scale. This is not only attracting existing vendors to e-tailing but also witnessing the creation of new businesses that are being established to catch the bandwagon. The country like India is a base for many vendors that cater to world-renowned brands and retailers. For instance, India is also a base for proprietary and ethnic merchandise products that have a vast global appeal and demand from the connoisseurs, because of its high aesthetic and artistic value. However, existing formats, structures, transaction systems, and costs do not allow these vendors to fully explore domestic and global opportunities. Hence, e-tailing is emerging as an enabling and promising platform for vendors to tap such opportunities, as cross-border tie-ups can either leverage e-tailing's reach to access regional markets, reach out to leading e-tailers for vendor opportunities, or launch own e-tailing routes and directly reach out to customers. The mention of an online Indian ethnic wear player is merited to support this argument. In its 10-year-long journey, this India-based player has managed to build a successful e-tailing business that focuses on nonresident Indians (NRIs) (i.e., Indian origin people living outside India). The player procures and customizes ethnic wear for women and men from over a 1,000 vendors, and sells these products directly to customers. The business earns foreign exchange, is understood to be profitable, and has successfully created a market with direct access to NRIs in over 30 countries. An evolved e-tailing business environment can thus serve as a strong catalyst for merchandise vendors to explore many such direct-to-customer global opportunities in a number of ways. Such opportunities will not only spur the demand for an increased vendor base but also catalyze the deployment of capital required to increase the capabilities needed to cater and endow this demand. Similarly, PepperTap has an inventory-light model where they tie up with local retail outlets and channel their orders through them. This empowers the local retail outlets and allows them to capture more customers from a wider geography. The delivery ecosystem is in-house and enables them to provide complete customer experience.

Such a range of possibilities can prove to be a boon, to the pockets of numerous local artisans who make a myriad of products ranging from fashion wear, accessories to gifts and from artifacts to home improvement and furnishings. For example, Amazon India's Seller University aims to bring on board more sellers through initiatives such as a YouTube channel, modules for web-based training, and local experts. Under the initiative, Amazon India runs a slew of programs, enabling new vendors to come on board in the online retailer's platform by either getting trained by professionals or engaging with fellow beneficiary vendors. A channel on YouTube teaches potential vendors about the marketplace model and how to sell through it. Teams at Amazon India also provide web-based training to vendors at remote locations, to help them understand the platform's functioning, and the benefits it can provide to small businesses. The company also has Amazon Trained Ecommerce Specialist (ATES), who are freelancers and work in remote locations with vendors. From all these examples, it is clear that the e-commerce wave is here to stay, and we can see its effects percolating to even the smallest of towns. In 2015, Amazon launched its Global Selling program for businesses in India, enabling local manufacturers access to millions of buyers across the USA and UK. Amazon is now extending two of its pioneering initiatives—Selling on Amazon (SOA) and Fulfillment by Amazon (FBA)—to businesses of all sizes to go global with listing on Amazon.com and Amazon.co.uk. Amazon offers businesses a good reach to customers around the globe. According to the company, their Global Selling program in India is designed to assist Indian manufacturers and businesses to grow their business by leveraging Amazon's world-class logistics infrastructure, state-of-the-art technology, and customer service expertise. Hence, FBA allows manufacturers and sellers to store their products in Amazon's warehouse, and Amazon packs and delivers the orders to customers, provides customer service, and also handles returns (reverse logistics). This infrastructure enables the manufacturers and local brands to seamlessly export products and increase business. Amazon claims that such initiatives have the potential to help businesses to effectively face the complexities of selling globally and develop an international footprint by leveraging the huge demand for their products across borders and thus may transform the way India makes and sells.

Creation of Opportunities to Build New Capabilities as Service Providers

We can see that some e-tailing interventions are similar to those of brick-and-mortar retail; however, the key difference for an e-tailer exists in the technology, marketing (branding), packaging, and logistics interventions. We have discussed how e-tailing is leading to the emergence of newer players in the logistics space. Here, one more thing that needs to be highlighted is that the growth of e-tailing also creates numerous opportunities for entrepreneurship in the technology, packaging, and marketing domains and verticals. In many instances, e-tailers require these functions to provide much focused, very specific, and nearly customized solutions, which may lack scale and thus not attract big service providers. For instance, the Chinese leading online player Alibaba.com is pushing all the limits to tap e-tailing space in India. Keen on content-making companies, they are also exploring strategic play in one of the largest media houses in India.

Also, there are cases wherein vendors simply do not exist to fill the gap and cater to such needs. Therefore, many innovator start-ups, enthusiastic freelancers, and small enterprises move in early to leverage this opportunity and close the gap. This scenario has fueled the start-up culture around e-tailing in not only mature markets but also markets that are in nascent stages of development (Table 3.1).

For instance, the online marketplace Flipkart has signed an MoU with "Common Service Centers" e-Governance Services India (CSC SPV) to help rural artisans and small enterprises, who sell through the CSCs across the country, and has provided them a platform and media to reach a larger market. As part of this initiative, the online retailer and CSC SPV have an opportunity to work toward development of ancillary industries like packaging and logistics, besides creating employment avenues in rural areas and remote areas. In India, under the National e-Governance Plan formulated by the Department of Electronics and Information Technology, the CSCs have been conceptualized to act as front-end service delivery points for government, social and private sector services in education, health, agriculture, fast-moving consumer goods (FMCG) products, entertainment, banking and financial services, and utility payments. Their main objective is to develop these communities and make them economically self-sufficient and also develop ancillary industries that will contribute toward

Table 3.1: *Services Provided to E-tailing Players*

Function/Vertical	Service Providers	Services Rendered
Analytics	Analytics firms/individuals/big-data services	Analyze consumer behavior and other information for insights and decision-making inputs
Marketing	Freelance blog writers, independent website owners, review sites	Attract new customers to the website/positioning and brand building
Content development	Content writers/copywriters	Write content and/or technical description for the website and for the merchandise on the website. Also to update it continuously and continually for relevance
Web designing and development	Web designing and web development agencies	Design and develop websites that are constantly upgraded for engaging the consumers and provide a superior experience to build the loyalty
Packaging	Packaging designing agencies and packaging manufacturing firms	Develop, design, and manufacture packaging solutions according to the brand image
Logistics	Start-up firms (like Ecom, Delhivery), e-commerce logistics arm and large logistics: courier companies	Pickup from sellers, packaging, warehousing, last-mile logistics, including same-day delivery, cash on delivery, reverse logistics

the employment generation. Hence, this tie-up has a potential to present the rural artisans and MSMEs with an opportunity to establish their brands nationally and access financial, marketing, and supply chain support. To cut a long story short, this partnership with CSC SPV can help the online retailer provide the rural artisan and MSME community with the support needed to market their products across the country, and has the potential to create the right environment for cluster development across the country. That can make CSCs a beehive of economic development, thus igniting the spark for the "Make in India" initiative.

Logistics is also becoming an information management business. Customers prefer to work with a single vendor for logistics, warehousing, and fulfillment services for seamless flow of information. However, for e-tailers, the priority is good service at the right price, even if that means multiple service providers. For instance, Holisol Logistics, which started in 2009, offers warehouse consulting solutions and later expanded its functions to deliveries. The company has set up warehouses for Jabong and FabFurnish at Jamalpur and Bilaspur in Gurgaon, respectively. The firm offers delivery services for e-tailiers like Jabong and Freecultr and off-line sellers such as Raymond and Biba Apparels.

Data Analytics: Decoding the Consumer's Mind

The e-retailers are facing formidable conditions that demand real-time insights and not just the casual data analysis. They face intense competition, shorter time to market, and very demanding customers, all of which raise the cost of acquisition and retention significantly. On the other hand, they have to comply with increasing stringent regulatory requirements and must adapt to the new demographic mixture with the dawn of millennial as new influential consumer segment and the social media as the channel. These retailers are increasingly requiring more customization and optimization to stay competitive and relevant. This and many other unpredictable human behaviors can undermine the best laid plans. So in this kind of business scenario, these online retailers strive to differentiate and clear the clutter by using the power of leveraging their data to attract and retain the customers. This essentially gives inputs regarding behavioral science and economics, sociology and psychology, and so on to address the real-life business problems.

Big data analytics refers to the process of collecting, organizing, and analyzing large volumes of data to discover patterns and other useful information.

With the world of business becoming complex day by day, many times the traditional research techniques do not reveal some of the insights that marketers are looking for, and here the tools of data analytics come to the rescue.

Data Analytics and Algorithms

Today, it is imperative for the marketers to make a clear distinction between customer experience and customer engagement. While experience is the interaction at a single point of time, customer engagement encompasses a continuing and continuous relationship of the customer with a product or brand.

Hence, customer engagement is basically the level of interaction that individual consumers have, either directly or indirectly, with a particular company or brand over the time. The term comprises all the interactions that occur along the customer journey, whether those "interactions" happen before, during, or after a transaction, and also include customer interactions that may be independent of specific transactions. Analytics is rapidly emerging as a crucial component of retail sector not only for online retailers but also for the brick-and-mortar players that have embraced the multichannel model of retailing. In the initial stage of evolution, the focus was basically on obtaining insights on consumer's buying preference, behavior, and patterns, but today, they are also accentuating on real-time analytics. As part of the process, retailers started paying attention to shopper's in-store activities as well as which categories and items they browsed during this period.

The next step is to make "precise predictions" about what the consumer would buy the moment she/he enters or perhaps before she/he enters the store. Today, the technologies like predictive analytics have enabled the retailers and brands to identify and reach out to the customers precisely and engage them across the touch points. The customer engagement is relatively more of a proactive approach. With increasing clutter due to advertising and marketing communication blitzkrieg, companies need to reach out to consumers to inspire purchases, build brand recognition, solicit feedback, and obtain insights. All this is aimed at maintaining a two-way dialog with customers that stimulate acquaintance and some level of emotional attachment to the retailer brand.

The simple goal of extremely complex algorithms is to enable the retailer initiate this two-way dialog and to understand consumer preference and expectations. It helps to understand the buyer's behavior and churn out products he or she is most likely to buy. Algorithm is basically the big-data analytics in real time. It processes huge amount of data that individual humans will not be capable of doing and helps users to arrive at smarter decisions. This data collection is not limited to a single site that a user goes to but scales up into creating users' social graphs, by capturing data across the users' browsing habits. These data include what a user searched for—age, gender, and location—what the person does on a site, and so on. Here the footprint churning is done by a proprietary code and that output makes the experience better each time the user visits the site. It is somewhere like how a search engine works, matching key words to what the browser might be looking for.

Today we can see that, more and more people are using smart devices for varied purposes like shopping, searching for jobs, paying bills, playing games, and social networking. During these activities, they leave digital footprints behind. Algorithms persistently track these prints and synthesize them to present user with astutely customized choices. Eventually, algorithms may be able to predict and preempt users' online behavior even better than them. By virtue of this, algorithms are not only helping companies manage inventory but also helping to decide what products and services users are likely to buy and also to offer personalized experiences. So the retailers today are increasingly focusing on getting algorithms that target users with precision and at scale. An intelligent algorithm will keep track of target audience's habits and preferences, to enhance the overall shopping experience. This leads to increased engagement, which eventually induces brand loyalty, and impacts user retention.

From global giants such as Alibaba, Facebook, and Amazon to leading domestic players like Flipkart and Snapdeal, and other start-ups, this piece of code—the algorithm—is increasingly becoming one of the most crucial tools to manage scale of operations, speed of execution, and complexity of human nature.

Other Benefits

Predictive analytics offers all possible variables that help the retailer devise the right strategy to achieve the desired customer satisfaction level. These insights can range from obtaining timely and accurate sales forecasting insights, to aligning them with opportunities to improve shopping experience and the design of their websites to accommodate the pressures of any shopping blitzkrieg. Hence, besides enhancement in the consumer engagement, there are many other benefits of data analytics to retailers. Analytics helps them predict the traffic on the website along with the possible conversion rate and also the amount of sales that is possible during peak sale seasons.

For instance, website of Amazon runs on the Amazon Web Services (AWS) cloud, this gives them the flexibility to scale up in real time. The company uses brand and SKU data along with the number of visits to various product pages to determine if the assortment will attract customers. These data are then shared with the listed sellers.

In addition, retailers are increasingly focusing on motivating the customers to download their app. The retailer can collect more consumer data through apps because it can access consumer data on mobile phones. This enables them to obtain more accurate information about their target audience, which eventually is very useful for obtaining valuable insights regarding their buying behavior and preferences. With the help of these valuable insights and inputs, the retailer can provide the consumers with better recommendations, which in turn lead to creation of higher number of loyal customers.

Employment Opportunities

This focus of online retailers toward the data has created a big demand for analytics resources in the e-commerce ecosystem. On the other hand, the business consulting has also undergone a paradigm shift from traditional tools of business assessment to business analytics and statistics. Over the years, these functional attributes, expertise, and knowledge of business analytics and statistics have become imperative to perform and survive in the consulting space. So the analytics and the business consulting firms are also relying on the same type of skill sets. This has eventually launched a healthy competition to attract new talents from the market. Both the sides of business are not only adopting innovative measures to hire the expert data scientists but also introducing attractive and lucrative schemes to retain them.

Hence, the upsurge of e-retailing has brought the opportunities for the people with skills like:

- The ability to scrutinize and analyze the business problems.
- Converting these business problems into a quantitative/mathematical problem.
- Solving these problems with the help of data analytics, other basic statistical tools/ functions, and their wide functionality.
- The ability to integrate and use unstructured sources to develop holistic and innovative solutions that are more precise and stand apart from traditional solutions.
- A fair understanding of performance management metrics in the business under consideration.
- The ability to differentiate between key performing indicators (KPIs) and metrics.
- The ability to visualize and foresee how the suggested solution/algorithm will impact and improve business performance.

In short, the data analytics helps the retailers to understand consumer behavior and buying patterns, through their digital footprint across multiple platforms, including mobile devices and social media. The technology not only helps them understand what the customers want but also highlights their pain points when they interact or transact with them. All these valuable inputs eventually help the retailers to make their online platform more efficient and user-friendly.

Hence, it offers data scientists with a lot of attractive opportunities available in the market, and the demand for them will continue to grow for an industry that is growing fast and heavily reliant on analytics. These data scientists are looking for not only the monetary remunerations but also a clear career growth plan from their employers. While the start-ups and e-retailers are providing them with a more hands-on experience, the consulting firms provide opportunities to work with multiple clients and at all levels of the project life cycle. This provides the data experts with more exposure and growth opportunities in different domains like implementation, maintenance, key account management, and client servicing. By virtue of this, they can experience the project life cycle through different phases. Understanding consumer behavior is the key to connect better with consumers, and its integration with digital, content, and data can give pragmatic solutions to many business challenges.

Entrepreneurship Start-ups in Logistics

Indian e-tailing sector is expected to touch approximately ₹2 lakh crore by 2020. But for this to happen in reality, the logistics sector—the link between e-tailers and customers—must keep pace with the rate of growth in e-tailing, and it is here that start-ups are playing a key role.

The rapid growth in the e-tailing sector can be gauged from the exponential growth of start-ups like QuickDel Logistics, which owns the delivery brand GoJavas. Its first client was the online fashion and lifestyle retailer Jabong.com, and today, it serves over 200 companies, delivers at over 2,000 pin codes, and covers over 105 cities. Another start-up, Gurgaon-based Delhivery, has witnessed the similar kind of exponential growth. All these start-ups work closely with the clients and have customized their services to suit customer needs. For instance, when Zivame, the lingerie e-retailer, asked them (Delhivery) to send only girls for deliveries, the logistics partner was open to accept their requirement. Meanwhile, GoJavas trained its delivery boys to pacify irate customers by showing them the proof of their effort to deliver the merchandise on time. Hence, these e-tailing firms are assured for the flexibility of these start-ups, because the survival and funding of a start-up depends on how it differentiates from its competitors. Though many times the new innovative ways of one logistics firm are copied by others, some are successful in maintaining their uniqueness and differentiation. For example, QuickDel was the first to launch open-box deliveries wherein customers could open and check the packet delivered to them before making the payment. But this model was later on copied and embraced by many other logistics players. But some features like tracking the delivery boy on Google Maps on the company's website have been hard to copy. Another start-up NuvoEx (Nuvo Express) opted for a different route and is primarily based on providing reverse logistics where merchandise is returned by the customer to the seller.

In addition to the start-ups, there are a few more players that are basically the affiliates or logistics arms of e-commerce players. For example, Flipkart runs its own delivery division eKart and online furniture seller FabFurnish started its own delivery service FabOne.

Start-ups are investing in automation to handle more volumes. For example, Ecom Express has started using robotics sorting technology instead of manual sorting of packages, which helps the company to increase the efficiency. Most companies are trying to fast become end-to-end service providers. Delhivery offers services ranging from last-mile deliveries, third-party fulfillment, warehousing services, to software solutions such as channel integration software for sellers selling across multiple platforms.

However, with the competition between start-ups and traditional courier companies increasing even at the order level, e-commerce companies have built strong algorithms to automatically allocate deliveries based on multiple criteria such as the logistics company's reach, efficiency in handling payments, and customer response.

Boost to Innovation Entrepreneurship

The novel digital economy is generating a whole new yield of entrepreneurs in India. The e-commerce wave is steering in a new form of democracy, where the only currency is the innovative idea. They are passionate and driven individuals who have the audacity to travel the paths that others have not. They are determined to build on niches and specialist online businesses. Most of these start-ups emanate from innovation and passion—a broad theme or an idea that one is confident and convinced about. They are set in motion by partnering with like-minded people and executed on a small scale. Gifted with the power of imagination, they are harbingers of change and enter the areas where the poster boys of e-commerce do not. This is resulting in creation of niches. Niche e-tailing or vertical e-tailing specifically deals with focus on a single-product category and provides huge range/assortments in that category—in short, acting as a category killer. This is in terms of both varieties within a product category and pricing. Due to better pricing and wider collection, these vertical or specialized players make money because of the good margin between the cost of acquisition and selling price.

It is relatively easy to establish and requires less capital when compared to a multiproduct marketplace model, which needs massive structuring and big funding. While large multi-brand e-tailers play on the numbers and on cost budgeting and schemes, the niche players have to focus on the quality, service, and customization, wherever applicable and possible. For example, an e-tailing venture that only stocks up on T-shirts or designer umbrellas or only saris. For instance, India Sari House sells saris online. According to its founder, while many e-tailers are focusing on discounts and a few on luxury (premium segment), Indiasarihouse. com is focused on the mass-premium segment of saris. Hence, these vertical models with specialized and focused approach have enormous potential as the markets and consumers are becoming more sophisticated and informed. However, a niche player needs to offer customers a good enough experience, so that customers choose it over horizontal and off-line stores and offerings. So here the key to success is differentiation that can attract a customer to go to a niche portal instead of a broad-based one that stocks a variety of products.

In the context of current market scenario, many more niches are expected to born, and they are good because that is where the market will move eventually as it will not be a one-size-fits-all scenario. Thus, niche players can appear more compelling by providing a customized user experience, so that customers make a true value purchase. The need for providing such a compelling user experience is also intensified by the fact that, unlike horizontal players that offer a wide range of products for which customers can revisit, niche players have to pull them back by casting a unique, compelling impression and winning their trust and loyalty. Hence for many vertical niche e-tailing shopping portals, the requirement is to be more value driven compared to bigger horizontal ones that are volume driven.

For instance, after electronics and fashion, home and furnishing is expected to emerge as a large category in the e-tailing market. Horizontal players like Flipkart, Amazon, and Snapdeal have not been able to make significant forays into this category, as it has emerged as a strong vertical in terms of barriers to entry. Hence, we can see that e-tailing by virtue of its ubiquity does not keep any segment untouched. Let us consider the example of ArtZolo.com, an online marketplace for art discovery and curation. It enables emerging and established artists to exhibit, promote, and sell their artworks to art lovers and aficionados. The online art retailer hosts number of reputed artists from India and abroad on its platform.

Encouragement and Support by Established Players

With an apparent increase in interest from investors and the buzz they have created among users, the online companies such as Flipkart, Zomato, and MakeMyTrip have made way for entrepreneurs looking to venture into other e-commerce verticals. The big online players such as Flipkart and Amazon do not have the time to concentrate on niches, and on the other hand, we have a lot of e-entrepreneurs with niche business ideas who have the passion but may not have the funds and financial resources to scale up. This is where a meeting ground is present and consolidation is happening. Be it services like education, health care, or delivery of essential items from your local shop, many of these start-ups are disrupting these sectors with innovative solutions. For instance, Touchtalent, a start-up that helps artists and content creators to exhibit and sell their work online, raised funding from Deep Kalra, founder of MakeMyTrip, and Sachin and Binny Bansal, founders of Flipkart, among other existing investors. Also Snapdeal founders, Kunal Bahl and Rohit Bansal, invested in an online travel start-up Tripoto along with IDG Ventures India. Online furniture segment has also seen an exponential growth, and players such as FabFurnish, Pepperfry, and Urban Ladder have become a household name in India. Urban Ladder, besides being just a brand on Facebook, has expanded to other digital platforms. The company launched UL Labs to work with other start-ups in the augmented reality sector to improve the user experience of its app users. Also the wave of acquisitions of such niche companies is testimony to this. Mahindra Retail, a part of the Mahindra Group, bought online baby products retailer Babyoye.com. Similarly, the Godrej Group acquired online grocery and daily essentials shopping store EkStop.com. However, many a time, an acquisition has also ended up in the niche portal being shut down as in the case of FashionAndYou buying up online beauty retailer Urban Touch and Snapdeal buying up electronics e-retailer Letsbuy.

Let us look upon the example of Chennai-based e-commerce start-up Flintobox. It started selling toys conceptualized by educators, prototyped by designers, and manufactured by top-of-the-line printers, all shipped in a box to little customers. At the heart of the venture was a simple idea: learning is fun. The idea behind this start-up was simple, that it would be great if they could curate new activities and ideas that would engage kids positively, at home, away from the television set and without need of parents' constant supervision. So they decided to take the idea forward and decided to do it in such a way that both parents and children should benefit from it. What they did was to bring in people with expertise in child development, game design, and education to build and test the first prototype. This was then tested with parents and children, and it was found that the parents and the children appreciated and liked the freshness of the idea and the quality of the product. This motivated and prompted the team to start and set up Flintobox as an e-retailer. They have adopted a very safe business model. They manufacture as per demand. There is no distribution cost as they sell directly to customers. There is hardly any inventory on hold. It is considered to be one of the smartest start-ups in India; Flintobox got the best start-up award in the education sector by the Confederation of Indian Industry (CII). It is also the winner of the Wharton India Economic Forum start-up competition.

Continuing with the education sector, with the large student population of India and growing Internet usage, e-learning has become one of the sought-after sectors for investors and entrepreneurs. There are more than at least 10 tech start-ups in India built around the model of online education. E-learning and related areas are growing and have started getting a lot of traction. Apart from education, health care is another vertical where investors are investing their money in. The spectacular increase in the usage of Internet has given a strong platform for entrepreneurs interested to explore and expedite into this relatively new and growing sector. The so-called "e-health entrepreneurs" have carved out niche business models to ensemble the online medium. One another service in the e-health vertical is maintaining electronic health record of patients, and has started to experience a lot of action from online health-care service providers. For example, My Health Records (MHR) maintains health records and other test results of its subscribers on their app. This start-up has seen steady growth, adding more and more customers every day. This is only because of the other online services like e-ticketing, online education, and e-application, people have become comfortable in transacting online now.

A Fair-play Platform for Women Entrepreneurs

As entrepreneurship, once considered "a man's cup of tea," is witnessing a sea change with many women taking the plunge, the number of women entrepreneurs in India is on the rise, and their start-ups, many of whom are in the booming e-commerce space, are showing the way for gender parity. Entrepreneurship is hard for men and women alike. A person needs a fighter gene and go-getting approach to be a successful entrepreneur. This qualification criterion makes entrepreneurship really a gender atheist. Hence, these New Age start-ups are seen encouraging female participation.

From Lijjat Papad, Amul, or other microfinance-funded small home-based businesses, women have been at the forefront, but this trend has slowly spilled over to white-collar jobs as well. Lately, women are also making inroads into senior management roles in many businesses corporations. And now with online retail start-ups like Zivame, Embibe, Grabhouse, The Lebel Corp, and LimeRoad, among others, they are making their presence felt in the e-commerce space too. The boom of web technology, Internet, and mobile commerce has helped not only men entrepreneurs in general to build more scalable businesses but also women entrepreneurs. And this has significantly changed the landscape, as we can see many examples of budding women entrepreneurs who are challenging the perception of entrepreneurship being "a man's cup of tea." As women make up half of society and control major consumption decisions in every family, across a range of Internet businesses from content to commerce, the women user base will drive growth going forward. Whether it is content or products that appeal to women, it is women who have a much better sense of the needs and hence can create much better solutions. For example, ShopClues' Radhika Aggarwal, Zivame's Richa Kar, Nykaa's Falguni Nayar, and LimeRoad's Suchi Mukherjee are respected names in the e-tailing industry, to mention a few. Twitter's first acquisition in India, ZipDial, was founded by Valerie Wagoner.

Nationwide women across various fields and domains are opening up to entrepreneurial opportunities and challenges, as the impetus level from government has dramatically risen with several women-oriented schemes and policies. For instance, Mahratta Chamber of Commerce Industries & Agriculture (MCCIA) has a special cell for women entrepreneurs. This shows that the business environment for women entrepreneurs has changed considerably in India. With a substantial market potential, there is government support as well. It is observed that at networking events, start-up and tech events, investor meetings, and start-up community gatherings and exhibitions, women are already making more of a presence, as they overcome forces of tradition, financial barriers, and structural bias to pursue their entrepreneurial ambitions.

Meanwhile, recent Global Entrepreneurialism Report conducted by international bank BNP Paribas has ranked India on top for the highest percentage of women entrepreneurs. The survey was conducted among 2,500 entrepreneurs in 17 markets spanning the USA, Europe, Middle East, and Asia. In this research, it is observed that 49% of the entrepreneurs in India were women. India performed better than Hong Kong and France, which were next on the list. In India, women now make up around 20% of the sellers on e-commerce platforms.

Challenges and the Way Out

There are no biases as such in finding finance and credit; both are often available these days. While women running small family businesses often find themselves rejected by banks for loans, there are more subtle barriers for larger-scale entrepreneurs in the race for VC. Though small, increasing number of women entrepreneurs is now circumventing the traditional boys' club barrier of VC firms to gain sizeable investments and valuations. But still there is a need for women-focused seed, angel, and VC funds, preferably by women investors. The investors typically try to understand the entrepreneur and want to check out important prerequisites. This may include the questions like whether entrepreneur (here women) is going to get married and have children, and whether she will be able to do a balancing act. Such kinds of funding have already materialized in the USA, and this would enable women-founded businesses to remain owned by women in most instances.

In this context and scenario of women entrepreneurship, some of the leading women entrepreneurs are proponent of a movement to fundamentally rethink the exceedingly time-intensive and hostile start-up environment, and make it more accommodating of other life priorities. Here the government can bring improvements by setting up more incubation centers where women can start a commercial activity and gain the confidence to take it to the next level. This will upgrade the entrepreneurial system to support different stages of women's lives. After all, an entrepreneurial setting has to give autonomy and flexibility to women for balancing their own personal and professional priorities.

A Boost for Social Entrepreneurship

Start-ups are increasingly partnering with nongovernmental organizations (NGOs) to market products and services offered by people from low-income groups, accessing the vast networks of NGOs and skilling marginalized youngsters in the process while taking their products such as handicrafts to international markets via online platforms. Megha Gupta, founder of Dharavimarket.com, realized the potential of marketing the products online. These products are made by the artisans from residents of Mumbai's large slum cluster Dharavi. Leather bags, shoes, costume jewelry, and accessories made in Dharavi are sold on the online platform, which was launched in August 2014. She realized the richness and variety of products made within Dharavi, and felt that if it could get an online platform, the reach could go international. This prompted her to start the venture with a self-investment of ₹6 lakh, before she was supported by an NGO called Asia Initiatives with grant money.

Collaboration with Asia Initiatives has helped them incentivize the workers there with social credits to hire women employees, open bank accounts, and so on, all further improving their living standards and lifestyle. They are also partnering with NGOs in Dharavi that are into soft skills, IT training, and women's education, as this helps them access more residents within the community for their platform. She has also approached e-commerce sites such as Snapdeal to sell more products from Dharavi.

Shop for a Cause, started in 2011, similarly looks to source products made by tribal communities, rural craftsmen, and other communities, and operates in both brick-and-mortar and online segments. They sell products across the home segment from organic food, kitchen, home décor, accessories, composting/recycling products to home gardening products and corporate gifting items. Shop for a Cause has allied itself with a number of NGOs, including Tripura Bamboo Mission, Kriti Social Initiatives, and FAME India. Their partnership with NGOs is a bit more than a typical retailer–supplier relationship as they provide their partners with feedback, new design ideas, and customer trends, which would enable them to expand their product portfolio.

Sudha Premnath, who runs the education and environment program for Kaigal Self Help Group supported by Krishnamurti Foundation India, has partnered with Shop for a Cause to sell products made by the tribal community in Andhra Pradesh. Their aim is to make the community, especially the women, independent with self-employment. So they help and train them to make products with materials sourced out of the local ecosystem. Their partnering with Shop for a Cause has helped them access a commercial outlet for these products. The online–off-line format helps them access a wider customer base, and over time, they are looking forward to improve their capacity and livelihood. Hence, Shop for a Cause and Dharavimarket. com are among the start-ups that are working with NGOs for their social enterprises, creating a bridge between nonprofit and for-profit enterprises.

Reduce Transaction Costs

One of the most important advantages of e-tailing's business model is its embedded ability to reduce transaction costs. Transaction costs here refer to the costs incurred in making an economic exchange/transaction, which, in retailing, involve three elements:

- Cost of distribution of goods
- (Un)certainty of tax receipts
- Use of leverage (credit) in the supply chain

Retailing in the infrastructure-deficient countries (like India) involves high transaction costs. The overall market structure and the infrastructure inadequacies and constraints are the key reasons for this high cost. A normal retail transaction in India involves the movement of goods through a multilayered distribution system from the producer/manufacturer to the ultimate customer. These layers of the distribution system entail distributors, wholesalers, dealers, and others who are located across geographies in a layered hierarchy. There are three challenges with such a structure.

The first challenge is that each and every layer of distribution adds an extra cost in making the goods reach the final consumer. In this process, the journey of the products through this structure increases the price of the product and hence the cost of the transaction not only for the consumer but also for the manufacturer.

The second challenge is the existence of credit in the system that puts pressure on the working capital of all stakeholders. Many a time, the layers in the system primarily act as financers to facilitate the movement of products from manufacturers to consumers. One of the major reasons for the presence of such a system/arrangement is the time lag between the sale at the customer end and the time the manufacturer becomes aware of it. For example, for the SMEs, one of the major problems with them is managing finances; that is, when SMEs work with online marketplaces, they are assured of payment within a specific period of time, which is otherwise not the case and has a bearing on their finances.

The third challenge is that most of the retail transactions at POS happen in cash. This may lead to the creation of a leeway in the system for tax leakages, namely under-invoicing and under-reportage of sales, whereas e-tailing provides an electronic POS that records sales and thus creates a certainty and gives assurance to the system about the actual volume/value of sales. Even in the scenario where customer decides to pay in cash (i.e., through COD), this eliminates any scope for under-invoicing and under-reportage. An explicit benefit and advantage of this system is that it increases the certainty/conviction of tax receipts (i.e., VAT, CST, etc.).

Hence, given that e-tailing uses the electronic medium of the Internet and web technologies, the immediate and real-time recording of POS data and payment receipts, and the absence of intermediaries in e-tailing chain, allows smoother and faster flow of money and information from the customer to the e-retailer and subsequently to the manufacturer. This has the potential to significantly advance the manufacturer's and the e-retailer's ability to manage the business with lesser working capital and reduces the credit levels in the ecosystem.

The projected growth of e-tailing has the potential to successfully address all the above challenges. The cost of distribution is in the declining mode because the multilayered distribution system is being replaced by an order fulfillment process developed and designed in a hub-and-spoke model. The layers of distributors are not required here as this role is being fulfilled by warehousing and logistics operations, which offer margin augmentation opportunities for manufacturers and better price points for consumers. The marketplace model of e-tailers like Amazon, Homeshop18.com and Flipkart allow individual sellers display their products, which is unlike the inventory model where the portal itself owns and stocks the products on offer. This system brings with it the saving of expenditures for retaining and maintaining the inventory levels that significantly brings down the overall transaction cost.

The benefit of transaction cost reduction is also very evident in the case of B2B e-commerce. There are three cost areas that are considerably reduced through B2B e-commerce transaction.

1. It reduces the cost of searching because here buyers need not go through multiple intermediaries to search for information about merchandise, suppliers (vendors), and prices as in a traditional supply chain. Hence, the B2B online marketplaces bring the buyers and sellers on a common platform that eventually reduces the search costs even further.
2. It reduces the costs of processing transactions (e.g., purchase orders, invoices, and payment models), as B2B e-commerce enables the automation of transaction processes and therefore the quick implementation of the same compared to other traditional channels.
3. The online processing improves inventory management and logistics.

In a nutshell, all these characteristics of e-commerce not only provide a transparent retailing environment for both the customer and the e-retailer but also offer a lucrative opportunity to reduce the transaction costs, which ultimately provide an increased margin for offering higher value. Also the increasing Internet access through affordable smartphones and efforts by online retailers to develop payment channels such as COD and mobile wallets and streamlining logistics infrastructure are expected to boost e-tailing growth.

COD is essentially a win–win situation for both the transacting parties, the customer and the e-retailer. This allows customer to receive and approve the product before paying for it. This ensures a transparent transaction without any financial impact. While in the case of the e-retailer, it gives them an opportunity to build a robust brand image by delivering quality products on time. This eventually helps to eliminate the trust-deficit and transaction-security factors, which are often associated with online transactions.

Growth of SMEs

Online e-commerce retailers such as Amazon, Flipkart, and Snapdeal have already started turning toward SMEs to find unique and exclusive products/merchandise to differentiate their respective marketplaces. India's e-commerce giant Flipkart has announced a tie-up with SMEs in India to promote manufacturing and entrepreneurship in the country. These SMEs present an array of assorted collection of merchandise, including clothing, handicrafts, jewelry, and accessories, among other stuff, and in return get a platform for selling their products, in addition: the training, infrastructure, logistical support, and technology from theses online retailers. Flipkart has signed an MoU with industry body promoting SMEs, FISME, and NCDPD, a body that promotes handicraft design in India. These agreements being mutually beneficial bring the synergy as the association provides two-way benefits to both the e-tailer and small entrepreneurs; the online player provides platform to SMEs and small entrepreneurs to sell their products directly to buyers across the nation, which in turn boosts entrepreneurship. These e-tailers can also enable MSMEs with the infrastructural support in data analytics, marketing, and customer acquisition to help them scale their business. Another advantage of going online is they can display thousands of products, which would not have been possible in the case of a physical store.

For e-commerce companies, it is imperative to have unique products and services on offer to differentiate from the competition. For those unique offerings, they have to go to the SMEs, who are small but exclusive and distinctive. In return, SMEs get to market their products to a worldwide audience without the need for intermediary sellers or wholesalers. This widens their exposure to the targeted audience, which ultimately increases the sales turnover. Also, this kind of association with established market players gives credibility to SME products, increasing consumer confidence in the offerings. Moving forward with the pact, the e-tailer helps SMEs in product pricing, payment automation, packaging, transportation, and brand building through its portal. E-commerce majors like Paytm and Snapdeal have launched chat applications (apps) for SMBs, where these merchants can list their merchandise and transact with interested customers. The online marketplaces also take care of issues like absence of back-end technology, packaging and logistics infrastructure, and dearth of finances.

The e-commerce technology helps the SMEs to not only market their products and for reaching to the wider audience but also procure raw material for production at competitive prices and rates, thereby decreasing their cost of production and hence in turn increasing their profitability. For instance, Ahmedabad-based Ingenius E-Commerce Private Limited launched an e-commerce portal—tradohub.com—to help SMEs to procure raw materials at cost-effective prices. The portal currently has many registered suppliers across the globe and offers various types of raw materials and machinery required in the agriculture, food processing, pharmaceutical, and chemical sectors. It works on a simple model: the e-commerce platform procures raw materials from its suppliers in bulk and offers it to small buyers at a discounted price.

Advantages, Limitations, and Challenges

E-tailing can be considered another form of non-store retailing. Its closest "cousin," in terms of other forms of non-store retailing, is catalog retailing. Catalog retailing still claims a significant part of all retail transactions pie. It is therefore instructive to compare e-tailing to catalog retailing to gain some insight into its potential impact. Catalog retailing, which evolved over a century ago, grew rapidly in its early stages (similar to e-tailing), and it was assumed to become a very important part of the overall retailing environment and market. It allowed customers to shop from home, when they wanted, at their own convenience. While this proved enticing and comfortable for some consumers and some types of products, there are some limitations that limited its growth further.

Advantages

1. Customers have a much wider choice at their fingertips (many e-tail sites, etc.). Thus, the web creates a global bazaar-style marketplace that brings together many consumers and many retailers and sellers.
2. With web search capabilities (which need further development), it is easier to find the different types and varieties of goods a customer is searching for.
3. Customers can execute transactions/put orders via the same medium the information is provided, so there is no disconnect between the *desire to purchase* and the *ability to purchase*.
4. Payment schemes are still evolving, and therefore, this advantage is likely to become more apparent in the future.
5. E-tailers can use price discrimination more efficiently than other retailers.
6. E-tailers can use previous transactions to identify the likelihood of products being purchased at certain price points.
7. Product placement: E-tailers can change the product placement (user display) based on previous transactions, to increase the visibility of goods that the user is more likely to purchase based on their close relationship with previous purchases. Thus, placement can be designed based on the context of the previous purchases.
8. E-tailing includes some advantages to the consumer that no other form of retailing can provide. The hypertext nature of the medium allows for more flexible forms of transactions—the growth of C2B and C2C highlights this point. It allows for ease of comparison across broad product categories with the evolution of shopping bots and allows for more flexible pricing mechanisms that lead to dynamic pricing.
9. This is giving benefit to marketers who provide products with real (perceived) value and consumers in general. It also penalizes the marketers who have thrived in marketplaces that had "information" barriers to entry, where lack of information for customers restricted their choices and led to inefficient pricing and localized monopolies.
10. Inventory-based e-retailers are known the world over for running highly automated and efficient warehouses, bringing new benchmarks in this function.

Limitations

1. All the customers may not have access to the web, as they do to the postal system. This is a temporary issue as the evolution of the web continues.
2. Ease of use may be an issue, as the web design may appear to be complex for some users or at sometimes a bit chaotic.
3. Online retail stores are not standardized in design in the way catalogs and retail stores (which use planograms for the same) have become.
4. Therefore, different user behaviors and patterns (navigation schemes) need to be observed for each online store. This is again a temporary issue as the evolution of the web continues.
5. Many times, trust deficit, security, and privacy concerns prevail. Consumers are concerned with the exposure of the data they provide/insert during transactions.
6. In Indian context, tax demands and regulatory hassles, coupled with low Internet density and sundry other problems, pose some other challenges.

Major Challenges

E-retail is very attractive in emerging markets due to various reasons. The first is convenience of not having to go to a physical store due to the traveling hassles and time consumption. Second, compelling prices and discounts are offered online. Third, for younger people, it is becoming a custom or fashion to shop online, as the whole "feel the fabric" obsession of the older generation does not seem to bother them.

However, on the other hand, the challenges that e-retailers have to overcome include delivering on the promise, concerns about security, addressing privacy vs. personalization trade-offs, meeting expectations, and so on and so forth. There is a big difference in the way e-commerce has evolved in India in comparison to the US evolution story. In the USA, people were already used to and quite comfortable buying through catalogs and switching to online was not a big change for them. However in India, the e-commerce cycle is being compressed and changes in shopping behavior, like reliance on touch-and-feel buying or credit card acceptability, took time to get incorporated. Thus, the big hurdle is not only trust but also comfort of the customer.

Moreover, profitability is also one of the major concerns. It is observed that the basket size goes down, because it is targeted shopping and there is no or very less impulse purchase, with no or limited opportunity to cross-sell and upsell.

Privacy Versus Personalization Trade-offs

There is a variance between the need for privacy on the part of the consumer, and the need to be able to personalize the offering on the part of the e-tailer. Finding the right balance is a challenge. E-tailing scenarios that can address this are likely to be able to make a significant impact, which in turn should provide a better experience for the consumer. As the payment (transaction) is the area where the data are exchanged, who should ultimately own that data (after the transaction) and what rules are established in terms of the use of that data are the questions that need to be addressed effectively. E-tailers need to develop schemes that enable them to develop a personalization program. This in turn enables them to take advantage of a wider scope of user behavior and to focus on personalization based on the user experience.

Other risks associated with e-tailing include the risk of the security of the transaction and the integrity of the business with which the customer transacts. In terms of security, there have been many highly publicized cases of crackers bringing sites down. Thus, the customer can become concerned with the security of the transaction data provided. As the e-tailing environment does not provide the same assurance as the physical world in terms of the integrity of the business, e-tailers need to make extra efforts to make sure the customer has confidence in the outcome of the transaction and with whom they are transacting, which in turn increase the ease of doing secured transactions. Companies such as eTrust are positioning themselves as intermediaries that focus on certifying e-tailers and their use of the data that are gathered from transactions.

Discount Trap and the Battle for Bottom Line

One of the leading online fashion stores posted a year-on-year revenue growth of 146% for the quarter ended September 30, 2014, but at the same time reported losses of ₹56.9 crore for the same quarter against a meager ₹4 crore in the year-ago period. However, the retailer with an optimistic view responded to these results by stating that there has been a lot of focus on branding and investment to build fashion properties and technology that will help them in the long term even though it impacts profitability now.

E-commerce has been a segment that has been under profitability pressure because there has been a big focus around acquiring customers, infrastructure, and distribution centers. A business has to make some upfront investment before revenue starts to come in. The Indian context is also different as it is a touch-and-feel economy; the e-tailing here is still in its early stages and is also a very price-sensitive market. Pricing is an important element of the marketing mix, and at times, it is the dominant feature that is played up. In India where consumers are very value conscious, even a premium brand needs to play the price card. And in case of online retailing, the rush to persuade the customer with deals and discounts is even more. Online retailers such as Flipkart, Myntra, Amazon, and Snapdeal have been running their sales periodically, and the discounts are anywhere in the range of 40–60%. They run high-powered full-page ads that pitch discounts and freebies. The reasons are manifold. It could be the year-end stock clearance, an entry of a new strong player, or a push in order to move consumers toward a new category. And the catcalls are only getting louder due to which all categories are getting "commoditized." While it may be necessary in some situations—a downturn in the economy is perhaps the most warranted—to reduce prices, discounting has risks associated with it. The major risk is that it can create a negative long-term perception of a company/brand/product in the consumer's mind. This impacts the brand value, ultimately leading to erosion of brand image, market share, and bottom line. It is somewhat like the street fight: if you need to survive this round, you got to slash your margins and offer the luring discount, but in exchange, you have to bear a massive hit in your perceived brand value. Customers spend their money in return for something that meets or exceeds their perceived value. When an aspirational brand turns into a brand "on sale," it results into brand dilution. From being a high-street brand, the brand can find itself bracketed with the "me too" brands with diluted brand image.

In this discounted economy like scenario, brand loyalty is the first casualty. As customers pick up merchandise with the price tags showing attractive discounts, brands lose their sheen. The difference between a brand and a product is this: you assign a certain amount of premium to a brand. People buy a brand for two reasons: either if it is discounted or if it is differentiated. So as prices are lowered continuously, the differentiation starts vanishing in this rush. The customer returns to the retailer only when there is an offer, or switches to another brand that offers a deeper discount. The Internet enables consumers to surf through a whole lot of websites, price-comparing sites for evaluating alternatives and selecting best deals, picking up coupons, and timing their purchases to flash sales.

Interestingly, e-commerce sites such as Flipkart, Myntra, or Amazon are many times seen as discount platforms; majority of the consumers perceive them as the marketplaces where brands are offered at discounted prices and sales drop when the products are being sold at regular price points. Sales spike only when there is a discount. At the same time, there is always the threat of new discount players emerging in the market. So here the consumer is not assigning any equity to the brand and hence not willing to pay a premium for the brand. The brand must have a certain amount of emotional equity in order to command a price premium and brand loyalty. The growth in e-commerce has not only brought in a never-ending season of discounts but also forced every other brand and category to play their hand and flag off the discounts. In order to compete, brick-and-mortar retailers are also forced to cut on their margins.

For instance, departmental stores like Shoppers Stop and Lifestyle have to hand out more attractive deals with extended EOSS (end of season sale) durations. This sort of price-centric, commodity-driven economy will be unsustainable in the long run because when there is a trade-off between the brand and the pricing, the price becomes the only way of promoting the brand and it is often to a brand's detriment.

However, to face this challenge, the online retailers have started pursuing the strategy of pushing high-margin PLBs and the brands with which they have exclusive tie-ups and arrangements, to increase the profitability. Because of PLs, the upside in terms of margins is relatively high.

Many times, the strategy of offering high discount frequently becomes a self laid trap for the retailer and the customer returns to them only when there is an offer; otherwise, customer switches to other retailer who is offering a deeper discount.

Photo 3.3: *High Discount Offers on Frequent Basis: A Golden Trap*

Source: www.mallmasti.com (accessed on 12 May 2016)

Hence, online retailers, particularly fashion e-tailers at the very least, seem to have found a savior in PLs, which help them build both profit margins and a differentiated offering. (PLs are the in-house brands, typically manufactured externally, under supervision, and sold exclusive on the e-store that creates it.) Not only do they build loyalty among fickle online customers toward the website, but also a strong private brand offering could possibly be taken off-line, maximizing the brand's potential in terms of profit and equity. Whether it is online or off-line retailing, today the PLs are not merely considered as category fillers, but each of these labels is treated as independent strong brands targeted toward a particular consumer segment, creating a long-term brand equity value, quite apart from their obvious economic value.

In addition, they also have started buying less than they had forecasted and are focusing more on costs and margin. With these deliberations, gravity is finally entering, and they are having the feel of the gravity as they are under pressure to ensure and increase the profit margins.

However, according to another school of thought, many of the online firms that offer heavy discounts were playing for time. They hope to build on the consumer franchise, before the market corrects itself and settles down over the next few years. They foresee and expect India to follow similar patterns as other developing markets, in particular China, where the e-commerce boom has already happened. For instance, e-commerce major Alibaba, which holds the leadership position in China's e-commerce space, sells premium products via a site called Tmall. Hence having spent the past few years on acquiring a customer base, e-commerce players are now moving into the next phase of growth, with profitability as the primary objective. For instance, some big players have started levying delivery charges on certain products, irrespective of the price, simultaneously reducing the discount levels, which is a way for players to generate revenue. With these steps, online players are now focusing on moving toward profitability after burning cash all this while in an effort to acquire consumer base. Many have started to decrease the level of discounts offered on various categories and have also started to charge for delivery. E-tailers have also started focusing more on their PLBs and are generating higher margins from them. These in-house brands tend to give at least 20% higher gross margins than external brands.

Logistics, Distribution, and Customer Service

As discussed earlier, though e-tailing increases the ease and convenience of transaction, a focused consideration needs to be given to the delivery of the merchandise. The next real growth is expected to be from Tier III cities, small towns, and rural areas, and the major challenge would be how to reach them, in terms of both connectivity and logistics perspectives. But this also gives a competitive advantage to online retail, as they can reach such small town and rural areas much better than off-line players.

On the other hand, time poverty of consumers is increasing and the industry need to manage the customer acquisition costs effectively. COD services impose substantial financial cost for online retailers, as unlike in developed markets, this continues to be a preferred mode of payment in developing countries like India. The e-commerce industry is at a nascent stage so obviously there are certain lags. Profitability for online retailers in the country was affected by free shipping offered to customers and a high rejection rate on COD orders. Moreover, customer acquisition costs are rising due to competition by companies with more funds. Many e-tailers have focused on integration of marketing and branding efforts to attract customers in order to increase the business; however, they also need to focus on the less glamorous, but equally important, aspect of this business, which is nothing but logistics. This in turn increases the loyalty behavior by offering seamless last-mile delivery. Most of the leading e-retailers such as Amazon, Flipkart, and Myntra have their own last-mile logistics units to have better control over the delivery time and experience, while Snapdeal works with third-party delivery service providers.

Offering huge discounts on dedicated days have been the tactic for boosting sales for most of the leading e-commerce players in the country. The trend started when Flipkart saw an unprecedented and overwhelming response to its Big Billion Day in October 2014. The company had said that it clocked revenue of US$100 million in only 10 hours on the day of the sale. After the Big Billion Day success, Snapdeal hosted a "Savings Day" in November 2014, while Amazon India had also hosted "Diwali Dhamaka" sale during the same period. Running deep discounts on dedicated "sale days" may have turned out to be a big success for Indian e-commerce players, but logistics and courier companies that support online retailers are left in a limbo with an "unstable and inconsistent" business inflow because of these events.

The following areas need immediate attention:

- Robust IT infrastructure
- Good coverage and penetration in Tier II, Tier III, and rural areas
- Greater, trained, and reliable workforce
- Transparency in merchandise delivery
- Seamless flow of information between e-retailers, it logistics partners, and end customers

Flipkart delivers 65–70% of its orders through its captive logistics unit, eKart; it works with logistics players for the rest. Amazon, which is also working on strengthening its delivery capacities, has set up a logistics company Amazon Transportation Services Pvt. Ltd in India to deliver products directly to consumers. It a subsidiary of US-based Amazon.com, which ship goods from sellers who transact on the company's online marketplace in India. The same service is offered by Snapdeal, which owns stake in delivery firm GoJavas and has signed a long-term strategic agreement—in order to get a long-term partner for last-mile delivery. While several e-commerce players have in-house logistics capacities, most of them partially depend on third-party vendors. These logistics players are also acting as consultancies for e-commerce players to provide optimized shipping at viable costs.

According to the logistics companies that cater to online retailers such as Flipkart, Amazon, Snapdeal, and Myntra, there are sudden spikes in demand from e-commerce companies during the two weeks after a sale day and during the festive seasons. During these periods, they want thousands of packages to be delivered within the time frame that they have promised to the consumers. During this period they want their logistic partners to deliver thousands of packages to the most remote destinations within a couple of days, because that is what they promise to their buyers. However, on regular days, the demand is much lower as compared to that of during the sale day and festive seasons. Hence, it becomes difficult and unfeasible for these logistics companies to serve this asymmetric demand pattern. So to maintain a good last-mile delivery experience, the logistics industry follows a model called managed marketplace. Under this model, in addition to its own affiliate, an e-commerce gets into a long-term deal with two or three logistics companies depending on their networks in different regions. The logistics companies understand the needs of e-retailers and are carving out special services to cater this promising business vertical in more effective and efficient way.

Let us take the example of MotaDeals.com. It is a hybrid site that retails both deals and merchandise online and caters the customers spread across the country. While the online retailer has its in-house logistics, it has also outside logistics partners. Hence, it has devised a multi-vendor strategy toward logistics partners. The online portal stocks all types of merchandise, which ranges from mass-market products, medium-priced items, and even the premium items. The retailer essentially works on the policy of keeping its inventory levels for not more than two weeks to ensure that consumers should get newer merchandise that have spent minimal ageing at its warehouse.

E-retailers are increasingly developing technology for integration with 3PL players to enable customers to track the status of the transaction and delivery. The process of merchandise delivery is one of the touch points of customer service, and it has the potential to create an interactive platform that allows customers to have a two-way dialog with the e-retailer. So it is not just a case of making the timely and quick delivery, but also enhancing the delivery experience.

For example, to address the expensive problem of failed package deliveries, Flipkart has set up collection centers for online customers to pick up their orders as per their convenience. These collection centers are also called as "experience zones" and essentially function in conjunction with its logistics arm eKart. This model is basically a solution to customer unavailability issues and allows consumers to adjust the delivery time and location according to their convenience. It also provides a smart solution to restrictions for entry into certain areas like defense establishments, tech parks, and gated communities. It is not only convenient to the e-retailer, its logistics arm or partner, and customer, but also helps to eliminate last-mile delivery costs. As these experience zones can also be used as a platform for offering many other services like open-box deliveries, product demos, spot trials, instant returns, and cash on return, and other third-party repair services can also be added to enhance the customer experience.

Once this relationship platform is created (via the transaction), the e-retailer can follow up with the marketing program to keep the customer engaged. It is so important, in this era of high growth and increasing productivity, to be careful with scaling customer service and overall experience. Customer service should be considered a profit center and not a cost center, as it has a significant impact on the long-term relationship of the customer with the e-retailer rather than the short-term transaction.

Logistics and Supply Chain Management

Supply chain, logistics, transport, warehousing, courier, and distribution industries are the pillars of a successful retailing business. Without these crucial components, goods would not move from supplier to buyer and will not reach the end consumers on time. Logistics has become a hot topic in boardrooms, as executives now understand that failing to deliver good service in a timely manner means consumers will take their business elsewhere. Warehousing and warehouse management are the vital parts of a logistics management ecosystem. Warehouse is no more viewed as just physical places for storage. In today's cost-conscious, efficiency-driven environment, many retailers are reevaluating their definition of warehousing by referring it as fulfillment centers. This has resulted in a renewed focus on the supply chain and logistics.

For example, Safexpress has developed and designed special services like express distribution, warehousing, and inventory management. By using such services, Safexpress ensures that the merchandise is delivered on time even to the most remote places. On the other hand, warehousing and inventory management ensure stocking and availability of the merchandise at the given point of time. In order to provide a good and timely service, Safexpress has its dedicated workforce for its e-commerce vertical as it requires a specific kind of mind-set while dealing with their customers.

For managing the online retail SCM effectively and achieving the lowest possible lead time (the time between date of order and date of last-mile delivery), logistics players like Safexpress has spruced up their services. These include enhancing the infrastructure for smaller deliveries, continuous training to the workforce, adding smaller vehicles to its fleet for ensuring higher mobility, systems and processes for odd hour, offer days, festival duration and holiday deliveries, developing cash collection and deposit systems, and setting up real-time order tracking systems.

With the immediacy technology has brought to life, customer service expectations are at an all-time high. No industry is immune from those expectations, including the logistics industry, where delivery services face greater pressure to get packages to their destination in the most timely and efficient way possible. Trends such as omni-channel retailing and same-day delivery pressured carriers to improve delivery systems or bear the risk losing customers. To meet changing consumer expectations and to make sure deliveries arrive on time, the retailer and logistics companies need to follow innovative/improvised practices with tried-and-tested procedures integrated with cutting-edge technologies.

Real-time Analytics and Predictive Analytics

As discussed earlier, the technologies like real-time analytics and predictive analytics are giving competitive advantage to the retailers, not only to online retailers but also to off-line players, those who have embraced the multichannel model of retailing. Retailers can leverage these technologies to effectively manage demand and supply and can successfully address the evolving consumer expectations. These technologies can enable the retailers to effectively collaborate with their suppliers and improve the efficiencies of their SCM operations. By using predictive analytics, retailers can obtain precise insights about shopper's purchase patterns, which can eventually be used to design customer-centric supply chain strategy. These technologies help the retailer for "demand sensing," which uses a combination of transactional data (orders and shipments) as well as point of sell and promotional and daily sales movements, among others, which is used to develop a daily statistical forecast. This forecast provides valuable inputs that are used to improve inventory management, supply chain cost, and customer service.

For instance, the technologies like real-time analytics can help retailers to bring effectiveness and efficiency in its operations that eventually results in providing value to the customer, be it in tracking shipments, returns, transportation routing, cost reduction, and price discovery in real time. The value can be interpreted in terms of:

- Analyzing the current inventory levels and demand patterns to automatically trigger price changes.
- Analyzing the geographic order pattern and warehouse proximity in real time to reduce end user product price.

- Analyzing the current transportation time for shipping, transportation cost, and predict approximate delivery time to the user.
- Detecting early logistics situations such as freight delay or loading time and sending automatic notification to the customer about the delay in shipping.
- Analyzing the geographic demand pattern and season loads to allocate/coordinate with idle delivery resources in real time.

As systems and industries become increasingly interdependent, it is difficult to discuss about logistics without talking about the retail supply chain, an important and inseparable component of any e-commerce business, which has prompted them to invest in that element. For example, taking a cue from transportation companies like Uber and Lyft, Palo Alto (California)-based Deliv is working with omni-channel and mall property owners to provide crowd-sourced same-day package delivery from stores. Deliv combines the technologies that retailers have in place to track merchandise with GPS-enabled smartphones to mobilize a driver pool. The same-day delivery services such as Deliv could be a game changer.

Walmart, with the help of predictive analytics, sensed that consumers start spending less toward the end of the month. So to address this type of situation, it began stocking several merchandise items across from different categories that are available at the price point of around US$1 during this period of the month. To execute this strategy effectively, it leveraged its efficient SCM and played a crucial role in providing better value to its customers.

Distributed Order Management

Retailers are adopting and implementing systems such as distributed order management (DOM) for a better handle and control on the real-time tracking of goods with the help of new technologies. In turn, carriers often use web portals to exchange information with retailers on the logistics process. For example, UPS provides an online tools service that retailers can integrate with their websites, offering tools such as tracking, rate and service selection, address validation, and time-in-transit information. The ultimate goal from a logistics perspective is to eliminate or at least reduce any black holes. Hence at any point of time, it can be tracked and they can know exactly where the product is, who has got it, and when they got it. Distribution being a vital pillar of the logistics business, established players such as Blue Dart and Gati are already ahead of the pack. E-commerce companies, despite running their own delivery divisions, depend on third-/fourth-party assistance because of their large network presence.

The logistics players tend to add more and more fulfillment centers, warehouses, and transportation vehicles in order to increase the coverage and speed. Logistics companies have also beefed up their efforts to scan products in and out of different substations across the country to increase visibility. UPS offers mobile apps that allow customers to find UPS locations for shipping or pick up, or to track packages they are expecting. A feature called UPS My Choice even lets customers manage delivery times when they are away from home or provide delivery instructions.

However, in the near future, carriers will eventually need to turn to GPS tracking in order to provide consumers with the ability to track a package's whereabouts at any given point of time, something that today's customers want and expect that level of transparency. The key to better delivery is better planning and increased efficiency in services. Carriers are tackling efficiency from a number of angles, from using data for better forecasting to deploying sensors to route optimization. Here the data also allow companies to make shipping decisions on how the packages can be routed based on the lowest cost shipping method and shortest amount of time so that the shippers can be more efficient and ship more things.

Photo 3.4: *A Fulfillment Center*

Source: www.businessinsider.com (accessed on 12 May 2016)

For example, UPS uses technologies like telematics, or sensor data, combined with algorithms to calculate optimized delivery routes for drivers. Truck data also provide insight into vehicle performance and condition, and find opportunities to coach drivers on safety, customer service, and efficiency.

Better sorting and organization are necessary to achieve the timely deliveries. In 2014, Amazon introduced the concept of the "sortation center," a warehouse where packages are sorted by destination or zip code before being handed over to the shipper for delivery. Traditionally, carriers have handled both sorting and shipping. Amazon opened such centers throughout the USA. UPS also has fully automated hubs in regions across the country where equipment can scan, measure, and weigh packages.

Therefore, in a nutshell, what needs to be worked upon in logistics is microlevel management. A robust SCM that delivers timely and that is cordial with the customers essentially ensures ever-growing size of orders and good delivery experience.

A look into some of leading inventory-based fashion online fashion retailers' warehouses

Some quick facts:

- By 2023, online retail is expected to become a US$56 billion (somewhere around ₹1,00,000 crore) industry and every single online retail transaction needs to be delivered.
- About 25% of the total warehousing uptake across the country in 2014 was taken up by e-commerce players. According to the report by global consultant CBRE, the emerging

retail segment took approximately 1.7 million sq. ft of warehousing space across Mumbai, Bengaluru, and Delhi-NCR in 2014. It has also been reported that the major share of fund-raising by e-tailers is also expected to get channelized into building warehouses.

With this exponential growth, advanced warehouses could mean the difference between success and failure for online retailers. Behind the glitzy online catalogs of clothes, perfumes, and apparel that are drawing customers in droves to e-retailer's portals, there is an organized network anchored by technology and manned by people with the task of ensuring the seamless last-mile delivery.

Let us look at the example of online fashion retailers. Fashion and lifestyle is the second largest category in online retail, with a 25% share after electronics. It is the domain of brands and specialists, unlike electronics, which is marketplace driven. So beefing up efficiency and effectiveness of storage facilities is crucial for these companies as fashion has emerged as the fastest-growing category in India's burgeoning online retail industry. These warehouses are essentially the very backbone of the e-retailing industry.

Warehouse Operations

As we have already discussed that the effectiveness and efficiency of operations of brick-and-mortar warehouse are crucial to the success of online retail, so it becomes imperative for us to understand how these warehouses function and leverage technologies to manage supply chain and operations from customer care to inventory and payments.

At the front end, customer-care executives can trace the journey of an item, while merchants can log in to see how quickly their stock is moving from the portal. On the floor of the warehouse, it is the software technology that plays a vital role by showing where items should be dropped and what path an employee should take to navigate the maze of storage places. As e-commerce players attract the prospective customers with deep discounts and same-day deliveries, faster processes become not only priority but also the necessity. These giant automated warehouses enable them to deliver the merchandise as per the promises made to the consumer. It is important because the online players are selling more merchandise in a small time frame. Here the fixed cost gets spread over more items, thereby reducing the cost per unit. Hence, deploying state-of-the-art technology to help manage day-to-day operations within a warehouse is the key to success.

For instance, when a customer places an order at Myntra's portal, say a pair of jeans, it makes its way out of the warehouse in less than four hours. At Zivame, it takes less than two hours. Zivame's warehouse in central Bangalore occupies two floors spanning 12,000 sq. ft each and soon expected to grow three times in size. While these facilities appear enormous, they would appear smaller in comparison to Amazon, America's largest online retailer, which manages over 80 warehouses, some large enough to occupy more than 28 football stadiums. Typically, warehouses in the USA are located in the suburbs and in close vicinity of airports to help companies take advantage of lower land, facility, and manpower costs.

In the apparel industry, gauging stocks is tricky, and software helps them decide what different people want to wear and which trend will disappear in the coming days. But there is only so much that software can do. It takes human ingenuity to find the right mix of technology and people to make sure that processes are efficient and cost-effective.

The process flows in the steps are as follows:

Step 1: The merchandise from various brands land at the warehouse days in advance.
Step 2: The received items go through a random quality check.
Step 3: They are recorded (entered into the system) in the database.

Step 4: The items are placed/deposited/stacked in the allotted grid until an order arrives.

Step 5: Merchandise is checked for quality again before shipping the order.

Step 6: Merchandise is packed compactly to reduce the cost and also gift wrapped whenever required/demanded.

Packing Methods

A separate station exists at Myntra for gift wrapping the items, and at Zivame, first-time customers are provided with a measuring tape. Also brown cardboard boxes are shrink-wrapped in plastic, so as to be discrete about lingerie purchase, unlike in Myntra's fashion range of products.

Step 7: The orders are segregated as per destination, and are handed over to the courier companies with destination details.

At Myntra, thousands of shipments are handled every day; the "pickers" who collect items are given a device much like the card-swiping machine carried by delivery boys. The device shows/displays which item should be picked up from which grid. The employees scan, pick, and deposit items in the grid, irrespective of whether all items belong to one single order or not. Globally, Amazon is known to have timers set within the handheld device, so the picker finishes the task within the time limit. It is a race against time and orders. During holiday seasons, Amazon uses robots, and we can see them deployed in the warehouse, helping employees complete multiple orders at once. Hence, greater volumes require more automation. In the warehouses of large e-tailers, conveyor belts and weighing machines, when automated and integrated with manual operations, can reduce turnaround time significantly.

Let us consider the example of FirstCry.com, which helps the parents to buy the world-class brands in the baby and kids products category. They not only focus on providing great variety but also ensure the quality aspect for all brands on their portal. FirstCry.com as a baby care multi-brand category specialist operates through its online and off-line stores and works with over 1,200 international and domestic brands to offer more than 90,000 products. The retailer provides a 32-inch touch screen kiosk at its brick-and-mortar stores where customers by their own can buy any merchandise that is not available at store at that moment but is available online. This offers a huge range of merchandise selection to order from without facing any hassles of online buying. They have built a very efficient delivery network to ensure timely last-mile delivery, which eventually enhances the overall shopping experience. They provide last-mile delivery services to over 14,000 pin codes nationwide. For creating an edge, they have also started the same-day delivery and next-day delivery to selected pin codes.

Following are the expected innovations in the near future:

- Fully automated warehouses where machines or robots will sort the parcels.
- Multiuser warehouses where logistics firms will pick up merchandise from multiple suppliers, stock, pack, and ship them.
- Customers can pick up or return a product from designated collection centers in cities and small towns, which will also be used as "experience centers."
- Specialized services like delivery person taking measurements of the consumer, going to a tailor, getting alterations done, and then delivering the altered garment.
- Lockers from where customers can pick up parcels using codes sent to their mobile devices.

Summary

Today, the retail industry as a whole is experiencing the emergence of Internet as a major factor influencing the consumer behavior. Consumers are more informed and educated about the brand and the model that they want to purchase, enabled by online research. Urbanization and the advent of e-commerce have played an important role in changing the lifestyle and spending patterns of consumers. E-tailing is an integrator of technology, infrastructure, and logistics and creates a relatively efficient marketplace not only for retailers, entrepreneurs, and other sellers, but also for consumers.

The industry is witnessing a rising appetite for online sales not only from metro and Tier I cities but also from Tier II and Tier III markets. We can see that the online buyers have emerged from cities such as Chandigarh, Patna, Jaipur, Ranchi, Surat, Baroda, Indore, Trichy, Leh, and Bhubaneswar, among others. This huge market potential essentially enables e-tailing to create new capabilities, which India needs, and to provide employment in its different forms to Indian youth. It has the competence to act as a catalyst, bring several synergies, and support the growth of new skills and industries. E-tailing has always been viewed through the same lenses with which the corporatized brick-and-mortar retail is observed.

However, though it is true that it serves the same end purpose, it also cannot be denied that the whole ecosystem within which e-retailing operates and flourishes is entirely different from the brick-and-mortar retailing. By virtue of its nature of doing the business of retailing, the e-retailing touches upon several sectors and serves many stakeholders across the functions, verticals, and components of the ecosystem. Therefore, instead of being clubbed with brick-and-mortar model, the online retailing deserves to be considered on its own merit while formulating the regulatory policies, as it has opened up more avenues as well as broken down barriers between a buyer and a seller.

Review Questions

1. Explain the meaning of e-retailing and its major features with appropriate examples.
2. "E-retailing is playing a significant role in the economy of country." How will you justify this statement with appropriate examples?
3. "E-retailing has proved to be a major opportunity for SMEs and other small businesses." How will you justify this statement with appropriate examples?
4. Explain the several initiative taken or innovations done by online players to woo the vendors with the help of appropriate examples.
5. Explain in detail about the initiatives that are being taken by online retailers for effective vendor management.
6. E-commerce has acted as a catalyst for development innovation culture. Justify this statement with appropriate examples.
7. Explain the e-retailing ecosystem in detail and how it is stimulating the employment generation.
8. Briefly explain the different functions associated with e-retailing and how they have created the new job opportunities with appropriate examples.

9. "E-retailing is acting as a catalyst for promoting entrepreneurship." Justify this statement with appropriate examples.

10. "E-retailing is a boon for women entrepreneurship." Justify this statement with appropriate examples.

11. "E-retailing is benefiting the social entrepreneurship initiatives." Justify this statement with appropriate examples.

12. "Established players in e-commerce are encouraging the new entrepreneurship start-ups in several ways." Justify this statement with appropriate examples.

13. Explain the major operational challenges faced by e-commerce players.

14. Explain in detail the supply chain and logistics management done by e-retailers by quoting appropriate examples.

Business Environment for E-retailing

Introduction

In recent decades, the retail sector has undergone a significant transformation. Due to deregulation of foreign investment, competition/monopoly policy, and land-use policy, alongside broader neoliberal reforms affecting consumer markets and trade, large retailers have managed to consolidate their power and expand globally. While small retailers still dominate in many parts of the world, transnational corporations are taking over larger shares of the market. As large companies seek to increase profits, they have reduced the risks of investment by subcontracting and franchising. These trends have impacted smaller firms, as well as suppliers, consumers, and employees.

Retailing is increasingly a global business. A more structured retail industry with more multiple retailers (those with more than one outlet) is a sign that an economy is developing, as organizations specialize and gain economies of scale.

Additionally, when disposable incomes rise, retailers play an active part in distributing increasingly discretionary goods to centers of population. Emerging markets are a real (although highly complex) opportunity for experienced retailers, especially if they are faced with high levels of retail provision and therefore competition in their traditional markets. As the artificial barriers to trade, such as import duty and quota restrictions, are removed from the global economy, many retailers will view the world as their marketplace and make sourcing and outlet operation decisions on a set of criteria that are relevant across the globe. However, regulatory scenarios, long distances, and political and cultural complexities are huge challenges too that retailers need to face not only in the global market but also in the domestic market. Globalization; reducing trade barriers; technological advancements and the related transformations driven by digital technologies, changing consumer behavior, and increased expectations; upgradation in SCM–logistics systems; and the changing geopolitical and world economic equations have brought many opportunities and challenges to the retail industry at domestic and international levels.

The arrival of digital technology has brought about major changes in shopping experience, globally. In the domestic market, online retailers have leveraged the growing Internet penetration and increasing use of smartphones to transform the Indian customer's journey.

Shoppers today want to use digital touch points throughout their shopping journey—from finding a product, comparing prices, and checking reviews to making the purchase and receiving deliveries at home to returning products—all from the convenience of clicking a button from their home or workplace.

They are not only availing attractive discounts but also getting wider selection of products, 24/7 customer support, and easy payment options like COD. These online portals have enabled the retailers to reach a much wider audience without the need to invest in brick-and-mortar outlets at multiple locations and the complex distribution networks. Digital technologies also help these retailers by providing them with the valuable inputs regarding consumer behavioral patterns by using the tools like data analytics and algorithms. While e-commerce has significantly affected off-line retailers, it has also reflected changing customer preferences, something which the off-line retailers are learning from. With digital media here to stay, brands/retailers would need to adapt to this new way of marketing and doing business. Today, digital tech is affecting in-store purchase behavior as well, and they need to integrate their physical and digital assets to create a seamless shopping experience for the shoppers. It is not only about selling online but also about creating customer awareness, customer engagement, imparting product knowledge in an interactive way, enhancing overall shopping experience, and providing post-purchase support through the use of digital medium.

Global and Domestic Environmental Factors

Globalization has reshaped our lives and is still leading us into uncharted territory. As new technologies drive down the cost of global communication and travel, we are increasingly exposed to the traits and practices of other cultures. When countries reduce barriers to trade, investment, and globalization forces, their industries need to deliver higher quality to be competitive and to survive. And as multinationals from advanced countries and emerging markets seek out customers, competition intensifies on a global scale. These new realities of international business are altering our cultures and transforming the way companies do business.

In recent times, the globalization business advances the retailers' interest, and the marketplace provides retailers the new scope of buying functions. Moreover, globalization connects the world's entire markets. Although nations historically retained absolute control over the products, people, and capital crossing their borders, economies are becoming increasingly intertwined. Globalization is the trend toward greater economic, cultural, political, and technological interdependence among national institutions and economies. Globalization is a trend characterized by denationalization (national boundaries becoming less relevant) and is different from internationalization (entities cooperating across national boundaries). The greater interdependence that globalization is causing means an increasingly freer flow of goods, services, money, people, innovations, and ideas across national borders. As its definition implies, globalization involves much more than the expansion of trade and investment among nations. Globalization embraces concepts and theories from political

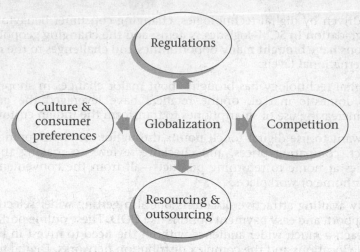

Figure 4.1: *Globalization Impacts: Culture, Competition, and Outsourcing*

science, sociology, anthropology, and philosophy as well as economics. As such, it is not a term exclusively reserved for MNCs and international financial institutions.

Global competition makes retailers source abroad. In order to expand marketplace rapidly, the successful retailers will be wise to search new marketplace. In the developing country, many retailers find a great price and quality to extend their global business. Recently, the clothing retailers focus on Asia market for growth. For instance, H&M, Europe's second largest clothing retailer, and Zara aimed the huge marketplace at Asian. H&M was opening stores in China more quickly than other locations in order to reverse falling profit. E-commerce players from the Europe, USA, and Japan are experiencing slower growth in home markets. They are increasingly looking to explore and enter developing economies of China, India, and Brazil, which have high or stable forecast growth rates in the coming years. Globalization impacts the retail industry in many ways, three of which are culture, competition, and outsourcing (Figure 4.1).

First of all, every marketplace has enormously different demands, regulations, culture, and customers' tastes and interests. Understanding the foreign culture is extremely difficult task for the global retailers. The successful global retailers spend time learning local market and consumers' customs. The global retailers try to understand the customers' tastes, preferences, interests, and their buying behavior in order to expand their business in emerging markets. At the same time, they need to study the regulatory scenario, FDI policies and foreign trade policies (FTPs) of the national economies, monetary policies, demographic attributes, competition, sociocultural factors, tax structures, political atmosphere (prevailing ideologies), and other legalities in order to formulate a comprehensive business plan. As far as retail industry is concerned, here we will discuss the globalization and major forces that are stimulating the globalization and creating a "global culture." Then we will discuss the domestic scenario in Indian context. In the last section of this chapter, we will look into how the Indian retail industry is getting influenced by current geopolitical scenario and how world economic power plays.

Globalization: A Historical Perspective

Globalization means different things to different people. A businessperson may see globalization as an opportunity to source goods and services from lower-cost locations and to pry open new markets. An economist may see it as an opportunity to examine the impact of globalization on jobs and standards of living. An environmentalist may be concerned with how globalization affects our ecology. An anthropologist may want to examine the influence of globalization on the culture of a group of people. A political scientist may be concerned with the impact of globalization on the power of governments relative to that of MNCs. And an employee may view globalization either as an opportunity for new work or as a threat to his or her current job. It is because of the different lenses through which we view events around us that the globalization debate is so complex.

History discusses about how civilizations have been shaped over the millennia with the turn of events and discoveries. Right from the Stone Age to the Industrial Age, the history has witnessed major changes to the culture of the human society with the new findings, leanings, and mélange of the people brought about by development of world economy by new trade routes, formation of new geopolitical equations (the wars), continuous inventions and innovations in the field of science and technology, and the sociopsychological impact of globalization. Migrations of civilizations and societies, travels, trade, and conquests have acted as catalysts for sociocultural change from time immemorial.

If we move forward across the timeline, starting from AD 1000, we will roughly find the chronological changes in the economic significance of developing countries. The first period, 1000–1500, was distinguished by the overwhelming significance and contribution of the three continents that are described as developing countries today. It was categorically attributed to large part of Asia, which was, in turn, attributable to two major economies of that era, China and India, which accounted for almost 50% of world population and income. These ancient civilizations (India and china) were virtually the business leaders and primary suppliers of manufactured goods to the world. In the second phase, spanning around 1500–1850, the three major developments in Europe—the voyages for discovering new continents and the colonization of the America, the mercantile expansion of trade that was encouraged by nations and naval powers, and the political, societal, cultural, institutional, and technological changes (i.e, the Industrial Revolution in Britain)—essentially created an "environment" for capitalist development. Britain's dominance in the 19th century was on account of the fact that it was not only the locus of economic activity based on new technologies but also the dominant military power.

The third period, 1850–1950, experienced the paradigm shift that can be attributed to the dramatic transformations in the world economy wherein the economic and political power was concentrated in Western Europe, North America, and Soviet Russia. The fundamental changes in manufacturing transformed the economic landscape of Western Europe, which spruced up productivity, output, and incomes. This was catalyzed by free trade imposed by imperialism and the revolution in supply chain, transportation, and logistics. The developments were also motivated by the intention to deindustrialize other regions. So during this period, the world witnessed a steep decline in economic significance of Asia (in particular China and India), Africa, and Latin America, and by the end of 1950, they were accounting for around two-thirds of world population and about one-fourth of world income. However, if we look at the contemporary history, the first age of globalization was suddenly halted by the arrival of the World War I, the Russian Revolution, decline of Britain, and the Great Depression.

So with the decline of Britain, the defeat of Germany, and the end of colonialism and the liberation of hitherto colonized nations, European nations witnessed their power and influence recede in the 20th century. On the other hand, the rise of the USA as a techno-economic and military power, and of global alliances that enabled it to project power around the world, ensured that America emerged as last century's dominant power. Hence, Britain and the USA dominated their centuries because the former had its colonies and the latter its allies.

The next phase, spanning 1950–2010, witnessed a substantial cover up by developing world, which was evident from the rate of their economic growth during this period. But it was only after the dawn of 1990s when this economic growth rate of developing world experienced a real momentum. The reason was simple, for 75 years, from the start of the World War I to the end of the Cold War, the world remained divided. There was a geographic divide between the East and West and an ideological divide between communism and capitalism. After the World War II, the West experienced steady economic gains, but international flows of goods, capital, and people were confined to their respective capitalist and communist systems and geographies. The pattern that prevailed in global affairs throughout most of the 20th century was transformed by a series of rapid simultaneous discontinuities that occurred in the late 1980s and early 1990s: the collapse of the Berlin Wall (separating East and West Berlin) and the rise of the World Wide Web (both in 1989), the sheer decline of the Soviet Empire and the end of the Cold War, and the market-oriented reforms undertaken in erstwhile "third world" countries. Gradually, central and eastern European nations got independence from communism, embraced freedom, and began to shift toward democratic institutions and free-market economic systems. The drivers of this second age of globalization—communication satellites, fiber optics, microchips, and the Internet—eventually lowered the cost of telecommunications and is still continuing to bind our world together.

Hence, the 21st century is different. The rise of several new postcolonial states around the world—called emerging economies—global prosperity, and power have become more dispersed. Today, no one nation can dominate the world, the way that Imperial Britain or postwar USA did, and the multiplicity of the sources of affluence and power are shaping an ever more "multipolar" world.

Major Forces: Stimulating New Age Globalization

However, if we study the contemporary history of world, the three main forces underlie the globalization of markets and production: *falling barriers to trade and investment, technological innovation,* and *the digital revolution of today's times.* These three features, more than anything else, are increasing competition among nations by leveling the global business playing field. Greater competition is simultaneously driving companies worldwide into more direct confrontation *and* cooperation. Local industries, once isolated by time and distance, are increasingly accessible to large international companies' base many thousands of miles away. Some small and medium-sized local firms are compelled to cooperate with one another or with larger international firms to remain competitive. Other local businesses revitalize themselves in a bold attempt to survive the competitive onslaught. And on a global scale, consolidation is occurring in many industries as former competitors' link up to challenge others on a worldwide basis. Let us now explore the pivotal roles of the six forces driving globalization in greater detail (Figure 4.2).

Falling Barriers to Trade and Investment

In 1947, political leaders of 23 nations (12 developed and 11 developing economies) made history when they created the General Agreement on Tariffs and Trade (GATT)—a treaty designed to promote free trade by reducing both tariffs and nontariff barriers to international trade. *Tariffs* are essentially taxes levied on traded goods, and *nontariff barriers* are limits on the quantity of an imported product. The treaty was successful in its early years. After four decades, world merchandise trade had grown 20 times larger, and average tariffs had fallen from 40% to 5%. Significant progress occurred again with a 1994 revision of the GATT treaty. A key deficiency of the original GATT was that it lacked the power to enforce world trade rules. However, the successful conclusion of the GATT's Uruguay Round and the creation of the World Trade Organization (WTO) in 1994 were the finale of a half-century of evolution, intensifying and expanding existing rules and practices while bringing whole new sectors, such

Figure 4.2: *Driving Forces of Globalization*

as services and intellectual property (IP), into the rules-based trading system. Membership also expanded dramatically over this period. Nations that had signed on to the treaty further reduced average tariffs on merchandise trade and lowered subsidies (government financial support) for agricultural products. The treaty's revision also clearly defined *intellectual property rights* (IPR)—giving protection to copyrights (including computer programs, databases, sound recordings, and films), trademarks and service marks, and patents (including trade secrets and know-how).

India caught the bandwagon since its economic reform and liberalization program, which began in the early 1990s, and shifted its stress to investment and exports as key drivers of growth. This enabled the Indian economy to catch up with much higher growth trajectory, almost double of the pre-reform era. However, India has been less successful in integrating itself into value supply chains, and this eventually become a key constraint on its exports. Though it majorly remains a mostly domestic demand-driven economy, it is invigorating itself as one of the attractive business destinations with the slew of economic and regulatory measures.

For example, India already has entered into FTAs with Japan, the Association of Southeast Asian Nations (ASEAN), Singapore, and Malaysia. It is about to finalize similar pacts with Australia and the 16-nation Regional Comprehensive Economic Partnership (RCEP). FTA negotiations with New Zealand and Canada are also in full swing, and we are looking at expanding the preferential trading agreement with Chile. New Delhi has preferential trading agreements with Chile and the Mercosur bloc that includes Brazil, Argentina, Uruguay, and Paraguay, but these cover just a handful of items. It is still a very limited arrangement, and both the sides are looking to move forward, toward deepening this engagement, adding value to it and really using it as a tool to be able to facilitate business exchanges with each other.

World Trade Organization

In the post–World War II period, the overall trend was toward creating an open, transparent, and rule-based multilateral trade regime. In the early years, the differentiation between developed and developing countries was taken as a basic principle, with relatively greater responsibilities and commitments falling on the former. However, since at least the Uruguay Round in the early 1990s, the focus began to shift toward reciprocity as the guiding principle, and the exclusive focus on goods trade and tariff regimes also began to give way to, including services and some nontariff provisions, as part of what is now the WTO regime.

The WTO is the international organization that enforces the rules of international trade. The three major objectives of the WTO are to assist the free flow of trade, help negotiate the further opening of trade, and settle trade conflicts among its members. It is the authority of the WTO to settle trade conflicts that essentially distinguishes it from its predecessor, the GATT. The various WTO agreements are basically contracts between member nations that entrust them for maintaining fair and open trade policies. Offenders need to realign their trade policies and practices according to the guidelines given by WTO or face fines/penalties and, perhaps, penalties in the form of trade sanctions. The WTO's dispute settlement system truly is the spine of the global trading system because of its ability and authority to penalize offending nations. The WTO launched a new round of negotiations in Doha, Qatar, in late 2001. The renewed negotiations were designed to lower trade barriers further and to help poor nations in particular. There are several changes that are apparent and will have significant impact on India.

According to the WTO, trade grew by 6% per annum between 1990 and 2008 while world GDP grew by about 3% per annum. Since 2008, this long-term trend has been broken as global trade has been rising at the same rate or even slower than global GDP. The trade slowdown is visible even in China. The 2007–2008 global financial crises transformed and are still transforming the global economic order. Some of the previous trends are being reinforced, such as the shift of global economic activity from the transatlantic to the transpacific, both in terms of proportion of global trade and investment flows. However, what still exists is the continuing domination of the global financial markets by the West, which continues to intervene even with the flows generated by emerging national economies.

The other issues, besides taxes, that need to be addressed are the legal positions with respect to use of data and rules for conducting business. While there are imbalances between these rules, around the world, it will limit the potential for a truly global marketplace, which the web, as a medium, potentially develops. Even today, there is a significant influence of West in determining the legal norms, standards, and regulatory frameworks, which govern interstate economic activity. More prominently, the West, and particularly USA, still continues to be the major source and repository of innovative technologies. As growth becomes highly driven by IT and knowledge in general, the West will continue to enjoy leadership position in the global economy. The WTO is working on developing standards for these areas. Legal standards, across states and countries, are as important as business and technology standards in terms of allowing markets to evolve. However, the decision makers need to keep these enduring factors in mind while designing an appropriate economic strategy for India.

Regional Trade Agreements

The WTO allows limited bilateral and regional free-trade arrangements, though such developments and arrangements diminish its role as the premier multilateral forum for worldwide rule-regulation formulations. In addition to the WTO, smaller groups of national economies are integrating their economies as never before by encouraging trade collaborations and fostering cross-border investment in mutually beneficial way. For example, the *North American Free Trade Agreement (NAFTA)* brings three nations (Canada, Mexico, and the USA) into a free-trade bloc. The more ambitious *EU* brings 27 countries on a common platform. The *Asia-Pacific Economic Cooperation (APEC)* consists of 21 member economies, coming together with a commitment for creating a free-trade zone around the Pacific.

Hence, WTO is increasingly becoming and also perceived as a forum for settling trade disputes, and this trend commenced before the 2008 crisis, which is being reinforced postcrisis as well. India itself has accomplished bilateral and regional trade agreements despite its commitment to the WTO and multilateral processes. It has also conceded the inclusion of services and a few other areas in its Comprehensive Partnership agreements with a select group of countries.

Objectives of each of these smaller trade pacts are similar to those of the WTO but are regional in nature. Moreover, some nations are placing greater emphasis on regional pacts because of resistance to worldwide trade agreements. However, the international trade and national output together with the WTO agreements and regional pacts have boosted world trade and cross-border investment significantly. Trade theory tells us that openness to trade helps a nation to produce a greater amount of output.

The emergence of East Asian, Southeast Asian, and Chinese economies took place in a global economic landscape dominated by the mature economies of the transatlantic zone. It is also the post–World War II expanding markets in this zone, joined subsequently by Japan, and the flow of capital and technology from the zone made the investment and export-led growth model a viable choice for the emerging economies. These countries also enjoyed a high rate of domestic savings, relatively cheap but increasingly skilled labor, and local entrepreneurship supported by the state.

For most of the post–World War II period, world trade has increased at a rate twice as fast as global GDP growth, as barriers to trade flows have gradually diminished. There has also been a significant increase in capital flows coming from the developed countries, which have encouraged and enabled export-led growth in developing countries. Typically, foreign investment has involved the setting up of local processing or manufacturing units for generating exports back to the home country or other foreign markets. The establishment of complex regional and global supply chains by international MNCs has reinforced this trend. Hence, acknowledging this trend and evolving a coordinated strategy to deal with it have become the need of the hour.

Technological Evolutions

Digital commerce is surely one of the tectonic shifts that happen once in few decades. This has changed the retail landscape not only globally but also in India. Over a decade ago, it was the malls and large-format retail stores brought the revolution, and today, it is the digital shopping platforms that are creating a natural evolution and redefining the way people shop and retailers sell. Retailers are constantly attracting new customer base, and the proliferation of personal computers, Internet, and smartphone has helped them to connect with these new connected consumers. Web technologies allow the e-retailers to bring together people having similar needs and demands across the geographies into the same online vicinity to fulfill to their requirements, which would never be possible in the physical world with the same ease. As far as brick-and-mortar retailers are concerned, the digital technologies have enabled them to track shopper's behavior both inside and outside the store. They can use this knowledge to offer relevant products, promotions, ease of interaction and transaction, and coherent in-store or online shopping experience to their target audience.

The Internet has made it easier to obtain information, which in turn has simplified the buying process. The marketplace models are acting as significant socioeconomic equalizers for small business in India. These SMEs and budding entrepreneurs are leveraging digital platforms to expand their current market beyond their immediate catchment area. Here the customers, who were underserved by off-line retailers, become potential online shoppers. It is happening for the first time that consumers living in the small town and rural areas of India have access to the same selection of merchandise as their counterparts living in big metro cities. Event the big brick-and-mortar retailers are leveraging the power of e-commerce to reach to the new markets and geographies where setting up physical stores is not feasible. This democratization of markets is assisting the SMEs, entrepreneurs, and other small retailers to reach customers globally and reducing the asymmetry of information and effectively distributing their offerings.

In addition, the once-in-a-decade shift driven by digital forces—including e-commerce and social, mobile, analytics, and cloud (SMAC) technologies, among others—as well as the incremental technologies are bringing industries and businesses at a junction. Retailers also use the Internet to achieve longer-term goals, such as sharpen their forecasting, lower their inventories, and improve communication with suppliers. The lower cost of reaching an international customer base especially benefits small firms, which were among the first to use the web as a global marketing tool. The pace of transformation and innovation is like never before. For instance, digital technologies such as cloud computing has rapidly evolved and is driving the delivery of business outcomes for enterprises. It has enabled the enterprises to access servers, storage, databases, and a broad set of application services over the Internet. With cloud computing, companies do not need to make large upfront investments in hardware and spend a lot of time on the heavy lifting of managing that hardware. Instead, enterprises can provision exactly the right type and size of computing resources they need to power their businesses or operate their IT department.

On the other hand, the new connected consumers can utilize the Internet and mobile technology inside or outside the store to interact with other consumers, friends, influencers, and peers to check references, validate their buying options, share their shopping experiences, and write reviews about a retailer's offerings using the social media.

Further gains arise from the ability of the Internet to cut postproduction costs by decreasing the number of intermediaries a product passes through on its way to the customer. Eliminating intermediaries greatly benefits online sellers of books, music, and travel services, among others. For instance, the Visa India's spend data showed 53% growth in the number of e-commerce transactions in 2014. The greater adoption of Internet and smartphones is the biggest driver of e-commerce in India. Internet penetration is rapidly increasing with around 300 million users in 2014.

As the smartphone and other mobile devices have become ubiquitous, they are fast becoming a new platform for retailers to increase their reach and interaction with customers. The e-commerce companies are focusing their efforts on increasing the penetration of their mobile apps for higher growth. These mobile applications are helping these players to reach more customers located even in remote and rural areas in a very short time. The availability of e-commerce applications on various mobility devices is helping to drive sales and revenue, and many big players in this market claim to have more than 50% of their revenue coming from mobile apps. Also these e-commerce companies have been able to bridge the service gap considerably by sending service updates and other communication via their mobile app, e-mail, and SMS (short message service). In addition, the digital advertisement industry is also growing fast as there is a growth in digital communication devices around the world. The increase in smartphones and tablets is enabling advertisers to reach a wider audience.

For example, Tesco operates a series of virtual stores that leverage the bar-code scanning technology in order to give an enhanced shopping experience to its customers. The Korean retail player's Homeplus chain was looking for ways to increase its market share without adding brick-and-mortar outlets and eventually came up with mobile shopping as a solution. Tesco has set up virtual grocery in subway stations in South Korea by plastering large-scale photos of store shelves that "displayed" merchandise just as they would be in a traditional Homeplus stores. Here each item featured a QR (quick response) code, which would be scanned by a shopper's mobile device and immediately added to a virtual shopping basket. A customer could then use his/her smartphone to pay for the merchandise online and have them delivered to his/her home. Thus, here the retailer brilliantly identified its customer's needs (ease-of-use shopping), pain points (time constraints), and paired these with right technology that can be leveraged easily with a promotion location that was central and routine for millions of South Korea (subway stations). Hence, here the key to success is to get all the components of marketing working together in a synchronized manner.

Advancement in Logistics and Transportation Systems

There is an obvious initiative among Indian retail enterprises to achieve global benchmarks in execution and customer service quality. They are focusing on the notion to "think fast" and "think forward" in order to fortify their relevance for the future. The ability to innovate—both for India and by India—is also higher because the retail industry today has become more complex and has built much broader capabilities. For instance, the e-retailing is not just about the sellers and buyers; it is also about the supporting businesses that are experiencing a phenomenal growth. A case in point is the growth of companies and start-up working in logistics (courier) sector. They ensure the timely last-mile deliveries of the merchandise purchased online.

For instance, there is a strong relationship between the low-cost carriers (LCC) from aviation industry and the growth in the e-commerce sector, and there is a significant contribution of LCCs in putting e-commerce on higher trajectory of growth. It has also created huge opportunities for other traveling-related intermediaries (holiday, hotel, events, etc.) to launch online business (B2B).

Innovation in the shipping industry is helping globalize markets and production by making shipping more efficient and dependable. The growing integration of production facilities across the globe and the rise of supply chains–logistics networks are essentially transforming the nature of trade and the way developing countries are connected to the global market. Resultant reduction in transport and logistics costs and improved ITs combined with more open economies have made it easier to operate businesses not only within countries but also across regions, continents, and so on. Some of the key business touch points that can bring in operational efficiency can be briefly summarized in the following points:

- The logistics service providers incorporate multiple parties, especially in the case of 3PL service providers. The resultant improvement in capabilities related to contracting, vendor management, scheduling, coordination, monitoring, and information sharing add significant value and eventually reduce the cost.
- Here transportation being one of the major components of the entire logistics ecosystem naturally gives rise to a host of related issues. The functions and systems like route plan fortification, scheduling, vehicle placement, transit adherence, and effective loss/damage/pilferage control improve the overall efficiency, which eventually results in growth of the business.
- Logistics management involves handling of disparate loads across different geographies/regions/sectors. So this essentially demands for meticulous planning of transportation vehicles and modes, process compliance, and adherence to the committed service quality–delivery experience.

So with the given complexities in terms of volume, scale, and geographic spread of operations of logistics service providers, any process implementation is a challenge and needs to be backed up by appropriate information and monitoring systems. For instance, operation of cargo ships is now simpler and safer due to computerized charts that pinpoint a ship's movement on the high seas using GPS satellites. Combining GPS with RFID technology allows continuous monitoring of individual containers from port of departure to destination. An RFID can show whether a container's doors are opened or closed on its journey and can monitor the temperature inside refrigerated containers.

The transport revolution that dismantled the barriers created by geography via distance and time provides the retail industry with opportunities to connect with the different national economies around the world and to expand in the emerging markets as well in the most effective and efficient way.

The Digital Age and the New Global Culture

We can see that in the past, the effect of changes took a certain time to become visible in the form of its impact on the societies and their cultural attributes. During this process of percolation of change to society, several subcultures got formed. For instance, if we look in the Indian context, over several centuries, trade and invasions by external armies have resulted in dynamic changes to our culture. These changes are evident in our eating habits, our food; in the way we dress up and the fashion we follow, giving up the ethnic clothing and preferring to adopt Western wears; or in our music preferences; and many other such things that we practice and prefer in our lives. Though these changes are big changes, they happened over a very long period of time, which can be measured in decades and centuries.

But it is not same with the digital age. Digital age is essentially a sign of new culture that brings sweeping and fascinating transformations to our everyday life at short intervals that are being observed and experienced simultaneously in more or less same measures throughout the world. Digital technologies have also led to expand the reach and penetration of new ideas, practices, and innovations, making some alterations to some cultures and also probably driving the evolution of common cultural code unconsciously throughout the world. For instance, the emergence of user-friendly mobile apps that have brought about changes in the way shopping is done, simultaneously in both the economically advanced and the developing countries around the world.

Therefore, here we can observe that what basically distinguishes the cultural change in the digital era is nothing but the speed of adoption of change at individual level, speed of the simultaneous adoption of changes at society as a whole, and the speed of expected impact on the traditions and heritage of the subcultures. As a result of such changes in the cultural fabric of the society, certain traditions would disappear and some others would get transformed for the better or the worse. In the digital age, the human values, beliefs, behaviors, and practices are being shaped by these transformations and eventually leading to social change.

The comprehensive understanding of the trends and the patterns of these transformations is crucial for taking cognizance of the societal evolution. It is essential for any industry or business because culture is one of the most influential factors that impact the customer behavior and mind-set. So it becomes imperative for retailers to meticulously analyze the influence of digital technology in their categories and create a relevant ecosystem to address this rapidly evolving phenomenon.

In the 1980s and 1990s, the global cultural changes were attributed to the medium of cinema and television, while in the recent decade, digital technology-enabled e-commerce and social media have expanded the scope and the penetration, and the society at large is impacted, creating the new social order. These cultural changes are primarily being brought about by two key developments: discovery and innovations from within the society and by importing and adapting to ideas from the outside. Technology is transforming the things faster than our imagination. The technologies such as the Internet and the social media integrated with the telecommunication technologies and the mobile devices are acting as change agents and are fundamentally transforming the social dynamics and driving the cultural changes.

Digital technology has enabled the retailers to make branding omnipresent. Brands are interacting with customers across platforms in a way comfortable to them without being perceived as intrusive. It enables brands to be a part of consumer community, for not just promoting their offerings but also enabling them to actively participate in communicative engagement. Hence, digitized world has become an integral part of our lives, influencing it like never before, simplifying it and fueling it too.

The Domestic Environment for Retail Industry

In this digital era, when it comes to the shopping, online seems like the future. The phenomenal growth in Internet connectivity through several mediums—the desktops, laptops, tablets, and none other than smartphones—is coinciding with the rise of upper middle class that has handsome salaries and more disposable income than ever before. Above all, there is an increasing demand for better standards of living and aspirations to live a life that qualifies as a "lifestyle" with higher propensity toward spending, acquiring, and indulging in lifestyle experiences. All these transformations in consumer psyche clubbed with increasing impact of technology and paucity of time have eventually transformed both ends of the market: the demand and supply. The e-commerce growth is essentially driven by virtue of wide selection offered by online shopping portals that are in sync with the prevailing global trends, consumer awareness, the augmented convenience, and coherent shopping experience offered by online shopping. The services like free and quick last-mile shipment return logistics and payment options like COD and easy returns along with the ease of shopping online as compared to in-store shopping are also helping e-retailing to gain the momentum. As we have discussed in the previous chapters, the e-retailing space has empowered not only the individual consumers but also the businesses by providing platforms designed to cater exclusively to the B2B model. E-commerce has gone beyond generating employment by encouraging entrepreneurship—which is evident from the growing entrepreneurial success stories in different forms and models like women entrepreneurship, social entrepreneurship, and innovation–start-up entrepreneurship—and is a boost to SMEs.

Although the e-commerce industry is growing at a phenomenal rate, there exist many challenges the industry is facing, which are as follows:

1. The current complicated tax structure (CST, VAT, etc.). There are many ambiguities regarding the current tax regime. The roll out of GST is the only expected remedy for all these issues.
2. The current FDI regulations and laws for e-commerce industry, which at times are debatable.
3. The quality, speed, and penetration of Internet are still an impediment in the expected growth of e-commerce.
4. The supply chain efficiencies are not of global standards. The logistics–warehousing–transportation infrastructure and delivery systems are not adequate and efficient. For most of the e-commerce ventures, the last-mile delivery is the first physical consumer interface and hence one of the key success factors.
5. Absence of any law for Internet and some other related ambiguities. The obsolete law, IT Act 2000, governs the e-commerce as well. There is a need for comprehensive law to

protect the interest and rights of both suppliers and buyers, as we can see that banking, logistics, and several other supporting functions and industries have become the inevitable components of the e-commerce ecosystem.

6. Heavy discounting models that are not sustainable in the long term and low customer loyalty.

Many of the e-retailers have developed strong PLBs, and these brands are helping them to create differentiation and in turn to improve margins. While some online portals are following horizontal business model with varied merchandise offering, other players have developed specialized merchandise category offerings. Many others are creating differentiations by developing efficient SCM and delivery management systems. Some are coming up with omni-channel strategies to offer hybrid shopping experience to their consumers. The use of tools such as data analytics and social media is providing them with valuable inputs to personalize the shopping experience and also to develop effective loyalty programs. While there are several challenges, there exists huge opportunities as well. The number of transactions, average time spent on the online portals, social media sites, the average ticket size of purchase (refers to the average bill value and is calculated as total sales/no. of invoices), and the average basket size (refers to the average number of merchandise units moving in one singe bill and is calculated as total units sold/no. of invoices), all of these are growing exponentially. Because of all these factors, e-commerce has been successful in attracting consistent investments across different categories, models, and verticals from various angel investors, strategic investors, and VCs and through Silicon Valley funding as well.

Quick Facts about the E-commerce Industry

Over time, Indian consumers are becoming more transactional online; this is only expected to grow. The credit for the creation of this vast user base goes to the travel portals, e-tailers, social media, and the migration of government services to the Internet like Indian Railways reservations and online filing of income tax returns. Over the past few years, they have invested time, money, and effort to ensure that consumers transact online through multiple means; they have offered convenient online interfaces, attractive offers and services like COD, EMIs, and hassle-free returns, and advertised in the mass media. These Internet users are proved to be the driving force for the growth of Indian e-tailing.

Today, we can see that e-commerce has become the fastest-growing business in the country, coupled with blockbuster massive funding from domestic and foreign investors. The high share of domestic consumption in India's economy, which is not expected to change much in the coming decade, also implies that India's retail growth rate will mirror the country's GDP growth rate. By 2020, India's online retail market is projected to grow to US$45 billion, from US$2 billion in 2013. Within this sector, fashion and apparel will grow faster, said a Motilal Oswal research report on e-commerce.

The key drivers for this high-growth segment have been the Internet user base of 278 million and mobile Internet base of 173 million, which is projected to double at 480 million by 2017. According to Nasscom, there is an untapped consumer market like 30% of the e-commerce sales coming in from the Tier II and Tier III cities. The local-level consolidation and presence of global players have also impacted industry dynamics. As per Technopak's estimates, India's GDP, in real terms, will grow at an average nearly to 6% over the next decade. This growth will therefore translate to an increase in merchandise retail market, from the current US$490 billion to US$810 billion by 2021 in real terms, and US$1.4 trillion in nominal terms (assuming a 7% inflation rate). The key reason for this disruptive growth lies in the fact that the market-enabling conditions and ecosystem creation for e-tailing will outpace the same for corporatized brick-and-mortar retail. This growth will offer many advantages to the Indian economy, besides bringing in immense benefits to consumers.

However, there is a flip side also; it has faced allegations of tax evasion and rule-breaking by major e-tailers. Also many traditional retailers, brick-and-mortar retailers, and consumer goods companies have complained that online retailers are involved in predatory pricing, selling below cost of acquisition to destroy their business. Recently, Flipkart had fueled a controversy when it unveiled its "Big Billion Day" sale, leading to complaints from consumers and allegations of predatory pricing. This incident led to traditional retailers lobbying against the online players. In this light, it is imperative to have an objective debate on e-tailing. The big boys of India's traditional retail finally came together to fight the onslaught of their online counterparts. In letters to the Ministries of Finance and Commerce, those with significant interests in the retail business such as Reliance Industries Ltd (RIL), Aditya Birla Group, ITC, Bharti, and Future Group complained against predatory pricing on e-commerce platforms. They have also sought clarity in norms for the e-commerce sector, as well as for the overall retail sector. The letters were sent by the Retailers Association of India (RAI), an apex body of major retailers whose members include RIL, Aditya Birla Group, and Bharti.

In this battlefield, one another front have been opened by Online Vendor Association of India (OVAOI), an association for parity among online and off-line players. The association has raised concerns over e-tailers undercutting them for products listed on their platform, which has impacted vendors who operate on thin margins. This added some more complications to the deadlock between brick-and-mortar retailers and e-commerce players over issues like pricing and preferential treatment to particular vendors. Vendors associated with OVAOI also alleged that expenses related to delivery and returns of products are borne by vendors, which are eating into their margins. Besides, the logistics services offered by the e-tailers leave a lot to be desired. E-tailers undercutting prices, thus impacting the business of brick-and-mortar retailers and vendors, have already been emerged as a contentious issue. Electronics manufacturers such as Asus and Lenovo have even cautioned buyers against purchasing from some leading e-tailers and denied their authorization as resellers of their products. Brick-and-mortar retailers had earlier launched an online forum called "We Will Act," condemning the modus operandi of some of the e-tailers. The forum, through its eponymous website, has appealed to the center to act against "unethical online retailers," alleging that "these unethical online retailers have been selling in losses and routing money illegally to kill the market." Some e-tailers were being investigated by the Enforcement Directorate (ED) for allegedly circumventing FDI rules, which bar any e-retailer with FDI from holding inventory. Indian laws do not allow foreign investment in e-commerce companies that sell directly to customers. They, however, allow such companies to set up online marketplaces, the model that Amazon India and later Flipkart adopted.

The ED has already found evidence against few of them for violating FDI norms. However, the hue and cry raised by off-line retailers or the ED hardly seems to have impacted the e-tailers, with the domestic e-commerce market poised to grow fivefold from the present by 2020.

Debate over Current Regulatory Scenario

Currently, there is no sufficient legal guideline to regulate, monitor and supervise e-commerce. Also, what is making monitoring a very challenging and difficult task is the lack of a mechanism of registration/licensing of online retailers. E-commerce activities are generally very complex and diverse to be kept under the jurisdiction of a single department or ministry. So to get over the ambiguity on regulation of the burgeoning e-commerce business and in a bid to effectively regulate the country's e-commerce market, which is going through an exponential growth, the government is considering a regime where there will be a clear demarcation of the different ministries and regulators. The Department of Consumer Affairs has moved a note for the consideration of the committee of secretaries (CoS) and sought approval for a proposal for clear allocation of business rules with respect to the sector. During any probe on online frauds, the government faces problems and constraints in accessing data from servers and data centers situated overseas. The government has made a move to ask e-retailers to set up data centers in the country, citing loss of business as most of these are located outside India. Hence, to get over the ambiguity on regulation of the increasing e-commerce business, a note prepared for a CoS has designated nine departments in the government with specific area and issues in the sector to handle and oversee.

Thus, according to the consumer affairs department's proposal, the Department of Revenue will handle taxation-related issues, while the RBI should look into banking and foreign exchange issues. The consumer protection issues will be taken care of by the consumer affairs department, while foreign investment and trade policy will be under the purview of the commerce and industry ministry. The Ministry of IT and Telecom will handle data protection, cybersecurity, and issues related to registration of server and website, while competition policy-related matters will fall within the jurisdiction of the corporate affairs ministry. Criminal frauds will be looked into by the finance, corporate, and home ministries. A database on the on the sector will be maintained by the statistics department.

Advertising and guidelines would be handled by the Ministry of Information and Broadcasting, especially as e-commerce companies have become one of the largest advertisers, on television, print, and the Internet, and are known for their aggressive stance. It has been observed that many of the rules governing the print and broadcasting business cannot be applied on Internet advertising because of the relative anonymity of the business.

The Proposed Web of Checks

According to the consumer affairs department's proposal:

1. RBI: RBI will look into banking and foreign exchange issues related to e-commerce.
2. Home Ministry: Criminal frauds by e-commerce will be looked into by the finance, corporate, and home ministries.
3. Department of Revenue: The Department of Revenue will handle taxation-related issues.
4. Ministry of Corporate Affairs: The competition policy-related matters will fall within the corporate affairs ministry's jurisdiction.
5. Ministry of IT and Telecom: The Ministry of IT and Telecom will handle data protection, cybersecurity, and issues related to registration of server and websites. Statistics department may maintain database on the sector.
6. Consumer Affairs Ministry: The consumer protection issues will be taken care of by the consumer affairs department.
7. Ministry of Commerce and Industry: The foreign investment and trade policy issues will be under the purview of the commerce and industry ministry.
8. Information and Broadcasting Ministry: I&B ministry will take care of advertising norms and related matters.
9. Statistics Department: A database on the sector will be maintained by the statistics department.

According to the consumer affairs department, this kind of system is now the need of the hour because most of the complaints related to the sector are being referred to the consumer affairs department on the contention that as the department looks into "internal trade" matters, it should handle e-commerce matters too, because such activities also constitute the "internal trade." However, the consumer affairs department has asked for more clarity in the meaning and definition of "internal trade." The department has opined that though it can take care of consumer protection issues and grievances, e-commerce has several other issues, including tax evasion, online frauds, predatory business pricing and practices, data privacy/cybersecurity, and FDI. Also as there is no list of genuine/licensed online retailers, consumers do not have any mechanism to distinguish between genuine/authentic and fake/fraudulent e-commerce players, and adding to this issue, many of the sellers do not provide proper contact information. The department also cautioned with the fact that many of the time consumers have been confused by different operating procedures and processes followed by online retailers for placing orders and for purchasing. The department is facing several complaints related to delivery of products and services as well as in canceling orders and getting refunds for returned items. The department also mentioned that SMEs with very limited resources are sometimes troubled by multiplicity of rules and regulations of e-commerce, and therefore are not able to make use of business opportunities.

Objections Taken by the Department of Industrial Policy and Promotion

The rapidly expanding e-commerce sector, which has been attacked by brick-and-mortar businesses over issues such as predatory pricing, has found support within the government against a proposal that seeks to impose control on the likes of Flipkart and Snapdeal that have disrupted the market. The consumer affairs ministry proposed to bring e-commerce under the purview of up to nine government agencies and regulatory bodies, including DIPP, the RBI, home ministry, law ministry, and Department of Revenue and Ministry of Corporate Affairs.

However, the DIPP opposed a plan to regulate the e-commerce sector, arguing that it would curtail innovation and the spirit of entrepreneurship. DIPP made it clear that the government must be at arm's length from entrepreneurship. According to them, if we put in regulation to the extent that the Ministry of Consumer Affairs is suggesting, it will kill e-commerce in the country.

Arguments Put Forth by DIPP

1. There should be minimal government interference and that e-commerce must be treated at par with brick-and-mortar industry.
2. If there are any specific complaints of consumers, then there are consumer courts to address them.
3. We need ease of doing business in the country and not to complicate it for entrepreneurs.
4. The move also does not seem to be in sync with the government's bid to attract investment to create jobs and help revive the economy.
5. In line with the "Make in India" campaign, aimed turning India into a global manufacturing hub, government departments have adopted a series of measures to reduce licensing and regulatory hurdles.
6. So, if we put unnecessary controls, e-commerce will not grow, arguing that it would curtail innovation and the spirit of entrepreneurship, and India must become a land of innovators to become an economic superpower.
7. Therefore, in order to turn "Digital India" and "Make in India" campaigns into reality, the government needs to work a lot toward improving the environment to promote and reward innovation.

Other Key Issues: Legal and Technological Infrastructure

E-tailing exists as a global bazaar. Rules for commerce, and its legal framework, have evolved within geographically limited borders (nation, state, and local laws and tax systems). For e-tailing to grow, a legal framework needs to evolve that makes sense for a global marketplace. India allows 100% foreign investment in single-brand retail and 51% in multi-brand retail, but not yet allowed in e-commerce. Marketplace model is common among ingenious Indian e-commerce companies: the e-retailer stocks no inventory and only provides a platform to bring together sellers and buyers. As it is a service and not retail, the government has found no reason to block foreign investment in it, at least until now.

Similar issues are faced by emerging economies the world over. Until a legal business framework is established, companies are not encouraged to do business. This is perhaps the one of the most challenging aspects to overcome in order to maintain the growth momentum.

In the absence of a uniform goods and services tax, there is the usual problem of billing the product in one state and shipping it to another. On the other hand, currently, there is a freeze on taxes (sales taxes) for e-tail transactions with businesses that have no physical presence. Clearly, this biases against traditional retailers and those that are adopting the web. Potentially, it is a major source of revenue loss for states and countries that would have received those revenues.

The other issue pertaining to technological infrastructure lies in low Internet penetration. The Internet penetration in India is among the lowest in emerging countries. A recent report released by the International Telecommunications Union said that only 13% Indian households had access to the Internet, which was way below China (44%), Brazil (42.4%), and South Africa (39.4%). A growing number of Indians have their first Internet experience on the mobile phone. For e-commerce to pick up, wireless broadband needs to be inexpensive. One of the key reasons for low Internet penetration in India is the huge delay in completing the government's ambitious national fiber network project to connect about 2,50,000 *gram panchayats* with high-speed Internet. The program, which was slated to be completed by 2014–2015, is now likely to become functional only by 2017. Also the government had decided to change the definition of broadband, increasing the minimum speed requirement from 256 kbps to 512 kbps. But still it could not be increased further because of infrastructural constraints.

The high cost of spectrum and the tariff wars have kept most mobile telephony operators from pricing wireless broadband aggressively. Also, state-owned corporations BSNL (Bharat Sanchar Nigam Limited) and MTNL (Mahanagar Telephone Nigam Limited), which control more than 80% of the country's fixed-line business, have not pushed fixed broadband and preferred to invest in mobility. However, the initiative and program like Digital India is likely to fill the gaps in infrastructure, which has traditionally been the biggest obstacle for the adoption of web tools in India. Projects like Bharat Net, a rural broadband connectivity project using optical fiber, solar-powered Wi-Fi system, and 100 Gbps optical fiber cable (OFC) link has brought a lot of optimism. The government leaders have made it clear that broadband highways are as important as national highways. Digital infrastructure is being adopted five times faster than electricity and telephony. The initiatives and programs like "Digital India" are expected to provide further momentum to the country's technological makeover. A digitized nation will help India leapfrog and be at the forefront of innovation and job creation.

Holistic Overview of FDI Policies in E-retailing Sector

E-commerce activities refer to the activity of buying and selling by a company through the e-commerce platform. As per present FDI policy, FDI, up to 100%, under the automatic route is permitted in B2B e-commerce activities. Such companies would engage only in B2B e-commerce and not in retail trading, inter alia implying that existing restrictions on FDI in domestic trading would be applicable to e-commerce as well. In recent months, there has been a lot of interest and debate around permitting FDI in B2C e-commerce. While its proponents perceive enormous benefit, there is no dearth of people who have serious apprehensions to this proposition.

A national-level body of Internet and mobile phone companies, stressing on the challenges as regulatory restriction to raise funds from foreign private equity/VCs, has suggested a caveat-based approach to allowing FDI in the sector. Another national body of software and IT companies has made persuasive case for allowing FDI in B2C e-commerce. It is stated that e-commerce can be aligned to the objectives of national development by providing thrust to manufacturing sector, order consolidation and distribution, facilitating and supporting SMEs, improving outreach and access to buyers/sellers, bringing traceability and transparency in transactions, empowering consumers with information and data, and, finally, creating employment opportunities. One body of industries has stated that MSMEs/traders are currently benefiting from e-commerce in India, and there is a huge scope of further involvement and growth of MSMEs/traders with further impetus to e-commerce. Even small traders have enhanced their coverage and reach by using e-commerce platforms such as Flipkart and Snapdeal. An international council has stated that India could garner enormous and nearly immediate benefits by creating an exemption from its retail FDI rules to permit the unrestricted marketing of retail goods through e-tailing.

However, on the opposite end of the spectrum, a national body of traders has strongly opposed allowing any FDI in e-commerce. They have stated that Indian market is not yet ready for opening up e-retail space to foreign investors. Small-time trading or opening corner stores still remains a large source of employment. An FDI in the sector will have disastrous impact on this domestic industry, leading to monopolies in e-commerce, manufacturing, logistics, retail sector, and so on, and causing large-scale unemployment. Because of scale of economic operations, e-commerce players will have more bargaining powers than stand-alone traders. Allowing FDI in e-commerce will provide e-commerce players with complete geographical reach, which will be against the spirit of FDI in multi-brand retail trade, that is, being restricted to cities with a population of more than one million in consenting states or any other city of their choice. Moreover, Indian e-commerce industry, which is at a nascent stage of development, will be seriously threatened.

Recently, RAI, country's largest group of brick-and-mortar retailers, alleged that there is lack of a level playing field in the foreign investment policy between them and e-commerce because of which these e-commerce players are making fast inroads into the country's retailing space through unprecedented discounts. While India restricts FDI in e-commerce companies selling products directly to consumers, it allows foreign companies to operate the so-called "e-commerce marketplace" that lends its platforms for other companies to sell their products. They gave example of some of India's largest homegrown e-tailers that have attracted billions of dollars in funding by operating such marketplaces. They also mentioned that US-based Amazon.com has set up a fully owned subsidiary here and demanded for parity in the policies. These brick-and-mortar players blamed that conditions such as foreign investors in supermarkets must invest US$100 million upfront with half of it in back-end infrastructure and such ventures must source 30% of the merchandise they sell from local vendors are the reasons for multi-brand retailer's failure to attract FDI, while there is no such restriction on e-commerce. They mentioned that because of these conditions, they have not been able to raise any funds per se as there are so many clauses and ifs and buts to it.

Some of the allegations made by brick-and-mortar retailers are as follows:

- Government is encouraging e-commerce without giving equal support to physical retail business, thereby promoting monopolization of retail sector by online players.

- The current FDI policy in retail gives by one hand but takes away by other.
- Distinction between B2B and B2C e-commerce has been removed by allowing firms to adopt the marketplace model even as it exists for brick-and-mortar players.
- The physical retailers are facing problems without access to the kind of overseas funds that e-commerce players have access to.

RAI, which represents hundreds of brick-and-mortar retailers including Future Group, Reliance Retail, Shoppers Stop, argued that marketplaces do more than just facilitate sales and the online retailers not only hold inventories on behalf of the sellers but also ship them to the buyers. They also alleged that though on paper FDI is not allowed in B2C e-commerce, on the other hand, a whole lot of marketplaces are coming up and retailing effectively. They are conveniently referred as "marketplaces" and can raise as much FDI they want. In such a scenario, it becomes extremely difficult for physical retailers to compete with online retailers as the former has to pay heavy rentals along with other establishment costs. RAI also alleged that this policy of encouraging to e-commerce without giving equal support to the (physical) retail business would warp the entire market, leading to closure of physical retail spaces and monopolization of the retail sector by e-commerce as e-commerce is not limited by physical boundaries, is not location specific and products specific, is not limited by the space on the shelf, and it can become free of all competition and kill the local shopkeepers.

Reacting to this petition, in May 2015, The Delhi High Court asked the government to consider the RAI's plea, seeking parity in the FDI policy vis-à-vis e-commerce players.

However, on the other end of the spectrum, the domestic online players argue on the basis of following points:

- The "third-party exchange marketplace model" adopted by them is more of a B2B model as they just create an online platform to help connect buyers and sellers.
- Their revenues come mainly from the fees for providing the online platform, data analytics, rent for facilitation centers, generating brand awareness, and commissions on sales.
- The sellers have full ownership over products and services and have freedom over pricing.
- The "marketplace model" players do not directly compete with MSMEs and therefore do not hurt entrepreneurship and employment.

Through this arrangement, the purport that is being given by such e-commerce players is that they are only an intermediary and facilitating a sale of goods owned by one to the purchaser without itself getting any element of ownership into such goods. Also representation from MNCs engaged in the inventory-based online retailing has opined that open and deregulated e-commerce sector would create new markets for small businesses/entrepreneur and help them scale at almost no cost and generate employment through investment/innovation in SCM, warehousing, logistics services, and other ancillary sector. However, the Indian government, after a stakeholder discussion on e-commerce, is also holding talks with states on "the manner in which FDI is needed or not needed, and on whether allowing FDI will affect the level-playing field of brick-and-mortar stores" besides issues such as definition of e-commerce and taxation.

However, as far as issues regarding taxation is concerned, the union government is of the view that the issues of erosion of tax revenue claimed by consuming states as a result of e-tailing would be addressed by the proposed GST, under which taxes on interstate supply of goods and services would go to the consuming state. GST brings uniformity to the taxation of e-commerce among various states in India. All supplies of goods, including stock transfer, will be taxed, and the credit chain will flow continuously across states. While in the case of VAT (value-added tax), it requires Form C for availing beneficial rates of CST (central sales tax), and the marketplace model of business of various e-commerce has been subjected to closer scrutiny with the intention of making the marketplace accountable for the transactions. Commenting on the issue, the RBI has also suggested that the country should develop a uniform and easy-to-implement model across states. Leveraging technology and plugging the gaps in the state laws will lead to reduction in the compliance cost and monitoring of e-commerce taxation.

Advantages and Disadvantages of FDI in B2C E-commerce

Major Advantages of FDI in the Sector

- Impetus to the infrastructural development: Increased capital will help to establish supply chain, distribution system, and warehousing.
- Boost to manufacturing sector: Growth in retail sector will have a cascading effect in the manufacturing sector, which will positively contribute to the overall growth of economy and employment generation.
- More efficient SCM will in turn reduce the need for middlemen, leading to lower transaction costs, reduced overhead, and reduced inventory and labor costs.
- Adopting best global business practices: Will lead to better work culture and customer service.
- Increased market coverage and outreach: Will provide increased access to buyers/sellers; allow MSMEs and artisans to reach out to customers far beyond their immediate location, both locally and globally.
- Traceability and transparency: Will not only empower consumers with information and data but also help in better compliance of regulatory framework.
- Reduced costs: On marketing and distribution, travel, materials, and supplies will benefit businesses.
- Improved customer service: Providing more responsive order taking and after-sales service to customers and competitive pricing.

Major Disadvantages of FDI in the Sector

- Works against the spirit of FDI policy in MBRT. Allowing FDI in e-commerce will provide e-commerce players complete geographical reach, which will be against the spirit of FDI in multi-brand retail trade, that is, being restricted to cities with a population of more than one million or any other city as per the choice of consenting states.
- Indian market is not yet ready for opening up e-retail space to foreign investors. It will adversely impact the small-time trading of brick-and-mortar stores. Small-time shopkeepers are not highly qualified and will not be able to compete with professionally managed e-retail business format.
- Because of scale of economic operations, e-commerce players in the inventory-based model will have more bargaining power than stand-alone traders and may resort to predatory pricing practices.
- The infrastructure created by major e-commerce players will be captive and government will not be able to achieve its objective of creating back-end infrastructure.
- Indian e-commerce market is going through the nascent stage of development. With FDI in e-commerce, global players will have adverse impact on this domestic industry. It will lead to monopolies in e-commerce, manufacturing, logistics, and retail sectors.
- Inventory-based e-commerce competes directly with MSMEs. Indian e-commerce B2C is growing in an ecosystem with Indian-owned/led companies offering open marketplace models that provide a technology platform to help MSME reach across India and even

globally. These marketplaces do not compete with MSME or retailers and allow everyone to trade. On the other hand, allowing the entry of inventory-based large foreign e-tailers may shrink Indian entrepreneurship and the MSME sector.

- MNCs may dump their cheaper products in the market, causing a negative impact on the Indian manufacturing sector in general and to MSMEs in particular.
- Small-time businesses/kirana stores/mom-and-pop store remain the largest source of employment in the country. Opening of B2C e-commerce on inventory-based model is likely to seriously impact these shopkeepers, leading to large-scale unemployment.

However, if we look at the global scenario, the global leaders in B2C e-commerce exports are the USA, UK, the Nordic nations, Germany, France, and the Netherlands. Their online retail cross-border exports, if combined together, are forecasted to reach 100 billion by 2020. Cross-border B2C e-commerce flourishes in Europe, supported by initiatives and measures taken by policy makers for creating a single online retail regulation and ecosystem. In the EU, more than a quarter of online shoppers have made purchases from other EU countries and with this share being higher in the euro zone.

But interestingly, none of the above mentioned countries impose rigorous restrictions on e-commerce companies, and do not perceive them as threat/competition whatsoever to brick-and-mortar retailers or even traditional retailers and SMEs. In most of the countries, e-commerce companies are considered just like any other professional business entity and are not treated like merely a technology platforms. Many such e-retailers across the globe and even in India are collaborating with small merchants/retailers/sellers as well as SMEs, not only to broaden their own merchandise mix and portfolio but also to enable these small players to enhance their market reach, customer base, as well as revenues through their medium.

Hence, putting things into different perspective, it may be more of a perception of threat than any actual threat that is compelling a particular model of retailing, some small businesses, and SMEs to protest allowing FDI in B2C e-commerce sector. Whatever may be the perceptions and opinions of players in retail sector and policy makers in the government, one thing is clear and true: today, the customer is the only king, and if one can offer a better product, at competitive price, with more convenience of shopping and acquiring it, and with a good shopping experience, it will be the winner.

Above all, there exist two distinct worlds in India: urban India and rural India, and the dream concept of "inclusive growth" is still rhetoric and not the reality. So this also extends to the rural consumers who now want parity in fulfilling aspirations and treatment as valuable consumers. Their economic status has improved, and they want to explore better options in terms of product quality and great brands. While the organized brick-and-mortar retail brands have limitations to expand in these markets, e-retailers are easily reaching to them with the whole gamut of high-quality products and brands. With the penetration of Internet, they have better access to the Internet and hence to e-commerce. In this sense, e-commerce is bridging the rural–urban divide and playing the role of a leveler.

Current Foreign Trade Policy of India and Retail Industry

Over the last few decades, the global trade regime has been moving away from a focus on tariffs and border measures to behind the border issues, which comprises rules, standards, regulations, and trading norms relating to IPR, quality, health, labor, carbon emission, and environment, among others. However, keeping some of these issues out of the WTO did not actually led to their elimination from bilateral and regional trade agreements. Traditionally, it is the tariff prism through which India continued to outline trade-related issues, and this influenced its negotiating strategies. Most of the time, India has joined bilateral or regional trade agreements for defensive purpose, majorly to protect market share or for preventing trade diversion rather than as instruments to encourage and endorse trade and investment. Because of this defensive mind-set, business in India has itself not been an active participant in formulating negotiations on FTA.

However, the Indian government has taken a step in aligning the FTP 2015–2020 with the global trading norms under the WTO. With this, the government has made efforts to bring exporters to the changing realities of the global trading paradigm. It has designed its first five-year plan for enhancing and accelerating India's international trade. The new FTP resonates the much-talked-about themes of the government—Make in India, Digital India, Skill India, and export from India—while easing doing business in the country. The policy will give a definite boost to the existing performers in international trade like the services sector, pharmaceuticals, agricultural and aquaculture, auto-ancillaries, and handicrafts, among others, and would potentially identify and support New Age performers like defense, high-tech, e-commerce, and many more.

In India, where the e-commerce sector is struggling with regulatory and taxation challenges, the central government's new five-year FTP is reason to applaud. The government has offered to provide incentives to e-commerce companies exporting products from sectors that create jobs. This policy is likely to provide a stimulus to the sector. The policy is recognition of the contribution to the exchequer made by small-time retailers and SMEs that export via e-commerce. For instance, eBay India has about 15,000 e-commerce sellers that use its platform to sell in 206 countries.

The policy provides a fillip to such retailers, as:

- They are able to ship small consignments via courier.
- They reduce their burden on transaction costs.
- The guidelines will also boost the Make in India campaign with a focus on handloom products.

Mainly, there two new schemes, Merchandise Exports from India Scheme (MEIS) and Services Exports from India Scheme (SEIS), that are launched by the government under the new FTP (2015–2020) for the benefit of Indian e-tailers. Under MEIS, companies exporting goods through the foreign post office or couriers using e-commerce of freight on board (FoB) value up to ₹25,000 per consignment and is entitled for rewards. If the value of exports using an e-commerce platform is more than ₹25,000 per consignment, the MEIS reward would be limited to a FoB value of ₹25,000. The goods entitled for benefit under the scheme are handlooms, books and periodicals, leather footwear, toys, and customized fashion garments.

The objective of MEIS is to compensate infrastructure inefficiencies and associated costs in export of goods, especially those having:

- High export intensity
- High employment potential
- High potential to enhance export competitiveness

The policy says that export of such goods under courier regulations shall be allowed manually on a pilot basis through airports at New Delhi, Mumbai, and Chennai. Department of Revenue shall fast-track the implementation of EDI (electronic date interchange) mode at courier terminals. The new FTP provides the specific fiscal support India Inc. was asking for. The simplified fiscal incentives proposed in the FTP (particularly the merged MEIS and SEIS schemes), coupled with the administrative reliefs on import and export of goods and services, should serve to underline the intention of the government to realize its campaigns like Make in India and Digital India and improve the ease of doing business in the country.

The FTP, which came into effect on April 1, 2015, spoke for the first time about global value chains and their relevance and significance in world trading order. Global value chains are fast becoming the most important aspect of any bilateral and multilateral trading arrangement. These global value chains are typically created by integrating goods and services from various countries into one compound production network to produce a single product or service. These are turning out to be an important attribute in mega-regional trade pacts such as the Trans-Pacific Partnership (TPP), the Trans-Atlantic Trade and the Investment Partnership, and RCEP. (India has bilateral trade pacts with many of the countries in TPP.)

The FTP states that the mega-agreements are bound to challenge India's industry in many ways, for instance, by eroding existing preferences for Indian products in established traditional markets such as the USA and EU and establishing a more stringent and demanding framework of rules. The Indian industry needs to spruce up to meet these challenges, for which the government will have to create an enabling environment.

This elaborates the intent and rationale that has gone behind framing the policy. The simplification of procedures could add to the ease of doing business, thus motivating the entrepreneurial spirit that can propel the engines of export performance. Government is relying heavily on entrepreneurship to unleash a growth momentum that also activates the next wave of reforms, and is more dramatic and pathbreaking. Rationalized export incentives can offer extra cash in the hands of potential export performers: businesses, products, or sectors.

Thus going forward, India will have to sign bilateral and regional trade pacts not only with countries that turn out to be lucrative markets for its produce but also with those which are crucial suppliers of vital inputs and have complementarities with the Indian economy. The focus is on providing higher incentives and benefits around creating a brand image for India in the global market, by promoting domestic value-addition and exports of value-added products. These mega-agreements give us a tremendous opportunity of creating an environment within the country for producing high-quality products for reforming our standards, for updating ourselves on value chains, and to strategize out trade relations. Quality assurance and branding can maintain a growth momentum, while competiveness can open new markets and opportunities. India needs to deliver on all cylinders simultaneously for growth to accelerate, and deliver the required growth rate.

A Transformed Geopolitical and World Economic Landscape

Today, India is one of the high-growth markets for the global players across the sectors and industries and continuously evolving as an attractive business destination. Over the last few years, "Brand India" has witnessed significant growth in retail, manufacturing, IT and ITES, service sector, and communications. The Indian economy is going through an interesting and promising shift point today that is fundamentally brought about by significant and far-reaching structural changes in economy, businesses, and technologies. In India, like elsewhere around the world, businesses are being supported by structural shifts because of globalization, ethical consumerism, strategic collaboration, consolidation, and the like.

The new rhythm of innovation, technology adoption, and entrepreneurial thinking clearly holds tremendous promise for the retail industry in India. Goldman Sachs' recent report on the tremendous growth and potential of India's e-commerce industry (US$300 billion by 2030) is majorly supported by the country's attractive demography of a young population. The country will have over 300 million new online shoppers in the next 15 years, making online retailing the largest online segment.

Today, the innovation cycles have compressed so dramatically that business leaders in India are increasingly thinking of driving innovation agility both within and outside the corporation. All these aspects and attributes of India as an economy triggered a series of developments in the global business canvass that are reflected in the formulation of new equations of geopolitical and world economic relations and changing dynamics of global power equations. While the Imperial Britain dominated the 19th century and the USA dominated the 20th, many economists and analysts have been in search of the defining power of the 21st century.

The visit of President Obama to India was laden with "symbolism," which can be decoded as the "US is now ready to acknowledge India's rising economic power." India is after all the third biggest economy in the world and is poised to grow at 7–8%, according to the International Monetary Fund (IMF). During the five-year period 2003–2008, even as the world economy was barreling along, three countries accounted for about half of the cumulative increase in global economic growth. These were China, the USA, and India. Over the next few years, the world economy is virtually certain not to repeat the same performance of that period. It is also a quite clear prediction, based on current and projected patterns, that these three economies will have a significant, if not larger, share of the global increase in GDP during this period. In this scenario, each of these countries should, logically, be searching for every natural and rational opportunity to expand economic linkages with each other. Hence, growth, trade, and investment are mutually reinforcing in a virtuous circle. The skewed pattern of global growth and its implications for bilateral relationships provide a useful context in which to understand the greater emphasis that all three growth partners appear to be putting on bilateral relationships within the triangle. India and Japan also see lucrative opportunities in India's booming e-commerce sector, which is growing at 40–50% every year. The Japanese e-tailing market looks saturated, and domestic demand is low, so the companies are looking to expand their presence overseas.

US president Barak Obama is the first ever American head of state to be the chief guest at India's Republic Day celebrations. The joint statement at the end of the meeting between Prime Minister (PM) Narendra Modi and US president Barack Obama, on the eve of Republic Day celebration of January 26, 2015, endorsed a new economic partnership that the two major economies that would be charting out for the future. The statement expresses confidence that India–US bilateral collaboration will increase opportunities for investment, improve bilateral trade and investment ties, and lead to the creation of jobs and prosperity in both economies. The two leaders brainstormed of their "shared commitment to facilitating increased bilateral investment flows and fostering an open and predictable climate for investment." The most significant outcome was their endorsement of the India–US Delhi Declaration of Friendship, which articulates tangible principles to guide ongoing efforts to advance mutual prosperity, a clean and healthy environment, and greater economic cooperation, among others.

Also, during the Barak Obama's visit to India in January 2015, two influential senators (the co-chairs of the Senate India Caucus, the only country-specific caucus in the US Senate) in a letter appealed to president to take up the issue of liberalization of the current FDI restrictions in B2C e-commerce sector with the PM of India. They opined that this (FDI) liberalization in e-commerce sector would benefit the Indian and US economies, and also the Indians will get access to cheaper goods and job opportunities. With expanded e-commerce, these consumers gain access to goods and services through retailers that currently lack brick-and-mortar locations.

They also mentioned that online generation of additional retail transactions would increase consumption, decrease consumer prices, improve market access for small and medium-sized companies, and create jobs across a range of professional fields like customer service, IT, logistics, transportation, and administration.

The statement stands out for the manner in which the USA has come forward to promise its support and mutual collaboration for a vast array of areas that form the core of India's development endeavors. The scope of this collaboration extends from strengthening India's digital platform by encouraging investment in the information and communication technology (ICT) sector to the upgrading of India's railways and civil aviation facilities. The USA has also promised to build on its existing partnership with India in the higher education sector and also to extend its support for skill development program and strengthen the innovation and entrepreneurship ecosystem, which is ultimately expected to boost the growth of many other sectors, including online and off-line retail.

His coming to India has given the American business community a signal that India is going to be important for business. Other reasons for Obama's visit could be that he is keen to tap India's economic potential, especially when China's growth is slowing down and the EU is facing a deflationary spiral that could turn into a full-fledged recession. India as an important member of BRICS (Brazil, Russia, India, China, and South Africa) is also close to both Russia and China, two countries that the Western powers are wary of.

The positive side of Indo-US relations is India enjoys a strong and warm friendly relations with the USA, founded on common commitment to democratic institutions, peace and prosperity, and a robust, expanding, and mutually beneficial economic cooperation agenda backed by close people-to-people links. India with its huge population of 1.2 billion of mostly young people is a future powerhouse of the world, and it is good to see the world's oldest democracy and the largest democracy looking to tango in a new global order.

Although the leaders of the two countries have charted out the future course of their collaboration in elaborate terms, the fact and challenge remains that governments of India and the USA have had considerable differences on critical issues of economic significance to both countries, and in bilateral and multilateral forums alike.

In December 2014, the US International Trade Commission (USITC) unveiled the report of its yearlong investigation of the effects of India's trade, investment, and industrial policies on the US economy. The investigation carried out at the request of the US House Committee on Ways and Means and the US Senate Committee on Finance concluded that a wide range of restrictive Indian policies have adversely affected US companies doing business in India. USITC reports that its investigations, covering a large number of US business lobbies, showed that two sets of policies, namely tariffs and taxes and financial regulations, have had the heaviest effects on US companies. According to a CII report on India's economic relationship with the USA, the perception in the USA is that India is curtailing market access for US companies. Other issues, including FDI and IP policies, have had large negative effects on specific industries (India accounts for only 2% of US imports and 1% of its exports). Companies providing agricultural products and food, financial services, and certain manufacturing products, including pharmaceuticals, were the most affected, with Indian policies having a substantial effect on the operations of US companies in these sectors. Reluctance to opening up multi-brand retail is also regarded as a hindrance to FDI inflows. The key message this report sends out to the Indian policy makers is that "if tariff and investment restrictions were fully eliminated and standards of IP protection were made comparable to US and Western European levels, US exports to India would rise by two-thirds, and US investment in India would roughly double." The message is crystal clear: India needs to undertake a significant change in its policy orientation so that it meets the expectations of the business interests in US and Western European countries.

This broad affront on India's economic policies by the USITC, which closely followed the investigation of India's IP laws by the US Trade Representative, seems to undermine the newfound warmth in the relations between the two countries. It is clear that the various wings of the US administration need to understand the spirit of the New Delhi dialog on economic issues between the leaders of the world's largest democracies, India and USA. Already, some of the leading US corporations have a setup of large-scale operations in India in the IT and consumer products space. The Indian business counts the USA as one of their largest export market, from IT/ITES to pharmaceuticals, garments, and jewelry. This engagement can surely get momentum as both countries move toward a long-term strategic engagement in other areas identified for mutual collaboration that include the "Clean India" project, engaging SMEs, development of industrial corridors, start-up and entrepreneurship development, joint research and knowledge sharing, investment in infrastructure and renewable energy, technology sharing and development, and smart cities, which, directly or indirectly, is important for the growth of both online and off-line retail. Because a week currency, high interest rates, and unfavorable foreign debt funding situations also remain key obstacles in Indian entrepreneur's funding needs. Hence, a bilateral investment treaty (BIT) can provide confidence and protection to investors from any discriminatory measures and shall foster a positive investment environment.

On the other hand, India's ties with Japan, which have strengthened after Mr Narendra Modi's visit to that country months after taking over as PM of India, are under the implementation test, over the substantial liberalization of the e-commerce sector. This sector and retail in general is one of the few segments in which the government administration is not too enthusiastic about entry of overseas players due to domestic political considerations. In India, as far as e-commerce is concerned, FDI is not allowed in the B2C segment, but 100% FDI is allowed at the B2B level. That is, this prohibits foreign businesses from selling items directly to Indian consumers without involving a "middle man."

However, the Japanese government wants India to open the e-commerce sector to foreign investment, seeking space for the Japanese online and off-line retailers. In the paper floated by Japan at the previous rounds of negotiations in New Delhi, it sought most favored nation (MFN) and national treatment to be accorded to the e-commerce sector. Rakuten, one of Japan's big online retail companies, has plans to become a global player, and also Uniqlo, a clothing retailer with a strong global presence both online and off-line, is also looking forward to expand in India.

Rakuten, Japan's largest e-commerce company, has requested the Prime Minister's Office and the commerce and industry ministry to allow inventory-led e-commerce in India. According to the sources familiar with the negotiations also confirmed that officials of another Japanese retailer, Uniqlo, which is a clothing designer and manufacturer, also met PM Narendra Modi and made a similar request. Uniqlo is planning to invest not only in retail but also in e-commerce and manufacturing. It plans to open 100 retail outlets, which is expected to take its investments past Swedish retail giant IKEA's ₹10,500 crore spread over several years.

Currently, the Indian government only allows a marketplace model in e-commerce, which is essentially a platform that allows retailers and traders to sell their goods through websites. The requests by the two companies were a part of the PM's talks with Japan to boost FDI into the country, which is a low 1.7%.

US e-commerce giant Amazon has also plans to expand beyond the marketplace model if FDI norms allow in the future. Globally, Amazon gets about 40% of its business from the inventory-led model, and companies like Rakuten are expected to have a similar mix. Rakuten sources from around the world and wants an inventory-based model because that will allow the company to continue to do so, stock in India and sell without the intervention of a retailer. While for Uniqlo, it is much simpler—it can sell what it makes to its customers online.

Similarly, the visit of Japanese foreign minister Fumio Kishida to New Delhi in January 2015 saw articulation of a consensus between New Delhi and Tokyo that India and Japan need to be linked by stronger bridges of economic cooperation that factors in the imperatives and future drivers of growth in both countries and mutual desire for comprehensive contribution to the entire Indo-Pacific region. To make the diplomatic dialog more comprehensive and committed, the foreign minister of Japan pointed out that the Japan–India Investment Promotion Partnership, which was agreed at the summit meeting between PM of India and Japan in 2014, seeks synergies between the two national economies. India on its part has been driving home its three great advantages that the Japanese economy can leverage on: democracy in the form of single-window clearances and speedy decision-making; demography cast in the burgeoning youth segment of India's population; and demand, huge capacity for private consumption. Hence either way, it is a win–win scenario of synergy for industry in India on both sides.

Likewise, Jack Ma, founder and executive chairman of China's Alibaba Group, China's largest e-commerce company, is eyeing a "significant play" in India's e-tailing segment. The online player is exploring strategic investments not just in online retail firms here but also in B2B e-tailing, logistics, payments services companies, and so on. By all these strategic moves, the group is looking to replicate its Chinese success in India, one of the largest consumption markets. Hence, the Alibaba Group is very interested in India, and their teams are spending a lot of time evaluating all options across the various segments and verticals. In other words, they want to be "ecosystem players" in India.

E-commerce in India is growing with a breakneck speed every year, and foreign retailers want to grab the opportunity. As per the current rules and regulations, they can sell online on a marketplace site like Flipkart or Amazon, but not directly to customers. This erodes margins for retailers as they cannot sell directly online. The restriction has also raised barriers for clothing manufacturers like Zara and H&M from selling online. If FDI in single-brand e-commerce or inventory-led e-tailing is allowed, it is expected to bring in a few billion dollars of investment into the country. However, the government is on the back foot and not allowing B2C e-tailing because of the opposition from off-line traders to e-commerce. The e-tailing industry is going through a discounting bloodbath, and the arrival of Chinese firm Alibaba and the Japanese firms is expected to start another round of discounting, which will only increase losses for Indian e-commerce companies. However, with new players entering the fray, consumers will benefit.

Developments Pertaining to RCEP

According to Japan External Trade Organization, e-commerce constitutes a big share of sales marketing in Japan and other developed countries, and big investors are expecting something concrete to happen in this regard. Tokyo has proposed this demand as part of talks at the RCEP grouping. RCEP is a proposed comprehensive free-trade pact among 10 ASEAN countries— Brunei, Cambodia, Indonesia, Laos, Myanmar, the Philippines, Malaysia, Singapore, Thailand, and Vietnam—and 6 partners with which they have FTAs, including Australia, China, India, Japan, South Korea, and New Zealand. Meanwhile, Australia and New Zealand have also joined Japan in trying to persuade India to open up its fast-growing e-commerce sector to overseas investment.

This huge growth is majorly attributed to the hyper-growth in affordable smartphones, improving infrastructure, and a propensity to transact online. Both countries have backed and endorsed Japan's proposal to include e-commerce in the 16-nation regional trade pact that is being negotiated. India opposed to this for various reasons. Among them is the need to ensure that homegrown online retailers are protected. Also the local e-tailers have strongly opposed Japan's stand for the sector's liberalization through the mega-regional pact called the RCEP agreement. The 16-member grouping of RCEP has set up a panel on e-commerce in response to a Japanese proposal on easing FDI in the sector under which member countries will exchange best practices linked to online commerce, which India may incorporate in its domestic policy. India has agreed for cooperation in e-commerce as part of the ongoing talks for RCEP so that all countries can exchange relevant information. Here the point that one needs to underline is the government has only agreed to "cooperate" and not "undertaken" any commitment in the e-commerce sector under the trade agreement.

However, the domestic e-commerce representatives, in RCEP stakeholder talks with the government, opined that we (India) should not "commit" to liberalize the sector through the "inventory model" as it amounts to B2C (retail) e-commerce, in which FDI is prohibited in the country. The analysts are viewing this as an attempt by these domestic e-tailers to create a vast business space using their fund-rich pockets to keep potential competition at bay. These online players have also objected to something unnoticed so far—India agreeing for a separate e-commerce chapter in the Comprehensive Economic Cooperation Agreement (CECA) with Singapore without adequate stakeholder consultation. E-commerce is increasingly becoming integral to FTAs, and the importance assigned to it is reflected in these pacts having a separate chapter for the segment. Article 10.1 of the e-commerce chapter of the India–Singapore CECA says both sides "recognize the economic growth and opportunity provided by e-commerce and the importance of avoiding barriers to its use and development and the applicability of WTO rules to e-commerce." In the previous round of negotiations in New Delhi, Japan has asked for MFN status and national treatment to be accorded in the e-commerce sector. Japan has not made a distinction between B2C and B2B, the way e-commerce is regarded globally. National treatment and MFN mean providing foreign companies the same treatment you give to domestic players. Hence, it has pushed for minimum barriers in e-commerce, seeking harmonization of the regulatory framework.

Hence, if India lifts these trade barriers, many foreign companies would enjoy greater access to India's US$4.9 trillion economy and growing middle class. Likewise, US companies can play a role in using India as a gateway for exporting to countries in Asia and beyond, leveraging India's FTAs in Asia. Hence, major transitions in the geostrategic sphere require elevation of the Indo-US, Indo-China, and Indo-Japan partnerships to a more intense and deep level. Clearly, India's economic rise and the emerging geopolitical scenario in Asia make it a partner of choice for the other superpowers, including USA. More importantly, its huge consumer market offers what is going to be one of the largest growth opportunities for businesses, including retailing, in all of its forms and formats in the years to come in the context of the future fact that India is about to enter a phase of digit-led growth. But at the same time, in the context of FTAs and mega-regional pacts, the government is holding more discussions on consumer protection and norms to prevent online frauds, privacy of customer information, use of low-tax regions by e-commerce firms, and the ability to seek information from online firms.

•

Summary

The growing interest of foreign investors in Indian e-commerce companies is riding on the back of high consumption and spending ability of consumers, higher Internet penetration, and the size of the untapped market in Tier II and Tier III towns. Today, India is the last billion-dollar market in the world and is going through revolutionary changes in technology adoption, consumption, and buying behavior. With the rise in level of affluence, there is a huge base of population that is moving from needs to wants, and technology is enabling them to access both basic and aspirational products in a very convenient way. As far as e-commerce is concerned, experts predict that India is expected to take 5 years to reach the stage where USA and China had reached in 20 and 10 years, respectively. That makes India the most exciting type of market because China has already gone through pretty much of that phase. However, regarding the entry of FDI into India, the government should learn from China and other Asian markets that have taken steps to ensure that there is not revenue or job losses.

At present, there is confusion and ambiguity around the operational structure of e-commerce companies, and this has created a situation where most of these enterprises are forced to operate like technology platforms. As the Indian market is too diverse for a single model of growth, states should be allowed to control their own fortune. The Center should act only as a facilitator and individual states should be left to compete with various policies. Historically, India has embodied proud cooperative federalism, ensuring harmonious functioning of the entire system. This has been true even in the case of introduction of the GST, rooted to be "the single most important tax reform after 1947," wherein the Center and the State would act in a harmonious manner to serve a comprehensive indirect tax system. The reservations about e-commerce have faded over a period of time, and the growing success of the model. Consumers have witnessed the power of competitive pricing, the convenience of buying at the click of a button, and the ease with which merchandise can be returned or exchanged. It is these aspects of e-commerce that have made it the next big thing to happen to the consumer retail industry, after the opening up of FDI. It is necessary that the regulatory framework in the country be conceptualized keeping in mind the larger interests of consumers in the country. If technology is available to cut intermediary costs on consumer products, it must be leveraged in order to bring down the retail price of many consumables and benefit the middle class, which is facing inflation. Hence, any regulation that restricts the open growth of this bridging medium will not only drive consumers away but also have an adverse impact on economy, business, and entrepreneurship.

Review Questions

1. Analyze the major domestic and global environmental factors with their impact of the business of retailing. Also discuss the "globalization in historical perspective" briefly and its impact on world as an "economy."
2. "Globalization is not a new phenomenon." Comment on this statement with your views.
3. Analyze the major factors that has stimulated the modern-age globalization and how it has influenced the retail industry.
4. Analyze the retail industry in the context of domestic environmental factors: political (regulatory environment), technological, and legal scenarios.
5. Capture the holistic overview of the FDI in retail industry with its plausible effects and implications.
6. State the probable advantages and disadvantages of allowing FDI in B2C e-commerce sector. Justify your views with appropriate examples wherever applicable.
7. Discuss the current foreign trade policy of India with its effects and implications pertaining to retail industry.
8. State your views on current foreign trade policy of India and its possible impact on retail industry. You can justify your views with the help of some related statistics and figures.
9. Discuss in detail the transformed geopolitical and world economic landscape and its possible impact on Indian retail industry.
10. Discuss in detail by looking at the larger picture of contemporary pressures from wider global economic, environment, and geopolitical factors, their impact on retail industry.

Chapter 5

Positioning and Promotion: Pragmatism with Romanticism

Introduction

Business success depends on building a growing body of satisfied customers. To succeed in business, retailers must first define their target markets and decide how they will be positioned in those markets. However, it must be determined if that ideal customer is the actual customer that is shopping at the site. One challenge for retail managers is the constant adjustment to this ever-changing customer base. The various ways for managers to stay in touch with the customer include working on the selling floor, listening to customer feedback from the company's staff, working with a focus group, and doing customer surveys. To better satisfy their customers, retailers develop and follow *merchandising policies*. These are specific management guidelines the companies follow to keep their inventory choices on track. Merchandising policies are adjusted regularly based on current trends and the needs of the target market. Retailers also have *operational policies*, which are designed to make customers feel good about shopping with them. These policies make the retail site appealing for the target market through physical appearance and customer services. Retailers' merchandising and operational policies complement each other to maintain the optimum marketing mix of product, price, place, and promotion. The policies are monitored carefully in relation to changing retail patterns, economic conditions, and the buying motives of target customers.

Understanding Buying Motives

Purchasing behavior is the way consumers act in the market. It is influenced by cultural, social, and psychological factors. To set it into action, consumers must have a want or need to be satisfied, and a desire to fulfill that want or need in a certain way. The response is a purchase based on *buying motives*, or the reasons why people buy what they buy. Buying motives fall within the extremes of rational and emotional responses. Rational behavior is a response to conscious reasoning. It is based on logical thinking and decision-making.

Important factors in a rational decision might be a garment's durability, comfort, quality, economy of use, and price.

Emotional behavior is based on feelings. A consumer who reacts emotionally will see a fashionable item in a favorite color and buy it just because he or she likes it. Factors contributing to an emotional decision include imitation, emulation, desire for status and prestige, sex appeal, desire for distinctiveness, ambition, fear, and personal pride. Consumers are generally unaware of the role these factors play in their choices. Sometimes consumers have rational reasons for *patronizing* certain retailers. They may shop where they know they are getting the best price. Other consumers have emotional reasons for preferring particular retailers. Perhaps they get an ego boost from shopping in a store that has a prestigious reputation. Most purchases fall somewhere between the two extremes of rational and emotional behavior. Some of each type of behavior is combined in varying degrees for different people, at different times, and for different products.

For example, fashion purchases usually involve higher amounts of emotional motives than rational ones. Thus, fashion marketers most often appeal to emotional buying motives in their advertising, VM, and sales training.

There are also product and patronage motives involved in consumer purchases. *Product motives* involve consumer purchases based on qualities or images of certain products. These product qualities might be materials, construction, style, fit, or guarantees associated with trade names, brand image, or reputations. Manufacturers try to instill this *patronage* in customers to encourage them to continue to buy their products.

Patronage motives involve customers who consistently buy from certain retailers or favor particular stores. The reasons why customers choose to shop at one store rather than another may be based on reputation, image, merchandise assortment, shopping experience or price, service standards, and so on. Other factors include convenience of location and customer services. Retailers try very hard to gain loyal patronage from their customers. However, less long-term loyalty exists among shoppers today. Patronage decisions now seem to be based on where consumers think they are getting the best value at the time. Product and patronage motives are based on a combination of rational and emotional buying behavior. Different consumers prefer different kinds of products and retailers. It is important for retailers to evaluate what customers think about their stores, catalogs, TV channels, or websites, as well as the products carried. Also, different consumers might see or use a particular retailer differently.

Positioning: Presenting an Image

Like any other English literature student, I too, swore by Shakespeare, quoting him whenever I need the last word in a discussion. But with his due respect, for once, I will have to disagree with his "a rose by any other name would smell as sweet...." It just does not work in retail industry. The brand is really what matters to a customer and, in many cases, to even the staff. What makes one brand different from the other, what does brand experience mean, and what does it take to generate a store loyalty? We got together with different concepts and strategies to get the answer and uncover some secrets to retail brand building.

A retailer's image is how the public perceives the company. An image represents how a given retailer is perceived by consumers and others. A firm may be seen as innovative or conservative, specialized or broad based, and discount oriented or upscale. The key to a successful image is that consumers view the retailer in the manner the firm intends. *Retail brand positioning* relates to where a retailer situates itself in the consumer's mind. This positioning guides all other decisions about how the retailer satisfies its target customers while differentiating itself from competitors.

Brands ultimately are closely linked with their environments, and this is where communication becomes so integral to the growth and positioning of the brand. Hence, brand positioning is nothing but establishing a space in the minds of an audience, and the point of brand positioning is to enhance your customer's perception of your value. With varied brand choices and minimal differentiation of product functionality and offerings, it is critical for a retailer to be well positioned and uniquely differentiated. This is done with a marketing mix that blends variables of product, price, place, promotion, people, process, physical environment: pervasive creativity, performance of retailer's offering on tangible and intangible fronts, PR communications, marketing by philanthropy, PLBs, patronage strategies, and positioning into an overall strategy for retailing success.

While all dimensions of store image inevitably contain both tangible and intangible elements, as any attitude statement is judged by customers on the basis of their own experiences, values, and priorities, the statements and dimensions were chosen to represent different degrees of tangibility. "Physical characteristics," "pricing policy," and "product range" were felt to be the more tangible dimensions, presenting customers with a higher proportion of primarily physical, immediate, clues upon which to base their perceptions, such as store cleanliness, décor, range, product quality, and price. From a management perspective, it was felt that this higher degree of tangibility would enable more rapid adaptation of these dimensions to host market conditions if need arose. The dimensions termed "customer service," "character," and "store reputation" were felt to represent less tangible dimensions of image, more reliant on customers' experience-based perceptions of staff helpfulness, kindness, trust, store appeal, and position. Organizations realized that intangible value for the shareholder. This was a paradigm shift in organizational thinking, turning marketing from a cost function to a profit center that added significantly to market capitalization.

It is like a personality, with different appearance and "mood" for each retailer. An image can be powerful in attracting and satisfying consumers. It is very important for retailers to develop and maintain distinct identities to set themselves apart from competitors. The retailer's image should realistically project the kinds of merchandise and operations it offers for particular types of customers. Its image of itself should match the customer's impression of it.

Retailer as a Brand and Retail Branding

When we start talking about brands, the first thing that crosses our mind would be the "logo" associated with a brand. It is not surprising to have a picture of a bitten apple when someone talks of an iPad or an iPhone. A brand is therefore a product, but one that adds other dimensions (both tangible and intangible) that differentiates it in some way from other products designed and developed to cater the same need. These dimensions (both tangible and intangible) are the prerequisites that define a brand and go a long way into building a "brand." Today, it is much more than just a logo that goes into defining a brand.

The retail branding is a strategy based on the brand concept and which transfers it to a retail company. A retailer's "products" are his/her stores that can be marketed in a similar way to any other branded good. Hence, a retail brand is nothing but a group of the retailer's outlets that carry a unique name, symbol, logo, or combination thereof. While all retailers constitute brands to some extent, some retail brands are strong, while many are not. Recognition and appreciation by consumers are the essential elements of a strong retail brand. Retail branding can be understood as a comprehensive and integrated marketing management concept, focusing on building long-term customer loyalty and customer preference.

The term "retail brand" has to be distinguished from the term "store brand." While retail brand refers to stores, the term "store brand" refers to the product level and is used synonymously with PL or own label. Often, the retail brand is also used to label the store brands, though this is not a universal characteristic. Retail brands are characterized by enormous complexity, which results from the service attributes of retailers as well as from the multiplicity of brand attributes and consumer retailer interactions.

Manufacturers frequently offer only a few products under one brand, and the industrial production process is completed through quality control, whereas the customer experience with the retail brand is often shaped by several hundred outlets, at different locations with uniform store designs, thousands of products, and dozens of employees in each store, who are also influenced by their service values, moods, and emotions. Though the rest of the experiences are uniform, the "people" factor plays very critical role in providing a uniform, consistent, and standardized performance and desired brand message.

For example, the sport shoes and accessories retailers such as Puma, Nike, and Adidas are strategically focusing on to hire people who are passionate about sneakers, sports, and servicing customers. They are recruiting athletes and intercollege to state-level players in their sales staff. The idea here is to create the right shopping experience for the targeted audience that is essentially sports enthusiast.

With the proliferation of Internet and web technologies, consumers can gather a lot of information at anytime and anywhere at just a click of a button. So according to the sports marketers, a typical sales-focused team is not enough to sell high-performance products to highly informed and demanding consumers. This heightened awareness has made it imperative for the sports retailers to scale up the levels of knowledge of the sales associates. Here the role of these sales associates is not just to sell the sports-related merchandise but also to act as an influencer and reinforce the brand image and brand value. Hence, these store associates embody and represent the standards of excellence and help to bring these sports brand to life in-store and online.

Therefore, to serve this purpose effectively, the leading sports brands—such as Puma, Nike, Reebok, and Adidas—are now hiring athletes and sports enthusiasts as their sales associates.

- Adidas–Reebok combined has hired over 200 runners as footwear specialists and the number is still growing.
- Adidas Group's franchisee stores are roping in the recruitment agencies to search active and sporty candidates from educational institutions.
- Puma has an internal marketing and HR teams that track runners and fitness experts and share their recruitment guidelines with its franchisee stores.

These sales associates perform various sport actions like sprinting, running, and jumping inside the store to influence and convince the shoppers to buy high-performance footwear by explaining and demonstrating its functionality and performance on the field. This increases not only the customer involvement in to the product but also the engagement in to the brand. They have also experienced an increase in sales figures after starting this hiring initiative. One other strategic benefit of such hiring initiative—from HR point of view—is reduction in the attrition because many athletes are excited to work for their favorite sports brands.

Establishing a strong brand is the key to long-term performance. It provides the retailer with some strategic advantages:

- An existing retail brand strengthens brand awareness and differentiation from the competition, because it can serve as an anchor for associations with the brand.
- From the consumer perspective, strong retail brands simplify the purchasing process because there is already some knowledge about the retailer, and buyers do not have to search for additional information about as merchandise categories, assortments, prices, service and so on. Strong retail brands also reduce perceived purchasing risk.
- Strong brands exert *halo effects*. A positive general attitude toward the brand in total positively influences the perception of all specific brands attributes. Considering the impact of these evaluations on the general attitude, a virtuous cycle can develop.
- Strong brands not only represent functional benefits but also serve as symbolic devices. They represent different values, traits, and characteristics. Shopping at a certain retailer might, therefore, allow consumers to project a certain self-image to themselves and others.
- If a retail company operates in different market segments, differentiated marketing with different retail brands facilitates approaching each market segment with a targeted approach. Cannibalization is easier to avoid, and each retail brand can develop its own image—without contradictory image transfers.
- Conversely, a strong brand can be used as a platform for expansion. This already occurs when retailers open new outlets, which, from the very start, are perceived with a certain image. Franchising concepts, in which the retail brand is transferred to independent shop owners, clearly illustrate this advantage.
- A strong retail brand can also facilitate diversification into new product ranges. This type of brand extension occurs when retailers use their image in one merchandise category to expand into additional categories.

Creating Brand Image

Once upon a time, a brand was an identifying mark burned onto livestock with a branding iron. Today, we can see a brand is the way to identify a product/service/company/firm and so on. Markers argue that a brand is a shorthand term for the sum total of the perceptions about company and the product and/or services the company offers. Advertising legend David Ogilvy described brand as the intangible sum of a product's attributes and these perceptions can be rational, emotional, or visual. Hence, a branding program is all about managing those perceptions by integrating the appropriate tools of marketing communications. Here we can say that brand is a promise of what the customer should expect from the retailer and a promise of how the retailer brand will perform. So a brand is not only a trademark but also a mark of trust that is endorsed, enriched, and undermined by the actions that are taken by the marketers. Walter Landor, a pioneer in the field of branding and consumer research, once said, "Products are created in the factory, but brands are created in the mind." By virtue of this notion of branding, if done effectively, it creates a point of difference (POD) in the consumer's mind and allows it to stand out and stand apart.

Establishing a clear brand image is a long-term process. Brands are established through consumer learning processes. Consumers store associations in their memory. Brand associations become stronger over time and must be reinforced by repeated exposure to the same brand messages, because they might otherwise fade away. The past investment in the brand building is at least partly lost if the brand marketing is changed. Thus, continuity is important. Also, risk reduction is one of a brand's main functions. Consumers trust a brand, because it entails a standardized and uniform offer under a certain brand-name. Some of the world's most successful brands demonstrate that retaining the same brand message and communication (with slight variations) for years and even decades is one of the key prerequisites of successful branding. The retail marketing mix includes all marketing instruments that a retailer can deploy. The term "mix" indicates that the instruments are not used in isolation, but that they jointly influence the consumer. In order to be successful, all marketing measures must be coordinated to ensure a close fit with one another and that all measures convey the same brand message. Because inconsistency makes a brand image fragile and consumers strive for internal harmony or congruity in their knowledge and information—(refer theory of cognitive dissonance)—creating coherence between all the different facets of the retail brand is crucial for success (Figure 5.1). Considering the complexity of the retail environment, ensuring synchronization among the marketing instruments and all brand contact points is challenging. IKEA, Sephora, The Body Shop, Boots, Zara, and others are examples of successful brands that succeed in projecting a uniform image with their store atmosphere, merchandise, pricing, communication, and service.

In the case of retailing, the appearance of a store's *physical environment* is very important. How stores please customers' senses forms an *ambience*, or atmosphere, that has a great influence on the image of the brand. The physical environment should match the image being projected. Upscale stores usually have luxurious surroundings, mid-priced stores have

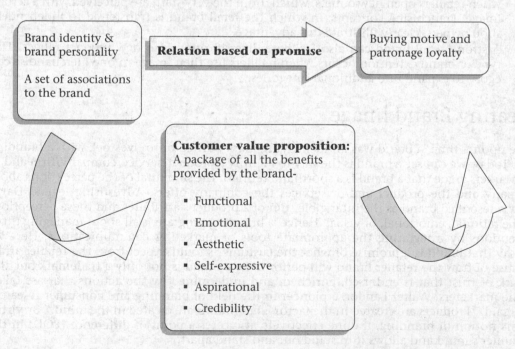

Figure 5.1: *Key Success Factors—Strong Buying Motive and Patronage Loyalty*

pleasing surroundings, and low-priced discount stores may not try for any particular ambience at all. So the key to successful VM is all about understanding the purchase logic of the target consumer and designing the visual aspects of the store around the same. This starts with the DNA of the brand, and the *visual brand identity* captures the brand's personality, mystique, and emotional values in a nutshell. The distinct and consistent orchestration of the identity is central to establishing the visibility, familiarity, and common identifiable brand imagery. The visual brand orchestration can manifest by way of its coherent application of its identity, the brand color(s), the other design elements like icons, the uniquely identifiable design, branded environment, and even the tone of voice.

A major influence on the success of Gucci in the 1990s was the appointment of leading designer Tom Ford. He joined Gucci in 1990 as the company's women's wear designer and became creative director of Gucci. With Tom Ford's vision, Gucci's image was reinvented. He was responsible for product lines, store image, and store design. In March 1995, Tom Ford's first collection which was inspired by "sex and glamor," caught the attention of the press and public.

The image and aura of prestige surrounding Gucci gives added value to the products. This is created through advertising, innovative designers, and the whole experience of buying Gucci. Gucci's premier position as a leading international luxury brand should also be attributed to the contributions of its design chief Frida Giannini, who joined Gucci in 2002 as a handbag design director, and has worked her way to become creative director (read design head) for all

Gucci opened the doors of its own museum in Florence to mark the completion of the house's 90th anniversary celebration. The persona of a luxury brand is largely a result of: first, its distinctive projection plus coherence of its applications across consumer touch-points and second, the brand communication through its advertising.

Photo 5.1: *Conveying the Brand Philosophy and Persona*

Source: www.guccimuseo.com (accessed on 12 May 2016)

product categories. She has been awarded the Lupa Capitolina by the then mayor of Rome Gianni Alemanno and Design Star Honor from the Fashion Group International. Frida's focus on the brand's rich heritage and her uniquely feminine and distinctly Italian point of view have enabled her to constantly design collections that have set trends and greatly influenced fashion across the world. Under her creative leadership, a new design montage for Gucci has emerged, one which celebrates the house's inimitable past and its expertise in luxury craftsmanship, all the while adding youth, color, and a playful extravagance.

The architectural and interior design environments—ambience—for Gucci's new store concept have been designed in line with its brand image, heritage, and persona. Frida provided creative directions for all advertising campaigns and worked with illustrious directors, such as David Lynch, Frank Miller, and Chris Cunningham. She also played a key role in bringing major celebrities to the brand, like James Franco, Evan Rachel Wood, and Chris Evans for fragrance.

The number of employees, and their appearance and attitudes, also contributes to image. Upscale stores are expected to have plenty of sales assistance available for shoppers. Hence, positioning is the most important and critical asset of any retailer brand. It is important to identify the "node" you wish to occupy in the consumer's mind. Do not try to be too many things for your target audience as you may end up being none.

For example, fashion retail brand ONLY is targeted as the edgy, young, and connoisseur of fun fashion who is willing to experiment with new trends and has her own distinct brand personality. ONLY is primarily a denim brand, with a focus on high-fashion denims in different styles, fits, and trends at affordable price points compared to many other international denim fashion retailers in the country. The ONLY collection embodies this spirit, and every single element on the ONLY product reinforces the brand identity. ONLY is positioned as the fast fashion brand, and the retailer brings the latest trends from fashions shows to the stores. In doing so, the retailer ensures that every new style is not only high on fashion but also something that will appeal to the target audience. ONLY has been able to carve a niche in highly competitive fashion retail sector, by understanding of market needs and product innovations accordingly. Over the years, with this product innovation and varied denim collection, ONLY has managed to attract an ever-growing base of loyal customers. For example the brand offers a range of linen products suitable to the tropical Indian climate specially designed for the Indian consumers.

In addition, the brand has successfully captured the customer loyalty by effective word of mouth. Word of mouth is very essential in highly competitive fashion retail sector due to the presence of many international fashion brands striving for market and mindshare. Though innovations and effective marketing campaigns are essential for brand publicity, the word-of-mouth recommendations from a trusted source often influence and make up a customer's mind. This eventually results in increased brand trials and brand popularity.

Today's Branding Scenario: Endorsing the Sensuality

Before jumping to the current branding philosophies and practices, let us go through the changing dynamics of "branding" over the years.

- In 1960s and 1970s, it was all about creating an apt logo and building a corporate identity.
- In the 1980s, it moved toward corporate branding.
- The 1990s actually witnessed the unleashing of "branding" and brands going all out to advertise and connect with their target audience.
- In 2000, the incubation of having a "big idea" evolved, which was more than just vanilla advertising.

- From 2010 onward, it became imperative for a brand to cite the purpose of their existence, the experience they were capable of delivering, and the change the brand had to undertake to make it more relevant to its target audience. A brand's success in marketplace was defined by the relevance and associations it created in a consumer's life. Then came the phase of defining a brand's unique advantage, with every category making room for newer and newer players.
- Brand valuation expert Jan Lindemann states that 30% of the stock price of companies (in The Economy of Brands) comes from their brand, thus furthering the argument to strengthen the brand.
- Finally, today, every brand's agenda is to create an emotional attachment or bond. This is not only to create takers and consumers for the brand but also to make them the advocates and endorsers of the brand. In this process, brands embody the consumers, and every step is to make the brand an integral part of their self-image and to help represent who they are. From instilling new value system to creating self-awareness, brands today are in pursuit of making better people out of consumers. In 1960s, it was all about establishing, but today, it is all about developing shared values.

Let us take a closer look at how they are doing so.

There was a time when brands would just show consumers the mirror of possibilities and how she could become a better or more desirable person with the brand performing the role of a catalyst. David Mackenzie Ogilvy, considered the father of advertising, has said that, "ANY damn fool can put on a deal, but it takes genius, faith and perseverance to create a brand." While this truth continues to be prevalent, there are categories that now, instead of asking their consumers to try and become better, inspire them to be just themselves. These brands celebrate the individual's sensuality and originality, thus bringing to the fore the real person. The more interesting thing is that the retailers in the categories such as beauty, fashion, and beverages, whose core comprises a fair degree of self-projection and imagery, are adopting the path of discovery of the real self, too. For instance, in the business of fashion retailing, sensuality can be defined as a "state of mind" that makes the person confident of himself or herself, and it is an expression that best captures and delivers the innate personality traits evident in the recesses of the mind of the customer. A consumer feels extremely confident and is able to express herself best, when the clothing she has done expresses her personality and captures her individuality in equal measures. Hence, sensuality is the physical expression of "grace," which is an integral part of every individual, and one of the most important components of brand creation and management.

A classic example of brand creation is Louis Vuitton's "Core Values" campaign. As a part of their "core values" campaign, Louis Vuitton used their website as the online medium to showcase their celebrity endorser's journey, their story to bring to life how the brand has been promoting the art of travel and inspiring legendary journeys. This travel message they give through personal journeys is a fundamental one for the brand. This campaign has led us to believe that brands today have chosen a new path to create empathy. From being conduits for improving your image to encourage you to be yourself, from benchmarks of progress being evaluated by the external to creating a new benchmark of progress, and from defining people by how much material wealth they have amassed to now encouraging them to lead a quality life, brands have traversed a long road. These campaigns today encourage people to journey inward to find a better life.

Finding a larger meaning to life, the new wave seems to bring with it the desire to find a purpose beyond the material, beyond the conventional. That has created a new world of validation, a validation from oneself. It is so now cool to be seen as someone having a purpose commonly

Hollywood actress Angelina Jolie strikes a pose in Cambodia for Louis Vuitton's "Core Values" campaign. Louis Vuitton's Core Values campaign revisits the brand's heritage with a completely fresh interpretation of the concept of travel in an emotional sense—viewed as a personal journey—a process of self-discovery. Core Values celebrates Vuitton's timeless classics in real situations on "real" people—meaning celebrities rather than models—and runs alongside their seasonal "fashion" campaigns.

Photo 5.2: *Conveying the Core Values and Sensuality*

Source: louisvuittonjourneys.com (accessed on 12 May 2016)

couched as passionate and youthful retailer brand. Today, particularly in fashion retailing brands, there are a world full of passionate young, discovering, trying, and experimenting to find "the meaning of existence and life."

A change has also set in the way brands showcase relationships. We can see brands embracing New World ideologies: women's empowerment, education, environment protection, sustainability and so on. The needle has now moved to the evolution of the thought process in the context of relationships. A higher degree of openness and acceptance defines the world of personal relationships, and this is increasingly being seen in brand communication. We can watch the new advertisement of Raymond in which a husband willingly staying at home to look after the baby so that his wife can manage her "working mother" world as seen in the advertisement. Relationships are being approached with high self-awareness rather than just playing to the galleries. The narratives of brands in the context of social relationships are also changing. Transparency and the courage to be yourself when the world outside expects you to don an image is the shift in this narrative across categories. Hence, the focus has shifted from the brands fulfilling a functional need to a need that will impact the way we evolve and change as people. By becoming more humane, these brands embrace and encourage "people growth" by creating a better world of people and for people. Linked to brands becoming more humane is a whole new world of values that brands propagate. These values open new way of thinking and being, especially in a culture that has been stubborn about its value systems, its rights and wrongs.

Brand Legacy

Many luxury brands have a rich pedigree and extraordinary history that turn in to an inseparable part of the brand's mystique. This mystique is generally built around the exceptional legendary founder character of the past, making up an integral part of the brand story and brand personality. The lineage of the brand has its role, keeping up the contemporary appeal and the newness factor is crucial for enduring brand relevance. Therefore, advertisement for luxury retailer not only needs to generate the desire for the seasonal collection but also, at the same time, must enhance the brand's cool quotient, thereby making it continuously desirable and aspirational. Hence, the passion points here are music, fashion, design, ambience, location, people, and the overall experience; it is the kind of thing that we call "bleisure"—a blend of business and leisure.

The luxury collection has hard brand deliverables as it is more of a celebration and a collection of indigenous experiences. So, when consumers buy, say a Cartier or a Chanel product, it is not only because of the product performance factor but also, subconsciously, because of the influence of the brand's rich lineage, heritage, and the years of mastery.

For example, Christian Dior, long regarded as one of the best fashion designers in the world, opened his doors at 30 Avenue Montaigne, which remains the house headquarters to the present day, in a dreary postwar atmosphere on 12 February 1947, and presented his first collection. His style created a fashion revolution and was renamed the New Look. Indeed, this new silhouette with flowing skirts and cinched waist turned the era's codes of fashion and femininity upside down. The designer immediately expanded his house by launching perfumes and accessories, while also moving into the international market, starting with the USA, as early as in 1948. His designs were more voluptuous than boxy; the wasp-waisted corsets and dresses flaring out from the waist resulted in a more curvaceous form. This New Look sparked a revolution that made Paris the postwar fashion capital of the world. This made Christian Dior the most celebrated couturier of his time by virtue of his avant-garde vision and sense of elegance live on through the house of Dior, which remains a leader in the world of fashion.

Christian's legacy and heritage has been carried forward by the label, now controlled by business magnet Bernard Arnault's LVMH, the world's largest luxury group. The brand's portfolio today includes ready-to-wear, leather goods, fashion accessories, footwear, jewelry, watches, fragrances, makeup, and skincare. It also retains the essence and persona of the brand as envisioned by its founder.

Let us consider the example of Hidesign, founded by Dilip Kapur in 1978. Hidesign is an Indian leather goods brand that made its foray into the global market in the late 1970s. It was the time when there was a trend of sophisticated and smooth Italian bags. Hidesign's rugged and rustic textures, accenting the genuine leather's natural scars and patterns, were a complete contrast, but that is what added to its appeal, and its brand persona was perceived as a rebellious attitude.

Coincidently, it was the age of the hippies, the young, and the rebellious. Hidesign strategically positioned itself as a rebellious brand with the earthy and rustic nature of its bags. Over a period of time, the brand covered a journey starting from selling in counterculture stores to upmarket premium international outlets globally to being the preferred brand of celebrities and who's who worldwide. Back to the home country, in the 1970s, Indians used to prefer plastic, jute, and nylon, and Hidesign was perceived as a very rough and uncomfortable product. But gradually, and especially in the 1990s, when the Indian economy opened and Indians started getting more exposure to the Western world, consumer's taste and preference changed. Globalization was knocking the doors of Indian market and Indians were increasingly inclined to follow the Western world vogue. In India, the company started selling only in 2000, but achieved a great success.

The company started with an objective to preserve traditional, natural, and eco-friendly Indian leather tanning techniques. It continues to believe in India's heritage and traditions, handcrafting each piece, unique in its own way, crafted with the same passion for creating artistically and aesthetically high-value designs. For 800 years, the greatest leather goods came from the Indian subcontinent, but the business was slowly declined after the colonizing powers took over the reins of Indian business. In this journey, Hidesign revived the dying Indian traditions of ecologically tanning leather and eventually evolved as a legendary brand. Hidesign products are sold in about 25 countries through exclusive boutiques and major stores. Hidesign, with its passion for a classic contemporary look, appeals to the savvy, sophisticated urban professionals and fashion connoisseurs. Its brand image is reinforced by its presence at premium international outlets such as John Lewis, Selfridges, and House of Fraser in the

Hidesign is a lifestyle group that redefined the vision of luxury in India through an ethos of high quality, ecological values and personalized service and created its positioning through its iconic leather brand based on strong legacy of innovation and craftsmanship.

Photo 5.3: *Portraying the Brand Image through Physical Environment*

Source: www.louisvuitton.com (accessed on 12 May 2016)

UK; Stuttafords and Edgars in South Africa; Myer and David Jones in Australia; Lifestyle, The Bombay Store, Westside, and Shoppers Stop in India; Parkson in Vietnam; and Robinsons in Southeast Asia, among others.

Brand Architecture

Brand architecture defines the different levels within your brand and provides a hierarchy that explains the relationships between the different products, services, and components that make up the retailer's portfolio of offerings. This architecture captures and reflects retailer's existing brand structure so that employees and customers understand the value of and relationship between its different parts and components. It also creates a roadmap for journey that guides how your brand can scale in the future. Hence, brand architecture is nothing but the logical, strategic, and relational structure for your brands, or put another way, it is the entity's "family tree" of brands, sub-brands, and named products.

As organizations grow through mergers and acquisitions, they are faced with many key decisions regarding brand architecture, including how many brands should be managed. Brand architecture addresses each of the following:

1. What the overarching branding approach is: master brand, brand/sub-brand, endorsed brand, stand-alone brands, or some combination of these?
2. How many levels of branding should exist?

3. What types of brands exist at each level?
4. How brands at different levels relate to each other, if at all?
5. What are the decision rules for creating new brands?
6. Which brands' identities are prevailing and which ones are recessive?
7. What types of names the organization uses—coined, associative descriptive, or generic descriptors—and in which circumstances (usually controlled by decision rules)?
8. Which brands are featured in each and every media, vehicle, situation, and circumstance (e.g., business cards, stationery, product catalogs, website, shipping boxes, vehicle signage, employee uniforms, building signage, etc.)?

Hence, brand architecture is the design and construction plan for creating the edifice of strong brand. If brand building is about creating an experience—an idea in the consumer's mind of why to choose your product over the competition—your brand architecture is the structural plan that makes sure everything fits together seamlessly.

For example, the department store fashion retailer Shoppers Stop has signed a strategic partnership with Bennett, Coleman & Co. Ltd (BCCL). Under this "co-create and co-own" partnership arrangement, BCCL will license Femina Flaunt to Shoppers Stop. Flaunt is basically the retail identity developed by BCCL for Femina. With this, Shoppers Stop gets the exclusive license to develop, design, and also retail the brand across all its stores, in the core fashion categories like apparel, footwear, accessories, and bags. The media company will extend *Femina*, one of its flagship magazines, into the consumer products space.

This strategic tie-up is essentially in line with BCCL's brand extension strategy to partner, with the retail player having potential to unleash the unexplored value in many of their marquee brands. Being positioned as premium brand, the Femina Flaunt range primarily targets today's progressive, perceptive, urban, and independent woman, who is in the age group of 25–35 years, working and living in the metros and other big cities. So if we talk about Shoppers Stop, the premium positioning of Femina Flaunt is a seamless brand fit into their diverse portfolio of premium brands. Hence, this strategic tie-up brings many synergies to both the partners.

Brand Hierarchy

Within the brand hierarchy, a retailer's brands can be divided into different levels. Retailers have brand names at the level of the retail company as a whole (i.e., corporate brand), and at store levels, the retail stores and the merchandise (i.e., the store brands), and specific retail services (i.e., banking services or loyalty programs). Besides the individual branding decision at each level, the interconnection between the levels has to be taken into strategic considerations. As in industrial multiproduct companies, retailers with more than one store have to decide whether the stores should carry the same or different brands.

Three general branding strategies can be distinguished at the level of the retail brand:

1. An umbrella brand strategy, where all the stores of the company carry the same brand, in most cases differentiated by a sub-brand.
2. A family brand strategy, in which groups of stores of the retail company (usually different retail formats) carry different brands, that is, the brands are strictly separated.
3. A mixed strategy, which applies an umbrella brand for some store formats and separates others by using different brand names.

The main topic in this context is brand image transfer versus brand image separation. Using an umbrella brand strategy, the common brand name leads to a substantial image transfer. Consumers transfer the associations they carry for Tesco Superstores at least partly to Tesco

Express stores. All stores are part of one large brand and have to convey the same message to the consumer, if the brand image is to remain strong.

A family brand strategy, on the other hand, is usually the result of market segmentation and an unambiguous brand focus with different brand attributes for each store format. Carrefour hypermarkets, for example, target a different market segment than Carrefour's discount chain Dia. An image transfer would, therefore, probably not benefit either of the stores.

When a brand extends across its product portfolio, it becomes more challenging to maintain the essence of the brand intact. The challenge is in scaling up the business to ensure it is sustainable and the promise of the large consumer base comes true. While doing so, it is extremely essential to ensure that brand credentials are kept integral.

One of the classic examples of expanding product portfolio is Titan. A JV between Tata Group and the Tamil Nadu Industrial Development Corporation (TIDCO), Titan Company Ltd (earlier known as Titan Industries Limited) commenced operations in 1984 under the name Titan Watches Limited. Titan is one of the successful retailers in the world because of the ability of the brand to cater to various consumer segments through diverse product categories and yet maintaining a clear positioning without any overlaps or confusion about who stands for what. Its product designs are contemporary and are aligned perfectly to the essence of each sub-brand, including Edge, Raga, Nebula, Royale, Fastrack, and so on. This is a disciplined brand owner with a good sense of strategy.

With a license for premium fashion watches of global brands, Titan brought international brands such as Tommy Hilfiger, FCUK, Timberland, and Police, as well as Xylys, Swiss-made watch, into the Indian market. In 1994, Titan diversified into jewelry with Tanishq and more recently into eyewear with Titan Eye Plus. In 2013, Titan entered the fragrances segment with SKINN. In the later part of the year, it ventured into the helmets category under its brand Fastrack. The crown jewel in the Titan brand league is, indeed, the jewelry brand Tanishq. Launched as a premium jewelry brand, Tanishq has traversed many boundaries and reached out to both ends of the consumers in the upper and middle class. Besides maintaining distinct brand identities, Titan products score high on design and their contemporariness even at the junctures when the attempt is to thrust upon old values and traditions. Hence, Titan's brand architecture is very clear, and there are roles and rules for sub-brands that never get vague. This makes Titan a disciplined brand owner with a good sense of strategic brand management.

Managing diverse brands is not the only virtue Titan holds, the company has a vast distribution network to make the last-mile connect with consumers. With over 1,110 retail stores, the Titan Company has a large network spanning across 220 towns. The company has over 400 exclusive "World of Titan" showrooms and over 150 Fastrack stores. It also has a large network of over 750 after-sales service centers and over 160 Tanishq boutiques. With right branding and distribution, the right pricing is another feather in the cap for Titan. Titan products are priced such that they remain affordable yet aspirational for consumers segments they target. Hence, Titan range scores for its innovative product design, reasonably good prices, great advertising, and increasing store footfalls.

Thus, it is imperative to maintain the core values, DNA, and perceived values of the brand during its extension.

Retail Brand Positioning

It is based on a set of fixed dimensions along which a retailer is perceived to be located. However, the retail brand is broader than the actual positioning. The total brand knowledge that a consumer associates with a brand is relevant to the brand strength.

The psychological model, associated network memory model, reveals how the human mind stores data and how the stored data can be strengthened. The associative network model views memory that is consisting of a network of nodes, representing stored information, and connecting links. Any type of information connected to the brand is stored in the memory network, including verbal, visual, abstract, and acoustic information. Retail brand image can be defined as perceptions about a retailer as reflected by the brand associations stored in a consumer's memory. The strength of the brand can be evaluated by analyzing the various relevant associations. Their uniqueness, favorability, strength, and the certainty with which consumers link the information with the brand are the dimensions to consider. The retail brand image is complex, and it is connected to an array of other images, both at a higher level as well as in the form of sub-images. The retail store format image (i.e., category "killer image"), service image, shopping center image, department store image, shopping destination image, high-end store image, location image, price image, merchandise image, and other components of the store or its context are all connected to the retail brand image and are part of the memory network of the consumer.

For example, Fendi said that a luxury label is not really a one unless it is located at Bond Street, London's real estate prime cut since the 18th century when it was the address for tony art galleries and antique shops. Expensive jewelry then made the way with their items, and luxury fashion retailers such as Louis Vuitton, Gucci, Christian Dior, Chanel, and Hermes followed the suit. Fendi is pretty much known as the inventor of the It-bag phenomenon with its Baguette, Spy, B Fendi, Peekaboo, and Silvana styles.

May 2014, finally, saw Italian fashion house Fendi stake its claim on its turf too. Here Fendi arrived on the stage with a bang and asked 10 influential lady Londoners to personalize its 2009 Peekaboo purse.

The Peekaboo embodies the essence of Fendi's spirit—the appreciation of rules alongside a truly unique creative ideology—and has been associated with iconic women in their fields of competence. Only three pieces will be released: one for the celebrity herself, the other for Fendi's archives, and the third piece will be sold at Sotheby's online auction with its proceeds going straight to UK's noted charity Kids Company.

The celebrities handpicked to customizing the handbag are performers Gwyneth Paltrow, Dame Helen Mirren, Adele, Cara Delevingne, Jerry Hall, and architect Zaha Hadid, among

Photo 5.4: *Strategic Importance of Location*

Source: www.fabindia.com (accessed on 12 May 2016)

others. The iconic brand gets associated with the women leaders in different fields to derive the prestige and find right identity through this brand promotion.

Now this celebration was particularly for the grand opening of the new outlet and also to connect with British community and give back to them. Each of the 10 handbags is truly a work of art and creativity. The new Bond Street store is located in a 19th century building with a brick and terracotta façade in the Flemish style. Besides, Fendi's bespoke and ready-to-wear lines, the three-storied store has an entire floor dedicated to menswear. The staircase hosts a 5,600-piece Murano glass chandelier. This store in London is also an art gallery for millions of Lagerfeld fans; several rooms here display photographs of Roman fountains taken by the auteur, along with the sketches he has realized for brand Fendi.

Prior to this, new Bond Street flagship store Fendi has opened its outlets at strategic locations such as Avenue Montaigne in Paris, Via Montenapoleone in Milan, and Maximilianstrasse in Munich.

Everything has to be smooth and perfect, delivered beyond expectation. And to underline that, retailers build a profile of what the physical product should look like, the kind of material, color schemes, and so on, how the service should be, and what are the passion points.

Strategic Retail Brand Management

In retail industry, we can see that some stores are positioned with the lowest possible prices and least amount of service, others are positioned for the best values for fashion forward apparel, while others coordinate the different variables and dimensions to position themselves in other ways.

The strategic brand management starts with a clear understanding of what the brand is to represent and how it should be positioned relative to competitors. Positioning is the deliberate and proactive process of defining and influencing consumer perceptions of a marketable object, with a strong focus on the competitive position. A product is thus positioned in the minds of the consumers. Positioning usually applies certain fixed dimensions along which the retail brand defines its position relative to its competitors. Market segmentation is often considered necessary for successful brand positioning. Market segmentation refers to the process of dividing a total market by certain attributes into (more homogeneous) partial markets. Segmentation criteria can be demographic, socioeconomic, lifestyle, geographic location, and many others. Segmentation therefore includes the selection of one or several market segments and targeting the marketing toward the purchasing behavior, motives, or expectations of these groups. However, segmentation is often considered difficult for retailers with given catchment areas and the need for high customer traffic in their stores that require appealing to broad customer groups. Successful positioning can be based on any retail activities, and a unique profile along the various dimensions yields a clear position, a prerequisite of a strong brand. At the same time, the advertising spending of retailers has increased strongly over the last few decades—as an indicator of the increasing relevance of retail branding—and in many countries, retail stores are among the most heavily advertised "products" in terms of media spending.

Another example we can discuss is of a fashion retailer where retailer's unique fashion image is formed by a combination of its merchandise fashion level, preferential marketing, trends and fads cycles, services and experiences offered, physical environment, people, promotion and PR campaigns, and communications. These components should be carefully combined to project its image to the public, and should be developed to appeal to the target customers. The merchandise fashion level is the emphasis of presenting goods in the early (introduction or rise) or later (peak and beyond) stages of the fashion cycle. For example, prestigious retailers that target affluent and fashion-conscious customers usually offer fashion goods earlier in the cycle.

Here advertisement is an efficient tool for highlighting the brand's best qualities and to draw attention to them through exposure. Advertisement accentuates the positive aspects and enhances the total image of the brand in a generally positive environment.

At an overall level, luxury advertising messages can be observed.

- As more emotional and sensual to distance it from mass-premium brands.
- To create a world and an aura that is truly exceptional to their brand signature.
- To generate major differentiation in its production and execution.

While the luxury brand's visual identity is a fairly stable factor, luxury brand *advertising* is a more dynamic and versatile marketing vehicle. Discounters emphasize fashion styles later in the cycle. Services offered also contribute to the image. Retailers with an upscale image offer better services than discount retailers. Higher-price/quality stores might include credit (charge) privileges, generous return policies, telephone ordering, home delivery, well-appointed rest rooms, gift wrapping, in-store restaurants, free parking, alterations, and jewelry repair. Discount "bargain" stores might operate strictly on cash-and- carry basis, and have limited refund policies.

Sometimes it is necessary or desirable to change a retailer's image. This might be done to adjust to changing demographics, the desire to attract additional customers, or to differentiate itself from increased competition. Companies want to keep old customers and add new ones, which might be done by changing the merchandise assortments, services, ambience, and promotion over time.

Caselet: McDonald's

McDonald's entered India in 1996, with the positioning—*value-for-money eatery serving burger and fries*—set to go premium by launching big-sized burgers for adults at almost 20% more than the existing range. The new form of burger, clubbed under the "Royal" category, is priced in the range of ₹130–₹135, while the US chain's existing burgers cost anywhere in the range of ₹25–₹115. The strategic move also helped Big Mac's archrival, American chain Dunkin' Donuts, to launch big-sized "tough guy" burgers at ₹130–₹170 as part of strategic decision to woo adults.

Here, the objective is clear to position the brand more than a value food chain and a family restaurant brand that has products available for everyone. This can be seen as a step Big Mac is taking to distance itself from being perceived as kid's hangout place, and step up profitability in the context of subdued economic environment to face the challenge of gentle demand and margin pressures. The move was basically aimed at increasing ticket size, which in turn leads to improvement in top and bottom line.

Working on the physical environment in line with the above shift in positioning, Big Mac started off large-scale revamp by shedding its red-and-yellow colors for more gentle and quite tones appealing to adults. The familiar red-and-yellow Mac logo and décor have been replaced with white and pale colors, in many stores across the country.

Since then the focus of the food chain retailer was on to strengthen the menu by introducing products at every level to find identity across all the age groups and income levels like McEgg in the value range, Masala Grill in the mid-tier range, and now Royal in the premium range.

McDonald's joint partners in west and south India provide flavors and product options based on detailed consumer feedback to get wide acceptance in the vast country with lot of variations in culture, eating habits, and taste–flavor preference.

On the other front, Domino's, the largest foreign fast-food chain in the country operated by Jubilant FoodWorks, launched kids-only meals in boxes along with a toy, named as "Junior's JoyBox", at ₹99, a price marginally lower than McDonald's Happy Meal. This new product was essentially modeled to take on rival McDonald's to counter its global property Happy Meal. According to the company sources, the kid's meal sub-brand "Junior's JoyBox" was aimed toward helping the company to tap a new segment and also to drive frequency of consumption. This strategic move was intended to boost the consumption from parents as children have a lot of say in their decision in this particular area. As kids influence family purchase decisions to a large extent, it would directly drive consumption from parents who might otherwise hesitate to buy pizzas frequently for their kids. Moreover, Domino's has positioned Junior's JoyBox as a complete meal that will include vegetables toppings on pizza slices, garlic bread sticks, custard desert, juice and a toy—a smart blend of health and entertainment for kids. Here, fries and aerated drinks have been completely dropped, use of which has caused McDonald's Happy Meal draw a lot of criticism from health activist from around the world.

Differentiation: Gaining Strategic Competitive Advantage

Achieving differentiation (in consumers' minds) is a central characteristic of a brand. Because of the huge number of retail players in the market, there is a strong competition among individual stores for customers' mind and wallet share. All retail marketing instruments affect the retail brand, as illustrated by the concept of the comprehensive retail brand character, which is made up of a fabric of interwoven associations. The brand character is the personality or image that is created for the product. It is the distinguishable quality that makes the brand different from others. Its function is to help the target group to distinguish the brand from the competitors over a period of time. The predictability that a brand image or brand personality provides, in terms of the experience, creates acceptance and trust among customers. This is a basis for creating brand loyalty. To become relevant and meaningful, the entire shopping experience needs to deliver value. The trendsetters in this space like Apple start by asking what experiences they could offer that customers would pay for. Then, explore that dimension where it becomes an inseparable part of their competitive rationale. For instance, Apple stores are the retail spaces where people would go to learn about new things they could do with their Apple product, and while on their way out from the store, majority of them would buy something.

To develop a strong and successful brand, three basic principles are generally followed:

1. Differentiation from competition
2. Long-term marketing continuity
3. Coherence of different marketing components

There are four types of retail competition.

1. The direct competition is between two or more retailers using the same type of business format. For instance, The Gap and The Limited are in direct competition because of their similar merchandise, customer service, prices, and locations. Another example is the department stores Lifestyle International and Shoppers Stop in India.

162

2. Indirect competition is between two or more retailers using different types of business formats to sell the same type of merchandise. For example, supermarkets and department stores compete in selling women's panty hose, but they are very different types of retailers.

3. Vertical competition is between businesses at different levels of the supply chain. The best example is apparel manufacturers who sell their apparel lines to retailers, as well as to the retailers' customers through factory outlet stores.

4. Lifestyle competition does not involve similar stores or products, but rather a fight for consumers' pastimes. Instead of consumers shopping as a form of leisure activity, spending discretionary income in the process, they may decide to use that time and money to dine out or watch a movie. Although restaurants, video/DVD rental services, and movie theaters are also consumer retail establishments, they are not apparel retail stores. Thus, they present a completely different type of competition.

Higher levels of differentiation from the competitor are expected to lead to higher profitability. Only brands that are well distinguished from their competitors can build up long-term customer loyalty and avoid store switching by the consumers. As shoppers have more choices today, retailers must select their target markets and marketing mixes very carefully. They should look at which competitors are satisfying which market segments. Possibly, several retailers are going after the same consumers, while other consumer groups are being ignored.

The fashion category is the most sought after online because of its high demand. However, the battle lines are clearly drawn. While players such as Myntra, Flipkart, Koovs, and Jabong are vying for the upper middle class, fashion-conscious consumer who goes all out for style, players like Snapdeal, ShopClues, and LimeRoad are trying to strike a balance between styles such as pricing.

In recent years, competition and changing consumer behavior have increased the relevance of retail branding tremendously. Such branding aims at enhancing differentiation, continuity, coherence, and the resultant customer loyalty. Retail brand management includes all components of the retail marketing mix and develops a strategic understanding of the intended positioning of the retail company. Developing a retail branding strategy helps to ensure the coherence of all marketing messages and market appearances of the company. Successful companies change over time, but considering the prerequisites of successful branding, the brand core should remain stable.

Let us see the example of online fashion retailer Voonik.com. Today, Voonik is an online fashion portal for women's personal styling, and that is the business model that Voonik.com has been building on. The app of Voonik picks up clothing for users depending on their tastes, preferences, body type, skin tone, and so on, and also provides suggestions from stylists on how to wear them and what to pair them with. Voonik was serving to both men and women initially but eventually realized that Indian men did not take to the concept as expected. Here Voonik tweaked its strategy and started helping user customer for selecting the best option. The founders observed that personal stylists were only catering to celebrities like film stars, businessmen CEOs, and other high-profile people who were hiring personal stylists to manage their wardrobe and looks. So it was a great idea to democratize these kind of services clubbed with appropriate range of selection. So here there was a gap (personal styling for mass consumer segment) or problem that can be filled by right product and technical expertise. This unique feature (personal styling) of this portal tries to make sure that customer is buying what suits to her. Voonik has strategic tie-ups with leading online fashion retailers such as Jabong, Zovi, Fashionara, and Snapdeal, among others, to ensure that the customer will get a wide range of merchandise to select from.

Voonik has leveraged technology, which allows the customers to buy all these retailer's offerings from their app. For instance, a customer can go buy the top from Jabong, bottom from Fashionara, and, perhaps, accessories from Zovi. Here customers do not need to install multiple apps, and the entire universe of selection is available through a single app.

Repositioning

We have seen that how the business of retailing has changed over the years and especially after the upsurge of e-commerce.

The entry of foreign players having experience of international market has also made a big impact on consumer's expectations. All these developments make repositioning essential to maintain competitiveness in a fast-changing environment (in the case of many players). A retailer's existing positioning base is vulnerable to continuous dilution because of evolving markets, changes in consumer's taste preferences, new entrants, innovations, emerging formats (models), some issues with the brand or aggressive competitors, and so on. In such a context, retailers are also focusing on customer needs along with trends in retail sector. They are increasingly emphasizing on customer-centric initiatives to bring some strategic changes and are "reinventing" themselves based on consumer expectations and "engagements."

Recently, we have seen an outbreak of activities among the established retailers to revamp and reposition their brand's image. Country's top retail chains such as Spencer's Retail, Café Coffee Day, Shoppers Stop, and many more are rebranding the stores, introducing new product categories, changing the entire physical environment and visual looks, creating new formats, and even changing the brand identity to adapt to the stiff competition and changing landscapes of the modern retailing.

Reebok's operations in India took a hit after the 2012 controversy that saw an alleged financial fraud come to the fore. This incident brought Adidas in the news as it owns the brand (Adidas had acquired the US-based Reebok in 2006). The German sportswear major (Adidas) took a series of strategic decisions in order to support the "re-emergence" of the brand—Reebok in India and the subsequent repositioning of Reebok as a "fitness brand"— that saw the introduction of Fit Hub stores. "Reebok Fit Hub" stores sell premium products and provide fitness consultation to customers and overall focus is on offering real value at different price points. It moved from a minimum guarantee-driven model to a cash-and-carry model for its franchise operations. As part of its omni-channel strategy, customers can now order a particular footwear model not available in the store through its in-store tab and get delivered at their homes. Adidas India had gone through an organizational restructuring— putting in place controls, along with checks and balances—with more involvement of the parent group in the day-to-day operations to correct the business practices of Reebok India and build a sustainable business model.

Spencer's Retail of RPG Group had left a perception of being a high-priced store in the consumer's mind. Eventually they changed their tagline. The retailer moved away from "Taste the world" to "Makes fine living affordable" as the new tagline. They complemented this with a strong in-store value communication on the lines of "Quality since 1863. Prices you can Trust." The retailer brand wanted to play this back to the consumer and reward his/her trust in Spencer's by working harder on providing value for what she/he buys. Hence with these initiatives, they have chosen to link quality, trust, and value in a more direct manner.

In today's retailing scenario, customer requirements are changing and are expected to change continuously because of many prevailing factors. The whole brand reconstruction, and planned dissociation from the past, is basically prompted by its previous performance in the market and its desire to rebuild itself in a completely new form and avatar. These changes create a need for image reengineering to alter the image with the aim of adjusting it closer to what target audience want. Hence, the entire reconstruction is based on what the retailer brand would like to be going forward and what exactly it wants to communicate to its audience. However, it should be done carefully, with lot of considerations at the back of its mind, because—though it is tempting for the companies to chase what they do not have—it may happen that the whole endeavor may land up devaluing what they do have. Such ventures may sometimes bring the jeopardy of dilution of focus and dissipation of valuable resources into areas where the company is essentially not so strong. This eventually may become an expensive pursuit. The second risk lies at the consumer level where a brand may finally end up giving out mixed signals and the consumer may not get what the brand represents anymore. The marketers here need to double-check that the brand component that is being eliminated has no significant residual equity or the brand component being added should have brand equity among the segment of consumers being addressed.

For example, Giordano was founded in Hong Kong by Jimmy Lai in 1980. In 1981, it opened its first retail store in Hong Kong and also began to expand its market by distributing Giordano merchandise in Taiwan through a JV. In 1985, it opened its first retail outlet in Singapore.

Responding to slow sales, Giordano changed its positioning strategy in 1987. Until 1987, it had sold exclusively men's casual apparel. When Lai and his colleagues realized that an increasing number of female customers were attracted to their stores, he repositioned the chain as a retailer of value-for-money merchandise, selling discounted casual unisex apparel, with the goal of maximizing unit sales instead of margins. This shift in strategy was successful, leading to a substantial increase in turnover.

During the late 1990s, Giordano had begun to reposition its brand by emphasizing differentiated, functionally value-added products and broadening its appeal by improving on VM and apparel. In 1999, the firm launched Bluestar Exchange (BSE), a new line of casual clothing for the price-conscious customers. Giordano's relatively mid-priced positioning worked well—inexpensive yet contemporary-looking outfits appealed to Asia's penny-wise customers, especially during a period of economic slowdown. However, over time, this positioning became inconsistent with the brand image that Giordano had tried hard to build over the years. As one senior executive remarked, "The feeling went from 'this is nice and good value' to 'this is cheap.'" As such, Giordano started to focus on establishing clear brand images and creating distinct identities between its brands. In September 2006, Giordano announced that it would rebrand BSE. This was to give BSE a makeover to sharpen its image, and decided to go outside the company to get a fresh perspective.

The newly revamped brand, now known as Blue Star Exchange (BSX), was unveiled at the launch of its first flagship store in Hong Kong in April 2007. The shift saw BSX evolve from price to "fun sell," targeting the key youth demographic. Expansion plans to bring BSX to other countries were made, following careful review and tweaking after its Hong Kong debut.

Additionally, having achieved success in its value-for-money lines, Giordano now wanted to penetrate the "upper premium" segment. This was done via the introduction of Giordano Concepts and its existing Giordano Ladies range. The lines focused on quality lifestyle and targeted the fashion-conscious consumer in the affluent market segment. In contrast to its unisex Giordano stores that carried a majority of items for women, Giordano Concept stores carry 60% of items catering to males. To create alignment between the new upmarket positioning and brand image, Giordano Concepts and Giordano Ladies stores were distinctly different from its mainstream stores. This included revamping store interiors and staff image to exude exclusivity, induce curiosity, and more importantly, appeal to an affluent target group.

Successful repositioning often demands unlearning a lot and abandoning the tendency of doing things in a certain way and framework. Organizations often have to disconnect themselves from the incremental improvement mind-set and managers need to be realistic about the finiteness of the brand repositioning or brand stretch.

For example, India's brick-and-mortar retail landscape has recently witnessed the addition of new storefronts, bearing familiar labels: Power and North Star. These stores, together with an expanded product portfolio, are part of Bata India's broader strategy to revamp the two brands. They are among the company's oldest and best-known brands. Bata India is revamping two of its oldest and best-known brands as a part of repositioning strategy to tap a fast-growing segment of the youth market: affordable luxury. The company hopes to leverage the inherent advantages of the domestic footwear market: low production costs, abundant availability of raw material, an ever-evolving retail ecosystem, and a huge consumption market.

The conception of "affordable luxury" here captures the idea of offering the product at the right value, which is a combination of price and quality. For Bata's buying and merchandising team, the objective is to broaden the customer experience and extend the product portfolio by adding trendy and quality products (based on trend forecasts) targeted at middle-income consumers. The objective is also to offer our customers a complete new look of vibrant colors, rich material constructions, and a comfortable product. "Affordable luxury" for sports shoes, for instance, brings the blend of technology (which offers traction, stability, cushioning, and flexibility) and style statement (which offers trendy and fashionable designs and vibrant colors) to meet the growing demands of the ever-more-aware, well-traveled consumer.

Indian footwear industry is in a strong position to deliver the kind of high-tech, high-fashion affordable brand positioning Bata is planning. So much of the repositioning strategy is formulated by a buying team that is young and fairly well-traveled, which is a right material to forecast trends, as the objective is to reposition Power and North Star and make them compelling choices for today's youth in the sports category.

But here the major challenge for Bata is whether the strategy can work, because Bata is revamping two legacy brands that were launched in the 1970s (Power in 1971) in a market that is saturated with new brands targeted at the emerging aspirational youth. The answer seems to be hidden in the question itself. Bata's legacy puts it in a strong position to take advantage of this market.

However, on the other hand, there are two broad trends that have emerged in the youth market over the past decade. One striking change is the orientation from long-term to short-term gratification. For instance, many young consumers tend to spend a month's salary on a mobile, and repeat the same after a year when new models enter the market.

The other trend is the result of evolution of mobile communications. Because of this communication revolution, there has been a convergence between brand aspirations of small-town and big-city India. The aspirational symbols of young consumers in metro cities like Mumbai and Delhi are not very different from that of in Tier II or Tier III cities. The difference between the two lies in the ability to fulfill those aspirations. This is the gap Power and North Star could fill with their positioning as affordable high-tech, high-fashion brands, adding, in the process, some youthfulness to their middle age.

Promotion of Retail Brand

At its core, every brand has a persona that is defined by its journey from the day of its inception. This personality is shaped by both internal strengths and external forces. Brands create storm and capture imagination of the consumers, but we see some brands fading away into oblivion because of lack of correct promotional strategies. For instance, retailers evaluate various opportunities for promotion and partnerships for brand building and take decisions based on the returns on investment from any such promotion, campaign, program, association, and the like. Thus by choosing right effective and efficient ways of promotional activities projected toward right direction at right time, the brands can captivate their audience in a feasibly convincing manner.

Sales promotion involves any activities that encourage consumer interest in the purchase of goods or services. Promotion activities include such things as advertising, publicity, discounts offers, VM, and special events. Special events may include fashion shows, trunk shows, personal appearances, and in-store art shows.

For example, Arvind Lifestyle Fashion that operate some of the marquee fashion labels, including Gant, US Polo Association, and Ed Hardy, among others, always used fashion weeks to launch new arrivals and brands but seldom considered the option of sponsoring such events. The reason is simple: these are very expensive deals, and it is a trade-off between cost versus value and benefit.

In today's marketplace, brand journey takes on an even bigger meaning as organizations connect with their audience through an ever-increasing and wide-ranging activities and initiatives. The rise of social media and the transparent flow of information have thrown up new opportunities and challenges. Brands are reevaluating their brand persona and are continuously and continually adapting to the changing landscape of consumer preferences. This constant shift makes brand promotion more challenging than ever, claiming more investment in both time and value.

The function of marketing being in focus across organizations, marketers face increased fiscal responsibility, which in turn means more focus on fine-tuning a brand's presence, promise, and promotion. This would mean a relook at the retailer's promotions to precisely coincide with customer's to buying decision. *Promotion*, such as advertising, should project the image appropriate to attract desired target customers. For instance, if a store attracts shoppers at a certain fashion level because of its advertising, but stocks merchandise different than projected, shoppers will likely leave without buying anything. *Advertising and promotional messages* should clearly define the store image to the target audience.

To achieve these precision, retailers go through a checklist in the form of a questionnaire: Who we are? And what do we do? Ones we find the answers to these two basic questions, we come to the next phase: What is our market? Who are our competitors? And, most essentially, what is our target audience? With these answer in hand, we move on and pose the question: What is that we are offering? Is it marketable/does it possess selling value? Is it better to what competition is offering? Are we clear and sure about how we are going to execute it? What makes us different? What is in our promotional program that will break the clutter and appeal to consumer? Is there a gap that we can fulfill? What may be the perception of our target audience toward this promotion?

Once we get a crystal clear picture of who we are, we must get to know who our customers are. Defining the target audience is an absolute must; a small mistake here can turn out to be very expensive and/or damaging in the long run. Once the target segment is well defined, the retailer needs to look into consumer decision journey. This would involve understanding of wants, needs, and desires of consumers and who the probable influencers and/or opinion leaders in this decision journey are. The goal of retailer's promotion and communication should be to help the consumers to distinguish them in terms of values, uniqueness, personality, and style. Hence by following this process in devising a promotional program, retailer creates a brand persona, a persona that consumer connects to and associates herself/himself to. The persona of a brand is largely a result of (a) its distinctive projection plus coherence of its applications across consumer touch points and (b) the brand communication through its advertising and promotion. This persona, when strategically integrated with the right communication and media vehicle, generates huge brand recall value for the retailer.

Let us examine the example of jewelry retailer Tanishq. A jewelry brand has to perform on multiple fronts, and one of the facets of the brand is the store associate's relationship with the customers. So keeping this key success factor in mind, the company launched a television campaign featuring four commercials. Each of the films features a member of the sales staff from the brand's outlets in different cities of India. The employee narrated what value and benefit is offered—as a real-life customer experience—to underline the value proposition developed by the jewelry brand. It strategically included the promise of transparency, the promise of great value (that accrues from the low making charges), the promise of purity (almost all Tanishq outlets across the country use the karat meter, nondestructive means of testing the purity of gold), and the promise of best exchange value. The imperative was to convey the brand messages through brand clues such as truth, transparency, honesty, passion, and best industry practices that essentially make any jewelry retailer the most trusted and preferred jewelry brand.

Hence, the campaign was all about conveying the brand message to the targeted audience and to convince them with a rational reason why they should go for Tanishq for buying jewelry that is typically a high-value deal. This campaign was also in line with what they have been focusing so far: celebrating relationships. Tanishq's advertising had always focused on relationships—between husband and wife or between parents and their siblings—and through this campaign, they focused the relationship between store associates and consumers. Hence by focusing on relationships, Tanishq has managed to attract young buyers and differentiate itself from the competition, in a more interesting and convincing way.

Caselet: Christian Dior

Over the years, Christian Dior has developed many styles that have left a strong imprint in the world of fashion. The Lady Dior bag, launched in 1995, got its name from Lady Diana. France's then first lady Bernadette Chirac gifted the Lady Princess of Wales the newest handbag from Christian Dior on the occasion of Lady Diana's visit to the Cézanne exhibition, sponsored by the LVMH Group, at the Grand Palais in Paris. The princess immediately fell in love with the black leather bag with elegant stitching. Her newfound obsession led her to order the designer purse in every style available. In November 1995, during her visit to a children's home in Birmingham, Princess Diana was photographed with the bag, holding a child in her arms. A few weeks later, during a visit to Argentina, she again appeared with her favorite bag, leaving the official plane. Following these two major appearances, a legend was born. The elegant and stylish bag became associated with the world's most photographed woman and was sought after by ladies the world over. In 1996, as a tribute to princess, the House of Dior decided to rename the bag "Lady Dior" with Lady Di's blessing. Since then, it has become one of the most iconic bags for the House of Dior.

The brand's new emblematic bags under the "Be Dior" collection blend pure elegance with fresh and casual style, making them "it" bags for urbanites. Renowned photographer Patrick Demarchelier, who captures the aura of the brand's muse Oscar winner Jennifer Lawrence with the bag, has put together the *Dior: New Couture* book for the brand, featuring his gorgeous photographic tribute to the House of Dior. The book is yet another addition to the brand's legacy of artistic expressions.

Hence, brands today have great opportunities for growth through innovation and can establish meaningful differentiation through strategic promotions, PR, merchandise mix, logistics, supply chain, customer service, brand architecture, communication, media, and so on. In a nutshell, differentiation must give way to differentiated brand experience. Promotion has become more important today because of increased competition, and all retailers make use of some sales promotion, choosing the most appropriate methods for their type of business and target market.

Caselet: Gitanjali Group: The Story of Glamor, Glitz, and Grace

- Parent company: Gitanjali
- Category: Product categories include jewelry, accessories, apparels, lifestyle products, cosmetics, and perfumes
- Tagline: Trust Forever
- USP: Trusted brand, innovative and creative designs, styles, patterns with the aesthetic values
- Target audience/customers: Urban upper-middle-class and upper-class young women those who are high on aspirations with fresh outlook toward life
- Positioning: Glamorous, creative, aesthetically brilliant, and smart designs that essentially incorporate the flavor of heritage that eventually exude a magnetic, energetic, and charismatic persona

With jewelry never going out of style, fashion, and trend, the Gitanjali Group outshines the industry by capturing the luster of a shimmering diamond. Mesmerizing generations with its aesthetically brilliant and smart designs with exquisite artwork, Gitanjali's cornerstone was laid as a diamond trading business in Surat, Gujarat, India. The group's logo epitomizes Gitanjali's glamor quotient, creativity, and heritage. Upholding the philosophy of integrity and commitment to the quality, its logo presents a unique amalgamation of maroon and gold and reinforces Gitanjali's magnetic, energetic, and charismatic persona at large. Its tagline "Trust forever" clearly speaks volumes about the faith and confidence that its patrons have reposed in the group.

Gitanjali was the pioneer in changing the way Indian consumers viewed and bought the jewelry. Gitanjali created ripples and brought about a revolution by launching the group's first diamond jewelry brand "Gili" in 1994 in Indian jewelry market that was primarily dominated by gold jewelry and largely characterized by the unorganized segment. Today, a market leader in jewelry, this brand highlights young woman's aspirations and outlook toward life. By virtue of these brand attributes, it resonates with its target audience in a sustainable way, empowering its patrons to have their own style statement. The group pioneered the retail revolution in the country with the launch of brand D'damas in 2003.

Adding another jewel to its dazzling crown, the group acquired the US-based jewelry chain Samuels and Rogers in 2006–2007, in addition to some leading Italian luxury brands—Stefan Hafner, Nouvelle Bague, IO SI, Porrati, and Valente in 2011—to its portfolio. To continue with its multi-branding strategy, Gitanjali has established the luxury retail store Giantti in the country in 2009. Gitanjali successfully rules the market with its most-sought-after brands, such as Nakshatra, Asmi, Diya, D'damas, Gili, and Sangini. The group also operates effectively and impressively in segments and categories of luxury watches, apparels, and high-end writing instruments. With a sizable bunch of brands in India and overseas, today the group owns the largest number of well-established jewelry brands under one roof in the world. All these brands cater to different price brackets, and the central idea is to offer "mass/affordable" luxury through its unique way of leveraging the multi-branding strategy.

Targeting customers of all the age groups, Gitanjali strives to impress them with its traditional, international classics and casual jewelry offerings. Taking this glam factor to the newer heights, its brands are promoted by celebrity endorsement route, roping in leading actors and actresses from Hindi film industry. With Shah Rukh Khan being Gitanjali's brand ambassador having significant popularity not only in India but also internationally, the group has got wide recognition across the globe. Shraddha Kapoor, a talented newcomer, has also come on the board. The brand ambassador selection strategy is partly driven by a switch in marketing strategy and partly by business realities. The jewelry retailer is essentially contemplating a new customer profile and is therefore revamping its product and brand portfolio. Jewelry brands like Gili and Diya have been extended to apparel. In addition, Gitanjali Gems is starting an affordable jewelry segment and paying more attention to ultra HNWIs.

Gitanjali also remains at the forefront when it comes to the award celebration nights, movies, or music album promotional events, blockbuster releases, fashion shows, and so on and consistently makes headlines. Gitanjali appreciated and applauded the hard work of women through its "Gr8 Women Awards," a salutation for women achievers. The group plays the role of host for many events, organized the Fourth Asia Cup Polo at Mahalakshmi Race Course in the financial capital of India, Mumbai.

Going beyond the conventional ways, the group aggressively employs social media platforms in order to make the brand resonate with the target audience and to keep in constant touch with its patrons. Enjoying a mass appeal and exploring these communication channels and vehicles, Gitanjali acquaints its prospective customers about its New Age designs and upcoming events through Facebook, YouTube, Twitter, LinkedIn, and so on. Gitanjali roped in superstar Salman Khan to promote its two lucrative gold and diamond saving schemes: Swarn Mangal and Shagun, a jewelry accumulation plan.

One of the relatively new trends within retailers brand communication is the use of the long-form commercials or the short-film videos to generate interest with the online audience. It is clearly a pursuit where retailer brands are looking to bridge the gap between the familiar world of print and the fast-evolving world of online. It has also proved impactful as, in a matter of few minutes, the viewer can have a clear understanding of the brand image or the story the brand is trying to convey or simply promotion of the new collection.

Quality, Style, and Design Considerations

Gitanjali, one of the largest integrated branded jewelry manufacturer and retailer of the world, rides high on the values of solidarity, credibility, and perfection that are aptly reflected in its transparent operations. Backed by effective CAD/CAM processes, Gitanjali's remarkable growth is a result of its artisans' cutting and polishing expertise and designers' finesse and passion to develop awe-inspiring creations. Giving preference to the diamonds category of its Indian and international patrons, the group offers a plethora of choices in the form of classic, ethnic, and contemporary patterns. Making fashion by weaving the threads of gold, platinum, silver, and stainless steel, Gitanjali's products bear a cachet of purity and authenticity. Being the first one to offer diamond-studded jewelry in different price brackets, the group is present in all territories, right from sourcing of the glittering stone to retailing its jewels through a far-reaching chain of stores.

Distribution Considerations

The group's strong distribution network is spread across the country with over 4,000 POS, which includes:

- MBOs and EBOs
- Franchisee stores
- Shop-in-shop (SIS) format in department stores
- Large jewelry outlets
- Retail stores owned by the group
- Exclusive distributor network for each brand to sell to jewelry retailers across the country

The group has strategically carved its global exposure by mitigating the international boundaries and spread its wings in USA, UK, Belgium, Italy, the Middle East, China, Singapore, and Japan. To expand the business in Europe, Gitanjali has incorporated a WOS in the name of "Gitanjali Resources" in Belgium in order to explore the jewelry market in the region. All these channels make it the largest jewelry house in terms of number of sales point globally with over 4,000 points in India and overseas.

The Way Forward

Treading strong on its future plans, the jewelry retailer is all set to transform the face of gems and jewelry retailing by setting up close to 300 stores in the country and approximately 250 outlets in the international market. This expansion is expected to be channelized through Tire II, Tire III, and Tire IV cities through franchise route and other retail channels such as e-tailing, ATMs for gold and diamond, and digital media.

Awards and Recognitions

The group recently bagged the Indian eRetail Award 2013 from Franchise India and Best Jewellery Award at the 19th Lions Gold Awards. In addition, it is also a proud winner of the national award of Best Employer in 2009 for its illustrious Saksham project.

Creating the Differentiation: The Promotion Route

The right message to the right group of consumers tells how the retailer will satisfy customers' wants and needs. The types of advertising and promotional activities chosen are the ones preferred by the retailer's target market customers. Advertisements in newspapers and magazines, and on radio and television, should sound and look like the image that appeals to those customers. This also helps the retailer to create the differentiation. Differentiation can also be achieved by effectively and precisely promoting the unique merchandise, such as *Private Labels* or confined national brand promotions that a retailer sells exclusively.

Stores can also differentiate with extended hours, during special promotional activities, campaigns, or with special sale events, which in turn result in the development of distinct image. By carrying out targeted promotions through their strategically designed campaigns, retailers build the correct image, whether it is budget, upscale, or somewhere in between.

Unless a promotion is targeted to the correct segment, it will only erode brand image and margins. While this is challenging for all retailers, it is particularly difficult for luxury brands, which tend to have less discounting experience. Because of this, such brands likely will struggle to balance the long-term image management, short-term financial gain, margin protection, and fulfill the preferences of traditional and new shopper segments. So by tailoring categories and assortments across each channel, retailer can meet customer needs without cannibalizing sales or eroding brand image for valuable boutique shoppers.

Ethnic retail chains Fabindia and Manyavar have emerged as India's most profitable apparel companies by avoiding discounts, staying away from prime locations and real estates, and making products in-house in a market where most international brands are looking to grab share of offering price cuts. Right from local boutiques to established traditional retailers and regional brands, every ethnic wear retailer is vying for a share of the consumer wallet in the market that is governed more by design and aesthetics than brand name. However, both Fabindia and Manyavar have over the years expanded across India. Now they are finding acceptance even among younger consumers, a new development in a category that was traditionally restricted to old-age buyers.

To build a sustainable business, they primarily focused on profits and cash flow and did not get into the trap of discounting to chase the sales volume. To boost bottom line, they avoided to open stores in prime localities or higher footfall zones or at malls that guaranteed higher sales volumes, as high rentals at these places would have impacted the margins and eroded the profits. In comparison, most apparel brands have been offering steep discounts to move unsold merchandise, resulting in the erosion of retail margins and more than a fifth of sales taking place during EOSS.

For Example, according to filings at the Registrar of Companies, Fabindia Overseas posted a net profit of ₹54 crore in the year ended March 31, 2014, while Kolkata-based Vedant Fashions, which owns ethnic wear brand Manyavar, made a made a profit of ₹49 crore. Levi's India was the only marquee international brand that could match them, posting a ₹49-crore net profit. This is the first time Levi's India has made a profit since entering India in 1994. None of the overseas brands, including Zara, Benetton, and Marks & Spencer, were able to come close to the performance of the Indian companies.

In addition, both retailers make nearly 95% of their merchandise in-house. This merchandising strategy helps them keep inventory tight and cost under control, which is another reason behind their strong bottom line. In fact, Fabindia runs every store as a profit center in an effort to democratize operations, while Manyavar either donates or destroys unsold stock, adding pressure on the company to keep designs relevant and sell products aggressively.

Leading department stores such as Lifestyle, Shoppers Stop and Westside are increasing the width of their private-label range and offer contemporary styling in the ethnic segment, fueling growth. This scenario demands both the ethnic retailers to reinvent their portfolio to sustain the top position in their segments. While Fabindia, which is positioned as organic and niche, has launched its western wear line Fabels, Manyavar is also expanding its occasion and wedding tag and is tweaking to offer more Indo-Western clothing that can be worn on more occasions.

To gain more profits, retailers must tighten their operations to lower expenses and try to lure customers away from competitors. Here the promotion comes for rescue. Retailers must set themselves apart or differentiate themselves from competitors. Some retailers have repositioned themselves in the market, such as going from full-line general merchandisers to limited-line apparel merchandisers. Retailers can set themselves apart from others in many ways. For instance, luxury brands have created extensions into a secondary line with relatively lower price points like Giorgio Armani's Armani Exchange, Roberto Cavalli's Just Cavalli, Prada's Miu Miu, and Alexander McQueen's McQ lines, among others.

Let us consider the example of Giordano. Giordano's management had launched several creative, customer-focused campaigns and promotions to extend its service orientation. For instance, in Singapore, Giordano asked its customers what they thought would be the fairest price to charge for a pair of jeans and charged each customer the price that they were willing to pay. This one-month campaign was immensely successful, with some 3,000 pairs of jeans sold every day during the promotion. In another service-related campaign, over 10,000 free T-shirts were given to customers for giving feedback and criticizing Giordano's services.

To continue connecting with customers, Giordano launched several promotions. Among its successes was the "World Without Strangers" slogan. First launched in South Asia as a means to raise funds for the 2004 Indian Ocean tsunami victims in Phuket, it gained popularity with its other markets and was launched across the region in 2005. The slogan extended to a range of T-shirts and rubber wristbands that promoted international friendship. The products came in a variety of colors and brought across the message through words like "Strength, Explore, Listen, Believe, Imagine, and Accept."

The words are designed to be personal watchwords, such as "have strength in your convictions," or "explore the world around you," almost reminders to live outside the box and experience the variety of life. The shirts are a sign of solidarity for fellow humans, spreading a message of peace, acceptance, and open-mindedness, which is something we can all use from time to time.

In light of international crises and fragile cross-border friendships, "World Without Strangers" served as a mediator and avenue through which customers could express themselves. The company has been able to act as a mouthpiece for society, championing various themes from environmentalism to community work, and even the economy. An example would be the "Cheer You Up" collection, produced in collaboration with Mr Jim Chim Sui-man. This collection aimed to lift the spirits of the people in the financial turmoil during the 2009 global economic crisis. The firm's skills in executing innovative and effective promotional strategies helped the retailer to gain public favor and approval.

E-tailer's Changing Promotional Strategy

As e-commerce companies are increasingly positioning themselves in the mainstream, part of their expansion strategy is to use the mass media vehicles and platforms like radio and television. This is to establish themselves not just in e-commerce but also to play host to off-line consumers. The aim is to capture a larger share of the market that has raised the advertising budgets of most e-commerce companies that on an average are pegged at 20% of their revenues. For instance, after making a debut as a sponsor of the Indian Premier League (IPL) Twenty20 cricket tournament to connect with customers, Amazon, world's biggest online retailer, keep on launching many television advertisement campaigns. Other e-tailers such as Quikr, Flipkart, Snapdeal, and Jabong are also going all out on 360-degree advertising, going beyond digital marketing. This is because according to the industry experts, digital advertising is silent advertising, and it cannot solely do brand storytelling for them. Category-specific e-tailers Lenskart (which sells spectacles) and FabFurnish (furniture e-tailer) are also running television ad campaigns. FabFurnish, which has a mixed format (as it also has off-line stores), uses mass media channels to reach untapped consumers or first-time buyers, primarily targeting the upper middle class; this led to increase in their traffic and ultimately revenue. This is becoming profitable because furniture is high-margin category.

Fashion e-tailer Jabong insists on optimal mix. Apart from TV campaigns, the company has sponsored leading fashion events, such as the Lakmé Fashion Week, to achieve desired brand awareness and identity. Rival Myntra was a sponsor for the Wills Lifestyle Fashion Week.

Television being a mass media with significant credibility factor addresses to wider audience, including those who do not use Internet. Hence, the two-channel television campaigning and digital advertising aid each other and go parallel in furthering the cause of a brand to consumers.

Price Promotion

A retailer that features intermediate quality usually sets some bottom limits that it will not go below. Retailers that emphasize lower "serviceable" quality tend to also emphasize their low prices. The class distinctions that have previously distinguished various price/quality retailers from each other are now eroding due to constant price promoting.

Price promotion is advertising special price reductions of goods to attract shoppers. To entice customers and perk up sales, retailers offer flat discounts, gift vouchers, and free merchandise. This builds traffic (numbers of retail shoppers) to buy other items as well. Shopping traffic has been shown to move up and down in direct relation to promotion pricing of merchandise. Upscale retailers seem less compelled and less inclined to indulge in price promoting than mainstream retailers because they continue to enjoy their own prestige and attraction. However, upscale stores have recently engaged in more price promoting than they have done in the past.

In the developing nations like India, customers always look for value. In such scenarios, retailers have to work hard to deliver better value to customers that may be in the form of price promotions. However, the sales promotions also tend to be handled differently by luxury marketers. While few have resorted to sales and discounts, most others play it by adding more value to the purchase like gift with purchase, gift certificates, or rebates for the next purchase, multiple item discounts, online or e-mail exclusives, more loyalty points, no shipping, and handling charges by online retailers. Luxury brands also use the channel of luxury retailers like Harvey Nichols and Saks Fifth Avenue, who offer annual sales by offering them slightly lower prices.

It is about understanding who is your customer and designing a right promotional offer for them. For instance, if the retailer finds out who their regular shopper is and which products she consistently buys, they can send her a message featuring offers for those particular products. The consumer will come back. It is about maintaining engagement by presenting relevant offers and proposition. Discounts definitely work, but they have to be relevant. So if a company is not offering a discount, there might be a possibility that they are devaluing their business. However, there are many luxury brands like Louis Vuitton and Prada that do not need to offer discount. They command such status. For them the task is to maintain the brand image and create differentiation, so that it does not appear arrogant. Discounts are an essential part of promotional marketing. If a consumer constantly shops with one particular retailer brand, it is essential that the brand respects the consumer. It should be done subtly, tactfully, and by keeping relevance in the mind.

Photo 5.5: *Price Promotion Generates Excitement*

Source: www.corallista.com (accessed on 12 May 2016)

Retail companies run discounts when they face a continuous fall in same-store sales or decline in the same-store growth rate. Same-store sales growth means the growth coming from stores in the business for a year or more. It captures consumer spending data, and falling growth shows lack of consumer confidence. Besides the trends like decline in consumer spending during the market slowdown cycles, today retailers are also hit hard by the heavy discounts offered at e-commerce portals. E-commerce has also hit the footfall at malls, and walk-ins have come down at many shopping destinations. This leads the retailers to resort to mid-season and EOSS offers to increase the footfalls and win back shoppers. In this way, they bring discount offers and promotions to cover the fall in sales.

EOSS Promotions

The EOSS has become one of the most promising promotion retail strategies for today's retail brands as it is their "trump" card when it comes to achieving the sales targets and/ or increasing the revenues. The phenomenal rise in the number of urbane shoppers with handsome spending power has created a lucrative opportunity for retailers to fulfill their needs and demands for variety of apparels, gadgets, lifestyle products and amenities, and so on. EOSS increases store footfalls, and the sheer attraction of getting high-quality branded merchandise at lower prices attracts customers and, in some cases, widens the customer base too. Retailers are therefore encouraging such customer base to buy the big-ticket items available at discounted prices, in good numbers (basket size), and also to shop for more by just advertising and running EOSS promotions or "stock clearance sale" (EOSS is also attributed as "clearance sale" as it is essentially held to clear the stock from earlier season). For instance, EOSS gives an opportunity to buy a Zara leather jacket at a discounted price to a college goer or medium-range salaried office goer and without making a big dent to her pocket. Hence EOSS presents a good opportunity to the retailer to reach to a wider segment of consumers and also to those who might just have started to shop for better store experience and in real low prices through this EOSS.

EOSS is a crucial component of the retail business, and it is essential for liquidation process. Many times, stores receive stock according to local demand that, at times, results in excess inventory that clutters a store, and EOSS helps in clearing up that space for the fresh arrivals. So far, it has been very effective from merchandising management point of view. It has also been observed that shoppers buy not only the merchandise on offer but also the fresh merchandise. After exploring and buying the merchandise on offer, shoppers often move toward the fresh arrivals. This eventually leads to significant rise in the sale percentage from fresh merchandise, during the EOSS.

However, today EOSS is not just a stock clearance sale or not just a promotional offer to boost the sales, but it is something more than that. It essentially provides a platform for the retailers to interact with their customers through various initiatives and programs undertaken by the marketing team to enhance the brand, increase brand awareness, or to create the brand loyalty. Moreover, during EOSS, retailers plan and develop special VM themes, which not only create an engaging shopping experience but also make the sale season more than just shopping by connecting with target audience, thereby eventually resulting in increased footfall and patronage loyalty. In a nutshell, EOSS is a win–win deal for retailers and consumers.

However, it also comes with some challenges that retailers need to address strategically and effectively.

- Sales and discount should not be the only motivation to keep the excitement and interest alive among consumers to visit the retailer's store. Therefore, retailers need to cautiously align such promotion practices in order to keep their bottom line sustainable.

175

- EOSS acts as a magnet for the stores to attract more customers, but eventually the majority of customers end up purchasing discounted merchandise that leads to erosion of margins. It also means that sale stock will take more effort to move at desired rates. (The average levels of discounting have grown substantially, specifically after the e-tailers started offering heavy discounts. So though the EOSS-related revenue has been increasing, contributions from this seasonal sale to overall revenues have been dropping consistently.)
- Ensuring that buyers attracted by attractive discount offers, purchase nondiscounted, or premium merchandise categories and that one-time customers make repeat (frequent) visits to lower costs of customer acquisition via EOSS.
- Strategic use of the targeted marketing to design the right promotional programs that will correct customer segments.
- Mitigating the pre- and post-EOSS decline and footfall contraction.
- Many times, customers are discouraged by long queues and average shopping experience during EOSS. Most of the high-spending customers have the perception that EOSS offer deep discounts on "slow-moving or nonmoving or outdated" stock and the store associates are not focused on their specific needs, preferences, and expectations.

Thus, offering higher discounts or just extending the EOSS period does not seem to be the right path in the long run; trying different and unique concepts becomes the hour of need. The solutions to these challenges are hidden in the customer data that retailers typically capture and other hints that customers leave along their journeys across different retail channels. Retailers can also leverage these inputs derived from the data to moderate pre- and post-EOSS declines. Mitigating pre- and post-EOSS plunge does not negotiation EOSS footfall. Customers have higher propensity to comeback within one month of purchase; hence, the probability of EOSS visits increases for customers who are also attracted and motivated to shop in the pre-EOSS season. The mall management teams also play a major role in supporting and promoting the EOSS. They strategically integrate or align the promotional offers run by tenant retailers with each other and also with some entertainment events, activities, and amenities in their malls. This eventually leads to the creation of an attractive proposition for shoppers to visit the mall, which also enhances the overall shopping experience provided by the mall to the visitors. This supports the retailers in significant ways by ramping up footfalls and increasing the revenues.

Summary

In summary, successful retailers attract customers with good image and location that is promoted effectively. They offer competitive prices and leave a lasting impression with professional salesmanship. This results in higher profit because customers return for repeat purchases.

It is imperative for retailers to deliver a relevant product assortment that connects with their customers' dynamic lifestyle. They create an image by creating a premium presentation in-store and online by telling compelling and interesting stories about the brands, categories, and styles they offer. By developing an engaging environment, they help the consumers easily navigate through the selection and find the product that is right for them. They create a clean presentation that is well organized and highlight the key products that attract the attention of shoppers. All these aspects work in integrative way to create the "positioning" of a brand and deliver the coherent shopping experience.

Review Questions

1. What do you exactly mean by positioning and how it is related to the buying motives? Discuss with appropriate examples.
2. Explain in detail: retailer as brand and retail branding. Justify your views with appropriate examples and instances.
3. Explain the major factors that strategically complement the brand image of a retailer. Justify your explanation with appropriate example.
4. Explain the various factors that are essential for creation of brand image of a retailer. Justify your explanation with appropriate example.
5. Explain how the branding as concept and practice has evolved to what it is today. Also explain the significance of "endorsing sensuality" in today's branding scenario with appropriate examples.
6. Share your views and ideas about the importance of "brand legacy" for creating a sustainable brand image. Justify your views with appropriate examples.
7. Explain brand architecture briefly.
8. Explain the significance of retail brand positioning and strategic retail brand management for creating sustainable competitive advantage.
9. How differentiation helps the retailer brand to enhance the strategic competitive advantage? Explain with appropriate examples.
10. State your views about the contemporary retailing scenario with the emergence of new business models and in terms of consumer buying behavior and consumer expectations. Are these new challenges being addressed by the traditional brick-and-mortar retailers? Explain the importance of repositioning in the context of this scenario with appropriate examples.
11. Explain the essentials for promoting a retail brand and how it enhances or reinforces the differentiating factors (associations). Justify your views with appropriate examples
12. What is the role and significance of promotional offers in today's retailing scenario? Explain the significance and limitations of EOSS briefly.
13. Write a brief note on EOSS.
14. "Strong and strategic positioning complemented with right promotional strategy enhances brand experience and consumer engagement that eventually results in increased loyalty." Explain the statement in detail with appropriate examples.

Chapter 6

Merchandise Management and Private-label Brands

Introduction to Merchandise Management

In retailing, products are either goods (merchandise) or services. Products and merchandise management is a crucial function in any retail organization. A company's product mix is its entire selection of goods and services. Retailers differ in terms of the product assortments they offer. Besides selling goods (shirts, jeans, suits, and accessories), they also offer services. For instance, sales associates of a fashion retailer also educate the customer regarding new vogue. Other services offered are convenient parking, entertainment (leisure) amenities, and clean restrooms, among others. Both goods and services must be considered when retailers evaluate their product strategy. Shoppers are more demanding than ever these days, seeking the highest-quality merchandise, at the lowest prices, with the best service. Hence, the product can be anything that is sold by a retailer to the end customer in a retail transaction. A product could be a tangible or an intangible entity like goods, services, events, ideas, traveling and tourism services, and consultations; for example, a furniture and furnishing retailer often offers the services like home delivery, fitting installations, interior designing, and consultation services. The product portfolio strategy is devised in order to cater both tangible needs (through merchandise and its functionality and pricing) and intangible needs (through brand imagery and visual cues) of the target audience. Hence, product portfolio and profile management translate the segmentation and positioning strategy of the retailer. So the selection of the product plays a crucial role in achieving customer satisfaction and gaining customer loyalty in sustainable way.

Introduction to Retail Merchandising

A term that is often used in retail sector is merchandising. This is part of a jargon that is related to retail trading. The term "merchandising" comes from the Latin word *mercantile*, which means "profit." Indeed, merchandising was created to sell. It is a sales tool, and its objective is to increase the loyalty behavior of the customers.

Merchandising is defined as a specific practice that retailer employs to accomplish the sale of product to a customer. The major objective of merchandising is to enhance sales through improving customer's purchase comfort. Hence, merchandising is more than simply the arrangement of products on the shelf. In today's competitive retail environment, a retailer cannot afford to consider merchandising as a "frill." Everyone is competing for the customers' money. There are more choices out there for consumers than ever before, and this scenario quintessentially makes merchandising and display the vital parts of the marketing plan. Hence, retail merchandising is the process of developing, acquiring, displaying, pricing, promoting, and communicating the retailer's merchandise offering with the right appeal.

If we look at retail store level, merchandising refers to the following aspects:

1. Range of availability of variety merchandise
2. Visual display of merchandise in an enticing way
3. Process of merchandise inventory planning and management

Therefore, appropriate management of merchandising typically leads to increase on ROI and thus profitability of a store. As mentioned earlier, merchandiser (retailer) needs to pay greater attention to all aspects of merchandising to ensure profitability of the retail outlet.

Some of these aspects are as follows:

- Types of *products* at outlet for sale
- Product accessibility optimization
- Optimum presentation of products and clear transmission of information to customer
- Consistency of segmentation in the store
- Determination of reasonable retail price of such products
- Improving ease of understanding and attractiveness of store offer
- Churning out (generating) purchase desire through attractive and compelling display and presentation
- Improving sales staff comfort by facilitating restocking and favoring additional sales

The first and foremost thing retailers do to narrow down on merchandising is they observe the customer pathway. In the initial days, the merchandising was a practice that was confined to physical format of retailing. However, now with the advent of online retailing, the same principles of merchandising also apply to the virtual or online formats. Retailers need to understand what the customer is doing and where they are going while roaming in the store. It is the general behavior of customers that they like:

- Easy access to product with free choice
- Shelf and fixtures that support browsing convenience
- Interesting store layout
- Discovery and choice diversity
- Store ambience linked to function, quality, price, and product definition
- Convenience and comfort of purchase

The point is that it is not enough to have unique, quality merchandise; retailers need to display it in a way that it should be very appealing to customers and should create an impulse to buy or own it. Hence, a meticulous space and display planning process enable retailer to design and implement ideal planograms and visualization.

Merchandise Selection and Planning

Merchandise planning enables a retailer to build the desired breadth and depth of product that perfectly matches the target customer's needs. It helps the retailer gain a control on merchandise inventory through the systems like open-to-buy (OTB) and also enables the retailer to achieve flexibility for responding quickly to emerging trends. In short, it effectively works toward inventory optimization across the categories to increase profitability of the business. Before discussing to the process of merchandise selection and planning, we will go through the factors that play crucial role in designing merchandise policy. These factors act as guiding principles and/or valuable insights for the merchandise buyers who plan, select, and buy merchandise for the retailer.

- Store's positioning (image)
- Targeted categories and assortment planning
- Demographic factors of current and potential customer segments
- Pricing strategy and merchandise quality levels
- Price point policy
- Store management practices and policies
- Desired profit margin
- Considerations for store layout and planograms

All these factors and aspects provide the merchandisers with a framework that helps in buying function. Effective communication of these policy factors not only provide the context and direction for merchandise planning but also help to drive the key decisions and perhaps improvisations at points throughout the merchandise planning process. The concept of merchandise planning is primarily based on a *process*-oriented approach.

Following are the steps that are involved in the retail merchandising process:

1. Developing the merchandise mix (planning and controlling merchandise variety and assortment). The retailers need to look into several aspects while preparing merchandise plan and buying the merchandise. The key factors are assortment, variety and quality, and the planned merchandise price points, which collectively are referred as the merchandise mix. The merchandise mix also incorporates the PLB offerings by the retailer. So, key to effective and flawless merchandise planning is to ensure that the merchandise mix enhances the customer satisfaction by providing them the expected and/or desired value that is mutually beneficial to both customer and retailer. Effective merchandise mix also creates the value proposition for the retailer's store—a rational reason why the customer should come to the store for shopping.
2. Establishing the merchandise budget (planning and controlling sales, inventory levels, purchases, shrinkage, and profit margins).
3. Build the logistics system for procuring the merchandise mix.
4. Price the merchandise offering (setting the price points). Price points are basically the range of prices for a particular merchandise line. Price point is a strategic tool to attract the target audience into the store and drive the sales.

5. Organizing the merchandise display in a way that will entice the customers and compel them to buy them.
6. Managing the customer service and store assistance.
7. Developing the retailer as a brand by advertising, promotions, and loyalty programs.
8. Developing the right ambience and visual cues that will reinforce the brand persona and support the merchandising mix strategy.

The obvious outcomes of such planning process are:

- Optimization of sales
- Optimization of merchandise and assortment performance
- Rationalization of merchandise categories
- Appropriate allocation of stock to each store
- Improvement in price realization
- Minimization of inventory holding costs
- Maximization of sales throughput
- Minimization of losses arising from either markdown or stockout
- Optimization of promotions and discounts
- Better control on shrinkage

Merchandise Selection

A retailer's array of goods is called its assortment. Assortment refers to the range of stock, or total selection, a retailer carries, whether it is full, limited, or specialty. Customers often patronize the retailers that offer the merchandise assortments they want. Included in assortments are the variety and types of styles offered: the colors, sizes, fashion, and quality level, as well as the price ranges of the goods.

Consumers prefer variety of assortment right behind location and price while deciding on to which store they should patronize and make them their favored shopping destination. Shoppers seek for variety because they are more likely to find what they exactly want when shopping in a store that offers more varied assortments. Also when tastes and preferences are not well defined or formed or are dynamic, the perceived variety matters even more because of customer's desire and tendency to become educated and well informed about what is available while maintaining flexibility. Hence, the variety perception takes the center stage and becomes crucial when variety-seeking motive drives the purchase decision. So here retailers focus on variety as the shoppers value the variety. This makes it essential to recognize how shoppers perceive the variety contained in an assortment and how these perceptions influence consumer satisfaction, shopping experience, and store selection. Retailers study their target consumer base in order to anticipate the variety and assortments their customers will expect them to have.

In the past, assortment strategy was restricted by the product/merchandise that can fit within the confinement of the physical store, but today, retailers have the opportunity to expand their assortment with no constraints of space. Retailers are taking the advantage of this reason to expand the assortment being offered by them. However, before increasing the assortment, a very careful consideration needs to be given to associated costs and impact on the brand image of the retailer. Larger assortments can create clutter and the possible confusion by providing too many options.

Assortment breadth (width) is the number of different item categories or classifications offered by a retailer, regardless of how many of each category is stocked. An assortment is said to be "broad" or "wide" when many different varieties of merchandise are available. For instance, there may be many different types, brands, and price ranges of dresses or suit styles offered in the store.

Assortment depth indicates the quantity of each item available in the assortment of merchandise offered to customers. An assortment containing an item in great numbers, in many sizes and colors, is said to be "deep." Thus, there might be multiple dresses and suits of the varieties offered. An assortment with only a few of each item is said to be "shallow."

Three different approaches to stock depth and breadth are:

- Broad and shallow
- Narrow and deep
- Moderate breadth and depth

Stores that carry a broad and shallow assortments stock small amounts of many different styles. Upscale, prestige retailers tend to stock broad and shallow assortments. They offer small stocks of many styles in limited sizes and colors because their customers desire exclusivity.

Retailers that carry a narrow and deep assortments stock relatively few styles, but offer them in many sizes and colors. Mass merchandisers focus on narrow and deep assortments of proven goods that are well into the peak of the fashion cycle. They stock the latest fast-selling items in large quantities and have high inventory turnover rates. Stores that cater to mid-range fashion and quality might stock moderate breadth and depth. These tend to be department and specialty stores. However, these stores usually stock broad and shallow assortments early in the season when new styles are being tested. When demand for styles has become clear, they concentrate on narrow and deep assortments of the most popular styles. As retail space and inventory costs must be considered, stocking a broad assortment may limit the depth to which those items can be carried. Conversely, if depth is desired, space and costs often limit the variety that can be offered. However, if the right items are not in stock when consumers want them, shoppers will go elsewhere. Also, assortments that are based on local customer preferences are easy to build and analyze, and retailer can profitably balance their most controllable investment, which is nothing but merchandise inventory.

Example: Giordano

Let us consider the example of Giordano. Simplicity and focus were reflected in the way Giordano merchandised its goods. Its stores featured no more than 100 variants of 17 core items, whereas competing retailers might feature 200–300 items. He believed that merchandising a wide range of products made it difficult to react quickly to market changes.

Giordano was also willing to experiment with new ideas and its perseverance despite past failures. It ventured into mid-priced women's fashion by introducing new product lines, such as the label "Giordano Ladies." This featured a line of smart blouses, dress pants, and skirts targeted at executive women. Reflecting retailer practices for such clothing, Giordano enjoyed higher margins on upscale women's clothing—typically 50–60% of selling price compared to 40% for casual wear.

Here, however, Giordano ran into some difficulties, as it found itself competing with more than a dozen seasoned players in the retail clothing business, including Esprit. Initially, the firm failed to differentiate its new Giordano Ladies line from its mainstream product line and even sold both through the same outlets. In 1999, however, Giordano took advantage of the boom that followed the Asian currency crisis in many parts of Asia, to aggressively relaunch its "Giordano Ladies" line, which subsequently met with great success.

Hence, merchandise planning is the scientific process of meticulous sales forecasting and inventory management strategically aligned with the art of identifying the merchandise that appeals to targeted customer base. The significance of merchandise planning is evident from the fact that while the retailer suffers from lost sales as a result of insufficient stock, it also suffers loss because margins are squeezed when unsold merchandise is marked down at the end of a season. So here the decision makers need to find the ideal balance between the two extremes. For this purpose, retailers are using the technologies that enable them to integrate their assortment plans with their shelf optimization system to ensure the right products are placed on the right shelves. They leverage technology to continuously compare the assortment plan with in-season sales and inventory performance to generate alerts when overstocks and understocks are forecast. So it eventually helps them by ensuring each assortment is attractive to the target customers and will support their bottom line. Here, company gets benefited from faster inventory turns, decreased lost sales, and fewer markdowns.

Hence, the essence of merchandise planning is enshrined in the following 7R model.

7R Model of Merchandise Planning Process

- Right product
- Right quality
- Right price
- Right quantity
- Right placement of the product in the store
- Right merchandise mix
- Right time

The whole purpose of merchandise planning is the optimization of the 7R (seven rights) so that the objectives of higher sales, lower inventory holding, and profit maximization are achieved.

Today, in the era of e-commerce, stores no longer need to carry the full range of assortment physically in store and can leverage technology to display the merchandise virtually through online channels. Retailers are increasingly adopting the formats like kiosks and also providing mobile devices like tablets to the store associates to show the extended assortment. In such cases, retailers do not need to carry stock for the full range of merchandise on the floor, with fringe sizes, colors, and so on. This leads to reduction in inventory levels and hence reduction in space utilization for stock rooms that can be added to the floor space. However, it has to be executed strategically because reducing stock in store can put pressure on the fulfillment capabilities where customer is asking for same- or next-day delivery with option to select a convenient location and time to receive the delivery.

Example: Chumbak

Chumbak is a Bengaluru-based lifestyle products start-up. The start-up has strong visibility both online and off-line at its exclusive stores and MBOs. After traveling for years and collecting souvenirs from different parts of the world, the founders of Chumbak, Vivek Prabhakar and Shubhra Chadda, realized that India has very little to offer its visitors in terms of gifts and souvenirs that represent the vibrant nature of this beautiful country in its true colors. The founders were a little fed up of the usual marble Taj Mahal replicas and handicrafts that were becoming the only option and thought that travelers deserve more options that should be trendy, fashionable, stylish, and colorful and still represented the soul of India. That is when the husband and wife duo decided to launch Chumbak in 2010 after understanding the growth and potential of the market with its first ever product line: fridge magnets. "Chumbak" means "magnet" in Hindi, and this inspired them to name their brand as Chumbak. Putting this idea at the center, they built strong business around extraordinary designed and crafted lifestyle products, including apparel and footwear, bags and wallets, souvenirs, key chains, and jewelry that are colorful and attractive.

They started with accessories in 2010, added "home" category in 2014, and added "apparel" in 2015, bringing the trinity of lifestyle under one roof. Meanwhile, they undertook an exercise to redefine Chumbak's design language itself. In this initiative, they transformed from the old India themed designs, which was more character driven, to what they call now "India inspired," which display different colors and design sensibility of India. The idea behind was well-designed and crafted products that could be used as accessories and gift items, which are always in demand.

Thus, the business model of spotting trends and developing products along those lines is a continuous process. As the new products are introduced, old ones, for which demand dips, are removed. The entire planning, designing, and production is in-house.

Example: Bombay Dyeing

No brands want to lose touch with the customer. And a strong legacy is not always a guarantee against that. Bombay Dyeing, the flagship brand of Wadia Group is now shaking off its reverie. Its home furnishing products such as bedsheets and pillowcases that were earlier characterized by pastel and flower prints are now sporting pops of bright colors complemented with the launch of new ad campaign. The 135-year-old Bombay Dyeing's bid to connect with the young customer is by customer survey that says the young shopper does not perceive it as modern or progressive. Bombay Dyeing has launched Neon Pops as its latest collection in soft furnishing, to talk to a much younger crowd than its previous catchments. It has launched seven collections to target men, young couples, and so on; also over the last six or seven years, it has been tying up with leading designers to launch collections that have always been priced at a huge premium. However this time, it is also overhauling the stores to give it a modern look and feel, better customer service, and right merchandising mix.

The new approach is more of a solution-based selling because earlier people would pick up whatever they felt like, but now when the customer buys a bedsheet, the salesperson in the store helps him to coordinate it with towels, rugs, and so on. They are majorly focusing on to add more stores to its company-owned stores fleet and revamping the existing ones with the core belief that they can do a better job than a franchisee in customer service and brand experience. With this brick-and-mortar presence, Bombay Dyeing is also present on e-commerce portals, the New Age shopping destination. Apart from selling on Amazon, FabFurnish, and Flipkart, its own site retails its designs.

Also as far as e-retailers are concerned, the leading fashion retailer Jabong has added three more international brands to its catalogs of over 1,000 brands. UK's high-street fashion brands River Island and Blue Saint have made their debut in India on the portal. The popular Mango, too, would be available on the portal, besides its own website. These brands are expected to stand Jabong in good stead as leading online fashion retailers are battling each other less over price and more over the exclusivity of their assortment. Myntra, Jabong's key rival, has launched the Dutch lifestyle fashion brand Scotch & Soda, adding to its pool of over 650 brands and designer collections. Earlier, Myntra had roped in Desigual and Harvard Lifestyle that sell exclusively through the portal. This is because of evolution of consumer choices and also attributes to increasing inclination of customers toward fast fashion and international brands.

Merchandise Hierarchy

The merchandise hierarchy defines the planning of the merchandise mix for a retail organization. The merchandise hierarchy is defined as the organized group of the merchandise mix at different levels, depending on the complexity of the retailer and product that it wishes to sell. The grouping can have up to seven levels as depicted in Figure 6.1. The definition of merchandise hierarchy establishes the fulcrum to develop a retail outlet merchandise mix. The hierarchy starts with the division of a large organization and percolates down to a specific SKU. Utilizing the concept of merchandise hierarchy to develop a store merchandise mix leads to the following advantages:

1. Quantification of merchandise mix elements at each level of merchandise hierarchy. It helps in concrete ordering and stocking information.
2. In case of any problem, analysis can drill down to rungs of hierarchy right up to SKU level.
3. Development of mix enables a merchandiser to add or remove mix elements based on real-time performance feedback.

This also helps in developing a decision matrix among the management hierarchy that is aligned to merchandising hierarchy, which, in turn, escalates remedial issues at an appropriate level.

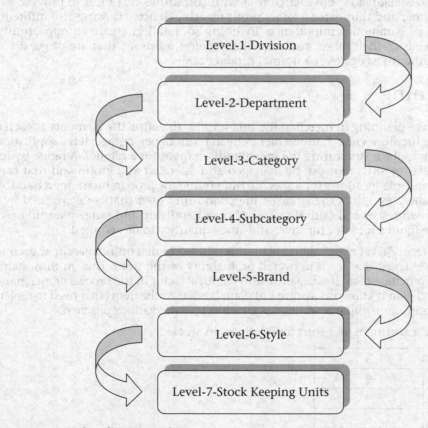

Figure 6.1: *Merchandise Hierarchy*

Improving Product Range and Stock Selection: A Small Story

Knowing what best customers buy frequently helps choose which lines to stock and which lines to expand on. The owner of a small suburban supermarket in the UK had some 12 months' notice that a large national supermarket was opening right over the road from him. He realized that without major changes he would not survive. What he did was simple but a smart move. The suburb in which he was situated was mixed, having mainly low-cost housing but also a very exclusive area. Many of his customers were low earners who bought their basic requirements every day or two from him—in essence, what they could carry home in a couple of bags. He knew that they would migrate to the lower prices and bigger ranges of the big chain. However, a considerable number of the more wealthy people would call in on their way home from work to pick up bread and milk and a few odds and ends. He started noting what they bought, and what they never bought. Over the months, he stopped ordering products that they never bought, and increased his range of things that they did buy. Over the year, his store slowly transformed from a small supermarket to a very big store selling ready-to-cook food, other delicacies, and exotic food items. His wealthy customers referred him to their friends and the composition of his customer base changed from mainly low earners to mainly high earners. When the supermarket opened over the road, his low earners did migrate, but he hardly noticed the difference.

Thus, the right bundling of product is more powerful than selling single products. For instance, Donut King offers its consumers a customized milk shake, converting a US$3 item to a US$9 sale. Also McDonald's sells French fries with soft drinks in a meal to provide added value to the consumer and thus earns a larger profit margin. Hence, knowing and influencing the customers are of paramount importance. By doing so, retailers create an opportunity to understand the needs of their target audience and develop solutions that are of great value, thus gaining a competitive edge over a normal product sale.

Range Planning

The concept of range planning in merchandise mix implies to define the elements at each and every rung of a specific store's merchandise hierarchy in terms of percentage. It is a sophisticated and highly flexible tool for structuring the merchandise ranges for a retailer. A range basically consists of a number of SKUs that can be managed and operated as a group and that can be allocated one or multiple locations for a specific time frame for procurement, merchandising, and sales. At the apex level, it is the strategic merchandising plan that is determined by top management and defines several critical factors of merchandising and range planning. These largely include the figures for sales turnover and stock quantity to be acquired.

Subsequently, a category-level merchandise plan is developed to determine margin at each level (right up to the SKU level) that leads to overall profitability of the store. This, in turn, helps in developing "OTB" purchase plan. It is usually the first critical factor in the process of merchandise planning. Next level plan is known as assortment plan. It refers to the items that need to replenish the store stock to minimum and maximum stocking level for the various products.

An example of the assortment of a shirt for 30 pieces in stock:

Small	3
Medium	9
Large	9
X'tra Large	6
X'tra X'tra Large	3

In the earlier example, the assortment ratio is built on stock turn of 30 pieces for a specific type of shirt. This results in establishing the replenishment cycle depending on the category of merchandise.

Stock Keeping Unit

- Every product available at the store has a unique code.
- This code that helps in the identification and tracking of the products at the retail store is called as SKU.
- The retailer feeds each and every SKU in the master computer and can easily track the product in the stock just by entering the SKU number.
- Assigning a unique code to each single merchandise unit avoids unnecessary searching.

Let us consider the example of Numero Uno, which stocks denims, shirts, and T-shirts and targets both men and women.

SKU for Shirts:

NU: M-40-FL-W or NU: M-38-FL-B

Here,

NU stands for Numero Uno

M for men

40 (collar size)

FL (full sleeves)

W (white, color of the shirt)

Similarly, the letter "B" in the second example would stand for "blue."

Thus, searching for NU-M-40-FL-W would let the retailer know whether the particular merchandise is available in the stock or not.

The Buying Process

Merchandise buying is a critical function for any retail organizations. Procurement takes top priority when profits are under pressure and competitors offer more. Purchase managers share best practices and map the future of this behind-the-scenes pillar of a retail organization.

As discussed earlier, the first step in this process is the development of OTB plan. Development of such a plan helps retailer to project and control future buying. Proper development of such plan leads to the right flow of merchandise to the store, aligned with anticipated sales levels at desired stock turn values.

Open-to-buy Control

As the name of the term itself suggests, OTB is the amount of unspent money that is available for purchasing merchandise that will be delivered during a given period of time. The fundamental aspect of OTB is to determine the amount of money that is to be spent on purchases of new (and existing) merchandise, which is essentially based on budgeted sales and budgeted stock on hand levels.

OTB is the retail measure as to whether forward orders are above or below the needs of the business relative to anticipated sales performance per merchandise category. OTB control (or OTB management) prevents over- or understocks, both of which are unfavorable to retailer's profitability. Hence, OTB numbers are generally maintained per department, but with the changing consumer behavior and preference, retailers tend to maintain OTB number by sub-department, brand, store, and so on.

> Open-to-buy (at the beginning of the month) = Planned purchases for the month – Outstanding orders that have to be delivered that month

The merchandise control can be worked out by effectively using the data that are available through the rupee planning procedures. A buyer is guided by the timing and quantity goals established in the six month of seasonal rupee plan for purchasing the merchandise. Hence, the buyer refers to a merchandising figure called open-to-buy (OTB), to gain even tighter control on the amount (volume) of merchandise received in a specific period and to prepare very precise sales and stock plans. This is the amount of money that has been allocated to purchases of the particular department (or brand, etc.) for delivery in the designated period. Hence, OTB basically shows the amount of unspent money that is available for purchasing merchandise that will be delivered during a given period of time.

For instance, if the retail business under consideration has long lead times, then the retailer need to update its OTB figures as supplier orders are placed in order to determine available OTB. Here the retailers need to update the available OTB figures for the current period as stock arrives.

It is usually calculated on a monthly basis and indicates that the buyer has not yet spent all the planned purchases or receipts for the period under consideration. Hence, it essentially represents the difference between the planned purchases for a given period and the merchandise orders placed already for the period under consideration.

While the planned purchase figure for a particular month indicates the sum available for purchasing merchandise during that month, it does not reflect the distribution of the money throughout the month. So buyers need to attempt to distribute the purchases over the entire month, and this enables them to:

- Replace or reorder fast-selling goods.
- Fill in stocks to make sure that complete stocks are offered.
- Gain competitive advantage by buying special purchases and/or interesting and new items as and when they are available.
- Explore the offering of new resources.

The unfilled orders, also called as open orders or "on order," are needed to be realized in or charged to in those months during which the delivery is expected. Because by doing this, the buyer is in better position to control by effectively correlating buying activities with selling activities. The function of this control is to identify the deviations between actual results and planned goals and hence the buyer can take corrective measures accordingly.

This process, if managed well, leads to positive cash flows. The benefits of OTB planning are:

1. Prevention of overbuying
2. Elimination of confusion
3. Enablement of a store toward profit maximization

OTB plan has the following characteristics:

1. Process of sales forecasting
2. Alignment of purchases with sales
3. Budget setting for sales
4. Determining merchandising inventory levels
5. Monitoring OTB amount outlay

This *process* also requires sales forecasts and efficient OTB plans. In a retail store, efficient inventory planning achieves the following benefit:

1. Optimization of purchase control
2. Achievement of planned stock terms
3. Ensuring freshness through "JIT" (just-in-time) concept
4. Achievement of customer delight through multitude of product offer

It is important for retailers to use an OTB plan, as most of the retailers tend to overstock when sales are on upsurge and, many times, understock when they feel sales are on downswing. In a sense, OTB helps a merchandiser to get a focus on the actual amount of stock that should be in his/her inventory at the start of a month as well as the levels that should be received during the month. Today, retailers are increasingly using the advanced and integrated IT systems and enterprise resource planning (ERP) solutions for having integrated OTB. Retailers just need to maintain the budgets by the OTB classifications they want (e.g., department or brand), and the system maintains the OTB figures automatically.

Example: Giordano

In order to maximize use of store space for sales opportunities, a central distribution center replaced the function of a back storeroom in its outlets. IT was used to facilitate inventory management and demand forecasting. When an item was sold, the barcode information—identifying size, color, style, and price—was recorded by the POS cash register and transmitted to the company's main computer. At the end of each day, the information was compiled at the store level and sent to the sales department and distribution center. The compiled sales information became the store's order for the following day. Orders were filled during the night and were ready for delivery by early morning, ensuring that new inventory was already on the shelves before a Giordano store opened for business.

Another advantage of its IT system was that information was disseminated to production facilities in real time. Such information allowed customers' purchase patterns to be studied, and this provided valuable input to its manufacturing operations, resulting in fewer problems and costs related to slow-moving inventory. The use of IT also allowed more efficient inventory holding. Giordano's inventory turnover on sales was reduced from 58 days in 1996 to merely 28 days in 2008. Its excellent inventory management reduced costs and allowed reasonable margins, while still allowing Giordano to reinforce its value-for-money philosophy. All in all, despite the relatively lower margins than those of its peers, Giordano was still able to post healthy profits. Such efficiency became a crucial factor when periodic price wars occurred.

Advantages of an Open-to-buy Plan

The advantages that a retailer derives from an OTB process are as follows:

1. Enables a retailer in estimating working capital requirement needed to be deployed in inventory, month on month.

Table 6.1: *OTB Terms*

OTB Terms	
Term	**Meaning**
Forward sales planning	The sales planning should be prepared for the entire year with month-wise details of sales. A good OTB plan helps in determining variations in sales
Forward cover	This implies quantities to be held on the planned stock turns for the retail outlet. Three-month stock is the ideal forward cover of "stock turns" for four times in a year.
Stock required	This is based on the forward cover planned for the store
Opening stock	The value of the opening stock is a merchandise inflow calculation. The first entry is an estimate for the first month. Subsequently, the opening stock is the closing stock figure of the previous month
Intake requirement	This is the difference between the required stock and the opening stock
On order	These are stocks that have been already ordered and due for delivery during the relevant period
Open to receive	This figure is arrived at by deducting the stock on order, if any, from the intake requirement. It is the inverse of "OTB" quantity
Closing stock to arrive	To arrive at this figure, one needs to take the opening stock, subtract the sales, and add the on-order and open-to-receive quantities

2. Attainment of best possible gross margin return on investment (GMROI) by ensuring right inventory levels.
3. Restrains a retailer on merchandise purchase commitment and enables a store to receive right amount of merchandise on right time.
4. Enables an inflow of fresh merchandise for a store during a particular sales season.
5. Provides a comparison of performance as per the established plan and remedial action to be taken in any specific area.
6. Assists merchandiser in getting his/her store maximum profitability.

The retail organizations that develop and implement efficient OTB plans are generally successful in their merchandising and buying activities. In most modern retail organizations, the merchandise management system software supports the quantitative approaches like OTB plans (Table 6.1). Retailers are increasingly focusing on adopting the technologies that enable them to integration between OTB plan and your purchasing system on real-time basis. However, at the end of the day, it is also the buyers' specific insight and decision-making capability that leads to optimal result.

Category Management

Category management is one of the crucial functions in retailing in which the total range of merchandise sold by a retailer is broken down into separate groups of similar or related products; these groups are known as product categories. In a merchandise group, a category is defined as a type of products that leads to fulfillment of similar needs and wants of a customer. For instance, examples of apparel categories may be formal menswear, ethnic women's wear, seasonal wear, and so on. Each category is then operated like a "mini business unit" in its own right, with its own set of turnover and/or profitability targets and strategies. Typically, the products in a category, in a retail environment, are displayed and, by and large, bought by customers in a group. So category management is also a process that involves not only managing product categories as business units but also customizing them (on a store-by-store basis) to satisfy the customer needs. That is why at grocery stores in India, all types of pulses and lentils are shelved together. Walmart's Store of the Community, implemented in North America, is one of the few examples where product offerings are customized right down to the specific store. This helps a customer in making choice faster and thus enhances their shopping experience.

Example: Aviraté

Aviraté is an international high-street fashion label that appeals to every woman's sense of style and sensuality. Aviraté (adopted from the Sanskrit word *avirati*, meaning sensuality), owned by a leading Sri Lankan apparel manufacturer Timex and Fergasam Group, introduced the brand in India in 2011. The brand leveraged its global fashion DNA and managed to expand over 14 stores in major Indian cities. The brand fulfills a growing demand for western wear by Indian women and forayed into the competitive Indian retail market, after having established a global reputation as a high-quality apparel manufacturer for over four decades for some of the most reputed international brands worldwide. Their target groups of customers are ladies who appreciate quality, are fashion conscious, well-traveled, and have had exposure to global fashion. In India, the popularity this category of western formal attire for women has increased significantly. The segment has seen a phenomenal growth rate and acceptance coupled with increasing popularity among Indian women shoppers. The triggering factors for the segment to grow are increasing number of working women, higher disposable income and desire to dress smart, befitting the occasion, and increasing inclination of women shoppers toward smart and comfortable western wear. Driven by such factors, Aviraté brought a range of formal dresses, aimed at crafting a new meaning to the personality of an Indian woman. From being a core dress wear brand, Aviraté has expanded its product portfolio to fashion tops, tunics, trendy bottom wear, lingerie, accessories, and footwear. This has been imperative product strategy to support the essence of complete wardrobe creation and addressing the lifestyle needs of the women customers. In the market like India where most of the international brands catering the segment are present, what Aviraté intends to do is to give a key differentiator in their product offerings. As the target customers are exposed to global fashion now and their aspirations are benchmarked against global giants, they are more demanding and seek for a greater value.

However, the language and grammar required for expressing the narrative posed by classy and westernized occasion are alien to the target audience. This is the space Aviraté operates in, to empower the Indian women to confidently express her in a fashionable, westernized dressing solution. As a larger number of women are choosing to dress up for every occasion, the strategic blending of category management in line with brand positioning has brought with it a multitude of occasions like evening dos, casual brunch, formal get-together parties, business meetings, business get-together, conferences, and so on. Hence by providing appropriate retail experience, service levels, and merchandise offering helped the expansion of the retailer brand across the chain.

Therefore, category management is an important part of the whole process of merchandising as was explained in Figure 6.1. It is formally defined as the process of managing categories leading to optimum profitability for each managed category. Many researchers feel that

Table 6.2: *Category Management*

Category Management	
Term	**Definition**
Category vision	This refers to the view of top management on each category, which is a must for leaders in order to achieve customer satisfaction or value offering and the differentiation
Category definition	This is based on customer segmentation and the specific SKUs belonging to the category. For example, a broad category definition can be "soft drinks," a subcategory can be "aerated soft drinks," and one of the SKUs within the same can be "Pepsi 500 ml"
Category assessment	The category assessment is done to identify gaps, if any, between the category vision and the existing SKUs contribution to the category. This assessment helps improve the category's business by identifying opportunity gaps in sales, stocks, and profits
Category balanced score card	This helps to measure the performance of the retail business. It establishes specific business targets to the category while reflecting on its performance
Category strategies	These aim at achieving the best of customer off-take from the shelves, ringing in the maximum number of transactions, earning maximum margins, and achieving certain subjective goals like excitement and sensationalism for customer satisfaction
Category tactics	Category tactics refer to the tactical requirements to achieve the score card targets. These tactics are compared with others to create a competition to attain the best advantage and edge. They are centered around the areas of assortment, pricing, space planning, promotions, and so on.
Category implementation and review	This refers to the store-level execution of the category business plan and strategies and monitoring category performance against the plan to take action on an ongoing basis

concept of category management in retailing is akin to group production in manufacturing industry. In both, product groups become the focal point for attention of the management (Table 6.2).

The fashion powerhouse Madura Fashion & Lifestyle, which operates brands like Van Heusen, Louis Philippe, and Allen Solly, among over half a dozen other marquee brands, has launched its online shopping portal Trendin.com. It is the largest online portal of any brick-and-mortar retailer in the country. Trendin.com is run by a completely independent management team and having dedicated warehouses and partnership with many tech start-ups. This gives a unique flexibility and agility to the platform, as the portal is basically built by in-house engineering team of Trendin. To bring the synergy among different functions and verticals, the search queries on Trendin are shared with Madura's merchandising team. This provides them with valuable inputs regarding the upcoming trends and preferred patterns, which eventually help them forecast demand better across the different categories and assortments. The merchandise that is moving faster or getting searched more online is stocked at the brick-and-mortar outlets too. All these strategic advantages give it an inherent strength of product mix and service, which is now crucial for success.

Financial Merchandise Management

In retail industry, it is relatively easy to showcase fast growth in revenues in the case of brick-and-mortar retailers while in terms of GMV in the case of e-retailing. These numbers can be achieved by opening new stores at a rapid pace or by discounting significantly and frequently. But when it comes to profitability, it is seldom sustainable in the long run. One of the most effective and sustainable ways to grow profitably in retail is by developing a robust inventory and SCM systems. There exists a direct relationship between inventory turnover and company turnover. This approach essentially enables the retailers to respond fast or to maintain low lead time, which is one of the key success factors of the business. By virtue of the importance of inventory management, retailers focus on financial merchandise management in a more organized way. There are numerous cases where reduced inventory cycles have resulted in better supplier, shelf space, and people management, and, eventually, in higher savings and better margins. This becomes even more significant in the case of the categories that are facing low margins, high value investment, seasonal, slow moving, and/or high levels of obsolescence.

Here the financial merchandise management comes for the rescue by helping the retailer to determine exactly which merchandise is to be purchased, when merchandise is purchased, and in what quantity to be purchased and repurchased. It helps retailers manage the merchandise planning process across the organization using top-down and bottom-up financial plans to drive earnings and financial results in line with corporate objectives. While the "dollar control" involves planning and monitoring, the inventory investment made during a given period of time, unit control relates to the quantities of merchandise handled in that period. Thus, the financial merchandise management incorporates methods of accounting, merchandise forecasting and budgeting, unit control systems, and *integrated dollar and unit controls*.

Merchandise forecasting and budgeting is a form of dollar control with six stages: designating control units, sales forecasting, inventory-level planning, reduction planning, planning purchases, and planning profit margins. Adjustments at any point in the process require all later stages to be modified accordingly.

1. *Selection of control units*: Control units are merchandise categories for which data are gathered. They must be narrow enough to isolate problems and opportunities with specific product lines.
2. By *sales forecasting*, expected future sales are estimated for a given time period. A key stage in the merchandising and budgeting process because its accuracy affects so many other stages.
3. Through *inventory-level planning*, a retailer sets merchandise quantities for specified periods; techniques include the basic stock, percentage variation, weeks' supply, and stock-to-sales methods.
4. *Reduction planning* incorporates expected (or anticipated) markdowns, employee or other discounts, and stock shortages.
5. *Planned purchases* are keyed to planned sales, reductions, ending inventory, and beginning inventory.
6. *Planning profit margins* are related to a retailer's planned net sales, operating expenses, profit, and reductions.

Hence, merchandise financial planning is a precise approach toward setting an organization's sales, margin, and inventory targets. Retailers can plan and forecast key performance metrics such as sales and inventory across multiple categories, selling channels, and time periods, and incorporate key attributes to align their planning process around consumer preferences. It is basically a initial (or high-level) step in the retail planning process wherein the merchandise planning teams can plan their business without getting caught up in the lower-level details of the merchandise hierarchy.

This tool also manages an organization's traditional OTB and offers the flexibility to choose their own planning calendar and manage strategic plan targets across any period within the time dimension. The merchandise managers can make changes or improvisations to merchandise financial plans at the highest and lowest levels within the defined merchandise hierarchy.

Benefits of Financial Merchandise Plans

Financial merchandise planning helps the retailers to enhance their merchandise and inventory planning processes and increases productivity for planners by helping them to:

- Expand enterprise-wide visibility to financial metrics, and adjust business goals in line with changing trends.
- Determine and study the inventory investment in relation to planned and actual revenues and to develop financial planning—key financial reconciliation, merchandising, channels, and finance.
- Effectively plan the value and amount of inventory in each department and/or store unit during a given period and to develop merchandise planning—key item planning and seasonal flow.
- Focus on attributes that matter most to their customer to align merchandise mix with customer preferences.
- Drive assortment planning, item planning, and store planning and manage OTB in season to increase sales, margin, and turn across all categories.
- Specify the amount of merchandise a buyer can purchase during a given period and to develop assortment space planning—logical assortments fitting into physical selling space.
- Estimate beginning-of-month and end-of-month inventory levels that help in determining the retailer's space requirements.
- Determine stock shortages and to uncover the bookkeeping errors and shrinkage.
- Classify slow-moving items, leading to increased sales efforts or markdowns.
- Maintain and keep an appropriate balance between inventory and out-of-stock conditions.
- Rapidly develop "what if" scenarios for key performance metrics to determine effective alternative strategies.
- Implement best-practice models that support financial planning process for physical retail, online retail, and omni-channel retail—configured to each channel's unique characteristics and demands.
- Rate buyer's performance and to set standards by using the measures.

Integrating Dollar and Unit Merchandising Control

Three aspects of financial inventory control integrate dollar and unit control concepts:

- Stock turnover and GMROI—when to reorder and how much to reorder. Stock turnover is the number of times during a period that the average inventory on hand is sold. GMROI shows the relationship between the gross margin in dollars (total dollar operating profits) and average inventory investment (at cost).

- A reorder point calculation—when to reorder—includes the retailer's usage rate, order lead time, and safety stock.
- The economic order quantity—how much to reorder. This helps a retailer in choosing how big an order to place based on both ordering and inventory costs.

GMROI brings together other KPIs (key performance measures) such as return on assets, asset turnover, sales, and profit margins. As discussed, inventory is basically an investment, and that way, it becomes crucial for retailers to keep a close watch on returns they are getting from their investment in inventory. For this, they assess the ROI from inventory investment. Hence, the gross margin percentage provides the retailers with insights into how much of the investment is being returned for each type of merchandise purchased. In short, "GMROI" and "inventory turnover" calculations give them a clear picture of how their inventory is performing, which is essential for more profitable and dynamic inventory decisions. Here the inventory turnover is a measure of how many times a store sells its average investment in inventory during a year, which gives them a clear idea about the productivity of the merchandise being purchased. In a nutshell, faster the merchandise turns over that is bought, marked, stocked, displayed, and sold, the more is the profitability of the retail outlet. Hence, it depicts how quickly the merchandise is moving.

GMROI = Gross margin percentage stock-to-sales ratio

Gross margin percentage = Gross margin ($) ÷ Net sales

Stock-to-sales ratio = Net sales ÷ Average inventory (at cost)

Hence,

GMROI = Gross margin ÷ Average inventory (at cost)

Inventory turnover = Net sales (at retail) ÷ Average inventory (at retail)

And

Inventory turnover = Cost of merchandise sold (at cost) ÷ Average inventory (at cost)

And

Inventory turnover (in units) = Number of merchandise units sold for the year ÷ Average inventory (at cost)

Hence, these simple calculations enable the retailer to measure the stock productivity, and it is the dynamic planning process and practice that enable the retailers to easily adjust their plans and forecasts to respond to changes in demand or other variables that impact margin and turn. Here the approach is that all physical planning and execution needs to be handled by the supply chain solutions in coordination with the planning imperatives. The current economic scenario has forced organizations to focus on increased cash flows. It is the reality of the market that, with the difficult credit markets, retailers are struggling to meet working capital requirements. These market realities reinforce the significant impact that company's SCM and inventory management can have on its cash position. Hence, this highlights the importance of ability to forecast, plan, and dynamically manage fulfillment, which eventually has an impact on both cash and costs. While inefficient supply chain adversely affects organization's cash position, lack of end-to-end visibility in supply chain results in inventory buildup and in turn increases cost.

Snapshot

- The lack of a dynamic inventory planning capability can result in excess inventory buildup.

- Ineffective expediting techniques can lead to degradation of supplier on-time delivery.
- The failure to benchmark freight rates and failure to monitor the use of lowest-cost carriers can increase freight costs significantly.

Each of these deficiencies in processes leads to loss of cash, which adversely affect organization's operations. The cumulative impact of this loss of cash affects company's strategic competitiveness and shrinks profitability. For instance, the potential to maximize margins by buying a fast-moving item is much more than the loss of sale due to nonavailability of the item.

Hence, optimization of end-to-end supply chain solutions brings in the operational efficiencies, which include:

- Improved forecasting and inventory management
- Effective sourcing and efficient supplier management
- Streamlined order fulfillment management
- Efficient and effective logistics management
- Enhanced aftermarket services (AMS)

Improved Demand Forecasting

In today's VUCA (volatile, uncertainty, complexity, ambiguity) times, challenging global economic scenario and rapidly changing consumer behavior, preferences, and patterns, there is a risk associated with the demand forecasting based on historical data. So when demand goes into a dark room, more accurate and meticulous forecasting process allows for faster responses and forecast corrections aligned with the demand fluctuations.

Benefits

- Improved service level and significant reduction in cost associated to inventory.
- Reduction in sourcing cost by synchronized demand planning and sales forecasting.
- Using market intelligence, data analytics, and a closed-loop approach to statistical output for improvements in forecast accuracy.

Inventory Optimization

Organizations are increasingly adopting a customized and dynamic approach to inventory management and planning, especially to those factors in variability within the planning cycle. This allows them to take calculated decisions and effectively manage the interface of risk and inventory.

Benefits

- Reduction in inventory by using a multilevel approach toward material and distribution requirement planning.
- Reduction in inventory through improved visibility of inventory across the supply chain.
- Reduction in inventory buildup through improved visibility on material scheduling.
- Reduction in total cost of ownership (TCO) by accurate and meticulous demand forecasting and space management.

Sourcing and Procuring

The sourcing and procurement process has direct impact on the retailer's profitability. So if managed effectively, it can reduce the TCO for the merchandise that the retailers buy.

Benefits

- Compliance-driven savings by analyzing contracted saving using spend analysis.
- Elimination of defective sourcing through process standardization and enhanced supplier communications.

Fulfillment and Logistics

An efficient fulfillment and logistics network is the essential for best-in-class supply chain. Thus, retailers are moving to periodic network redesign and are increasing focusing on benchmarking their carrier's cost and performance. They are leveraging technologies and implementing processes to achieve greater visibility into their in-transit inventory.

Benefits

- Improvement in consolidation and efficient utilization of assets by monitoring metrics.
- Improvement in savings in freight costs through periodic network analysis and monitoring key metrics in a dynamic environment.
- Reduced usage of spots and expedites by monitoring LLC usage and benchmarking.
- Minimization of contracted penalty payments using initiatives to reduce payment leakages.

Aftermarket Services

AMS or after-sales services is a tool for providing a great last-mile delivery experience and hence a great overall shopping experience to the customer. This eventually helps the retailer to satisfy the customers and increase the customer loyalty. The retailers that perform on this parameter can successfully retain the customers on a long-term basis and also reduce cost and improve productivity within their AMS operations.

Benefits

- Reduction in service cost and improvement in asset uptime by using remote monitoring.
- Reduction in warranty costs by auditing majority of claims through an efficient audit reasoning matrix.
- Improvement in customer response time and delivery time through consolidation.
- Improvement in supplier warranty recoveries through efficient management of reverse logistics function.

Caselet: Vaibhav Global

In this challenging global economic environment, the one online retail company that deserves to be mentioned here is Vaibhav Global Limited (VGL). VGL is a Jaipur-based online retailer of affordable fashion jewelry, watches, bags, and home décor in the Canada, USA, Ireland, and

197

UK. Vaibhav Global basically targets middle-class consumers in these countries. VGL is listed in India and was incorporated in 1982 and went public around 1995. It started reworking on its strategy around 2010 and decided to bring down the price points of its merchandise to an average of US$18–20 per piece as compared to an average price of US$100 per piece after the 2008–2009 global financial crises, which significantly eroded the buying power of its target customer base in the USA.

This can be worked out effectively only because of its exceptionally efficient merchandise management, marketing management, sourcing and other procurement strategies and operations, and supply chain and inventory capabilities. Vaibhav Global's sourcing infrastructure is spread across the major procurement hubs of the world (like China, Bali, Bangkok, Thailand, and Indonesia) and extends to its low-cost, high-quality manufacturing facility in Jaipur. It possesses over 65,000 designs comprising fashion and fine jewelry, fashion accessories, and other lifestyle products (office and home décor). Its in-house PLBs comprise Rhapsody, ILIANA, J Francis, Elanza, FH, Karis, Geno, Strada, and Eon1865.

Today, it is one of the world's few exceptionally profitable online discount jewelry and lifestyle accessory retailers. This is evident from the numbers given here. VGL recorded consolidated gross revenue of around ₹1,376 crore for the year ended March 31, 2015 (registering an increase of 6% on a year-on-year basis). It reported a gross profit margin of 60%, a profit after tax of about ₹103 crore in FY15, return on employed capital of 43%, and return on equity of 40%. During 2014–2015, the company's cash profits enabled it to rationalize debt and emerge as a net zero-debt company.

The company claims that it maintains an average price point of US$18–20 per piece for its products (it generated average per product realizations of US$18–20 in 2014–2015) and thus generating volumes. VGL has leveraged major satellite television providers and television distributors (like AT&T, DishTV, DIRECTV, and Verizon, among others) to access the US market. This facilitates VGL to reach millions of households 24×7, which is further complemented by a web presence (www.liquidationchannel.com) and its call center for fast customer service and response. VGL progressively expanded its US coverage of TV households, improved the positioning of its home-shopping TV channels, and migrated to HD broadcast signal. Around 75% of their merchandise is sold through television channels, while the remaining is through the online portal. Around 70% of its revenues come from the USA, and the remaining from UK. This essentially enabled it to consolidate and leverage its scale economies across procurement, last-mile delivery operations, and advertising (procuring airtime), and eventually to reduce costs. It ships around 95% of its orders within 48 hours of order placement.

VGL implemented a number of technology initiatives that enhanced customer proximity. It implemented an advanced TV business management platform across its US operations. It adapted to an SAP-based HR information platform. It initiated the process of launching an SAP-based web platform on the Hybris framework that intensifies and expands its web customer engagement. It is also leveraging the mobile app technology in the USA, extending its access to new customers on a sales channel that is gaining traction rapidly. Simultaneously, it is looking for some other mature markets for television sales and evaluating entry into markets like Japan, Korea, or Germany, among others, in near future.

The company also performs well on the CSR front. For this, VGL has partnered with Akshaya Patra, a not-for-profit organization, that works extensively for the causes like hunger and malnutrition in India. The Akshaya Patra Foundation encourages organizations and individuals with philanthropic values to collaborate with them, in order to fight the dual issues of hunger and illiteracy among children in India by implementing the Mid-day Meal Scheme in the government schools and government-aided schools.

This collaboration has given a boost to Mid-day Meal Program in Jaipur initiated for offering quality meals to underprivileged students across schools in the area. This program covers over 140 schools in Jaipur with logistics support for the entire operation feeding to around 15,000 students in a day. The CSR model is based on a very unique concept in itself. For each unit of merchandise (e.g., one piece of jewelry) sold in the retailer's UK-based home-shopping television channel, two meals are provided in India. Hence, instead of spending certain percentage to the cause from the overall profit base, the company donates a fair share on every chunk of revenue the company generates on continuous basis. The company is intending to expand the span and scale of the program continuously and gradually.

All these initiatives, whether related to business or social cause, reinforce that VGL is not only committed toward a business model that creates an economic value but also contribute toward the society. This eventually results in enhanced shareholder and stakeholder value and leads the path toward a sustainable development.

Private-label Brands

The definition of private-label branding has evolved significantly over time. Some would argue the term "private label" is a misnomer of great proportions. There is no question that the words "private label" acknowledge the birth, history, and existence of generic and store brands. Yet, the term does not adequately capture the extent to which PL has progressed. Today's retail marketers are managing their proprietary brands with the same combination of care and innovation as manufacturers of national brands.

In recent years, retailers have been liberating themselves from the traditional definition of private-label marketing as being the poor relative of national brand consumer goods, and, in doing so, opening up huge opportunities for private-label branding. These opportunities require the adoption of a different set of marketing and branding practices to support and propel the retailer's business and marketing ideals for its PLBs.

The key to successful marketing management for today's retailers is to understand the contribution and role of their proprietary or "own" brands in the long-term business strategy and marketing mix of the retail store and consider both the supply side and the demand side of the equation. Effective category management can enable retailers to solidify and optimize supply chain relationships. Strategic brand management goes hand in hand with these endeavors to establish sustainable PODs in each aisle and segment within the store. It also spurs decisions about how to appropriately define the retailer's "own" brand portfolio in order to galvanize consumers to connect and reconnect with its franchise in a compelling manner.

Historical Marketplace Dynamics

The private-label phenomenon has leapfrogged in India compared to other Asian countries for many reasons: the value-conscious Indian shopper, their familiarity and comfort with unbranded/generic products, and the focus on quality of private-label products on behalf of the retailers. The Indian market can stand testimony to successful business models for PLBs.

PLBs were traditionally defined as generic product offerings that competed with their national brand counterparts by means of a price–value proposition. Irrespective of the route to the market, the introduction of PLs is essentially centered on the principle of offering a product with quality comparable to a national brand at an affordable price. Retailers continued to push more and more of private-label products into different categories of the marketplace because they represented high margins and the promise of profitability with little to no marketing effort.

199

Historically, private-label retailers appreciated that it was important to tout certain category and product benefits to incite consumers to purchase. Yet, rather than look at the consumer directly to understand his brand and product selection criteria, they took their cues from the national brand competitors that had already identified and manifested some of the category's salient attributes and benefits through advertising, packaging, and other brand messaging. The result was often a series of "me-too" private-label positioning that strived to emulate the category leader. Most importantly, these examples underscore a need for private-label marketers to be cognizant of how their initiatives play a role in the overall marketing mix and the long-term definition and impact of their portfolio.

Meaning

1. Store brands or PLs are simply defined as the products owned and branded by the organizations whose primary objective is distribution rather than production.
2. Hence, PLBs are the brands created and developed by retailers themselves in tie-up or association with product developers or, in the case of garments/apparels, designed by fashion designers and sourced directly from contract manufacturers or producers.
3. They typically give higher margins to retailers because there is no brand equity outgo, and they can price them lower than national brands as they spend less on promoting such brands.

According to the Private Label Manufacturers' Association (PLMA), "[private label] products encompass all merchandise sold under a retailer's brand. That brand can be the retailer's own name or a name created exclusively by that retailer. In some cases, a retailer may belong to a wholesale group that owns the brands that are available only to the "members of the group." This suggests two things. First, it is the retailer who owns and controls the brand, whereas this was traditionally the role of the producer. Second, the retailer has exclusive rights over the product. This means that different retailers do not sell identical PLBs, which is not the case when retailers sell name brands. Thus, the development of PLBs does not only alters the relationship between producers and retailers but also affects competition between retailers because PLBs become an additional way of differentiating between retailers.

This approach to private-label management had resounding impacts on a category as a whole as well as the individual product offerings within it.

The Shift in the Private-label Paradigm

PLBs have clearly become a more instrumental priority for today's retailers. They are starting to diversify their offering beyond the expected, enabling them to compete more effectively in existing product categories and foray into new and different product categories that have traditionally been dominated by national brand players. Today, the way in which consumers are buying has changed too. We are buying more via the Internet, which has opened a vista of information and choice, allowing consumers to research and buy from anyone at any time. Democratization has altered the balance of power in favor of the consumer. Whichever way it is viewed, the dynamic has changed in the way in which retailers are organizing themselves in response is changing too.

In many instances, PLs have surpassed a national brand's capacity to deliver on visibility, consumer interest, involvement, and appeal. Proprietary brand decision makers are often able to command close to parity or parity pricing for their products, without articulating cost as the differentiating factor. This represents a point of departure from the past: there is an acknowledgement that today's proprietary brands have the ability to transcend the negative baggage and problems of traditional store brands, creating unique, resonant benefit propositions for consumers.

Retailers are beginning to recognize that they cannot simply rely on national branded products to draw consumers into their stores and sustain loyalty. This is due to the fact that manufacturers' product brands often have the ability to transcend geographic location, distribution channel, or retailer (e.g., Peter England shirts are available at a wide array of multi-branded department stores and exclusive showrooms across the country). Due to this pervasive presence of national brands, consumers need not have a strong relationship with a particular brick-and-mortar store setting to have access to these products. It is only the proprietary brands, exclusively available at a specific retailer that can be a magnet to draw people into its store versus others and accrue direct meaning and loyalty to the overarching banner.

Brands Take a New Approach to Private-label Branding

In today's highly competitive scenario, it has become imperative for retailers to create a persuasive consumer connection. In order to accomplish this objective, retailers have had to elevate themselves above competitive retail outlets by having a comprehensive offer in the form of strong and unique in-house brand exclusively available at retailer's outlet.

There are certain contemporary brands that have been either placed on a pedestal or carefully noted by retail marketers and consumers alike. Their situations and strategies start to lend insight into a more compelling definition for a retailer's proprietary brand offering, and, more importantly, a sense of how to optimize success as an exclusive, proprietary brand and to develop their portfolios and provide proprietary products in categories where national brand manufacturers' offerings did not suffice.

Perhaps the strongest success story in this regard was that of the Marks & Spencer brand in the late 1980s and early 1990s. This was a clothing retailer known for good basics that complemented its offering with proprietary branded food products. Quality was the cornerstone of the food product range, and the only brand provided was its proprietary label. Mainstream retailers could emulate neither Marks & Spencer's premium quality nor its price.

Sainsbury's is another interesting retailer to consider in understanding how to develop an appropriate proprietary brand strategy. In the mid-1990s, it became the first mainstream UK supermarket to have more than 50% of its turnover accounted for by PL. Let us look upon the classic example of "Classic Cola," a PL made by Cott Corporation for J. Sainsbury Supermarkets in the UK. Classic Cola was launched in April 1994 at a price 28% lower than Coca-Cola's. Today, the PL accounts for 65% of total cola sales through Sainsbury's and almost 15% of the UK cola market. Yet, despite previous accomplishments, Sainsbury's faces an uphill battle today.

Another example is fashion retailer Globus, which has compelled to give up a fourth of its revenues and shut down its biggest stores in Delhi and Mumbai because they were losing money and decided to tweak the strategy. Its rival fashion retailers like Forever 21 and Vero Moda, for instance, are churning out new designs every fortnight at similar price points and bringing more selection for customers. Here, Globus plans to counter the competition with its PLs that typically bring in better margins. Also Globus needs to reposition itself in terms of the product mix, prices, and designs. There is more focus on party and evening wears and less on day and office wears, which is possibly why it has not been able to compete with fast fashion players or even the pure-play Indian PL players. The higher price points might be another reason for keeping customers away.

Pantaloon Retail India Limited, which was acquired by Aditya Birla Group in 2013 from Future Group, makes 50% of its sales from its PLs.

Shoppers Stop value brand Stop garners the highest volume sales, more than even third-party brands. According to Kabir Lumba, MD, Lifestyle International, their PLs are gaining large-scale acceptance among customers, to the extent that these have become key differentiators vis-à-vis other stores.

For the retailers with PL contribution of less than 20% (i.e., 16–17% for Shoppers Stop), investment would be mainly in advertising to build the brand image, while for retailers who get more than 70% of revenues from them would need to make supply chain investments imperative. The Tata-owned Croma, a durables and electronics chain competing with Reliance Digital, is investing in the back end. Now Croma's sister concern, the Tata-owned private-label-led fashion chain, Westside, gets most of its revenue from in-house brands that account for around 85% of its merchandise.

Let us have a look on the PLBs' scenario of consumer durable retailers. Top durable retailers in India such as Croma, Next, Reliance Retail's Reliance Digital, and Future Group's Ezone seem to have finally cracked the private-label business. They attribute the success to differentiated researched products, sourcing from multiple location, inventory management, and brand building. The sole focus is on quality of private brand with value that will ensure good brand recall and business. In their earlier attempts to push in-house brands, the retailers were stuck with products that did not match up to leading brands and had issues with service support and unsold inventory that impacted their profitability.

The retailers have addressed these issues and are now aggressively chasing a bigger pie of the consumer electronics market dominated by multinationals such as Samsung, LG, Sony, Panasonic, and Whirlpool. Their USP: quality products with desired functionality level at a 10–30% discount to leading brands. Next Retail, whose PLs account for around 30% of total sales from its outlets, attributes its success to greater penetration in Tier II–VI markets where 80% of its 500 stores are located, because consumers in these markets want good value for money and does not fancy the brand value, which is a reason for high sales. Reliance Retail gets 18% of sales from its famous in-house brand Reconnect in categories such as flat-panel television and air conditioners. The company has extended the brand to almost all electronics categories, including washing machine, smartphones, and tablets. Future Group too has reported good response to its PL Koryo in categories such as air conditioners, microwave ovens, and small appliances like iron, sandwich, and tea makers. Besides air conditioners, Croma has got excellent response to its tablet. Rising sales of in-house brands help improve consumer electronics retailer's profitability as the margins (which are 15–30%) are significantly higher than established brands (which are 8–12%).

A key learning from this retailer's situation is that it grew its PLB according to the industry's traditional approach and failed to build proprietary products on the platform of a real consumer need, which enforces how the myopic approach toward development of PLBs can lead to disaster. It is conceivable that retailers who reached this point were taking private-label success for granted and not being fully cognizant of the resounding long-term impact of their PLB development. The fact that they were providing branded products that emulated manufacturers' product in terms of quality and price and, at the same time, were delivering much better margins fueled their portfolio expansion.

Concurrently, Tesco created an organics line, a kid's line, and, perhaps most impressively, the Tesco Finest sub-brand. Tesco Finest started in ready meals and chilled foods, where the retailer has a natural advantage (these products are difficult to prepare and distribute). Integral to its success was its very high premiumness. The exceptional price and quality were well received by the higher-end consumer. It was also evident that Tesco Finest was an encompassing proposition and could stretch into other categories. But rather than trying to rule the world, Tesco selectively ventured into those specific areas where it could add value.

High-end cookie tins, which are popular Christmas gifts, are a good example. Tesco was smart to recognize that manufacturers were struggling to add value in this seasonal, yet, premium playing field because branded products deemed suitable for everyday consumption dominated the category. Tesco Finest was able to compete here because, as a brand, it had more permission to extend into the premium sector. In view of that, its Tesco Finest cookie ranges have been a big success.

Underpinning Tesco's winning private-label strategy was spectacular packaging design across the entire range. For instance, Tesco Finest packaging was in silver boxes that were very premium looking with first-rate product photography. There was also a section of the aisle dedicated to the range. It was well marketed and supported from start to finish.

Of course, Tesco was not baking its own cookies. Here, it was playing a strategic ball game. It was sourcing them from those manufacturers with who Sainsbury's was looking to compete. However, Tesco was offering to buy at wholesale those products that the branded manufacturers would struggle to sell.

Similar to Tesco in the UK, Loblaws, Canada's largest food retailer, is also a trailblazer in the private-label arena. It too perpetuated a segmented strategy for its two proprietary brands. Together, it is No Name and President's Choice (PC) proprietary portfolios that have over 5,000 SKUs. The No Name brand is its multiple category, competitively priced value range of products. PC, on the other hand, is a complementary higher-end PLB that has premium imagery and a commitment to taste appeal and quality that inspires unquestionable loyalty to its retailer.

Retail marketers often cite PC as a shining example in the area of exceptional private-label product quality. The signature PC product was the decadent chocolate chip cookie, which had nearly 40% chocolate by volume and contained real butter. It was many times better than its competitors and served with the President's Blend coffee, a passion-fruit sorbet, and special Belgium Biscuits to demonstratively show that PC was actually better than existing options.

This is evidenced by Loblaws' commitment to the innovation and creation of a superior tasting, excessively chocolaty chocolate chip cookie that fulfilled a marketplace desire for a rich and indulgent consumption experience. By looking at consumers' needs, wants, and desires rather than manufacturers' existing products for success cues, PC was able to develop its own unique cookie product that carved out a niche in the category by resonating with consumers in a way that its national brand competitors had not considered. This visible shift to a consumer-centric brand definition gave PC a believability and a POD that enabled it to stretch to new and different product categories. The PC brand was backed by the personal involvement of the CEO Dave Nichols, who placed his signature on the package. He wrote his *Insider's Report*, which provided a quirky, humorous take on food in a comic book format and relentlessly promoted the innovation and quality of the brand and, in doing so, provided ongoing energy and credibility to it.

There has been a rapid shift in the mind-set about the role and requirements for today's PLBs. Retailers are evolving to a new definition and greater focus for these proprietary offerings to elevate their stature and influence on the current and future business strategy. Today's PLBs need to embody the attitude and demeanor of an "own" brand. "Own" brands are relevant to the broadest set of audiences. The trade feels an affinity and desire for the "own" brand to prosper. The consumer is loyal to "own" brands and seeks them out as an integral part of his/her lifestyle. The retailer celebrates and nurtures the "own" brand as a vital embodiment of its brand proposition that will build and sustain a greater degree of loyalty. This new paradigm of private-label thinking requires that retailers consider an arsenal of often overlooked business and branding tools to further success.

Private-label Brand Through Retailer's Strategic Perspective

In order to be truly successful, retailers must advance from the generic or store brand mind-set of the past to a new private-label paradigm. Many retailers have begun to describe their PLBs as "own" brands because there is a recognition that these proprietary, exclusive offerings are tools that represent momentous power and potential for the retail store.

The term "own" brands acknowledges that today's visionary retail marketers have powerful proprietary portfolios that they control and manage and there is a potential to reap bigger and better rewards by taking a closer look at the way they orchestrate the role and expression of these brand offerings in the eyes of consumers in each product category. Those retailers who appreciate the magnitude of this brand opportunity have created a new industry standard in their realm of influence and activity. "Own" brands are articulated and developed in a way that they not only fit with the brand promise of the retail store, but also, if effective, give consumer drivers a key point of departure to enhance and celebrate the overall retail brand proposition to keep consumers coming back for more.

A New Outlook to Private-label Branding

Profitability Perspective and Collaborative Category Management

"Show me the money," the famous dialog from the Tom Cruise starrer *Jerry Maguire*, has always been the mantra for the retailers whether online or off-line behind their "look toward private labels" strategy. As manufacturers' (producers') brands have large advertising expenditures built into their cost, a private labeler is able to buy the same goods at a lower cost and thus sell them at a lower price and/or at a better profit margin. In addition, private labelers have more control over pricing (promotions) and are able to advantageously display their own brands for maximum impact. Margins in PLs can range from 30% to 50%, more than the usual 20–25% on other brand. Hence, it becomes more interesting to invest in PL because during sales or discount period, PLs can experiment with new ranges as the footfalls would translate into more shoppers pursuing it at the stores.

For example, a grocery store can quickly reduce the price of its own PLB in order to meet or beat a competitor's price. Or the grocery store can create a special POP advertising display and/or give its brand predominant shelf space in order to boost sales.

Strategic category management is instrumental for a retailer to realize its "own" brand goals and aspirations. It requires the development of a symbiotic relationship with manufacturers and/or suppliers to elevate relationships and further a mentality of partnership.

For example, Big Bazaar now runs 230 stores versus 40–50 stores during its early years, which also implies that its buying volumes have gone up. So while pricing will pretty much stay the same, Big Bazaar plans to get higher margins from its suppliers, justified by bulk buying. According to an insider having direct knowledge of the development, Big Bazaar's profit margins from its in-house brands are higher now and about 15–17% of Big Bazaar's total sales come from its PLs.

In this new way of thinking, the retailer and trade partnership become more about cooperation and less about the retailer negotiating with the manufacturer or supplier on price and listings. By working together, the parties involved can solidify trade relationships and ensure that the category as a whole remains profitable and emotionally appealing to the customer so that both private-label and branded goods win. So overcoming the challenges and ensuring long-term sustenance in the business of PL is basically dependent upon carefully devised strategies in the

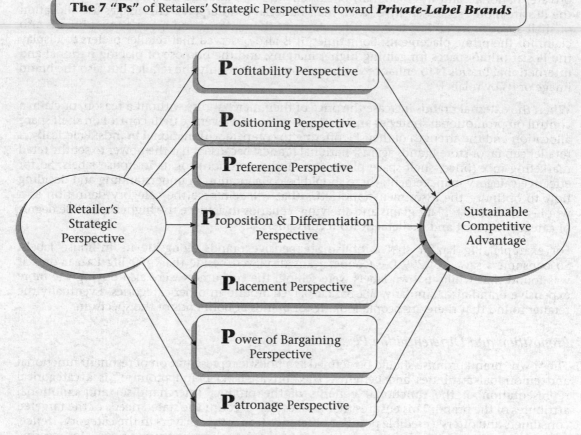

The 7 "Ps" of Retailers' Strategic Perspectives toward ***Private-Label Brands***

Figure 6.2: *Looking Toward "Private Labels" through Retailer's Strategic Perspective*

area such as product design life, branding, merchandising, cost control, and the pricing–value equation. The continuous and continual optimization of the PLB portfolio helps the retailers to ensure the business focus and investment are perfectly aligned with the goal of maintaining a well-differentiated and hence a profitable brand (See Figure 6.2).

Placement Perspective

Shelf space is a place that is allocated to different merchandise items on the shelf. Shelf space is a valuable asset for any retailer, and it is a challenging task for the retailer to allocate appropriate space to the merchandise items of different brands. Shelf space allocation directly impacts the retailer's profitability, and they often tend to allocate more space and/or prime places to those brands that garner higher profits for them. It is also often alleged by national players that retailers offer more space and/or allocate prime spaces to their PLBs and hence tend to give biased treatment to the national brands. They also assert that PLs occupy more space disproportioned to their market share. They alleged claim that the retailer replaces the national brands from the prime places when the new in-house brands are introduced.

Shelf placement is not only a critical resource for the retailers but also an alternative to concede in negotiation with national brands. The retailer displays all types of brands on the shelf (e.g., private, national, and international) but often wants to allocate prime places for its PLB as the PLs are more "space sensitive" than their national counterparts. This makes the allocation of shelf space more critical task for the retailer as the national and international brands also claim for the prime placements. Sometimes, it is also observed that retailer prefers to display the PLs at prime spaces for gaining higher margins, and the purpose of placing national and international brands is to enhance the brand image of not only the retailer but also the brand image of its own label.

When the external brands increase the price of their merchandise without a reason, or claim a control on promotional strategies and tactics, retailers can leverage their control on shelf space allocation and the strength of their PL offering to compete with national brands. Practically, a retailer can favor store brands against national brands, because it has the power to set the retail marketing mix (price, shelf space placement, and promotion) for its in-house labels. So for effective category management, there should be collaboration in understanding and deciding how to optimize the assortments and SKUs that will reinforce the category definition as a whole and establish planograms and shelving scenarios to achieve the highest possible degree of category interest and excitement from consumers.

For example, Big Bazaar started housing expensive brands alongside its in-house labels. So consumers saw a ₹1,299 Lee Cooper jeans displayed beside the ₹499 Big Bazaar one. It was found that while its own labels were selling, the consumers were also buying the more expensive brand also. Similarly, Big Bazaar played around in other categories. Eventually the retailer found that there are people looking for brands at both ends of the spectrum.

Proposition and Differentiation Perspective

The "own" brand promise should be defined as a holistic representation of resonant functional and emotional attributes and benefits. The "private-label brand promise" is a categorical representation of the functional benefits of the product (merchandise) and emotional attributes of the brand. This ensures that it takes into account the stated needs of the targeted consumers and offers a credible point of difference from other players in the category. Hence, it becomes necessary for the retailers to understand the salient consumer needs, for creating effective private-label brand proposition.

Once the brand proposition is solidified, the brand architecture strategy enables decision makers to promote this promise at the retail store level in order to engender a sense of familiarity, recognition, and trust. Private-label packaging has become more beautiful and functional. Whereas earlier, PLBs use to scream "I'm poor" from the cart, now they say "I'm savvy."

The major advantage coming with a PL to retailer is that is the factor of differentiation that a retailer can have with PLs. E-tailers are also choosing to raise the bar on their differentiation to get around the price conundrum. But in order to create such differentiation, the retailer should be successful in positioning the PL against the national brand in such a way that a PL should be considered as equivalent as or better than the national brand. The majority of retailers in India have introduced their own PLs driven by increasing consumer acceptance and associated economic benefits. Retailers such as Spencer's, Future Group, Reliance Retail, and Bharti Walmart have been working continuously to create a spectrum of private brands in order to restructure their product portfolios in coming years.

Shoppers Stop offers Kashish, Haute Curry, Vettorio Fratini, and Elliza Donatein PLs in its products offerings. Life' offers T-shirts for men, while "Stop" as ladies western wear. This new development may be seen as a new strategic move to have an operational edge over competition, as well as to retain their customer base. US retailer Kroger Company believe that strong in-house label programs can successfully differentiate their stores and cement shopper's loyalty, thereby strengthening their positions with regard to national players, which in turn increases the profitability.

With fashion and lifestyle quickly becoming the largest category in India's fast-growing online retail industry, Myntra and its rival Jabong are increasingly focusing on global brand partnerships and designer-led in-house brands to attract and retain customers and to create global standard PLs in fashion apparels and accessories space. Myntra tied up with Italian fashion house Parabellum, led by popular Italian designer Vanni Lenci, to create a special line for its Roadster private brand.

Jabong.com has set up a design-cum-branding office in London to take its private brands to the next level and hired global talents from Asos, River Island, and Zara's parent Inditex. The purpose of setting up this design office is not just to develop the designs but also to position itself as a smart and contemporary fashion label, with the help of people who have worked with the best of fashion houses. These offices are also assigned with the job to lead the partnerships of the fashion e-tailer with brands in UK and Europe, liaise with European design studios, spot global fashion trends, and generate fashion content.

Private brands are a big strategic play for any retailer, whether it is online or off-line. These online players are not looking at it as a business for filling category gaps through their own stable, but it is actually a fashion brand business for them that present an attractive opportunity to create a value proposition. The two leading fashion online portals first sold their own locally created brands; then they went heavy on global brands such as Mango, Dorothy Perkins, and Steve Maddens; and now, they are trying to create global standard lines of fashion and accessories to tap the growing market for such products in the country.

Positioning and Promise Perspective

By crystallizing a differentiated value proposition, an effective "own" brand considers the approach that national brands use to arrive at a holistic benefit proposition rather than the specific positioning they use. Many store brands are now designed to elevate the brand promise and offer a credible POD from other category players. This furthers an "own" brand promise that has been informed by the competition, but is clearly not a "me too" expression. It is also successful because it demonstrates a commitment to offer consumers multiple options and varieties with distinct attributes, benefits, and price points.

In today's retailing scenario, it is very essential to strike the right balance of similarities and differences with brand messaging and portfolio offerings. Brand architecture is a critical consideration for "own" brand marketing as it is becoming more and more important to differentiate an "own" brand's attributes and benefits. Brand architecture and design expression can help the consumer navigate the breadth of the "own" brand portfolio and understand its depth of expertise in different areas of the store.

To raise its inspirational quotient, retailers create a personality for pls, and there needs to be a distinct style of VM and brand ambassadors. Now Shoppers Stop and Lifestyle, two national anchor store chains, are sprucing up their PLs with power of stars. Lifestyle, belonging to Dubai-based retail and hospitality conglomerate Landmark Group, recently signed up the actress Deepika Padukone to model for its print ads. Shoppers Stop had earlier signed up actress Soha Ali Khan for its ethnic wear Kashish, and recently signed up Shruti Haasan for its fashion wear Haute Curry.

For example, Melange is a private-label brand of Lifestyle International (P) Limited which is one of the leading department stores and is a part of Dubai based Landmark Group. Melange from Lifestyle is a contemporary ethnic wear brand for men and women. Its wide assortment includes kurtas, salwars/churidars, dupattas, and kurtis for ladies that can be liberally mixed and matched. The collection at Melange possess designs inspired by traditional Indian crafts such as block printing and delicate hand embroideries on cotton, silk, and other fine fabrics. The collection is ethnic yet it offers modernity through the designs and style. These product and brand features successfully associates Melange with the modern Indian Woman. Melange also has an exquisite range of sarees. Melange for men offers shirts and kurtas in cotton, blended silks, and silk jacquards, perfect for the casual look or for an occasion.

By developing relevant store environments, in-store messaging like signage, merchandising systems, and packaging as well as external messaging like media news/stories, social media postings, catalogs and advertising, and other PR vehicles in a congruent manner, the retailer is able to create an enduring impression in-store, at shelf, at the time of purchase and during usage.

Repositioning efforts often go hand in hand with packaging redesign and sub-branding initiatives. These are critical tools that help to visualize and verbalize what the "own" brand stands for and demonstrate its expertise and PODs in various product categories. These brand executions are the vehicles through which "own" brands deliver on category-mandated functional and emotional virtues, spurring consumers to select the retailer's brand over others.

Let us consider the example of Bollywood actor Hrithik Roshan-promoted HRX ventures. The brand is a mix of his supreme style and passion, and is being sold exclusively on Myntra. com. The brand of fitness wear is a mix of his supreme style and passion, and was launched in 2013 exclusively on online fashion portal Myntra. The brand persona of HRX leverages this association with Hrithik Roshan by reflecting his passion for fitness, his work ethics, and his image as one of the most stylish actors in Bollywood.

When the concept of creating and developing the brand HRX was originated in 2010, the founder spent the next two and a half to three years in carrying out research about what are the personality tributes and traits that audience relates to with Hrithik Roshan. This market sensing was very crucial for obtaining inputs on what categories they can explore and eventually how the brand can be positioned. The research highlighted that things like fitness, dance, and fashion resonate with Roshan in the audience's mind and thus a fitness and lifestyle brand made sense. As a result, the range includes extreme casuals and easy actives in apparel

Bollywood superstar Hrithik personifies fitness and the brand HRX aims to capitalize on Roshan's image, which drives consumers to embrace fitness.

Photo 6.1: *Celebrity Brand Endorsement—By Celebrity*

Source: http://hrxbrand.com/ (accessed on 12 May 2016)

along with sports footwear for men. These outfits are lightweight and made of premium fabrics designed with a fashionable slim fit and available in vibrant colors. The brand has been built with the purpose of creating a platform that endorses the philosophy of inspiring people to bring out their best and to never give up. The huge fan base of the star is a major advantage for the brand. The brand image of HRX is in sync with the brand philosophy of Myntra and is one of the attractive propositions in its PLB portfolio.

Patronage Perspective

An effective private-label strategy can allow a retailer to create a genuinely unique offer for shoppers. This pervasive presence of national brands eliminates the "dependency" of consumers on a particular brick-and-mortar or online store establishment. Consumers can very easily access these (national) brands through multiple retailers. So it is only the PLs that are exclusively present at a specific retailer's store that develops them.

Besides this, the PLs typically allow retailers to fix the gaps in their merchandise assortments that have been neglected by the national players. They also use PLs for reinforcing the store image and to get a distinct share of mind. This eventually helps the retailer to create a kind of exclusivity that eventually results in extension of loyalty from the brand to the store. Hence, the retailers often use their in-house brands as a crucial tool to drive shopper patronage loyalty.

They have recognized that they cannot simply rely on national brands and the merchandise offered by them to pull consumers into their stores. They have taken cognizance of the fact that they need to offer something exclusively to achieve sustainable loyalty. This is due to the fact that national brands often have the ability to transcend geographical boundaries, distribution channel, or retailers.

A strong in-house brand literally has the potential to possess the consumer connection and increases customer engagement with the store brand. If it is broadly defined, it has the capacity to strike a chord with consumers in multiple merchandise categories. Unlike national branded products, PLBs are exclusively available with a specific retailer and can often transcend specific product categories because they are high on consumer orientation rather than just product focused in terms of their brand foundation.

In today's retailing scenario, the consumer needs are changing and expectations are increasing like never before. Consumers have become more fickle, rebellious, and demanding, and the "universal shopper" of today is far less brand loyal and is ready to buy from different sources (e.g., a pair of Gap jeans with a Prada handbag and other accessories from an online shopping portal).

Hence, the inclusion of strong PL across multiple categories offered enables the retailers to improve its margins without any huge investment on marketing and advertising activities. Besides this, the PLs also enable retailers to gain consumer loyalty, which can be attributed to the exclusive presence of these brands in that retailer's store. Hence, they have the right potential to act as magnets to attract customers into the respective retailer's store and build up a strong patronage loyalty.

Let us consider the example of Macy's. It is one of America's largest retailers with sales of over US$25 billion, through over 850 Macy's and Bloomingdales stores. Macy's is recognized as a retail industry leader in developing PLB merchandise that differentiates its assortments and delivers exceptional value to the customer. Each private brand, available "Only at Macy's," is developed to appeal to a certain customer lifestyle and is supported with marketing programs that create a precisely defined image. Macy's also develops private-label goods to meet specific customer needs and to fill gaps in the assortment. Sales of private-label apparel, accessories, and other items have outperformed other merchandise categories for years and now account for over 20% of sales. The company states the reason they are strong is that "we develop and market them just like branded goods," and points out that PLBs grew when the economy was weak or strong. In fact, Macy's derives 35% of its annual sales from its private-label goods and designer items exclusive to Macy's by celebrities such as Martha Stewart and Tommy Hilfiger.

Walmart appreciates the role of its exclusive brands like Ol' Roy for dog food or ReliOn for diabetes for its success in the business of retailing. These brands claim such a trustworthiness and adherence from their loyal consumers that Walmart is their intended retail source whether they are running low on dog food or diabetes medication. The exclusive brands may be the reason that consumers are initially drawn into the store, but once they are there, retailers also have the opportunity to encourage them to spend more on incidental or impulse purchases.

When the in-house brands are appropriately developed and operated, they have the potential to reach their pinnacle of success. In doing so, they create a seamless persuasive connection with consumers, drawing them into a retail store, but, more importantly, becoming an essential, experiential, and indispensable lifestyle choice that they embrace over the long term. Therefore, exclusivity through in-house brands not only reinforce enduring loyalty and positive feelings for the overarching retail brand but also often enable the retailer to capture a significant share of the consumers' wallet, heart, mind, and lifestyle.

Preference and Promise Perspective

Merchandise quality and innovation are the essential functional groundwork for a PLB offering. A perfect combination of national brands and the PLs can build a strong brand equity in terms of consumers' preference toward the retailer as a brand over time. This is the reason why PLB development is often synchronized with merchandise mix rationalization as it essentially helps to calibrate the in-house brand's promise that it is making to the consumer. So retailers perform on both the fronts (preference and promise) and are increasingly focusing on quality of the PLs and other cues like the attractiveness of packaging (labeling), brand image, brand ambassador, and all the aspects that are associated with the positioning of the brand. In addition, the image of the retailer itself may be leveraged and extended to influence consumers' perceptions toward private-label quality. Hence, both the brands—the retailer and its PL—can leverage and extend each other's brand image to achieve the synergistic effect on consumer's perception.

Hence, it is imperative to consider how package design, nomenclature, quality parameters, and product strategy can propel and support the retailer's vision for the in-house brand promise. Retailers are increasingly taking cognizance of how various aspects of their in-house brand marketing mix work together to create a strong, consistent brand message and preference. In order to have a consistent and compelling brand voice, retailers need to understand the contribution and role of PLBs within their business and also within the lives of their consumers. Hence, retailers are striving for not only to introduce PLs but also to make them achieve a high "shopping cart share" and consumer preference.

Let us take the example of Target. One of the many reasons Target resonates with its consumers is by borrowing equities from design and lifestyle personalities like Michael Graves, Isaac Mizrahi, and Cynthia Rowley in various parts of its store. The retailer has lines from each of these individuals, and their allure and expertise provide a sense of contemporary relevance for consumers. Like an exclusive or proprietary brand, these brand personalities infuse meaning into the overarching Target promise and experience.

Done by None, which is basically a pure-play private-label portal that sells clothes, shoes, and accessories under its own name, resorted to stylized photography and presentation of its offerings in order to reinforce its brand promise and to position itself as a chic option for young buyers.

Power of Bargaining (Private Label Versus National Brand): Balancing the Power Play

The three main advantages derived from the adoption of PLs are:

- Higher margins.
- Better control on marketing mix components.
- Increased store loyalty that results in strategic bargaining power and relative market position vis-à-vis national and international labels.

The strong PLs give the retailer the greatest disagreement payoff in negotiations with manufacturers and other national brands, leading to better terms in negotiations. Hence, these strategically developed and positioned PLBs can be used as the BATNA and acts as generals on the negotiation army that fights in favor of the retailers in negotiation with national brands/manufactures.

PLs are generally launched by retailers to gain higher gross margins than it earns from national brands. They differentiate the retailer's own product from the branded ones and aim to gain and sustain consumer loyalty. They provide a competitive benefit to the retailer over branded players. They also offer a platform for the retailers to negotiate with branded players. In order to have a consistent and compelling brand voice, retailers need to understand the contribution and role of proprietary or "own" brands within their business and also within the lives of their consumers. The in-house brand products, branded communication, and expressions should all be developed in accordance with this thinking to obtain a sustainable negotiation power and platform. Hence, PLs allow retailers to control prices points, retain margins, and, of course, experiment even when the consumer turns stingy.

Retailers combine PL clothing with national brands. They create their own brands and sell them in their outlets along with other national brands at a 40% cheaper price. Stores like Sears and JCPenney opt to combine 50% of their apparels with 50% of national brands like Adidas and Sag Harbor. This way, sourcing and cost advantages are passed on to the consumers. Retailers who sell their own PL apparels have appropriate control over product development. The apparels are created by an internal design team. Through adequate market research, they are able to customize their outfits to target specific groups of consumers.

However, in totality, these trends may seem daunting for national/international players, but they tell only half the story. The increased strength of PLs does not mean that we should write an obituary for the national brands. Actually, they are alive, reasonable healthy, and, in most of the cases, are thriving also.

According to the top brass officials of the national brands, the renewed focus of multi-brand retailer on their in-house brands is not going to make a big dent on their pocket, as more consumers are shifting from unbranded to branded products and modern retail. The sheer numbers will insulate the national brands from any adverse impact. Industry experts also point out that it might be easier to launch PLs, but it is equally difficult to assure quality and after-sales services, especially in the categories like clothing. There is a need to develop expertise in handling after-sales trouble. With new assortments, there might be disappointments, and ensuring the quality would be a tall task.

Brand-names exist because consumers still require an assurance of quality when they do not have the time, opportunity, or ability to evaluate and inspect the alternatives at the very POS. National brands shorten and simplify the selection process in cluttered product categories for the time-pressured, affluent, dual-income households with higher purchasing power, and increased disposable income opt for national brands. Here they prefer comfort and security; sometimes relatively higher trust factor and perceived value make them prefer national brands over the PLs. Here "the better value with lower price" card played by PLs to woo "the price-conscious customers" do not work. Perceived risk factor plays against the PL—perceived risk which is the feeling of uncertainty faced by customers when they cannot predict the consequences of the purchase decision that they are going to make. The perceived risk factor overpowers the "price-consciousness behavior," which results in the urge to play safe by purchasing national brand.

Hence, the national brands enjoy a running start by virtue of its solid foundation, their brand equities they have built rather earned over decades of advertising, strong imagery- desired positioning, and through delivery of consistent quality and performance year-on-year.

For year to year, there is little or no change in consumer's perceptions and rankings of the strongest national brands. Retailers cannot afford to cast off national brands that consumer cherish for and expect to find widely distributed. When a store does not carry a popular brand, consumers are put off and may switch stores. This makes essential for retailers to not only stock but also promote the national labels. Theoretically, even if retailers make more profit per unit on PLs, though they act as magnets to pull consumers, those product—single-handedly—just cannot have the traffic-building power.

1. Benefits: The drive behind exclusive and private brand label product development is twofold: (a) increased profitability and (b) differentiation. In increasingly crowded markets, a well-crafted exclusive and PL product proposition can form the basis of a range architecture that provides clear PODs for the retailer, and compelling reasons for picky consumers to shop. The benefits to the bottom line for the entire business are compelling.
2. Growing Share of Wallet: An exclusive or PL product proposition, which is well constructed, can provide opportunities to extend the reach for retailers to a bigger market of new customers and also grow the share of wallet from current customers.
3. Higher Margins: Typically, 10–20% better than established brands.
4. Greater Retailer Brand Equity and Loyalty: Standing out in the marketplace is crucial: too much similar "stuff" provides no compelling reason for the consumer to visit your store. Send out the message that you have a great range of things that are different and what your customers want and you reinforce the equity of your brand. This results in greater loyalty. Successful PLBs will be able to create better sales opportunities for retailers. The customization of store brand labels—such as to logos and taglines—can personalize a customer's shopping experience that can lead to higher customer loyalty.
5. Change the Balance of Power between Retailer and National Brands: PL assortments or range allow the retailer to leverage their negotiating power with their branded counterparts to improve overall contribution. As with anything, there are upsides and downsides. Potentially, there are significant margin, sales, and brand benefits in any well-organized and executed exclusive and PLB product program. But there are risks. Key among these is the costs and investments required to develop exclusive and PLBs, combined with the skills and capabilities of the teams necessary to create them. On top of this, the financial risks in controlling large and complex branded product inventories are high if not managed correctly.

Example: Koovs

Let us take the example of online fashion retailer Koovs that listed on AIM (formerly Alternative Investment Market) in 2014, a submarket of the London Stock Exchange, thereby becoming the first Indian e-commerce company outside of travel to go for an initial public offering (IPO) abroad. It focuses on current trends, prevailing vogue, and bringing the best of international collections to the astute Indian customers at competitive price points. Koovs majorly targets the fashion-conscious, well-traveled, and "connected" customers who maintain a continuous exposure to the international vogue. Koovs has adopted a three-pronged strategy—developing Koovs PLs, a high-street fashion collection of leading international and national labels, and exclusive designer collaborations with the who's who of global fashion space—that helps the online fashion retailer to differentiate from the other players in the category. Koovs PL is basically a collection designed in London and made in India and presents a line of affordable runway fashion. Some major brands from Europe like Timberland and Glamorous from UK sell exclusively on Koovs and have international designer names like Patrick Cox and Melissa Odabash along with a team of 12 designers in London. The collection is inspired by the celebrity looks, best of latest trends, designs, patterns, and styles. Koovs also has a selective list of international and national labels in its brand portfolio that is managed by cross-continental team of buyers who ensure the best collection will be available on the portal. As displaying best collection and developing strong PLs is not sufficient, so Koovs ensures that shoppers will get seamless navigation (browsing experience) from its well-designed portal throughout the shopping journey. The website also offers bespoke fashion content and dedicated blog to educate shoppers and drive the shopping experience to the next level.

Private-label Brands by E-retailers

PLs have become an essential component of e-commerce space worldwide. Earlier, only niche PLs dominated the market, but now even mainstream e-commerce players have introduced their in-house brands. Much like its off-line counterparts, e-retailers also taste the sweet water of PL and experience the magic of consequent high margins. PLs are dominating segments that are filling up a need gap. For instance, home furnishing products as beyond the Portico and Bombay Dyeing, it is difficult to extend the list to the fifth or sixth known brand in the category. Clearly, PL is the buzzword in the online space, especially when it comes to the apparel and the footwear categories. There is a huge business opportunity in the space. In-house brands are going to be a key differentiator in the industry in terms of high margins, revenues, and the range they can offer. The price differential in case of PLs is in the range of 20–25%. UK's largest online fashion retailer Asos gets around 50% of the revenue from its PLBs. Indian online fashion retailers are getting around 20% of business from its in-house brands. The Indian branded apparel market is fragmented and the options that consumers have are still limited. So if an e-retailer can identify the potential gas and come up with high-quality trendy PL, there is a lucrative business opportunity. Consumers are always in search of great offering at the right price point. So here a strategically developed PL can make a good proposition for an already captive audience.

Primarily, a few product categories such as fashion and apparel, food and wellness, footwear, and home furnishings come to mind when one considers the possibility of launching a PLB. Another category may be electronics. For instance, Croma and Ezone have been selling certain electronics items under their own brand labels. A PL requires building a brand from scratch, handling the manufacturing and supply chain. As discussed earlier, point of friction that could emerge between e-retailers and manufacturers would be in the event of the former selling the latter's products at a price point lower than the market operating price.

Margins from PLs can be higher than the net margin on the branded retail range. In fact, a PL breaks even much faster as the margins to play around with are higher with less cost incurred per acquisition. However, unless a portal has a clear vision about the in-house label and how to position it in the market, it should not launch it. PLs can be promoted by e-commerce players by using an effective search and recommendation platform to enable better product discovery. With the relevant search, navigation merchandising control, and accurate recommendation, e-commerce sites can promote specific groups of products through on-site search and navigation results.

Flipkart has its own range of electronic and computer accessories like headphones, speakers, and pen drives under its PLB Digiflip, launched in 2012. These products are mostly sourced from original equipment manufacturers in locations such as China, Hong Kong, Taiwan, Korea, and India. Also Flipkart is in the process of launching the tablet computers soon under the same brand-name and which will be available soon on its portal. The tablet is expected to boost margins in the highly competitive electronics retailing space. Retailers typically launch the PLBs to fill the gaps in categories or to improve margins. According to the industry estimates, margins of PL electronics products (which is also the largest category for e-tailers sales–wise) could be about 20% higher than branded products in the same category.

Flipkart also have PL fashion apparel range to improve the bottom line. This is in line with its acquisition of fashion portal Myntra, which has expanded its in-house brand range. Beyond the high margin offered by selling PLs, online fashion retailers are looking to create online-only brands. For instance, fashion e-tailers like Jabong and Myntra are positioning their PLs as recognized brands through celebrity endorsements and designer tie-ups to be sold across marketplace and targeted at entry-level consumers.

Myntra retails over 1,000 brands, also sells 10 of its own brands, including Roadster, Dressberry, Anouk (ethnic range for women), Mast & Harbour, Kook N Keech, Yellow Kites (for kids), Invictus, and HRX (by Hrithik Roshan). This merger also enabled both the brands to leverage each other's strength in building strong consumer relationships with brands and use of technology. With merchandising tool, category managers can promote their PLs in search results and even create filtering/sorting rules to make sure users find and see them. Some brands like Roadster, Dressberry, and Mast & Harbour have grown significantly and are already category leaders on Myntra. Hence e-retailers can use the traffic coming to their sites to promote their in-house brands, create touch points, and tie up with celebrities. For instance, Myntra has a tie up with actor Ranveer Singh for their in-house brand Roadster.

As far as apparel is concerned, the category has emerged as online success mainly due to easy and free returns, innovative visualization tools, and the presence of customer reviews. For instance, one of the leading online fashion retailers is in the process of acquiring three-dimensional (3D) technologies in an attempt to offer better visualization to customers on its mobile app and website. It is looking for 3D visualization and print technologies that will help augment the shopping experience of its customers on its mobile app as well as help the e-tailer speed up its PL offerings. In the case of online buying, the customer can only view (merely on mobile or on website) the product but cannot touch and feel. So, if they have a 3D view of the product, it will help customers to understand the product better, resulting in faster decision-making. Such technologies can also be useful for production of fashion and accessories because it generally takes weeks for any fashion idea to reach the production stage: from sketching of the product designs to prototyping. The fashion industry generally spends a significant time in prototyping, in visualizing what the idea is and from the line sketch to the final product. Hence with the 3D technology, the e-tailer plans to reduce the time taken in sketching and prototyping to merely few hours, which could help the online retailer to design the new fashionable range for its PLs and produce the apparels at faster rates.

Hence to develop a PL, it needs to make sure that the brand has good visibility, has right price–value equilibrium, design, and range. Besides all this, the e-retailer needs to work on getting the sourcing right, building capability to work with multiple manufactures, identifying quality vendors, and right investing in in-house design team. Because the design team needs to closely work with manufactures, they need to understand the trends precisely to avoid the risk of sitting on high inventory. The current scenario is there are some challenges such as regulatory compliance. As players with FDI investment are not permitted to take on their books any inventory, how can they offer PLs and still stay compliant with all the norms is a big question mark at the moment. The decision to launch PLs is mostly tactical in nature. Most of these brands still are price worriers hoping to capitalize on the consumer's high propensity to experiment online. But that is only the beginning; holding onto these customers is a bigger task. To perform this task, there has to be a focused brand building, and strategic efforts have to be in the direction to build these brands outside the ecosystem of the platform with higher degree of differentiation.

Summary

In a nutshell, effective merchandise management and planning help the retailer to minimize inventory carrying costs, stockouts, and emergency replenishment costs. It identifies negative margin and stockholding trends. It also helps to monitor stock movement and highlights liquidation opportunities. It assists the retailer to manage perpetual and promotional inventory. So in order to be able to control the business, the decision makers define the critical success factors (CSFs) of the business. Retailers are focusing on improving profitability through improvement in revenue throughput, as fast-changing consumer behavior is driving many retailers to rethink their business models. Achievement against these is basically measured using KPIs. The KPI typically is the components of high-level plans that provide strategic direction. In the recent times, after the upsurge of e-retailing, brick-and-mortar stores are increasingly focusing on profitability—even in some cases it means, moderation in revenue growth. They are constantly enhancing operating efficiency, which includes exiting unviable merchandise categories, rightsizing stores, increasing focus on PLs to boost profitability, and embracing cluster-based store expansion strategy.

There has been a rapid shift in mind-set about the role and requirements for today's PLBs. PLBs have obviously become a more instrumental priority for today's retailers. They have started diversifying and differentiating their offering beyond the expectations, which in turn enable them to compete more effectively in existing merchandise categories and venture into new categories that have traditionally been dominated by national and/ or international brands. Retailers are increasingly feeling an affinity and desire for the in-house brands to prosper. The consumers are increasingly preferring to the PLBs and are often loyal to them. They seek them out as an integral part of their lifestyle, which nourish their association and connects them with the brand persona. The retailer, in turn, celebrates and nurtures the PLB as a vital embodiment of its brand proposition that will build and sustain a greater degree of loyalty. Hence, retailers are evolving to a new definition, and greater focus for these proprietary offerings, to elevate their stature and influence on the current and future business strategy.

Review Questions

1. Briefly explain the concept of "merchandise management" and "merchandising."
2. Briefly explain the merchandise planning and selection process. Also explain its strategic significance in the business of retailing by the help of appropriate information.
3. Briefly explain the merchandise hierarchy and range planning with its significance.
4. Explain the "open-to-buy process." Quote some appropriate examples to justify its importance and functionality.
5. Briefly explain the process of "category management."

6. Briefly explain the concept of "financial merchandise management" with its strategic benefits to the retailer.

7. Explain in detail the meaning of "private-label brands." Give some examples of successful private-label brands developed and created by retailers.

8. Explain how the growing challenges in current retailing scenario have increased the importance of private labels in the business of retailing.

9. Briefly discuss the shift in private-label paradigm in the context of growing challenges in the retail industry.

10. Explain the importance of private labels through retailer's strategic perspective. Justify your explanation and view with appropriate examples.

11. Explain the 7 "Ps" of private-label brands that reflect the significance of private labels through retailer's strategic perspective with appropriate examples.

12. "Private-label brands are equally important for e-retailers as they are for brick-and-mortar retailers." Explain this statement with appropriate examples.

13. "Overall merchandise management, including private-label brand strategies of a retailer, is the reflection of its marketing, branding, and positioning strategies." Explain this statement with appropriate examples.

14. "Private-label brands: a gateway to strategic and sustainable competitive advantage." Explain this statement with appropriate examples.

Chapter 7

Retail Pricing: Strategies and Techniques

Learning Objectives

- Pricing strategies in retail
- Pricing techniques
- Markups
- Markdowns

Introduction

Determining the exact retail price for an item is an important step in selling merchandise. In very simple terms, price is the result of a transaction or exchange that takes place between two parties (here, the retailer and the customer) and refers to what must be given up by one party (the buyer) to get something offered by another party (here, the retailer).

The retail price of an item affects its salability, the store's image, and the overall profitability of the store. The retail price of an item needs to be established before the merchandise is placed in the store, which further adds to the risky and speculative nature of the pricing decision. Although past records, current pricing policies, market conditions, expenses, and other factors are considered, the final decision in establishing a retail price also depends on the judgment of a person. Underlying all the previously described pricing methods is the need for the buyer or merchandiser who sets prices to possess knowledge of the merchandise item, the store's image (retailer's positioning), the market, and the consumer.

Hence, pricing is one of the major components of the marketing plan, which is a part of a full business plan. Assigning merchandise price is a strategic activity. The price retailer assigns will impact how consumers view the products and whether they will purchase it. Price also helps differentiate the retailer from its competitors. However, the price retailer assigns must be in line with its other marketing strategies and the merchandise offerings. Here market research and competition analysis are imperative for developing a marketing plan and also to decide on the pricing strategies the retailer is going to implement. The insights gained from the research help in assigning appropriate prices to the merchandise or services. Hence, the quality and attributes the merchandise items and services offered by the retailer are eventually reflected in the price points that the retailer sets.

Pricing Strategies in Retail

Pricing policies determine the price levels or price points at which retailers sell their merchandise. Retailers' price points indicate the amount of money at which merchandise items are offered for sale. A retailer's pricing policy has to be coordinated with its brand image as the price points of merchandise play a significant role in creating and influencing customers' perceptions toward the retailer's offerings. Hence, pricing is a key component in developing the positioning factor and needs to be decided in relation to the target market, competition, and other marketing mix factors. Price is a strong motivation in consumer buying behavior, and it is a competitive weapon, and many times, it is the only way to appeal the customer patronage when merchandise assortments are comparable or if they are identical.

Therefore, this makes essential for the retailers to select the most appropriate pricing strategy to develop the desired competitive advantage and differentiation. Choosing the correct approach to pricing has a large effect on profits. While some retailers emphasize low price as a major appeal to customers, others accentuate on the aspirational merchandise and brands with high prices. Research shows that many a time consumers patronize a retailer on the basis if its pricing policy and the price points are one of the major factors that retailer are using to increase the loyalty behavior. For instance, price-conscious consumers actively compare prices by several retailers, both online and off-line, in order to get the best deal. The brand-conscious customers prefer the image and positioning attributes of a retailer brand and are ready to shell out premiums for acquiring the merchandise of that brand. Hence, the price–value relationship has become a powerful buying incentive.

Offering the Right Price Points

Here are some factors and aspects that retailers consider before arriving at a pricing policy.

- Purchase price and all other costs associated with a product.
- Number of competitors sell the same or similar products.
- Brand image and positioning in the market—premium products at premium prices, discount value store, and so on.

Moreover, equipped with modern retail systems, retailers can also study how similar items performed previously and they can find answer to some of these following questions:

- Is there an opportunity for a price increase while still maintaining strong sales?
- Does the product need to be a bit cheaper to achieve the required sell-through rate?
- When should the item be marked down and to what price in order to clear the product before its "right time" runs out?

Here the retailer may consider adjusting the price of an item per store or per region based on local factors such as economic demographics or the strength of the local competition. Hence, "pricing" is an art and science and, if employed strategically, can enhance the value proposition of the retailer. In the case of retailing, pricing is referred as "price points." This is the prevalent practice of predetermining the retail prices at which an assortment of merchandise will be carried. A retailer offers a merchandise assortment to the consumer at a specific price point such as ₹500, ₹1,000, and ₹2,500.

A buyer in the retail company creates a stock assortment by considering what price lines, which depend on many factors like the image of the retailer, the merchandise category, the merchandise assortment, quality level, and the value it is planning to provide to its target audience. The emphasis of a stock by price points depends on the composition of the consumer segments that the retailer plans to target. It eventually plans the depth of assortment offered at the various price points. Hence, the number of price lines and those particular price points in the assortment, in turn, help the retailer to present its image.

For instance, a fashion retailer may sell a shirt for ₹1,000. Now this price point may cover a variety of designs, fabrics, and sizes. Here the retailers with the help of research on buying behavior of its target customer segment know that the customers visiting their stores will buy the shirt for ₹1,000. Another retailer may stock a variety of shirts that retail from ₹500 to ₹4,000. This is referred as price range, which is nothing but the lowest to the highest price point carried by the retailer. Many times, customers prefer to go for either one price point or several price points that are relatively close to each other. Sometimes, customers may even prefer to buy multiple merchandise items being sold at very distinct price points. Most of the time, different customer segments prefer to buy the merchandise at different price points. So taking all these possibilities into consideration, a retailer brings different price zones, which refer to a series of price lines that are likely to appeal to one segment of customers that the retailer is targeting. Hence, when the retailer stocks more than two price lines, a price zone situation emerges.

For instance, a retailer can stock shirts in three different ranges: ₹800–₹1,500 (lower zone), ₹1,500–₹3,000 (middle zone), and ₹3,000–₹5,000 (higher zone).

The Key Pricing Strategies in Retailing

High–low Pricing

High–low pricing is a method of pricing for an organization where the merchandise or services offered by the retailer are regularly priced higher than competitors. However, through promotions, advertisements, and other offers (programs), lower prices are offered on other key items consumers would want to purchase. The lower promotional prices are designed to bring customers to the organization where the customer is offered the merchandise on promotional prices as well as the merchandise at regular higher price points.

High–low pricing was born, and fairly quickly became the norm. This strategy was used as another element of differentiation; some retailers started reducing the prices of key merchandise items, in order to pull customers into their stores, where they used to buy other merchandise along with the reduced-price merchandise. The retailer made little profit, or even a loss, on the price-reduced products, but recouped the lost margins in the increased sales of other profitable lines. High–low pricing also introduced an element of excitement into shopping and enhanced the shopping experience. Shoppers get encouraged with the feeling that they have bought an exceptional bargain, and this would tend to motivate them to return.

High–low pricing is a type of pricing strategy adopted by companies, usually small and medium-sized retail firms. The basic type of customers for the firms adopting high–low price will not have a clear idea about what a product's price would typically be or have a strong perception that "discount sales is low price." High–low pricing is extensively used in the fashion industry by retailers like Reebok, Nike, Adidas Lifestyle, Westside, Shoppers Stop, Macy's, and Nordstrom.

Everyday Low Pricing

EDLP, another strategy for retail positioning, promotes the idea that consumers can shop in the store at any time, knowing that they will get a fair price that gives good or great value for the money. This strategy has been used recently by some discount chains. It tries to instill a sense of trust and consistency toward pricing, while providing a reasonable profit to the retailer.

EDLP is a pricing strategy promising consumers a low price without the need to wait for sale price events or comparison shopping to appeal to the more price-conscious shopper and to simplify shopping for the time-poor shopper; other retailers adopted a pricing strategy wherein they charged a fair but low-as-possible price for all the merchandise items. In this case, there are not only high seasonal markups but also the bargain prices during promotional sales are also eliminated. This leads logically to the idea that a brand that is consistently priced as the cheapest in the market and can have an incredibly strong position. Profitable and sustainable price differentiation can be more than a tactical maneuver; it can be a winning strategy for a brand. EDLP has been an acknowledged part of grocery retailer positioning for many years. But Walmart's strategy in the USA has echoes in Lidl and Aldi in Europe, Ed in France, Kopeika in Russia, and Shoprite in South Africa. Similarly, the international players like Walmart, Food Lion, Gordmans, and Winn-Dixie and Indian retailers like Big Bazaar, Easyday, D-Mart, and Reliance are the retailers that have implemented or championed EDLP.

Stores that use this strategy may enjoy more credible pricing, reduced advertising costs, a steadier flow of sales, and better partnerships with vendors, which can be attributed to more regularity in the stock turnover. EDLP also saves retail store's efforts and expenses needed to markdown prices in the store during sale events, as well as to market these events and, also believed, to generate shoppers' loyalty. EDLP is the perfect solution to those for whom shopping is a "task" to be handled as painlessly and quickly as possible. Here, there is no need to shop around, no need to watch for best deals, no need to waste time, simply buy what you need from the same place every week and know that you are getting a square deal.

A classic example of a successful brand that uses the EDLP strategy is Trader Joe's. Trader Joe's is a PLB that conducts a niche marketing strategy, describing itself as the "neighborhood store." Apart from the many strengths of Trader Joe's, the most prominent is their commitment to quality and lower prices. The retailer has been growing at a steady pace, offering a wide variety of organic and natural food items that are hard to find, enabling the business to enjoy a distinctive competitive advantage. At Trader Joe's, EDLPs are available to everyone. The retailer works on the brand philosophy that goes like this: "every penny we save is every penny our customer saves."

The company has successfully managed this economy-affordable and "value for money" image, which eventually became its value proposition. Trader Joe's developed a distinct image in the minds of its target audience because it does not market itself like other grocery stores do, nor does it require its customers to take out a membership to enjoy its low prices.

Pricing below the market is a policy in which retail prices are set below those of the competition. Price-cutting policies were originally introduced by supermarkets, and then spread to apparel and other product sectors. Retailers may use this below-market pricing policy if they:

- Are in an inconvenient location
- Are a self-service organization
- Concentrate on high-volume sales
- Stock PL merchandise
- Lower their costs by using innovative technology to receive floor-ready merchandise from manufacturers
- Forego some promotional efforts

However, EDLP presents some challenges also. In the absence of other differentiators, any loyalty exhibited is to the prices charged, not to the business. Higher sales volumes and lower operational costs may not match the overall reduction of prices. Also, the many shoppers who shop sales events and enjoy "the thrill of a bargain" may be disenchanted by this approach. EDLP shoppers will defect to a competitor who begins to charge slightly lower prices.

Profit Up Front

After high–low pricing and EDLP, profit up front (PUF) was a new approach that was adopted by retailing firms to create differentiation on the basis of pricing. PUF pricing is seen in the warehouse club industry (e.g., Costco, SAM's, and BJ's) where qualified customers pay for the privilege of buying items at rock-bottom prices, which include extremely low profit margins. Usually, customers buy membership by paying an annual fee in advance. This membership makes them eligible for buying merchandise at "wholesale" prices at the warehouse. The operator can sell merchandise at these low prices because the revenue from these up-front membership fees account for about half of its pretax profit.

Psychological Pricing

As is the case with certain other elements in the marketing mix, price has multiple meanings beyond a simple functional statement. One such meaning is often referred to as the psychological aspect of pricing. Elucidation of quality of product from its price is a common example of the psychological aspect of price. Psychological pricing strategy is commonly used by retailers in establishing price for their products. For instance, ₹1,899 is psychologically "less" in the minds of consumers than ₹2,000. Though the difference in price here is too minor but has a potential to make a big impact on consumer psyche.

Another manifestation of the psychological aspects of pricing is the use of odd prices. We call prices that end in such digits as 5, 7, 8, and 9 "odd prices." For instance, many times we see the price tag that bear the numbers like ₹1,579, ₹1,879, and ₹4,999. Odd prices are intended to drive demand greater than would be expected if consumers were perfectly rationale.

Psychological pricing is one cause of such price points. For a long time, there have been long discussions and many research carried out in order to explain why odd prices are used and what its impact on consumer buying behavior is. Perhaps one of the most often observation made is the psychological impact of odd prices on customers. It seemed to make little difference whether one paid ₹1,959 or ₹2,000 for an item. But the difference is that customers perceive even prices such as ₹1,500 or ₹2,000 as regular prices. Odd prices, on the other hand, appear to represent bargains or savings and therefore encourage buying. Though even pricing is widely used, odd pricing is still very common. The psychological pricing theory is based on one or more of the following hypotheses:

- Consumers ignore the least significant digits rather than do the proper rounding. Even though the cents are seen and not totally ignored, they may subconsciously be partially ignored.
- Fractional prices suggest to consumers that goods are marked at the lowest possible price.
- When items are listed in a way that is segregated into price bands (such as an online real estate search), the price ending is used to keep an item in a lower band, to be seen by more potential purchaser.

Product Bundle Pricing

This strategy is used to group/bundle several items together to sell the slow-moving items. This is a useful pricing strategy for complementary, overstock, or older products. Customers purchase the product they really want, but for a little extra, they also receive one or more additional items. The advantage of this pricing strategy is the ability to get rid of overstock items. This strategy essentially motivates the customer for impulse buying. A somewhat related pricing strategy is combination pricing, such as two-for-one or buy-one-get-one-free. Consumers tend to react very positively to these pricing techniques with the feeling of getting more.

On the other hand, customers not wanting the extra items may decide not to purchase the bundle. This strategy is similar to product line pricing, except that the items being grouped together do not need to be complementary.

For example, retailer may have remaining stock of some festival-related merchandise items after the festival is over. So if the retailer prefers not to carry this inventory until next year, they can make an attractive "package or bundle" of variety of merchandise items and put the entire package on special offer with attractive discounted price. Product bundle pricing can be employed with the objective of revenue maximization or basket-size maximization or turning the slow-moving or nonmoving stock. Here value proposition can be achieved as some customers will appreciate having the opportunity to purchase a group of merchandise items at a discount.

Anchor Pricing

When consumers are unfamiliar or clueless with a merchandise category, they will use the highest priced model within a category as an anchor. PLBs in the supermarket are a good example of this strategy. They are placed close to the branded product and the price is typically 10–20% lower (approximately).

Multiple Pricing

Multiple pricing is aimed at getting customers to purchase a product in greater quantities by offering an attractive discount offer on buying more quantity. In this case, a price for the purchase of single merchandise item is displayed along with the price for a larger quantity. This automatically compels the customer to compare both the offers, and it is likely that the customer gets attracted toward better offer, ending in purchasing more. This eventually increases the ticket size and hence the revenues of the retailer. The multiple pricing strategies works well with the profit maximization and quantity maximization objectives.

For instance, a fashion retailer may price one T-shirt at ₹500 and two at ₹900. Pricing in this way offers the customer an apparent discount (now in this example, ₹100) for purchasing the greater quantity. Customers think that if they are getting a good discount what is the harm in buying more. Here the retailer is not actually offering a very big discount but still can manage to sell more. On the other hand, customer however would have to spend ₹1,000 for buying two T-shirts, but he is saving ₹100 with this offer. This gives the customer a feel of getting good deal and hence an enhanced shopping experience. Hence, a customer purchasing a single item will pay more for the item than what retailers would typically charge if they were not using a multiple pricing strategy.

If the retailer thinks that majority of their customers will purchase the greater quantity, they plan to go for these kinds of offers wherein they can cover the costs and, at the same time, profit margin is maintained. Here the customer enticed with the feeling that they are "indirectly" paying more by not purchasing more. In addition, multiple pricing strategy, if employed effectively, has the potential to increase the quantity of merchandise items being sold, hopefully resulting in regular stock turn or fewer unsold items and hence less items to be marked down at the time of EOSS.

Prestige Pricing

Prestige pricing is a policy of setting high prices on merchandise items to appeal those customers who want high-quality products and aspire to buy top-end brands (luxury brands) or the status of owning expensive and exclusive merchandise. Many luxury retailer brands set prices above those of competing retailers to create an image of superior product quality or image as a "prestige-luxury brand." This approach to pricing reinforces the image—positioning—differentiation of the in the retailer brand in the minds of target customers. Retailers who follow this pricing policy usually have stores located in affluent localities, high-end shopping centers, or at high-street area of the city. They typically offer a high level of service, carry exclusive labels, and may also offer high degree of personalization.

Pricing plays quite a big role in the way consumers perceive luxury brands. Consciously or subconsciously, consumers tend to generate a mental luxury stature or image with the price range that the brand operates.

The brands like Gucci, Louis Vuitton, and Cartier have created a unique positioning and the imagery for their products to appeal to the high-end market. The prestigious pricing of their products creates a high-quality image and positions the brand in the mind of the consumer as a status symbol.

In an effort, to maintain the prestige image of a Louis Vuitton product, the company operates a pricing integrity strategy among its entire distribution network; that is, a Louis Vuitton bag is never reduced in price, and there are no sale periods.

Hence, a brand's price is just as important and integral to a brand's equity as any other association. Price is a source of meaning and identity for a brand, not a separate countervailing factor. When price is recognized as a critical element of a brand's association set, it is usually in relation to a luxury brand. The status of a brand such as Louis Vuitton, Prada, or Armani is underpinned by the price at which it is sold. Its high price sets it apart and makes it exclusive; it is an integral and crucial part of its equity. The high price is part of the badge value that the brand's customers enjoy.

Premium Pricing

Premium pricing is employed when the merchandise offered is unique and of very high quality. Here the focus is not on the revenues generated but on the aspirational value of the merchandise and brand. The resultant high brand equity of the brand is leveraged to garner a high premium. Perceptions about a brand's values, personality, and heritage all factor into consumer sentiment toward a brand. Typically, price is seen as something separate and distinct from other elements of brand equity, a factor that consumers weigh against their feelings about a brand. By virtue of these functional and aspirational attributes, a high premium is justified. Therefore, it is important for luxury brands to price themselves right, as setting the price lower than the consumer expectation and willingness to pay can potentially harm the brand value. Buyers of such products typically view them as luxuries and have little or no price sensitivity. The advantage of this pricing strategy is that retailer can price high for the merchandise it is offering and earn a large profit to make up for the small number of items being sold and can also recover the investment made in building the brand.

Premium pricing strategy establishes a price higher than the competitors. It is a strategy that can be effectively used when there is something unique about the product or when the product is first to market and the business has a distinct competitive advantage. Premium pricing can be a good strategy for companies entering the market with a new market and hoping to maximize revenue during the early stages of the product life cycle.

Hence, premium pricing can be employed with the profit margin maximization or quality leadership pricing objectives. The premium price charged for the uniqueness and quality of retailers' product allows them to generate large profit margins on each item sold. The product will also demonstrate the commitment of the retailer to quality, and customers will think of the brand when they desire such quality.

The pricing strategy in luxury brands gained spotlight in the recent past not only because of the challenging economic environment but also because of more informed-and-exposed consumers who are more discriminating and demanding, for whom premium pricing without substance does not imply luxury. A recent research by Unity Marketing suggests that affluent shoppers will not spend ten times more for something only three times better. The luxury brands must, therefore, justify their price through the interplay of the marketing mix elements pertaining to the business of retailing, thereby keeping up and maintaining a higher perceived value.

"Privileged" Pricing

Most pricing strategies clearly appeal to one category of shoppers but not to others. EDLP, for example, would appeal to time-poor/value-seeking shoppers who have little to spend or seek more value for every penny spent or want to avoid the hassles of searching and comparing the deals. It would make sense for them to choose a solid EDLP store and do all their shopping there. High–low pricing would appeal to cherry pickers that fall into the time-rich/stiff bargainer category. The "premium pricing" would appeal to those who are looking for high-end products with high aspirational value and have little or no price sensitivity.

But "privileged" essentially appeals to all categories of shoppers. "Privileged" pricing is nothing but a loyalty-based pricing technique and its unique feature is that it allows a retailer to differentiate prices between regular customers and occasional shoppers in an open, transparent way. It is ultimately fair-tiered pricing system that is one of the most striking features of privileged pricing. Up until now, it is been difficult to offer higher prices for occasional customers and lower prices for regular customers within the same retail store, without offending some customers. But "privileged" pricing, by using new technologies and a points-based loyalty card program, now makes it very easy. Customers gain loyalty points on every purchase, which can be redeemed eventually on the next purchase. Here, pricing is done at two levels: the price that a merchandise item would normally sell for, and a very much lower price that is available in exchange for some of the customer's loyalty points.

Modus Operandi

Customers collect points on their purchases, using a seemingly standard points-based loyalty program. Throughout the store, key items are priced at two levels: the price that the item would normally sell for and a second price lower than the first one, but supplemented by some of the buyer's loyalty points.

For example, as expected, a merchandise is usually priced at ₹1,000 could be bought off the shelf for ₹1,000. But alternatively, it could be bought for ₹600 plus some of the loyalty points that the customer has already collected. Here ₹400 discount is earned by spending an amount in the previous purchases. It may or may not be counting the bonus points; even then, it is a substantial reward. This means that the customers have control of the prices they pay, and how they spend their loyalty points. They gain this control by being loyal to a particular retailer or few retailers. This is a win–win situation as it helps the customer to earn rewards for her loyalty and assists the retailer to enhance the loyalty behavior of its customers. It also maintains member interest, and gets customers interacting with the program on a frequent basis (every time they go shopping) and thereby enhances the shopping experience.

Predatory Pricing

Predatory pricing is a pricing strategy that is undertaken by businesses in order to damage or eliminate a competitor. The practice is generally taken to mean selling certain key products at a price that is lower than the prevailing price points for those products. Furthermore, it is believed that selling below invoice cost is predatory; that is, to reduce prices below invoice cost for a sustained period can only be motivated by predatory tactics.

In a typical scenario, a large retailer engages in selling below cost on a persistent basis, and in so doing, the company attracts customers away from other players that are unable to compete with the unreasonably low prices. This can eventually force the smaller players out of business or they may face losses and the predator, left with the market to him, can increase prices to whatever level he/she likes. The customer, with nowhere else to shop, has no choice but to pay up.

The predatory pricing has been interpreted in different ways by different jurisdictions and discipline; for example, economist define predatory pricing as "A price reduction that is profitable only because of the added market power the predator gains from eliminating, reducing, disciplining, or otherwise inhibiting the competitive conduct of a rival or a potential rival. Hence, predatory pricing is a price that is revenue maximizing only because of its exclusionary or other anticompetitive effects and implications."

There are a number of criteria that must be met before a retailer's pricing strategy can be considered predatory. Selling below cost is one such criterion and, therefore, finding an acceptable or agreed definition of "cost" is a critical factor. "Below cost" is regarded by some as a price that is below cost plus a margin that reflects the need for all business to make a profit, but we do not find this to be a commonly held view.

It is generally accepted, however, that "cost" is greater than simply the purchase price paid by the retailer for the merchandise in question. It also includes the operating/overhead costs incurred by the retailer in actually bringing the merchandise to the store. Furthermore, the predator may have certain level of confidence that once the competitor has exited the market, he will not reenter or, alternatively, that he will not be replaced with some new entrant.

Selling at a price representative of invoice cost less discounts (in other words, at a price less than the true purchase price of the product) would be a predatory tactic. We cannot agree with this assertion because, as we shall see, we consider that there are many legitimate reasons for selling a product below cost.

For example, Walmart was alleged with three separate charges of predatory pricing. Government officials in Wisconsin and Germany accused the retailer of pricing merchandise below cost with intent to drive competitors out of the market. In Oklahoma, Walmart faced a private lawsuit alleging similar illegal pricing practices. The Wisconsin Department of Agriculture, Trade and Consumer Protection filed a complaint with an administrative law judge accusing the retailer of violating the state's antitrust law. The complaint alleged that Walmart sold butter, milk, laundry detergent, and other staple products below cost in stores in Beloit, Oshkosh, Racine, Tomah, and West Bend. This was alleged to be aimed at forcing other stores out of business to gain a monopoly in local markets, and ultimately regain its losses through higher prices.

In Germany, Walmart was charged with similar predatory tactics. The Federal Cartel Office accused Walmart and two other large supermarket chains of selling goods below cost and ordered the companies to raise prices immediately.

The items in question included staple products like milk and vegetable oil. A common Walmart strategy was alleged to price such staples, known as "corner products," very low. Corner products are items for which consumers know the going price. By setting prices on these items very low, Walmart allegedly created an overall impression of having very low prices, when in fact much of its merchandise may not be such a good deal.

In Oklahoma, a supermarket chain filed a predatory pricing suit against Walmart. The suit argued that Walmart sold goods below cost at its store in Edmond in order to force that supermarket out of business. The supermarket chain also alleged that Walmart employees, including some top officials, regularly visited the supermarket to monitor prices. According to the suit, Walmart then targeted price cuts to undermine the competition, often reducing prices well below its own costs to take on its rival. Such tactics are illegal under two state laws, the Unfair Sales Act and the Antitrust Reform Act.

The Online Retail Onslaught

The rapid growth of online retail over the past years has worried the traditional brick-and-mortar retailers (both organized and unorganized).

Internet has transformed the retail experience for consumers by activating their emotions and sparking the desire to buy through imagery, videos and virtual try-on, huge selection choice, real-time feedback, free home delivery, so on. With online shopping gaining momentum among the middle class, the threat of physical stores getting cannibalized is clear and present. Foreign investors have been looking for opportunities to make inroads. They found one in e-commerce where business was growing leaps and bounds. Now under the extant policy, 100% FDI is allowed in B2B transactions in e-commerce, whereas it is prohibited in B2C. However, there was no robust framework and clear-cut rules to regulate e-commerce companies. There was no clear demarcation for what exactly constitutes B2B and B2C in the context of e-commerce.

It was alleged by the off-line retailers that the e-commerce companies have taken advantage of these loopholes and ambiguities in policy environment to have free access to foreign funding and yet claim that they are in full compliance with extant regulations. The RAI argued that e-commerce companies have presented their business as "marketplace model." They contend that they are merely providing a platform to sellers and buyers for conducting transactions, that they are mere facilitators or service providers and are far removed from being a party to these transactions. In other words, they are apportioning themselves to B2B classification where 100% FDI is permitted. RAI also argued that some top e-commerce players were following the deep-discounting models in India aided by "foreign funds" and the country's brick-and-mortar retailers were facing tough competition as there was no level playing field (Figure 7.1).

They alleged that online players used this money to offer heavy discounts, which will have a serious devastating effect on brick-and-mortar players in retail space. Even the unorganized

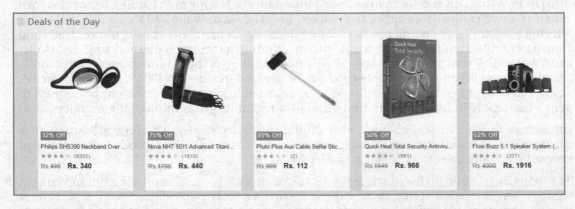

Figure 7.1: *The Price War*

Source: www.snapdeal.com (accessed on 12 May 2016)

players will not remain unaffected. Customers find virtually anything they need online at heavily discounted prices and have them delivered for free. They save money, fuel, time, and get more work done in same time frame.

Opening another front against pricing policies of e-commerce firms, the Confederation of All India Traders (CAIT) complained to the Center that some online marketplace biggies are violating the consolidated FDI policy circular, 2015. CAIT alleged that these e-commerce portals are circumventing the law and engaging in B2C activities, which are prohibited for them, as these companies have received foreign investments. This allows them to undertake only B2B, and not B2C e-commerce activities, according to the FDI norms, as no FDI is allowed in B2C e-commerce.

Referring to the "sale" events announced by these online retailers, CAIT alleged in a letter to the Center that the advertisement campaigns addressed to the general public are equivalent to retail trading. It further urged the DIPP in the commerce and industry ministry to issue directions to these firms, restricting them from offering "sales" and "discounts."

While the aggressive pricing strategies of e-tailers is the biggest reason for their growth, increasing customer confidence in buying online is playing a major role in the growth of e-commerce. The biggest USP of e-tailers has been their prices, and their pricing policies have ranged from aggressive to predatory.

The retailers have appealed to the government to take action against "unethical online retailers" who are using their money power to sell products at below cost price to attract customer and killing the whole market using foreign VC money. The retailers have also alleged that while VC funding is not allowed in e-commerce, some online retailers are floating parent companies outside India and routing the money to India.

E-commerce Companies Respond

To these allegations, some of the leading online retailers responded with the argument that they are operating on "marketplace model" wherein they connect thousands of sellers across India to millions of buyers. They also argue that they do not carry any inventory and that retailer and manufacturers list and sell their products directly to consumers via the platform. They also stated that this model is helping the small sellers to scale their business and that also at a fraction of the traditional selling cost. They said that they are providing the online retailers with all the support in terms of a more well-known brand name, technology, market reach, logistics, and customer support. These online retailers also argued that the prices of merchandise being sold on these marketplaces are decided not by them but by the sellers. The online players state that they also provide analytical reports to the retailers/sellers pertaining to their sales performance and suggestions on how they could increase the sales. They argue that the sellers leverage these insights to determine the optimal price at which they should sell their products for higher revenues. In most of these cases, these small retailers have seen a double-digit month-on-month growth in their business after listing on their marketplace—a relatively simple business model.

However, CAIT in a letter to the Center argued that as these companies claim to be marketplaces, they can provide only a technology platform for the sellers who are registered with them. But these companies invite the general public to their respective sales through big advertisement campaigns on print, electronic, and social media. Here they posed a question that if these e-commerce biggies are only doing B2B business, where is the need for big advertisements addressed to the general public, adding that as marketplaces, they can only provide a technology platform for the sellers registered with them. They also added that as the ownership of inventory does not hold by the said companies, they cannot offer "sale" or "discounts" in totality on their online portals, but they are doing so, which also establishes that they are not only marketplaces but also the violation of FDI policy.

According to RAI, the DIPP asked the state governments to give their inputs on the country's e-commerce situation, including their views on deep discounts being offered by some major e-retailers, in order to formulate a "consolidated" policy on retail.

Pricing Techniques: Markups and Markdowns

Retail pricing is fundamental to the retail sale of merchandise, to the satisfaction of the consumer, and to the profitability of the business. To maintain the sustainable profitability, retailers need to follow the appropriate pricing techniques. Price also plays a significant role in retail marketing, where it is one of the variables in marketing mix that retailers use to develop the marketing plan.

With many items, the primary focus of the buyer's decision-making is on the selection of the item based upon the style, color, size, and other features that will be in demand by the consumer. Style and color are the first characteristics noticed by the consumer when shopping for many items and are often the characteristics that give appeal to the merchandise item when displayed in the store. When it comes to India, fashion, style, and the best price on a sustainable basis are what customers are looking for.

Selecting the right merchandise items for that will appeal to target consumer, and offering it at right price is key to success in retail. It is very difficult to sell the right item at the wrong price. In today's retailing scenario, assigning a right retail price seems simple, but it is as difficult as determining the right item. Pricing decisions involve three basic elements: the cost of the merchandise, the retail price, and the difference between them, which is referred as markup (MU).

Concept of Markup

All retailers would like to sell large volumes of merchandise at high prices for greater profits. However, the marketing triangle has shown that price and quantity sold are inversely related to each other. Most retailers either seek high unit markups on low volumes of merchandise, or low markups on high sales volumes. The overall profits of each might be similar, but they are selling to different target markets and offering other differences in the total marketing mix. In developing a pricing strategy, the retailer must price merchandise low enough to generate sales but high enough to cover costs and make a satisfactory profit.

Markup is a standard technique used while pricing merchandise, and it is the amount that is added to the cost price of merchandise to arrive at a retail price. Hence, this amount has to be large enough to cover the cost of the merchandise, the expenses incurred for selling it, and the desired profit. The retail price must contain the wholesale cost of the item and the markup assigned to the item. Here the cost of the merchandise is generally called cost of goods or "wholesale cost," a generic term that will be used regardless of the type of merchandise item that is purchased. This cost is the price of the item charged by the wholesaler, manufacturer, or other distributor, and it represents the price that the retail buyer paid for the item. Cost of goods includes the invoice value of the item, which is also called the list price, the transportation, and often the cost of insurance to cover the merchandise while it is being shipped by the vendor or manufacturer to the retailer.

Retail price = Cost of merchandise + Markup

Markup = Retail price – Cost of merchandise

Markup is based on cost and is expressed in percentage terms.

Markup = Percentage of margin calculated on cost added to arrive at the maximum retail price

The retail price elements can also be viewed as percentages. Percentages are useful for making comparisons across items, across departments, and across stores. The retail price is the base of the relationship and represents 100% of the price. Using the retail price as a base is common for many retailers. The formula for retail price percentages is:

Retail % = Cost % + Markup %

Hence, markup serves as a guide in pricing merchandise and in providing the desired operating profit.

- Markup includes operating expenses, retail reductions (that are markdowns, discounts, and shrinkage), and profit.
- Markup is the difference between the retail price and the cost of goods sold.
- Markup may be established by one of several methods, for example, component addition, price lining, and market pricing.

    1. With the component addition method, markup is built from the value of needed expenses.
    2. In price lining and market pricing, markup is the result of the difference between cost and the established retail price.

- Markup may be set as a single amount for every item, regardless of type or classification of merchandise; however, a fixed or single markup is usually used only with like or similar items within a merchandise classification.
- Markup may also be fixed as equal to the cost of the merchandise. This method is known as a *keystone markup* or a markup that doubles the invoiced cost of the item to achieve the retail price.
- Alternatively, markup may vary across the same classifications and/or other merchandise categories.
- Markup, within one store, may be different for many items.
- Markup may also change for an item as the season and the level of sales change or during price adjustments such as markdowns, special promotions, or other price changes.
- Many methods are used to find markup, but the formula, which represents the relationship among the price elements, is the same in each situation.
- Markup is the percentage amount (calculated on cost) added to cost in order to arrive at the maximum retail price for a product.

Hence, the formula is:

Example 1

What is the markup percentage for a jacket that costs ₹2,000 and retails for ₹4,000?

Markup (%) = Difference between maximum retail price (MRP) and cost
(₹4,000 − ₹2,000) ÷ Cost (₹2,000) × 100

= ₹2,000 ÷ ₹2,000 × 100

= 100%

Example 2

A retailer purchased a lot of T-shirts. Each T-shirt has a merchandise cost of ₹150. A keystone markup is used by the store, and hence the markup on a shirt is ₹300. So what will be the retail price of the T-shirt?

Retail (₹) = Cost (₹) + Markup (₹)

(*Note:* Keystone markup means that the markup is the same as the cost)

Retail price (₹) = ₹150 + ₹150

Retail price (₹) = ₹300

Example 3

A retailer purchased some home furnishing items at a cost of ₹10,000 per unit for a suggested retail price of ₹15,000 per item. What is the necessary markup for one item?

(*Note:* Here, we need to make the algebraic changes and formula can be rewritten to compute the markup)

Markup (₹) = Retail (₹) – Cost (₹)

Hence

Markup (₹) = ₹15,000 – ₹10,000

Markup (₹) = ₹5,000

Example 4

In order to explore the multiple sales opportunities, the retailer decided to purchase fast-fashion denim jeans to complement it with the T-shirts in Example 2. The denim jeans were retailed with a keystone markup on US$1,800. What is the cost of each denim jeans?

Cost (₹) = Retail (₹) – Markup (₹)

(*Note:* Keystone is doubling the invoiced cost of the merchandise item. In this situation, calculate markup (₹) by finding one/half or 50% of the retail price.)

Cost (₹) = ₹1,800 – ₹900

Cost (₹) = ₹900

Retail Price Elements as Percentages

Example 5

A small artifact item is assigned the markup percentage of 45%, and the cost percentage is 55%. By applying the formula, a retail percentage of 100% can be confirmed.

Retail (%) = Cost (%) + Markup (%)

Retail (%) = 55% + 45%

Retail (%) = 100%

Hence, by adding cost percentage and markup percentage, the retail percentage of 100% is confirmed.

Example 6

A leather jacket has a cost percentage of 40% and the retail percentage is known to be 100%. What will be the markup percentage for this product?

Retail (%) = Cost (%) + Markup (%)

After the algebraic changes, Markup (%) = Retail (%) – Cost (%)

Markup (%) = 100% – 40%

Markup (%) = 60%

Example 7

The standard markup percentage for the furniture retailer is 43%. A four-chair dining set is sold in the store at ₹30,000. What is the cost percentage of the dining set?

(*Note:* Retail percentage is 100%.)

Retail (%) = Cost (%) + Markup (%)

Cost (%) = Retail (%) – Markup (%)

Cost (%) = 100% – 43%

Cost (%) = 57%

Concept of Markdown

It is one of the most common and widely followed price adjustments and is technically referred as markdown (MD). As the name itself suggests, it is the act of reducing or lowering the original or the previous retail price on one item or on a group of merchandise items. Original (list) retail prices are often higher than actual selling price points. Value pricing is the selling of merchandise items below the price suggested by its vendors. This price-cutting policy is used by discounters, those that generally follow the EDLP. However, some vendors and retail stores imply that list prices for merchandise are higher than they really are. The merchandise item is then marked down to a normal level, but with value pricing implied.

For example, a vase article was retailed for ₹1,000 when it was received in the store but eventually reduced to ₹750, as there were some minor scratches on it. This price adjustment (here, in order to make the defective article more salable) is called a markdown because the retail value of the merchandise was reduced. This difference between former price (₹1,000) and the new selling price (₹750) is (here ₹250) referred as markdown. Hence, markdown is nothing but amount by which the retail value has been lowered, and this figure is very critical for any retailer.

Retailers would prefer to sell most of the goods at the original retail price. However, the reducing the prices becomes sometimes necessary to provide successful merchandising options. Markdown is the amount reduced from the MRP to arrive at new retail price. Markdown is calculated as a percentage of MRP.

Markdowns are done when:

- Merchandise sales are low or the season draws to a close and the related merchandise inventory needs to be cleared from the shelves.
- Inventories are high, saleable merchandises get damaged or shop-soiled, or certain price-off promotions are done.
- Merchandise has minor manufacturing defects but is still salable, and it is found at the floor level or found by customer when picked at.

Higher frequency of such incidents or practice can cause retailers to lose credibility with consumers.

Retailers often express the markdown as a percentage of net sales of all merchandise during a specific period, monthly or yearly. It is essential to keep the markdown percentage at the lowest, as it directly affects the returns on gross margins in a retail store.

Markdown merchandise (%) = Net sales at markdown ÷ Total net sales × 100

This is the percentage of marked-down merchandise to sales. If the ratio increases, the retailer may need to take a closer look at merchandising practices, particularly pricing.

Example 8

What is the markdown percentage for a vase article whose original MRP is ₹1,000 and the new retail price after markdown is ₹750?

Markdown (%) = Difference between old MRP and new MRP after markdown

(₹1,000 – ₹750) ÷ old MRP (₹1,000) × 100

= ₹250 ÷ 10

= 25%

The Purpose of Markdowns

Retailers often prefer to sell merchandise at regular prices and avoid the markdowns. Markdown leads to reduced sale prices that limit the profit potential and cash flow on sales. However, despite these financial concerns, there are several advantages that a retailer can achieve by marking down merchandise prices at the right time.

Sometimes, marking up prices only to put the merchandise on sale at a more reasonable figure might be manipulation, but many times, it also tends to work, though the customer realizes the retailer's tactic. It is a general tendency of customers to enjoy the "perceptual discount" that comes with the pleasing feel of getting great bargain. Retailers often play the markup–markdown game to attract and motivate customers, as the feeling of getting good offer is also a component of shopping experience.

However, the markup–markdown strategy is not so easy to execute and needs to be implemented very carefully because if it goes wrong, it can be harmful to the image of the retailer. It requires meticulous study to determine the extent to which merchandise should be marked up and should be discounted eventually and the percentage off it takes to move slow-moving items.

One of the major reasons retailer markdown merchandise items is to clear out the slow-moving or nonmoving stock. For instance, at the end of the festive season, a department store typically marks down the festival-related merchandise before the buying season ends. Sometimes, the merchandise may not be sold for desired profits or may be at no profit, but it clears the inventory and also the space. Here the lost profit may eventually be recouped from the sale of stock at the beginning of the festival and also from the other items that are sold during the markdowns.

- To simulate the sale of merchandise toward which customers are not showing desired interest.
- To attract customers to stores by offering "best buy" deals.
- To meet competitive price points.
- To act as a source of open-to-buy money to purchase the fresh stock of merchandise items.
- To design special promotional offers/campaigns like festivals, celebrations, special offers for employees, and so on.

However, the disadvantage of markdowns is that they can decrease the retailer's profits if the markdowns are excessive or are done when it is not necessary. Markdowns can also make accounting more complicated as the retailer have to account for the different prices of the merchandise items at different times.

Reason for Markdowns

The retailers need to analyze the reasons for markdowns in order to minimize it. There are several causes of markdowns.

Buying Error

- Overbuying in quantities that eventually results in the slow-moving or nonmoving inventory.
- Buying wrong sizes/designs/colors/patterns/out-of-vogue fashion and style.
- Issues related to quality of the merchandise or damages.
- Wrong or inappropriate timing in ordering merchandise or the retailer receives the shipment of merchandise late.
- Wrong pricing of the merchandise. Sometimes, the merchandise is priced with wrong markups, which eventually results in slow-moving of the stock because customers perceive it costly vis-à-vis the perceived value. It also includes errors like deferring the markdowns for too long or calculated risk of carrying "prestige" merchandise.
- Merchandising errors: The merchandise is not displayed rightly or not at the right location.
- Improper handling of the merchandising that led to damage or soiling; it is also called as "forced markdown."
- Sales associates did not presented (preached) the merchandise in the manner that will appeal to the customer.
- Remnant merchandise items from the broken merchandise stories, sets, and assortments.
- Remainder merchandise items from festival sales or other special offers or remaining merchandise from the summer–winter collection.

The Amount of Markdown

Deciding on correct markdown percentage requires the business acumen of a professional that is based on experience, skill, and expertise. As the reasons for markdown may be different at different point of time and situations, it is difficult to devise a generalized formula for computing the amount of markdown. Here the "right" depends on the circumstantial factors and reasons that essentially depend on the:

- Reasons that led to reduction in price (markdown) of the merchandise
- Nature of the merchandise and/or its current form
- Inventory of the merchandise in hand
- Obsolescence level of the merchandise
- Level of damage or defect
- Initial (original) markup
- Nature, degree, or intensity of the circumstantial factors that are responsible for markdown

However, following are some general guidelines that are generally considered while marking the merchandise down:

1. The first markdown needs to be sufficiently sharp so that it will allow a significant volume/quantity/amount of merchandise to move (sold out). The prime objective of markdown is to rapidly sell the merchandise, under question. So, here the amount of markdown should be set optimally so that will help the retailer to achieve desired results.

2. Markdown should be sufficiently big enough. Large markdowns often ensure that the customer will be attracted toward the offer with the feeling of getting good bargain/value. But it does not mean that it should be large always or too large because such things may lead to generation of a feeling of suspicion in the mind of consumer.

3. Small markdowns are often not effective enough to drive the sale and movement.

Example 9

A men's fashion retailer had a stock of 50 jackets priced at ₹2,250 each. It was a slow-moving item, so to stimulate the sales of this slow-moving item, the retailer decided to reduce the price of the jacket to ₹1,750. This markdown eventually resulted in the sale of 40 items in a short time. After a certain time, the retailer further reduced the price of the jacket to ₹1,250 each to clear the remaining stock of 10 jackets. At this price, all the remaining jackets were sold out. Compute the total markdown that retailer had taken in this case.

Here the first markdown for the item = Original retail price – First markdown price

= ₹2,250 – ₹1,750 = ₹500

The amount of markdown per piece of merchandise item = ₹500

The total number of piece sold with the first markdown is 40.

Hence,

Total markdown = 500 × 40 = ₹20,000

The second markdown on the merchandise item is

First markdown price – Second markdown price = ₹1,750 – ₹1,250 = ₹500

The amount of markdown per piece of merchandise item = ₹500

The total number of piece sold with the first markdown is 10.

Hence,

Total markdown = 500 × 10 = ₹5,000

Thus,

Total markdown = ₹20,000 + ₹5,000 = ₹25,000

Summary

The "right price" is the amount consumers are willing to pay for certain products and retailers are willing to accept. It is the price that is satisfactory to the customer both before and after the sale. In summary, it is a price that brings about the sale, generates a profit, satisfies customer expectations, and meets competitive situations.

The effect of changing prices can also be studied, for example, which customer segments buy significantly more or less. To help with differentiation, some retailers reduce the prices of key products to attract new customers (hoping they will buy other products as well as the reduced-price ones). Other retailers try to "buy loyalty" to low pricing (EDLP). Yet others use PUF pricing, where the customer pays to be a shopper but gets low prices all round. Recently, a fourth way, called "privileged pricing," has emerged, allowing customers to use loyalty points to "buy" extra discounts on selected items in store (e.g., shirt for ₹3,000, or ₹1,500 plus 500 loyalty points).

Items sitting on the shelf as obsolete inventory are simply dead capital. Keeping inventory up to date and devoid of obsolete merchandise is another critical aspect of effective inventory control. This is particularly critical with style merchandise, but it is also crucial with any merchandise that is turning at a lower rate than the average stock turns for that particular business.

Markups are usually highest when a new style first comes out. As the style fades, efficient sellers gradually begin to mark it down to avoid being stuck with large inventories, thus keeping inventory capital working. They will begin to mark down their inventory, take less gross margin, and return the funds to working capital rather than have their investment stand on the shelves as obsolete merchandise. Markdowns are an important part of the working capital cycle. Even though the margins on markdown sales are lower, turning these items into cash allows the retailer to purchase other, more contemporary merchandise, where they can make the desired margin.

Keeping an inventory fresh and up to date requires constant attention by any organization, large or small. Style merchandise should be disposed of before the style fades. Fad merchandise must have its inventory levels kept in line with the passing fancy. Obsolete merchandise usually must be sold at less than normal markup or even as loss leaders where it is priced more competitively. Loss leader pricing strategies can also serve to attract higher consumer traffic and thus creating opportunities to sell other merchandise as well as the obsolete items. Technologically, obsolete merchandise should normally be removed from inventory at any cost.

Review Questions

1. Briefly explain the pricing strategies in retail.
2. What is the meaning of predatory pricing? What are the effects and repercussions of heavy discounted pricing by e-retailers?
3. Explain the concept of markup in detail.
4. Explain the concept of markdown in detail.

Managing People: HRM in Retailing

Introduction

Strategies might vary, focus and brand inclination may differ, and corporate philosophies could be unique, but the one thing common to all retail players is that people remain at the center. This is one of the crucial differentiating factors that attract customers toward the retailer. The terms like "globalization," "process management," and "value-based management" are the buzzwords in the boardroom discussions in retail companies. There has been an increasing realization that people are one of the key assets of any organization. The days have gone when HR department was considered just as a nonprofitable department of an organization. With changing times, additional responsibilities, and innovative practices, HR departments have now become an integral profit-making part of any company that is in the business of retailing. In retailing, customers are served in the direct way and at the personal level, which naturally demands special attention from retail companies to fulfill the demands of an increasing number of well-informed and sophisticated consumers.

On the other hand, one of the significant developments shaping the HR today is the rise of the millennials. This assorted generation that grew up with a mix of the laid-back 1990s and the transitional 2000s is driven on technology with a strong desire to connect and find meaning in their work. They flourish within flexible, collaborative, and passionate workplaces where their views and voices are respected and appreciated.

In view of all the changes in both national and international contexts, it is absolutely crucial to have the right people to ensure the success and sustainability for any retail organization. As mentioned earlier, retailing is majorly a labor-intensive function. Therefore, companies are continually challenged to reorganize and improve the human part of their structures to become more efficient. Emotionally, the workforce needs orientation and vision in changing times. HRM has to provide a "guide" not only to organize but also to support employees and management mentally and professionally in fulfilling their tasks and to channelize their efforts toward organization's goals. People are the driving force behind all transactions that occur in retailing outlets. In the future world of retailing, there will be an increasing need to adapt and change toward a more formative and proactive style of HRM. HR management guru, Dave Ulrich, says human resource needs to shift focus from inside a company to outside and concentrate on end customer alignment when hiring and mentoring talent.

Major Changes in Business of Retailing

The formats of retailing have been evolving continuously over the last 100 years, and individual retailers have changed tremendously in the products they sell and in the manner in which they operate. Initially, HR was seen as a support function and used to majorly concentrate on hiring and managing the exit of staff. With the opening up of FDI, entry of large retailers, and upsurge of e-commerce, there are lot of tasks in front of the HR teams such as retention, innovative hiring, increase productivity, and reducing attrition created due to competition. In addition, the volatility in the economy has a direct impact on organizational growth, and most retailers are constantly adapting to the changes in the market. This volatility has made organizations to make effective decisions, especially related to human capital management. In response to these business pressures, retailers are reevaluating their strategies around HRM. HR departments are expected to provide insights that are appropriate and aligned to the trends in the overall business environment.

For instance, retailing of lifestyle products has a direct impact on the changing cultural patterns of our societies. In order to provide an expanding product and service range, retail has had to alter and amend its approaches to satisfy ever-more-insatiable and increasingly educated and information-rich consumers. The changing face of India's retail has also experienced sea changes in the way HR department functions. If we think in Indian context, we will find that within a very short span of time, India has emerged as a favorable destination for international retailers, outpacing UAE, Russia, Indonesia, Brazil, South Africa, and Saudi Arabia. The sector employs around 7% of the total workforce; this is the second largest employer after agriculture and continues to increasingly provide employment opportunities within the country. The retail formats in India have evolved without any past blueprint or precedent to refer back to. Therefore, India's retail industry has been defined by experimentation, risk-taking, and trial-and-error methods.

On the other hand, the manpower-intensive nature and unique requirements have resulted in HR deliberations taking on supreme importance for the sustainable growth of the sector. Over these years, the primary focus of every retailer was on sales and brand building along with expansion strategies. But this causes big challenges with respect to dealing with the short supply of qualified (skilled), future-ready talent, capable of performing at high standards and retaining key talent. Here the key task for the retail industry in India is to find solution for how organizations can sustain high performance while dealing both economic challenges and skilled manpower shortages. To face the challenge of increasing competition that has resulted from liberalization and globalization, Indian organizations have to initiate adoption of innovative HR management practices to foster creativity and innovation among employees. The future HRM has to find a practical approach that will lead to the right balance of organization's and employees' needs in terms of remunerations, training, working hours, and service guarantees for their customers.

Today, organizations are expecting the HR department to act as a strategic partner. So once designed primarily as a compliance function, today's HR needs to be business-integrated, agile, data-driven, and skilled in attracting, retaining, and developing talent. Environmental factors such as economic, social, political, cultural, technological, and other demographic features are driving the rapid changes in the retail business. The top management and HRM department of any retail organizations have to be aware of all these changes. It is necessary for any organized retailer to collect and structure all experience and knowledge from different staffs, stores, and countries (markets). Today, the crucial task for the management of a retail organization in general, and HRM in particular, is to ensure the availability of right knowledge at the right time and in the right place. Hence, exchange of knowledge is one of the basic prerequisites. Hence what is most important is the transfer of learning and percolation of the knowledge up to floor level. When there is a transfer of learning, all the resources invested in training yields a high return. Retailers need to encourage this (transfer of learning) by cultivating a culture and by providing positive reinforcement, rewarding those who practice what they learned.

Changing Role of HRM

Fast-changing retail trends are heavily influencing the HR strategies in retail, which started off as operational function and soon became a strategic partner in the business. HR departments very initially were called as payroll departments. Then renamed as staff management, followed by another metamorphosis to personnel and then to HRM, which have been in the frontier of change management in retailing. From a retail organization's point of view, if we go into the flashback mode and rewind the memories to few years back, we think about the words such as "employee retention," "talent matrix," "succession planning and manpower budgeting," "resource optimization," and so on. These are the notions that were good to hear in the annual meetings or during HR planning meetings in many companies. However, with changing times, now the retail industry itself has changed so drastically within these few years that managing the "people factor" requires a lot of attention from every department. HR's key performance indicators were designed purely on hiring, payroll/staff administration, and so on and so forth, but now, with the changing business environment and more exposure to HR functions via education, the role has emerged to be a business partner. HR leaders' influence is becoming increasingly strategic, and the top priorities in retail sector are talent acquisition/recruitment, talent management, employee retention, and performance management and employee engagement.

The growing needs of retail industry can only be matched up with the innovative and creative HR practices. Though retail calls for having the right product at the right time and in the right place, still it is highly dependent on the right people at various levels. Proper planning, organizing, and strategizing along with perfect execution are vital to the success for any retailer. Here the execution is purely dependent on the teams and their capabilities, and many retail organizations have recognized that HRM is a vital component in achieving the long-term success. Areas such as the recruitment process, selection, induction, retention, performance monitoring and evaluations, staff training, development and motivation, decision-making, and resourcing for expansion are the fundamental functions of the HRM. People in different kinds of businesses have to adapt and change in response to emerging trends. Here training plays a crucial role. Employees (the people component) should be courteous, knowledgeable, helpful and passionate for serving customers, tech savvy, and presentable. For instance, the staff of any fashion retailer should be dressed in such a way that it should reflect the fashion level of the merchandise for sale in the store.

Even the most sophisticated training program will not guarantee the best customer service. People are the key. They make exceptional service possible. Training is merely a skeleton of a customer service program. It is the people who deliver that give it tangible form and intangible meaning. The success of any player in this sector depends not only on understanding target market and implementing marketing mix strategies but also on how effectively a retailer develops systems of high-performance work practices, including comprehensive recruitment and selection procedures, reward policies and performance management systems (PMS), and extensive employee involvement and training. HR people are the backbone of any company, and the success of retail business depends a lot upon the kind of HR strategies it is following and how people are managed. Because of the increasing competition among organized retailers, the retail industry is facing challenges and hurdles from different areas.

Growing Significance of Corporate Culture

Research shows that today, consumers are concerned about the culture that drives a company, and company's business ethics and practices also play a key role while deciding what brands they would buy or which retail stores they would patronize. A thriving corporate (workplace) culture enables the organizations to maintain appropriate business practices, enhance employee engagement, offer great customer service, and improve financial performance. This is because a great corporate culture seamlessly integrates goals of organization with that of individuals. In the process of achieving goals, the company should make sure that high performance should lead to employee engagement not to employee burnout.

It is also observed that many shoppers had stopped supporting a retail company/brand because of something that should not happen (in the case of) to its corporate practices or ethics. For instance, among some instances of this type were with Amazon, Walmart, Reebok, McDonald's, Gap, and so on. The corporate culture and business ethics of a company—or even the public representation of it—is as important as branding or advertising efforts of that company.

Additionally, the purveyors of corporate culture are its people. So it is essential to hire right people for building a great corporate culture, and vice a versa is also true. Because many times, the corporate culture plays the most important role in attracting the right talent because people often prefer good corporate culture and business practices over the remuneration package or growth prospects. Hence, talent retention, employee well-being, and high performance coexist in organizations with good corporate culture. This necessitates the organization to put right people at right place, and it all begins with its hiring process. Hence for building a great corporate culture, it requires for an organization to take an integrated and consistent approach toward hiring right talent, continuous learning, collaboration, innovation, and retention of right talent.

Developing the "Service Culture"

Customers shop with retailers that provide services comparable to the prices they are paying. The amount of service corresponds with the price/quality level, whether self-service, limited service, or full service. The services mix is one of the key non-price tools for setting retailers apart from each other. In the modern marketplace, customers are empowered through peer advocacy and social media. Everything is up for public scrutiny, from product reviews right down to the small experience of service. Consequently, retailers need to look into customer satisfaction/delight as a key ingredient of their business models.

It is high time that HR departments move beyond just creating a culture of keeping employees contented and meeting their expectations. The changing customer expectations call for flexibility in service models. Today's busy lifestyles and smaller families have narrowed the window of opportunity to service customers, so retailers need to offer services as per customer's convenience. The customer needs to be treated as a major stakeholder in the workforce strategy, the workforce guiding principles, and the workforce technology, besides the work culture. For instance, companies might decide to extend their credit payment terms or stretch their evening hours to differentiate their store from their competitors. Discount stores, featuring low prices, offer only basic customer services, such as free parking, credit, and merchandise return privileges. Traditional department stores provide additional customer services, such as gift wrapping, repair services, and alterations. Exclusive stores might provide special services, such as a store employee delivering an evening dress and making sure it fits the customer properly, or helping a customer coordinate a dress, shoes, and jewelry. Services encourage customers to stay in the store as long as possible. The store provides all the needed services to keep customers there to make more purchases.

Keeping the customer at the center, retailers need to focus on employees, investors, and social frameworks. We have entered into the third phase of HRM evolution, while the first phase of HRM was about process and policy compliance and second revolving around talent and technology. Now in this third phase, the primary task is to bring the customer at center stage. Hence in a customer-centric organization, the attitude of servicing the customer percolates at every level, from top to the front line and from the back office to the storefront. Here every employee's role is aligned to the customer's expectations by channelizing their efforts toward acquiring clients or focusing at delighting the customers.

For instance, METRO Cash & Carry India is operated through the cash-and-carry format and opened its first wholesale center in 2003 in Bengaluru. Cash-and-carry wholesale is essentially defined by its customer base and the unique business model it follows. In this format of retailing, registered business customers visit a cash-and-carry outlet, select their purchases by their own, and carry the merchandise by themselves instead of placing orders with multiple vendors. To inculcate the service culture, the store HR announces Sewa Champ of the day for his/her exceptional performance on a daily basis (*Sewa* means service in English). The employee who receives, rather wins, the maximum number of Sewa Champs in a month is declared as the *Anmol Ratna* (meaning precious gem in English) of the month.

To help customers find out what they are looking for, some fashion retailers like Gucci have rolled out smartphones for their sales associates so that they can locate detailed information about clothing lines, obtain a customer's purchase history, and allow payments to be processed anywhere in the store. Hence, smart use of technology to help salespeople provide a more personalized shopping experience, and brands can retain the high level of customer service standards that people expect from luxury labels, while also offering new services that mimic what shoppers previously have found only online. In high-end fashion, what people value most is well-informed and available staff. If technology can help, that is icing on the cake. Let us have a look at some of the pivotal ways in which customer delight ought to be woven into the fabric of a retailer's service strategy, not just as a customer satisfaction tool but also as a retention and advocacy tactic.

Giordano's commitment to service began with its major customer service campaign in 1989. In that campaign, yellow badges bearing the words "Giordano Means Service" was worn by every Giordano employee, and its service philosophy had three principles:

1. We welcome unlimited try-on.
2. We exchange—no questions asked.
3. We serve with a smile.

As a result, the firm started receiving its numerous service-related awards over the years. It had also been ranked number one for eight consecutive years by the *Far Eastern Economic Review* for being innovative in responding to customers' needs. Furthermore, proving its expansion success in the Middle East, in 2006, Giordano received double awards for exceptional service and customer centricity from the Government of Dubai.

Strategic HRM in Retailing

In the businesses like retailing with multiple points of interactions and engagements with customers, the "people" factor is very important and critical in obtaining the desired perceptual outputs. The former global chief marketing officer of Kellogg Co. said, "Unless you have clarity of what your brand stands for, everything else is irrelevant." Successful branding not only generates customer engagement but also attracts talent, as potential employees perceive the organization as an innovative, enriching, and promising workplace. Retailing means working in a global context but simultaneously adjusting to local needs, service requirements, and expectations. In the near past, major retail companies decided to invest globally to explore markets having greater potential and ensure the sustainable growth. Several retailers have identified internationalization as a huge opportunity for growth. For instance, the American retail giant Walmart, France's Carrefour, and Britain's Tesco are the organizations that are aggressively pursuing international expansion to increase their global footprints.

The HR strategy hinges on the business strategy of the firm. The HR persons in charge need to act as business partners for management, providing strategic and practical operational solutions in the form of HR functions and solutions based on thorough knowledge of the business. Walmart's initial attempt at expansion in Germany failed—as did Marks & Spencer's—because neither of these companies realized the fine distinctions of German culture. The extreme evidence was that Walmart trained its female employees to smile when customers walked in: now this welcome gesture works in America, where there are specific norms that guide interactions with consumers. In Germany, when female employees smiled at male customers—though it is for greeting and salutation—the latter developed the wrong idea. In addition, they also underestimated the local competition and, especially, the price sensitivity of German customers. If an image is correctly interpreted by a company's own employees, it spreads to the customers and reinforces itself in the marketplace. Carrefour's foray into the UK likewise ended with a strategic retreat. From these examples, it is evident that retailing is nothing but responding to culture. Here the HRM function plays a crucial role in assisting corporate management to understand and adapt to local cultures. For instance, the Swedish retailer IKEA, when entered into China, realized that Chinese consumers did not want DIY but instead wanted "do it for me."

Hence, the strategic tasks of HRM, the key strategic tasks of HRM of a retailer, include:

- Cross-cultural recruiting and training: All cultures have their own unique behavioral attributes and preferences, some of which are obvious while others are more subtle and harder to detect. HR departments need to be able to not only offer advice and professional preparation to local managers but also ensure that individuals appointed to these positions are aware of company policies as well as sensitive to the local culture. For instance, in international settings, individuals need both a common language and intercultural sensitivity.

- Assisting the retailer's top managers who need to face and negotiate countless complex issues in a competitive marketplace, cope with stress arising from rapid changes, fierce competition, cost pressures, time management problems, and pressure of making quick decisions.
- Keeping up to date with continuously developing technology and being able to optimize its usage so as to achieve the right balance between productivity gains and service gains.
- Dealing with demography (e.g., an aging workforce in Western Europe, China, and Japan but predominantly young and inexperienced employees in other areas of the world, such as Asia, particularly India and the Middle East). Strategically, this poses one of the hardest challenges for HR professionals who are required to recruit and develop skilled staff, offer training for all age groups, ensure a well-balanced age structure, and build up a working climate, enabling employees of all ages to buy in and show suitable results.
- Identifying and retaining highly qualified, highly motivated individuals and improving their skill sets on continuous and continual basis.
- HR for HR: HR executives need to ensure they invest time and money on developing the skills of the function. Re-skilling HR is becoming necessary across organizations, and HR leaders need to have a budget resource for this. While there may not be many lead indicators of impact, there will be clear lag symptoms of impact in the long run around company's readiness for business challenges. The one who will initiate will certainly harvest the rewards.

Operational Tasks of HRM

Some key HRM tasks and responsibilities that have to be performed to enable the workforce to meet the service needs of customers nationally and internationally include:

- Reshaping and restructuring the workforce so as to broaden their experience by the acquisition of new skills. For instance, developments like automatic stock replenishment, new methods of conducting transactions, compliance with the key merchandising principles and innovations, in the way merchandise is displayed, have increased employee training requirements in the retail industry.

Besides that employees must learn to serve increasingly demanding consumers while maintaining high productivity, which is essential for high-volume, low-margin players. So retailers need to train employees on how to balance these oft-conflicting demands for high staff productivity and great customer service.

- Today the critical resource of most businesses is no longer financial capital, but rather their human capital. Hence, it is an important task for HR managers to gather the data and identify the tools to analyzing this data for human capital valuation and assessment of the return on HR investments.
- HRM has evolved to its new role as a strategic business partner and building the basic structural foundation that will enable retail organizations to organize and optimize their return on HR.

Thus, thinking from the organizational behavior perspective, there are two major factors the HR executives need to consider for building the future-ready organization. First is related to the leadership and its relation with the employees. Leader is the first person that affects the behavior of the individual (besides inherent characteristics of the employee). The other decisive aspect that affects organizational behavior is the culture of the organization. Increasingly, companies are looking to tweak the environment or culture to align it with their business objectives. There has to be a right fit between people strategy (HR policies) and business strategy to reap maximum benefits to emerge as winners in the highly competitive marketplace. If there is a mismatch, it could prove disastrous for the company.

Hierarchy is undoubtedly essential as there has to be a strong sense of accountability. However due to globalization, organizations have become flat in terms of hierarchy with mangers expected to coordinate and collaborate with employees across various functions and verticals. Today's retail organizations are more horizontal in their working style, and employees have to work in a networked environment spread across the nations and regions. This requires effective collaboration and coordination skills to obtain synergy. Hence, it is imperative for retailers to intrinsically motivate employees so that everybody is committed to the organizational goals and perform their respective responsibility without the need for continuous monitoring. In this way, coordination challenges can be overcome with intrinsic motivation. Not only HR executives but also the organization leaders should be able to cultivate intrinsic motivation of the employees and make them feel that they are part of the organization. So, organizations have to work more on the internal part of motivation by interacting and collaborating with employees, understanding their requirement, valuing their work, and so on. This requires lot of efforts, practice, and experience in managerial skills such as listening to people, interpreting people behavior, followed by action in order to motivate them intrinsically. Intrinsically motivated people are more likely to provide innovative solutions, which is a key to success in the uncertain and highly competitive marketplace. It is not only challenge but also an opportunity.

Let us consider the example of Giordano, a Hong Kong-based retailer of casual clothes targeted at men, women, and children through its five company brands: Giordano, Giordano Concepts, Giordano Ladies, Giordano Junior, and Bluestar Exchange. Giordano was operating more than 1,800 retail stores and counters in some 30 markets worldwide. Its main markets were Mainland China, Hong Kong, Japan, Korea, Singapore, and Taiwan. Other regions in which it had a presence were Australia, Indonesia, Malaysia, Middle East, and North America.

Giordano maintained a flat organizational structure. The company's decentralized management style empowered line managers and, at the same time, encouraged fast and close communication and coordination. For example, top management and staff had desks located next to each other, separated only by shoulder panels. This closeness allowed easy communication, efficient project management, and speedy decision-making, which were all seen as critical ingredients to success amid fast-changing consumer tastes (preferences) and fashion trends.

Giordano successfully repositioned itself in 1987. From a retailer who has sold exclusively men's casual apparel, it repositioned the chain as a retailer of value-for-money merchandise, selling discounted casual unisex apparel, with the goal of maximizing unit sales instead of just focusing on the bottom line. This shift in strategy was successful, leading to a substantial increase in turnover. Another factor that contributed to the firm's success was its dedicated, ever-smiling sales staff ever ready to serve the customers at their best. Giordano has always considered frontline workers to be its customer service heroes.

Building the Performing Team

Organization Strategy and Goal Congruence

In today's retailing scenario, it is vital for HR executives to understand the "customer brand" and align it to the "employer brand." HRM has to align and integrate its entire program with company's overall vision and strategy. These strategies connect people to the company's growth

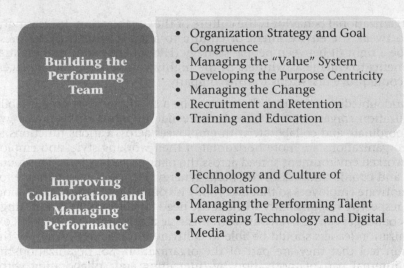

Figure 8.1: *Strategic Human Resource Management in Retailing*

story, develop a sense of ownership among them, and eventually improve their performance. This approach enables HR professionals to be "business oriented" along with "people oriented." This two-pronged strategy is categorically described as keeping the end customer in mind while taking care of the employees who are the internal customers (Figure 8.1).

Customer centricity is the capabilities of an entire organization (and not just the customer associate staff) to "collectively and collaboratively" keep customers at the center of the scheme of things with the intention of adding value. It has been proved that the retail organizations that practice customer centricity generally create considerably more stakeholder and shareholder value than others.

The HR is not just a department but also an internal business partner who can learn from the past, see the current trends, and analyze the future trends and requirements to build a future-ready team for its organization along with contributing to the industry practices. For HR to integrate with the business as a strategic function, leaders need to be clear on the strengths and opportunities that HR can build upon and simultaneously be aware of weaknesses and threats that can pose new challenges to HRM. A well-designed strategy will go waste if not executed properly, and on the other hand, if a strategy is not right, it is not going to work however precisely it is executed. Hence, strategizing and execution go hand in hand.

The journey starts with being able to mobilize talent around business objectives. This is far more critical today than it has been ever before. It is necessary to articulate the vision of the organization and then communicate with impact and empathy as this can help create optimism, clarity, and certainty within the organization and externally also. As the business environment becomes increasingly global, cross-cultural, and networked, the HR teams need to find ways to inspire a company's talent using creative and collaborative methods. The following factors therefore become important.

- It is therefore important for well-designed practices and highly efficient HR functions to be aligned and coupled with the business goals of the company concerned.
- Planning and strategizing are done with deep consideration for the organization's goal in a long-term perspective.

- A well-designed and well-executed functional agenda can make the challenges easier and the rewards greater.
- Hence, HR strategy must be "comprehensive" in the sense of catering all the different personnel and HR activities need to be contributing to the long-term development of the organization.
- It can help the entire HR team become true business partners and better contributors to the overall success of the business.
- HRM functions have to conceptualize and design business plans in such a way that the individual goals have to be in congruence with the organization's mission, vision, goals, and common values.
- The significance of human capital and the goal congruence is especially significant in the case of a merger. The success of a merger depends much more on the competencies of the staff and management than on other components, such as finance, IT, and production.

In the next step forward, HR develops a people-focused strategy that is in congruence with and supports the foundation of the company's goals and values. So here HR needs to devise a well-defined plan that clarifies what kind of talent it needs—both for the present and for the future. The retailer should be able to create and maintain HR systems that enable it attract select, position, develop, reward, and retain this talent. Finally, it not just the talent that can do, but it is also necessary to ensure how people perform the assigned job. This helps the HR department to develop an ethical organization culture, which in turn helps attract the right talent.

For example, some of the leading online retailers have replaced annual employee appraisals with biannual or trimester reviews, wherein employees go through performance appraisals and goal-setting every six months or four months. This is in line with online retailer's own way of fixing its business targets, as one year becomes too long a period to evaluate staff performance in an industry that is growing with an exponential rate. The industry also faces rapidly changing priorities and challenges in the form of consumer preferences and shopping behavior.

In the context of such business environment, it becomes essential for the retailer to pursue a biannual- or trimester-based approach to business planning and eventually to align the workforce toward that approach. The system involves setting organizational goals at the beginning of the appraisal period. Every functional head then determines his or her goals and links them to the organizational goals. A similar method is eventually followed to percolate the functional goals to team functions and performance to achieve goal (congruence) by bringing business goals in sync with individual goals.

These new systems are also based on employee feedback, which is essentially designed for frequent and continuous engagement with the young staff (the average age of employees is less than 30 years in most of these companies) and retention of high-potential employees. The assessment brings monetary and nonmonetary rewards for employees based on their performance. This also helps the company in effectively managing expectation of a young staff and to keep attrition under check.

Hence, such systems are enabling these organizations to foster an environment that drives innovation, transparency, agility, regular review and feedback, employee development and up-skilling and/or re-skilling, and eventually the culture of meritocracy.

Managing the "Value" System

Organization culture is a system of beliefs and values as apparent in the attitudes, behaviors, and motivations of employees. Hence, work culture and values are not something that can be force-fed into people. It takes time for people to get absorbed and settle in a new environment, and eventually, people gravitate toward a better culture. It is not a quick process, but building a healthy culture means the organization must recognize and address the "people needs." The ability to value diversity and dynamism within the workforce is strength, provided that this is backed up by continuous training and continual improvements. Many retail organizations conduct courses and programs on this aspect, usually under the title of "Increasing Self-awareness," as the aptitude to value one's impact on others is an influential skill.

Giordano works on the philosophy that the only way to be relevant and to keep abreast with cutthroat competition in the retail sector is to know the customers' needs and serve them well. Customers pay our paychecks, so they are our bosses. Giordano considers service to be a very important element (for attracting customers) and service should be given the prime importance and preference.

Similarly, United Colors of Benetton has designed a program referred as "Core Values Champions Award," which is conducted annually with objective to identify, appreciate, and honor the employees who demonstrate Benetton India's core values and beliefs in the best way.

From the above examples, we can state that the HRM has to decide what actions add measurable value to the business. All the actions of HRM need to be strategically focused toward setting the right tone within the organization for defined values to flourish. Here the commitment in the form of personal engagement and belief in the organization and its concepts is important. HRM has to support this by elaborating concepts and criteria for their evaluation, some of which should be revised gradually to bring dynamism. The following behavioral aspects of the workforce should be incorporated in the HRM concept:

- Personal integrity and honesty
- Self-motivation and professional entrepreneurship
- Ability to communicate the values, beliefs, and benefits
- Developing people by training, coaching, and mentoring
- Developing the purpose centricity

In the context of retailing where "people" factor is very important, many retailers consider people as brands. There are similarities in the brand relationship spectrum that can be used to describe what is happening in the culture. This is important to consider because it is a move that aligns to the way more and more people work. When a brand works the way people work, it is easy to grow and nurture a relationship at the personal level. The core values of any organization do not matter in real terms, unless and until the entire organization is "committed" to those core values. Hence, the most valued thing is successful alignment of value system of HR around the values and vision of the respective organization. Apart from technology, organizations need to instill the company's core values among the employees to build a collaborative culture. Creating an environment of continuous learning and upgrading each employee's skill sets through various training modules and working on projects in cross-functional teams (CFTs) strengthen it further.

Let us take a look at the example of Zappos. It was founded in 1999 when there were very few online shoe retailers in USA. Still the company differentiated itself from other e-retailers by providing customer-friendly services like free shipping both ways and a 365-day returns policy. The service representatives at Zappos put their heart and soul to help the customers, and also delight them. This highly motivated staff are able to offer high levels of customer service due to the prevailing culture in the company, where employees are presented with a working environment that helped them realize and perform to their potential.

The culture at Zappos was categorically defined in terms of its "core values." The company was highly committed to those core values. For achieving this, the HR policies and practices were designed to appreciate and reward behaviors that reflected the core values, which helped the organization to strengthen the unique features of its culture. Hence, it was imperative for Zappos to recruit people whose "purpose" was similar to that of the company to preserve such a culture. All this was attributed to their unique recruitment process. Apart from technical interviews, prospective candidates were screened based on their aptness to Zappos' culture and values. Also the training for the new recruits was designed to introduce them to the culture of the company and make them understand and inculcate it. The new employees were trained on customer service, irrespective of their position in the company. The training was a continuous process, and every session and module of it were designed to reinforce the values of the company. The appraisals were based on an individual's ability to perform in the framework of the core values. This ability of Zappos to uphold and endorse its unique work culture is attributed to its continuous emphasis on its core values. Zappos continued to operate as an independent entity, maintaining its unique work culture even after it was acquired by another leading e-retailer, Amazon.com, in 2009.

Developing the Purpose-centric Workforce

The key task for HR is to help shape a highly skilled, engaged, and performing workforce that is passionate and oriented toward a common purpose—in short, building a purpose-centric human capital. Purpose-centric workforce is a team of people that is motivated by a shared sense of purpose and vision and committed to achieve it together and share the values that the organization holds cherished. As the sense of purpose evolves, people start putting their heart and soul into achieving the purpose. This can be found in organizations and in other kinds of groups, such as nonprofits, sports teams, military-armed forces, and so on. For instance, some of history's famous armies were high on purpose centricity. What makes this purpose centricity so important is the SCA it creates for the organization. Technology can be purchased or acquired in no time; new strategy can be adopted as soon as it is described in a case study, business journal, or blog; capital can be raised from several sources that are available today like never before, and in the era of web-based e-commerce procurement, any retailer can acquire goods and services for the best price at click of a button. Even efficiency and productivity are broadly understood and eventually achieved by benchmarking, and hence they can offer only incremental advantage.

But the sense of purpose cannot be coded; it needs to be instilled. When people are connected by this sense of purpose, the whole organization gets synchronized and moves forward in tandem. So it is only the "purpose centricity" that can create sustainable and unbeatable value. Retailers should be very careful in hiring the right people and, more importantly, groom them to imbibe the sense of purpose. The purpose centricity inspires people, and inspiration is the origin of all innovation, achievements, invention, improvements, and so on, which eventually is followed by enhanced efficiency, effectiveness, and profitability. Though there are many advantages to such cultures, we will discuss a few in particular.

They Are Very Good at Attracting Talent and Retaining It

To attract right talent, grooming them as per the demands of the company and then retaining them are the biggest and ongoing tasks in front of any retail HR today. The smartest and most passionate people like to work in places that not only reflect their values but also are abundant with other smart and passionate people. In an organization, employees value intangibles as much as the tangibles. Though money is very important for entry-level staff, there are various factors that affect the person's intent to be associated with a particular retail organization. Simple aspects such as candid communication, access to management, and internal celebrations go a long way in enhancing the environment to work in. so here a strong corporate image is one that effectively communicates the company's brand and philosophy. In order to recruit and retain right talent, a company needs to be able to project itself and provide a good idea of what it really represents. We have seen a shift in the focus of HR practices from just recruitment to nurturing the talent. So we can see that retailers are coming up with innovative policies and program to motivate their staff.

Let us discuss the example of department retailer Lifestyle International that increased the employee engagement by taking various initiatives across the fronts of HR management. The retail company is a part of the Bengaluru-based Landmark Group that owns and operates several of brands across the categories like fashion, apparel, and home furnishing such as Lifestyle, Max, Splash and Home Centre. The company after essentially focusing on maturing products and processes subsequently shifted its focus to enhancing the people engagement in order to get the right people to stay and grow with the organization. With this purpose at the core, they started with a program "Corporate Theatre," an innovative and informal learning technique designed and developed on the street play methodology that is being used to educate, entertain, enlighten, and engage the employees. To implement this initiative effectively, their trainers have been certified on Corporate Theatre by professional theater artists through a certification program. These trainers enact policies of the company to employees.

Lifestyle motivates and encourages its young talent by involving the interns at minute levels of business operations, and also seeks insights and feedback from them. The interns are involved and exposed to different aspects of business as a whole, which in turn impart a pragmatic learning experience. This motivates the young talent because they feel significant as they are being consulted and listened to. This is applicable to the floor staff too as Landmark has not left the bulk of its workforce out and is receptive and sensitive to the physical and emotional labor involved on the front end. The staff at the store is also provided with a good pantry, training room, and yoga in the mornings. The company has introduced flexible working hours (with a two-hour window in the morning and evenings), as a manifestation of its belief in work–life balance. All these initiatives have eventually brought the attrition rate down significantly.

They Create Economic Value

It is true that companies that are not driven by quarterly results have a substantial advantage in creating cultures of purpose centricity. This is because people who are passionate are constantly looking for ways to express that passion, and they will do so with a drive and innovativeness that cannot be mandated in a job. Therefore, the purpose-centric HR are invincible because they are high on customer-centric approach. So the HR executives of retail organizations are not leaving any stone unturned to create a dynamic, energetic, and collaborative work environment where the staff are encouraged to experiment, innovate, participate, learn, grow, and, most importantly, enjoy the work that they do. Hence, the focus is on enriching the quality of life of employees with improved work–life balance to develop their potential and maximize their productivity.

In Giordano, to ensure customer service excellence, performance evaluations are conducted frequently at the store level, as well as for individual employees. Internal competitions were designed to motivate employees and store teams to do their best in serving customers. Every month, Giordano awarded the "Service Star" to individual employees, based on nominations provided by shoppers. In addition, every Giordano store was evaluated every month by mystery shoppers. Based on the combined results of these evaluations, the "Best Service Shop" award was given to the top store. Customer feedback cards were available at all stores and were collected and posted at the office for further action. Increasingly, customers were providing feedback via the firm's corporate website.

Thus in this case, the retailers need to perform on the parameters like trust, transparency, demonstration of vision and leadership, learning and development, performance management and reinventing HRM, perceptions of company product and services, workplace environment and operating style, and culture and engagement.

They Live Their Values

People want to be associated with organizations that resonate with their values. They want consistency between what they believe/care about and where they work/shop. They want evidence of a company's commitment to its products, services, and ethics. Hence, the ability to collaborate productively with others—employees, peers, stakeholders, customers, and even competitors—is swiftly becoming a keystone skill for thriving in the increasingly interdependent, diverse, and dynamic workplaces. Organizations need to internalize these intangibles in their culture to motivate the employees and create an environment of belonging and ownership.

Initiatives that are being implemented and are very effective include celebrating events such as birthdays and anniversaries of employees, organizing social gatherings during nonworking hours, encouraging interactions outside work and helping employees maintain a work–life balance, encouraging the employees to get to know each other on a personal level, and lending a helping hand during personal or professional crisis. These gestures and initiatives not only strengthen the purpose centricity but also help in building a conducive and friendly workplace environment where the employees understand each other better. To develop an effective purpose-centric workforce, mutual trust between people at every level of the organization is essential.

Today, the retailers are adopting many innovative strategies and techniques to motivate their employees and build the efficient purpose-centric and customer-centric human capital, which is essential to face the ultracompetitive environment in the retail industry. For example, a growing number of firms in India have started using unusually idiosyncratic titles for their young workforce.

The e-tailer company Jabong addresses its product management team as "Bob the Builder." Bob is a protagonist of children's animated show *Bob the Builder*. In this British animated television show, Bob the Builder uses the catchphrase "Can we fix it?" as a dialog, and this invites "Yes we can!" in response from the other characters of the show. This is extremely imperative for young e-commerce companies to attract young and dynamic talent. These exciting designations keep employees full of energy and dynamism. They avoid old titles and establish a new work culture that is all about enthusiasm and performance. Such rule-breaking and interesting designations are being adopted to create a team spirit among the employees and to infuse the purpose centricity among teams.

Likewise, Pepperfry, the furniture and home products e-commerce marketplace, calls to its back-end support team as "Ninjas" in a motivating tone. The idea and rationale behind calling company's back-end support team "Ninjas" is when their Champions (front-end customer support team) are not able to resolve issues at the customer end their Ninjas step in with remedies and improvised solutions.

The online furniture seller Urban Ladder refers to its customer service employees as "buddies," the term associated with relation of friendship. When their customer service executives go beyond transactional communication with the customers, the e-tailer expect the customers to treat these customer service teams as buddies too. Here, the notion behind calling customer service executives as "buddies" is to make the customers comfortable to receive their call and converse in a friendly manner with the staff for any queries/questions or suggestions.

In the same way, Amazon India refers its consumer business team "cowboys," which symbolize the high energy levels and adventure. These "cowboys" come up with out-of-the box ideas, go above and beyond their regular roles (boundaries), break through the barriers erected by external environments, infrastructure failures, or resource constraints but are always be committed to the common goal and purpose. To promote this culture further, the company has even instituted a "Cowboy Award" to appreciate various team members who put their heart and soul to counter the challenges to unleash new opportunities for its customers and sellers. One more classic example we must discuss here is of Jabong. The e-tailer instills its operation intelligence team with unbeatable powers of inference, calling it "Sherlock Holmes." In addition, it also refers its designers as "design dolphins," its HRM team as "One HR," and its content writers as "wordsmiths."

Managing the Change

In the context of retailing, the most important drivers for change are:

- Globalization, geopolitical, and world economic forces.
- Technological advancements and proliferation of smartphone technologies.
- Impact of e-commerce on consumer buying behavior.
- Consumers who are well informed, tech savvy, and increasingly relying on knowledge-based decision-making.

All these sea changes in the retailing landscape demand for redefining firms' performance less in terms of cutting cost and more in terms of profitable growth. HR managers have to be able to empower their own staff. Because it is only through true empowerment that staff can really contribute to the changing needs of a business. Change management recognizes the need to reflect on the manager's role in the management of change, the identification of challenges, and the ability to steer changes in either a programmed or a nonprogrammed manner.

Above all, today we are in a New Age where our world is experiencing a digital transformation that has never been seen before. Today, people have access to unlimited amount of information and they can instantly share that information with anyone around the world in a fraction of a second. There is a huge choice of companies that they can do business with. This digital reality is not only liberating but also empowering. Today, when people choose a retailer, they expect that the retailer should know them, listen to them, and serve them flawlessly. If find that the company is not fulfilling their expectations, they will go for another one. Switching another option is as simply as clicking on their smartphones or tapping their tablets. Gone are the days when business decisions were always clear or forthcoming. So now onward, the HRM function of any retail organization will have to be agile and flexible in their ability and capacity to respond quickly to the changes and challenges. Above all, they need to deliver this without being overwhelmed by emotions. It will require a very pragmatic but emergent attitude and mind-set. Hence, volatility is the truth of New Age retailing, and if you are going to be able to absorb volatility, you are going to be able to manage the change successfully.

So here the question is, whether your organization is ready to adopt these changes. This question is posing various challenges not only to the retail industry but also to every other industry. Business leaders recognize that this new set of customers is putting tremendous pressure on them, on their strategy, and the values that they provide to their customers. Today, HR executive of any organization in the business of retailing has to recognize that many of its services and methods of functioning have to be radically redefined in order to stay buoyant and also take hold of the opportunity to rethink how they can lead the change and transformation.

Transforming the business has three areas for action:

1. Embracing the disruption
2. Building shared values
3. Fostering collaboration

Embracing the Disruption

Due to the factors discussed above, the dynamics of working in a retail company have changed. Previously, the staff used to bring mobile devices at workplace and eventually they brought social networks inside. This led to completely new ways of working, the social business. Most recently, a term is gaining popularity and that is "sharing economy," where individuals trade with different companies (it may be a big organization or a start-up) and also with each other for everything from different products, places to stay overnight, business services, or perhaps just booking a taxi. This has created a new construct for commerce. To cater to this change, many industries, including retailing, have started implying innovation and leveraging technology not only for external audience but also for internal employees. Organizations have adopted social business and transformed the ways how their employees connect, communicate, and collaborate to drive greater workforce productivity and setting higher benchmarks. Deploying a secure and highly customizable enterprise social platform allows the organizations to create a flexible environment that is able to capture valuable insights and more easily engage all key stakeholders—employees, customers, partners, and suppliers—to accelerate innovation and deliver results.

The digital innovation is attributed to converging technologies. However, the biggest disruption most often happens at the intersection of the digital and physical technologies. As social, mobile, analytics, and cloud technologies intersect and amplify each other, entirely new opportunities, possibilities, and challenges take shape. In this phase of the transformation journey, it is crucial to make dynamic changes based on the insights that could be tapped from the social interactions and the new communication channels that have opened up. The HR strategy needs to prioritize continuous iteration and to make room for omnipresent experimentation and a human force that can adapt to this transformation to capitalize on them.

Building Shared Values

To create a consumer-first strategy, a retailer has to know its customers better and deliver personalized experiences. While many organizations are facing disruption from new entrants, a growing number are inviting their customers to disrupt them first. As it is essential to know and adapt transformations, sharing the values and wisdom can make the entire working system agile. So in this kind of scenario, organizations are left with two options:

1. Explore the opportunity created by mobile and social technologies to understand your consumers and serve them better than competition to win an edge over or
2. Lose those customers forever before you could even serve.

Social collaboration and digital experience are the vital resources to enable real-time knowledge sharing, increased productivity, improved and improvised processes, and faster innovation via introduction of an integrated set of tools. The value of sharing and hence the efficiency of an organization increase when they put people at the heart of the system and derive value out of each other's experiences. This facilitates them collaborate real time, making faster decisions and delivering desired value to the consumers, which in turn increases their loyalty behavior toward that retailer. With the abundance of data and information that is now potentially available for use, it has become easier for the retailers to predict the individual expectations of the consumers. By accessing and sharing all these inputs, retailers can better understand customer behaviors and personalize products, services, and overall experiences. Being regarded as the business partners, the HR leaders are looking for new ways to proactively engage their customers in the process and get their direct input—not just on their products or services, but also on every aspect of their organization.

Fostering Collaboration

It is often observed that, with growth of an organization, several departments and verticals are created that are driven by fiefdoms. This led to creation of silos, which eventually become the standard; data is shared but information, ideas, and innovation sharing become exceptions. Here employees are rewarded on the basis of productivity in terms of proficiency in their functional areas.

However, with the implementation of appropriate systems and procedures, professionals today can collaborate and communicate across the regions, overcoming the barriers once inflicted by geography and time. Smartphones are fast becoming the preferred device to felicitate all these transformations and activities. Consumers are also accessing a range of services, including surfing the Internet, browsing various e-commerce sites, sharing photos or videos, e-mails, downloading apps, accessing social networking sites, and so on through their application-packed phones. The proliferation and popularity of social media are a main contributor to this trend. So retailers need to find a way to integrate and foster this effectively within their systems for a better and exciting way of to collaborate and manage business operations, communication, and improve connect among the human-ware. In this scenario, there is a need to move away from operating in silos to working on a collaborative mode. The benefits of collaboration have long been apparent and discussed in the later part of this chapter. The "pragmatic art" of collaboration is just emerging. This will ensure an open and transparent culture, building immense trust in the system. We have also started to understand how collaboration works in a better way—how to foster human connections across complex networks and create new models of engagement and cultures of transparency.

If social business is a coin, in many respects, trust and data are its two faces. So it is very crucial to democratize the data to facilitate both facts-based (pragmatic) improvisations and data-driven innovations. It is widely experienced that the most analytically sophisticated organizations share data more freely. This approach modifies the power structure, effectively flattening the organization and creating a culture of collaboration, transparency, and openness. In this era of runaway innovation, expanding partnerships to deepen innovation capabilities will speed the application of new technologies and business models. Retailers that understand the benefits of collaboration and identify new ways to serve customers holistically will define new business ecosystems and generate maximum benefit.

Recruitment and Retention

Employee recruitment (and selection) is one of the most important and fundamental HR functions. However, as far as recruitment is concerned, the retail industry has been facing difficulties in attracting highly educated people. On the other hand, the dynamic and volatile business environment requires retailers to equip their people with the right skills to stay ahead of the curve, drive change rather than react to change, and constantly practice a customer-centric approach. The communication mechanism, the incentive and reward system, and the overall employer value proposition (EVP) are the means and media to attract the right talent and ensure result-oriented performance. Retailers that are high on EVP are strong employer brands, which enable them to garner reputation as an employer—how good is the work culture at that particular company.

Retailers with good EVP do not have to engage in the rat race for attracting the talent, and they need not have to pay a premium to acquire it. On the contrary, the talent with right skills is almost always attracted to them. Hence, a good EVP is the driver of recruitment, retention, and employee engagement.

It is vital for retail companies to start building a strong leadership pipeline to fuel growth and insulate the organization against the volatilities, uncertainties, complexities, and ambiguities of the future. For building leadership, a retailer has to reorient its HRM processes and plans around the customers' needs. Hence, today's HR teams are expected to play the role of strategic partners for future growth. So once they are reoriented and re-skilled accordingly, they partner with and support business and the end customers in the desired way.

The key to successful business is talent acquisition, their management, and, most importantly, talent development.

Retaining staff in retail industry is very difficult because it calls for:

- Long working hours.
- Working on weekends when footfalls are comparatively more than other days of the week.
- Working on festival, as these are days when shoppers flood the retail destination for shopping and retailers run most of the promotional offers.
- Working without a robust career path.
- Working on relatively less attractive compensation packages.

These are the typical issues the HR department of any retail company has to face. On the other hand, retail industry is one of the largest employers of staff in its sales team, and the demand continues to increase with the expansion of modern retailing. In addition, the industry is coping with high attrition rates, and this will continue as more players enter the market, creating more options and greater choice for the skilled workforce. As the competition in acquiring the right talent will increase, it will become more challenging to attract and retain high-potential people. It is this competitive quest for high-potential talent that is redefining how organizations look at their people assets and how they can best harness the power of that talent to pursue growth opportunities.

Therefore, here the challenge for HRM is to present the attractiveness and dynamism of the retail sector and to ensure appropriate training and careers, so that this sector can take a leading place in the competition for available talent. Also, it is not easy for HRM to offer a concrete succession plan to the employees. This often impacts the employer brand equity of retail organizations when they explore for talent. Thus, it is again the responsibility of the HR team to match the expectations of retail employees and illustrate them their career succession plan. Next agenda of retention focuses on the efforts to keep performing staff in the organization and to increase and leverage their loyalty. This hinges not only on interesting work, fair compensation, and a motivating climate, and management culture, but also on job security and transparent career succession paths combined with a supportive management that provides mentorship.

As far as *compensation component* is concerned, the retail industry operates with thin margins, and it is very challenging to manage the compensation expectations in a situation of scarce talent, especially about the entry-level staff, who are keen about their pay package than about the organization. They tend to switch jobs even for insignificant sundry salary hike. Hence, it is key task for HRM to design an effective compensation mix—a blend of fixed and variable components—that is collaborative and leading to win–win situation.

One of the major reasons behind the high attrition rate in retail companies is the feeling of *job insecurity* among the employees. There is often high level of job insecurity among the retail staff, especially at the entry level, as retail is a target-driven job. HR department has to play a very important role of a catalyst and as an internal training department by which employees can meet their desired productivity and performance level. With this purpose, HR departments come up with various incentive plans, motivating employees at various levels. Hence, building a sense of belongingness and ownership is a vital part of the HR agenda.

Over and above, HR departments are coming up with out-of-the box ideas and practices and adopting new ways of recruiting and retaining the talent, including social media such as Facebook and LinkedIn, where the retailer is promoted as the preferred employer in the industry, and to attract fresh talent. HR departments across retail organizations are trying to adopt innovative practices to attract and engage employees. Various motivational experiences are being experimented and performed at various levels such as celebrations at store levels, weekend gatherings, and address by leaders, recreational events, infrastructure and facilities, awards and incentives, flexibility in working hours, internal and external trainings, sponsoring further education, special employee discounts, and celebrating the retail employee day.

For example, Giordano practiced stringent selection procedures to make sure that the candidates selected matched the desired employee profile. Selection continued into its training workshops, which tested the service orientation and character of a new employee.

The retailer offered an attractive package in an industry where employee turnover is high. Giordano motivated its people through a base salary that probably was below market average, but added attractive performance-related bonuses. These initiatives and Giordano's emphasis on training resulted in a lower staff turnover rate. Giordano not only believed but also invested heavily in employee training and has been recognized for its commitment to training and developing its staff by such awards as the Hong Kong Management Association Certificate of Merit for Excellence in Training and the People Developer Award from Singapore, among others. Giordano's philosophy of quality service could be observed not only in Hong Kong but also in its overseas outlets. The company has been honored by numerous service awards over the years.

Training and Education

This is one of the major challenges for most employers, especially for retailers and those who employ staff in large numbers. Retailers invest in comprehensive and structured training and skilling of their teams in each area and discipline of customer value that eventually form the essential framework for customer centricity. These key disciplines are customer insight and foresight, competitor insight and foresight, strategic alignment, peripheral vision, and cross-functional collaboration.

Staff has to take retraining in order to adapt to a constantly changing external environment and consumer behavior/expectations. Here, HR executives needs to understand the business, the ingredients, functional components, and skills the business requires and make sure the right people join the company. It is a matter of mind-set, working environment, and attitude toward self-responsibility and taking ownership. Let us take the example of online retailer Housing.com. The average age of employees of this online retail company is about 25 years and most of them are fresh graduates or having an experience of couple of years. Now the major challenge in managing such a young and dynamic workforce from HRM context is that they expect to see an accelerated vertical career growth. To address this challenge, Housing.com has charted out a "snake path" of career competency. This takes them laterally across functions and verticals, in order to move them up gradually. In this way, they are exposed to cross-functional skills and enable them for multitasking that are of relevance. During this journey across multiple or cross functions, they gradually pick up these skills and eventually move up the ladder. As they are looking for a workplace to exhibit their skills and work as a professional entrepreneur of sorts, the company allows them to take full ownership of their functions and converts their energy into motivational force.

Hence, the future will be characterized by the following needs, among others:

- The need to handle increasing complexity in the business and working environment.
- The need for continual enrichment of the management skill sets known as "lifelong learning" (i.e., the ability to adapt to changing environments, challenges, and technology).
- The need for a positive attitude toward emerging changes and opportunities: employees themselves have to come up with the self-motivation and enthusiasm to become lifelong learners. The process can be aimed, for example, at obtaining further business qualifications, such as an MBA, executive management programs, qualification in HRM, or attending training courses/workshops on market research, key skills, such as leadership, communication skills, personal development/grooming, and other soft skill development programs. Some universities/institutions are offering courses on work-based learning in which live projects are offered to work upon that are directly related to the learning environment of the individual student's workplace.
- The need to communicate effectively and precisely, and transmit meaning and values: While the organization will provide support, it will be the individual managers who have to "campaign" their own learning and also that of others in phases of extreme change. This can be channelized by using technology such as video conferencing or e-learning modules. HRM needs to consult and coordinate with leaders on how best to use the modern methods.
- The need for creative and innovative management: This can be the way to inculcate new insights into common view or to introduce new issues or ideas as an area for development. Many times, people are confined into their own reality, thought, and beliefs or imprisoned into their own version of their world. In such cases, they are allowing themselves to be trapped into a mind-set of either success or self-perpetuating failure. So managers need to ensure that they are not getting entrapped in an "intuitive prison" of their own thoughts, causing them always to see things in one dimension only.

For example, Lifestyle International, a part of the Dubai-based Landmark Group, identifies high-potential employees and starts working with them by providing them with self-development programs and also works on functional and behavioral competencies that are required for respective role. They evaluate employees based on these competencies, identify gaps, analyze the gap, and eventually address them with development plans. Employees are sent to premier institutes, classroom trainings, and open programs within the organization.

Further, functional inputs are offered by "EEE" training methodology: *experience* (on the job training), *education* (assistance for further education), and *exposure* (sending them to the overseas offices/outlets). This methodology of career development is referred as a "career passport" for each employee. With this program, the employees go through LIFE methodology: *learn*, *implement*, *fast-track* (training program), and *expert* path, supplemented with various training programs during each of these stages. Lifestyle also posts/advertises on its intranet about the internal job vacancies available at various levels to different roles, for employees who are interested to move to other departments/roles. It also runs mentoring program where the identified mentors act as guide for store-level staff. Hence, the entire journey designed in such a way that it effectively helps the employees to move up to superior levels.

Similarly, in late 2006, Giordano opened Giordano University, located at Dongguan in China. At its initial stage, the university trained staff located in Hong Kong and Mainland China.

There are plans to offer training to its other markets and even franchisees and authorized dealers. Giordano's efforts on staff training and development reaped results as was shown by the many service awards it secured. The bottom line is that instilling the purpose centricity in an organization is important. But it is not easy because the organizations having this sustainable competitive purpose-centric human asset are either founded with a purpose at their core or evolved over a long period of time.

Improving Collaboration and Managing Performance

Technology and Culture of Collaboration

HRM in retailing has transformed in recent years, and customer centricity has come under the limelight. Customer-centric HR is now being recognized and practiced as the next level of HRM, as discussed in previous section of this chapter. This transition is due to the paradigm shift in the way retail companies, especially the e-tailers, are delivering their offerings to their consumers. What this scenario demands is, building a culture that encourages strategic collaboration and transparency and ensures synergy. So here the culture of collaboration comes into the picture and plays a significant role. Collaboration is of the major capabilities that enable people working in a team to achieve not only personal growth but also the outcomes benefiting the whole organization. It is a very effective way to deal with complex challenges. This is attributed to its unparalleled potential to tap the team creativity and unleash innovation in a collaborative atmosphere. The power of collaborative culture lies in the knack of bringing people together to work toward a common goal, overcome the volatility and ambiguity that differentiates the external environment, and drive organizations toward success. Hence, the culture of an organization portrays how it conducts its business. It defines the behavioral style as to how an organization caters its various stakeholders, internal as well as external. Companies strive incessantly to inculcate an appropriate culture to achieve optimum organizational effectiveness and efficiency. And this makes culture a very significant aspect for the success of an organization in long terms.

As companies grow exponentially and expand into different regions and geographies, it becomes even more challenging to have a common culture of collaboration across all wings. In a globalized economy, one of the valuable skills a team can have is the ability to work with people of varied cultures and nationalities. As a part of diverse team being located in different nations, it requires the collaboration of open minds with right attitude to work together toward a common goal. Today, global corporations are trying to incorporate this culture of collaboration into their leadership development programs. Some send their high performers to work at a foreign subsidiary, with the idea that living abroad will broaden their horizons, while some organizations send their executives for programs conducted by international business schools, which assure to impart the experience of working in diverse teams in the classroom. These are tried-and-tested techniques; however, the growing demand for professionals with a global mind-set is such that new and innovative programs are always welcome. This is applicable to not only multinational retail companies but also national players. For instance, in the context of country like India that has a huge cultural diversity, it is of prime importance for any national-level retailer to manage this diversity and maintain a standard code of culture across all the stores, outlets, and franchises.

In all this exercise, technology is playing a significant role in connecting people far and wide. While planning on creating a culture that motivates employees to be open and communicate freely across various channels, an organization need to have strategically set outcomes and common goals. At this juncture, HRM is expected to reflect upon how to adopt technology actively in its functioning and create a new environment for employees at the workplace, because it is crucial to connect employees internally and enable them to collaborate effectively with external stakeholders for better performance of the organization at all the levels of performance pyramid.

Benefits of a Collaborative Culture

- Strategic, comprehensive planning that supports systemic success in the long term.
- More clarity for all involved about what is needed for the organization and its people to grow over a period of time.
- Inclusive and collaborative decision-making that benefits the whole by win–win outcome.
- Bringing new ideas and innovative solutions for vexing challenges.
- synchronized actions in service of shared, measurable goals.
- Effective time and talent management.
- Increased autonomy and sense of ownership among staff.
- Sturdy relationships, expansive engagement, accelerated learning, higher trust levels, valuable knowledge sharing, heightened sense of collective purpose and flourishing purpose-centric organization.
- Technology platform leveraged creatively provides several ways of enhancing employee engagement. The scope of employee engagement has got widened as everyone in the organization being connected somehow by some kind of technology platform or forum.
- Counseling and mentoring for career advancement are two dimensions of employee engagement that employees eagerly look forward to and can be promoted by creating forums that will nurture it.

Smart technology is also helping organizations to upgrade the HR function itself and align it with the constantly evolving sociocultural trends—all based on rich data gathered from diverse businesses and talent domains. Though technology is becoming extensively embedded in HR functions, we must remember that "personal touch" should not be lost by being solely dependent on the effectiveness of virtual platform because it is the people who make all the difference.

Managing the "Performing Talent"

The high-performance-driven organizations have to constantly focus on building a talent pool to support the business vision. These include focused endeavors to build a robust talent pipeline, extending the employer brand beyond the national and regional borders, achieving the distinction of becoming an aspirational employer for professionals, and augmenting talent on the technical side. Social media when used effectively have tremendous potential to assist organizations fortify their employer brands, compete aggressively for top talent, and engage and retain employees. They can also use this as online tools to hire, manage, and retain high-performing employees. As retailers embrace globalization of talent, we see that frameworks to manage "performing talent" are cohesive and aligned across geographies, with the flexibility to customize and implement the framework as per local needs. This amalgamation of alignment with agility and flexibility is important to build an internal pipeline that caters the needs of the retailer at large and not just the immediate job profile. Talent-rich companies not only look at individuals but also look at cadres of talent at different levels.

Step 1: The HRM department ensures that they have a pool of employees having high potential and relevant experience with an aim to continuously raise their performance benchmark higher.

Step 2: From this pool of "performing talent," the company then selects "leadership material" that can be groomed to be the organization's leader or leaders of specialist functions within the organization.

This is the essence of a larger "performing talent" management process in which leaders identify organizational needs and critical job roles and capabilities. These perspectives provide a balanced view of an employee's skills and growth areas. This acts as a gateway to the successive "career succession plan."

Now here again, technology comes into picture because companies cannot implement efficient HR strategies without it. It captures systematic data about the complete life cycle of an employee, from pre-hiring, to hiring and induction, training, performance management, and exit. This makes the talent management process more transparent and swift. Plus, HRM gets the leverage to implement standardized and integrated talent acquisition and management strategies across global markets. This in turn gives impetus to employer branding. So, the right HRM technology with a user-friendly presence on job portals, company websites, and social media can be a deciding factor for the kind of talent an organization attracts and acquires and hence a decisive input in its performance.

Building Up Performing Workforce

As discussed earlier, HR executives of any retail company has to ensure that the workforce is motivated and trained with a common purpose to satisfy today's demanding consumers. For achieving this, retailers have to develop the employee value proposition. This means an attractive position with the fulfillment of employee expectations and need and building a prospective, superior and unique image in terms of recruiting, training, managing, and developing human capital. In simple terms, it is nothing but creating a cogent reason, why the employees should work for that company. Here we discuss some approaches to assure desired HR quality but for this investment is must. Such an investment has to be justified in monetary and fiscal terms and must therefore be constantly reviewed and improved.

- Planning the HR costs and expenditures for the annual business budget and forecasts.
- Supplying key data needed for planning the workforce at all levels and providing benchmark data on KPIs, such as average working hours per store opening hour, turnover per working hour, and profit per working hour.
- Elaboration of systems to measure the work involved in and results of HRM (training investment per employee, rate of internal job placements, etc.).
- Conveying and inculcating common and communicated values of the organization to provide a strategic framework and common mind-set to the workforce.
- Creating and developing a transparent internal job market.
- Giving perspective for the future and showing a clear career paths to the employees to increase the loyalty.
- Flexible models of working times, such as part-time working concepts, annualized hour contracts, and balancing of professional and personal life with the aid of sabbaticals.
- Ensuring appropriate processes, adequate tools, and sufficient budget to achieve their objectives and goals.
- Continuing education of executives and employees within actual training programs and a corporate university.
- Providing soft skills trainings and professional mentoring to ensure proper alignment of their values with the organization's values and beliefs.
- Initiation of an employee suggestion/inquiry system for continuous improvements.
- Recruitment of talent from exchange programs with universities worldwide.
- International education within internal exchange programs, with participants from different countries.
- Apprenticeships and relevant education in new professions to build up the workforce with updated knowledge and skill sets.

- Sharing company success and achievements with the staff (incentive systems at all staff levels, based on parameters that are accessible to employees).
- Offering fringe benefits, such as discounts for shopping at the employer's stores, company cars, equity programs and stock options, retirement arrangements, club membership, and other social benefits.

For example, the feedback system at the online retailing company Flipkart is dynamic, informal, and spontaneous. The sense of ownership and independence provided at the company is unique. Their approach to employee interaction is not confined and restrictive. Flipkart gives them the independence to work and prefers to involve them in key decisions. The management encourages crowdsourcing, from deciding on a holiday to the names of PLs to be launched by Flipkart. This helps the online retailer in development and nurturing a value culture based on belongingness.

Leveraging Technology and Digital Media

Every organization needs to understand the evolution in technology and use it to their advantage. Today, the world is moving at an amazing pace in technology where no particular device or operating system is dominant.

Our personal and professional domains have started overlapping in an extensive manner. With the phenomenal upsurge of e-commerce, the physical retailers need to offer more flexibility to their employees. The introduction of smartphones, tablets, and laptops has revolutionized the way professionals and enterprises are functioning. In some of the new and emerging markets, management has to decide whether to implement an integrated system with all branches aligned with the parent company. However, it can be prohibitively expensive for a branch at the periphery of the organization to lock into a global IT infrastructure that is geared to operations in Western countries where labor costs are at relatively higher levels. Retailers operating internationally rely on common platforms and IT structures, so the decision for investments has to be made at the right time.

A major change in retailing in the future will be the worldwide use of RFID technologies. The success of the Metro Group in developing and running their "Future Store" in Rheinberg as a closely controlled experiment has had a strong impact on the application of new technologies in "real business," as Metro has shared the results with industry and with its suppliers, as well as its IT and logistics providers. The scientific research involves customers' reactions to the new shopping methods, and also staff training in the use of intelligent technologies and introductions to available information and changing processes for customers.

Thus, there has been, and continues to be, a great deal of activity surrounding staff appraisal. The management of progression, or performance monitoring, continues to exercise HRM executives, who wish it to be as fair as possible to individuals, but also want the company to obtain maximum benefit from the efforts and activities. The strategy should be not only systematic but also continuous, with a fully implemented set of key metrics. A panoramic view at each individual's future, which can be a position as well as a set of personal goals, should be carried out at regular intervals. Hence, it becomes imperative for HRM professionals to ensure that line managers can perform this function. Organizations oftentimes do not have the financial resources or the inclination to research software and find budget-friendly options for implementation. People are sometimes uneasy and/or skeptical about new technology. However, the best retail companies embrace technology and find the right technology application for their businesses. There are thousands of HRM software options that can make the HRM processes faster, easier, and more effective. A comprehensive strategic plan addresses this aspect. Data mining technology, HRM tools, and statistical modeling assist in HR trend analysis not only at the microlevel (organizational) but also at the macrolevel across industries and geographies. All these resources give a clear vision to HRM teams and help them to understand where they actually stand and where they need to head. It also assists the HR leaders on how to systematically plan future workforce strategies or modify the current ones.

Now as far as recruitment and training are concerned, technology has brought a lot of changes and has increased the effectiveness and efficiency of these HR functions. Video interviews and web-based training programs are increasingly used by HR executives to increase the functionality. For example, interview on Skype. Skype is a hybrid instant messaging and voice chat application that allows free video calls by connecting users to one another from any global location with Internet access. It is very cost-effective also as it saves the expenses on traveling and brings a number of significant advantages in the form of flexibility and mobility to both personal and business communication.

Besides all these disruptive technological developments, the real action today is also happening in the virtual world, the hub of millions to connect. The penetration of smartphones and the exponential growth in Internet usage are also changing the dynamics of the online job market. Through these media, the job seekers are reaching out to their colleagues in previous or current employers, to the competitors, industry professionals, and corporations, while thousands of recruiters are watching and pursuing them closely. The gap in the right talent demand and supply, constant global and local economic pressures, volatile emerging markets, and the proliferation of technology is forcing HR executives to stand back and reevaluate the way they function. In a way, technology has democratized the functioning of HR departments. Easy access to information on virtual platforms has broadly expanded the horizon of talent acquisition and employee management and taken its scale of operations to a global level. Putting things in a nutshell, technology has now become the backbone for all HR functions. Hence, it is imperative for HR managers to be "online" if it wants to keep the door "open" to a gamut of talent, business and management opportunities.

Social Media Recruitment: A Subset of E-recruitment

Recruitment is a process of searching potential candidates and attracting capable applicants for employment. E-recruiting is the use of Internet technology to attract potential candidates and support the recruitment process. This usually means using recruiter's own company website, a third-party job site or job board, a CV database, social media, or search engine marketing. Social media recruiting (social recruiting) is the part of e-recruiting. The use of smartphones and social networking has impacted HR, as many companies now disseminate information to employees via these platforms. As the technology is developing at the breakneck speed and changes are happening constantly, the methods used today will likely be different one year or even six months from now. Also the market is so competitive that recruiters need to innovate and find unconventional ways to search and source talent. Today, it is social media—the enormously popular, nonintrusive but still attractive, approachable, and casual platform—that has captured the momentum and is one of the major instruments for both talent and job hunts. Relatively, a low-cost recruitment solution is its added advantage.

For example, in the context of recruitment in retail industry, using social media is about getting engaged and having conversations with people before they are even thinking about the concerned retailer as an employer. As a recruiter, the retailer needs to be present where the most qualified, talented, and largest pool of applicants are. In this way, the HR executives can leverage social media to tap in to potential recruits. This is not restricted to entry-level openings; retailers are using social media like Twitter to tweet about critical/senior roles also, because they are getting wide response on such platforms. Companies today are interested not only in active seekers who are registered with job portals but also in those who are not seeking jobs actively, the passive talent pool. Social recruiting allows a two-way dialog between candidates and prospective employers that provides the recruiters with a comprehensive view of the individual. Recruiters not only ask questions but also allow candidates to ask their queries regarding the company, job profile, and so on, and senior management reply to it in real time. This approach leads to a more engaging and transparent conversation. This type of head-hunting is nothing but social recruiting. It is about engaging with users and using social media tools to source and recruit talent. The social networks like blogs, microblogs, and online video communities through "social sourcing" also facilitate tapping of passive seekers. Recruiters like and prefer those easy reference checks through referral engines of social media platforms or company-specific referral apps.

For instance, Twitter is a microblogging social networking service where messages are known as tweets. It is a simple tool that helps connect businesses more meaningfully with the right audience at the right time. To make the job-posting tweets standout, recruiter can use hashtags (#). The hashtags are used as a way to filter and find information on Twitter. The recruiter just needs to include the hashtag with a keyword in their tweet and it becomes instantly searchable. For examples, the hashtags the recruiter might consider using #job, #employment, #hiring, #career, #salesjob, #merchandiserjob, #visualmerchandiser, and so on. According to the estimates, 5,00,000 social job announcements are released on Twitter every month. HCL was the first company to run an end-to-end recruitment process on Twitter.

Now for searching the potential candidates, the recruiter can just preach a quick search on Twitter (search.twitter.com) for anybody discussing a specific keyword and they can get hundreds of contacts. The HR executives can also search for people they know, by industry, location, interest and preferences, hashtag, popularity, time, and more. For example, Snapdeal has extensively used Twitter to broadcast open positions. Very often, these are senior positions within the organization. This also enables the recruiter to expand the talent pool exponentially and the company gets to connect with its audience/followers. In this way, social recruiting also becomes a good branding opportunity for companies. Snapdeal has hired 800 people through pure-play social strategies, a third of its total headcount addition, and the count is growing.

Similarly, LinkedIn offers tools that help recruiters manage all their talent leads in one place. It offers them a strategic platform of building their brand among employees and also for searching special skill sets. It has also developed a differentiated pricing model for many of its offerings such as Talent Solutions, a mass hiring platform, and LinkedIn Recruiter, which allows recruiters to search and target profiles. The reason for developing this business model is simple. They cater a very different audience from what a typical job site caters to. They provide services ranging from assistance for purely accessing professional content to providing career opportunities and providing a platform to network with peers in the industry. The company is also viewed as a communication platform. It operates long-form content publishing platform where several India-based leaders have joined the platform as "Influencers."

Likewise, Facebook is a social platform that connects people with friends and others who study, work, and live around them. Its objective is to connect friends, family, and business associates. The model has eventually expanded to incorporate connections to organizations, businesses, and interests and not just individual people. Hence, Facebook is increasingly becoming a very easy and yet affordable way to build a pool of applicants. This Facebook directory is widely used to search for groups, users, pages, and applications. Facebook permits free job postings in Facebook Marketplace, and the company Facebook page can also be used as a recruiting tool. The advertisement requires very basic information such as title, job category, subcategory, job location, and job profile. Many times, individuals even use their personal Facebook page to post status updates, register job opportunities, and invite people to reply privately if they are interested. For example, Snapdeal ran a contest on its Facebook page for the most innovative solution to a real business issue the company was facing. In this contest, the applicants were asked to formulate a case study and solve the problem. The applicants who stood in the top 10 were then interviewed. Such a type of recruitment drives are targeted toward a specific talent pool.

Strategic Advantages of Social Media to Human Resource Management. These sources provide not only information regarding the professional skills but also inputs related to personal and behavioral aspects of job seekers. It becomes possible because on these platforms, the job seekers usually let their guard down—things that are necessary for evaluating their cultural and ethical fit in an organization. Plus, there is an added advantage of a significant reduction in the recruitment cost attributed to posting/sharing job advertisements with various "talent networks" or "talent communities." However, in recruitment via social media, employers need to be a lot more rigorous when it comes to credentials of the applicants if the person is being sourced directly from the social platforms.

The job seekers are also quick and eager to take advantage of social networking services because:

- The social media presence may help them to find desired job opportunities; in some professionals, virtual dossier may turn out to be a prerequisite to prove their track record and skills.
- The contacts given in social networking services may help them to obtain valuable information and knowledge (e.g., by sharing experiences), get the inputs to their queries or assistance in looking for solutions to their problems.
- These services are a valuable resource of knowledge about potential employers and also for preparing for job interviews (fan pages, microblogs, topic-related forums).
- This pool of information helps them to understand the recruiter's organization culture and also to create and present their own image.
- Social media also provides an attractive environment for job seekers, by giving them an opportunity to present their experience, expertise, skills, and competencies.

Both traditional companies and New Age start-ups are communicating with the hashtag generation with hiring videos or hirals (portmanteau of hire and viral on YouTube that are going viral). Hence, YouTube, Facebook, Twitter, LinkedIn, MySpace and so on are exceptionally good places to derive a media presence to attract a variety of talent pool. They have taken recruiting back to its grass roots of networking, but for a digital age.

The objective of using social media as a recruiting tool by retailers is also aimed to create a buzz about them not only as an employer brand but also as a talent brand. While employer brand is an organization's reputation as an employer, talent brand is the public version of employer brand. That is, it is the public's perception that is reflected in what the talent thinks, feels, and shares about the organization. It also includes what people are buzzing about the organization on social media platforms, apart from employees of the organization. Hence, a company's talent brand is a direct outcome of its talent value proposition or the actual set of experiences of people who work for the organization. The employer organization shares stories of successful employees, and advertises an interesting culture. The career sites also feature employee stories of what it is like to work at a particular organization.

On the one hand, the role of talent branding and employer branding are crucial in attracting right human capital that is required by the organization. On the other hand, potential recruits can refer talent branding developed through social media marketing, personal experience (reviews, blogs), word of mouth, and their perceptions of the brand to support their decision-making while evaluating potential employers. Hence, it becomes imperative for the organizations to have a continuous scan of the viral content present in blogs, other media platforms, or online communities and sensibly and cautiously handle the crisis communication, if any.

Even smaller companies can explore this technology by posting job openings as their status updates. This technique is relatively inexpensive, but there are certain things that need to be taken care of. For example, tweeting about a job opening might spark interest in some potential candidates, but the ploy is to show your personality as an employer early on. Though tweeting may be an effective way to recruit people who are open about their job search, still the platforms such as LinkedIn might be a better way to acquire more seasoned candidates who cannot be open about their undercover hunt for a new job, because of their current employment situation. LinkedIn is an interconnected network of experienced professionals from around the world, representing hundreds of industries and countries. LinkedIn has given people permission to put their résumé online without fear of objection or retribution from the current employer.

Let us consider the example of Zappos.com, an e-retailer based in the USA. It was established in 1999 to offer online shopping experience for footwear. Eventually, the selection has grown to include not only footwear but also clothing, accessories, bags, eyewear, and many more categories. Zappos is one of the many organizations that use YouTube videos to promote the company. There exists a link in those videos that channelizes viewers to the company's website to apply for a position in the organization.

Hence, social media are becoming an important tool in recruitment of future employees for retailers. They offer an easy and simple access to people having required talent and experience at a low cost. Though social media recruiting requires some patience and efforts, it is an investment with long-term benefits for the company. An effective social media presence is also a cost-effective way for improving employer branding score. In a nutshell, companies are also converting their talent acquisition program into a marketing blitzkrieg focused toward employees who are in search of a competitive work culture, which is also called "recruitment marketing."

The fast-changing nature of technology not only presents opportunities but also creates challenge. As new technologies are developed, employees may be able to implement innovative ways of performing the assigned job responsibilities with improved output. HR managers are also responsible for developing policies and disciplinary guidelines dealing with cyberloafing and other workplace time wasters revolving around technology. Human stress levels and lack of work–life balance are also greatly influenced by the cutting-edge technology (Figure 8.2).

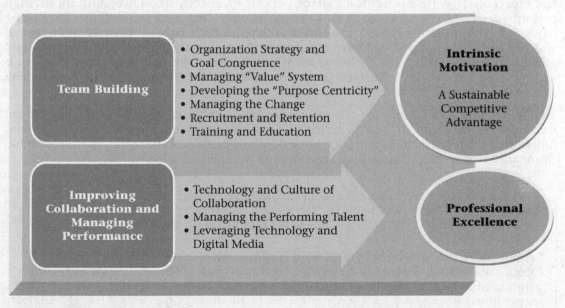

Figure 8.2: *Outcomes of Strategic Human Resource Management in Retailing*

The Future of HRM in Retailing and the Way Forward

Future of retail is very certain with major retail expansion, shortage of right talent, and competition between organizations to attract the best of the available talent, creating new talent to meet their demands and retaining them. HR's role has changed with times, and it will adapt and improvise itself in the coming future as well. HRM has to keep an eye on such constraints, as the retail trade is anxious to attract the best employees.

Future HRM will concentrate on supporting management and workforce and outsource administrative tasks to contractors. In future, there will be more intensive collaboration and networking with external parties. Professions in retail, such as that of IT specialist, are developing. HRM must also emphasize on ethical working conditions, safer working environments, and equal opportunity policies (ending sex/age discrimination, inclusion of minorities, etc.). In any company, HRM has to build up trust and commitment among all persons working in that organization. Continued reliance on traditional processes is definitely no longer a recipe that promises much success. HR management has to assure fast and market-oriented actions that are appropriate to complex market situations. HRM will have to set priorities on the HR strategy and its realization, but will be viewed on the operational side more in the role of a service center. In the future, the issue of management development will gain even greater importance.

To sum up, HRM has to be aligned with the business strategy of the company, to work in keeping with all of its corporate objectives, and to be prepared not only to help in implementing all changes necessary but also to instigate and be at the vanguard of change programs. Further, HRM should be aware of employee interests within the organization yet conscious of its place as the "powerhouse" when controversial business decisions, such as downsizing, have to be implemented. Lastly, it plays a key role in ensuring that constant retooling and retraining takes place in the operation to meet ever-evolving challenges. Lifelong learning should be an integral part of any business, to enable it to respond to its rivals' activities with fresh initiatives within the company.

HRM specialists have to ensure the long-term performance of "their" retail organizations. High performance has to be an outcome of working smartly, leveraging technologies, and being passionate about the "purpose," and this also requires right balance between professional and personal life. Today's workforce is increasingly multigenerational, multicultural, and globally dispersed. It is a big challenge for HRM to meet the future needs, and the task is wide ranging. How well HR managers perform their function will determine whether a retailer registers a sustainable success in the future.

We have tried to understand the comprehensive and central role of HRM in retailing. Retail has been and will continue to be an exciting field of business throughout the world. The main function of the retail sector is to work with and for people all over the world, so that retail has the chance to give people interesting and fulfilling workplaces.

Summary

With increase in use of Internet technologies and search engines, consumers can find any information on their smartphone, anywhere and at any point of time. They are increasingly gaining knowledge about the products they intend to buy and this has increased their expectations from the sales associates of the retail store. It has been observed that a knowledgeable sales associate increases their likelihood of making an in-store purchase.

They also expect sales associates to be knowledgeable about products; they should help them check out quickly, let them know about loyalty program benefits and promotional offers in detail, and should greet them promptly with a welcoming attitude. In terms of in-store technologies, consumers believe that store associates can provide a better shopping experience when equipped with the latest mobile technologies. So here, HR executives need to understand the changing needs of these New Age customers to design a development program that will equip and brush up the store staff accordingly. To achieve this, the HR executives need to bring the culture of "service" and culture of "collaboration" by effectively imbibing the purpose centricity in order to develop the organization peopled by purpose-centric workforce.

Now this is regarding the service part; let us visit the culture and collaboration part in the next paragraph.

Many times, there is a confusion between non-changing culture and values and inevitable change any organization needs to make to remain relevant in the market. The leaders of retail organizations have realized that they should contemporize the products but not the culture with changing times. If company culture is to respect the individual and create non-hierarchical culture, then there is no reason to change it for decades. In fact, it would be unfavorable to company's growth. While transformation is considered as the goal for many retail organizations, it is imperative for the HR executives to outline exactly what it means and the nature of the transformation they are actually seeking. The reality of any kind of change is that it puts forth an adaptive challenge for an individual at deeply personal level. Change comes with shift in the mind-set, different roles and responsibilities, new cultures, and a changed set of expectations, because business transformation is all about being able to do the things more effectively and efficiently—rather, in today's terms, more smartly. Retail organizations need to possess the ability to recognize the risks that accompany change such as attrition, skill gap, and legacy systems that reinforce status quo, increased cost, and low engagement. So in order to transform, the retailers need to look at how they need to change and fundamentally reframe the business and HR processes in the context of digitization to derive the optimum value for the stakeholders.

The concrete foundation of change management is built by understanding the value of value. The values that are critical to organizations and individuals evolve cultures that are resilient during change, help moderate risk, and align the behaviors. At times, the values are perceived even more important when the change is sensitive in form and nature. When the values assume a shared form, they are transformed into culture; this can eventually play in two extremes: either as an enabler or as a barrier to the change. So if the adopted culture is characterized by integrity, excellence, transparency, and collaboration, it is more likely that the change will be viewed through this paradigm and be espoused.

Review Questions

1. Briefly discuss the changing environment in the business of retailing and implications on the role and function of HRM of a retail company.
2. "With the changing environmental scenario of retail industry, the role of HRM has also changed." Comment on this statement.
3. Explain in detail the how the "service culture" is being developed in the retail organizations with the appropriate examples.

4. Explain the strategic HRM with appropriate example. Also present the major components of strategic HRM.

5. Briefly explain the importance of goal congruence for effective HRM.

6. "Managing the 'value' system is essential for building performing team." Comment on this statement and justify your views with the appropriate examples.

7. "The 'purpose'-centric workforce is a key to building performing team." Comment on this statement and justify your views with the appropriate examples.

8. Explain how the modern HR managers in retail industry can successfully adapt to the change? Justify your answer with appropriate examples.

9. Briefly explain the various factors that the HR managers in retail need to consider in order to increase the effectiveness of recruitment and retentions.

10. "Continuous and gradual training and education are of utmost important for the employees working in a retail organization." Comment on this statement and justify your views with the appropriate examples.

11. How the technology is being leveraged by retailers to develop and build the culture of collaboration among the employees?

12. How the "performing" talent can be successfully managed by HR executives of a retail organization?

13. Explain the significance of technology and digital media in strategic HRM with appropriate examples.

14. "Today, social media has become one of the most significant components of strategic HRM." Comment on this statement and justify your views with the appropriate examples.

Chapter 9

Physical Environment and Pervasive Creativity: Bringing the Retail Store Alive

Learning Objectives

- **Introduction to the concept of visual merchandising**
- **Purpose of visual merchandising**
- **Creating right atmospherics, ambience, and environment**
- **Components of exterior environment**
- **Components of interior environment**
- **Key merchandising tools**
- **Key designing principles**
- **Brand image and visual merchandising**
- **Pervasive creativity**
- **Pervasive creativity and perceptual process**

Introduction

Virtual merchandising is the art of creating visual displays and arranging merchandise assortments within a store to improve the layout and presentation and to increase growth, sales, and hence, in turn, the profitability. VM helps to attract the customers toward the displayed merchandise and also improves the shopping experience for customer by sending the right message about the merchandise and presenting it in a unique manner with effective creative quotient.

Visual impact is a huge component of retail merchandising. Customers entering a store are greatly influenced by the visual information they gather in the first split second. One simple visual element, such as color, can catch a shopper's attention and also greatly affect their mood. In today's ultracompetitive marketplace, it is of paramount importance that retailers understand the basics of VM.

Definition and Meaning

VM is the way one displays "merchandise for sale" in the most attractive manner with the end purpose of making a sale. "If it does not sell, it is not visual merchandising." VM is the art of implementing effective design ideas to increase store traffic and sales volume. VM is a technique that is applied and practiced in any retailing environment.

VM is an art and science of displaying merchandise to enable maximum sale. VM is a tool to achieve sales and targets, a tool to enhance merchandise in the store, and a mechanism to communicate to a customer and influence his decision to buy.

VM, briefly defined, is the presentation of a store and its merchandise in ways that will attract the attention of potential customers and motivate them to buy the products. The role of the visual merchandiser in this effort is to carry out the merchandising concepts as formulated by management. These merchandising plans include what items are to be featured and in which locations they should be housed. The products change, but the identity of the brand does not. It is vital to have the product, merchandising, and store design aligned with the identity of the product. The visual merchandiser, guided by these decisions and using all of his or her creative talents, sets out to present the best possible visual effects.

The aim of a successful merchandising is to address the needs of today's consumer. The retailer should understand the purchase motive, rationale, and display the merchandise accordingly. A thumb rule is to place impulse-buying products in the left zone, planned purchases in the right zone, and appealing (hotcakes) merchandise in the central zone. VM today forms a crucial element and component of retailing. Visual merchandiser uses season-based displays to introduce new arrivals to customers, and thus increase conversions through a planned and systematic approach by displaying stocks available. The façade and window displays attract passersby and increase walk-ins. Consumer behavior studies have confirmed that the lure of eye-catching window display and a tastefully decorated façade, more often than not, prove irresistible as they walk in to check out what is on offer. There is in-store décor as well, which is essentially designed to enhance the customer's desire to buy, increase comfort and convenience while shopping, and offer a superior shopping experience.

Therefore, the concept of VM is also referred as the art of retailing. In the world of VM as we know it today, artistic talents play a major role in creating an atmosphere and ambience that motivates shoppers and converts them into customers. Unlike the fine artist whose creativity is a statement of feelings, today's visual merchandiser must create displays with an eye on function and artistic expression that ultimately increase the store's profitability and maximize the aesthetics of the merchandise displayed with the intent to increase conversions, which eventually translate into sales.

VM can also play a role in imparting the look, feel, culture, image, prestige, and positioning to a brand. When executed effectively, it can create magic while simultaneously increasing brand loyalty. Most importantly, it can act as a magnet that draws customers inside the store and drive sale—all based on the aesthetic quality and appeal of retailer's way of displaying the merchandise. It also ensures exclusivity as no two stores should look alike. Besides these factors, when the mood and theme of such displays change at regular intervals, VM ensures that the store remains at the top of mind. Loyal customers have often been known to anxiously wait for the next display, which acts as a motivational factor in catalyzing the impulse-buying behavior. This visual communication is enforced by blending it with the imaginative use of colors, lighting, space, furniture, visual elements, and other factors of store ambience with regard to in-store displays. Once customers walk in, it is but imperative to ensure that they enjoy their first encounter with the store. After all, repeat visits will only happen if a customer's first visit is a memorable one with good experience. The logical arrangement of counters, with clear passageways, allows for easy access to merchandise.

Physical environment does not stop at VM and great-looking window displays, it is more than this. It includes ambient factors ranging from in-store layout and merchandising, to housekeeping, color, lighting, scent, product information, sensory inputs such as smell, touch, and sound/

Rather than getting lost in the clutter that most large stores are, the customer feels more comfortable in balanced product displays. Space is allocated to various product categories strategically and tactically coordinated taking into account the number of SKUs stocked, and shelves/counter space requirements are worked out accordingly.

Photo 9.1: *Balanced and Visually Appealing Merchandise Display*

Photo credit: Amit Kumar

music, as well as technologies such as digital displays and interactive installations, price tickets, posters and graphics, window display and props, right through to the color of walls and the fixtures used—all of these elements and how the retailers visually organize and harmonize these elements and how often they rotate these elements within the retail space is VM.

Hence, by synchronization of all these elements and inculcating retail atmospherics in evaluating customer value help the retailer to reinforce its brand image/store image and to enhance customer loyalty behavior. The associations due to environmental dispositions in and around the retail store will help positioning and communicating value in terms of points of parity (POPs) and PODs in the consumer memory. The practice of VM requires creativity, inspiration, logic, and organization and coordination. It has been quoted on numerous occasions as being a mix of art and science.

Though advertising or other promotional activities are crucial in building the brand, in the context of retailing, they are not sufficient to create the desired brand image that leaves a lasting impression on the consumers. The atmospherics and ambient factors are crucial for crafting and reinforcing the desired brand image of the retailer. When a physical environment with right blending of sensory and visual cues makes a "visual sense," a customer will be naturally attracted to the space, enticed to come in, convinced to stay and shop, and, most importantly, wants to buy!

The Purpose of Visual Merchandising

For generating expected revenues and desired profits, a "retail space" has to be the most productive. Now one of the best ways to optimize sales space for maximum revenue is to employ the art and science of VM. VM is the discipline that essentially employs a sense of aesthetics, to garner desirable customer response to the retailer's store and its offerings.

- To make merchandising desirable
- To make merchandise easy to locate in the store
- To introduce and explain new products

- To promote store image
- To cajole customers into the store
- To show merchandise assortment

VM helps in:

- Educating the customers about the product/service in an effective and creative way.
- Establishing a creative medium to present merchandise in 3D environment, thereby enabling long-lasting impact and recall value.
- Setting the company apart in an exclusive position.
- Establishing linkage between fashion, product design, and marketing by keeping the product in prime focus.
- Combining the creative, technical, and operational aspects of a product and the business.
- Drawing attention of the customer to enable him to take purchase decision within shortest possible time, and thus augmenting the selling process.

Visual Merchandising Placement Process

Where the products are located and how retailers arrange it around the store can be placed based on shoppers' buying behavior. For their easy access and reach, the ultimate VM is liable. A proper VM can affect on consumer decision to make a buy from prompt to multiple.

- Prime locations
- Eye-level and hand-level arrangements
- Customer entrance
- Window displays
- Store layout
- Customer space
- Store interior
- Store decorations
- Props

Shelf Displays

Here the retailers need to plan how they are going to use shelf displays to feature the merchandise, and how much shelf space each merchandise item will get. Here the retailers need to:

- Be careful for not to clutter the shelves by stacking more merchandise than capacity of the fixture.
- Place a striking or appealing merchandise in plain view of their entrance.
- capitalize on spaces at the end of shelves.
- Place their popular or targeted merchandise between eye level and knee level.
- Place the most profitable items at eye level.
- Place merchandise for children at children's eye levels.

Stock Displays

Retailer groups the related stock items together, and uses the premium spaces—for example, the ends of the aisles—to feature profitable merchandise. Here the retailer needs to:

- Group similar products together to encourage add-on sales—for instance, we may place crockery with cutlery.
- Group different but related merchandise together to help make companion sales—for instance, include all components of bathroom accessories in a set (also referred as "story").
- Change the displays regularly and keep them clean and well ordered.
- Feature a few merchandise items, including merchandise advertisement and fliers, at the POS space.

Components of Visual Merchandising

- Merchandise the focal point
- Right choice of colors is vital
- Display themes to appropriately support the product
- Display should complement the retailers' other strategies
- Cleanliness
- Change the display settings in frequent intervals

Creating Right Atmospherics, Ambience, and Environment

Retail atmospheric cues may generate sets and subsets of associations related to attributes, benefits, emotions of pleasure (or displeasure), attraction (or distraction), high (or low) confidence, self-actualization, and other basic human desires. The retail atmospherics consist of physical environmental elements such as bright or dim lighting, classical or familiar music, attractive window displays, sales staff appearance/dressing styles and layouts, magnificent architectural design, freshness and fragrance, appropriate temperature to make it cozy and comfortable, soothing and trendy color, attractive logo, and gentle crowding. These are ideal conditions that can affect the current and future behavior of consumers. The entire retail environment that includes store ambience consistently throws brand messages that the consumer experiences throughout the shopping endeavor. The retail environment is harmoniously designed in order to communicate brand persona and image of the store. In order to add depth to the perceptions encapsulated in the atmospherics and communicate the retailer's brand value and promise, each element of the retail environment is transformed so that it is differentiated from the competitors, standardized, and stimulates consumers' purchasing behavior.

The purpose of interior display is to develop a desire for the merchandise, show what is available, and encourage both impulse and planned buying. Three major goals of a store should be to motivate the customer to spend money, project the image of the store, and keep expenses to a minimum. It is been observed that nothing influences the consumer's purchase decisions more than advertising used where the sale is actually made—the point of purchase.

Let us consider the example of Tommy Hilfiger Denim stores. Tommy Hilfiger has launched this sub-brand Tommy Hilfiger Denim to target the youths who just love their indigo denim and prefer it as their most stylish outfit. The line essentially focuses on denim-passionate millennials and has created an image that is much casual and modern than the parent brand itself. The objective is to make the brand resonate with teenagers, college goers, and even the professionals who prefer to put on denims during weekends. The store design is contemporary with huge racks that display wide variety of denims in a very persuasive way. To connect with the target audience in an engaging way, the seasonal apparel, shirts, jackets, and other formal and casual wear other than the denim jeans are generally hung by wall or stacked neatly on

The contemporary look and rustic feel of the store is in line with the brand name "Tommy Hilfiger Denim" and the overall ambience–through its casual and laid-back feel–gives it a 'denim-ish' attitude.

Photo 9.2: *Look of the Store Matches the Nature of the Brand*

Source: www.global.tommy.com (accessed on 12 May 2016)

wooden chests, just in front of the denim's display, which create a rustic look. This rustic look perfectly complements the rugged feel of the denim jeans. The accessory section at the end is given an Old Worldly or antique feel with the help of stylized chairs (used as props) and racks to display the merchandise, which make the things more interesting. Mannequins are placed at the places where they can get maximum visibility, and sections for "He" and "She" are well demarcated. Besides all this, the bare walls and its creatively exposed red bricks seamlessly complement the ambience of the store. The overall display of the merchandise creates a feel of as if one is just looking at his or her wardrobe to dress up. Hence, perfectly clubbed VM and the store ambience eventually enhance the shopping experience.

The Components of Exterior Environment

A customer's first impression of a store is often created by the store's exterior. Store exteriors can help bring in new customers and retain existing ones. The best store exteriors attract, stop, and "invite" customers to shop. Considerations about store exteriors include their position on the site, architecture, and signage. Façade is one of the most significant components of the exterior environment and also very important space for branding of the mall or stand-alone store. Façade branding plays major role in catching the attention and attracting targeted audience. The visibility factor makes it an impactful space for branding and helps in enhancing and uplifting a brand's image by reinforcing the positioning the brand strives to create. By virtue of all these factors, it essentially defines the look of a retail store, brand, or shopping mall, making these brands more prominent, visible, and appealing.

Similarly, store's position is how and where it is placed at the location. The best store position and best façade design offer visibility, compatibility, and convenience.

- The store is clearly visible to vehicle and/or pedestrian traffic, using the most advantageous setback, angle, and elevation. A visible store becomes part of a consumer's mental map of where to shop for certain products. It attracts impulse shoppers on first visits, as well as long-term customers who are reminded of its products by continually noticing the store.

- The store is compatible with its surroundings, fitting the contour of the land and natural habitat. The design and construction materials are harmonious with the environment. The size of the facility is also in proportion to the size of the lot.
- The store is convenient for consumers, offering ample parking that is easy for vehicles to negotiate, possibly near public transportation, safe for pedestrian movement, and accessible for people with disabilities.

A store's architectural design should appeal to the targeted consumers. The design can reflect a retailer's size, prestige, product mix, and affiliation. Also, a store's architecture should be functional and allow the store to operate efficiently. Functional considerations include construction and maintenance costs, energy use, security, and customer convenience. Operational efficiency encourages easy movement of customers and sales personnel, and maximum merchandise exposure. A store's signage is the total of all the signs that attract consumers' attention and identify the store and its offerings. The main store identification sign should indicate who the retailer is, with an identifiable name, logo, or other symbol. Exterior signs also may inform consumers about the store's type (department store, supermarket), its product line (food, greeting cards), its service and price levels, and when the store is open.

Signs

A sign is a silent salesperson, and part of a shopper's first impression of a store. Signage should reflect the image of the store, generate interest, and invite consumers to try the store. Retailer can make different signs around the stores that help to grab customers' attention. This certainly helps to boost up the sale, especially when retailer called a discount on the specific products. An effective sign will communicate what type of business is being conducted. Off-premise signs provide information and direction, especially for travelers and new residents. Signs can also help effectively communicate a poor location. A sign's design conveys a great deal about the business inside. A stark design and limited materials may suggest discount prices and no frills. Elegant and expensive sign materials may suggest luxury products and brands. Signs may also be used to target a specific market segment such as youth, women, senior citizens, and singles. Where many signs compete for customers' attention, design and logo become even more important. They should be unique, noticeable, and readable. When preparing a sign to draw the customer's attention, consider size, shape, materials, lettering, height, placement, and structure. For example, among several rectangular signs in close proximity to one another, construct an oval or circular sign that will stand out. Also consider a sign's relationship with its surroundings.

A sign may look good on an individual storefront, but very unattractive when viewed in conjunction with other buildings on the street. Simple, brief, well-designed, well-lettered, and easy-to-read signs will convey a feeling of welcome. Design graphics appropriate for the nature of the business, and create a message that is clear and simple. Focus on one or two key words to describe the business. A clean, clear message will have more impact. Brick-and-mortar retail brands are taking on their online counterparts by investing more in efficiency and in-store and outdoor design to enhance customer experience—after realizing that they cannot compete with online players on discounts. To overcome this trend and continue attracting customers in big numbers, prominent malls and retail stores have started several initiatives such as boosting the experiential and service aspects with increased focus on design, creativity, food, and entertainment. Mall owners, who typically have a revenue-sharing arrangement with retailers, are bringing in rare and newly sought-after brands. They are also ensuring that the brands innovate on display and design features to give a seamless experience of rich and compelling designs to their customers. Most international brands prefer popular shopping malls to open their stores in India mostly due to lack of quality high-street destinations.

For example, The Armani store at Mumbai's Palladium Mall has had a 50-feet-tall eagle installed on the shop floor. The bird, which is an integral part of Armani's signature logo and signifies the brand's premium quality, makes the store stand out. While setting up the store, they brainstormed the idea of installing the eagle to make Armani clients indulge in a never-before design innovation and experience of creative display (aesthetics). Foreign brands are designing the stores by bringing in local innovation because the objective is to give consumers an engaging brand experience, which they cannot have online. High-end brands, such as Zara, Mango, Aldo, Marks & Spencer, and Steve Madden, are the leading clients of the Palladium Mall, which also houses the biggest names in luxury retail like Jimmy Choo, Burberry, and Gucci. As luxury brands focus on display innovation, the brands with a more mass appeal are ramping up in-store presentation, creativity, and experience. Hence a store's sign is its *signature*. It is personal, original, and continuously recognizable to the public. It should create an image that is consistently carried throughout the remainder of the store and its business actions.

Marquee

This special type of sign is used to display the name of a store. An effective marquee must stand out from the other businesses to attract attention. A marquee on some older buildings is a permanent canopy projecting over an entrance that provides protection from the elements. It can be used to announce a change in seasons, a special event, or a promotion. The top of the permanent canopy (marquee) provides an opportunity to showcase seasonal displays or special promotional banners.

Banners are used increasingly as an inexpensive but colorful, eye-catching means of promotion. A new and interesting appearance can be offered by changing the banners frequently. Consistency is an important aspect of retailing used to maintain a businesses' image and identification. The design concept used on the banners will be more effective if an attempt is made to carry the colors and graphics throughout the store, and on promotional materials and newspaper ads.

Store Entrance Lobby

It is been observed that the first-time customers remember a store's entrance, which provides the first and last view of the store's interior. Picture walking up to an expanse of wall whose flat surface is pierced only by a plain glass door, as opposed to the protective feeling offered by walking under a porch or canopy. A properly designed canopy or porch not only protects the customer in bad weather but also adds to the aesthetics of the building. When adding an entryway, be sure it is designed to blend or be consistent with the architecture of the building. A cluttered entryway causes shoppers to indefinitely postpone entering a store, while an attractive, well-designed entrance is inviting to the customer. Entrances that allow shoppers to come into a store without being aware of their entering are also becoming more popular. An example is a V-shaped window display that funnels window-shopping traffic into the store.

Windows Displays

It is very important for the retailing, regardless whatever products the retailer offers. This is the first place where a customer gives their concentration at a glance. Retailers give utmost importance to it. Special emphasis is generally placed on a store's window displays because they are the information link to the potential customer. The golden rule for window display is to remember the three-second attention span it has on the passer-by. Within the span of three seconds, the window should be able to pass a single, clearly understandable message. Hence, window displays can be as important, if not more important, than advertising.

The quality of a storefront is a major determinant for a customer, particularly a new customer, and should not be underestimated. The exterior appearance of one store, a block of businesses,

Properly lighted window displays can help sell specific products or ideas that promote a store's image. Window lights should be strong enough to overcome the reflections from outside objects, such as parked cars and buildings. At night, additional lights on overhead marquees and projecting cornices can make the window area look larger.

Photo 9.3: *Artistically Illuminated Window Catches the Eyeballs*

Source: www.gabrielasalgueiro.com (accessed on 12 May 2016)

or a cluster silently announces what customers can expect inside. Good exterior VM attracts attention, creates interest, and invites the customer into the business. The exterior presentation can offer a conservative, progressive, and lavish or discount image to the customer.

Visual merchandisers create themes for window displays that reflect the store's style and personality. Retailer brands use their window display to make a statement about their business and brand image. Window display must compel the passers-by to step inside the shop. Some of the guiding principles for window design include the following:

- A window display must feature the star products or very selective offers.
- It must be regularly updated.
- It must be very well linked to other communications of the company.

For instance, let us say that the retailers want to convey an image, that is elegant, sophisticated, edgy, or contemporary. Then the window display will:

- Be modern, relevant, and seasonal.
- Use props, images, signage, and products to convey an idea and message that will help the customers to connect with the merchandise/brands.
- Change the window displays regularly and also make sure products in the display are easy to find inside the store but not necessarily at the front, where the customers will need to explore no further.

275

- Change the window display theme, and here they need to remember to change the store's interior in such way that it will match the theme.
- One small but very expensive mistake that should be avoided is displaying something in the window that is susceptible to sun damage or fading, if the store frontage is exposed to direct sunlight.

Clear passages are provided for products, which require touch and feel. All impulse purchase-driven products are also clearly displayed so that the customers can reach them without any hindrance. Also, it has been observed that when a person enters a room, the human eye moves in a Z pattern (i.e., from rear left of the room to right rear, followed by front left of the room to front right). Care should be taken to do up the rear left end of the room in an appealing manner so as to guide the direction of vision and keep a shopper visually interested. Window displays are more successful when a dominate theme is carried throughout the display, regardless of whether the featured products are fashion-oriented, institutional or promotional in nature. Suggested window treatments that have proven successful include the following:

- Merchandise displayed as it would be utilized in a realistic setting
- A theatrical setting using fantasy and drama
- Straight merchandise glamorized with props
- Animation, such as in holiday windows that draws crowd of shoppers
- The use of sculpture, paintings, or art objects for a touch of class
- Media tie-ins, with current area activities, films, stars, or best-selling books

Window displays should be in harmony with the entire surroundings; a *whole* is being created rather than a fragment. When planning a window display, consider the building façade, street, people and their perceptions, color harmony, lighting, and viewing angle. Closed-back windows require a high level of general illumination. Massed window displays are often lighted with overhead fluorescents, which are supplemented by closely spaced clear incandescent lamps. Miniature portable spotlights are used to accent small display areas, price cards, and specific items in a massed display. Compact footlights help relieve shadows near the bottom of vertical displays.

The key areas that need to be targeted are the ones that are in direct view of people when either passing by the store, or when they first walk in. It is also important to bear in mind that VM and store design go hand in hand. One of the most important elements of VM is the placement of products. The most attractive and best-selling items should always be placed in direct view of a person. At the same time, it must be handled in the most effective manner possible. Working in opposition to this idea could lead to being detrimental for the business.

The Components of Interior Environment

Selling space should have a friendly, welcoming atmosphere that is inviting and convenient for customers. It should also provide a functional and safe atmosphere that boosts employee morale and allows for smooth store operations. Appropriate layout, fixtures, lighting, color, and space utilization all play a role in designing selling space. Well-planned stores always sell more than stores that are not well thought out. Shopping is encouraged with good traffic flow through the store. Good sight lines allow for customer viewing of various departments and merchandise. The walls, fixtures, ceilings, and flooring are a backdrop for the merchandise. They should define and accentuate the environment without detracting from the merchandise presentation. Interior décor should be psychologically pleasing to the store's target market to put customers into a buying mood.

Color

Color contributes significantly to people's impression of a display, as well as a store's overall appearance. Color in a display can catch the eye and make people pause and look. The color combinations of the ceiling, walls, floor covering, and the overall décor can affect the atmosphere of a store. Changing the color scheme can change people's attitudes and perceptions of a store, and can increase (or decrease) business.

Color can change the shape and add interest to a dull room, and can direct attention toward a specific object or away from problem areas. People tend to respond a certain way to different colors; these responses are outlined in the chart on the following page. Warm colors (red, yellow, and orange and colors with red or yellow hues such as yellow-green, beige, peach, brown, and orange-red) are stimulating and cheery. They make a room feel warm and intimate. Warm colors make a room seem smaller while making objects in the room appear larger. A warm color on the end walls of a long narrow room will appear to shorten the room. Blue, green, violet, and the colors containing blue, such as blue-green and violet-blue, are cool colors. These help create a relaxing atmosphere. Rooms decorated primarily in cool colors tend to appear larger and more spacious. Cool colors are especially pleasing in smaller rooms.

Photo 9.4: *Sample for Home Décor Store Showing Use of Color*

Photo credit: Marthy Bermejo

Colors and their emotional response

- Blue: A cool color (makes room seem cooler). Calms and relaxes excited people. Tends to stimulate thought processes and encourage conversation.
- Green: It is easy on the eyes, a cool color, restful and tranquil. It stimulates conversations.
- Red: Excites and stimulates and induces aggression.
- Yellow: A cheerful color creates a feeling of warmth and happiness, draws attention, and boosts morale.
- Orange: It is a friendly, warm, vibrant, and exhilarating color.
- Violet and purple: A cool color that tends to lend elegance and sophistication with a royal touch and appeal.
- Brown: It is relaxing and warm.
- Gray: It is cool, rich, but subjectively having the depressing effect.

Understanding color preferences of customers can help in communicating and building the brand image of the store. Consumers have learned to associate meaning with different colors or color combination that are imbibed into the culture and social norms they belong to. Understanding color prejudices and their meaning beyond the textual context on a local scale can help in adding value to the store's core brand image and clearly define the brand personality. Brands opt for different colors in order to communicate their uniqueness, functionality, value, category membership, and to stand for a single-minded proposition/promise. Consumers often associate brand and store image with their color, so this focused proposition helps the brand to resonate with the target audience. Brands like McDonald's use red and yellow color to communicate leadership and happiness. Colors have differences in their significance, with changes in cultural context. For example, the color black has different significance in Western and Eastern cultures. Universally, the color pink is used to communicate feminine attribute; green is used for freshness, natural, and vegetarian; and so on. Moreover, the color preferences of consumers change with change in fashion, fad, and trend.

Lighting

Lighting is the key ingredient of any store's ambience and plays a strategic role, including creating the "right" ambience for shopping, as well as helping to "define" a store to its target audience. It also reinforces store's positioning and complements its décor in an aesthetic way. Lighting is an important determinant of retail environment and is essential in calling attention to merchandise in a display. A shopper's eye is drawn automatically to the brightest item or area. Lighting treatment may be used to draw attention to part of the display area, a specific item in the display, or to coordinate parts of the total display area. Lighting at malls and the allied retail spaces always play the significant role of serving as a key differentiator by creating pleasant, bright, and enjoyable shopping atmosphere.

Lighting can also be used to direct shoppers through the store, attracting them to various displays along the way. Because of this tendency to follow a lighted path, display lights should be two to five times stronger than lighting in other parts of the store. The objective of lighting is not only to highlight a particular brand or logo but also to play a significant part in influencing consumer purchase decision. Lighting makes shopping a "sensory" experience, and encourages them to examine the merchandise displayed. Coming up with good lighting to the window display is very essential for the success of the VM.

Also the effects of in-store illumination on shoppers' cognition, value, and consumption behavior can be seen in reference to consumers' arousal and vision as these are two important

Photo 9.5: *Sample for Home Décor Store Showing Use of Lighting*

Photo credit: Marthy Bermejo

outcomes of lighting effects. It changes consumers' mood, creates excitement, and gives thematic appreciation to the store image and retail brand positioning. It is also important to understand that whether customers feel more comfortable in bright light or soft light and does lighting preference change with store image. Hence, the issue of "image" versus "function" is highly critical in creating an appropriate atmosphere. However, discussion with retailers in India revealed that lighting affects customer's attraction and choice of retail store and visibility in evaluating products' features, price, ingredients, labels, and so on. Research has suggested gender differences in optimal lighting requirement in presence of romantic partner. It is no surprise that across categories of retail, including fashion and consumer electronics, lighting is making a key contribution in branding and allied activities.

There are three types of lighting used in store illumination: primary, accent, and atmosphere lighting.

Primary Lighting

Primary lighting is the overall level of illumination of the store using fluorescent or incandescent light sources. Exterior lighting includes basic window lighting, marquee lights illuminating the sidewalks, and lighting for the general lobby area. Inside the store, primary lighting is that which fills the selling floor from overhead lighting fixtures and provides the bare essentials of store illumination.

Accent and Secondary Lighting

Accent or secondary lighting provides illumination for designated display areas. Flat, shadowless, overall lighting can create a tiresome selling floor. Accent lighting provides change from light to dark or highlights to shadows, to prevent this boredom. This can be accomplished with downlighting from the ceiling, showcase lighting, and valance (drapery or canopy) lighting.

279

Atmosphere Lighting

Atmosphere lighting is used to play light against shadow to create a distinctive effect on specific displays. Generally, this category includes the use of color filters, pinpoint spotlights, and black lighting to create dramatic effects.

In addition, architects and interior designers highlight that international retailers are utilizing the contrast theme in-store, which involves a suitable combination of light and dark areas, along with ambient and accent lighting. This blend would help to ensure that a store appears larger in size but, at the same time, "familiar" to consumers and encourages them to stay longer at an outlet. The products in an outlet should be displayed in lighting that appears natural, and the ambience should also appropriately reflect the season. Each store has its distinctive style and character, and its brand positioning, and the lighting solution should also reflect the same.

Most retail spaces are finished out with commercial fluorescent lighting fixtures, which usually give a good level of light but do little to add to a warm atmosphere. Generally, fluorescent lights are used for primary lighting, and as they cannot be focused or directed toward a specific object, they wash an area with light in which no accents or shadows are made. Here spotlights play vital role and are good for merchandise displays. An incandescent floor light can be used to illuminate lettering that identifies a store or a department within a store. A light and dark pattern can be created by highlighting the important parts of the display and letting the shadows create depth and pattern. Spotlights can be used on a larger scale to add excitement to merchandise racks. Turning off the lights in the aisles on either side will allow the spotlighted areas to stand out even more.

While planning lighting, retailers need to pay suitable attention to finding the right balance between illuminating a store window, merchandise displayed, and an appropriate ambience. The lighting conditions influence consumers' time perception, visibility, and, most importantly, the store image through associations created in the consumer memory at a post-purchase stage. It can be used to draw consumers' attention to strategic pockets in the store or it may help in downplaying less attractive areas. The lighting highlights the merchandise displayed, color- and season-wise on the window. Hence, a balanced approach between decoration and functionality has to be maintained while designing the lighting.

Music

Music variations such as fast, slow, classical, instrumental, and hit numbers influence consumers' mood, time spent, impulsive behavior, unconscious thought process, and emotion. Research has scientifically proved that the time spent in the retail store or shopping is correlated with the type of music played and relative familiarity with music. Changing music in different parts of the store was found as an influencing factor that can alter consumers' mood or appeal to different consumer segments. It is also observed that the customer value increases when customers' shopping time increases due to music familiarity or specifying special occasion and festivity. Music may increase or decrease stimulus-seeking behavior among customers, affecting their actual shopping time, product selection, shopping volume, and impulse buying. Shopper's time varies due to loudness and softness of music. Relative to "no music" or "unfamiliar music," playing "familiar music"—or the music that appeals to the targeted audience, or the music that creates the nostalgia, or the music that psychologically helps the customer to associate herself with "desired self"—acts as a catalyst to positively swing the mood of the buyer, increases consumers' attention to products and service by emotionally connecting and creating identification with them. Hence, music can potentially increase consumer value and shopping volume by providing relaxation and calmness to the consumer so that beneficial associations can be churned out in the mind. The consumers' interest in shopping, pleasure, and time spent depend on the nature of these associations.

Wi-Fi Internet

Public Wi-Fi is becoming as ubiquitous as lighting, heating, and air-conditioning in public spaces; today, it is only the absence of such amenities that would remark upon. Globally, more than half of the world's Internet users access the web through mobile devices and the count in increasing day by day—a fact reflected in the rising sales of mobile devices. Mobile devices have become the number one information source for receiving (and sharing) everything from current affairs to celebrity gossip to exploring and comparing options on e-tailer's portals and so on, and public places equipped with Wi-Fi hotspots have become fundamental to this trend. Today, not only in India but also all over the world, we can see the increasing number of Wi-Fi hotspots located at commercial places like retail outlets, shopping malls, cafés, hotels, colleges, and education centers, while it is almost taken for granted in hotels and coffee shops now; retailers are likely to follow the suit. For instance, Nordstrom has installed Wi-Fi at all of its full-line stores.

Previously, some retailers seemed to be reluctant to develop a network inside the stores with the inner fear that this may lead customers to use mobile devices for comparing prices online that may result in customer buying products from some other online store. While some retailers found that providing a Wi-Fi network actually increases the probability of purchasing and hence increase in the conversion rate, some research surveys observed that while some revenues are lost from comparison shopping. It has been recommended that this is more than offset by connected customers being less likely to leave without buying, and hence spending more in totality.

Today, visitors at retail outlets and shopping malls expect and consider Wi-Fi access in the same way as air-conditioning, music, or lighting. This newfound behavior has given birth to the concepts like "magic hour," which reflects the time that typically customers spend waiting at billing counters or while roaming in the store, while accompanying their spouses, friends, peers, and so on when they are browsing the store, or maybe at the time of having some quick refreshment break during the shopping and so on. The retail sector considers this time period as "magic hour" as the customers are effectively a receptive and hence captive audience primed to browse shops and make purchases—per square meter and per time unit available.

There are many benefits of Wi-Fi:

- It helps to develop a pool of customer data, and by using this information, retailer can offer personalized targeting of future visits. One thing here noted that this depends on the privacy agreement.
- Retailers can keep a track on customers' online behavior. This includes the information regarding which competition they are visiting and delivering communications customized according to their browsing behavior.
- The Wi-Fi network allow shoppers to conduct personal activities and transactions, which means more time in store, and this increases the possibility of more impulse buying.
- This also facilitates push applications such as localized targeting of offers, promotions, other information, and up-selling to shoppers' mobile devices.
- It also provides real-time access to stock status, which can free up sales associate's time to spend on more valuable activities such as customer assistance.
- In-store Wi-Fi network can enable the retailers to deploy interactive screens where the customers can browse other offerings by the store and also do the bill payment.

Thus, first identified within the retail sector, the airport "magic hour" reflects the time—typically "airside"—that passengers spend waiting to board their flight. Airside shopping, conducted during this magic hour, has helped to establish airports as some of the most prime retail real estate locations in the world. In fact, such behavior has become a "default" for many travelers who actually reserve this time specifically to do shopping and making purchases. Shoppers Stop, India's largest department store, also plans to offer Wi-Fi in its outlets to help customers navigate the stores, find brands and offers, and shop online from the store itself, as part of its efforts to woo customers to its shops at a time when more and more Indians are taking to online shopping. These trends means that not only the volumes of data are increasing but also the type of content being shared and quality of service expectations are also rising at the same rate, thereby creating considerable infrastructure implications for the same. This captures the reflection of a wider trend of behavior where real-time communication and supporting infrastructure will be given, whether you are shopping, sipping a coffee, or, indeed, about to board a plane.

Hence, in order to further capitalize on this opportunity to its fullest, retailers will need to develop better applications to improve the shopping experience and invest in their web connectivity. However, the big challenge here is customers' privacy for online tracking, which is a very tricky and social issue, rather sensitive issue, and therefore the retailers need to work on the trust-deficit factor. They should develop the technology infrastructure and systems that will ensure that there will not be any breach in customers' privacy.

Fragrance and Temperature (Olfactory and Tactile Factors)

Olfactory factors, such as scent and freshness, and tactile factors, such as temperature, complement with other ambient factors and help in creating a holistic atmosphere in a retail store. These cues create holistic atmosphere in a retail store through aesthetically pleasing and sensitive dispositions, signal store's merchandise quality, clientele, and comfort and act as a vehicle to communicate store brand image through associations in the consumers' memory. Congruency of consumers' age, gender, aesthetic sense, and ethnicity with olfactory factors can be used in appropriate departments to influence consumers' buying behavior. Fragrance intensity varies with consumers' gender, age, aesthetic sense, personality factors, degree of indulgence, and ethnicity. Hence, the ambient scent and product class have a significant impact on the store's perceived image. The tactile factors such as temperature and smoothness of floor create aesthetically sensitive environment that potentially increases customers' value due to personal comfort and aesthetic values. These factors quintessentially increase customers' exploratory tendencies and sensation-seeking behavior.

Key Visual Merchandising Tools

Fixtures and Merchandise Display

Store fixtures are one of the most significant element of VM and the retail store's décor irrespective of the type or format of retail store. These fixtures help in displaying and arrenging the merchandise in an organized manner. Apart from this, store fixtures also help in creating a customer-friendly display to attract more potential customers. Right positioning of the merchandise is vital to VM.

The right retail fixtures are flexible enough to accommodate the specific design and layout of an individual retail store. They enable the store personals to do readjusted and improvisations rapidly, in order to adapt to changes in inventory, such as changing fashion trends or seasonal retailing cycles. It is observed that customers shop at eye level, so it is neccesary for the retailers that the store fixtures and retail shelving take advantage of this narrow spatial window of selling opportunity. Facing out the merchandise is also essential in positioning the merchandise to achieve the greatest selling impact as it has more buy appeal. Facing refers to the number of identical merchandise items (or same SKUs) on a shelf turned out toward the customer. It is the act of pulling each item to the front edge of a shelf with the label turned forward. This not only gives sufficient exposure to merchandise items but also creates an appearance of store being full with merchandise. A fixture should not only complement the merchandise but also create an atmosphere in the store. Each fixture should present the merchandise to the shoppers and thereby act as a silent salesperson.

Merchandise can be effectively displayed on a variety of fixtures such as shelf, gondolas, tables, cubes, mannequins, waterfalls and other racks, display cases, and manufacturer POP displays. One of the most common fixtures in stores are gondolas: movable shelving approachable from all sides used in self-service retail stores to display merchandise. They can be lined up in rows as in grocery, hardware, and drug stores, or used separately to create an island. Endcaps are units at the end of aisles. Endcaps are important selling locations and should be used for high-profit impulse or seasonal merchandise.

Different Fixture Types

While deciding on store fixture's selection, the retailers need to think about functionality and flamboyance. Store fixtures should be trendy, smart, eye-catching, and, most importantly, they should match with the retail culture and overall retail experience that the retailer commits to the target audience. Different types of fixtures serve distinct purposes, enhancing the appeal of the merchandise in unique ways. Hence, retail fixtures chosen correctly serve as a powerful component of VM strategy, helping the retailer to generate inspiring retail displays that ignite consumer desire and drive sales.

- *Straight rack*: long pipe suspended with supports to the floor or attached to a wall.
- *Gondola*: large base with a vertical spine or wall fitted with sockets or notches into which a variety of shelves, peg hooks, bins, baskets, and other hardware can be inserted.
- *Rolling racks*: one of the most widely used fixture for apparel display. Rolling racks can easily and efficiently hold many clothes and can be easily browsed by the customers when they want to pick any apparel for trial. The wheels attached to the base of these racks make them easy to move. The store associates can easily shift many apparel from one place to another conveniently on them.
- *Four-way fixture*: two crossbars that sit perpendicular to each other on a pedestal.
- *Round rack*: round fixture that sits on a pedestal.
- *Gridwall and slatwall fixture*: While gridwall contains grid systems that can be linked with diverse display hardware, slatwall uses portions of hardware and grooves. Accessories such as shelves, baskets, and hooks are some of the accessories that often accompany these displays.
  These fixtures, by virtue of its functionality value, effectively add space along the walls of the retail store and very useful to keep the apparel orderly. Racks and hooks can be attached to these wall fixtures for neatly displaying clothes and accessories on them.
- *Mannequins*: Humanlike figures to display clothes are one of the fixtures to attract customers to any apparel/fashion store. Mannequins bring life to the clothing by exploring its design, style, and shape, enabling the shopper to visualize the on-body appearance of the apparel. Hence, apparel stores can not give complete shopping experience without mannequins that are wrapped with the most fashionable outfits that the store have to offer.

- *Hangers*: The design and material of hangers is chosen as per the quality, aesthtics, and brand image of the merchandise that is being displayed. Hangers are available in different materials like wood, fiberglass, metal, and plastic.
- *Display cases*: They are very useful for displaying expensive merchandise items, such as jewelry, watches, and artifacts. They not only keep the high-value merchandise safe but also enhance the visual appeal of the merchandise in a flamboyant way. Display cases can be half-vision, full-vision, countertop, and so on. They are generally available in different variety of materials such as wood, metal, and acrylic and essentialy reinforce the elegance value of the merchandise displayed.
- *Other common fixtures*: tables, large bins, and flat-based decks.

Wall Fixtures

- To make a store's wall merchandisable, wall usually covered with a skin that is fitted with vertical columns of notches similar to those on a gondola, into which a variety of hardware can be inserted.
- Can be merchandised much higher than floor fixtures—ensures the optimum utilization of the available vertical space.

Merchandise Display

- Shelving: It is flexible and easy to maintain.
- Hanging: easy to manitain and also easy to browse.
- Pegging: small rods inserted into gondolas or wall systems. It may be labor intensive to display/maintain but gives neat/orderly appearance.
- Folding: suitable for softlines that can be folded easily and stacked on shelves or tables, and creates high-fashion image.
- Stacking: suitable for hardlines that can be stacked on shelves, base decks of gondolas or flats; easy to maintain and gives image of high volume and low price.
- Dumping: large quantities of small merchandise can be dumped into baskets or bins, highly effective for softlines (socks, wash cloths) or hardlines (batteries, candy, grocery products), and creates high-volume, low-cost image.

The fixture types and style talk more about the retail brand, the store, and essentially express the ambience that the retailer wants to create to reinforce its positioning and brand image. The choice of fixures, the planograms, and other ambient factors convey the brand message in an effective manner. The use of right store fixtures such as tables, gandolas, platforms, and risers encourage the "touch and feel" mentality that is essential for getting the customers to buy. Right fixtures help in creating a neatly arranged and visibly appealing presentation of merchandise, which eventualy create an interesting shopping atmosphere and hence the shopping experience. The attractive presentations, right fixtures, stunning store displays, and pleasing retail shelving enhance the art of VM. Hence, the store fixtures that both visually complement the retailer's merchandise and enhance the merchandise's appeal to customers. The quality and elegance of display fixtures add value to the merchandise while also enhancing and adding to the overall look of the store.

Let us consider the example of Nashville-headquarderd Johnston & Murphy stores. The brand came to existence way back in 1850 and has stores spread across the USA, Canada, and the UK. US presidents, right from Abraham Lincoln to Millard Fillmore to Barack Obama, have some or other time have purchased shoes from this iconic brand. The brand is often percieved and regarded as the epitome of workmanship and for the unique American style. In India, the

Right fixtures help in creating a neatly arranged and visibly appealing presentation of merchandise which eventualy creates an interesting shopping atmosphere and hence the shopping experience.

Photo 9.6: *Fixtures—A Crucial Component of Visual Merchandising*

Source: www.pantaloons.com (accessed on 12 May 2016)

brand opened its first of its outlet in Mumbai. The store merchandises footware and related accessories and products that are essentially sourced from their authorized vendors, globally.

The brand brings the same "American legacy" to its Mumbai-located outlet as well. As a part of its key merchandising strategy and to retain its "bridge to luxury" positioning, the retailer has sourced all the fixtures and related tools of VM from USA. The heritge frames displayed inside the store highlight the brand's well-known and high-profile customers. The customers can also easily view portrait of US presidents and the shoes from this brand that the presidents have selected. This unique approach appeals to the targeted audience, the high-end customers. The customers feel a sense of pride to be associated with the brand and get connected with at emotional level.

Planograms

The physical representation of merchandise assortment is termed as planogram. Planogram is a visual representation that depicts how products or merchandise should be presented on various types of retail displays/fixtures. Arranging the assortment of modular units and fixtures, along with merchandise placement, is among the most critical aspects of planning a store. Planogram is basically a visual plan or a guide that shows how different merchandise assortment is arranged in the store so that it can get more eyeballs. Planograms are essentially based on demographic insights; they make it easier for retailers to fine-tune their merchandise, display the right assortment (mi)x for customers in a particular area, and enable the retailer to take a more active role in customers' purchasing decisions. It not only ensures the attractive arrangement/display but also involves some scientific considerations that give enhanced exposure to the merchandise. In the case of multi-store retailers, uniformity of display is achieved with the help of planograms. It is also necessary that the store design is universal not just in terms of the store layout but also in terms of the fixtures, number of aisles, bays, and the number of shelves in each of the fixtures. Planograms are an illustrated setup that shows where products or merchandise should be placed on a shelf or other sort of display.

Hence, the planogram is a visual drawing or diagram that provides details regarding placement of every merchandise category in a retail store. These schematics not only present a flowchart for the particular merchandise departments within a store layout but also very meticulously depict on which aisle and on what shelf an item is placed. A planogram should also illustrate how many facings are allocated for each SKU.

A Planogram is a meticulous plan that guides the store managers about merchandise placement; the depth, width, and height of the Planogram; and also the placement of promotional materials whenever required (Figure 9.1).

The different dimensions of merchandise placement that need to be given a carefully considered are as follows:

- Location and size (dimensions) of modular units and fixtures within a store.
- Shelf height: depending on the size of merchandise item to be displayed and ease of reach for the customer.
- Merchandise placement: location of the shelf and the place on that shelf a merchandise item should be placed.
- Merchandise facing: the number of merchandise units or orientation of merchandise item that is exhibited to the customer.
- Shelf depth: the number of merchandise units that are positioned behind the front-facing merchandise.
- Shelf tags: visually spontaneous strips that indicate item description and placement on the shelf with other related information.
- Price strips: strips giving information for identifying price points (by employees) and the sell price (for customers).

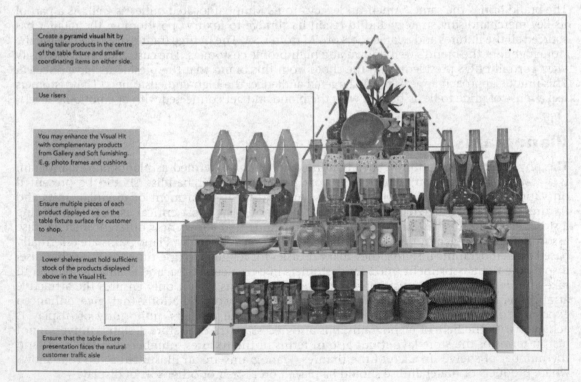

Figure 9.1: *Planogram: Instructional Model*

Photo credit: Marthy Bermejo

Photo 9.7: *Planogram: Sample from a Home Décor Store*

Photo credit: Marthy Bermejo

The planogram schematics are typically developed and designed centrally (the corporate level) and are followed across all the outlets of the retailer. This ensures the uniformity of shopping experience across all the stores of the retailer. However, the designing team may invite some suggestions, feedback, or inputs from the store personnel to develop the store-specific planograms. To assist the retailers in achieving their twin objectives of optimization of merchandise display and growth in sales revenues, some of the more evolved suppliers have also started developing planograms for retailers. In this case, suppliers send the planograms to the retailer even before they deliver their products. Such planograms give suggestions to retailers as to exactly where a particular supplier's products can be placed and displayed once they arrive. Hence, all the possible sources can be tapped to collaborate and share information on planning store space, which could be incorporated while designing the planogram.

The whole idea behind developing planogram is to optimize sales of a retail outlet by providing right exposure to the merchandise and making the display more attractive ad compelling. This is achieved by maximum utilization of shelf space. There are determinants affecting merchandise on display:

1. Absolute quantity of merchandise on the shelf.
2. Visual appeal to attract potential customers' attention.

A fixture or shelf set is considered perfectly compliant when the merchandise is arranged according to the planograms. This ensures the merchandise items are at their right (strategic) locations, in right quantities, with adequate facings (exposure), and with shelf tags displaying accurate information about the merchandise and its price. On an average, store displays receive shoppers' attention for only a few seconds. Hence, it becomes imperative for the store management to comply with the set planograms, and any deviation (or noncompliance) can lead to:

- Losing a sale that result in reduced revenues
- Out of stocks due to less control o stock replenishments

- Improper utilization of shelf space
- The retailer, without compliance, not evaluating the effectiveness of their planograms

Different types of planograms are utilized at different segments of retail sectors. For example, FMCG organizations and supermarkets use planograms to achieve the following:

1. Optimization of shelf space
2. Faster inventory turns
3. Higher profit margin

Such planograms are known as "text and box"-based planograms. However, in apparel merchandising and clothing stores, the planograms must provide the visual look, so as to analyze how such merchandise be displayed and identified. Therefore, they generally use pictorial planograms. The major advantage of a planogram is that it moves a step beyond pure numeric type of planning to a visual orientation. Software packages for store space planning support planogram methodology. This involves stock mapping, utilizing graphic representation. This, in turn, leads both ease in replenishment and optimal store space utilization.

Planogram: A Plan for Effective Merchandising

Analysis of the shopping basket helps the retailer to identify what merchandise lines are bought at the same time, particularly by the loyal customers. The insights obtained from this analysis are used to design planograms, which eventually can encourage the cross-purchasing (Figure 9.2). For instance, some retailers discovered from basket analysis that men who buy denim jeans also look for a T-shirt or a smart-casual shirt to complement with. A lady customer who has bought a top may immediately look for leggings or some other accessories to complement with.

Key Benefits

The whole purpose of developing planograms is to increase customers' loyalty to a store by providing him an ease in selection. The planograms also lead several other business benefits, some of which are as follows:

Figure 9.2: *Planogram: A Plan for Effective Merchandising*

Source: http://insider.asdonline.com/wp-content/uploads/2015/05/Step-by-Step-Guide-To-Visual-Merchandising-470x330.jpg (left); accessed on 27 April 2016
http://s3images.coroflot.com/user_files/individual_files/original_448162_RJs90a2sYr3e1LEJaBKT1T4mt.jpg (right)

1. Planograms helps retailer to ensure the right SKU in the right quantity, at the right location, and in the right orientation, which eventually lead to increased sales.
2. One of the major tangible results of the planograms is that both the planning and streamlining of display space are achieved. They increase space productivity of stores and provide optimization of the capital investments.
3. Planograms assign selling potential to every square foot of space and satisfy customers with a better visual appeal.
4. Planograms lead to an accurate visualization of product display in a store. It leads to conformity between the various stores operated by a large retail chain.
5. Tighter inventory control and reduction of out of stocks as it allows easier merchandise replenishment for staff. This eventually results in higher availability of merchandise to customers.
6. Reducing restocking activity and improving on-shelf availability can increase the inventory efficiency.
7. Allows better planning for related product positioning and acts as an effective communication tool for staff-produced displays.
8. Market strategies, specific merchandise for particular consumer, and new product's launch can be evaluated by a planogram that is designed specifically for such purpose.
9. Planograms also help the retailers and brand owners during seasonal and promotional periods, when selling opportunities for many merchandise categories are augmented.
10. Planograms also help in maximization of supply chain efficiency. This achieves to most efficient space utilization, maximization of inventory stock turns.
11. Planograms can be customized and arranged for assortment for a particular store. It helps in meeting the true local demand and better financial result.
12. In addition, utilization of a planogram technique leads to the following:

    • Increased sales and profitability
    • Optimum stock turn and reduction in operational cost
    • Optimum supply chain efficiency
    • Lower inventory carrying cost and reduction/elimination of excess inventory
    • Overall maximization of bottom line

Props

A prop is something used with a product in a display that clarifies the function of the merchandise being sold or the story being told. Props are an integral part of a display. They are used in VM to tell a story about the product, the merchandise concept, or the store itself. A display prop may be something that is not for sale, such as floor coverings, wall treatments, backgrounds, mannequins, shelves, and steps. Props may also be merchandise that is for sale, but is not the theme merchandise, such as golf clubs used in conjunction with golf wear. Merchandise from other departments used to highlight salable items can lead to multiple sales. Visibility is provided for the original theme merchandise, in addition to the prop merchandise.

When using salable merchandise as a prop, be sure it is appropriate for the theme of the display and in sufficient quantity to meet an increase in demand arising from the display. Prominently, display theme and prop merchandise in their respective departments for easy access by the customer. If a store does not have merchandise available that can be used in a display, use display props from non-merchandise categories. Non-merchandise props used for their original purpose can assist in telling a story. Examples include while designing a show living room in a home furnishing store, we can complement the sofa set display with available merchandise catagories like end tables and center tables, a TV unit, vases, photo frames, antiques, murals, and so on, for decorative purpose to make the display more tempting, and a non-merchandise category like TV to create a real feel of a living room, to give a visual idea to the prospect about how the sofa will actually look in his or her living room.

Interior Signage

Signage is a critical part of interior display and POP promotion. Store signage that communicates a sales message to the customer can make up for lack of sales personnel. A good POP sign, properly placed, acts as a salesperson without wages. Signs were originally used to identify a store, name various departments, and announce sales and sale merchandise. Although this is their primary purpose, signs also commonly advertise vendors, colors, styles, quality, and prices. They can be used to explain customer benefits and describe merchandise features. Benefit signs, or a combination of benefit and price, are one of the most effective merchandising tools. A good sign provides the most information in the fewest possible words. POP signs or shelf-talkers should:

- Draw the customer's attention to the product.
- Identify the merchandise item being sold.
- State a customer benefit.
- Tell something about the product that they do not know or understand.
- State the price of the item.
- Communicate the brand image in a very subtle manner.

Signage and window dressing are the face index of the store that can attract or repel customers from the store. Customers may develop associations of trust, value, quality of merchandise and services, price, warranty and guarantee, and so on as they come across visuals such as signage, window dressing, and logo, based on past shopping experiences. Signs and graphics used in the store act as bridge between the merchandise and the target market. Design factors create theatrical effect, add personality and beauty, and communicate store image.

Design Aspects and the Key Designing Principles

Design factors can create attraction and uniqueness to appeal to people at a focal point by signaling a pleasant and worthwhile experience. The design aspects of retail stores are an ideal convergence of artistic ideas, instinct, and business in a planned and profitable manner. Selling space is the most important part of a store, and therefore, efforts to utilize each square foot will help to maximize sales. One proven way to do this is through interior displays that effectively show merchandise to the customer. When planning interior displays, remember that the theme and image presented on the exterior must be carried throughout the interior of the store to provide consistency for the customer. Consistency becomes the key factor when information is available just on clicking of a button, and this in turn necessitates that the message of the brand is well articulated through VM. In addition, the new trends are also need to be brought in VM and window display. The purpose of interior display is to develop desire for the merchandise, show what is available, and encourage both impulse and planned buying. Three major goals of a store should be to motivate the customer to spend money, project the image of the store, and keep expenses to a minimum.

Promotion and advertising dollars are less effective or even wasted when efforts are not made *within* the store to effectively merchandise the products. Well-designed displays and in-store promotions are essential for a consistent theme and to help the customer find advertised items.

Although the percentage of in-store purchase decisions may vary by type of store and product, nothing influences the consumer's purchase decisions more than advertising used where the sale is actually made—the POP.

Essentials for Designing an Effective and Relevant Display

An effective way of attracting customers to a store is by having good displays, both exterior and interior. A customer will be attracted to a display within three to eight seconds, which is the time a customer spends to determine interest in a product. This is why it is critical to have a properly designed display. Every display should be planned and have a theme. Good design makes a visual presentation come together. This means the design attracts attention in a way that strengthens the store image, as well as introducing merchandise to the customer. One of the most effective VM is by coming up with a theme that incorporate with the seasons. So if it is currently winter or holiday, then try to come up with some holiday and colorful theme for window display. If it is summer, then the theme should be such kind of beach or related with the summer.

Before designing good displays, answer the following questions:

1. What is the store's image? Select an image to present to the public. The customer will identify a certain look with a store and expect that look to be carried throughout the business, be it trendy, elegant, off-price, or discount. Do not mix images within one store; it will only confuse the customers.
2. What type of customer is being attracted? Use a display that reflects the targeted consumer. A display that works well in one community may be ineffective in another community.
3. What is the concept of the merchandise to be presented in the display? Display and highlight the merchandise, do not merchandise an attractive display. Items should be displayed as they are meant to be used or worn. If formal wear is combined with day wear and kitchen accessories, the consumer is confused and sales are lost.
4. Where is the display going to be set up and how will the location determine the design? There are many types of locations for display in every store: windows, walls, cases, gondolas, or islands. The principles of display should help make the location work for the display.
5. Why is this merchandise being put on display as opposed to other merchandise? This reason will determine the visual presentation and design. For example, if the merchandise is on sale, it will be displayed differently than regular price merchandise. Keep in mind there should be enough backup stock to warrant a display. If not, do not display it. Retailers generally place sale or promotional merchandise in the front of the store for short periods of time only. If the sale or promotion lasts for several weeks, they move the merchandise to the rear of the store. Interested customers will search out a bargain. Retailers always look for introducing the customers to new, exciting, and creative merchandise with a display at the front of the store.

To execute a display that will sell merchandise, it is necessary to have a working knowledge of the principles of design. The primary principles of design used in display include balance, proportion, rhythm, emphasis, color, lighting, and harmony. When applied appropriately, all parts of the display are pulled together to create a purposeful, effective, and aesthetically pleasing presentation. An understanding of these principles will make it easier to design a display for all types of merchandise.

Brand Image and Visual Merchandising

The retail store atmospherics is an array of tangible and intangible dispositions interwoven into a web of meanings, subtle cues, and brand messages that touches the social, psychological, economic, cultural, and religious lifestyle of consumers, due to concordance with current fad, fashion, and trends. Retail atmospheric cues may generate sets and subsets of associations related to attributes, benefits, emotions of pleasure (or displeasure), attraction (or distraction), high (or low) confidence, self-actualization, and basic human desires. In the retail atmospherics, environmental elements such as bright or dim lighting, classical or familiar music, attractive window dressing and layouts, magnificent architectural design, freshness and fragrance, appropriate temperature to make it cozy and comfortable, soothing and trendy color, attractive logo, and gentle crowding are ideal conditions that can affect the current and future buying behavior of consumers. The entire retail environment that includes brand design consistently throws brand messages that the consumer experiences throughout the shopping endeavor. The retail environment is harmoniously designed in order to subtly communicate brand personality and image of the store, in order to add depth to the perceptions encapsulated in the atmospherics and communicate the retailer's brand value. This brand value and identity then percolate into each element of the retail environment in such a way that it is differentiated from the competitors, standardized, and stimulates consumers' purchasing activity.

Components

VM is not an isolated and one-off phenomenon but rather forms a significant component of retailing. Besides the window displays, which are designed with the purpose to attract walking-by consumers and encourage walk-ins, there is also in-store decoration that is designed to enhance the customer's comfort and convenience while shopping. The overall aim is to enhance the consumers overall shopping experience. VM to a retail chain is known to be literally one of the last steps of the selling process. Product is sourced, purchased, delivered; marketing campaigns are executed; and staff are developed and trained, leaving the VM to ensure that the customers' in-store experience aligns with brand standards and expectations. And when done well, VM will always assist and encourage customer purchase; remember, we use VM to develop, maintain, and increase sales. And make no mistake, the VM competition within this group is fierce. From one brand to the next, we are always checking to see what it is our competitors are selling and how good their stores look; a retailer cannot afford not to have a VM strategy and program in place.

Success factors of VM include the store's appearance, signage, lighting, uniforms, menus, POS material, color, shapes, textures, packaging, ticketing, presentation, and the "wow" factor each of these elements bring together in a retail setting. When these elements come together to showcase a brand, it enriches the customer experience, leading to a positive shopping experience and increased sales.

Brand Experience

Customers expect a certain standard from a retailer brand that is typically unique and reinforces its brand values. Retailers try to offer a consistent brand experience, starting from the merchandise and services they sell, the website, loyalty campaigns, POS material, and so on. It includes its staff, right down to how they treat their windows, and in-store selling space. VM enables retailers to "visually" play out their brand strategy on the shop floor. In today's retailing scenario, it is of utmost importance for every retailer to have its "own and unique"

VM identity that visually aligns with their "own and unique" brand strategy. Customers must be able to experience their brand through the visual components that surround their offerings. It is essential for the retailers not only to enhance brand experience through VM but also to connect with the targeted audience by engaging with them through "storytelling." "Storytelling" enables the retailers to resonate with their customers at emotional level across the touch points. Brands are coming up with many innovative ideas to achieve this. For instance, retailers create buzz around the brand with the help of influencers by encouraging them to explore the merchandise displayed in the store. Here the influence may be a film star, celebrity, fashion icons, models author, and so on, depending on the category. This kind of activity makes a profound impact on consumers' perception toward the brand and eventually enhances their engagement with the brand. For example, a famous department store in Paris regularly invites high-profile celebrities from various fields like sports, art, fashion, literature, and films. The retailers then ask the celebrity guests to identify and gather their favorite items from the store and also to organize the selected merchandise items in a "story" (or formation). This kind of activity gives an opportunity not only for "storytelling" but also to connect with the targeted audience by getting associated and identified with personalities (or influencers) invited. This kind of emotional connect with the brand eventually encourages the consumers to be loyal with the brand.

Creating a "Theme" or "Look"

Brands can better execute VM strategies by implementing themes into their displays. Themes tell a story and create customer buy-in. They generally accompany a new product launch. Most importantly, themes allow a brand to reinvent itself with new colors, layouts, fonts, design, pictures, and photographs at the time of a new product launch. Theme ideas can range anywhere from coordinating colors to grouping products to individual motifs and anything in between. There are not any rules when it comes to themes, but it is a good idea to consider the store, season, new product, overall look and feel of the brand, and how the theme will tie into any current in-store promotion.

Creating an effective theme also requires the identification of current trends, which is usually done through keeping one's ears and eyes open while traveling, at the movie halls, and so on. This is very useful at the conceptualization phase. In the next step, designing of the theme is done, which is also called as "decoding the concept." Here, design means appropriate blending of colors, material, shapes, finishing or textures, and graphics. So instead of mixing all sorts of displays in the store, it would be better served to establish an overall theme that will unite the merchandise. All displays need not look exactly alike, but they should be complementing each other and compatible or blend with each other. This theme can explore many options and directions, from eccentric and idiosyncratic to very conventional and formal, and anything in between. It is determined mainly by the products the retailer is selling and the targeted audience.

By adopting a VM program, retailers have the opportunity to "pack a punch" through strong, eye-catching, individual window displays, giving customers a reason to enter their stores and shop. In addition, by conducting VM activities on a regular basis, the product offer is kept fresh, inviting, and in constant rotation. This is extremely important, as many independent retailers suffer from this syndrome of "set and forget." This creates a stale, boring store and, without a doubt, will lead the retailer to lose sales. Through regular VM activities, retailer will be challenged with rotating product around the store, merchandising to complement key retail promotional events (i.e., Diwali, Valentine's Day, Christmas, etc.), and strategically marking down product and moving it on when necessary. Hence, VM keeps the store not only attractive but also organized, and infuses life to it.

Tonality

Tonality refers to a brand's consistency throughout all marketing materials, messages, and communication and communication vehicles. It also can be referred to as the brand personality or voice: It means conveying the look, feel, and completeness of the brand within all existing marketing elements. That is, VM must be consistent across all platforms, including in-store displays, the retailer's website, and on third-party websites. VM must not be seen as an one-off thematic or sales activity. It is rather an ongoing, continuous, and continual process to ensure that VM is effective, contemporary, and relevant. This ensures customer brand loyalty and also ensures that brand is going to deliver. In turn, the emotional connection a customer has with the brand is strengthened. The general ambience of a shopping center environment, including music, lighting, smells, sounds, cleanliness, and general appearance, must all work together to inspire and convince the customer to stay and shop—at the same time, retailer must ensure that VM is executed to a level that keeps the customer interested, entertained, and inspired to shop from one store to the next.

To become a shopping destination of choice, VM principles are key because when a retailing environment makes "visual sense," a customer will be naturally attracted to the space, enticed to come in, convinced to stay and shop, and, most importantly, wants to buy! This leads the retailers to devise "key merchandising principles" to adopt uniformity in the physical environment across all their stores.

We have heard the phrase "a picture is worth a thousand words." VM is based on the same principle. Retailer designs a display that communicates with its customers, conveys the brand attributes to the targeted audience, and reinforces the brand image. VM works great for retail stores as people have a propensity to do some window-shopping before buying any specific product.

Pervasive Creativity: A Pragmatic Approach to Design Thinking

Creativity and design thinking are no more mysterious concepts today. It is now the lifeline of all the businesses cutting across scale and specializations. It not only offers simple, ingenious, and insightful solutions to complex issues in business of retailing, but also plays a key role in presenting positive attitudinal changes in the society. So the imperatives of design thinking in this VUCA (volatility, uncertainty, complexity, and ambiguity) age and today's fast-paced ecosystem is design thinking, which includes the ability to multi-sense, to see patterns that are not so obvious to others, and the ability to create something that can potentially influence the buying behavior of people and, in a sense, lead to pervasive creativity. Pervasive creativity is a tool that can configure new design models and patterns, improve customer experiences, and trigger decisive game-changing moves in VM and creating overall visual experience. It has a potential to immerse shoppers into a context, to provide them with a unique experience or convey a unique brand message, and to act as a unique touch point that could result in conversion of that shopper into a buyer.

Visual merchandisers face a challenge in bridging the gap between creative and critical thinking. Both creative and critical thinking are necessary components for developing successful merchandising campaigns. Good merchandisers not only make products look good but also know what makes consumers tick, and what will create a compelling purchasing context.

Some people think that VM involves displaying the product itself in a window. This is not true; VM or window dressing is much more than simply putting a product on display in a glass window. Hence, passion for design and creativity is essential to be a good visual merchandiser.

Here the focus is to understand the important factors of pervasive creativity in window display that influence consumers' perceptual process, buying behavior, and in-store promotion activities.

The window display, if used effectively, can bring the retailer new customers, create customer loyalty, enhance the brand image, promote certain merchandise lines, and, above all, be a major selling tool in increasing sales. As discussed in VM, it is vital for the retailer to understand the importance of display and the message they are conveying to the customers.

In fact, it is never advisable to put the merchandise item alone on display. If you think that it is essential for the merchandise item to be a part of the display, then it should always be accompanied by reference materials like banners, artworks, and informative models.

Definition and Meaning of Pervasive Creativity

Pervasive creativity can be defined as the impulse to create, generate, coordinate, innovate, and execute everything (scientifically artistic creative work) the customer sees, feels, and experiences—both exterior and interior environment and atmospherics—that attracts consumers and gives an image to the retailer or to the brand, to which customer desires to get associated and/or want to identify with, which in turn results in attention, attraction, interest, desire, and action on the part of the customer.

To execute a display that will sell merchandise, it is necessary to have a working knowledge of the principles of design. The primary principles of design used in display include balance, proportion, rhythm, emphasis, color, lighting, and harmony. When applied appropriately, all parts of the display are pulled together to create a purposeful, effective, and aesthetically pleasing presentation.

It gives the retailer a sustainable edge over competition. When strategically used, VM can even create a brand identity, right image that leads to a *sustainable positioning*. It sets the context for the merchandise in an aesthetically pleasing fashion, presenting them in a way that would attract the window-shoppers convert them into prospects and ultimately buyers of the product and/or service.

In today's VM practices, pervasive creativity in window display plays a central, rather than a pivotal, role of the retailers' marketing strategy. Besides the window displays, which are clearly designed with the purpose to attract walking-by consumers and encourage walk-ins, there are also in-store decorations located at various focal points that are designed to enhance the customer's comfort and convenience while shopping, and overall to offer the consumer a better shopping experience. Taking into account the importance of VM on retail businesses today, the single and most important reason for adopting pervasive creativity is to attract, engage, and associate with prospects to *churn out desire* and inspire shoppers, to encourage them to buy more of the products the retailer is selling, to increase sales, make margin, and generate a return on floor space. Window display, if used effectively, can bring new customers; help to position the brand in desired way; create customer loyalty; enhance the image, prestige, and brand promise; promote certain product lines; and, above all, be a major selling tool in increasing sales. In order to persuade today's "SOLOMO" (social, local and mobile) consumers, who are willing to explore both online and off-line markets, companies need to come up with innovative techniques, such as touch screen display and viral marketing.

Hence, it is essential to make perfect blend of merchandise to display with related accessories, cross-merchandise, accompanied by reference materials like props, visuals, touch screen interactive display, banners, artworks, and informative models. With the revolution in photography technology, retailers are working to redefine the shopping experience with new technologies like 3D holograms. Brand value has increasingly been defined, not through the narrow lens of price but in terms of the total experience that consumers have when they interact with a given brand.

A case in point here is the lingerie hologram from lingerie brand Empreinte; the brand made waves in Paris and further proliferating on social media. Empreinte made use of a holographic model to window-display its lingerie collection and draw walkers' attention also to promote the new concept store in Paris, L'Atelier lingerie. To capture the eyeballs of the shoppers, they placed a full 3D hologram mannequin wearing L'Atelier lingerie in the shop windows.

The idea of the campaign was to create a real buzz around the brand and their new concept store. The hologram was actually just one piece in an otherwise global communication strategy, which had two main objectives: create awareness and drive people to the store. This global strategy also included interacting with bloggers, advertising on fashion blogs and with social media insiders, posting a hologram video on YouTube, and a PR strategy targeting consumer's magazines. This creative initiative helped the brand in two ways:

1. Using technology in this way helps create a new brand experience that eventually allows customers to interact and engage with the brand and its products in a sensorial way.
2. They received positive response because consumers are looking for innovation, online and in real life too.

Pervasive Creativity and the Perceptual Process

Pervasive creativity is a scientific (art) form in itself, and when in the right hands, it can make that all-important difference between customers or no customer, profit or loss. True, it is only one component of the whole shopping experience, but it is arguably the most influential one. Here are a few indispensable ideas when it comes to making of shop's displays stand out from the rest and creating that all-important wow factor. From creating the window display that the prospective customers first see to the visual graphics and signage and the layout that retailer decides on, to channelize the customer in an ongoing traffic to ensure appropriate exposure to the merchandise, are all taken care by store interiors.

For instance, an up-and-coming cosmetic brand can better showcase its product through colorful displays with bold signage and edgy models to convey a sense of youth. On the other hand, a conservative cosmetic brand can use pastels, script writing, and soft imagery to appeal to a mature audience. For example, the layout of Bobbi Brown cosmetics store in Delhi highlights its brand philosophy of "helping women to look their best." In line with this strategy, the store provides substantial scope for consumers to try various products of this brand. The store also has vanity mirrors that are placed at the strategic points in the store. The store also has makeup artists working in the store as beauty consultants, and they consult the shoppers on skin care, cosmetics, and other related products. In addition, classic- and rustic-textured wooden furniture complemented with chrome chairs helps to enhance the elegance of shopping atmosphere.

These subtle strategies not only attract the targeted demography toward the brand, but also open up the customer to the brand experience and engagement. This, in turn, fortifies brand loyalty and increases the chances of a customer to visit the store frequently in the future.

Pervasive creativity transforms shopping in an experience that excites and arouses all the senses, so why not take advantage of the sensory possibilities of all the departments in the shop to create something unique and unforgettable (refer to Figure 9.3). For example, think about how the store sounds, smells, and even feels, the various sections of the store, and how you can

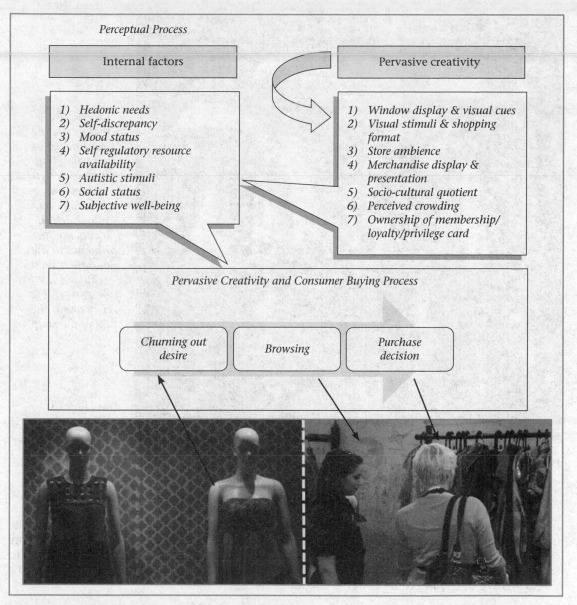

Figure 9.3: *Pervasive Creativity and the Perceptual Process*

Photo credit: Amit Kumar

manipulate the retailer's image and environment to gain the maximum impact. Consider the messages you are giving out through music, aromas, and window displays.

Window displays, one of the most evident manifestations of pervasive creativity, are perhaps the most obvious yet still one of the most impactful ways of getting shoppers through the door. So the window display should be interesting and compelling enough to encourage shoppers to enter the store and see what else is there for them. On the other hand, it should not be much

Pervasive creativity is the scientific art of implementing effective design ideas and executing every minor detail. If eyes are the windows to the soul; then shop windows are just as revealing. They reveal the soul of the shop.

Photo 9.8: *Pervasive Creativity Acts as a Magnetic Field*

Source: www.hc-display.com (accessed on 12 May 2016)

revealing, and potential customers should not be able to see everything in the store from the front window or else they may be reluctant to come inside. Window displays should capture customers' attention and should stimulate customers' interest and churn out the desire to explore a little further by coming inside. After all, it is the luring finger enticing them into a treasure trove of the heavenly delights beyond.

The perceptual process starts with a sensory exposure. In VM, the sensory exposure is most likely sight as it has such a high importance to consumers as it is the beginning of the perceptual process. This exposure leads to attention and subsequently to the comprehension. Sensory exposure, such as a signs and window displays in a mall, needs to be at or above the absolute threshold. The absolute threshold is the minimum level of stimuli a consumer needs to experience, a sensation that produces vibrations in the strings of desire. If these attributes are not at the absolute threshold, it will more than likely go unnoticed by the shoppers. While the level of stimuli is a subjective matter, it becomes empirical for retailers to consider while planning and developing different elements and attributes of VM.

For instance, in the case of multi-brand retail store, the point to keep in mind for window display would be to have a concept that enables groups to create links between the brands and favor a trans-generational consumption. However, it is necessary to avoid piling up of different brand names, as DNA brands must be respected in any multi-brand retail store. Here the key success factor would be to create a global concept that federates the whole brand's portfolio while expressing a genuine personality without any dilution).

The design of physical retail space has a huge impact on consumers' perceptions toward the brand or retailer, at both the conscious and subconscious level. Compelling physical environment supported by senses gratifying pervasive creativity results in arousal of desire for acquiring the things in consideration. Arousal is the state of physical wakefulness or alertness experienced by a consumer in the conscious and subconscious mind. Arousal is low when sleeping and high during exciting events. Arousal is an important consideration when evaluating the performance level of stimulation a display possesses. With too little stimulation, arousal remains low and consumers retain little information. But if stimulation is very high, consumers become overstimulated and essentially shut down. Their arousal also becomes too high, resulting in comparatively little retained information. This goes against assumptions that an overly stimulating display is memorable. In fact, consumers remember the most about a display when their arousal is subtle.

Among these factors is self–discrepancy, which is incongruence between actual self and ideal self. Actual self is the representation of the attributes that a person believes he or she actually possesses, or that person believes others believe they possess. The "actual self" is basically a person's self-concept. It is one's perception/perceptual judgment of own attributes (intelligence, athleticism, attractiveness, and other personality traits).

Ideal self is a person's representation of the attributes that someone (the person itself or another) would like to have in that person, ideally, to possess and usually motivates individuals to change, improve, improvise, and achieve. Hence, different types of discrepancies between representations of the self are related to different kinds of emotional vulnerabilities that lead to formation of different behavioral patterns.

It is found that the shoppers who are high on this personality trait of self-discrepancy may become excessive shoppers, who are highly motivated to buy, in order to support the intended improvisation of their actual self. In this way, they try to fill up the "gaps" between how they see themselves (actual self) and how they wish to be seen (ideal self). Also the shoppers who are low on self-esteem are also a source that leads to impulse buying as a mean of psychological relief from the self-discrepancy. Here, pervasive creativity if executed in right way acts as a catalyst to the process of filling the "gap" between actual self and ideal self.

Another internal motivator is the "hedonic needs." This term is defined as "those facets of consumer behavior relating to multisensory, fantasy, and emotive aspects of one's experience with products and services." Typically, hedonic consumption is tied to imaginative constructs of reality. What consumers desire reality to be is what hedonic consumption acts are based on, rather than what consumers know to be real. Pervasive creativity plays a major role in arousing this "desire" and makes consumer experience and feel this (desired reality) factor on the psychological grounds. This motivator can be related to the concept of self-discrepancy described earlier. This dissimilarity between the real and desired could play a role in invoking impulse. Hence, pervasive creativity of an effective theme influences consumer buying behavior in a very compelling manner toward impulse buying.

A good theme will lure the customer with a shopping mood into the store. Themes mainly depend upon the retailer's imagination and creativity. Focusing on the right theme rather than creating a display with expensive raw materials is the key to successful window display. A shoe store theme can be a group of elves buying shoes. A theme for display of casual wears can be a group of mannequins sitting casually at a get-together in different poses. Related themes will tug the heartstring of the customers and will pay off. They can be romantic, wild, or capricious, and capture not only eyeballs but also people's imaginations.

Hedonic Versus Utilitarian Products

Hedonic products are consumed for luxury purposes, which are desirable objects that allow the consumer to feel pleasure, fun, ecstasy, enjoyment, and a sense of indulgence. Under the study for hedonic motivation, there is quite a bit of research carried on how this type of motivation can influence people's shopping habits. This is completely different from utilitarian products, which are purchased or consumed frequently/or on regular basis for their practical uses/functionality and are based on rationality. Utility products are items that are purchased frequently and are an inevitable part of the consumer's daily life, which leads the consumer to be more sensitive to price factor toward these products because they are purchased and used frequently. These items can be cleaning grocery items: laundry detergent, regular clothing, toilet soaps, or other items that a consumer uses regularly, bought out of necessity and do not necessarily bring any joy to the consumer.

Because of this reason, the consumer is generally willing to spend more on luxury, hedonic items because here they can rationale that these items are more associated with their ideal self, and will not be purchased very frequently, which allows the buyer to be less price sensitive and more impulsive toward these items. This impulsive behavior is essentially the result of the strong aspirations for acquiring these products or brands that are influenced by the attributes or benefits that consumers strongly associate with a brand (brand association).

These products could constitute anything from luxury brands, high-fashion apparel brands, to artistic furniture to luxury watches (jewelry) to luxury bags (perfumes) to fine chocolates or candles; basically, anything that a consumer desires to acquire, earn, and get indulged in. Hence, a luxury store targets and is focused on high-net-worth consumers and are more about the class, the category of target audience, their specific needs, expectations, preferences, self-esteem, lifestyle, perceptual associations, and behavior. Such stores typically have wide range of products across varied categories, but all in the luxury (premium) range. The environment, design considerations, and ambience for such stores utilize the typical category codes, clues, and luxury quotient to which the consumer wants to associate with. On the other hand, premium brand stores tend to create their own character, philosophy, value, and identity by creating a luxury experience and hence complementing the brand and the products.

Let us consider the example of Swarovski, a leading designer, producer, and retailer of fashion jewelry. Swarovski especially lays emphasis on unique store ambience and VM. The luxury retailer has developed a unique concept for its stores that is based on the theme "Crystal Forest." This concept accentuates on the endless possibilities of crystal and reinforces company's deep affinity with nature. The objective is to engage with customers through spectacular store ambience-created exceptional store design. Its innovative and creative "Crystal Forest" concept highlights its merchandise, the crystal jewelry and accessories.

This unique concept is created through stainless steel prisms, which catch light and reflect from outside the store. Also the textured walls featuring reflective white prisms surround the space to create the illusion of an organic crystal forest. This interaction and congruence of light from different materials enhance the glitter of the store. The rapid changes of seasonal offerings by the brand get highlighted with the help of creatively designed thematic window graphics and showcases. The thematic pieces of the season are strategically positioned in the front area of the store. The Swarovski Crystal Forest Boutique on Dam Square 6 in Amsterdam has received a platinum LEED certificate.

Photo 9.9: *Floating Window Boxes that Allow for Unique, Eye-catching Displays of Swarovski's Crystal Accessories*

Source: www.swarovski.com (accessed on 12 May 2016)

The positive hedonic influence comes from the buying of luxury products for enjoyment and indulgence, which ultimately influences the buying behavior in a positive rather than compelling way, which in turn increases the footfalls and ticket size.

Now another important stimulus pervasive creativity influences in motivating impulse purchases is autistic stimuli. Autistic thoughts are resulted in response to internal impulses and are self-contained and self-serving. They do not follow rationale and are frequently associated with emotional urge and sensuality. Consequently and quintessentially, autistic stimuli can have strong and aggressive suggestive power and can result in impulsive-buying behavior.

Another factor that pervasive creativity vigorously reacts with is mood states. Mood also plays an important role that leads to impulse buying. Some people indulge themselves in impulse purchase in order to relieve unpleasant mood but also to cheer up themselves. Pervasive creativity acts upon the positive and negative feeling states that are potential motivator for impulse buying. In decision-making, consumers experience a "balance beam" effect between affective (emotional) desires and cognitive (reasoning) willpower, triggered by internal and external stimuli. It is been observed that pervasive creativity, in the context of negative rather than positive sentimental state of mind, generates driving force toward chronic impulse buying.

In totality, a good window display should get shoppers' eyes popping and should generate a desire to browse the store. Here the urge to enter the store should be uncontrollable. In essence, a good window display should set a mood for an event, a sale, or a general "feel" of what the shop is all about. Retailers often create the themes based on emotions and feelings like fun, family, excitement, alternative, and romance.

Now, external factors are those that retailers can influence and can enjoy greater control over by aligning them with window displays. Here, consumers' impulse purchasing behavior is influenced and triggered by many shop-related environmental factors such as visual cues and visual stimulus, shopping format, service and experience, store environment and ambience, offers and discounts, merchandise display, shelf space, aisles and endcaps, ambient factors, sociocultural factors, perceived crowding, and ownership of membership/loyalty/privilege card.

Visual stimulus encountered accidentally by the shopper can generally be the merchandise itself, suggesting that consumer impulse buying is driven by the environmental stimulus and is followed by an unexpected urge to obtain it/own it/acquire it or simply a desire to buy it, which acts as a very powerful trigger to the act of impulse buying. Hence, pervasive creativity plays the right cord in such a way that it becomes hard for consumers to refrain from the urge in the moments following their encounter with it by watching, feeling, experiencing, touching, tasting, and sniffing, or just by physical proximity—in all the abovementioned forms.

Sociocultural factors, which embrace store employees and other customers, are considered as external factors that influence impulse buying as well. Employee behavior, helpfulness, attire, and total presentation skills enhance the willingness to buy. However, some other schools of thought through light on some different angle of this social factors concept. According to them self-service environment is an impulsive purchase factor. Indeed, it enhances the shopping pleasure, and as a result, the shopper, who is free to move around, free to act, and unwatched, is more likely willing to try on "new things and styles and fantasize, wrapped in the indulgence of a self-service environment." However, a contrast has to be made between self-service environment and in-store browsing. In-store browsing is considered as creating encounters with desirable products that may evoke an appeal to buy. This urge gets harder for shopper to refrain from due to physical proximity of the merchandise. Consequently, malls and retail stores have come up with a list of "things to focus on," which includes specific roles that different forms of in-store signage have to play, in order to effectively increase sales. One of the major reasons that urge people to buy more is "looked well on shelf," that is, VM. This has a significant impact on impulse buying. There is a direct proportional relationship between customers' buying behavior and in-store form/mannequin display, promotional signage, and window display, which are the most visible manifestations of pervasive creativity.

Pervasive creativity stimulates the store environment and consumer senses, and this increases the likelihood of impulse buying because it creates impulsivity that leads to a momentary loss of self-control and rational buying behavior.

Summary

The world of retailing is changing, and appearance is so important in a retail shop that one should put a great deal of thought into planning and executing the displays. The more distinctive the store is, more the customers will remember and engage with it. In today's world, shopping and leisure are more of an experience. With the evolution of e-tailing, it has changed the name of the game and shopping is more of an "event" today. Stores are increasingly becoming galleries where objects or merchandise at the store are displayed, rather presented, as pieces of art. Once the consumer is inside the store, there is a lot to be tapped into by connecting the subconscious consumer motives. Pervasive creativity offers many techniques and means to bring alive the power of VM as the silent salesman and the science of store design. They also reinforce the essence of the brand and products inside the store, which go together to offer customers a delightful multisensory experience and resonate into deeper brand loyalty and bigger purchase baskets. Retailers are focusing to offer a consumer an option to "just be out there" and not push sales to them.

The focus from a marketing perspective is on improving the experience of consumers walking into our stores. This will be done by delightful in-store ambience and VM, with a clear emphasis on key products and story building around the categories. Imagination is the key ingredient to planning eye-catching and appealing displays. Today, retail spaces are "being" spaces for consumers where they come to hangout, escape, learn, and try out, and all of this then eventually leads to "consumption." This is all about transforming a "plain vanilla" into a "hot fudge sundae" with power of imagination and creativity.

Review Questions

1. Define the concept of visual merchandising and briefly explain the meaning of it.
2. What is the meaning and purpose of visual merchandising?
3. Briefly explain the importance of store atmospherics, ambience, and environment with its impact on consumer buying behavior.
4. Briefly explain the importance of components of exterior environment in visual merchandising.
5. Briefly explain the importance of components of exterior environment in visual merchandising.
6. Which are the major tools of visual merchandising? Briefly explain the importance of each component with appropriate examples.
7. Explain in detail the role and significance of fixtures in merchandise display and in overall visual merchandising of the store.
8. What is the meaning of planograms? Briefly explain its role and importance.
9. Explain in detail the role and significance of planogram merchandise display in overall visual merchandising of the store.
10. Briefly explain its role and importance of props and signage in visual merchandising and physical environment of the store.
11. "The design aspects and key merchandising principles are very essential for visual merchandising and in developing the right store ambience that eventually reinforces the brand image of the retailer." Comment on this statement and justify the views with appropriate examples.
12. What is the meaning of "pervasive creativity"? Briefly explain its role and significance in influencing the consumer buying behavior.
13. Explain how the "pervasive creativity" influences the perceptual process and eventually ends in influencing the consumer buying behavior through its different components.
14. Explain how the "pervasive creativity" works across the different consumer touch points and influences the consumer buying behavior.

Location Strategy

The Current Scenario

Place strategy relates to site location and physical site design, which should complement each other. Place for catalogs is in homes or at working places where they will be read. Internet retail sites must be easily entered and used by online shoppers. These are very important determinants of retail success. They directly relate to retail positioning for particular target markets, establishing retail images, and differentiate from competitors.

The challenge in India has not been the existence of customers as much as reaching them. E-commerce is increasingly becoming a significant channel of fulfilling demand created by mono-brand stores, which are playing the role of being "brand temples." If we compare online shoppers with buyers at brick-and-mortar stores, it is found that majority of the first group consisting of new customers. Hence, e-commerce is clearly fueling customer acquisition in India. That is why retailers and brands are encouraged to start selling online even if they do not have a physical store presence in India. The growth of online retailers is of great concern to traditional modern retailers as well as mall operators. Earlier, consumers would generally conduct initial product research before buying goods from physical stores. Now exactly opposite is increasingly happening, and this new trend is known as "showrooming": consumers seek to experience products in brick-and-mortar stores before looking online for the cheapest price. That is prompting many retailers and mall owners to consider reviving the marketing mix and also to adopt the hybrid way by making migration. This is a clear signal that the retailer sector is under pressure. Three major factors are putting huge pressure on organized off-line retail. These are as follows:

1. Need for capitalization
2. High real estate prices
3. Emergence of e-retail

Various surveys and projections show and predict that although e-retail is still a small part of the market, it is, and will be, growing at breakneck speed. This is attributed to the growing Internet usage on mobile phones and the services like cash payments on delivery and free returns. Its burgeoning popularity has surprised not only the conventional physical retailers but also made them ultra-conscious for any significant investment. Though such disruptive service innovations may not be sustainable financially, as long as they are being supported and nourished by optimistic private equity funds, e-retailers are expected to pour money into them, as well as into more strategic and dynamic pricing and deep discounts in order to gain higher share of wallet. As a result, this many consumers go to retail stores to physically view, touch, and experience a product but eventually place the order online. The e-tailing initially started with books a few years ago, and today, it has expanded to products like mobile phones, garments, accessories, laptops, electronic items, furniture, and even groceries. Adding to the woes of physical retailers is the challenges of managing the skyrocketing rentals for physical spaces and stores. In the countries like India, the leases for brick-and-mortar stores are very high in many cities and, many times, even totally out of sync with relatively lower purchasing power of their catchment area. As retailers are suffering losses at some locations, in recent times, many malls have experienced a huge turnover among stores. It has affected not only the retailers but also mall developers, and some of the developers have converted malls into offices, some have even been shut down and a few developers have downsized or shelved their mall plans. If the physical retailers have to address these challenges, they need to be sufficiently capitalized. However, many times, most of them are facing the capital crunch. Under such circumstances, given the uncertainty over the business, it is not easy to raise money from the market, either from private investors or from the public. Hence, all these factors make the process of selection of location more crucial, as once it is done, there is no scope for retake because retailers consider location mistakes to be among the most costly and complicated to rectify.

Strategic Store Location

While the terms "location" and "site" are often used interchangeably, there is a distinct difference between the two. In the context of today's retailing scenario, "location" is a marketing term, while "site" is a physical, real estate term. A strategically prime location is very essential for attracting enough customers to make a good profit. Customers have a general tendency to choose and patronize a store that is situated near work or home, or with a group of other stores that can complete and complement all of their purchases. The selection of a location type must emphasize the retailer's strategy and reinforce retailer's positioning. The location-type decision needs to be consistent with the shopping behavior of the target customers, size of its target market, and the retailer's image. While deciding on choosing the site locations, large retailers will first evaluate a wide area that acts as their catchment area, such as a specific part or parts of the city or country.

For instance, national chain retailers evaluate market growth and need for their stores in various regions of the country before deciding to expand into those areas or open more stores in that region. Regional retailers must determine the right state or town in which to locate.

A certain population base, with target market composition, is necessary to support different types and sizes of stores. For some retailers, small local markets of their target market segment, which have less competition, are better than heavily populated areas that have more

305

competition. On the other hand, mass merchandise "megastores" draw from a larger area of heavy population. Even if there are already similar stores in that area, they may be able to take business away from the competition and be very successful. So once the right area-wise location has been selected, a decision is made about the most suitable shopping center, mall, or street location. Large retailers sometimes stand alone, able to draw customers by themselves. Many other retailers prefer the pulling power of a cluster of stores grouped together for more convenient one-stop shopping, which also acts as destination centers. A tenant mix is the particular assortment of different stores grouped together in a cluster, shopping center, or mall. Most of the brick-and-mortar retailers rent their store spaces from commercial real estate companies that develop and own the sites.

For example, with stand-alone stores outnumbering Big Bazaar's mall stores, the strategy is atheist of format. Big Bazaar, because of the cross section of audience, has to be accessible by private vehicles and public transport, has smooth movement inside, parking, washrooms, and so on.

Hence, there are three major types of shopping situations: convenience shopping, comparison shopping, and specialty shopping. The optimum location for a retail store is one which offers high customer traffic, minimum competition from stores in the same category or carrying the same merchandise, and good infrastructure facilities for transportation, including public transit lines, easy access to mass transportation system, or private transport arrangements and parking.

- The site should have a good visibility to passing traffic, and it should be easy to approach, enter, and exit with a comfortable parking space.
- It is an eye-catching and prime section of town—one that enjoys a good reputation and considered as symbol of status among shoppers and tourists, if tourism is a significant aspect of the area under consideration.
- It should be safe and sound that is relatively protected from crime and other potential problems.
- It should also be compatible with customers' shopping needs. For instance, the luxury fashion stores are generally located at high-street areas of the city, and grocery centers are usually found nearby market areas or near the high-density residential zones. In all the cases, retailers try to place their stores for the convenience of their target markets.

Market Coverage Strategies

Retailers are internally and externally driven to open new stores and outlets. While externally, they are faced with significant pressures from competitors to expand their network of stores, internally, shareholders expect tangible financial outcomes of expansion and growth. Fundamentally, retailers strive for to increase sales revenues, market share, and profitability to better service their customer base, to counter the uncertainties of the market environment, and to obtain economies of scale in branding, promotions, advertising, and distribution. This eventually results in expansion of their network. However in today's scenario, retailers are increasingly forced to justify the existence of their network of stores. As the traditional retail model changes, retailers will need to reassess their store portfolios. The increasing cost of operating stores, changes in consumer behaviors, and the growing online multichannel opportunity indicated that retailers will require fewer stores in the future. Many are coming to the realization that they grew too fast and should scale back, if not halt, new store openings. For those retailers able to grow, the site selection process has become increasingly important. Thus, selecting a site for a new store is no longer an act of making marks on a map, or choosing a site on an intuition. Site selection process for retail companies includes devising the market coverage strategies in with all the details. In this case, retailer chalks out a plan on how concentrated a presence the company wants to have in a specific geographic area.

The loyalty card and patronage motives enable the retailer to profile the demographics of best customers, and because it is often likely that the best prospective customers generally have similar demographic characteristics, this makes selection of new locations much more precise. In addition, if the addresses of existing customers are known, they can be targeted geographically and sites can be chosen where there are faraway pockets of customers or gaps in coverage. The main market coverage strategies include the following.

Intensive Market Coverage

This involves selecting and utilizing as many retail outlets as are justified to obtain blanket coverage. This approach tries to serve all customers of an entire market area. A typical example is convenience stores, for example, Big Bazaar and D-Mart.

Let us consider the example of Van Heusen owned by the Aditya Birla Group's Madura Fashion & Lifestyle in India. It has improvised its marketing strategy to increase the brand awareness and recall about the international lifestyle brand in Tier II and Tier III cities in the country. Van Heusen's target customers are mostly in the 35–45 age group, and the smaller cities are increasingly becoming attractive markets for fashion wear and branded clothing because of exposure to digital media and growing disposable incomes. After realizing the fact that consumers in Tier II and Tier III cities are becoming more aware of style and branded clothing, the brand started going to smaller cities in a big way by opening new stores, thereby opening franchisee outlets and going slow on EBOs. This strategy typically gives intensive market coverage with comparatively less capital investment.

Selective Market Coverage

This involves choosing strategic locations to ensure adequate coverage of selected target markets. Chain apparel retailers and department stores often do this by locating a store in each of the major shopping malls of a metropolitan area. For instance, the department stores like Lifestyle, Shoppers Stop, and Pantaloon.

For example, German sportswear firm Puma has always adopted a balanced approach for its expansion in India. It has opened new stores in Tier II and Tier III cities and going selectively while adding new outlets to existing developed metro city markets. The dependence on metro cities is decreasing as the other cities are growing with a fast pace. Meanwhile, the brand is also working continuously on making its online platform Puma.com richer in terms of contents and offerings. Puma started to make profit within four years of operations as the coexistence of both—online and off-line—channels is supporting the revenue and overall growth.

Exclusive Market Coverage

This involves using one location to serve either an entire market area or some major segment of that market. Prestigious specialty retailers can use this approach as customers tend to travel a long distance for their unique goods and shopping experience. Typically, the luxury retailers adopt this kind of market coverage strategy.

Example: Vertu

The company has established flagship stores in exclusive shopping districts, so that it was close to other exclusive brands, thus benefiting from a halo effect. Vertu announced the opening of its first stores in Paris and Singapore in October 2002. Vertu has since opened new channels for distribution and intends to continue to build these globally. Along with their stores in Paris and Singapore, Vertu has client suites in London, New York, Hong Kong, and Singapore and also has POS located in some of the world's leading department stores and fine jewelers. The company was extremely selective when choosing suitable retail channels. They sought department stores that catered for an international client base, and who target very affluent shoppers. The stores must have a global reputation of offering quality and luxury across all product ranges and whose philosophy of high product knowledge and excellent personal service are consistent with that of Vertu's.

The General Guidelines for Location Selection

Before we start to discuss this topic, let us have a look on a classic example of how wrong location can scramble the ambitious retailing ventures. The New South China Mall in Dongguan was a grand vision of impressive proportions. Symbolically called as the "Great Mall of China," it was one of the largest malls in the world—twice the size of the Mall of America—with a whopping 5 million sq. ft of shopping area. It was designed to offer a unique shopping experience with a grand Arc de Triomphe, long canals with gondolas, and entertainment facilities like indoor and outdoor roller coaster. But, unfortunately, rather surprisingly, the mall did not live up to its pledge. Since opening in 2005, to the nightmare of shop owners, the mall could attract stipulated footfalls, save for a handful of outlets serving a trickle of walk-ins. On the contrary, Dongguan is one of the upcoming industrial cities in China. It is strategically located in the Guangdong Province, which is one of the largest exporting regions after Shanghai and Shenzhen. Though there seems to be no reason for the debacle, when the founders investigated for the failure, they found that most of its inhabitants are workers migrated from other area and having very limited income. These people migrated there to work in factories and could not afford the time or the money for shopping or enjoying the roller coaster. Another issue with the location was with its accessibility: It was not convenient to drop in the mall because there was no train or direct bus. The mall was also not located near a major highway, and reaching by bus could easily take more than two hours. In addition, there was no airport in Dongguan, which makes the mall inaccessible to visitors from neighboring regions.

This case study of the New South China Mall once again highlights the importance of devising a comprehensive location strategy, before taking off a new retail investments or expansion decisions. The cost of investing in the wrong location, combined with the opportunity cost, necessitates the need for a thorough research of market developments, the retail landscape, and consumer characteristics. In the case of emerging markets, a top line consideration is not always sufficient in providing a clear picture of all the business opportunities and associated risks. So, acquiring in-depth local market knowledge and insights through market research, on-site assessment, and engagement with industry players would therefore becomes essential. Because there is no retake once an action is taken and no money back guarantee for the wrong location selection. Hence for a retailer, brand owner, or property developer, it is imperative to select retail location that would present the most attractive revenue potential, or a platform that will strengthen the company's brand positioning in the market. So a robust location assessment methodology, backed by on-the-ground insights and certain guidelines, is critical in helping a company while selecting a store location.

Define the Goal or Objective

A store location strategy demands a full consideration for firm's policies, goals, and objectives regarding expansion or change of store location. These policies include the type and size of store desired, merchandising appeals, merchandise mix, and customer services to be provided. The criteria for evaluation would depend on the company's business profile and objectives. Profile refers to aspects such as product category, target customers, positioning, and merchandise mix. Objectives could be market entry or penetration, establishing a flagship store or new branches, acquiring an existing firm and so on. Following are the major points that need to be checked thoroughly:

- Type of store desired and optimal mix of retail stores/channel formats
- General location desired
- Potential revenue generating or branding opportunity for a particular location
- Specific type of location desired (shopping center, high-street area, etc.)
- Desired size of the store (square footage)
- Merchandise mix (categories in product lines to be carried)
- Merchandise appeals to be used
- Level of customer services to be offered
- Expected catchment area and expected footfalls of target audience
- Total cost, expected walk-ins, and desired business considerations

Analyze the Market Dynamics

For a retailer that is new to a particular market, the decision makers start off by analyzing the market attractiveness in order to justify potential market entry/investment.

- Developments in emerging markets are usually dynamic where economic activities such as foreign and government investments or industry development are expected to generate employment, thereby spurring consumer demand and spending. There are several factors like FDI policies and FTPs that affect the market's economic base, which in turn has an impact on income levels and purchasing power.
- An influx of foreign investments, developments in tourism, development as education hub or manufacturing/service hub, and so on may transform a city or a region into a potential retail hot spot.
- The emergence of new special economic zones or industry developments may stimulate local consumption.
- Hence, market dynamics and consumer behavior are likely to vary across cities and regions. City-level macro indicators (such as GDP per capita) may be postulated by the presence of a few industries, and may not be representative of the average consumer's propensity to spend.
- It is therefore essential to assess the sustainability of economic growth and the stability of drivers that affect the future outlook.

Analyze the Economic Base of the Catchment Area or Targeted Population

The economic and demographic characteristics of the area play a vital role in the long-term success of the location under consideration. The factors like population size, disposable income levels, and consumer expenditure patterns determine a market's addressable economic base and spending power. These aspects need to be examined in the context of consumers' shopping habits, as higher incomes may not necessarily lead to more purchasing in the home market. Hence, it becomes imperative for any retailer to do a market research and obtain following information about that location:

- Demographic information like age, income, disposable income, and population density.
- Income/employment stability.
- If any major employers moved out of the area. If such things have happened, which are those factors that are responsible, and if any other employer is in the process of moving out, and so on.
- What are the major sources of income/employment and what are the future prospects.
- The unemployment rate.
- Other factors like specific shopping behaviors, local cultural and societal characteristics and features.
- The total disposable income within the market are the average per capita income and the average per family income, the current rate of change in income (per capita and per family), and the projected rate of change for the future.
- Comparison of the rate of change in income in this market area with the rate of change in the nation as a whole and in similar markets.
- The distribution of income and purchasing power by income class in the market.
- Other demographic characteristics such as education level, gender ratio, age breakdown of the population, the proportion of double-income or multiple-income families.

Let us consider the example of Arvind Lifestyle Brands Ltd, which runs more than 800 stores in India across a portfolio of over 30 brands that include leading brands like Gap, Calvin Klein, Arrow, US Polo, and Tommy Hilfiger. It is a subsidiary of denim and branded apparel major Arvind Ltd, one of the largest integrated textile and branded apparel players. Arvind Lifestyle Brands Ltd has signed a strategic license agreement with the US-based Aéropostale Inc, the specialty retailer of casual and active apparel for men and women. The New York-headquartered brand is also popularly known as Aero. Aero, Abercrombie & Fitch, and American Eagle are also known as the "3 As" in the USA. They are well known in their home market for hoodies, jeans, and T-shirts, mostly for teenagers.

The US-based youth retailer has presence in over 1,000 locations across the USA, Canada, and through licensing JVs (partnerships) in Asia, West Asia, Europe, South America, and Mexico. One of the striking features of this tie-up is the license agreement covers not only the physical (brick-and-mortar) retail locations but also e-commerce portal.

Aéropostale has successfully positioned itself as a youth-focused retail format and is very optimistic to be popular and successful in India, because 40% of India's population is below the age of 20. According to the CEO of Aéropostale Inc, it is a very strategic move to bring the Aéropostale brand into India as this has helped them expand their international presence amid the stagnating sales in the home market (USA). This optimism lies in the fact that they perceive India as a truly exciting retail market driven by its growing economy and vibrant youth culture.

Retail Business Centers

After established a particular market is feasible for entry or investment, the next step would be to proceed to identify the potential retail hot spots. If the retailer is looking for space in the retail business center/mall, the company has to look into factors such as the availability and growth of retail space, as well as likely developments in the pipeline. So the following points are taken into consideration:

- Retail mapping: Retail mapping is nothing but identify locations with a high level of economic or retail activity. Retailers map out the distribution of existing/upcoming retail spots within each zone and select areas for in-depth assessment. This includes the evaluation of benchmark-selected malls/retail areas in terms of revenue potential and brand "fit" and the current/future revenue potential that it represents.

- Mall/retail area's positioning, perceptual image, and shopper profile.
- The existing and upcoming retail business centers in the area.
- Consumer drawing power of the existing retail business center and the expected customer pulling power of the upcoming one, if any.
- The centers having highest potential for a retail floor shop and analyzing their walk-ins.
- The players that are already present there: The tenant mix and presence of relevant crowd-pullers (e.g., anchor tenants, attractions)
- Quality of current/potential catchment areas
- If the prime floor is available or it is already occupied? If it is occupied, who is occupying it?
- The other players present there and competitive intensity within the area or in the vicinity.
- Other considerations include the depth and breadth of retail offerings, average price points, as well as the presence of international brands or retail chains.

Other Infrastructure-related Considerations

- The road network, accessibility of the location, and convenience to reach the store from various residential areas/market area/major catchment area.
- Projected road networks, flyovers, and any other infrastructural developments that may affect the potential of the location positively or negatively.
- The accessibility and distances from major highways, railway stations/local railway, or metro stations.
- The hourly traffic flow patterns across the location area.
- One of the most important factors is the visibility of the store itself and signs/signage.
- New and proposed highways or other major infrastructure developments can potentially change current traffic flows and patterns. So all these possibilities are carefully checked as it has the potential to drastically affect the footfalls and eventually the business.
- However, the traveling convenience of locations is not always important for retailers with unique, differentiated offerings than for retailers with an offering similar to other retailers. For such stores that offer a unique merchandise assortment, store atmosphere and shopping experience customers tend to travel to wherever the store is located, and its location becomes a destination.

Legal Considerations and Zoning Regulations

Legal considerations need to be examined when evaluating different location types. Laws regarding how land is used have become so critical that it has to be retailer's first consideration in a site search. Legal issues that affect the location decision include environmental issues, zoning, building codes, signs, and licensing requirements. Zoning determines how a particular site can be used and for what purpose it can be used. For instance, some parts of a city are zoned for residential use only; others are zoned for light industrial, commercial, and retail uses. Zoning regulations have a significant effect on the kind and size of floor shop the retailer may develop. The regulations also play a decisive role in designing the parking spaces and the size and kind of signs that can be used. Restrictions on the use of signs can also impact a particular site's desirability. Sign size and style may be restricted by building codes, zoning ordinances, or even the shopping center management. Environmental factors comprise considerations such as political stability (any impact on business confidence), sociocultural characteristics of the region, technological and infrastructure development (how will this affect accessibility), and climate change (risk of operational disruptions). For example, convenience retailer 7-Eleven provides crucial support to its franchisees to get operations up and running. 7-Eleven as a franchiser takes care of several operational issues like scoping and buying the real estate, handling the zoning approval process, bearing the ongoing costs of rent, real estate taxes, utilities, certain building maintenance, and equipment replacement.

Competition Analysis

Here, competition means all of those retail establishments that compete for the same type of business and target the same customer base. The study of competition requires a market research that will yield information about the physical characteristics and type of each store, the merchandise offered by the stores, level of customer services provided by them, and a reasonably good estimate of the store's sales. Other than the information regarding the sales, business, and average footfalls, a consideration for the following aspects is necessary:

- The competitive analysis starts with identifying key players who operate in similar retail segments or product categories.
- The extent of competitive threat posed by these players hinges on aspects such as firm's existing retail coverage, relative market share, and profitability.
- Their connections with major distributors or retail chains, aggressiveness of marketing activities, and so on.
- The historic data about the firm, its origin, and growth.
- Average weekly walk-ins and the footfalls on weekends.
- Brand positioning, image, and other perceptual associations and whether the company's current retail outlets are well-positioned vis-à-vis competitors.
- Evaluation of its executive management: ability, motivational level, leadership quality, service quality and efficiency, customer feedback and general perceptions, backup management, so on.
- Evaluation of store personnel (staff): efficiency, motivational levels, working conditions, length of work week, average working hours per week, use of part-timers, morale, selling skills, creativity, and the quality of service provided to the customers.
- Strength of the organizations: growth rate, aggressiveness, financial resources and standing, creativity of displays, key merchandising principles and the policies of compliance, promotions, advertising, PLBs, loyalty program, gift card business, social media marketing activities, PR, digital marketing, CSR initiatives in the locality, and so on.
- Future expansion policies: projected and upcoming new stores, remodeling, acquisitions, flexibility, types of locations, ownership, and lease agreements.
- Store facilities and infrastructure: size, age, quality, condition, efficiency, design, layout, fixtures parking space, availability of food courts, presence of recreational, and entertainment facilities.
- Supporting facilities: warehouse facilities, central and separate designing, delivery pools, affiliation or tie-ups with buying groups, corporate/institutional business, and so on.
- Merchandising policies: merchandise quality, categories, variety, assortment, depth of SKUs, pricing, PLBs, specialty departments, and sources of supply, advertising, and promotion.
- Operating policies: store management systems and standard operating procedures, return policies, store hours, layout and design, standards of customer service, store maintenance, customer services, and so on.

Analysis of Retailer's Own Market Coverage and Penetration

If the retailer already has presence in that area, then there is the possibility of cannibalization. So it becomes important to determine the precise trade/catchment areas, market penetration, customer shopping behavior, and loyalty behavior toward these stores. So the results of this component of the study should provide basic information for:

- Evaluating current sales performance of each store in relation to market potential.
- Outlining and targeting areas of under penetration.
- Estimating the effects of new location strategies on existing company stores.
- Evaluating the possibilities for leveraging the brand image and other tangible things like warehouse, loyalty programs, and gift card program.
- Expanding (one of the key barriers) in emerging markets, where the lack of retail establishments that have the appropriate size and positioning to house these international brands for many international high-end retailer brands.

Analyzing Store's Performance

- Here the retailer analyzes the sales and profit records of each store, including a detailed assessment of recent financial statements. Retailer also analyzes the factors such as present investment in each store, rent and lease terms, store management, current catchment area, and loyal customer base.
- By selecting the right location, companies have been able to increase their average unit volume (AUV) of new stores.
- Special efforts that have been made in the form of ATL (above the line) and BTL (below the line) activities to promote the store.
- The findings should be evaluated in relation to all other relevant information obtained from the preceding step.
- From here, the retailer needs to proceed to a review of the present performance of each store in relation to the market potentials.

The economic pressures are there to be, and critical assessment of the store portfolio is now essential for all retailers. It is not only about the closing of the noncontributing stores but also about the size and shape of other outlets. Hence, the retailers need to focus on understanding the optimal future size and penetration. The implications that are arising from reduced ranges in store can eventually be complemented with extended virtual (online) ranges and flexible fulfillment solutions, for instance, delivery anytime and anywhere.

Evaluating Store Facilities and Locations

- At this step, the retailer reviews the adequacy of all existing stores and also appraises the possible locations for the immediate and future expositions.
- Here, strategies and plans are formulated for possible store location moves (such as enlarging, relocating, and closing) for those stores that are obsolete or poorly located (or which will become so in the near future), and for those stores whose leases are going to expire in the near future. These plans are tentative and are subject to reappraisal after the next step is completed.

Studying the Locations of Under Penetration

- The retailer ascertains the potential of locations and areas that are not presently served or underestimated or served inadequately (areas of under penetration).
- Then it determines the walk-ins and business potentials for all areas of under penetration.
- After that the retailer assigns areas for possible sites if they present desired business potential.
- The retailer makes an estimation of the effect of each new store location expansion into the area of under penetration on the sales of company's other stores.
- This is done with the objective to avoid any type of cannibalization. And if it is unavoidable at all, the overall impact has to be assessed vis-à-vis the total business potential, expected market share, expected total footfall (all stores combined), and ROI.

For instance, as metro and Tier I cities are rapidly heading toward saturation, the large retailers are increasingly looking toward Tier II and Tier III cities for further expansion.

Competitor's Likely Location Moves

- The retailer gives a deep consideration for competitor's probable expansion plans and plausible strategies, or at least ideas for immediate and future growth. Here many times, corporate intelligence is used.
- Retailers determine the possible location moves competition are likely to make by analyzing the store facilities and locations of each significant competitor, their marketing strategies, mergers and acquisitions, historic pattern of store expansion, and their financial and managerial strength.

Identifying the Right Store Format

- Once the key hot spots have been shortlisted, the next step is to determine the right retail format that would provide the best "fit" with the location's characteristics. Here the decision makers will decide on whether the company should establish a single-brand store, partner with an MBO, set up a factory or discount outlet.
- This needs to be evaluated in the context of the company's profile and objectives. For instance, a site that falls under "high revenue potential–low brand fit" could still be an acceptable consideration if the company plans to offer a merchandise mix that caters to this segment (e.g., setting up a factory or discount outlet).
- Alternatively, a "low revenue potential–high brand fit" site could provide a suitable location for the establishment of a concept stand-alone store.
- On the basis of the information crystallized, the retailer then identifies the right store format.

At the end, we need to admit that large, financially strong retailers have the greatest chance of expanding in this marketplace and are able to allocate considerable resources to their site selection process. These large retailers have considerable real estate holdings, routinely open new stores, and have sizable internal real estate departments to manage their real estate needs. These retailers practice to make location selection decisions with increasing skill and sophistication, but it is not clear that any of them are simply following a set formula. If they were following a formula, it would be easy to determine where all the future stores would be located, but this is far from the way things work. Retail experts employed at the large retailers insist "there is no set formula," yet it has been found that much can be derived from a model based on a large number of their past decisions. In fact, such models give an excellent prediction of where future stores are needed.

Showrooming: A New Challenge for Retailers

In today's retailing world, technology has been one of the biggest disruptive forces for the retail industry. In the form of e-tailing, it has given the shopper more than one channel to shop with, convenience of shopping from home, driven down cost, saving of time, and shifted the center of gravity of customer experience from provider to the buyer. Today, the well-informed customers:

1. Research online to explore options
2. See, try, and feel the product in the store
3. Place the order online
4. Pay online through credit/debit cards or by Internet banking or pay COD

This has given rise to the term "showrooming." The top two reasons for this behavior are convenience of online shopping from home or office, doing so 24/7, and the advantage of cost. On the other hand, people who shop in-store do so because they like to feel the product, experience the shopping atmosphere, get instant delivery, and like personalized services. Also a large part of India shops in store because they do not trust the delivery system, are skeptical about product quality that will be delivered actually, and are worried about data security or do not own a credit card or do not have easy access to Internet or maybe do not have a data connection. While with the deep penetration of data and credit services, the last three reasons will become less and less important over a period of time, so it is time for brick-and-mortar stores to plan for a sustainable business model.

In the debate of retailing vs e-tailing, the truth today is somewhere in the middle. While e-tailers worldwide are growing at a scorching pace with the help from technology and analytics that help them understand consumer better, off-line retailers have so far little data that they could use. However, it is also true that the e-tailers are increasingly feeling the need of getting into physical formats with strategic locations where customers can walk in, feel and see products, and then order online, shopping walls, or lockers for convenient delivery. Amazon, eBay, and Tesco are the classic examples of e-tailers. On the other hand, brick-and-mortar retailers are upping the game by going the multichannel route, and we will see somewhere the line blurs between e-tailing and retailing, and a new business model emerge for the industry.

First and foremost, today more than ever, it is important for retailers to cater to multichannel formats. This will also help to drive down the infrastructural issues and location cost but, on the other hand, also offers the customers with more options. It is becoming important for the off-line retailers to take the multichannel option as a big drive for growth. This requires a change in operations, the way marketing and branding is done, and a business model that will cater all these factors.

While showrooming is a growing phenomenon, it is also true that online is driving sales in-store in a number of categories. There are categories such as computer, electronics, furniture, home ware, and household appliances segment that are researched online and bought off-line in the physical store. Now this behavior would mean that shoppers are today walking into stores to buy certain categories more than the others. The retailer hence needs to strategically devise the category mix and realign them to drive sales in-store.

Finally, retail is all about people, their behavior, and what drives their loyalty. One of the biggest reasons people shop in physical stores is social interaction, so stores need to evolve to become destinations and places where customers not only shop but also get-together and "hangout." The classic example here we can quote is of IKEA, which has developed their stores not only as shopping but also as social destinations. Finally, here we can conclude that place/location will be a strategically very important factor for brick-and-mortar retailers, but what is equally essential is and true is that they will need to reinvent themselves continuously to stay relevant and cater to the changing trends.

Therefore, some off-line retailers are also venturing into the virtual space to take on their online rivals. In fact, the Internet has provided a new sales channel for global and domestic brands like Shoppers Stop, Puma, Aldo, Charles & Keith, and Mango. The brick-and-mortar retailers need to expand their footprint by having more stores so that shoppers can access the products and buy multiple products from them. They also need to provide more services, such as returns, exchanges, home delivery, and bonus/loyalty points, to be able to counter the e-tailers.

Brick-and-mortar retailers, in a bid to compete successfully against e-tailers would need to leverage their omni-channel strategy along with demand-driven and location-based fulfillment services, and simultaneously optimize their SKUs to local consumer behavior.

Brands like Mango, which are already present in brick-and-mortar shops, associating with e-commerce platforms is not a matter of choice anymore but a necessity. We can see a lot of international brands striking up exclusive tie-ups with portals like Jabong and Myntra because these e-commerce platforms have already established a brand value. So there is an online environment that has already been created and ready for these brands to take advantage of. The international brands do not fear that their brands will get diluted in any way by listing online with these portals.

Foreign high-street labels also have some of the obvious advantages such as avoiding high real estate rentals if they choose to test the waters by launching online in India, as also other entry hurdles in getting a Pan-India access. The brands can also learn more about the taste of the Indian market to know whether they are likely to get enough traction or not. But players like Jabong would have to account for the costs that exclusively brings with it when launching fashion brands online. The exclusivity-driven models of most online fashion retailers is that of a "buy, stock, and sell," which involves large inventory and its concomitant cost.

The Key Trends

Reverse "Showrooming" Boosts Footfalls

As mentioned earlier, from the growing number of smartphone users and increasing Internet access, it is evident that "digital" technology has become an inevitable part of consumer behavior in India, and the propensity to embrace digital is increasing day by day. E-commerce organizations have already leveraged this digital wave, which is quite evident by their growing GMV. So here the million-dollar question is: How do brick-and-mortar retailers ride this wave rather than consider it as a threat to their business model to counter the consumer behavior of "showrooming"?

The solution lies in the consumer behavior itself because though consumers are increasingly preferring to purchase online, a significantly big percentage of consumers still continue to use a combination of physical and digital technologies during the shopping journey. While customers are increasingly becoming tech savvy and prefer the convenience of shopping anytime and anywhere, they still value the "touch–feel–try" experience provided by brick-and-mortar retailers.

This shows that even though customers become more comfortable with purchasing online, the brick-and-mortar retail stores will never lose their relevance and continue to play a significant role. This is reflected in the consumers' inherent propensity to touch, try, and feel the product before finalizing the purchase decision. So with the strategic management of variety and assortment of products across the categories carried by store can reverse showrooming. The retailers that adapt to consumer preferences with array of products in-store, along with attractive prices and location-based offers, will benefit from increasing number of footfalls at their outlets. In addition, many times, shopping is considered as an entertaining and sociable pastime, by many, and the focus on instant gratification would help the retailers to keep their cash register ringing.

Hence, the off-line retailers have the opportunity to score over the e-tailers in terms of leveraging this consumer behavior, by offering them a seamless experience across both off-line and online channels. This means offering flexibility in buying and receiving delivery.

For instance, the consumers can:

- Buy online and pick up the delivery in-store
- Buy from one store and pick up from the other
- Buy in-store and take the delivery at home
- Browse free Wi-Fi in-store to order

All these options could be offered realistically only by a retailer having both physical and digital presence. This hybrid shopping experience developed across integrated channels is called as "omni-channel" system. This suggests that omni-channel is a strategic way for the retailers to leverage the trend and achieve exponential growth.

Personalized Recommendations

Retailers today need to enable and empower their sales associates to connect with customers and provide a personalized experience. Several studies have highlighted that one-in-three consumer purchases at leading online sites emanate from recommendations, and traditional retailers also have the opportunity to recreate this kind of service experience via Apple's iBeacon. As customers are increasingly well informed, they expect, rather demand, more from the service they receive in the store. They enter the store armed with a capital of information and store staff is expected to not only match this enhanced level of knowledge but also add to it and provide additional value. It is also observed that consumers today are willing to share information with retailers, if it results in personalized, timely, and relevant offers, bundled with incentives and loyalty points. This effectively puts CRM into the hands the store associate to create a coherent and personalized experience for the customer.

Use of Social Media

Retailers need to ensure a suitable presence via mobile applications and social media, which facilitate greater personalized interactions between brand and consumers. In addition, a growing number of consumers expect to complete their online shopping from social platforms without browsing on an online retailer's site.

Supply Chain and Fulfillment

Online retailers like Amazon and Zappos are able to offer the same-day shipping and fulfillment because of their effective and efficient supply chain infrastructure. So the traditional retailers also need to optimize their back-end operations in order to achieve a similar objective. Here, it is the demand of the hour is to improvise their operational flexibility and agility, and a transaction to cloud-based systems will certainly assist in that process.

Omni-channel (Multichannel) Strategy: A Hybrid Shopping Experience

The consumer behavior of "showrooming" is defined as shopping in-store and then searching for the best price and making the purchase online. While this prevalent behavior still presents a potential risk for traditional brick-and-mortar retailers, it is worth noting that there exists the reverse behavior also. There are many consumers who are doing just the opposite of showrooming. They browse the portals of online retailers, look at different items online, but go to a physical store, touch–feel–try similar items, and then buy there in the store itself. This reverse behavior to showrooming is called as webrooming.

Despite the fact that webrooming is favorable for off-line retailers, an online presence is also highly essential for attracting and driving consumers to the storefront and increasing their frequency of visits and purchase. So developing an appealing and compelling online presence—across all digital screens—is a vital component of the entire shopping journey. The retailers that essentially provide an engaging and efficient online and in-store experience—with consistent assortments and coordinated promotional offerings—could stand apart and break the clutter. Furthermore, retailers that can capture and integrate data across both the digital and in-store channels to build "a single view of the consumer" have the opportunity to use that data to design a more personalized shopping experience for each customer.

Today, the technology and the technology-enabled retailing models, referring here to omni-channel or multichannel, have completely changed the meaning of location. While we can see many off-line retailers launching their online portals or tying up with the marketplace portals to build their online presence, there exist many online players that have made their off-line foray and have discovered the benefits of having a brick-and-mortar store. With this, the facility of online shopping being provided not only by the e-retailers but also by the brick-and-mortar retailers, and consumer can transact with a retailer through her or his mobile device from anywhere and at anytime as per her or his convenience. So here the location means not only the physical place where the retailer's shop is situated/located but also the channels through which it can be accessed by the consumer for shopping transactions.

For example, when online jewelry retailer BaubleBar opened a brick-and-mortar outlet in Manhattan, it realized that how its in-store shoppers are different from its online customers. The retailer observed that shoppers suddenly started paying more attention to unflashy pieces that were often overlooked online. More women customers bought multiple necklaces that could be worn together, which in turn created an opportunity to increase the cross-selling. The in-store shoppers typically purchased more merchandise as compared to the online BaubleBar customers.

Let us now consider the example of Nykaa. It is an online beauty and wellness retail company and launched its operations in 2012 through the online platform that went live in 2013. Subsequently, Nykaa has already made its way to be an omni-channel player with a physical store at the T3 terminal of Delhi's Indira Gandhi International Airport. The beauty and wellness retailer is in the process of opening more mall-based brick-and-mortar outlets in other metros of India.

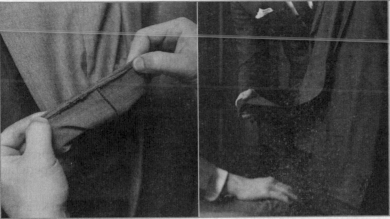

Having the opportunity to touch, feel, try the product is a big value and has some unique advantages. Using the brick-and-mortar outlet these online retailers are creating a memorable, one of a kind experience. Hence providing an in-person fashion consultation and shopping experience can't be imitated on the gadgets like tablets or smart-phones.

Photo 10.1: *To Touch, Feel and Try the Merchandise Is an Experience*

Similarly, Bonobos is among the online-first retailers that started to have brick-and-mortar store. At the Bethesda store of Bonobos, shopper can touch–feel–try on clothes and then order the items online. These physical places are branded as Guideshop(s); these are small showrooms where customers can try on suits, blazers, dress shirts, and so on and then place the order online with the help of a sales associate. The product is then delivered to them at their place.

Some online retailers have forayed into brick-and-mortar spaces by partnering with existing stores, and the brick-and-mortar players that want to go online tend to go to a marketplace initially and then launch their own portal as it is common practice and behavior that buyers go to marketplaces, compare, and then buy. The success of a store, whether online or off-line, is judged less on how much revenue it pulls in and more on its ability to function as a marketing tool for the brand.

These market dynamics are changing the retailer's approach toward the overall location selection strategy, and they are simultaneously giving considerations to their off-line and online presence, which is driving them toward adopting the hybrid way and omni-channel strategy.

Chumbak, a retailer of gift and souvenir, is a classic example of how the retailers are adopting the hybrid way. Chumbak categorically follows a hybrid business model where they operate both online and off-line presence. Founded by a Vivek Prabhakar and Shubhra Chadda in 2010, Chumbak came to limelight by offering a slice of India to its visitors and shoppers by adding a bit of quirkiness, humor, and fun to the Indian souvenir market.

The exciting journey started with Facebook, where majority of their marketing and advertisement was done. Soon, they gradually started retailing in MBOs like Crosswords, other small boutiques, and bookstores. It was 2012 when they decided to open their own store and launched their first kiosk in Forum Mall in Bengaluru to cater the increasing demand. After receiving their first round of funding from VC firm, they started expanding more, and today, they have over 30 kiosks across the country. By mid-2014, they started venturing into the vast category of home and décor when they raised their second round of funding. Chumbak also entered into a strategic partnership with PVR to set kiosks inside their multiplexes, in the metro cities like Delhi, Mumbai, and Bengaluru, and also partnered with international players in order to expand in overseas markets. However with the strategic plans on to increase the retail store count, the company eventually closed many of its pop-up stores and kiosks in high-traffic areas like malls. These formats were not able to showcase their entire range of products, which have grown from accessories to home category and eventually to fashion apparel, all under one roof.

Meanwhile, they were simultaneously focusing on their comprehensive online presence and striving to build an effective Chumbak web store that is high on experience and quality, besides their presence on marketplaces like Flipkart and Amazon.

As a result, today, they have market presence through their flagship retail stores in cities like Delhi, Mumbai, Bengaluru, Hyderabad, Gurgaon, Kochi, and Jaipur. Besides their own web store Chumbak.com, they have online presence through the online marketplaces such as Flipkart and Amazon and fashion apps like Wooplr and Roposo. While the online presence brings them scale, the off-line presence is helping them to build and enhance brand experience and engagement across the touch points.

However, though it is true that retailers are continually evolving their omni-channel systems, they are also well aware of the fact that going omni-channel cannot be a one-size-fits-all approach. So before boarding on the omni-channel bandwagon, retailers need to develop clarity on its own positioning, define its own omni-channel vision, and build its own road map.

Retailer's Self-evaluation Before Embracing Omni-channel

While these examples suggest that omni-channel is a new way of life for the retailer, it is not that easy to embrace it. We need to revisit and look into what is omni-channel and what does it take to implement at a retailer's end, as it is not just about opening a new channel but also reevaluating the entire retail architecture. Hence, a holistic approach is to be given to all business functions, separately and also as integrated units, in a comprehensive manner. As discussed earlier, omni-channel essentially integrates many cross-functional components and elements comprising operations, technology, transactions, and management systems. So retailers need to think and act about changes required across operations, technology, and available resources in order to develop, design, and deliver their omni-channel road map effectively. Here are few of the key areas, among others, that need to be revisited and evaluated before going omni-channel.

Structure and Mind-set of Organization

For effectively implementing the omni-channel strategy, it requires a change in the mind-set—it is the transformation from selling through channels to selling across the channels in an integrated way. So retailers need to relook at the organization structure, and the key objective could be enabling strategic collaboration across channels, and not working in silos. Hence, implementing omni-channel requires the retailer to bring some strategic changes in structures and hierarchies, incentive schemes, and PMS.

Omni-channel Experience

In the omni-channel arrangement, stores need to act as the interface in providing a seamless experience to the consumers. So retailers need to appraise and improvise the physical footprints and formats to effectively cater the changed consumer preferences and expectation. Thus, in order to provide a coherent omni-channel experience, the role of store associates needs to be relooked and redesigned. Here the role is modified from simply selling and processing in-store transactions to providing services to continuously connected consumers at several other facets of an integrated ecosystem.

Supply Chain Management

SCM is already a very crucial component of retail management, and in the case of omni-channel experience, it becomes more complex. So retailers need to reevaluate their current supply chain and distribution capabilities to support the change in consumer purchasing trends and last-mile delivery services. Here the inventory ownership may need to shift from channel specific to enterprise owned, and that is quintessentially with clear visibility of inventory across all customer touch points.

Technology

Technology infrastructure is the very foundation for developing omni-channel shopping system and needs to be leveraged as a key enabler across functions and systems. So retailers will need to ensure the real-time connectivity between the front-end brick-and-mortar store/website and the back end. Enhanced in-store technology and applications are essential to offer a new level of coherent service/shopping experience to customers.

Analytics

In short, leveraging advanced analytics to derive and develop precise consumer insights across consumer touch points and applying those insights across functions like designing loyalty programs, marketing, and supply chain have the right potential to develop significant differentiation and unique proposition for the retailer.

In addition, Indian retailers have to face their unique challenges, which need to be addressed with certain improvisations. Most of these challenges are already discussed in the first few chapters of this book. Moreover, a significant number of Indian-organized retailers operate on a franchisee model, and most franchisees operate on a stand-alone basis. In such cases, retailers may need to offer an attractive incentive structure that will encourage the franchisees to embrace omni-channel systems. While omni-channel is a new way of life, embracing omni-channel is not a choice but going to be an imperative in near future.

Thus, taking these challenges into consideration, the brick-and-mortar retailers are developing the omni-channel system into phases:

1. In the first phase, they strengthen their online platform by increasing options/categories/varieties/assortments available at the website and by improving the user experience.
2. In the second phase, operations of online and physical stores are strategically integrated. That is, the integrated system will enable the consumer to access the store through online as well as physical store route, though here the experiences might differ.
3. In the third phase, the company would move to the omni-channel infrastructure and arrangement where it develops a single view of the customer and inventory, which, in turn, offer a truly omni-channel experience.

Summary

In today's highly competitive environment, choosing the correct site location for a retail outlet ranks among the top factors in determining that outlet's success or failure. The most frequent response to the question "what are the most important three things in retail" is location, location, and location. Location is a very important element for customer to prefer a store. Location also has a competitive advantage, which is not easy to simulate. The critical side of channel strategy is the location of a store. While other elements of retail marketing mix can be changed, improved, or acquired easily, it is very difficult to change the location of the store with such ease. Second, location decisions have strategic importance because they can be used to develop an SCA. If a retailer has the best location, that is, the location that is most attractive to its customers, competitors cannot easily copy this advantage and are relegated to occupying the second-best location.

Retailers are very sensitive while choosing location. Especially features like demographic features of the catchment area, retailer's target audience, location economy consideration (cost, income, from productivity point of view), traffic features, neighborhood establishments, competition considerations, and brand image of the retailer need to be considered. The location of the store is also the manifestation of its positioning and brand image. Research in this area has also proved that location of the store is one of the factors that essentially play a major role when shoppers decide on which store to patronize. Hence, the right location increases the shopper's loyalty toward the retailer.

With the changing retail landscape, omni-channel has become a growing phenomenon. Online players do not have the physical location, but physical retailers have that option. In many categories like apparels, fits and sizes are important. Here, omni-channel retail enables shoppers to check online and buy from stores and vice versa. As we discussed earlier that location is a crucial element of contemporary retail marketing mix, and it has gone beyond simply being as a physical place. Today, location also represents the different channels across which a shopper can transact and interact with the retailers. Hence, the concept of location has essentially evolved to the "channels" both online and off-line (hybrid). This ubiquity or omnipresence of the retailer allows the customers to browse the merchandise offered by a retailer online, touch–feel–try off-line, purchase online, and get the delivery off-line, all irrespective of the physical location of the retailer's store.

Review Questions

1. Explain the importance of strategic location in the current scenario of business of retailing.
2. Briefly explain the market coverage strategies with appropriate examples.
3. Explain the general guidelines that retailers follow while taking decision on selection of store location.
4. Explain how the technology and emerging models of retailing, referring here to omni-channel, have essentially changed the "concept of location."
5. What is the meaning of showrooming? Explain how the brick-and-mortar retailers are addressing the challenges posed by showrooming behavior.
6. Explain the key trends in retailing with the innovations done and initiatives taken by both online and off-line retailers.
7. Briefly explain the omni-channel model of retailing. Also explain the essentials for developing and building an effective and efficient omni-channel shopping experience.
8. Briefly explain the key trends in consumer shopping behavior and how they are addressed by retailers.
9. Briefly explain the meaning of hybrid shopping experience. Also explain the essentials for developing and building an effective and efficient hybrid retailing model.

The Pyramid of Performance

The Performance Pyramid: Creating a Coherent Shopping Experience

The way consumers are shopping and interacting with the retailer brands is changing rapidly. Consumers are very demanding, and the propensity toward overall shopping experience, personalization, virtualization, mobile platforms and applications, and the interactivity have brought about sea changes in consumer expectations toward the retailers. The difference between "good" and "outstanding" players in the retail sector is increasingly becoming more visible and akin to the performance of a sportsman. This scenario has changed the consumer behavior and driving new strategies that define customers' engagement, with their favorite retailer brand.

Over the past few years, while retailers have become responsive to the changing needs of consumers with various tech-based solutions and apps, the need is for them to "stay ahead of the curve" and anticipate customer buying preferences and trends in purchasing behavior.

The metrics of organization performance have transformed significantly; the merchandise (product) quality, brand, and service efficiency are just primary things in today's retailing scenario where delivering a unique and coherent experience is the only way for achieving an SCA. To achieve this objective, retailers need to view each aspect of their businesses from "customers' lens" and deliver a relevant experience at each exposure and transaction, both in-store and online. Retailers need to utilize demographic and psychographic factors, including consumer preferences that contribute to the individual identity. Hence, the ability to transform from "responsive" to "adaptive" business model has been emerged as the key theme to performance in the contemporary retailing scenario.

Consumers are increasingly demanding an array of features while making their purchase, and it requires retailers to respond appropriately, whether it is a mobile wallet or home delivery of products and allied features.

Of course, e-retail discounts hurt physical stores, but the real problem is, over the long run, this is trying to change the consumer behavior—once those consumers become accustomed to shopping online in these categories, why should they have to walk into a store? So the brick-and-mortar players need to counter it by achieving desired product and service-level performance with possible level of customization, overall shopping experience, and the level of personalization. Performance refers to the delivery of superior experience of a retail store brand at four levels: first at a product level, second at a customer preference level, third at an experiential level, and fourth at the personalization level (Figure 11.1). So, for brick-and-mortar retailers, the major source to build SCA is found in the performance and the value addition it generates for the consumers. This value added must be firmly based upon customer needs and values, and may comprise both tangible or functional and intangible or symbolic elements.

At a *product level*, fundamentally, performance must satisfy the functional and utilitarian characteristic as well as deliver on its practical physical attributes: a recipe of quality or design excellence ingredients like craftsmanship, precision, materials, high quality, unique design, extraordinary product capabilities, and technology and innovation. In today's retailing scenario, we are working in a world dictated by customer preference. Preferential marketing means scanning the desires and needs of your target audience by getting inside the minds of your prospects and understanding their world. Brands will need to create the perfect marketing mix to reach customers at the right time, and across every device with relevant content.

Here, product is one of the most significant factors to retain the customer as it establishes quality. Marketing and branding may attract a lot of shoppers, but if the assortment is not right, they may not convert and also may not make a return visit to the store. Here one thing that is to be noted is, value is created through the marketing mix that includes the product as one component. Today's consumers are well traveled and observing the evolution of retail

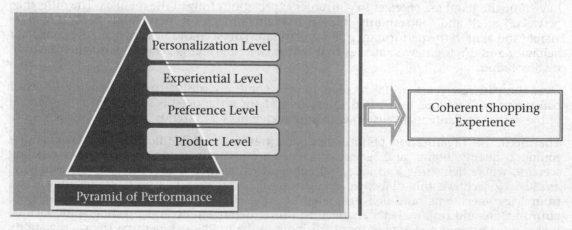

Figure 11.1: *Pyramid of Performance at Four Levels*

internationally; the demand made by them in India has also evolved with greater expectations. They have access to information at the click of a button and are well aware of price. They are no more reluctant to discussing with strangers the merits of a product or service online, and they are not even afraid to criticize what is not good and of value. Although consumer preferences have changed with time, they still buy products high on value. In a nutshell, competition is high, expectations are even higher, and a strong value proposition is a must.

Other than CRM data, companies are also experimenting with behavior data within the store to uncover actionable customer preference insights. This enables them to devise a comprehensive, cohesive, and cross-functional implementation strategy to improve the performance and win loyalty. Newer technologies have come up that create opportunities to provide superior value propositions.

FabFurnish.com targets urbane homemaker, in the age group of 26–45 years, who is tech savvy, well informed, and has a taste for good living. The online retailer in furniture and home-improvement segment claims its customer satisfaction rate to be around 90%. This level of customer satisfaction is attributed to the practice of seeking regular feedback from customers after every purchase, across products, customer service, new features, and offers. It eventually uses the inputs derived from feedback to make likewise changes, whenever necessary, so as to offer a better shopping experience. They extensively engage with customers through social platforms such as Facebook, Twitter, Google+ and Instagram. The top management regularly conducts customer interviews, mystery shopping, and similar initiatives to identify improvement areas. This approach enables the retailer to keep on adding products with new design attributes and functionality benefits. It helps them further to discontinue the non-appealing merchandise items and hence keep them abreast with the latest designs and technology that is congruent with the demands of their target consumers. The retailer successfully identifies niches that are not easily available off-line, which helps it to create differentiation and enhance customer satisfaction and in turn increase loyalty.

The Preferential and Experiential Retailing

Everything from acquiring new customers to reengagement with dormant customers and existing active customers will mean that brands can market to individuals based on real insight. Hence as retailers, they deal with inspiration, emotion, and sensory-based aesthetic products. This demands that these retailers to provide their target customer with information that helps them better understand their own world. They deliver them value and preference, "preference … is built over time." *We cannot buy preference; we need to earn it.*

Entering into new markets is challenging for unknown brands, but by focusing on the market they want to reach and those customers' *preferences*, they can find the right marketing strategy and marketing mix to work with.

For example, Marks & Spencer has updated its iPhone app with My Offers, which will offer customers exclusive content and deals relevant to their shopping preferences.

Traditionally, businesses have been structured in various functions or silos like the marketing department, customer service, buying, merchandising, finance, HR, and sales. So what is required is nothing less than a fundamental change in how businesses think and work and to orient entire operations and functions toward building a customer-centric organization. Retail organizations need to look afresh at what the customer journey looks like today, how customers *engage* with brands, and how they can fulfill their needs in a meaningful way to gain sustainable loyalty. Increasing adoption of technology by consumers has compelled the retailers to review and revisit the ease of use of technology in stores to cater the new connected consumer. Retailers are meticulously mapping out the customers' journey, which essentially involves stepping into their shoes to know exactly where they are engaging with the brand and then ensuring that the customer experience is flawless, simple, effective, and elegant. This eventually leads to improved in-store and online conversion and enhanced customer *experience* with their offerings and brand. Hence, technology is becoming instrumental in helping the retailers for extending a preferred approach to customers and to create a seamless shopping experience that works as one to fulfill the needs of modern customers.

This kind of experiential marketing is increasingly turning out to be a new brand-building tool for retailers all over the world. Experiential marketing is fast gaining currency for high-engagement categories, namely apparels and luxury lifestyle products/services. Advertising is increasingly becoming very expensive and is like carpet bombing. However, there is a direct correlation between higher level of customer engagement with brand to conversion and preference for the brand.

Experiential marketing primarily focuses on motivating, luring, and helping consumers to experience a product, brand, service, and so on with the aim to create a memorable and emotional connection between the consumer and the brand. This is where customers are treated as both rational and emotional individuals who seek "experiences" from products. The key is to engage customers in a memorable experience around the product/service, developing a relationship with customers, and creating an affinity with them. To catch the public's eye in a marketplace overflowing with choice, forward-looking retailers are giving people more exciting things to see and do in their store, positioning shopping as a leisure "experience." The central aim of experiential marketing is to create an emotional attachment between the brand and the customer.

Take an example of Spice Retail, which recently launched India's first smartphone spa, a one-stop destination that offers customization, accessories, and servicing of handsets, irrespective of brand. The smartphone spa claims to offer high level of customer experience, engagement, and swift service by trained mobile engineers who act as and called as smartphone therapists. Spice Retail has also developed the service menu designed on the lines of a typical spa brochure and offers services as deep body cleansing, screen guard facial, fresh skin rejuvenation, and holistic healing services.

Experiential marketing works best when it acts as a showcase for something that is already there in the brand. Gucci, Louis Vuitton, and Vertu provide this experience through their unique product image and features, their outstanding service, their exclusive retail environment, their pricing, their selective channels of distribution, and complete with their distinct packaging. But above all, the benefits associated with their unique brand images. To promote a product to the high market, it is important that the customers have the right experience so that the desired feelings, images, and perspectives become linked with the product/service and their marketing program. Here, experiential marketing comes into picture as it reaches to the opinion leaders, who are the innovators and early adopters in the category. They act as prime influencers, the enthusiasts, who in today's retailing scenario—in the context of changing buying behavior, with online retailing and social networking—are more important than ever. They create a viral buzz that quickly reaches a wider audience. This is a very effective and equally sustainable strategy to build brands beyond conventional route of advertising.

Increasing technology adoption in-store has also allowed retailers to provide store associates with detailed product information, real-time updating on stocks and inventories, and access to the product experts, which they can further pass on to the customers and serve them effectively. The mobile devices such as iPads and tablets are proliferating and can serve both as an easy-to-browse catalog that is updated on real-time basis and a POS device, to provide personalized assistance to the customers.

For example, consider the Apple Store, which has changed the landscape of how we shop these days. Apple Store associates are using mobile POS to bill the payments and provide customers with e-mail receipts of the transaction. There is no central cash register, but stores have roaming sales assistants, an interactive genius bar, and an EasyPay self-checkout instead. All this makes for a much more engaging experience, and it is fair to say that the Apple Store has become, for many, the main destination in a shopping trip. Faced with increased online retail competition and witnessing the success of the retail innovations introduced by the Apple Store, brands are intending to transform the retail shopping experience by enhancing the in-person retail experience. This trend is now referred to as "experiential retailing."

Augmented Reality: For Enhanced Online Shopping Experience

The ubiquitous use of smartphones, tables, laptops, and desktops has contributed to the rapid growth of online retailing and also the mobile retailing. Though the online shopping is gaining momentum, it has some limitations vis-à-vis traditional off-line shopping at brick-and-mortar stores. Naturally, the biggest challenge for online retailers is to bridge the gap between customer and the merchandise experience. The gap is created as the consumer cannot touch–feel–experience the merchandise, the way she or he can do in the case of shopping off-line. Here the technologies like augmented reality, virtual reality, and 3D technologies are bridging the gap by enhancing online shopping experience.

Augmented reality enables the online retailers to deliver 3D visualization and enhances interaction by letting consumer select merchandise item, examining them from all possible angles. This technology enables the consumer to move (rotate) the merchandise object virtually for better view. This eventually creates a compelling digital replacement of a physical interaction. For instance, if a consumer wants to buy sunglasses online, the augmented reality technology helps them to see themselves virtually wearing those glasses displayed and then to choose the most suitable design option.

Let us consider the example of Mad Street Den, a Chennai-based start-up that helps online retailers to display apparel that is exactly what customers are looking for, when they click and upload a picture of a preferred garment on the search engine of the website. The technology empowers a site to recognize the cut, color, texture, and gender of the apparel and help it to instantly bring back similar results using a mix of artificial intelligence and computer vision. This type of technology requires new user behavior, which is very difficult thing to develop and which is one of the main reasons why they chose the e-commerce field to start with, because incorporating this technology into the online stores would demand only an extension of the existing user behavior rather than creating a new one.

Similarly, a user can try an apparel item virtually with these technologies and broadly imitate the experience of a brick-and-mortar retail store. Here a virtual person wears the apparels, as if it is displayed on a mannequin in brick-and-mortar store. This enhances the merchandise experience and helps the buyer to take right and more confident purchase decision.

The point is to make the customer purchase once and for all, and not depend on the "trial and error" or "gut feeling" method. This is happening not only in the case of products like clothing and apparel but also across the categories like furniture and home décor. Furniture and home-improvement category is emerging as a significant segment in online space. For instance, online furniture retailers like Lamya & Tanya's and Urban Ladder are also leveraging augmented reality applications in order to enhance the experience of buying furniture on their portal. Urban Ladder has developed an augmented reality mobile app, named as "Living

Spaces." The app allows consumers to view in real-time virtual life-size models of furniture in their homes. That is, when we walk into an empty house, we can visualize how we want it to be exactly even before we buy it, all with a click of a button. Urban Ladder has also launched "UL Labs," an initiative for digital start-ups to develop virtual reality technology for them.

Virtual reality allow the consumer to see a panoramic view of a sofa set with center and end tables, for instance, and augmented reality allow the consumer to place the entire set of sofa into their hall to see how well it fits with the rest of the background. This is the beauty and functionality of this technology, which is being used by these online retailers to provide a unique shopping experience to their target audience.

For example, online furniture marketplace Pepperfry has developed a visualization tool for their users. With several other retailers, IKEA is also using such technologies on their online portals that allow the users to choose a sofa virtually, change its color, design, or styling. It also allows the consumers to view it in different areas of their home. HomeLane, another online portal, launched a virtual reality device "Kaleido," which is provided free to customers to "try" furnishing options.

Along with online retailers, the traditional brick-and-mortar retailers are also increasingly coming up with such technologies to create more compelling experience and to encourage shoppers to complete the purchase decision in the store itself. The strategic objective of using such technologies by the off-line retailers is to counter the showrooming trend among the consumers, wherein the consumer touch–feel–view experience the merchandise in physical stores but buys it online, to get a better offer.

Hybrid Shopping Experience

The Gen Y wants seamless shopping experience, irrespective of the touch point they use to connect with brands. These new shoppers are also referred as SOLOMO, and they are very much linked to the Internet. They use social media to find out about brands and products and also get opinions from friends before making a purchase. So inspired by the insight that these consumers prefer shopping with friends and family in stores and do not enjoy the same companionship when they shop online. Flipkart launched a new chat feature called Ping. Built within the Flipkart app, this feature allows users to talk to their friends and share product images while shopping.

These consumers extensively use their smartphones and tablets to search information about products or brands before buying it. So the retailers need to think on how to connect and engage with them. They also need to study consumer behavior and leverage new and emerging technology to engage with them in this fast-moving environment.

Hence, a retailer brand must perform at an experiential level as well, that is, the emotional value of the brand the consumers buy into—beyond what the product *is* to what it *represents*. Going forward, the world of retail is rapidly heading toward an omni-channel marketing. E-commerce and brick-and-mortar stores will have to coexist. Smart omni-channel marketing is about understanding your consumers' tastes, preferences, and matching the products and overall shopping experience according to their requirements and convenience. This enables the consumers to shop seamlessly, online and off-line. The stores are getting digitized. Here the consumer will just key in the size and design that she or he want, and an app will help her or him to get exactly what she or he is looking for.

For example, L'Oreal Makeup Genius is a mobile app that allows consumers to upload their picture and virtually try makeup looks, receive suggestions, and purchase products for these looks. This helped L'Oreal bring its in-store customer experience online. Similarly, Myntra, through its app, informs the customers about new trends and even makes recommendations based on their past purchases.

Brick-and-mortar stores will become more like showrooms where the shoppers will experience a brand, and they could be buying it online. Many retailers are establishing an omni-channel capability across brands and formats. All formats will be getting digitized soon.

For example, a leading sportswear retailer announced that it would let its shoppers order merchandise online from its stand-alone stores. The revenues would eventually be split between the e-commerce partner and the franchisee from where the order has been placed. Their clear omni-channel strategy that allows revenue sharing will have a strong impact on delivering a coherent brand experience to consumers.

It is not only Gen Y that is tech savvy. Technology impacts nearly every consumer, not just in how they acquire information about brands and how they choose to buy but also in how their use of technology has influenced their psychology. For one thing, we simply get bored more easily and desire richer, more engaging experiences and products. So, brands need to "ramp up" everything that they do—more product turnover, more exciting campaigns, more intense and largely visual messaging and so forth. It heightens the authenticity of a brand message and reinforces the brand differentiation.

For example, the off-line retailers are creating a virtual platform for shoppers at their brick-and-mortar stores. These are the latest trends that brands are incorporating to entice customers. They are hiring technology start-ups to bridge the gap between online and off-line retailing. The features like "virtual reality," "unlimited product stock," "similar searches," or "related products" options are being introduced. From Satya Paul, Being Human, Walmart, Nike, USPA, Bata to Freecultr, almost all off-line retailers are trying to give customers the advantages that online retailers offer. These technology-based solutions, gadgets, and tablet-like devices installed in the store allow customers to browse across the categories. This happens in the similar way if they would be browsing an e-commerce portal. It also allows customers to mix and match various products and view; how they would look in the ensemble. For instance, they can see how a shirt and trouser would look if paired together. Technology is gradually changing the world into virtual reality. For instance, in the world of modern luxury, it is not all digital, but it is human touch that plays the decisive role. Luxury fashion brands, like Hermès and Louis Vuitton, build and design flagship stores that are exceptionally beautiful, where the consumer can actually like to just browse around before they buy. Hence, those are emotional places indeed. Even for younger tech-savvy customers, this side of a retailer brand is extremely important to connect with them as they want seamless integration between the physical side and the digital side. Hence, today we can see that consumers have already become omni-channel. They are using several "digital and connected" devices such as mobile, tablet, and laptop to connect with the retailers, which means consumers will be entering and exiting multiple channels at different points in time. So in this scenario, the retailers need to ensure sharing of the data effectively and efficiently among various departments and functions such as customer support team, marketing, and store managers. All of them need to collaborate to orchestrate an omni-channel user experience. Here technology industry is playing a key role in the transformation. The brick-and-mortar retailers have realized the need for omni-channel offerings, and they have started working in this direction by investing more on technology and omni-channel strategies to take on the growing threat from e-tailers. The omni-channel strategy implies that a retailer's customers get the same buying experience and treatment in both physical stores, online and through mobile devices. It requires significant investment in the back end to tie in inventory and logistics to make it work.

Hence, in today's ever-connected multi-device world, more and more retailer brands are striving to adopt an omni-channel strategy. The brands that blur the lines between online and off-line channels will truly be successful. The retailer brands like Titan's Helios, Louis Philippe, Future Group, and Lawrence & Mayo work with Nifty Window, whose technology allows brick-and-mortar stores to display their inventory online, and update the inventory information and make offers in real time. The Future Group has partnered with SAP to drive its omni-channel venture. Shoppers Stop, Reliance Retail, Pantaloons, and Tata Group are investing to acquire the slice of online shopping space by providing the omni-channel experience to their customers. Hence, the hybrid retail concept is nothing but a place where people "live" and are not at the store just to purchase or shop. It is a place that invites people to stay a little bit longer, offers additional services to the consumer, and eventually provides them with coherent shopping experience. For example, apparel brand Weatherproof has opened its concept store in New York. Here, almost no products are available for sale. The central idea is to recreate an apartment ambience for brand loyal customers and allow them to have a good time within that space—watching television, chatting in large comfortable sofas, sipping a coffee, and so on. Similarly, on the service side, Sephora Boutique uses mobile devices for payments with personal shopper assistance.

Personalization

Retailing today is undergoing enormous change. Competition has never been as fierce, and the complexity of doing business never greater, but retailers have the chance to prosper as well if they focus on what makes their business possible: the individual consumer. The phenomenon of personalization can be understood across different perspectives like consumer technology, business, and human psychology.

With the proliferation of globalization, we have entered a new era of mass personalization of products and services. This has resulted in the rise of an ecosystem that is essentially empowering the consumer, who is now truly "the king." In this digital age, the invention of wireless Internet and mobile applications has led the entire world of retailing to an information revolution where the hitherto universal principle of "one size fits all" is being rejected by the New Age consumers. This is particularly true for the so-called millennial consumers who embrace products or services based on their novelty value and desire a personal experience. On the other hand, the new digital tools are facilitating digital imagination of businesses, and also corresponding reduction in the cost of acquiring technologies. From the business perspective, those acts fast and embrace personalized retailing strategies now are poised to be tomorrow's greatest success stories, and expectation setters for the future. So personalization is being driven by customer engagement, which leads to increased customer patronage loyalty and eventually helps the brand to gain higher market share and mindshare. On the human psychology perspective side, personalization resonates with the intrinsic human needs and expectations to feel engaged, and it can be fulfilled by involving them in the creation of product or services. When customers get involved, they get more engaged with the brand and its offerings, which eventually make them see more value in that product or service.

One thing that is essential for customization is the availability of demographic information of consumers. So, here e-retailers have upper hand to their off-line counterparts with the resources to obtain consumer's demographic information, behavioral patterns, and preferences by using the tools like data analytics. E-retailers are utilizing these information resources and providing customized offerings, intelligent analytics-based product suggestions and so on. Amazon today is setting consumers' expectation that all retailers have to compete with. Its explosive growth is due in large part to its commitment to positive customer experiences. It has been the leader in website personalization, tailored e-mail recommendations, over-the-top shipping responsiveness, and other customer-facing innovations and has been rewarded with ever-increasing customer loyalty.

One thing that Amazon does very well is personalizing the shopping experience to each user. While browsing Amazon's home page you will see different sections such as "Related to Items You've Viewed," "Inspired by Your Shopping Trends," and "Recommendations for You in...." Amazon knows that the more relevant the product is to the user, the more likely the users will purchase.

There are some key things brick-and-mortar retailers can learn from online sites, and vice versa is also true. This is a gold mine of opportunity for retailers. In September 2008, the reinforced "Giordano Ladies" focused on a select segment—the "office ladies, but dressier" market, with 46 "Giordano Ladies" shops in Hong Kong, Taiwan, Singapore, Malaysia, Indonesia, and China offering personalized and exceptional service as one of its core offerings. Among other things, the employees were trained to memorize names of regular customers and recall their past purchases. In a nutshell, customers want the easy sorting, fast price comparisons, inventory transparency, and ratings capabilities in stores. They want to go to a store, want to touch merchandise, and make immediate purchases, but they find the experience very (time) consuming because it is less interesting and slow compared to online shopping. There are many platforms that can be incorporated into brick-and-mortar stores such as the digital signage, interactive ratings devices, faster checkout, and many of the other things that consumers like about online shopping. The retailers that do this and act toward personalization of product and/or experience—even in a minimal way—are truly admired by consumers.

We need to understand some important points:

1. Shoppers expect that their favorite retailers understand them and know their preferences, tastes, and interests. According to a recent research, consumers are more likely to purchase from a retailer again if that retailer provided them with offers targeted to their interests, wants, or needs.
2. While consumers expect personalization, they do not expect to have to tell retailers what they want. This sounds like a paradox, but it is not. Consumers are pretty astute, and they recognize that retailers already have a wealth of data on them, including recent online and off-line transactions, user-generated reviews, blogs, e-mail logs, and other online interactions.
3. Consumers may not know how this data should be used, but they know that this data can and should be used by a retailer to know them better.
4. Personalizing the retail experience—whether it is greeting customers as they walk through store doors, having products recommended online based on customers' tastes and interests, or tailoring deals based on previous purchase behavior—is critical for cultivating loyalty. And loyal customers are the crux of a retailer's success.
5. While targeting customers over multiple channels, brands need a complete picture of their shopper. Many retailers are now trying to take a single customer view, ensuring that the pieces of their marketing campaign are working more efficiently together.
6. The use of first- and third-party data to "super" target the customer base will grow in the coming years so that brands can change the way they engage with customers as individuals.
7. The past few years we have seen the rapid rise of personalization in marketing, with brands using data in increasingly sophisticated ways to develop tailored content and target customers based on their preferences and online behavior.
8. Though it is difficult to provide personalized experience if you have millions of customers, it is a critical deviation—because if you do not do it, your competitor will.

Today, consumers' almost insatiable appetite for technology is continuing to blur the lines between brick-and-mortar stores and online shopping. As a part of this change, the retailers, along London's Regent Street, have designed a smartphone app that is linked with beacon technology, or small transmitters that interact with mobile devices. As people shop and/or move around the Regent Street, which houses brands like Hugo Boss, Barbour, and Karl Lagerfeld, their cell phones receive messages from the stores that they passed, offering online promotions, product information and/or reminders, and other sales-related information. This Regent Street app is developed by autoGraph, a Seattle-based digital marketing company. They have installed sensors at their entrances that can communicate directly with nearby phones and other mobile devices carrying the app. App users must select what type of information they want to receive, and the technology allows brands to build a detailed profile of customers who redeem online special offers, respond to mobile advertising, and even enter the physical stores. Such data, until recently, were available only to online retailers, which typically have greater access to consumers' digital information. If the retailer ping people with messages indiscriminately, it quickly becomes a frustrating spam, but if it is selective, the retailer can build up level of trust directly with each consumer. This is just one example of the changes in luxury retailers approach to consumers.

For many retailers, the push comes in response to the growth of luxury e-tailers such as Net-a-Porter and Yoox, which have taken the online retail techniques pioneered by Amazon and eBay and have brought them to the business of fashion retailing. This can just be called as the *beginning of retail revolution*, and in the future, there will not be any differences between physical and online retailing. Retailers are investing more resources in new campaigns and products that interact with shoppers and adopting a "personal touch" to promote their private-label ranges and their company brand as a whole.

Another recent example that is really impressing is from German drugstore DM. Taking a different approach, it linked up with ProduktDesigner to create "Foto Paradies," a website that allows consumers to design their own packaging across a range of private-label products. Shoppers were able to change the text on bottles and even include photos, bringing excitement to the category. This scheme took personalization to new levels, allowing shoppers to create products that are completely unique to them.

Leveraging the Technology

At a time when online shopping is catching up the momentum by using the cutting-edge technology, the brick-and-mortar retail brands have also geared up to attract the shoppers to their physical spaces. They are increasingly looking at leveraging technology to customize and even personalize their offerings and thereby adding the unique appeal to the off-line shopping experience. For instance, fashion retailing is one of the happening spaces in terms of customization and personalization.

For example, Pepe Jeans has brought the concepts of "Custom Studio" and "Magic Mirror" to its brick-and-mortar store, which enables the consumers to customize designs and embellishments for their denims that include using laser technology to print messages in a few minutes. The "Magic Mirror" captures multiple images of the products as consumers try them on and help them compare the looks on one screen.

Burberry, the British heritage label, is acknowledged in the fashion world as a leader in digital outreach. In September 2014, its customers watching a live stream of its runway show to order items directly through Twitter. Since Burberry opened its flagship store on Regent Street, it has been refining in-store features in an art deco (44,000-sq. ft space). Almost all the items on sale are tagged with small microchips that interact with monitors around the store to display extra information about the coats, bags, and dresses. When prospective customer enter the store's trial rooms, videos of the apparel they are trying on seem to appear magically on floor-to-ceiling screens, along with more photos/images of the product. This experience plays a vital role in converting a prospect into a buyer. Companies such as Ralph Lauren, for example, have created smartphone apps that allow users to customize their own cloths and makeup and then share the items on social media, large monitors at the brand's stores around the world, and even on interactive billboards in places like Times Square in New York.

Hence, these retailers are increasingly investing in technology for making the physical outlets more vibrant by providing enhanced shopping experience and brand engagement. Here, they are leveraging the technology and strategically bridging the gap between the online and off-line models.

Caselet: Vertu

One can buy a watch for few hundred rupees, yet one is willing to spend several thousands and lakhs for a luxury watch. It is the same with cars. One can get a basic model, which will get him/her from one place to another, but not as lavishly and luxuriously as a Ferrari. So people who inhibit "that space" want to be different. They generally appreciate the finer things in life. And Vertu believes that there is a place for a telephone in that as well. Within the Vertu life, they have privileges such as access to fashion shows, or hard-to-get tickets for sporting events, music concerts, and so on. When you pack all these services together, it is very unique in the marketplace, and it hits the right spots with the right type of audience.

Vertu is a new unique luxury brand specializing in top-of-the-range, deluxe mobile phones. For its parent company, Nokia, the Vertu brand is/was a different business game. Nokia was the world's most successful mobile phone manufacturer developed this new brand as a way of creating an exclusive luxury brand in mobile telephony. It was a strange move in that Nokia does not publicize the linkage between Nokia and Vertu, and therefore does not gain from any brand linkages or associations. In essence, their products are jewelry-like mobile telephones. Vertu headquarters is located in the UK with several offices situated worldwide, including Paris, New York, Hong Kong, and Singapore. As Vertu was a new entrant to the market, their main focus has been on creating product awareness among the elite and to create a brand that is exclusive and luxurious. Vertu utilizes craftsmanship, precision engineering, high-end technology, and a unique personal service dimension, to create a distinctive luxury brand.

A big selling point associated with these phones is the Vertu Concierge service. Vertu Concierge provides specialized travel assistance, allowing users to access and reserve restaurants, hotels, concert tickets, and much more. Having a Vertu mobile phone allows users to access this exclusive concierge service, 24 hours a day from anywhere in the world, where they will try to assist the every whim of the user. Vertu also offers a customization service, thus truly differentiating itself and allowing the firm to earn even higher margins. Also the company offers free upgradeability when new technology emerges, such as color screens and Bluetooth. Vertu phones are also available to purchase through their website. With the aid of this distribution channel, customers can now personalize their mobile phone to their own individual tastes. By offering a first-class personal service combined with extensive product knowledge, Vertu has enhanced their image of reliability and expertise.

Caselet: Arvind Limited

Arvind Limited is the manufacturer of garments under brands such as Flying Machine, Colt, and Excalibur. The company also has retail brands such as Megamart, Next, and Club America. In near future, Arvind Internet, the online arm from Arvind textiles, is in the process of launching several business models under its e-commerce foray. The company has announced the launch of Creyate.com, which uses the omni-channel strategy, including online, off-line, and kiosks.

With Creyate.com, Arvind Internet is trying to merge personalization and mass consumption. As personalization is global phenomenon, they are trying to use the latest technology to give users the personalized products, and they have a factory at their disposal that company has built and that can provide thousands of designs in a day. It is also supported by an automated warehouse that takes care of the delivery. User by using creyate.com can schedule a home visit with Creyate's "Style Stewards." These Style Stewards not only take a customer's measurements but also give them style and design advice and also guide them the complete wardrobe solutions. These Style Stewards are well trained and have good experience in retail. Other than a home visit, consumers can also avail of Creyate retail outlets, which are on the lines of Apple Store(s). At Creyate, users can get access to fabric that Arvind provides or even opt for international brands. Arvind Limited is also the authorized seller of products of several global brands such as Arrow, Elle, and US Polo Assn, and has a JV in India with Tommy Hilfiger. Similarly, Van Heusen's My Fit concept brings a unique personalized experience to its customers by allowing them to order online after visiting an outlet to check for fit and feel.

Caselet: LVMH

LVMH stands to serve the taste and preferences of premium brand lovers, and it serves its purpose by catering "preferentially" to these market demands. The famous brand started out back in the 1850s. The founder was made famous for crafting the luggage for Napoleon. From these roots the brand has become synonymous with luggage and in particular handbags. Louis Vuitton is very much the envy of the industry, is famous for its handbags, but also sells a range of wallets, briefcases, eyeglass cases, and so on. In recent years, the brand has tried to modernize its image by utilizing the talents of young designers and artists in rejuvenating the image of some of their products while maintaining the classic designs. This reinvention has attracted younger buyers into the brand. However, no one designer for Louis Vuitton has eclipsed the powerful brand image of Louis Vuitton itself, unlike other design brands.

LVMH conducts marketing exercise on the basis of requirements of the target segments and the brand. It is indeed not made by masses, and its target audience is the upper segment of the society. But it is believed that this norm is applicable for all true-blue luxury labels in the world, which focus only on certain segments or a niche of the market. They are their preferred customers, and they work on the business philosophy that apart from low purchase products, everybody has a certain target audience, where they act in a preferential way and want their offerings to do well.

Louis Vuitton stands out from its peers through its relentless focus on product quality. All products are extensively tested to make sure that they can withstand wear and tear, and that there are no imperfections. The company has blended mechanization and handmade craftsmanship into their products, boosting their productivity, maintaining that high level of product quality, while still holding on to the allure of handmade quality.

Louis Vuitton's quality emphasis the following requirements:

1. Extensive laboratory equipment test products (e.g., opening and closing zippers 5,000 times).
2. Leather is sourced from Northern Europe, as they tend to have fewer insect bites, thus less blemishes.
3. The company offers a lifetime repair guarantee.
4. Integrates manufacturing initiatives such as "quality circles" in the production process.

To perform on the personalization level, the company offers customized products such as personal engraving on hand luggage pieces, boosting its appeal further. Furthermore, the company sponsors elite sporting events such as yachting and motorsport events. This is in effort to match the audience of sponsorship property with the target audience of the brand itself.

In India too, this market is growing phenomenally well. This is also tempting luxury brands from all over the world to foray into India. For example, the elite watches market is growing at an awesome rate, and for a brand like Tag Heuer, they target not only the elite class but also "generation next" who can afford such price levels. So depending on the product & brand, LVMH preferentially adopts a strategy.

The Way Forward: Future of Retail

The Retail Industry Is in the Midst of a Customer Revolution

The collision of the virtual and physical worlds is fundamentally changing consumers' purchasing behaviors. Consumers are seeking an integrated shopping experience across all channels, and expect retailers to deliver this experience. Failure to deliver puts retailers at risk of becoming irrelevant. The key drivers of this customer revolution are the rapid adoption of mobile devices, digital media, and tablets equipped with shopping apps. Traditional retailers must find opportunities to seamlessly embed the virtual world into their retail strategy by developing in-store and online technologies that allow them to create and maintain meaningful and sincere connections with customers across all channels.

The Future of Retail Has Arrived

The retail paradigm has shifted from a single physical connection point with customers to a multipronged approach that crosses both physical and digital channels. The traditional bricks-and-mortar retail store is no longer the dominant medium for purchasing goods. Instead, it serves as one of many potential connection points between customers and a retailer's brand. As one industry observer has noted, "While physical stores may have once enjoyed the advantage of crafting cool shopping experiences, the aesthetics of the iPad and all the social sharing surrounding online shopping today are now shifting that advantage to online retailers." However, many retailers are struggling to take advantage of the increasing number of channels available to them for connecting with customers. Further, they are neglecting to make appropriate investments in technology, operations, and talent that would better equip them for seizing control of these channels. Retailers' technology can be disparate and fragmented, and multiple physical locations can drive an unsustainable cost structure that is not flexible and often underperforms. Additionally, employees often lack the knowledge, training, and tools necessary to facilitate a shopping experience that engages customers across a variety of channels and extends beyond the traditional shopping experience. As a result, many retailers are falling behind in the race to offer a unique and comprehensive experience with their brand that keeps pace with customers' ever-evolving attitudes and expectations.

Retailers are faced with the challenge of engaging customers on more than just price. They must make shopping across all channels a more stimulating and satisfying experience, rather than simply a way to find the lowest price for a particular product. New competitors are disrupting the market and capturing valuable market share through innovative business models. Many companies are now seeking to become vertically integrated by controlling the whole supply chain. As a result of a vertically integrated value chain, a new generation of e-commerce players is bringing high-quality products from the warehouse directly to consumers at significantly lower prices. Hence, retailers must respond to new competition by enabling digital experiences that improve both the store and virtual experience for the customer. Equally important, they must find a path to success that not only addresses the needs of their customers today but also flexible enough to continually evolve with customer interests and expectations. The customer revolution and the future of retail have arrived. Retailers must respond now or risk facing obsolescence.

Retail's Path to Relevance

Adopt a Single Strategy and Vision Across Channels

Today's consumers are increasingly connected to both the physical and digital space and able to interact with retailers through multiple channels simultaneously. To stay competitive in this ever-evolving landscape, it is imperative for retailers to deliver a seamless customer experience across all channels and provide the right services and products at the right time. Specifically, retailers must develop an integrated strategy that aligns talent, physical space, processes, marketing, and merchandising to meet consumer demands. This strategy should be supported by emerging technologies and continually adapted to remain relevant to the customer of tomorrow.

A robust retail strategy must include:

1. A strong vision of the experience the customer desires across all channels.
2. A nimble operating model that can adapt as the retail environment changes.
3. A deep understanding of how to support the vision through inventive digital solutions and retail technologies, such as playbooks, to operationalize the omni-channel strategy.

Creating a Relevant Customer Experience

The transformation of the retail store begins with a deep understanding of the customer and a strategy to personalize the experience at every point of interaction. The most appropriate technologies should be leveraged to enhance the experience in both the physical store and digital world.

Mobile commerce is an important channel for many retailers; however, its application can and should be extended from merely an online sales alternative to a tool that drives meaningful connections between the brand and the consumer. Social commerce is another critical part of the customer experience, and digitally savvy retailers will devote task forces to supporting their social media strategy. Proper management of Facebook, Twitter, and other media is vital. To keep customers engaged, retailers should also consider including a social element in their mobile apps. The successful retailers will maintain locally relevant Facebook, Twitter, and other social media pages, and will also look to the next big development in social media.

How Do Retailers Prepare?

Investing in the Core

Addressing today's connected consumers may require structural changes to the retail organization in order to deliver a seamless experience across channels and drive competitive differentiation for your brand. The key is flexibility. With the increasing occurrence of channel overlap and the pace at which new applications and devices are brought to market, the future leaders of retail will be those who can quickly embrace operational changes brought about by new technologies and anticipate integration of emerging solutions that have not yet been invented. A flexible IT infrastructure needs to integrate existing and emerging applications and devices, and should be channel agnostic. With 60% of smartphone owners reporting their use in in-store shopping, retailers that invest early in flexibility and in aligning their business around the customer, rather than the channel, can become leaders in an environment in which it is becoming increasingly harder to play catch-up.

For example, online marketplace portal Snapdeal.com acquired Doozton.com in 2014. Doozton.com is an online—social product discovery technology—platform in the fashion and lifestyle category that helps people search trending products and designs from online stores.

Doozton.com provides fashion and lifestyle product suggestions that include clothes, shoes, and accessories for men and women. The technology platform earned popularity among its users by making shopping not only easy and social but also entertaining and fun.

The technology developed by Doozton.com provides a personalized and artful way of listing and suggesting fashion merchandise on Snapdeal. Hence, it is very helpful for not only buyers but also sellers on the platform. On the other hand, the technology of Doozton. com gets a wider and more established platform like Snapdeal, which provide a much larger canvas for their objective of enabling intuitive and fun merchandising of fashion products. This eventually enhances the overall shopping experience.

Constant Performance Evaluation

There is no silver bullet or single solution. Retailers must commit to making change the "new normal" in their operating model, and this means continual evaluation and analysis of their business to determine if they are delivering on the customer experience. Thorough collection and analysis of customer data will give retailers the best chance to understand, anticipate, and adapt to the continuous change that comes with the connected consumer. Information is king, and the use of predictive analytics can help retailers gain deeper insight into the value that is being generated for their customers through their own operating model, and provide them with leading indicators of the experience desired by the constantly evolving connected consumer. While online retailers are growing with the help of technology and analytics that help them analyze and understand consumer behavior better, the brick-and-mortar retailers have so far had limited data that they could use. However, the situation is changing with physical retailers increasingly using targeted advertising, analytics, and other innovative methods to get customer data.

For example, Lifestyle International, a multi-brand department retailer, has over five million members under its loyalty program, which is branded as "The Inner Circle." The off-line retailer has roped in a technology firm for an analytics solution. This technological support enabled Lifestyle International to obtain further insights into the shopper behavior. Using analytics, they track consumer purchase behavior through their credit card, e-mail address, or mobile number and use the information to target precisely only those customers who are likely to respond to a promotional campaign. These inputs help them to design and develop customized offers, accurately evaluate the impact of their promotions, and even create opportunities to cross-sell their product categories on the basis of shoppers' history. With this focused effort to increase cross-selling and creating customized offers, the retailer can increase the basket size and frequency of visits of the customers, resulting in increase in the revenues and the loyalty behavior, respectively.

For instance, if someone is regularly buying their in-house brands like "Code" shirt and "Forca" denim, with the help of analytics, the technology solution can predict what is he most likely to buy next and the retailer can then target the customer accordingly. Now these solutions can be integrated with the social media platforms as well. This eventually saves costs for the retailer who would otherwise send messages to its entire database of customers for every promotion.

Innovation

The brick-and-mortar retailers have just started warming up to the idea of technology. But many things need to be done around customer data. The loyalty programs need to be dynamic, and this is the time for retailers to push the boundaries in delivering a connected customer experience.

They can start with three key areas:

1. New talent strategies

   • Position your talent as brand ambassadors.
   • Equip them with smart gadgets/phones and train them to be technology savvy.
   • Empower them to use social media or messaging services to connect with customers.

2. Change the physical space

   • Evolve the physical space as a primary point of brand contact to one of many points of contact.
   • Embrace the virtual environment as a connection point to your brand from anywhere and at any time.
   • Transform the physical space to a compelling customer experience instead of a place to transact.

3. Emerging solutions

   • Embrace technology and be an early adopter.
   • With developments today in technology, solutions can and should be "user friendly" and have the "flexibility" to meet a "retailer's specific needs".
   • So it becomes necessary for retailers to undertake not only a thorough research on what the company needs from the technology to be deployed, but also, equally important, a thorough research on the IT partner before bringing them on board.
   • Enhance the customer experience and support sales associates in delivering desired service models.
   • Use real-time data to provide relevant real-time promotions to further personalize the shopping experience. Hence, shoppers can avail real-time deals and dynamic pricing with personalized messages from the retailer, which gives them a better shopping experience.

Caselet: Livspace

Let us discuss the example of Livspace, a Bengaluru-based online home design and décor portal, one another niche player in home furnishing segment. It is the first mover in the end-to-end home design experience and marketplace for homeowners and designers. It provides new homebuyers with select interior design for their homes through a catalog and also allows them to buy the combined sets. For building these catalogs, the company has an in-house design team and selected designers. Livspace's idea of selling complete looks for homes is disruptive, as opposed to only selling furnishings only, which has encouraged new consumer behavior.

Designing a home highly involves visual and personal experience—unlike buying a piece of chair or table online, which many furniture e-tailers offer, and by nature is typically a low-involvement buying experience—so to offer a compelling, unique, and specialized experience, a key to success in this category, Livspace acquired DezignUp—a dynamic design community and marketplace for design professionals—and Dwll—a network of interior designers and home furnishing stores. With this, Livspace uses designs, proprietary algorithm, data science technology, and in-house exclusive catalog to create numerous pictures for every home, which in turn can help homeowners visualize their homes before making an online purchase. It also acquired YoFloor, a mobile platform that offers a virtual trial room for home design decisions. The YoFloor app basically helps the users to visualize how different home designs, furniture, and furnishing items (designs and dimensions) would look like in their home. Hence, the app enables Livspace to offer high-quality home designing experience by bringing more scale and choice to homeowners supported with 3D visualization tools to in-house designers and users. This strategic acquisition is in line with the company's focus on building creative tools for their designer community. Above all, this technology offers the overall design experience on real-time basis, eliminating the hassles of lengthy exchange of frequent changes in design and feedback.

Home design in India is a huge market but has remained segmented, and according to the industry experts, there is a huge potential for innovation in this category on different fronts. First, the product itself because perfectly designed furniture customized as per the room designs/areas with good quality is not easily accessible, as about 90% of the furniture market is unorganized in India. Second, technology is drastically changing the way the product is visualized. Third, material handling, as logistics of furniture is very different because of the size and nature of the product. So the key opportunities for Livspace are to remove the pain of the customer, associated with getting one's home designed in India, and visually communicate with the customer.

The concept of an end-to-end service with a focus on personalized design, supported by technology, which reduces turnaround time and offers free design consultation throughout, is very promising. Hence, the synergies of the technology, design expertise, and execution capabilities of Livspace, coupled with the designer network and consumer-centric focus of Dwll.in's platform, make it a complete package to transform the home design space. Livspace has pioneered a unique approach, and with DezignUp and Dwll.in, it is expected to further accelerate the continuing growth and market presence.

Summary

Today, when it comes to customer experience, things have completely changed. Retailers have realized that the traditional methods are no longer sufficient and efficient because the New Age shopper demands more than ever before and wants the shopping experience to be delivered on their terms and not the brands'. Hence, it is evident that creating a unified customer brand experience is imperative for most retail businesses, especially given the nature of retail where innovation is essential and customer tastes and preferences are dynamic and fast changing. In this connected era, digitally savvy customers are expecting shopping experiences that are device agnostic, socially integrated, and consumed on the go. Creation of a standout customer experience is critical for a brand in today's marketplace because of the influx of more channels, more clutter, cutthroat competition among the players, more players crossing borders, more competitors coming out of more places and formats, and so on, so it is important than never before to offer a complete brand experience, which will make their retail business stand out and maintain its brand's differentiated positioning. Technology has emerged as a key differentiator, and retailers are leveraging data analytics as a reinforcement tool to redefine consumer experience.

Also the mass personalization is an opportunity for brands to not only develop and strengthen relationships with each customer but also make them active coproducers and partners. The capability to track a single consumer's journey across multiple devices has enabled the retailers to customize their offerings and create a loyal customer base in the long run. This strategy has the right potential for converting them into loyal brand patriarch.

Therefore, today, personalization is a source of substantial strength for brands in the future. This postulation is based on two pillars. The first is the increase in unequivocal expectations of today's millennial generation. Second is the increasing inclination of this generation toward sharing their lives on the social media. By virtue of this behavior, a vast amount of data is available to collaborate and cocreate products that offer a distinctly personalized experience. In short, personalization stands as one of the most important brand promise of them. This heightened focus on in-store experience could be a sign that the definition of successful store is changing in the retail industry.

Hence, performance of a company at all levels of the "performance pyramid" demonstrates brand confidence. This helps the retailer brand to drive brand equity and loyalty, which eventually enhance all aspects of the business value chain. It not only enhances the brand loyalty among customers but also creates sustainable differentiation.

Review Questions

1. Briefly explain the importance of loyalty program and CRM in enhancing the customer loyalty.
2. Explain the essentials for designing an effective CRM program with appropriate examples.
3. Explain the strategies for ensuring the success of a loyalty program with appropriate examples.
4. Explain how the retailers are leveraging loyalty programs and CRM programs to win back the lost customers.
5. Briefly explain the strategy the retailers are using to win back the lost customers.
6. Briefly explain the retailer's "gift card" as a business opportunity and branding tool with appropriate examples.
7. Explain the benefits of gift card to retailer and consumer.
8. Briefly explain the major factors influencing the gift card business.
9. Explain the strategic considerations for enhancing gift card business in detail.

Chapter 12

Patronage Loyalty and Customer Relationship Management

Introduction

The loyalty of customers stems from building relationships with them and that edifice of relationship have to be built on the strong foundation of patronage loyalty. A good loyalty program has the power to transform a business into a customer-centric profit machine. Every employee in an organization with a customer-centric role, right from a retail sales executive to senior managers, needs to pay attention to find new ways to add "value," and that could be achieved by additional complementary services or experiences. Here, we will discuss major factors that directly impact the success and profitability of a customer loyalty program. The objective is to increase not only customer retention but also customer lifetime value (CLV) and profitability by means of a long-lasting customer relationship.

Many researchers and consultants argue that there must be strong "attitudinal commitment" to a brand for true loyalty to exist and flourish. This is seen as taking the form of a consistently favorable set of stated beliefs and behavior toward the brand purchased. These attitudes may be measured by asking how much shoppers say they like the brand, feel committed to it, will recommend it to others, and have positive beliefs and feelings about it—relative to competing brands in the same segments. The strength of these attitudes is the key predictor of a brand's purchase and repeat patronage. This is what Oliver (1997) has in mind when he defines customer loyalty as: "A deeply held commitment to re-buy or re-patronize a preferred product/service consistently in the future, thereby causing repetitive same-brand or same brand-set purchasing despite situational influences and marketing efforts having the potential to cause switching behavior."

Loyal customers spend more, purchase more profitable products and services, try other brand offerings, and are more likely to refer customers to their preferred brand/business. In other words, loyal customers are a company's most valuable asset. It is vital for the marketing department to contribute to the profitability of the business, and it has to be able to measure and demonstrate its contribution to profits, despite the common misconception that marketing is a cost center, not a profit center, as they identify potential high-value customers and then cultivate them to become loyal consumers.

But at the same time, the marketplace is changing because of burgeoning threats from e-tailers: customers are becoming more demanding, and competition is becoming more intense. It is becoming increasingly difficult to differentiate one business from another. Technology is providing some answers, but each answer brings more choices and more decisions to be made. However, it is sensible to:

- Focus on the best customers that you already have.
- Optimize the profit that can be made from them.
- Increase the duration in which they remain customers.
- Be able to produce measurable results of success.

Every business must develop and deliver a consistently branded experience for its customers. The essence of the brand should be apparent in every interaction a customer has with the company, enabling customers to form an emotional attachment with the brand. This includes training and enabling frontline employees who interact with customers, developing high-impact marketing campaigns, defining the brand's "promise," and segmenting customers on the basis of value. The loyalty program provides a truly multichannel vehicle through which to communicate this brand experience, and through which the consumer can become more attached to the company and its brand, which in turn increases the retailer's share of wallet. In addition, new features to a loyalty program would be far more viable vis-à-vis promotional strategies over the long term, and it would help to not only retain customers but also attract new ones.

CRM and Loyalty Program

Today, customer expectations are higher than ever before, because there is so much information freely available and can be easily searched. So when a consumer enters a store, she/he may know more about the product than the person who is selling it. It is, therefore, a challenge for any business to keep up with consumers' expectations. To engage this new breed of consumers, retailers have to first understand who the customer is and segment them and try to know them at the individual level. After precisely segmenting them, target and cater them in the right way and perspective. This is nothing but the CRM. It is not only about loyalty points anymore. It is not necessarily about transactions. It is about allowing interactions to happen between the customer and the brands, and among customers. This perspective essentially distinguishes CRM and loyalty. Here, it is also essential for retailers to identify their most profitable customers—perhaps those who buy high-margin products, those who pay full price without negotiating for discounts, those who place a small number of large orders (ticket size) rather than many small orders, and do not demand extra service.

Hence, a loyalty marketing program is the continuous process of identifying and creating "new and enhanced value" with "individual customer," essentially aimed toward delivering incremental profit.

Here the first stage is to obtain insights regarding the customer behavior–preference–buying patterns through the data collected from several sources. The next stage is to engage with the target audience by leveraging the insights and realize the objective of augmented value creation for individual customer.

CRM is about communicating with customers and engaging them with the brand. Loyalty is about looking at the transactions between the consumer and brand. But those transactions need not be just related to "accumulation of points," and it can also be non-transactional. As discussed earlier, the loyalty of customers originates from building relationships with them and that edifice of relationship have to be built on the strong foundation of patronage loyalty. This is the point where CRM comes into play.

The purpose and execution of CRM and customer loyalty programs have to adapt appropriately to the changing buying behavior. If the objective of a loyalty program is to create new and increased value to grow beyond the rewards for purchase scheme to a more comprehensive solution for greater brand involvement.

Importance of a Loyalty Program

1. A well-designed and well-run loyalty program can do all of these things. But it is just one aspect of a comprehensive marketing strategy. However, if a loyalty program is used to full effect, it should be the central pillar of that marketing strategy.

2. The theory of customer loyalty is quite simple: a retailer that retains its customers for longer usually makes more revenues and profits from them at lower cost than one that is constantly paying to acquire new customers.

3. Logically that makes sense, but building customer loyalty is hard, especially when your competition is just a mouse-click away. The customer today has access to greater information and more control over the communication that reaches her/him and the channel through which she/he communicates with brands.

4. Today, consumers are exerting greater influence on other shoppers through online discussion forums, reviews, and ratings. These activities impact the marketer's brand and reputation, and yet are outside his sphere of control.

5. So the basic fundamental is to know your customers, find out what exactly motivates them to patronize your store, and only reward them for behaving in the way that you want. A loyal customer base is any retailer's biggest "asset," and it would be necessary to plan and evaluate any marketing activity in terms of contribution to a company's financial objectives.

6. Through a loyalty program, customer and transactional data can be collected, and the intelligent use of that data will provide a much clearer picture of the customer base, and this will lead to more profits from the beginning.

7. A good patronage loyalty program is quintessentially customer centric and will pay back from the very beginning. Those who have realized the value of a customer-centric approach have thrived: examples are the Tesco Clubcard program in the UK, widely regarded as one of the best and biggest loyalty program in the world, actually made money from Day One.

8. Again, the data obtained from the loyalty programs is already customer centric by its very nature, and hence the implementation of a loyalty program presents a vital opportunity to merge and integrate cross-department data silos.

Essentials for Designing an Effective CRM Program

Unlike the past, when CRM was regarded as being synonymous with huge, costly IT systems, today, retailers are accentuating more on explaining the benefits of the system to both employees and customers and streamlining meticulous processes for data collection. Some of the key errors that can cause CRM projects to fail or prevent delivery of the expected ROI are a reliance on technology as a global "cure-all" and downplaying the importance of management-level buy-in.

Loyalty program execution normally includes all forms and variety of BTL ad under it, as retailer brands engage their best set of customers. Hence, an organization will get maximum bang for the buck if it were to bring in direct marketing, events, and social media engagement budgets under the aegis of the loyalty program and utilize these to increase engagement. The list of issues to address and their span of influence while designing a loyalty program are long and wide.

Indeed, any failure to address some of the more important points could result not only in a failed program but also in unrecoverable expenses and losses, lost consumer goodwill, legal issues, and lasting brand damage. Also to ensure the long-term *relevance* of an organization among consumers, attention needs to be paid on an appropriate segmentation of shoppers, whether it is based on lifestyle or buying patterns or frequency of visits to various retail formats, among others.

Some other important issues to be handled with utmost care are loyalty program ecosystem, infrastructure, and objectives; strategy (program type, proposition, commerce, partnerships, infrastructure, etc.); objectives, key process flows, KPIs, rewards, benefits, financials, and timelines; desired behavioral changes; benefits and rewards, type, tracking, communicating, bonus and incentives, reward currency, breakage, and liability; partnership details; tiers (both thresholds and management); financial and administrative controls; legal aspects; staff requirements and training; ROI; program rules; system functionality; fulfillment process and costs; data requirements and usage; and the list goes on. Also the frequency of transaction should be recorded and measured and is a key element in designing a loyalty program.

However with the advent of new technology like data analytics and the use of information obtained from it have enabled efforts around customer loyalty to be tracked and measured where the impact of a program and ROIs are no longer a black hole. The results of this analysis combined with demographic information can provide valuable insight on a potentially large customer base, which would be viewed as key to the future growth of a retailer brand. Hence, having the correct focus and commitment can significantly improve a CRM initiative's performance.

Strategies for Ensuring the Success of Loyalty Program

The "7"-point Program

The rationale for spending on the loyalty program is that, over a period of time, organization can make their spending on marketing more effective, as they can afford to reduce the expenditure on ATL advertisements, where they are not able to measure the response. There are various elements that are critical to the long-term success of any customer loyalty or relationship marketing initiative. First, these programs are definitely not a "quick fix" for an ailing corporate bottom line. It takes time to build loyalty because loyalty is based on trust and relevance-based relationships with best customers. Precisely targeted marketing is a benefit of loyalty data, and is essential if the program is to be seen as "relevant" by its members. The metric to measure the effectiveness of the dollars spent on the loyalty program is to evaluate the average additional value that customers have contributed, post launch of the loyalty program, vis-à-vis the money spent per customer. Hence the budgeting for loyalty program should also be determined by cost per customer, assuming that the outlay will be restricted to the best set of customers.

Hence for increasing the effectiveness and throughput of the loyalty program, retailers are increasingly focusing on the following factors.

Obtaining Consumer Insights, Not Just Frequency and Number of Visit

No two customers are the same, nor do they want to be treated as such. Customers want to feel special, and to build the right loyal customer base, retailers develop offers and rewards that are tailored to their individual needs and preferences. A "loyalty program" if not designed as per the customer's expectations cannot buy true loyalty—or even repeat visits—in any lasting way. Previously, it was thought that the reward would be enough to bring customers back, time after time. But it did not take long to become apparent that they were not on the right track. Customers simply carried many loyalty cards and collected points wherever they shopped. They were just as promiscuous as before. However, the retailers started using the loyalty programs not only to increase the frequency of visits but also to obtain information from their customers in order to derive more insights about their customers. This enables them to identify the most profitable and least profitable customers, what they want or expect, and what changes or offerings would be most likely to make them truly loyal.

They can make the process of obtaining these valuable insights easier by allowing customers to choose the way, the channel, or the platform of their preference, for communication. Though e-mail remains a staple, mobile-centric programs are in vogue now, and experts suggest that let the customer choose the channel, be it e-mail, Facebook, Twitter, SMS, Pinterest, and so on. It is really important to give customers the choice because if you give them the choice, they are more likely to continue the engagement. Besides that, brands also need to focus and invest in a consistent cross-channel communication strategy. The right cross-channel strategy would involve knowing your customer and asking her/him how she/he wants to be communicated to: in-store, SMS, WhatsApp, hike, Viber, and so on. Also do not underestimate the power of social media. For instance, if a consumer likes a page on Facebook, the gesture shows that she/he wants the brand to communicate with her/him on the medium. So a brand must keep to that.

As the sales through mobile devices is growing, companies operating in the consumer loyalty program space have started replacing the plastic cards with mobile application-based trackers to make redemption of the loyalty points for online and off-line transaction easier. Such strategic move to mobile application-based loyalty program has another advantage: it opens up an alternative channel for the off-line retailers to get deeper understanding of the user behavior. Off-line retailers have realized the need to provide relevant offers to high-value customers using the loyalty app as a marketing channel. Hence, being on-app helps the brick-and-mortar retailer brands to send out the location-based push ads to consumers with offers, also to track the preference (interest) and intent of the user. To increase the adoption and to motivate the consumers to download the app, they cross-link it to their SMS notifications.

Shoppers Stop invites customers through its promotional activity of Shoppers Stop Loyalty Program. The loyal customers are called as "First Citizens" of Shoppers Stop. As one of the early adopters of digital media, Shoppers Stop also launched its First Citizen mobile application. After this initiative, their customers have to no longer carry around their plastic cards. The First Citizen mobile app (available on Android, Apple, and BlackBerry platforms) takes the First Citizen experience mobile. It offers good discount to its loyal customers through this program. The objective here is to attract more footfalls, increase revenues, and enhance the shopping experience.

Customer Acquisition by "Recognize and Differentiate" Approach

A loyalty program should act as a magnet to attract new customers to the store. How effectively it does so will depend on how exciting and how valuable the rewards are perceived by their target audience. Acquiring customers is no doubt essential to any business, but it can be expensive if compared to nurturing existing good customers. However, the quality of new customers acquired can be raised by careful use of the existing data from a loyalty program, which can be used to establish the demographic and psychographic profiles of existing "best customers," and then to target prospective customers with similar demographic and psychographic profiles in acquisition campaigns. Hence, a good understanding of customers can help both retailers and brands to increase their sales exponentially. The more they know about customers and their needs, the easier it is to identify opportunities to sell them new products and differentiate, or at times customize new offers to suit their requirements.

For instance, today the mobile technology is helping retailers to deliver more personalized communications and recommendations as they are based on an individual's profile. They also represent a way to communicate with the consumer all the way through the purchase, while remaining connected to any pre-visit behavior exhibited by the customer. This essentially enables the retailer to understand a customer's entire path to purchase and eventually to initiate a conversation with the customer, offering the right information at each stage of their decision process.

Let us consider the example of Shoppers Stop, which starts by calling its loyal customers "First Citizens." The Shoppers Stop Loyalty Program is one of the largest in the industry with over 3.5 million members who contribute to over 70% of sales annually. Shoppers Stop is successful in generating a significant amount of incremental business by simply activating insights gathered from the First Citizen data.

For instance, to capitalize on the festive shopping extravaganza during Durga Puja, it identified Bengali surnames from its First Citizen database in Bengal and in other markets. The retailer then sent a promotional offer to these shortlisted customers. The promotional offer was linked to their festive purchases. This exercise led to additional revenue to the company's top line.

Increasing the Consumer Spending

Many times, loyalty programs are symbolic. Such programs urge shoppers to collect points, but the spend-to-points ratio under such programs is not so attractive. They are often designed in a tempting way, while the true benefits are restricted or missing because of the many criteria and riders. As a result, redeeming these points at times becomes a tedious process, diluting the objective of providing the customer with a great experience. Loyalty points are only but just the glue that sticks together various activities that a company needs to undertake to create loyalty among their consumer base. Hence, the effective loyalty programs create incentives that are lucrative to customers and go beyond accumulating points to actual purchases and eventually to engaging them as well. By giving rewards (e.g., offering extra points for exceeding a specified spend threshold in a time period), customers can be moved up from one rung of spend level to the next. This means that the loyalty cards can be used to create the first level of engagement with the customer. This, coupled with analytics and interactions outside the store, leads to a long-term relationship.

There are many ways in which it pays to earn the true loyalty of customers. When retailers successfully engage customers, they can convert them into advocates of the company or the brand. This activates the whole set of chain of actions and results. These loyal customers acting as the advocates of the retailer tend to refer it to others, resulting in the retailers' saving on the marketing and advertising costs for acquiring new customers. Loyal customers buy more, and are often willing to pay more. This means not only increased revenues but also improved margins. Loyal customers are more forgiving when the retailer makes any mistake—even big one (especially if the retailer has a system in place that empowers employees to correct the error immediately, in such a case, even greater loyalty is usually earned because it becomes an "experience").

A loyal customer's endorsement is more powerful to their family and friends than any advertisement campaign. Companies with high customer and employee loyalty levels are generally seen to outpace their competitors. The resultant increase in customer retention can boost bottom-line profits significantly.

Also the data from a loyalty program can play crucial role in formulating pricing structures. If enough best customers are happy to buy a product at a particular price, there seems little rationale in reducing that price simply to attract cherry pickers.

Let us look at Tata Starbucks' loyalty program, My Starbucks Rewards. It is a reloadable payment card that awards customers with stars for their purchases. Customers get membership at different "levels" depending on the frequency of purchase and get benefits that vary from complementary beverages to birthday treats, free customization, and so on. Putting things into right perspective, the Starbucks program is also a tool for customer engagement; the company's loyalty program is designed to make tracking rewards fun and exciting, just like a game. This is what loyalty programs should ideally be—more than "a point for a purchase."

At Lenskart.com, they have data to know each customer's purchase in terms of quality or price of frames and types of lenses used, CL (contact lens) purchased, and when are they due. It is followed by a feedback call for reminding and reassuring the search and purchase. This provides the company with an opportunity to upgrade the customer to a better product using the previous data.

Going Beyond Points and Improving Customer Engagement

Not all the new customers of a retail company are same, some will be profitable, but a larger slice of the pie will not. Hence, the retailers' ability to make the customer spend more depends on their understanding of the customer. In retailing, it can be more profitable to lose bad customers than to gain new ones. "Cherry pickers" (customers who buy only discounted lines and nothing else) cost them, as does any low-spending customer. It costs the retailers more money to serve them than the revenue they generate for the retailer. And the best way to identify the "cherry pickers" is to analyze the data that the loyalty card holds. Then designing a loyalty program that rewards better and genuinely loyal customers without rewarding this segment at all gives these "less" desirable customers less reason to stay. Some of the retailers are actually practicing this process. For instance, Shoppers Stop, which has one of the oldest running loyalty programs in the industry (started in 1994), has systematically invested in maintaining customer data and slicing and dicing it for consumer insight. It is also experimenting with integrating and consolidating social media data with its own card—data to target customers better.

Louis Philippe, another retailer, is one of the retail brands that has been able to make the most of its loyalty program membership. The brand has been able to build strong engagement with its core customers through customized red-carpet events at its stores. These special events are designed to enable the company's management and sales teams (floor staff) to interact with their most profitable set of customers to understand their needs and aspirations better and transcend these into their products, service, VM, and overall shopping experience. The repeat loyalty program members (i.e., members who have been in the program for more than one year) contribute about over 50% to its total sales.

Hence, any business can run a loyalty program, and that loyalty program does not necessarily have to be about giving points or discounts. It is also not about low-margin or high-margin retailers. But it is certainly about recognizing individual consumers who give them repeat business. So in return, the retailer should award them special treatment. That might be through CRM, if they do not have the opportunity or resources to return value to the customer through discounts or points.

Enhancing the Customer Lifetime Value (CLV)

A business can make its loyalty program more effective by first focusing on the customer buying experience and service standards and then layering the loyalty program on top of it. Many businesses get this sequencing wrong. Unless there is a consistent customer experience across all the touch points of the business, loyalty will not be built and CLV cannot be earned. CLV is increasingly being recognized as one of the most important measures of the worth and value of a customer. As each customer contributes a varying proportion to a brand's profit or loss, there should be considerable emphasis on ensuring that this customer's evolving needs are fully understood, and met. It takes into account not only the customer's value to the date but also the expected value over their projected lifetime as a customer.

For instance, if the goal of a retail chain is to increase a consumer's "lifetime value," emphasis needs to be placed on suitable factoring gross margin assumptions, and this would enable the necessary investment required each year for serving her/him. It is undoubtedly the best way a marketer can demonstrate unequivocally that a program is working in the direction, that is, rise in CLV of targeted customer value. Being able to identify customers through a loyalty program means being able to monitor the long-term CLV, and being able to identify the demographic, psychographic, social attributes, cultural features, and even purchase profiles that define the most profitable customers—and that knowledge enables the retailer to target and develop more of them. Different sectors should focus on different aspects of the customer experience.

For instance, an apparel brand should exhibit its knowledge of the customer segment, tastes, and preferences by mining past purchase patterns and providing offers or discounts on relevant categories to make the customer buy more. Hence, the focus on delivering the next "level" of experience to a shopper would help a retail brand to "engage and connect" in compelling and profitable way with their target audience.

At American Swan, they, with widgets and features, recognize a repeat user and offer product recommendations based on browsing and purchase history. The sophistication that technology solutions offer is truly admirable in making the entire experience highly personalized.

Building Strong Customer Relationships Based on Relevance

Building a strong and sustainable relationship with customers can lead to improved patronage behavior and loyalty and thus to increased bottom-line profits. If we examine the human elements, a long-lasting relationship will find several elements, all of which can be approximated by careful collection and analysis of loyalty program data. Knowledge about the customer is supreme today. It is leveraged to foster better loyalty with customers by treating each customer as an individual. Here the CRM program plays a vital role by enabling the retailer to learn about the customers, applying the right insights to that data, and activating upon that data to deliver relevant value to each customer. Retailers eventually use these insights for delivering the specific and relevant value to each customer or to each customer segment.

The key element, trust, can be built up by always excelling at customer service, customer experience, preferential customer-centric actions, and correction in the areas where customer issues lies, and also by providing consistently good products and services that suit the customer's unique needs. Surprise and delight can be achieved by delivering personal offers such as birthday or anniversary discount shopping days for the most profitable loyalty program members.

For example, when Titan Company wanted to offer customers the best shopping experience with the widest selection of products, it launched Encircle in 2013, which combines three of Titan's loyalty programs: Vista for Eye Plus, Anuttara for Tanishq, and Signet for the World of Titan. This allows customers who shop from any of the Titan Company stores (World of Titan, Tanishq, Helios, Fastrack, and Titan Eye Plus) to earn points while shopping, which can be redeemed across all brand stores. The retailer also offers special discounts in the form of extra points to their loyalty cardholders on their birthdays or marriage anniversaries. By virtue of this, the retailer can provide its consumers with the personalized experience and relevant communication, which in turn helps Titan to understand the consumer behavior in a better way. This cross-redemption of points has also come out as the key differentiator.

Leveraging Coalition Program

The idea of cross-redemption that the Titan Company has introduced can also work when linked across companies across sectors. This can enable the consumer to buy things at a department store and redeem the points at a retail outlet of a petroleum company. There are already enough examples of brands coming together to get access to a wider or newer set of customers. For instance, banks offering freebies on credit card spends of customers in coalition with retail partners. The bank does not pick up the tab on behalf of the customer, it is the retail partner that offers the gift to be able to extend its message to a wider audience. Another shared benefit of coalition is the reduction in cost of technology and infrastructure for all the partners, and since most of the players that enter in a coalition do not compete with each other, there is little chance of cannibalization.

Partnership in a coalition loyalty program is often thought of (quite rightly) as a quick method of entry into the field of customer loyalty; however, there are disadvantages that must be weight up first, such as the ownership and usage of loyalty program (customer-specific data), and potential competition of other program partners in future markets they plan to expand into.

Successful coalition programs have a major partner in several of the key consumer sectors in order to quickly capture a significant proportion of consumers' spend. Ideally, this would be a major grocer, fuel retailer, bank or credit card, department store, and mobile telecom service providers.

Experts feel a strategically designed loyalty coalitions can be a game changer. A comprehensive combination is expected to have at least one major bank (credit or debit card), one petroleum company, and one major retailer with a Pan-India presence. The presence of these categories in the coalition is essential for the customer to see value as these are the categories that bring in high-velocity transactions. By this way, a significant proportion of the target market can be enrolled very quickly. This also leads to maximization of the share of each consumer's wallet. Technology is enabling brands to gather and analyze data, in real time. It also provides with a "window" to understand and predict consumer preferences. Most importantly, new partners joining the program, after it becomes established, automatically gain the same degree of market penetration as the existing partners. This co-marketing and co-branding activity with the program's operator puts consumer awareness on higher growth trajectory.

Let us consider the example of Payback, which offers multi-brand customer loyalty programs, both online and off-line. It ran a joint promotion with Big Bazaar and Hindustan Petroleum, where customers got a chance to earn loyalty points and redeem them at both the places. If the customer used an American Express or ICICI Bank credit card, then they could further add to their points.

Winning Back Lost Customers: The Two-pronged Strategy

The retailers have the advantages with lost customers, which they do not have with prospects. This includes information about their past purchase history, where and how to reach them, and their preferred communication channels. Moreover, these parted customers know about the retailer they left and had dealt with them sometime. So if they separated from these retailers, that means they are somewhere not happy with them and may be in some cases irate with them. Hence in this scenario, it becomes top priority for the retailer to win them back. Because if it not done, they may spread a negative word of mouth for the retail brand/store. Also if they are in opinion leader category of customers or influencers, then the consequences of such separation can harm severely to the company and damage will be bigger. But building back the lost loyalty and developing relationships with these departed customers who are worth keeping are not so easy. Meticulous planning and unflinching patience are vital in the journey. Anticipating customer needs and consistently delivering great experience will go a long way in establishing a business relationship that is based on trust and respect. Today, retailers are focusing on developing a two-pronged strategy, designing counteraction to the challenges posed by competition and retargeting the separated customers. Here, e-retailers specifically are widely using the cross-channel retargeting strategy for improving the lost customer reconversion rates.

Designing Counteraction to Competitive Challenges

Today, we can see that lot of innovations and experiments are happening in retail industry for customer acquisition. A good loyalty program's ability to tie purchases to individual customers allows quick and accurate identification of customers who move away when new competition emerges or when the competition comes up with new offers. With the upsurge of new retailing models and formats and emergence of new players across these models and formats, the loyalty is under high pressure. Customer can move to other players, though they are getting a satisfactory shopping experience from a particular retailer to explore something new or to get something extra. They can then be enticed by the competition with customer-specific special offers or maybe better or unique experience.

In this scenario, a well-binding loyalty program should be in place before the customers move to the competitors, or the retailer should work on very strong customer touch points that will strengthen the patronage behavior that will resist her/him from defecting away. For instance, prices on online portals and off-line stores can vary. However, if a physical retailer has an attractive loyalty program, consumers may end up buying from that retailer.

The retailers that possess the highest levels of sternly loyal customers have built that loyalty not on card program or gimmicks, but on a solid, dependable, core offering that appeals to their customers. These retailers have focused intently on what they know appeals to the type of customers they want to attract, and have determinedly concentrated on delivering what is expected every time. Online retailing has raised consumer expectations. So brick-and-mortar retailers need to empower their staff with better product knowledge, to make the right decisions under given circumstances. They should be trained to keep the customers updated and educated about the program.

For example, the North American retailer Nordstrom is well known for the extreme loyalty of its customers. They built this loyalty by understanding what its customers wanted and then empowering its employees to deliver those needs consistently. Hence, retailers are always looking at the changes in consumer buying behavior to formulate new strategies to seize their attention.

With the fierce competition among value retailers that practice EDLP in Indian retailing context, Big Bazaar launched the Big Bazaar Profit Club in 2012, a prepaid loyalty program, which offers benefits against an upfront payment by the customer. Customers who pay ₹10,000 to sign up are entitled to shopping worth ₹1,000 every month over the next 12 months. This offers them to buy goods worth ₹12,000 in the year. The value to the customer is apparent; what the company gains may not be so evident but is no less attractive. It was eventually observed that for the most part, consumers end up spending more than ₹1,000 per visit, giving the company a far bigger share of wallet than they had deliberated for. The company claims to have added over 1.5 lakh new customers by promoting this program.

Cross-channel Retargeting Strategy

If window-shopping is a problem for brick-and-mortar retailers, shopping cart abandonment is one of the biggest challenges the online retailers are facing. Some visitors browse the site for a short while and then move on, while some others add items to their cart but abandon it without going through the purchase process. So here the first priority for both the types of retailers is to make the shopping experience so compelling for consumers that they complete the purchase loop. And even after that, if they do indeed exit, the retailer needs to find ways to bring them back to the site. At this juncture, retailers are following the retargeting strategy. In retargeting, e-tailers try to bring back lapsed customers by showing relevant ads on other websites so that they come back to the original e-store for their next purchase. Traditionally, retargeting had been strongly associated with performance marketing and the ROI. But the notion is being redefined today. It has become a customer value management program. Retargeting helps in extracting the value of the data generated and investing it back into the system to engage dormant or active customers.

Today, marketers are using retargeting in new ways: brand awareness, social engagement, customer retention, and driving the sales. Hence, retargeting forms part of the monthly digital budget of most e-tailers and run throughout the year, just like search marketing. Retargeting generally helps convert users at 1.5–2.5 times the website's standard conversion rate. This makes retargeting a high ROI campaign. A retargeting strategy would vary depending on the category and sector the retailer operates in.

Stage 1. Understanding Consumer's Needs and Analyzing Why She/He Was on the Said Portal in the First Place

The interest of the user could be defined in different ways during the customer's journey. Some parameters to look at are: how many times the user has visited the site, which categories, how many products did she saw, how deep she/he went into the website (cart vs home page), buying history, and so on. In this review, if a customer has shown a greater propensity to convert, then the e-tailer retargets her/him more aggressively. For this purpose, e-tailers first segment the audience under groups such as abandoned users, product viewers, category viewers, checkout users, and so on. Because after segmenting, they can design different communication plans for each segment to retarget them precisely.

Stage 2. Working Out the Optimal Retargeting Frequency

Retargeting is a process through which, over a period of time, we come to know which audiences are more likely to convert. So to work out optimal retargeting frequency, retailers find out those consumers within a target audience segment who do not buy at all and couple them with those who take a longer time to be persuaded to buy or more efforts to get converted. In this way, retailer can work out the optimal retargeting frequency. This strategy also saves them from being far too specific in retargeting and avoids the risk of being seen as a quasi-stalker.

Stage 3. Communicating a Predetermined Action-oriented Message to the User with a Clear Call to Action

The key to successful retargeting lies in creating a customized message. Here, the e-tailer may show a "static ad" of a product, a "semi-dynamic ad," which will include price, discount, and so on, or a "fully dynamic ad," where other relevant products with their prices are shown. In a campaign, there can be multiple elements to entice a user to respond. Hence, retargeting potential buyers with different styles of communication and channel is important.

For example, Lenskart's first-frame-free offer was not shown to visitors who have already made a purchase from the site. Such repeat visitors were rather shown the latest collection of its eyewear. The "right timing" is also very crucial in the retargeting. For example, if someone has ordered monthly disposable lenses, then Lenskart starts reminding the user with messages to change her/his lenses before the expiry date. They keep a close check on the performance of each segment and measure metrics like click-through rate, conversion rate, cost per action, and ROI on a daily basis.

Retargeting is also helpful in a category like furniture where the purchase cycles are longer. If a customer is looking to buy a sofa or bedroom set, she may take 10–30 days to make a decision. Hence, by effective targeting and retargeting, the e-tailer can stay relevant and interesting in customer's decision-making frame. The e-tailer can further modify the offers depending on how far the customer has progressed in the purchase cycle.

Stage 4. Determining the Effectiveness of a Retargeting Strategy on Two Metrics: Conversion and Return on Investment

The focal point of retargeting is to ensure that consumers return to a brand or an online portal to buy a product or service of interest. The reason retargeting works for the marketer is fairly easy to understand. First, it is about building a funnel of consumers who have already interacted with the brand and shown interest in a product/service. Second, it steers these consumers through the conversion funnel by bringing the message back in their view. So retargeting is integral to the marketing mix. If we can create additional sales at no or little cost, then we are achieving the best possible ROI. Here the retailers also need to ensure that if the campaign is projecting higher-margin or lower-margin products.

It is easier for online retailers to determine their ROI because any retargeting activity can be flawlessly linked back to the sales generated online. However, for the brick-and-mortar players who do not have any e-commerce presence or any such kind of platform, this becomes a little complicated. In such cases, they have to find ways to close the loop at stores and counters to determine the effectiveness of retargeting.

Now when it comes to the improvement in conversion, in the e-tailing space, the focus is moving to apps. App retargeting is making more business sense, and companies have been investing heavily on data-led retargeting via apps. Because it has been observed that there is better conversion ratios in apps compared to mobile web.

Besides this, the retailer needs to ensure that the retargeting efforts should not prove to be a spoiler because there is a thin line between following up, reminding or retargeting, and spamming. For this purpose, companies are finding ways to identify the customer they are retargeting and stop at the right time. The decision is mostly based on mature algorithm and judgment that help to determine that we are not moving in the direction of spamming, and it does not become a noise. At the same time, it is crucial that we are not compromising on the privacy of the consumer while retargeting. It has to be a controlled strategy to ensure that we do not oversell or reach out on too many channels, creating a lot of noise in the process.

Gift Card Business

Corporate retailers are now effectively utilizing different customer acquisition and intimacy initiatives like gift cards, gift vouchers, loyalty programs, and e-coupons to increase customer engagement and lifetime value. The concept of gift card business is being practiced by retailers in order to develop sustainable relationship bonds not only with the individual customers but also with the institutional/corporate customers. The gift card business also acts as an extra source of revenue generation for the retailers, which comes with added value to the entire shopping journey and overall experience.

There are mainly three levers for the gift card programs:

- The retailer gets more customers
- Or the retailer gets its customers to come more often
- Or it makes existing customers to buy more

We can see that across all the categories of organized retail chains, shopping mall, food chains, restaurants, hotels, entertainment, spas and salons, and so on are having some sort of gift cards that are offered to individual customer for personal gifting or institutes/corporate for corporate gifting purpose. Typically, there are two kinds of gift cards in the market. A closed-loop card is retailer-branded one and can only be used at the issuing retailer's store or chain, such as the ones issued by Lifestyle, Shoppers Stop, and so on. Retail chains like Lifestyle Stores, Shoppers Stop, Pacific Coffee, Pizza Hut, Benetton, Tanishq, Pantaloons, and many others are leveraging gift card business to drive incremental revenue through new customer acquisition, increased frequency of visit, and increased average ticket size. They also keep on adding new variants to their gift card offerings continuously and gradually.

Then there is the open-loop card, which can only be issued by a bank along with a credit card company like Visa or MasterCard. These can be used across all stores.

Technology is creating new benchmarks in the art of gifting. With the advent of the digital medium, the market has evolved from manual (old-fashioned paper vouchers) to electronic transactions (prepaid gift cards) because store vouchers can limit the choice for the other person. The prepaid service to customers is like a barometer of customer trust on a particular brand. Here the consumers pay in advance for the gift card offering, and therefore, the entire ecosystem and technology backup plays a very crucial role. While traditionally, the giver decided what they wanted to gift, in due course of time, with the upsurge of e-commerce, access to social media, item search and breaking of geographical boundaries for gift delivery has brought the recipient in the center stage of gifting.

The reasons behind this shift are:

- Improved control
- Increased consumer accessibility
- Availability and acceptance
- Reduction in incidences pertaining to fraud
- Greater flexibility
- New revenue opportunities

After all, vouchers are for one-time use and have to be redeemed for the entire amount. This is why gift cards make for a more savvy choice. These are prepaid cards, which can be charged for a certain amount. Similar to debit cards, they can be swiped at any brick-and-mortar outlet or used at online portal accepting plastic. Another benefit is that the recipients can swipe a gift card only for a partial value and use it multiple times until it is valid (e.g., Citizen Loyalty Customer program by Shoppers Stop and "The Inner Circle" by Lifestyle International).

Gift Card Business Opportunities

Today, retailing has changed drastically and emerged as the ecosystem where many experiments are happening. Retailers today are focusing not only on selling more but also on engaging more through program and offerings like loyalty card and gift card to provide higher intangible value to the customers. These offerings eventually help them ensure long-lasting relations. While gift card helps to acquire new customers, loyalty programs play a significant role in retaining them and in turn enhancing lifetime association and value.

Traditionally, in India, gifting has been given a center stage during festival season and occasions like birthdays, wedding, and anniversaries. India is a country where people are very passionate about festivals, which repeats round the year. Today, it is the growing phenomenon of presenting gift card to the loved ones during such festivals as a token of love, appreciation, and so on. The rationale here is to affirm relationships and enhance the personal connection between the giver and recipient. Hence, the personal gifting is a very lucrative business opportunity for the retailers.

As far as corporate gifting is concerned, in the industries like IT and ITES, manufacturing, and hospitality, corporate gifting is today done through gift cards to employees. Previously, cash prices/incentives were given to employees on the occasions such as timely completion of projects or achieving targets/deadlines or for longer years of service and so on. Gifting is also done to employees on the occasions of festivals, anniversaries, birthdays, appraisals, and so on. These businesses use the retailer's gift card/gift vouchers for gifting not only employees but also vendors, government officials, media personnel, customers, and so on. Here gift cards offered sincerely and subtly act as cost-effective ways to build a sense of partnership with valued associates and clients.

Today, gift cards or gift vouchers have emerged as a great option with many value additions. The trend is actually changed and appreciation is expressed in the form of gifting a gift card or gift voucher. Research in this field suggests that carefully timed and appropriate gifts not only make people feel appreciated for their performance but also increase the chances people will feel motivated for putting extra efforts in the future. These gift cards can be used like almost in the same way we use credit/debit cards. These cards are easy to use/redeem, very handy, and are easy and safer to carry. Hence, corporate/institutional gifting is also providing lucrative opportunity for the retailers to increase their revenues through this gift card/gift voucher business. Retailers today are competing for grabbing higher chunk of corporate gifting market and to build a strong corporate customer base. At times, they are also offering customized gift card programs and/or loyalty incentives.

Value Addition by "Retailer's Gift Card" to the Gifting

First of all, the recipient can buy anything of his or her choice from the whole array of selection the retailer provides across the categories and assortments. Though it is true that a "gift" is basically a physical form of emotions, many times, it happens that the recipients get straddled with unwanted gift objects that go unused. Here gift card becomes the best solution as the recipient can buy what he or she wants or suits to the recipient's taste, preference, and choice.

Next, a gift card brings not only a gift to the recipient but also a whole set of different experiential factors. For instance, when a recipient gets gifted with a gift card, he or she goes to the retail store/shopping mall; enjoys the atmosphere and ambience of the shopping place, crowd, music, lighting, temperature, colors, scent, visual effects, and merchandising, maybe some entertainment events/activities; and indulges in the association with brands, maybe in the company of their spouses, friends, peers and so on. Hence, a gift card provides the recipient with a complete package of tangible gift and intangible experiential factors. These factors touch upon various behavioral and emotional attributes of human psychology, providing the recipient with a coherent and memorable (memorable because it is derived from a gift) shopping experience. Technology can help create a bridge between the aspirations of the gift recipient and the giver. Today's consumers are high on aspirations; they are inclined toward branded products (merchandise or service) and resonate with great shopping experience and atmosphere. Here the gift givers may satisfy the recipients by gifting them with gift cards of retailers that have high brand image and strong PLs and offer rich shopping experience (ambience). This eventually motivates (delights) the recipients by making them feel recognized in a desired manner.

All these tangible and intangible benefits make these gift cards the best gifts for any occasion or no occasion at all. Retailers are increasingly promoting the gift cards among their corporate clients as an effective "gifting instrument" to make their internal and external customers feel special.

For example, "The Inner Circle" is Lifestyle's exclusive rewards program that is now valid across over 100 Landmark Group stores in India. The Inner Circle is an exclusive club providing exclusive privileges and exclusive rewards. The Inner Circle offers its members reward points for every purchase made at Landmark Group stores in India. That is not all. There are special periodic offers and discounts, and The Inner Circle members get special invites for exclusive previews of new season collections and EOSS. The members get personalized updates and information on in-store promotions, launch of new brands, and exclusive offers from partner brands like restaurants and health clubs. Landmark Group stores in India are Lifestyle, Home Centre, Splash, Bossini, Max, SPAR Hypermarkets, and Sanjeev Kapoor's The Yellow Chilli.

Benefits of Gift Cards to Retailers and Customers

For Retailers

- A great way to showcase your brand
- Front of wallet visibility
- Boost profit margins by reducing return- and exchange-related costs

355

- Data and visibility: connecting retailer's users and products with targeted solutions
- Customer acquisition: both gift buyers and recipients become new customers
- Increased revenue turnover: Through upselling and reducing cart abandonment
- POS display: no value on card until activation
- Increase brand awareness, purchasing frequency, ticket size, and patronage behavior
- Secure and durable
- An interactive marketing tool
- Redeemable in-store and online
- Can be reloaded
- Reduces overhead costs: voucher storage, print, money transfers
- Benefit from the "float": remaining money on card
- Retailer can design the targeted e-mail gift campaigns and reminders. Focus on personalized and preferential gift sections that act as a curator
- Scope for contextual gift upselling and cross-selling
- Meeting your customers' gifting needs can create a good business driver for the retail store

For Consumer

- Perfect solution for that last-minute gift
- No need to guess size, color, design, and so on
- Delightful and personal gift redemption experience for recipients
- Recipients enjoy flexible store credit options
- Recipients select the color they like, size that fits, and design and aesthetics they prefer
- A great way to give a gift
- Fits into a purse or wallet
- Secure and durable
- Easy and convenient
- Redeemable in-store and online
- Can be reused
- Balance enquiries: in-store, online, telephone, message

Major Factors Influencing the "Gift Card Business"

Retailers give a special emphasize on educating its customers about its CRM–loyalty program while preaching for their gift cards. It is also regarded as one of the strategic components in promotion of gift cards for their corporate clients. The strategic blending of gift card programs and CRM–loyalty programs creates instant, relevant, enhanced, and perceived value for the customers, which needs to grow from being a simple "rewards for purchase" scheme to something more engaging, by way of recognizing customers and better experience.

Retailers are also leveraging their strong PLBs as a USP for enhancing their gift card business, as the recipients can use these gift cards to buy their favorite PLs. Strong PLBs positively influence the purchase decision process for gift cards as these brands are exclusively available with that retailer only. PLs are developed according to the taste, preference, and choice of target audience of the retailer and, many times, fill the "gaps" left by the national brands. This approach makes PLs relevant to the broadest set of targeted audiences. They perceive them (PLs) as a part of their lifestyle, which in turn nourish there association and connect them with the brand persona. The retailer, in turn, celebrates and nurtures the "PLB" as a vital embodiment of its value proposition that will build and sustain a greater degree of loyalty. This also helps the retailers in creating a value proposition for its gift cards and adds the "exclusivity quotient" to the gift offered.

There is a significant impact of brand image, VM, ambience, and physical environment on the purchase decision process of gift cards. While VM helps retailer to lure the shoppers, toward the displayed merchandise, physical environment and ambient factors enhance the shopping experience. Both combined together convey the retailer's brand message and help reinforce its image with the help of effective "creativity quotient." This in turn helps the retailers in creating a value proposition for its gift cards and adds the "creativity and experience quotient" to the gift offered.

Retailers' brand image (positioning) and brand differentiation also play a vital role in the decision-making for purchasing the gift cards. Retailers' positioning is nothing but its perceived image in the minds of the consumers (shoppers). Hence, retailers' brand positioning relates to where a retailer situates itself in the consumer's mind. A firm may be seen as innovative or conservative, specialized or broad based, discount oriented or upscale high-end luxury brand and so on. This positioning guides all other decisions about how the retailer satisfies its target customers while differentiating itself from the competition. A unique and perceived brand image helps the retailers in creating a value proposition for its gift cards and adds the sense of pride, achievement, and a feel of image association to the gift offered.

Strategic Considerations for Enhancing the "Gift Card Business"

Here, we have looked toward the major factors that influence the buying behavior of individuals and corporations toward the gift cards of retailers. These factors are essential for the retailers to consider these behavioral factors, also with the changes in consumer lifestyle, new gifting trends, and recipient's changed expectations and usage behavior toward the gift cards. Here we will try to understand the rationale behind some major strategic factors that retailers focus on to enhance their gift card offerings.

- Retailers develop and convey their gift card sales message that is consistent with their brand image and positioning. They keep it consistent across all marketing channels: in-store, online, on social media, and in print. They also promote the gift card during the ATL or BTL promotional activities/events.
- Retailers need to ensure that the message (advertising copy), design, and visual form (presentation) of the gift card are in line with the overall brand image. This eventually evokes an emotional response—appealing to their customers—as they receive the same message consistently. This in turn enhances the brand recall for the retailer's gift card offerings as the target audience starts developing positive and deep association with them.
- Retailers are giving wide exposure and promoting their gift card across the customer touch points. This POP display, visuals (banners) at different locations inside (or outside) the store, eye-catching window signage, badges on salespersons' shirts, and so on can help spread their message throughout their brick-and-mortar establishment.
- Retailers can also extend their message to their online store by adding it to the checkout process—"would you like to add a gift card in your shopping cart?"—or maybe within their order confirmation and/or delivery confirmation/schedule e-mails or in the form of profile picture on the social media account of the retailer.
- Retailers are training their store sales associates to preach for the gift card to the customers during the checkout process and also motivate them to educate and guide the

customers regarding the gift card program. Retailers are also incentivizing them to perform on this front. Also for driving gift card business in corporate/institutional sector, retailers have dedicated store or region-level sales manager.

- Today, retailers are blending loyalty program with the gift card. By doing so, they can obtain valuable insights regarding purchasing done on the gift card. This information can eventually be very useful for designing a targeted and focused marketing campaign that will entice these former gift card purchasers to purchase again. Hence, this "gold mine" of customer data can be used to expedite over the duration of building profitable and long-term relationship with customers. Besides this, the retailer can offer loyalty points on top of the incentive to maintain, reward, and delight their loyal customers.

- In today's era of man-to-man marketing when personalization (customization) is rapidly becoming the buzzword and one of the key success factors, gift cards are no exception. With increased aspirations, people like to be gifted something that is created exclusively for them. Recipients feel delighted to receive personalized gifts, and a personalized gift card helps to achieve the desired effect. It can be simple personalization, such as just a personal message on the cardholder or a name embossed to the face of the card, or may be more complex, such as allowing the customer to upload an image online and that will be printed on the card. In the case of corporate gifting, retailer can personalize the cards by providing prepaid cards that allow companies to brand the card body with company logos, occasion wishes, congratulatory messages, the names of winners, and so on. Though there are some limitations in this area, retailers are partnering with technology supporters that provide this kind of innovative solutions.

- Service consideration: In the case of the prepaid gift card program, retailers are very much conscious about the related service level. Here the store-level employees need to take cognizance of the fact that customers have chosen them over others to receive a service by "prepaying" for the service, which shows the level of trust they are putting in the brand. The customer has given up the right of choice and so expects a lot more for this "preference" that they have given. Hence, the retailer may have the best technology and system that can be leveraged to cater to the needs of the regular customer. However, when they have a prepaid customer, they are morally obliged to offer a stellar service to the customer.

Hence, it is very easy and clear to interpret that gift cards foster loyal customers who keep coming back. Selling a gift card means not only getting business but also winning a repeat customer. Blend a loyalty program to that and retailers can virtually guarantee a long-term customer relationship if the perks (tangible and intangible, monetary and nonmonetary) are planned properly.

Summary

Today, loyalty program has become the significant component of retail marketing mix, as it enables the retailers to build strong and sustainable relationship with their customers. The changing consumer behavior, expectation, preferences, and new emerging models of retailing have changed the dynamics of business. This scenario suggests adding six new "Ps" to the well-known "Seven Ps of Marketing" (those being product, price, place, promotion, physical environment, people, and process). The six newcomers that stand to benefit the customer loyalty are positioning, PLBs, PR, philanthropy, pervasive creativity, and performance. The *performance* of the entire enterprise, and its quality and consistency therein, is increasingly critical to delivering performance and desired functionality and focusing on preferential, experiential, and personalization marketing; in a way, it engenders patronage loyalty and repeat purchasing behavior. Other critical success factors in the development and management of successful loyalty initiatives include strategy and economics, the features and benefits offered by the program, the methodology of the reward component, and the metrics and measurements used to track the effect of the program. It would not be surprise to point out that successful retail organizations have built an "emotional" loyalty with their customers, and word-of-mouth recommendations have helped to keep the shopping momentum on and the cash register ringing.

Loyal customers help retailers to grow even during the slowdown, and that is because their favorite brands offer them "value" as well as utility. And, it is becoming increasingly imperative for both the online and off-line retailers to introspect and ensure that they remain relevant to consumers. By virtue of a good loyalty program, retailers obtain an opportunity to transform the way business is conducted and the entire customer experience, both in-store and online, and subsequently, it would require retailers to get a "deep" understanding of their customer needs. Also in this era of proliferation of smartphones and allied tools (applications), consumer attention is rather limited, and brands would need to ensure that they understand evolving purchase patterns of their target audience as well as focus on a profitable long-term relationship.

Review Questions

1. Briefly explain the components of "the pyramid of performance" and how the performance of the retailer across these components leads to creation of coherent shopping experience.
2. Explain the importance of preferential and experiential retailing and how retailers are leveraging new technologies to enhance overall shopping experience and consumer engagement.
3. Explain the importance of personalization or customization in retailing and how retailers are leveraging new technologies to develop the personalized shopping experience.
4. Briefly discuss the future trends in retailing and how retailers are preparing themselves for facing challenges in future.
5. Discuss the essentials that retailers need to work upon for being future ready, in the context of rapidly transforming retail landscape.

Chapter 13

Public Relations and Strategic CSR

Learning Objectives

- **Introduction to the concept of PR in the context of retailing**
- **Objectives and scope of PR**
- **Role and significance of PR in retailing**
- **PR a gateway to social relationship and community engagement**
- **Benefits of PR in the business of retailing**
- **Social media: An influential PR tool**
- **Content creation and extension**
- **Evaluating the success of social media campaign**
- **Social listening through social media analytics**
- **Philanthropy and strategic CSR**
- **Leveraging strategic CSR for branding and positioning**

Introduction

PR and corporate communication was considered as the media relations until end of first decade of this century. Its existence, specifically, through the eyes of the top management, has been quite cosmetic and was lacking impact. This is evident from the fact that in most of the companies, the communication team's output was measured in terms of the quality and quantity of press it managed to secure. However, today, and more specifically after the social media revolution and its proliferations across the globe, we can state that corporate PR communications by no means equals media relations. In real terms, a media relation is just a subset of corporate communications, albeit a minor one. In this scenario, the PR and corporate communication professionals cannot confine themselves in the boundaries of journalists, bylines, the value of coverage secured. They need to think beyond pitching story ideas to journalists or write "good and favorable" press releases.

The corporate communication and PR is a big ocean of specialties, and media relations cannot do any justice to the scope and variety of output that such a function is capable of churning out. Corporate communication and PR involves a permutation and combination of wisdom, knowledge, and skills across brand communications, business administration, data analytics and research, social science and psychology, and anthropology, among other such domains. A PR team should be able to build and sustain relations with employees, customers, trade, investors, government institutions, and agencies along with several other stakeholders. This is because of the fact that a corporate brand's reputation is critical to its acceptance among these stakeholders. Whether a brand is perceived as trustworthy and creditable is totally dependent on how that brand manages its reputation in the market and social conversations as well. And this principle does not apply to retail companies and brands, and even to those in the purely B2B domain. Today, retailers need to be careful about their reputation, and keeping it intact is a primary responsibility of the PR and corporate communications team.

Public Relation

PR is the management function that evaluates public attitudes, identifies the policies and procedures of an individual or an organization with the public interest, and plans and executes a program of action to earn public understanding and acceptance. New media and its use as a marketing tool are becoming more and more relevant every day. Consumers are now leading conversations that can define a brand.

What the public wants to hear is a good story. Good PR is about telling a good story. The better the story, more will be the acceptance by the public and the stronger will be the PR. Of course, if the story is especially appealing to those that could be your clients, then you could have a PR home run. In this case, it is communication with your target market that may or may not be very public. A retailer can find a variety of avenues to keep him constantly in the news. Everything the retailer does can be turned into news if pitched correctly, from a grand opening or 10th-year anniversary, to a new product launch or special events the retailer may be holding. As the industry value chain is becoming more and more digital, it is essential to understand the major drivers to a successful new media strategy.

For example, in 2015, to celebrate the opening of their new flagship boutique in New York's Madison Avenue, Fendi brought together five celebrities to work on their iconic 3Baguette bag and to give it their own interpretation. The desirable and fortunate lineup, and also the representative of New York's creative spirit, boasts of musician Rihanna, actor Sarah Jessica Parker, model Jourdan Dunn, artist Rachel Feinstein, and blogger Leandra Medine. The fashion connoisseurs endowed their personal touch to the bags, be it in the choice of colors or textures. Each 3Baguette has been realized in three pieces: one for the celebrity, one for the auction, and one for the Fendi archive. Also as part of philanthropy, all five celebrity creators chose a charitable organization to receive the proceeds from the sale of their customized bag. Actor Sarah Jessica Parker—in her formal release regarding her association with the luxury brand—mentioned that Fendi was integral in the storytelling of *Sex and the City*, and also said that it was the first big luxury house that worked with them. Her design for the 3Baguette features a mix of colors and textures with smooth black velvet, rich purple satin, gold galuchat, and shades of blue and cream. According to her, during the selection of color, texture, and materials, she thought on many facets of the brand like its heritage and past, about what Fendi has done, and about the DNA of the house and the bag. Commenting on her design, the actor opined that it reflects her personality and the high regard she is having for the fashion house.

Hence from this example, it is evident that PR describes the various methods, strategies, and tactics a company uses to disseminate messages about its products, services, or overall image to its customers, employees, stockholders, suppliers, or other interested members of the community. While the public part implies inclusion of things like public affairs, community relations, investor relations, public press conferences, media events, internal communications, and crisis communications, it also involves a lot of behind-the-scenes, nonpublic activity. It could involve simply the writing of a press release, but it could also involve coordinating media contacts for an event or conference, securing credentials, lobbying for article placement and the like. It is also a sophisticated branding machine for maintaining ongoing relevance and dialog with the customers and consumers, especially so in fashion, technology and seasonal trends driven categories. At a tactical level, PR is utilized to generate buzz and convey the brand news, point of views of inspirers and influencers (celebrity talk or the designer speak), a crucial support for brand activation (like the fashion weeks, sport events, and themed previews).

PR Versus Advertising

When you advertise, you create a tightly controlled message. You know exactly what your advertisement will say, but with publicity, you have no idea how the message will be conveyed to the public. For example, a reporter can quote you out of context; the resulting publicity may not necessarily advance your business goals.

PR plays an enormous role in image proliferation of the retail brand, thereby subtly influencing public opinion. It is also employed to convey other supporting messages and attributes of the brand that cannot be explicitly captured in advertising, but by no means are less important to create brand's personality, mystique, and emotional values. Also you need not pay for media-generated publicity. This can make it more credible and influential than a paid advertisement.

Although advertising is closely related to PR—as it is also concerned with promoting and gaining public acceptance for the company's products—the goal of advertising is generating sales, while the goal of PR is generating goodwill. The effect of good PR is to lessen the gap between how an organization sees itself and how others outside the organization perceive it.

PR involves two-way communication between an organization and its public. It requires listening to the constituencies on which an organization depends as well as analyzing and understanding the attitudes and behaviors of those audiences. Only then can an organization undertake an effective PR campaign.

The country where having great product knowledge on self-esteem is India. It is a burgeoning tendency of people in which they derive a lot of joy and fulfillment in their lives, by being experts in a product category. We are finding an increasing number of people getting a lot of personal satisfaction from brands. These experts are fairly easy to find because of chat rooms, websites, blog post and so on, so the retailers and their clients can create an army of people out there, to tell their brand story, in essence for free, and they go out and tell their family and others. It is a coming together of forces. So it is totally different from the marketing campaign of the previous years. Let us make a television or print ad and go for lunch. It takes the brand away from propaganda, and what you are really doing is being the Sherpa and helping people make the right decision.

Gucci has experienced many changes since it opened its first luggage company in Florence in 1921. At first, it mainly sold only luxury leather goods. Within a few years, the store became popular among international and affluent clientele. By the 1950s Gucci's global presence was established with its first store in the USA, a store in New York. Soon Gucci's products grabbed the attention of many powerful celebrities, including Jackie Kennedy, Grace Kelly, and Audrey Hepburn. Gucci went so far as to name a bag in its range the "Jackie O," after the former first lady Jackie Kennedy. These women represented elegance and style, which enhanced the prestigious aura of Gucci. The cult of celebrities had begun, through PR film, television, and magazines.

Many small business owners elect to handle the PR activities for their own companies, while others choose to hire a PR specialist. Managers of somewhat larger firms, on the other hand, frequently contract with external PR or advertising agencies to enhance their corporate image.

Objectives and Scope of PR

Some of the main goals of PR are to create, maintain, and protect the organization's reputation, enhance its prestige, and present a favorable image. Studies have shown that consumers often base their purchase decisions on a company's reputation, so PR can have a definite impact on sales and revenue. PR can be an effective part of a company's overall marketing strategy. In the case of a for-profit company, PR and marketing should be coordinated to be sure they are working to achieve the same objectives.

Another major PR goal is to create goodwill for the organization. This involves such functions as employee relations, stockholder and investor relations, media relations, and community relations. PR may function to educate certain audiences about many things relevant to the organization—including the business in general, new legislation, and how to use a particular product—as well as to overcome misconceptions and prejudices.

PR is communication in many ways with your target market. Maybe instead of PR, we ought to call it target market relations (TMR). You may be communicating about a new product, spreading news about your company, or making a major announcement. You want to communicate publicly, but the only people you care about are potential prospects, customers or investors, in the case of a partnership or a public company.

PR is a multifaceted activity involving different audiences as well as different types of organizations, all with different goals and objectives. As a result, there are several specific areas of PR. However, one exception may be communication to a group that you are trying to influence for the best interest of your company and target market. For instance, besides the target customers and general public, it includes relationship enhancement with other stakeholders like employees, investors (financial institutions), suppliers, government officials, and lobbyists.

Let us consider the example of Walmart. Though the company had been ranked as the most successful and admired brand in the USA by *Fortune* magazine, public criticism and some serious allegations by human rights groups (regarding its HRM and predatory business practices) toward Walmart's business practices spoiled its image considerably. Over the issue of alleged discrimination against women in pay and promotions, the retailer was involved in the largest class action suit in US history.

To tackle this critical situation and to regain the lost consumer confidence in the brand, Walmart, in 2005, hired Edelman, one of the largest PR firms of USA. They aggressively ran a PR campaign named "Candidate Walmart," which essentially highlighted Walmart's new low-cost generic drug product and how it contributed to Hurricane Katrina relief. Through this campaign, Walmart also conveyed its vouch and efforts toward becoming environmentally responsible organization. Living to its promise, Walmart significantly reduced its global plastic bag consumption (approximately about 16%) by 2010. It also made a strong commitment to reduce the emissions of greenhouse gases, which are very harmful to environment. Encouraged by Michelle Obama, Walmart announced a five-year plan to reduce salt and sugar in its products and also to reduce the prices of nutritious (healthier) food products. In addition, the retailer continued to focus on achieving efficiencies through better HRM and practices and by adopting cutting-edge technologies for enhancing the effectiveness and efficiency of various operations.

Other Initiatives to Enhance PR

Other types of programs that fall under the umbrella of PR include corporate identity programs, ranging from name changes and new trademarks to changing a company's overall image. Special events may be held to call attention to an organization and focus the public's goodwill.

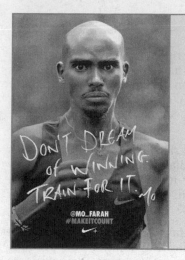

Their objectives in this social media campaign was to make people really think about what "making it count" really meant to them and to committing to trying to better themselves or their lives and to become active on Twitter and Facebook, to join the social media world of tons of other people with the same goals or desires. The, "Make It Count" campaign really took off. When Nike originally came out with this campaign, they merely wanted to promote their new FuelBand; however, it spread quickly, and even though Nike was not the official Olympics sponsors like Adidas, they stole the social media by promoting and sponsoring individual athletes in the Olympics by using their "Make It Count" campaign.

Photo 13.1: *Nike's "Make It Count" ad*

Photo credit: Nike Inc. Created by Wieden + Kennedy London and AKQA. Here the campaign includes a series of posters shot by photographer Adam Hinton

These include anniversary celebrations, events related to trade shows, special exhibits, or fairs and festivals. Speakers' bureaus and celebrity spokespersons are effective PR tools for communicating an organization's point of view. Speakers' bureaus may be organized by a trade association or an individual company. The face-to-face communication that speakers can deliver is often more effective than messages carried by printed materials, especially when the target audience is small and clearly defined.

Nike: Make It Count Campaign

Nike used all forms of social media marketing; they used television advertising and massive advertisements throughout their stores and branches. They also used both Twitter and Facebook. They used the #make it count, all over Twitter. Find your greatness was pointed more at the everyday person who is trying to achieve and meet athletic goals they never thought before.

Puma's Faas shoes were modeled on Jamaican athlete Usain Bolt. This was in order to attract the target customers to this range. The campaign for this launch was strategically accompanied by Faas test wherein users were invited to wear the Faas shoes and asked to demonstrate how fast they can run.

Steps in PR Campaign

Effective PR requires a knowledge, based on analysis and understanding, of all the factors that influence public attitudes toward the organization, while a specific PR project or campaign may be undertaken proactively or reactively (to manage some sort of image crisis):

Step 1: In either case, PR involves analysis and research to identify all the relevant factors of the situation. In this first step, the organization gains an understanding of its various constituencies and the key factors that are influencing their perceptions of the organization.

Step 2: Organization establishes an overall policy with respect to the campaign. This involves defining goals and desired outcomes, as well as the constraints under which the campaign will operate. It is necessary to establish such policy guidelines in order to evaluate proposed strategies and tactics as well as the overall success of the campaign.

Step 3: Organization outlines its strategies and tactics. Using its knowledge of the target audiences and its own established policies, the organization develops specific programs to achieve the desired objectives.

Step 4: Involves actual communication with the targeted public. The organization then employs specific PR techniques, such as press conferences or special events, to reach the intended audience.

Step 5: Organization receives feedback from its public. How have they reacted to the PR campaign? Are there some unexpected developments? In the final step, the organization assesses the program and makes any necessary adjustments.

Define what your public or target is in your PR effort. This is best done by defining your target market and then any subsegment. Lining up publications and broadcasts with the market and the segments will define what the public is for your PR.

Major PR Tools

1. *Press Releases.* These short documents detail what is new, different, or exciting about your business. Press releases make it easy for journalists to understand how their audience might benefit by learning more. A tight one-page press release that captures the most newsworthy information about your firm can persuade key media contacts to write a story and mention your business favorably.

2. *Press Kits.* A press kit or media kit often includes a press release along with background information and your business card—all packed neatly in a snazzy, eye-catching folder. The folder might also include photographs, product information sheets, articles from other publications, customer references or testimonials, financial data, your biography, and a list of questions you are prepared to answer (also known as a "cheat sheet" for radio and TV hosts).

3. *Tip Sheets/Newsletters.* A tip sheet is a page of snappy advice or information that helps your customers. Newsletters provide short articles and practical information that is of interest to your target audience.

4. *Bylined Articles.* The advantages of writing articles about your area of expertise and persuading editors to publish your submissions are twofold: you can advance your agenda while arranging for your name, phone number, website, and a few sentences about your business to appear at the end of the piece.

5. *Awards.* Applying for industry or local awards provides great visibility if you win or earn recognition as a finalist. Many trade journals, government agencies, and professional associations sponsor annual "best of" award programs for entrepreneurs.

6. *Online Outreach.* Smart, media-savvy entrepreneurs use chat rooms, their own websites, and other Internet-based tools to launch awareness-building campaigns of their companies.

7. *Special Events.* Examples include fund-raisers, contests and drawings, public celebrations of your company milestones such as your firm's anniversary, book signings, and client parties.

8. *Trade Shows/Conferences.* To maximize your presence at a large event, you may want to pay for a centrally located booth that is guaranteed heavy "foot traffic." Or you can save money and strategically prowl the aisles to spread your message, perhaps by

introducing yourself to key contacts or participating in "breakout" sessions that relate to your business.

9. *Speeches.* Deliver a speech on your business to community groups, local schools, or nonprofit agencies.

10. *Social Media.* Social media touches every stage of multichannel retail from the early influencing stages to after-sales service. Bringing transparency to buying (whether "liking" products on Facebook or re-tweeting unhappy reviews) as well as the fulfillment process, your social media channels are expected to react to stock queries, delivery times, and returns issues. Retail marketing management today is a dialog between brands and consumers wherein brands highlight their value proposition and consumers share their experiences in the form of reviews and testimonials. Even when in-store, consumers are sharing their buying experiences, both positive and negative, on social media.

Significance and Role of PR in Retailing

PR: A Gateway to Social Relationship and Community Engagement

India is going through a lot of change, and the Internet and web technologies have liberated us in a lot of ways. It has also democratized us, and people are not constrained by age, gender, or social class. There is a lot of aspiration among people today, and brands are striving to capture a place that celebrates this optimism. A comprehensive, ongoing community relations program can help virtually any organization achieve visibility as a good community citizen and gain the goodwill of the community in which it operates. Banks, utilities, radio and television stations, and major retailers are some of the types of organizations most likely to have ongoing programs that might include supporting urban renewal, performing arts programs, social and educational programs, children's programs, community organizations, and construction projects. On a more limited scale, small businesses may achieve community visibility by sponsoring local sports teams or other events. Support may be financial or take the form of employee participation.

Retailers have the opportunity to improve goodwill and demonstrate a commitment to their communities when they open new outlets/stores. One of the more sensitive areas of community relations involves store/outlet closings. A well-planned PR campaign, combined with appropriate actions, can alleviate the tensions that such closings cause. Some elements of such a campaign might include offering special programs to laid-off employees, informing employees directly about proposed closings, and controlling rumors through candid and direct communications to the community and employees.

Fashion portal LimeRoad is one of the e-commerce ventures that strategically leveraged celebrity endorsements and associations. LimeRoad roped in former Miss India and Bollywood actress Neha Dhupia as their style director. They are focusing on building a community by allowing Neha to lead the community engagement, bring in fresh style ideas and interact and encourage the users. The site that focuses on women's fashion along with home décor includes social aspects in shopping with consumers creating and sharing scrapbooks. Scrapbooks are "visual looks" created by putting cloths, footwear, and accessories together. The e-tailer has added its trademark scrapbooking feature to its mobile application for better engagement with customers.

Similarly, Jabong also get connected to youth through fashion and sports to convey brand message and eventually to reinforce its brand positioning, while Myntra, its rival, is sponsoring a women's marathon event and fashion shows.

Organizations conduct a variety of special programs to improve community relations, including providing employee volunteers to work on community projects, sponsoring educational and literacy programs, awareness campaigns for a cause, celebrating anniversaries, and mounting special exhibits. Organizations are recognized as good community citizens when they support programs that improve the quality of life in their community, including crime prevention, employment, environmental programs, health and medical programs, cleanup and beautification, recycling, and restoration. Other programs offer political education, leadership and self-improvement, recreational activities, contests, and safety instruction.

Let us take the example of unique and interesting promotional program undertaken by FirstCry. com, wherein it offers a GiftBox to the mother of a newborn baby. The gift box basically contains all the essentials that are required to take care of a newborn baby in a better way. The merchandise includes items like lotions, diapers, and baby wipes, which is offered to the mother as a present, after she delivers. FirstCry.com has tied up with thousands of hospitals, in over 50 cities where parents receive a FirstCry.com GiftBox as a token of congratulations on the birth of their child. This promotional program connects the brand to thousands of new parents every month through these hospitals. The program creates a perfect win–win situation, by benefiting all the stakeholders.

- The brands get opportunity to present their offerings to the potential customer very precisely and that also at the very start of their customer life cycle. This eventually enhances and simplifies the buying of baby products for parents also.
- The hospitals get an opportunity to give a complimentary gift to these new parents and a platform to express their feeling of care for the infant.
- The mothers gain awareness of quality brands and receive informative literature that becomes a good guide for them in the journey of their motherhood.

With the constant focus on value addition, innovation, and quick last-mile delivery of merchandise, FirstCry.com has grown to be the clear market leaders for baby product market in India. FirstCry.com launched one-of-its-kind community website—World of Moms— that provides a platform and space for every digitally connected mother where she can get everything that she needs to enhance her experience and journey of motherhood.

Major Benefits of PR

- **Increase Sales:** By targeting a pool of potential buyers, retailer can build visibility and thus grow its client base. Each time people get exposure to the brand name of the retailer and associate it with something positive, it will reinforce their awareness and brand recall for the retailer's brand and help them differentiate the retailer from its competitors.
- **Build Credibility:** Business start-ups often need to build their credibility quickly to compete with more established rivals. By positioning as an expert in the business, the retailer can attract media attention and serve as a quoted source in published articles. As the company officials give interviews and get quoted, professional associations may ask the retailer's representatives to give speeches or participate in panel discussions, thus solidifying their credibility.
- **Build a Strong Customer Relationship:** In today's retailing scenario, it is not enough to win a new customer. Retailer needs to convince the customer to come back and buy more. By aligning PR campaign with the goal of attracting repeat business, retailer can build consumer confidence and trust. Here the retailer can leverage the PR initiative—campaigns—efforts to increase the loyalty behavior, which eventually leads to enhanced relationship with the customers.

For instance, by profiling some of their best customers on its website, the retailer can send a message that they value their customers and share a stake in their success.

- **Penetrate New Markets:** When retailers enter a new market or launch a new brand or store, they inform the potential buyers through different channels of communication and attract them toward the new outlet or the new collection/brand launched. Effective PR can draw them in and educate them about what the retailers are offering.

- **Attract Investors:** Strategically designed and managed PR can introduce the retailer to a range of investors. It is especially very essential for the new start-ups and ventures. Better yet, an ongoing PR campaign helps the company to create an image as a long-term player in its business domain, rather than someone who is testing the waters and may not stick around. Investors like to see this type of commitment.

- **Connecting with the Target Audience:** Getting the public to discuss about you is thus becomes the ultimate goal of PR. When their interest and awareness about what the brand is selling or what the brand stands for, the target audience start relating (associating) to the brand on many levels. Publicity can come and go, but with a robust PR campaign, a retailer brand can connect with its audience over the long haul.

- **Emotional Connections:** Apart from these, with the intent of enhancing the "emotional connections" with discerning mind-sets, brands have been exploring the digital space by engaging them in their activation programs. The objective is to generate a genuine affinity with the brand that transcends beyond the product, to an extent where the consumers feel that they have found a soul mate.

When people buy a Vertu, they are buying a badge of exclusivity, luxury, and uniqueness. It was believed that if watches, pens, or even wallets can be transformed into luxury brands, why not a mobile phone. With awesome rise in mobile phone penetration; the phone makers need to develop new strategies to get people to buy newer phones. Newer technology was a prime motivator in consumers buying a new phone; now Vertu wanted their phones to become status symbols. For a technology product, this is a first as due to technological advances, products lose their value very quickly, when some new and improved product feature becomes available.

Instead of launching their new product range at technology shows, as per the general industry practice, Vertu instead prefers to become associated with fashion shows, launching, for example, their new range during Paris Fashion Week. Thus, this brand is aiming to create a fashion brand rather than a technology brand, trying to woo people through its fashion status. The bottom line is to get word out about you, your company, and your products and services to those who could potentially buy from you. PR is just one part of marketing, as marketing is made up of many things. The good news about PR is the cost and the effectiveness when it is in front of your target market.

Social Media: An Influential PR Tool

In today's retailing scenario, the approaches used for mapping customer's needs, expectations, and their experiences have been undergoing transformations. Social listening is the new mantra for understanding and analyzing customers and their buying behavior patterns. Social media has become a livewire platform for conversations and sharing of ideas, expectations, and experiences. Hence social listening is the new art of listening to the target audience with objective to the customers with the objective of knowing who the customers are and profiling them accurately.

Most of the retailers are utilizing the social media. The objective may not necessarily be, as deep as, engaging the audience in their storytelling, but it has been done largely to generate the desire or the lust for the brand or the product. It is also an effective tool to keep up the contemporary (appeal) and the newness (factor) by having a continuous dialog. The movement of brand building from mass marketing to social marketing requires new approaches and different goals. Instead of acquiring the customer, the aim becomes starting a conversation with (and maximizing the value of) that customer over time.

At present, we are in the age of storytelling. Today, the consumer's thumb is more powerful than the Roman Emperor's once was. If they like the work, they will tweet the appreciation and share and you prosper. If they do not, they will ignore you. With the rapid rise of social media resulting in an phenomenal surge in digital interactions with customers, both positive and negative brand experiences spread like an epidemic to millions across geographies in minutes. Television and print commercials can spread awareness, but the "customer speak" performs a crucial part of creating interest and converting the interest into purchase decision. Instead of the goal being mass impressions, it is to go deeper with fewer people and create customer evangelists. Marketing has to catch up to this new psychology. The concept of "customer as brand ambassador" or "endorsement by customer" is becoming big in retail industry. Market share becomes share of customer lifetime; share of customer voice and communication of improved service offerings takes on the added dimension of enhanced customer relationship. Businesses need to encourage consumers to champion their products and brands to others through social media, representation on websites and social media platforms, contests, and through ratings and reviews.

The Influencers

At the end of the last century and in the beginning of this century, the rising competition among suppliers/retailers tilted the bargaining power in favor of the customer. With the intensification of competition, the purchase decisions of the customer started deciding the fate of the brands/products and hence the suppliers. This resulted in the creation of marketing jargon "customer is king."

The power of the customer was further expected to multiply manifolds with globalization, deeper penetration of Internet, and proliferation of social media sites. The ever-expanding consumption basket of the consumer and the abundance of alternatives/options and associated information put an intense pressure on consumers' decision-making capability. However, the abundance of information, coupled with large number of alternatives, as expected, did not increase the power enjoyed by the customer. But it further reduced the power of the supplier. So here the question arises: Where the power is gone?

When marketers analyzed this scenario, they found that this power moved to a new class of market players: the influencers. The consumer is increasingly using inputs from third parties, consultants, search engines, personal trustees, peers, and so on. They also follow celebrities, lifestyle bloggers, and creative thinkers and share and re-tweet their posts. After passing through the surfeit of information, bombardment of advertisements, and the maze of options, these third parties help her/him in decision-making. In one sense, influencers have become the "BPO for decision-making." Social networking sites provide a platform for consumers to exchange their opinions. People today want better product, better value, better access to channels and better experience. A lot of it can be attributed to the growth of the middle class in developing economies. The middle class is developing significantly in this country with their increasing purchasing power and so the demand. This market scenario, with all the information available on the single click with many options and channels to buy them, attributes to growing importance of the trust factor. This means people are placing greater value in information sources that they can trust. Using this information, technology identifies what is trending and also influences subsequent trends. The former helps these sites understand consumers' mind and the latter makes them a large-scale influencer.

Win–Win Situation

Social media enables retailers to understand whether a particular merchandise brand or recently launched merchandise collection or promotional campaign has achieved the desired success (in terms of awareness) and that also very quickly and at low cost. On the other hand, browsers are interconnected with social media, so a marketing (promotional) campaign is easily communicated with a large customer base and that also very quickly and at low cost.

Also, social networking sites provide a platform for consumers to exchange and share their opinions and experiences. Using this information, technology identifies what is trending and also influences subsequent trends. Hence, the former helps these sites understand consumers' mind and the latter makes them a large-scale influencer. Friends and family continue to the most valued source of communication in terms of making decision. In India, there is a dramatic increase in the percentage of people valuing independent sources of information. People are looking at brands that communicate trust. So retailers need to take actions that help communicate trust through the product experience and also putting across the right image through social media and social values (CSR).

Deeper Relationships

- Events and dialog applications both support and create brand experience; people feel part of the brand, addressed as valued customers.
- Conversation and learning (from both customers and experts) increase category interest, making newcomers comfortable and creating a path to involvement.
- Customer satisfaction levels rise, based on the perception that the company is present and responsive.
- Improved understanding of customers and their product preferences clears a path toward more successful products/services.

Increased Revenue/Productivity per Community Participant

- When people engage in a site's structures for a dialog, they tend to stay around much longer.
- Loyal to a conversational site and what it offers, community members take greater advantage of calls to action, including product purchase.
- Page views from community participants are far greater, as their interest and connections lead them to explore opportunities the site offers.
- Conversation draws them back again and again, as relationship grows.

Reduced Costs, Based on Network Efficiencies

- One-to-many or peer-to-peer support lessens the needs for employee support staff.
- Product reviews/testimony support lower-cost customer acquisition and conversion.
- An engaged customer audience creates (and returns to view) content that they themselves add to the site, limiting the need for editorial staff.

Today, customers are increasingly using social media to stay informed, stay connected, and stay up to date on brands, offers, sales, and more. We are using our mobile phones for shopping, making flight reservations and interacting with our favorite brands. And when we are on our favorite social networks, we are in contact with brands throughout our day. We all know that one person who seems to do nothing but post Facebook updates and tweet whatever random thought pops up into mind. As the use of social media sites continues to grow, so does the importance of a social media strategy for retailers.

With the exponential rise in the number of social network users, Internet penetration, and smartphone adoption rate, retailers are increasingly customizing their strategies to accommodate the influence of social media on the entire purchase journey from searching to final purchase. According to a research, approximately 80% of *smartphone* users access social networks on their devices, and 55% of those users visit social networks on their devices once per day, and 96% of smartphone users have researched a product or service on their phone. These statistics reestablishes the power of social media as an effective tool for branding building. It is increasingly imperative to make sure brands fully optimize their customer retail mobile and social experience. Spontaneous, real-time word-of-mouth publicity for a retailer brand influences the purchase decision for a prospective consumer. The significance of consumer reviews can also be underlined by the fact that many retailer brands have formed online communities where they promote consumers to share their views (experiences) about their category and brand.

For example, Sephora, retailer of cosmetics, owned by LVMH, has created its own interactive shopping social space by launching its online Beauty Talk community. It has brought its customers together and encouraged them to discuss their passion for beauty. Sephora found that by creating a community and by opening itself to its customers, it was flooded with people highly interested to talk to each other. This initiative not only put the brand at the heart of the community but also makes them buy more. While a Beauty Talk community user spends around 2.5 times more than the average Sephora customer, the most active community users—or "superfans"—who post the most of the content and are highly engaged spend 10 times more. Sephora has created a social community where they do not push their products at their customers, but customer discussions lead to them recommending products to each other instead.

Let us consider another example of online fashion retailer Yepme. Yepme is an online retailer that specializes in men's and women's apparel and accessories and is one of the biggest online fashion brands. The brand essentially targets fashion- and style-conscious men and women in the age group of 20–29 years residing in Tier II and Tier III cities. The target audience of Yepme residing in these cities has high level of vogue awareness through Internet, TV, and movies, but has no access to high-fashion brands due to low retail presence of these brands in these small-town areas. On the other hand, the current sets of fashion brands that are available through online marketplaces, due to high premiums (hence high price points), have low appeal and penetration with the target audience of Yepme. Here is the gap that has been strategically filled by Yepme and successfully created a favorable brand image among this customer base. It has millions of fans on Facebook, and with this huge fan-following, the online fashion retailer has created a benchmark in the online fashion industry. It was rated—as one of the top five start-ups to watch out for—by *Forbes* for revolutionizing the online retail industry. Yepme was also awarded "Web-only" Brand of the Year in 2014. Among all the leading fashion brands, Yepme has one of the highest social engagements on Facebook and has been ranked as top 20 fashion brands in the world (as per Stylophane).

Content Creation and Extension

No other technological change ever has empowering customers like the social media has done. It has enabled the users not only to consume information but also to produce it very easily. Content is rapidly becoming key to maximizing social media's engagement with consumers and crucial for an effective social media marketing. However, content should be relevant and appealing to the target audience, should be easily accessible, and should catch the attention and hold the interest of browsers. Mobile technology or the mobile applications are also helping retailers to leverage this customer-driven content. One of the major aspects that need continuous attention is the amount of data (content) consumers are producing through social media and its impact on the relationships they develop and maintain with retailers and brands. Consumers are increasingly sharing their purchase and post-purchase experience with a brand on discussion forums, blogs, reviews sites, and other online platforms.

It should lead to building and maintaining ongoing relationships that would be tracked under social listening. Content that is developed should attract the intended audience, and it should be so influential that the user would like to share such content with their networks and that is how the multiplier effect of relationships will be realized. It is therefore of utmost importance to see how people react and respond with suitable actions and adds to the overall customer experience with the product/brand. Social media strategies can be used to promote the retailer's offerings, showcase the company talents, highlight their CEO's pursuits, and humanize the organization. Interacting with customers in the hope of increasing sales can also play a part. The challenge lies in making sense out of what being shared "one to one" and/or "one to many" and converting key phrases from such conversations that are in unstructured format into structured database and obtaining insights from the mélange of data and multifarious formats, which will be the key to making social listening strategy successful. This underlines the importance of content and context in any social media initiative. The retail organization can then act upon such formations in a timely fashion.

Showcase for New Products/Arrivals

Social media helps the retailer to give wide exposure to the new arrivals and to share the information about it with their customers. They can post pictures/images of the new arrivals, describe something engaging, and post it on social media platforms.

For instance, a fashion retailer can post images of new outfit or design for sale in the store, a user may re-post that photo, commenting "I love this dress!" This may give the retailer even further reach outside their existing fan base and followers.

Promote Exclusive Deals and Offers

Retailers are emphasizing on exploring the ways to leverage their off-line and online presence to obtain more of the inputs from social media content in order to:

- Deliver a more personalized experience for their customer.
- Offer special promotions and deals to loyal fans and followers.

Posting a discount code on social media sites like Twitter or Facebook can result in an immediate impact on footfalls and sales figures and also make for excellent shareable content. Sharing good deals with friends, that is what people do! Posting a special offer can result in re-posts on Facebook and re-tweets on Twitter. If a brand backs that up with some searchable terms (e.g., hashtags on Twitter), that will make it easier for the users to find the retailer's offering.

Share Employee Recommendations

Sharing "employee picks" with customers via social media has multiple benefits for retailers. First, it makes an employee feel that their opinion is valued. As any business owner or manager knows, employee morale is always good for business. Second, this puts different products in

GAP has successfully kept their high numbers of Facebook fans engaged by continually updating their content, thereby sparking conversations in the form of "likes" and "comments."

Photo 13.2: *Social Media: An Effective Channel for Engaging Customer*

Source: www.facebook.com/gap/ (accessed on 12 May 2016)

front of your customer that they may have not otherwise known about. Finally, customers love recommendations, which could result in a purchase.

Hence, it should also be remembered that while social listening is often connected with customer, their aspirations and expectations, product portfolio management, and marketing, it is immensely beneficial for HRM as well. It allows the HR executives to understand their employees' aspirations and expectations better as well as to map the brand equity with the ex-employees and potential employees and devise an appropriate communication strategy. Also, investor communication strategy is another area that can be addressed effectively with this tool.

For example, some of the luxury brands have also utilized the social media.

Jimmy Choo organized a real-time treasure hunt around London via Foursquare to engage fans both online and off. The idea was to track down a brand representative who checked in on Foursquare into some of the most famous places in London. He published hints and tips about his hideaway on Facebook and Twitter. This representative carried a pair of Jimmy Choo shoes with him. If you could track the shoes down and catch them while he was still checked in at a venue, then they were yours. The Idea of this campaign was to make customers their brand ambassadors.

Evaluating the Success of Social Media Campaign

The starting point for social listening is that there have to be adequate awareness about the brand offerings and also engagement with the retailer brand itself. To start generating the responses and making voices louder and insightful, placing the right content constantly and creating the "buzz" is an art that retailers need to develop and implement tactfully. Hence, it is crucial for any enterprise in the business of retailing to understand how to write for, share with, and connect to customers on the social media platforms.

Thus, merely counting "likes" that a retailer or brand have on their Facebook page or number of followers on Twitter will not work. But a business outcome cannot be justified solely on the basis of just that. It is undisputedly a good measure, but eventually, it has to be converted into marketing ROI. While Facebook or any such social networking sites are a very effective engagement platform, it sometimes can be difficult to measure ROI. For instance, consumer may like the product she/he views on a platform but does not immediately buys it. It may happen that the same consumer later searches for the same product on Google and goes on to purchase it from yet another online retailer site. So in the context of such behaviors, a retailer has to be really thoughtful as to what is working from the investment point.

By measuring the social media metrics, a brand starts to recognize that what is working and how the customers are responding. So the enterprise here can get the most out of its social media efforts. Creating a positive image through that media is crucial in achieving competitive edge. PR, sometimes referred to as media relations, is perhaps one of the most cost-effective and efficient communication vehicles the company could leverage to garner the new clientele. Retailers have always been carried out research from time to time to understand consumer perception about their brands and offerings. However, social listening is different from such marketing research as it enables the retailers to actively listen to their target audience and markets in real time. Retailers need to not only communicate effectively in the social media age but also listen and respond, aligning with both brand and customer expectation on an ongoing basis. Experts suggest the following social media metrics:

- **Fan/follower growth:** How many new fans the brand gained during a select time frame?
- **Engagement rate:** The number of user interactions (likes, comments, re-tweets, replies, and shares).
- **Response rate:** The percentage of user posts or questions that the administrator responded to.
- **Response time:** The average amount of time it takes for the administrator to respond to user posts or questions.
- **User activity:** Identifying the hours and days of the week your users are engaging most frequently.
- **Shareability:** The number of shares and re-tweets a post gets.
- **Interactions:** The number of interactions that a page or post receives and the types of interactions (likes, comments, re-tweets, replies, and shares).

Hence, organizations are recognizing the need to build a sound social listening strategy that would enable them to identify the right strands of customer conversations to follow, analyze, and act upon. Social networks give retail brands the opportunity to form a relationship with millions of customers and also speak to them individually. And as more people shop and spend money online, retail brands need to get their online social strategy right. Retailers are increasingly giving importance to creating and maintaining online communities to deepen relationships, spot problems, and stay abreast of trends by monitoring the feedback and gathering useful insights at each stage.

The decision to build online social marketing venues requires a set of clear strategic objectives. In most cases, goals will involve particular user volumes, demographics, and actions that either contribute to and support the brand or provide a specific type of customer support. This enables the brands to sharpen their business strategies to fight back in the highly competitive market of retail. Retail has certainly reacted to the social age, and almost every brand has some form of presence on social media, whether it is a Facebook page, a Twitter handle, or a Pinterest board. Hence, a strong implementation is expected to result in a foundation of loyalty that maximizes customer value and return over customer lifetime.

Social Listening through Social Media Analytics

Of all the windows through which a business can peer into an audience, social media has emerged as most appealing. The breadth of subjects, range of observations, and, above all, the ability to connect and draw inferences make social analytics hugely exciting for the brands that are interested in understanding and influencing past, present, and potential customers, employees, or even investors.

Let us discuss an incident happened with Revere, by a mass-based candy maker NECCO (New England Confectionery Co.) when a customer tweeted that she could not find a new line of Sweethearts at Walmart. The heart-shaped candies were stamped with phrases like "Bite Me" and tied to a popular young adult vampire romance series *Twilight*. They were due out by Valentine's Day, but fans were hunting them earlier. They immediately informed this to Walmart, they released the candy, and it sold out like hotcakes.

This incident shows that a page dedicated on Facebook or an alert on Tweeter would have been considered adequate to pull in the ideas and feedback of customers. Brands may be drawing millions upon millions of people to their Facebook page, but just because people are "liking" or "re-tweeting" does not mean they are buying. And that is surely the end goal of brands developing and maintaining a social media presence. A social strategy needs to create a community and generate engagement that will lead to increased desire for products and hence increased sales. So people need the right social environment to engage with a brand and then be encouraged to buy its products.

Here the social analytics comes into the picture. As individuals leave traces of their activities—personal, social, and professional—on the Internet, they allow an unprecedented view into their lives, thoughts, influences, and preferences. Social analytics attempts to draw useful understanding and inferences, which could be relevant to marketers, salespersons, HR managers, product designers, investors, and so on. Thus, as social tools like Facebook, Twitter, LinkedIn, WhatsApp, and many more host a plethora of social activities of many people, a humongous amount of data is generated about people's behavior, sentiments, and preferences. Like any other conventional data, it can also be analyzed to gain useful insights.

The two simple steps are as follows:

Step 1. The first and the most vital step in a social analytics initiative is to identify the business goals that the analysis might contribute to, and the key indicators that relate to those business goals.

For example, the typical objectives include increasing revenues, influencing public opinion, reducing customer service costs, and improvement in products and services. Some key variables that may be relevant in a business context could be, thus, audience reach, customer engagement, product-related sentiment, public awareness and acceptance, and so on.

Step 2. The next step would be to see if these variables can be measured fully or at least in parts, in terms of inferences from social media. For example, customer engagement might be measured by the numbers of followers for a Twitter account and numbers of re-tweets and mentions of a company's name. At the same time, for a company offering specialized products for a niche audience that is not active on Twitter, this could be irrelevant.

Importance of Social Media Analytics

1. As marketing is increasingly shifting online and digital and social marketing is becoming a bigger part of the marketing efforts, the most common use of social media analytics is to mine customer sentiment in order to support marketing and customer service activities.

2. Social analytics can help the retailer to listen and analyze customer interactions about the products or services and address customer concerns and preferences promptly.

3. Certain online behavior can, for instance, indicate preference for a product or a brand, or help identify the right influencers. Blogs, community postings, and so on can reveal about the influence levels. All of these can lead to identification of specific product opportunities and purchase drivers.

4. Social media analytics helps to measure the impact of most of the retailer's social media activities. And by virtue of those insights, these initiatives can be optimized for maximal impact.

5. It provides the retailers with a window to view and observe relevant happenings on a social platform leading to recommendations for social media intervention (e.g., to respond to an influential negative chatter), or for product development, or for marketing (i.e., what messaging could be more relevant, target group characteristics, etc.).

6. Social analytics is quite useful for sales enablement and support, as this data are very helpful to analyze and identify target customers and unleash focused sales effort. It can be used for lead assessment and qualification and content targeting, based on this, and can accelerate conversions.

7. Social analytics can be used for making targeted offers. For instance, many online retailers have used correlation between certain social media behaviors with preferences toward certain product bundles or payment methods and so on. Such predictive analysis combined with continual multivariate testing can lead to robust social analytics models, driving in sales and aiding marketing.

8. In B2B scenarios, social analytics can lead to highly valuable insights and profiling information about an account. This prosperity of information about an account can be garnered by looking at the activities of various individuals in that organization's ecosystem: employees, suppliers, buyers, competitors and so on. Retailers track conversations to identify leads and business opportunities. A Twitter interaction about, say, issues with a competitor product could lead to a sales opportunity.

   For instance, the e-commerce players in B2B segment have built sophisticated processes. These processes are built on domain and product knowledge to listen, organize, and analyze this data. This in turn enable and accelerate sales by providing sales teams with relevant information about their key target accounts, thereby exposing new business opportunities.

9. Activities on these happening social media portals can signal new initiatives, hiring, projects, or investments. The job postings and people profiles on professional networks can provide information about products being used, extent of usage, and so on.

10. Companies with highly complex and specialized products can also get deeper market intelligence based on the professional activities of the target audience, leading to actionable information about the relevant business opportunities and threats, thereby implementing relevant marketing tactics to engage and convert these into tangible business.

11. Social analytics is highly relevant for individuals also, it may be a celebrity, businessperson, entrepreneur, blogger, and so on. They can build their online presence by using social media analytics tools. It is important to know, for example, how many people did your post reach or what kind of links do your followers like best or, even, does anything you do online even matter? There is an assortment of analytics tools available where one can assess and get a score, about one's social presence.

Limitations and Challenges

However, with all its potential, there are challenges associated with social analytics. The users need to address these challenges carefully on the grounds of ethics.

- There are critical issues of privacy and reliability that to be handled with utmost care.
- Use of personal data for targeted marketing can be interpreted as violation of one's privacy.
- Also there lies a risk related to hyper-personalization, which may irate and estrange customers.
- It may create negative opinions, if messages are wrong (after all, any analytics is prone to some errors) or intrusive or not sensitive to the person's context (which is a very subjective factor).
- Trust in social analytics must also be tempered with recognition of the divergence of online and off-line lives. This may create a serious error in interpretation. The "real" personality could be very different from what is projected by the online persona, aspirations, and behavior.
- For many businesses, substantial portions of the relevant population may not be generating adequate social data. So here, care must be taken whether data derived from social media sites are plausible enough to influence business decisions.

Besides all these challenges and bottlenecks, if applied correctly, social analytics can yield enormous benefits to an organization's objectives. It is essential that the models correspond to the business context and the intervening mechanics are accounted for.

Philanthropy and Strategic CSR

Any business in the world operates in the context of a community. By the very nature of the business, retailers have a unique opportunity to play a significant role in supporting the communities where they do business. Not all the members of the community are investors in the company or its customers. But they are impacted by what the company does. Business operates in a social, cultural, and regulatory context, a lot of which is not directly in the value chain. If that is the context in which the business operates, it is absolutely important for retailers to have a philanthropic CSR strategy.

Over the years, business has taken many benefits from the society. Society accepts new concepts, products that are being showcased by the businessmen. Therefore, it becomes obligation for the enterprise to return to society as well. A business cannot succeed if society fails. This, therefore, clearly establishes the stake of a business organization in the good health and well-being of a society of which it is a part. Retail companies can make a significant tangible impact nationally and globally by contributing help and resources locally. It is almost impossible to make a purchase these days without being asked to contribute to a charitable cause. Whether it is saving the rain forests, helping to find a cure for a disease, or providing relief for a natural disaster, businesses are in lockstep with charities. Corporate philanthropy and profits are positively related in industries with high advertising intensity and high competition and high involvement. Perceived retailer attributes are more important for consumers' patronage intentions, while retailers' philanthropic activities are more important in terms of their impact on purchasing behavior of their target customer, which in turn has significant impact on companies' market performance. Globalization and universal expansion of the economies enhance the consideration of image and reputation among organizations. An organization's image and reputation can be ruined in days through unregulated and unethical practices. So, imbibing CSR practices becomes the strong foundation in image building.

Lessons from Ancient Indian Scriptures

India has had rich tradition in giving back to society in various forms, which has been manifested not only in her ancient text, scriptures, and philosophies, but also during the independence movement, where philanthropists of all hues played a catalytic role. In India, the concept of institutional and individual social responsibility has been discussed and practiced since the ancient times. The traditional belief system in India has always been rested on the notion of "Daan" (giving), which is directly linked to "Karma" (it is all about what a person has done, is doing, and will do in future. It is the principle of cause and effect of our actions). So the "Karma" eventually affects and influences the "Moksha" (emancipation). According to the ancient Indian scriptures, it is basically a cyclical act that benefits us as we benefit the world. Hence the ancient Indian scriptures have always propagated the importance of charity and philanthropy to the world. If we have something to give and donate, let's give it with love and compassion, and with this we can make the world a better place. *"Krishna"* called it as *Lokasangraha,* which upholds the need to contribute our share to the welfare of the society in order to make the world a better place. The great Indian economist and philosopher, *Chanakya*, in his seminal work *Arthashastra;* has categorically highlighted the importance of philanthropy and good governance. Though it may be referred by different terms or concepts, from ancient scriptures to medieval and modern time literature in India; has always endorsed the modern philanthropy. When we all perform little acts of service and small deeds of kindness, the world will become a place full of happiness, satisfaction, and peace.

Meaning of Charity, Philanthropy, and CSR

With the surge of globalization and resultant proliferation of MNCs majorly after mid-1980s, questions on equity and concentration of wealth are raised; it is gratifying to see that a new era of "giving back" has begun. The word "philanthropist" is derived from Greek words *philas*, which means "loving," and *anthropos*, which means "man." In other words, the basic meaning of philanthropist is "a loving man."

Though the nature and role of charity and philanthropy gets equated to each other, there lies a fundamental difference between both concepts. Charity emerges from compassion and it is spontaneous response to social distress or any other form of sufferings. Philanthropy means utilization of some share of one's wealth in a more integrated and strategic manner to bring about "sustainable social change," which acts in the direction of society's betterment in the long run.

Corporate philanthropy mirrors individual philanthropy, except for the fact that a corporation, not an individual, is donating funds, time, or talent. Although done on a larger scale, corporate philanthropy is still done without any expectation of direct commercial gains, but usually involves indirect gains (such as enhancing a company's brand, engaging employees, recognition, and so on). It is essential for any organization not just to convince their stakeholders about their commitment but also to sincerely do business as a responsible corporate citizen for their own sustainability.

Big companies have CSR programs, but that is different from having a CSR strategy. CSR strategy in its proper context is beyond giving, and here the company needs to look beyond donations and charity. However, these ad hoc philanthropic projects or short-term initiatives may well be unrelated to their business and have little value in building the resilience needed to truly enhance reputation among stakeholders.

However, the CSR strategy requires the company to think very carefully about its business purpose. In this context of thinking, when the organization measures business impact, they also have to measure the social impact of the CSR initiatives they are going to undertake. By this approach, they can create a strategically differentiated offering for all stakeholders by adopting CSR initiatives that are in natural alignment and in line with their business expertise. Hence, the real objective of CSR is to address the well-being of all stakeholders, which is built on the strong foundation of philanthropy. Here, philanthropic activities act as a significant component of CSR. This is basically a strategic shift from periodic social service initiatives (having a short-term impact) to strategic CSR programs (having a long-term impact). Hence, CSR essentially constitutes a much larger set of activities involving strategic business responsibility and sustainability.

Attributes

- Like standard philanthropy, corporate philanthropy focuses on treating the cause of a problem or issue instead of the symptom.
- Unlike standard philanthropy, corporate philanthropy must be done through a corporation directly or a corporation's own nonprofit entity.
- Funding for corporate philanthropy mainly comes from the company's contributions and is usually treated as a business expense.
- Funding can also consist of individual donations if, for example, someone wanted to donate to a corporation's nonprofit.
- Companies are allowed to deduct up to 10% of pretax income for direct charitable contributions (this includes giving to the company's foundation).
- The retailer enhances the diffusion of private-label (own-brand) products and directly steers ideation, production, and trade, leading to the retailer's natural channel leadership, which also results in the uplifting of local producer (suppliers).
- Hence, the CSR is all about stakeholder accountability, transparency in all dealings, and sustainability.

For example, Big Bazaar India's biggest value retailer controlled by Future Group has been taking lot of initiatives to support the cause toward women empowerment. Initiatives had been taken to build the platform for distribution and marketing of women-led organization engaged in producing food products, textiles, and handicraft. An immensely successful initiative of this nature was "Yatra," a joint effort between Big Bazaar and Yashaswini, a self-help group platform. The purpose was to encourage the efforts of underprivileged women traders through establishing a channel for them to sell their produce in a profitable manner. The idea was to serve their customers, in an authentic manner, the rich, diverse, traditional cuisine and food items from each geographical region within the state of Maharashtra. Similar initiatives with self-help groups and local indigenous communities have been initiated in the states of Assam, Karnataka, Kerala, and Delhi and have met with very encouraging responses from customers and the communities.

Some of the common forms of corporate philanthropy are:

- **Cash donations:** including grants, donations, sponsorships—whenever money exchanges hands.
- **In-kind donations:** such as donating products, access to employee volunteer groups, the use of a company's facilities, property, or services as examples—whenever nonmonetary support is given.

For example, one of the leading coffee retailers in the world, Starbucks, has more than 15,000 coffee shops in more than 35 countries. Starbucks donates nonperishable food products and gift and novelty items from its facilities throughout the year. Items help stock food in pantries and other resource centers for needy individuals.

Similarly, The Home Depot, one of the world's largest home-improvement chains and second largest retailer in the USA, donates building supplies and materials from its more than 2,150 stores to nonprofits focused on affordable housing, neighborhood revitalization, and rebuilding communities. Through its best-in-class retail donation program called Framing Hope, needy families and impoverished neighborhoods affected by disaster, neglect, and economic downturn will be empowered and enhanced.

CSR is of high topicality in business practice across all industries. Even though CSR is not a new idea and there are several retailers that have always cared for socially responsible behavior, CSR activities such as ethical sourcing, corporate philanthropy, cause-related marketing, or socially responsible employment have been introduced or intensified by retail companies mainly in the past several years.

Leveraging Strategic CSR for Branding and Positioning

"Doing well by doing well" has become a familiar motto in the business community, which acknowledges that the motivation to "do well" is at least partly self-serving. The reasons why retailers engage in philanthropy initiatives are not only routed in legal rules or accounting regulations. Retailers are also aware that their customers more and more evaluate them according to their socially responsible behavior. It is observed that consumers do remember those brands that value them as humans; they will remember what they bought in the past. Thus, the question of whether to act and practice socially responsible or not is not only an ideological one but also an economic one as it imprints positive image in the minds of key stakeholder and public. It is thought that consumers may prefer to "purchase products from companies with high ethical standards." If that is true, then "companies may increase profits by acting as upstanding corporate citizens."

Once involved in philanthropic endeavors, businesses should not be shy about their efforts. Many marketing experts opine that "the true definition of PR is to do good things and broadcast it." You have every right to have some publicity, because that way you are doing some kind of charity and performing your responsibility toward your community in which you are operating. Today, companies are increasingly aligning their CSR initiatives and activities with their brand to reinforce the brand image, which in turn help them obtain good value from investing in CSR.

A strong brand gives many strategic advantages, ranging from the image as a good employer brand to customer loyalty to better corporate image and so on. All these strategic advantages eventually translate into better mindshare, market share, profitability, and better valuation. Companies that perform the philanthropic activities and CSR are perceived as having character and strong values and trustworthy.

For example, Gucci roped in Madonna, Jennifer Lopez, and Rihanna for philanthropy initiatives (nonprofit organizations) Raising Malawi and UNICEF projects. Frida Giannini, the creative director of Gucci, is deeply dedicated to and instrumental in Gucci's continued partnership with UNICEF. In February 2011, the US Fund for UNICEF recognized its efforts with the inaugural Woman of Compassion award. Frida is also on the board of directors of PPR Corporate Foundation for Woman's Dignity and Rights (now known as Kering Foundation), an organization that fights violence against women and promotes their empowerment.

Many times, it is observed that usually negative aspects of retailers' behavior are discussed in public and favorable behavior get less coverage in the media. The negative behavior of companies, which violates social norms, is believed to exert higher influence on consumer behavior. One of the most valuable assets of any company is its brand. Philanthropy and CSR influence perceptions positively and make the stakeholders feel good about the brand, which is the ultimate purpose of good branding too.

Hence, communication of philanthropic activities, both at the POS and in general marketing communications, is important to keep consumers informed about the companies' activities. However, various research study results accentuate the honesty, sincerity, and credibility of communication activities that are of key importance. Aligning the philanthropic CSR initiatives with the brand can be more fruitful because it engages consumers on values. Many times, consumers view the commercial advertisements with skepticism; they are more likely to accept and respect communication of social initiatives. In some cases, they even seek out or subscribe to updates to achieve a sense of satisfaction by being aware and responsible toward social causes. Hence, this provides a cohesive channel to the brands for being in touch with their consumers and other stakeholders. Hence, it has been progressively projected because organizations have recognized that besides growing their businesses, it is also important to shape responsible and supportable relationships with the community at large.

The Two-pronged Approach

Companies are taking the two-pronged approach for building a strong brand (Figure 13.1).

- Establishing perceived retailer attributes: First, the retailer establishes the unique positioning and perceived brand image in terms of merchandise mix—quality, service, ambience—store environment (location), and overall shopping experience.
- Establishing the image of socially responsible organization through strategic CSR: With this approach, they establish themselves as responsible corporate citizens. When a company works for a particular cause or works toward the betterment of society—through a strategically designed CSR program—it helps the company to build a credibility and reputation. It provides a platform of moral uprightness and establishes a retailer's reputation in the minds of customers and employees.

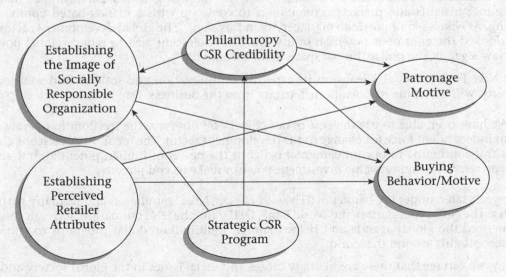

Figure 13.1: *Building a Strong Brand: The Integrated Approach*

Hence, the CSR program, when designed in conjunction with regular branding activities, positively influences people's perceptions. In order to create a holistic impact, retailer can seamlessly blend brand building and strategic CSR in an integrated way into the processes and systems and which is continuously evaluated and actively managed from within. This enhances their bonding (engagement) with the brand and eventually increases the patronage (loyalty) behavior. All this creates a "responsible" aura around the organization and helps the retailer not only to provide a satisfactory shopping experience but also to build respect and credibility.

Tata Trent Ltd, corporate sustainability at Tata Trent, integrates economic progress, environmental concerns, and social commitment. As retail organization, having a trained talent pool with a strong orientation for customer service is very important to business. Trent decided to address this challenge by tapping into the huge pool of talent available from the underprivileged sections of society. This initiative called Saksham (Sanskrit for "capable") was pioneered, which aims to enhance the employability skills and provide gainful employment to these sections of society. This program encourages and recognizes equal employment opportunity to underprivileged sections of society also. These programs enrich the quality of life and opportunities for all. Also every year, a special fund is created from the sale of diyas and stars from the stores during Diwali and Christmas, respectively. Trent has initiated 23 projects that are aligned with areas of "Child, Education, and Nutrition."

Another example is Starbucks, which has openly declared its commitment to conducting its business ethically. The company's Business Ethics and Compliance program supports the Starbucks' mission and helps protect its culture and reputation, by providing resources that help its employees make ethical decisions at work. This program develops and distributes awareness materials, including the standards of business; facilitates legal compliance and ethics training; investigates sensitive issues such as potential conflicts of interest; and provides additional channels for partners to voice concerns.

Strategic Focus

In 2004, after deciding on the importance of a high leverage approach to philanthropy, the Nike Foundation conducted a "business analysis," applying Nike's core competencies in consumer insights and market segmentation to come up with a market-based approach to giving. As Nike's senior portfolio manager Adam Day says, "The global development sector had overlooked the enormous potential of investing in adolescent girls to reduce global poverty. We saw a gap in the philanthropic space that we could fill."

The Nike Foundation also leans on its expertise in innovation and scale to find solutions to poverty, while keeping its operations separate from the business. Day says:

> We have been able to use the best of our Nike DNA, but have the freedom to operate as an independent force for change in the development sector. The focus on adolescent girls is truly authentic to our fundamental belief in the power of human potential, but also represents the highest value investment you can make to end poverty.

Five years later, under the banner of "The Girl Effect," Nike Foundation and its many partners, such as the NoVo Foundation, the World Bank, DFID, and the UN Foundation, have successfully influenced the global agenda and helped launch multimillion-dollar programs to empower adolescent girls around the world.

Today, we can see that there are so many causes and social issues in the global society and also so many brands in the global market. We can say that there is availability of a brand for every social cause and a social cause for every brand. These brands gain high levels of brand equity in terms of preference. This eventually results in increased customer loyalty, word-of-mouth recommendation, and enhanced marketing effectiveness, leading to higher profitability. So, retail companies are increasingly looking at moving from ad hoc philanthropy to strategically powerful brand-oriented CSR.

For example, global retail major Walmart, in line with its global women's economic empowerment program, works in association with a nonprofit organization WEConnect International to market and promote the products made by women-owned businesses. The retailer has also launched a "women owned" logo in collaboration with this nonprofit organization to identify and brand the products made by women-owned businesses. Under this initiative, the certified businesses that are at least 51% women owned, operated, and controlled by women can display the logo on their product packaging to be sold across Walmart stores in the country. The objective of this program is to help bring recognition to products made by women-owned businesses and to provide them a platform to market and sell these products. Sourcing from women-owned businesses contributes to their reputation for great assortment and quality local products. The idea behind increasing sourcing from women-owned businesses is to develop a strong base of women suppliers, as they are expanding their stores in the country. Hence, this has created a win–win situation for both: the women-owned businesses and Walmart. Besides this marketing support, the company also has a host of other initiatives such as training women for retail sector, in factories, and farming with partners. Hence, the company, in collaboration with partners, works toward identifying women-owned businesses, making them part of the supply chain, and training them to develop capacity and scale up their businesses.

Summary

Today, consumers are actively looking for information on social networks regardless of the stage consumers are in the purchase cycle. Brands highlight their value proposition explicitly or implicitly and to influence and motivate the consumers to make a purchase. On the other hand, consumers are increasingly sharing their purchase and post-purchase experience with a brand on discussion forums, blogs, reviews sites, and other online platforms. Social media has emerged as a strong influencing factor in the sales funnel. The purchase journey of consumers begin with several brands, research for a few with regard to the merchandise mix and overall shopping experience on the brand's owned social media properties (Facebook page, YouTube channel, Twitter handle, Pinterest boards, and other platforms). After that, they go through consumer-generated content on review sites, blogs, forums, and testimonials and then do shopping with regard to a brand. Once they have decided on the brand, they choose a channel of purchase (off-line or online) based on past experience, convenience, and overall shopping experience.

Hence in the ever-evolving world of multichannel retailing, while the traditional marketing and communication channels like advertisement, promotion, and PR are being used for increasing brand awareness and building strong brands, the social media platforms are being used to amplify consumer-generated content, facilitate the dialog between brands and consumers, enhance brand engagement, and improve loyalty.

Also as far as the CSR is concerned, the need of the hour is that it should be approached in the holistic way and needs to be integrated (collaborated) with the core business strategy for addressing social, environmental, and economic impacts of businesses. The form of CSR is not only important but also crucial for the retailer to understand what its brand is all about, what is its brand philosophy, and hence what they need to do, to reinforce the brand image and positioning. So if designed, developed, and implemented with right approach and in a right way, brand building and CSR can perfectly complement each other.

Review Questions

1. How will you evaluate the PR campaigns vis-à-vis advertising in the context of retailing? Justify your views with the help of appropriate examples.
2. Discuss the objectives and scope of PR in the context of retailing with appropriate examples.
3. "PR: a gateway to social relationship and community engagement." Comment on this statement. Justify your views with appropriate examples.
4. Discuss the role and significance of PR in today's retailing scenario.
5. Social media has emerged as a very influential tool of PR. Comment on this statement. Justify your views with appropriate examples.
6. Explain the role and significance of social media: content creation and content extension in PR campaigns.
7. Briefly explain how the retailers can evaluate the success of their social media campaign in the context of enhancing PR.
8. Briefly explain the concept of social media analytics with its importance in the context of enhancing PR.
9. Briefly explain the importance and challenges of social media analytics.
10. Explain in detail the philanthropy and strategic CSR with its importance in the context of today's retailing scenario.
11. Explain in detail how retailers are leveraging the strategic CSR in enhancing the patronage loyalty of customers.

Store Management

Introduction

Today, with the growth of e-tailing and in the era of multichannel shopping experience, the retail industry is experiencing a paradigm shift. Consumers today have very high expectations toward the quality of merchandise, service, and overall shopping experience. The nontraditional retail players are leading the way, providing innovative customer journeys and exposing and exploring gaps in offerings and service provided by the traditional retailers.

Hence, in the context of this new reality, incremental adjustments to the store format and product portfolio can no longer be sufficient to satisfy the demanding consumers. So a thorough rethink of the purpose of the store in the consumer shopping journey and the number of stores required to reach the target audience are necessary. Today, retailers need to redefine the store proposition and need to develop a convincing reason: why the customer should come to them or patronize their stores. They need to create differentiation and identify the ways to address the changing needs of the customers in the best possible ways. The retail organizations need to focus on whether or not its stores are performing in terms of customer service, in line with the brand promise and generating expected revenues and profit at the unit level. As far as branding and positioning are concerned, major responsibility lies with the flagship stores, and they act as the benchmarks and role models for other group stores. The flagship stores are aimed at brand building and creating aspirational value that get propagated to other outlets of the retailer. The money spent on flagship stores should be construed as advertising and marketing expenses, and the spending should be defined by one's P&L statement.

However, while managing the stores, it is also imperative to respect the regional preferences because just replicating the stores across cities without considering the city- and region-specific flavor may not work. Going forward, the stores need to be a "manifestation" of the brand image and a "destination" for the consumers where they will get much more than simply shopping, browsing, and transacting. Today, we can see that retailers are offering a dedicated space to create new customer experiences in store that entertain the shoppers. For instance, fashion retailers are increasingly leveraging video content, large display screens, and interactive display interfaces in store to attract and mesmerize shoppers. The idea here is to offer fresh experiences with relevant and regularly updated digital content to increase footfalls and boost revenues. The brick-and-mortar retailers are also leveraging stores to conduct learning and community events that increase the customer engagement with the brand as a whole. Hence, they need to act as an integral part of the multichannel shopping experience and cannot be confined as silos.

Store Management: Major Functions and Operations

It is necessary to start with the consumer and understand how the store is going to cater the customer requirement and meet their expectations. So a clear view on consumers' shopping behavior across the channels is crucial to determine and shape the proposition in each channel and in particular the store. The consistency in execution in terms of relevant ranges, price points, and service offering is very critical to run an effective and efficient business model.

Some significant features of retail operations, which help a retail store in its functioning and performance, are as follows (Figure 14.1):

- Customer service and selling process
- Store staffing and scheduling
- Retail floor and shelf management
- Store administration and facilities management
- Warehousing and SCM
- Loss (shrinkage) prevention
- POS/cashiering process
- VM and displays

As today's consumer do not distinguish between channels, the stores need to develop a seamless integration with all other channels, providing access to full assortment, customers preferences, order information, and so on.

For example, Burberry turns their London store into an entertainment destination, at the beginning of each season for getting engaged with customers through an audiovisual experience featuring huge screens and iPads. The regular customers are invited to the store and provided with an exclusive opportunity to buy the latest range of the season. Customers enjoy the view of new collection through catwalks broadcasted (showcased) on the big screens in the store. They are then enabled to purchase the selected items via iPads. This is how the retailers are offering a coherent shopping experience to their customers to increase their patronage behavior, which in turn gets translated in to the increased revenues and profits.

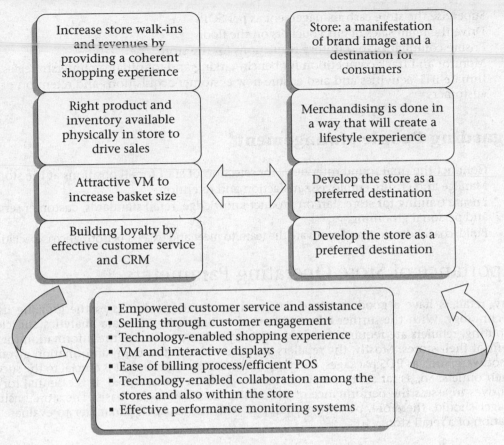

Figure 14.1: *Scope of Store Functions and Operations*

Key Responsibilities/Functions of the Modern Store Business Managers/Management

Regarding Store Operations

- Finalize and drive store-level sales to achieve the budgeted revenues and bottom line
- Analyze brand/category performance with the territory category managers to ensure the right product mix for the store
- Ensure adequate facilities, store ambience, and services for staff and customers
- Create effective checks to track utilization of store expenses
- Ensure adherence to retail standards
- Regularly review stock status and monitor timely replenishments (from warehouse to the store)
- Implement and adhere to the standard operating procedures (SOPs) for all retail operations
- Track and minimize shrinkage, damage, and pilferage within norms

- Supervise the store cash management as per SOPs
- Drive the retail sales of gift vouchers on the floor
- Ensure compliance to statutory regulations for the store
- Monitor and track competition for benchmarking and to initiate counterstrategies.
- Initiate BTL activities and also ensure new customer acquisitions and retention of TIC customers

Regarding People Management

- Conduct the final round interviews for selection of staff for all positions at the store.
- Manage and ensure employee satisfaction and retention.
- Ensure training for store staff on product knowledge, retail standards, customer service, and personal grooming.
- Build, coach, develop, and motivate the team to meet and exceed performance expectations.

Importance of Store Operating Parameters

Today, retailers have a good access to data and information, thanks to the growing usage of technology. With the further advancement of technologies like data analytics and cloud computing, retailers are required to acquire the expertise to optimize the information for the benefit of their stores. Mostly, the retailers are piled up with too many information given by ERP software, such as POS packages, and they think over as to find what is crucial to the success of their outlets. So, as far as the front-end retail operation is concerned, it is essential for the executives to assess the performance of the outlets on a day-to-day basis. The store business manager should, therefore, be always equipped with the dipstick parameter to evaluate the operation of a retail store.

Dipstick Parameters

Dipstick parameters assist to identify the strengths and weaknesses of certain facets of retail operations at a given point, such as customers, space, finance, and staff. These facets are discussed in detail in this section.

Customer Transactions

Customer conversion rate is the percentage of the customers that actually purchased/billed something out of total walk-ins (footfalls). So the store managers need to analyze the following: Has the conversion rate gone up? How many customers visited the store (walk-ins or footfall) as compared to the corresponding period last year? How does the day-to-day average cash memo value or ticket size be compared with the average value of last month or last year? How much has this gone up during a promotion and hence what is the threshold ticket size that should be considered to boost sales for the forthcoming promotion? The analysis of these parameters will help achieve the store's objectives.

$$\text{Customer conversion rate (\%)} = \frac{\text{No. of customer transacted}}{\text{No. of customer Visited}} \times 100$$

The percentage shows retailer's ability to convert a prospective customer into a buyer, which is also called as "percentage yield rate" or "walk to buy ratio." A small figure points out that the marketing efforts are not being turned into business sales. It essentially suggests the marketing and sales efforts that are required to put.

Returns to Net Sales Ratio

Before discussing this ratio, we need to understand the term "net sales" here. Net sales are the total sales for a given period of time after customer returns and allowances have been deducted from the gross sales figure. So by showing the value of returned goods and allowances as a percentage of net sales, this ratio is a window that shows customer satisfaction toward the quality of product offered by a retailer that includes both quality of merchandise and service or effectiveness or may be clarity of the offers and promotions. So, any rise in this figure gives an early indication of caution to the retailer. This could mean that customer expectations are not being fulfilled, and therefore, the quality of the merchandise needs to be reviewed.

$$\text{Return to net sales (\%)} = \frac{\text{Total return and allowance}}{\text{Net sales}} \times 100$$

Transactions per Hour

It is the ratio of number of transactions to the number of hours. This information can be obtained from the cash registers, as it maintains a record of the time of transaction. It enables the store manager to keep a close track on the number of sales transactions happening (closing) per hour, day, week, or season. This information is very crucial in order to schedule store opening hours (especially during promotions) and preparation of staff roaster, especially for cashiers.

$$\text{Transaction per hour} = \frac{\text{Number of transaction}}{\text{Number of hours}}$$

Sales per Transaction

For any product category or SKU, this ratio can be computed by evaluating in terms of percentage of the quantity of that specific product or SKU sold from the stock.

$$\text{Sales per transaction} = \frac{\text{Net sales}}{\text{Number of transaction}}$$

Hourly Customer Traffic

The number of footfalls per hour at a given time (hourly customer traffic) is observed for the whole store or for particular department to order to ensure that sufficient number of staff is available to serve them at that particular point of time and also to plan store working hours. Store managers apply this method to work out the graph of customer traffic on an hourly, daily, weekly, or seasonally basis.

$$\text{Hourly customer traffic} = \frac{\text{Customer traffic in}}{\text{Number of hours}}$$

Stocks and Selling Price Comparison

The control on total value of goods sold or cost of merchandise sold is vital for profitability. The buyer when decides on what merchandise to buy, he or she also makes decisions regarding the cost, transportation, and credit terms as they are related to these purchases. It is the actual practice that the accurate cost of goods sold is determined on the basis of complete calculation that represents the total cost of goods purchased, beginning with an invoice or billed cost to which other factors are adjusted as shown below.

Total cost of merchandise = Billed cost (Invoice) + Charges for inward transportation − Workroom costs − Cash discount

Now to determine the strength of one's stockholding, the average selling price is required to be drawn out compared to the average stock price. The situation is considered to be quite ideal if in case both occur to be near to the same value. This evaluation essentially helps the store management to determine whether the store is overstocked or understocked, in any given category.

$$\text{Average selling price} = \frac{\text{Total value of goods sold}}{\text{Total quantity sold}}$$

Stock Turnover Ratio

The stock turnover ratio is the rate at which the average inventory is replaced or turned over, throughout a predefined standard operating period, typically one year. Stock turns or turnover is the number of times the "average" inventory of a given merchandise is sold annually. It helps to determine what the inventory level should be to achieve or support the sales levels desired or predicted and hence gives a crucial insight regarding the performance.

When the store managers turn more stocks, they are able to generate more returns. Hence, turning stock around efficiently generates better profits. This can be established for any category or SKU any time by checking the proportion sold from the stock of a specified category or SKU.

$$\text{Average stock price} = \frac{\text{Total value of merchandise in stock}}{\text{Total quantity of stock}}$$

For example, in the category where the dipstick is employed, if daily sales account for 4% of stock, it will take 25 days to sell the entire stock. Then, dividing the number of days in the year (365) by 25, we get the number of stock turns for the year (14.6 times). This enables store manager to compare it with the store's target for stock turns and start corrective measures, if required. So here we can conclude that it is the GMROI (gross margin return on inventory) that is crucial.

Hence, stock turnover is basically the way retailers make money. Though it is not the profit per unit of sale that brings money for the retailer, it is the sales on a regular basis over a period of time that eventually results in profitability.

$$\text{Stock turnover/inventory turnover rate} = \frac{\text{Net sales}}{\text{Average inventory at retail (sales)}}$$

$$\text{Stock turnover/inventory turnover rate} = \frac{\text{Cost of goods sold}}{\text{Average inventory at cost}}$$

If the inventory is recorded at cost, stock turn equals cost of goods sold divided by the average inventory. And when the inventory is recorded at sales value, stock turn is equal to sales divided by average inventory.

One of the concerns to retailers is the number of times a year most items in an average inventory are sold out. More often an inventory turns over, the less is the need for a high markup. On the contrary, the lower is the number of stock turnovers, the higher the markup to make a profit.

Let us suppose that a fashion retailer who sells men's and women's wear experiences that for menswear, the stock does not turnover as compared to that of women's wear. This is because men do not buy cloths as many times as women do. So men's items are often marked higher than that of women's wear as they purchase more items and hence turnover of the stock with higher frequency.

Similarly, too frequent inventory turns can be as great a potential problem as too few. Too frequent inventory turns may indicate the business is trying to overwork a limited capital base, and may carry with it the attendant costs of stockouts and unhappy and lost customers. At the same time, they must be balanced against excessive inventory because of carrying costs.

This also enables the retailers to examine the performance of each supplier in terms of:

- Maintained markup (the measure of how much profit the company was able to garner over the cost of the merchandise).
- The number of returns by customer.
- Stock turnover (the measure of the average time it took to sell the items).
- The reliability of shipments (whether the given orders were received on committed time and quality.

Evaluating the Store Performance

The last decade is characterized by events that marked the unprecedented change. Due to both the severity and magnitude of change, retail organizations are now being compelled to include "change management" as one of the key competences in their competency framework. With the growth of e-commerce, the consumer behavior is continuously being refined and retail organizations redesign to be compliant and relevant with the new rules of retail business and, at the same time, cater the ever-growing expectations of the consumers. Hence, retailers increasingly need to develop an understanding of how consumer behavior is evolving and the impact of these changes on consumer expectations both inside and outside of the brick-and-mortar store. As consumers become more tech savvy, they tend to take the charge of their own shopping experience, identifying and leveraging many different sources of information and channels to optimize the different elements of their shopping journey. But before designing the PMS, we need to first understand the key parameters that are measures of performance of a store.

Store Performance Parameters

Over the years, several models have been built to understand the performance parameters of retail outlets and regarded as a management tool for assessing and improving productivity and financial performance in retailing. However, the three very basic but very important tools for measuring the performance of a retail store are inventory, space, and people. While gross margin percentage, inherently reflective of the retailer's initial markup decision, is a central component, productivity of these three aspects eventually becomes the base for performance evaluation.

- Retail inventory (GMROI)
- Retail space (square footage) (GMROF)
- People or human capital (GMROL)

The biggest benefits of these parameters is the insights they provide to the retailer, which is very essential for planning, executing, and benchmarking the inventory, space, and people strategies in an integrative way.

GMROI Percent Inventory Carrying Costs

Today, if we talk about the multi-store retailers, the biggest working capital investment is in inventory. So to monitor and control the profitability, the retailers need to analyze their ROI. GMROI is a simple formula that combines the stock turn rate and gross profit percentage of merchandise to arrive at a figure that shows the ROI for that inventory. The GMROI equation is generally known as the sales to inventory ratio or the S/I index, and it is "reflective" of the inventory turnover ratio of any retailer. The ratio "cost of goods sold" divided by "average value of inventory at cost" is also being used by some retailers. Excessive inventory is a possibility provided by one of these ratios decline.

GMROI is especially useful for comparing the relative ROI of high turnover, low-margin items and low turnover, high-margin items. It essentially shifts the focus from sales to the ROI of the merchandise items.

$$\text{Percent inventory carrying costs} = \frac{\text{Inventory carrying costs}}{\text{Net sales}} \times 100$$

However, over a period of time, with the changing market dynamics, the high interest rate has resulted in increase in inventory carrying costs, and therefore, the ratios have become more significant. To reduce obsolescence of stock and to prevent blockage of working capital, this measure is used. The fixed costs of maintaining inventory indicates net sales. This measure is used to track the percentage of their net sales.

$$\text{Gross margin return on inventory} = \frac{\text{Gross margin}}{\text{Net sales}} \times \frac{\text{Net sales}}{\text{Average value of inventory}}$$

$$\text{Gross margin return on inventory} = \frac{\text{Gross margin}}{\text{Average value inventory}}$$

With modern retail ERP systems, GMROI for every item stocked can be reported "at the click of a button." Expressed in monitory terms, the parameter GMROI provides comparison of the margin on sales vis-à-vis the original cost of merchandise. This computation provides the value of return one achieves on investments in specific merchandise item. So with the help of GMROI analysis on all items in all stores, retailers can rapidly identify the items that give best and worst ROI in them. Hence, it becomes easy for a retailer to address the problems with the items giving the lowest ROI, or to replace them with products similar to one giving much better ROI.

Though inventory can be evaluated at (a) retail price and (b) cost price, most retailers tend to use the value at retail price because it is more easily available. However, limitation in this is that it may not give a realistic picture of investments in specific merchandise.

The two parameters that can bring about huge changes in GMORI value are:

1. Gross margin
2. Inventory turnover

This clearly indicates that there are two "ways" to a higher GMROI:

1. Change (e.g., increase) the gross margin percentage and/or
2. Change (e.g., increase) the sales to inventory ratio or the S/I index

Hence, GMROI simultaneously measures the ability of the retailer to achieve a target margin and a target turnover number. Reducing markdowns is another strategy for improving GMROI.

For instance, a multi-store retailer may continuously track the sale of a merchandise item store-wise. Let us say Store A is selling that merchandise item faster than plan and will sell out early. Store B is selling slower than plan but a markdown may help it along. Store C is performing really poorly in case of that merchandise, and even a large markdown may not be enough to clear the inventory. In such a case, the retailer may consider moving merchandise from Store C to Store A, where it can still sell at full price. This meticulous approach toward applying markdowns selectively and transfer merchandise judiciously is an important component in increasing gross margin.

GMROF: Managing the Space with Profitability

For brick-and-mortar retailers, space utilization in a productive manner is the key to success. With the phenomenal growth of e-retailing and the heavy discounting done by them, the margins of brick-and-mortar retailers are under pressure. Retailers are reevaluating the use of retail floor space, with space being focused not only on driving the sales but also on engaging the shoppers.

Therefore, these retailers are increasingly focusing on the parameters that assess space productivity. One such parameter is nothing but GMROF (gross margin return on footage). This parameter basically measures the gross profit margin achieved by a specific retail store divided by the total square footage of the sales area or of the store.

Space being a key element, its productivity can also be measured using various other elements of retail costs:

1. Stock
2. Customer
3. Employees
4. Facilities

In monitory terms, these performance parameters can convert occupancy cost into a money value per unit of selling space. These parameters give an idea of the quantum of gross margin in money value for each unit of space that is deployed for retailing to achieve full coverage of occupancy cost.

$$\text{Occupancy cost per square feet selling space} = \frac{\text{Occupancy cost}}{\text{Square feet of selling space}}$$

Whether expressed in quantity or value, this parameter is useful to compare alternate allotment of space to different merchandise lines. It is also useful to compare performance of different departments within store by applying a standard benchmark. This ratio will change depending on the variety of merchandise and the models used for retailing. This parameter is utilized by retailers to work out the percentage of total space that is actually used as sales space.

Net Sales per Square Foot

Inventory per selling (square foot) in retailing is a widely used measure of merchandise intensity, and its multiplication with the S/I index gives the measure of space productivity in retailing, which is net sales per square foot. While the merchandise intensity is defined as "inventory per square foot," its multiplication with the "margin on inventory" computes the space productivity result.

$$\text{Net sales per square foot} = \frac{\text{Net sales}}{\text{Square feet of selling space}}$$

$$\text{Stock Per Square Foot} = \frac{\text{Net stock}}{\text{Square feet of selling space}}$$

$$\text{Percentage of Selling Space} = \frac{\text{Selling space in square feet}}{\text{Total space in square feet}} \times 100$$

$$\text{Gross margin return on footage} = \frac{\text{Gross margin}}{\text{Net sales}} \times \frac{\text{Net sales}}{\text{Selling space in square feet}}$$

$$\text{Gross margin return on footage} = \frac{\text{Gross margin}}{\text{Selling space in square feet}}$$

Because of the rising property value, increase cost of lease/rent, and growing competition from the e-retailers who do not have to bear the space cost, analyzing the "productivity of space" employed is of utmost importance to all the brick-and-mortar retailers. The most effective way is to use sales/sq. ft/month (or day), as most retailers pay the rent on monthly basis. This measure when considered along with the rent/sq. ft/month gives the actual productivity of the space (Table 14.1).

Let us, for instance, consider a department store where sales of a specific department is

Sales = A = 60,00,000

Area = B = 10,000 sq. ft

Then the sales per sq. ft = C = A/B = 60,00,000/10,000 = 600

And per day sales = D = C/30 = 600/30 = 20

Here, we can also measure the productivity of staffs by just assuming the number of staff is 10.

Sales/staff/month = 60,00,000/10

= 6,00,000

And per day = 6,00,000/30 = 20,000

As discussed, efficiency is the ratio of effective output (referred as gross margin earned) to inputs. So if output is referred to the net sales, then the effective output is the gross margin earned in amount. So using the above example, returns/sq. ft and returns/staff can be considered as the respective efficiency measures for the productivity measures of sales/sq. ft and sales/staff.

Hence,

Sales = A = 60,00,000

Gross margin (%) = B = 30%

Gross margin = C = A × B = 60,00,000 × (30/100) = 18,00,000

Area = D = 10,000 sq. ft

Then

Returns/sq. ft/month = E = C/D = 18,00,000/10,000 = 180

And returns/sq. ft/day = F = C/D/30 = 180/30 = 6

Example: Trader Joe's

In the USA, Trader Joe's is a prime example of a retail brand that uses multiple best-practice strategies for its proprietary portfolio offerings. While Trader Joe's may be considered small in reach when compared to other food retailers, it is clear that this brand has been developed around its target audiences because it galvanizes a cult-like following of loyal gourmet food enthusiasts.

The supply side of the coin is as interesting to note as the consumer demand side. Trader Joe's should be admired for its ability to manage and sustain powerful relationships with manufacturers and suppliers. It purchases in bulk from manufacturers whenever possible and does not mandate slotting and promotional allowances from partners.

In addition, a clear commitment to superior merchandise mix, merchandise quality, a store environment that furthers the brand proposition and well-defined merchandising strategies help in outlining the strategic direction of the retailer. Trader Joe's private-label offering contributes powerfully to its brand proposition; approximately, 85–90% of store offering is PL, and there are about 2,000 SKUs in the portfolio, and sales per square foot are more than twice that of supermarkets and three times that of other specialty stores.

Table 14.1: *SPF (Sales per Square Feet) Analysis*

A sample worksheet of a department retailer showing how the SPF analysis is done (month till date (MTD) analysis) and the growth over last year (GOLY) is computed (SPF: sales per square feet)

Dept Name	Area	Budget	Budgeted SPF	Last Year (LY)			Current Year (CY)			Growth/Degrowth		
				Sal Qty	Net Value	SPF	Sal Qty	Net Value	SPF	Sal Qty	Net Value	SPF
Ethnic MNM	2142	4119393	62	10062	4053809	61	6046	2784581	42	-40%	-31%	-31%
Ethnic Sarees	1408	901117	21	662	1071996	25	215	435537	10	-68%	-59%	-60%
Ethnic SKD	918	514924	18	819	1239346	44	376	684889	24	-54%	-45%	-45%
Western casual	3024	3218276	34	10982	4691933	50	3900	2102890	22	-64%	-55%	-55%
Denim	740	1544772	67	2241	1948786	85	1381	1340138	58	-38%	-31%	-31%
Formal	292	643655	71	1830	1142074	126	644	492673	54	-65%	-57%	-57%
Sports	27	64366	77	240	119737	143	123	95555	114	-49%	-20%	-20%
Winter wear	101	257462		1026	858386		1038	826624		1%	-4%	
Night wear	101	347574	111	824	224687	72	321	120873	39	-61%	-46%	-46%
Under garments	702	1158579	53	2293	876479	40	2261	867566	40	-1%	-1%	-1%
Total	8921	12873104	47	32035	17166069	58	16307	9751707	35	-46%	-37%	-23%

Table 14.2: *GOLY—Growth over Last* Year

Dept	Jan'2015	Jan'2016	GOLY	Jan'16 Tgt	Ach(%)	Area	SPF
Brand Style	159185	112042	–30%	133015	84%	80	45
BS-Accessories	184230	57108	–69%	92475	62%	124	15
BS-Clothing	4183444	2340710	–44%	3400297	69%	2604	29
BS-Infants	750092	287771	–62%	303587	95%	1112	8
BS-Nursery	521391	268849	–48%	425265	63%	0	0
BS-Winter	75959	3604	–95%	29203	12%	131	1
BS-Toys	2258395	748841	–67%	1700453	44%	2081	12
Grand Total	8132696	3818925	–53%	6084295	63%	6132	20

GMROL: Managing the Productivity of Investment in People

As discussed earlier, retailers need to enable and empower their staff to connect and build relationship with the customers and provide them a personalized shopping experience. This implies a change in the role of the sales associates. They now have become the brand advocates and are live form of interface of the brand with their customers. So they should be trained and motivated to execute the shopping experience that reflect the brand image of the retailer.

The usual way to measure employee productivity is to assess with the sales turnover that is achieved. Such parameters are normally divided by total sales of a day by total number of salespersons deployed. In free access format, the parameters generally used divide total number of cash memos/customer handled by a specific salesperson. It is again the gross margin return on labor (GMROL) employed for that matters. Today, retailers continuously evaluate their talent management strategy and the implications on aspects such as training and pay structure.

$$\text{Net sales per full-time employee} = \frac{\text{Net sales}}{\text{Total full-time employees}}$$

Expressed either in terms of quantity or rupee value, this measure represents the average sales generated by each full-time employee. It is also used by many retailers to set target of performance for sales personnel.

$$\text{Labor productivity} = \frac{\text{Total labor cost}}{\text{Net sales}} \times 100$$

This parameter computes the productivity of labor by evaluating the labor cost component to achieve a targeted sales turnover.

$$\text{Gross margin per full-time employee} = \frac{\text{Gross margin}}{\text{Total full-time employees}}$$

Expressed in monetary terms, this ratio represents the gross profit generated per employee. It can be used to find out the sales employees' performance. Though this is not the only measure of an employee's performance, it can provide a starting point for closer examination. To improve the performance and hence the profitability, the store associates need to adapt the changes that will cater the changes in consumer behaviors. So the store employees need to be trained on the skill sets that will enable them to provide a coherent shopping experience supported by technology. It is observed that conversion rates increase when customers are assisted by employees who possess and continuously develop a high degree of product knowledge and demonstrate strong interpersonal skills.

In a nutshell, the "cost of store space" is often very high, and it includes all the items that make up total occupancy costs, including rent, depreciation, security, taxes, facility (property) management and maintenance, interest on a mortgage, and so on. For some retailers, especially mall-based specialty stores, occupancy costs can very easily surpass the cost of manpower, which is usually considered to be the highest expense of being in a labor-intensive service business like retailing.

Perhaps an equally important reason for accentuating on "productivity of space" as the key model metric is because retail store space is basically a relatively "rigid" investment decision that is quite difficult to reverse in the short to moderate time frames. Many times, retailers tend to get into fairly long-term lease agreements that may come with a burdensome conviction. This may eventually trouble them with high fixed lease payments for many years to come. So maximizing the productivity of an expensive (and scarce) input, that is, retail space is practically more crucial goal and priority followed by maximizing the productivity of a relatively inexpensive input in inventory. Hence, the key to maximizing profitability in retailing would be to maximize GMROF and set an optimal target for GMROI and GMROL.

Essentials for Designing a Performance Measurement System

Designing of performance measurement system is an extremely important task for an organization. Success in designing the right PMS would be critical for organization's success. As can be seen from the framework, numerous factors would impact the PMS of an organization. A number of internal and external drivers like changing customers, market situation, legal framework, actual performance, market situation, competition, and uncertainty may support and facilitate the evolution of PMS (Figure 14.2). But a number of constraints like organizational culture, technology, resources, and lack of motivation can work against the process. To address this challenge, many retail organizations are initiating a digital revolution and marketing change, embracing social media and mobile applications for branding, data analytics, and cloud technologies to increase the efficiency and hence the performance.

Development of a PMS is important for a retailer to track and monitor a retail outlet's performance over a defined period of time. Several of the retail start-ups fail due to lack of well-defined performance measurement program. It is important for a store not just to have variety of reports and information but also to analyze accurately with defined standards or predetermined goals. In case of any variance with the standards or goals, rectifying action should be taken immediately. Management accounting tools are used for measuring performance, providing inputs for decision-making and thereby managing performance. Decisions would be based on the basis of organizational goals, its strengths and weaknesses, and the business environment.

Management accounting information would enable the managers to take more accurate decisions and make the decision-making process more objective, transparent, and professional.

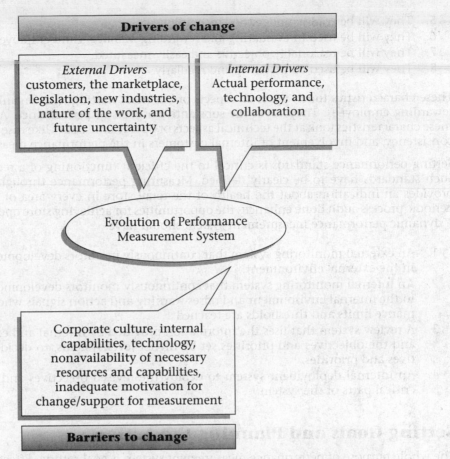

Figure 14.2: *Evolution of Performance Management System: Framework*

It can be obtained from varied functions within an organization, such as information management, treasury, efficiency auditing, marketing, valuation, pricing, and logistics. For a growing sector like retail, drawing the right information from various functional areas across the value chain is extremely important from the point of view of increasing efficiency in operations, enhancing profitability and sustainability under volatile business conditions.

For instance, large brick-and-mortar retailers have aligned their business models to Tier II and Tier III cities to drive growth. With the changing times and with the emergence of new business challenges, they are increasingly focusing on smaller stores with a limited assortment of products—based on price points—to achieve faster breakeven and control inventory.

Therefore, for a store to grow and prosper, a well-defined performance measurement program is absolutely essential.

Effective performance measures will have the following characteristics:

1. They will relate to the goals of the organization.
2. They will balance long-term and short term concerns.
3. They will reflect the management of key actions and activities.
4. They will be affected by actions of managers and employees.

5. They will be readily understood by employees.
6. They will be used in evaluating and rewarding managers and employees.
7. They will be reasonably objective and easily measured.
8. They will be used consistently and regularly.

These characteristics touch upon all aspects of business, starting with organizational goals to rewarding employees. They cover the substantive aspects of performance. At the same time, these characteristics look at the technical aspects or operational issues like ease of measurement, consistency, and involvement of internal customers in the performance measurement.

Setting performance standards is critical to the efficient functioning of a retail organization. Such standards have to be clearly defined. Measuring performance through defined reports provides an indication about the health of the retail store in every area of its operations. A periodic process audit done enhances the opportunities for achieving store operating efficiency. A dynamic performance measurement system should have:

1. An external monitoring system that continuously monitors developments and changes in the external environment.
2. An internal monitoring system that continuously monitors developments and changes in the internal environment and raises warning and action signals when certain performance limits and thresholds are reached.
3. A review system that uses the information provided by internal and external monitors and the objectives and priorities set by higher-level systems, to decide internal objectives and priorities.
4. An internal deployment system to deploy the revised objectives and priorities to the critical parts of the system.

Setting Goals and Planning the Action

The whole purpose of performance measurement system is goal setting. Effective performance measures are essential for all organization. Most organizations have multiple goals and therefore multiple performance measures are necessary for measuring and monitoring those goals. Not all measures are expressed in financial terms. A good performance measurement system would thus include both financial and nonfinancial goals.

The system focused on the following nine "key result areas."

Financial Key Result Areas

- Profitability
- Performance and productivity
- Market position

Nonfinancial Key Result Areas

- Preferential portfolio leadership
- Personnel development
- Employee attitudes
- Collaborative work culture
- Public responsibility
- Balance between short-run and long-range goals

Financial measures are objective in nature and are easy to measure and compare. But they have some limitations like their short-term focus, past orientation, and focus on external appearance rather than internal processes. Traditional performance measures based on cost and financial accounts have been criticized for having a short-term focus. Hence, relying completely on financial measures is not sufficient and can be harmful for several reasons:

1. It may encourage short-term actions that are not in the company's long-term interest.
2. The more focus given to meet current profit levels, the more likely the business manager will be to take short-term actions.
3. This short-sighted approach can drive the business to myopic situations, which is not favorable in such dynamic times, especially for the business of retailing.

With this understanding of the limitations of financial measures, a number of nonfinancial measures were designed.

Balanced Scorecard

The balanced scorecard is a tool, developed by Kaplan and Norton, to articulate, execute, and monitor strategy using a mix of financial and nonfinancial measures. It is designed to translate vision and strategy into objectives and measures across four balanced perspectives: financial, customers, internal business processes, and learning and growth.

A balanced scorecard is a performance measurement and reporting system that strikes a balance between financial and operational measures, links performance to rewards, and gives explicit recognition to the diversity of organizational goals. It thus takes care of most of the limitations of financial measure and fulfills the criteria for being a good performance measure.

The balanced scorecard translates mission and strategy into objectives and measures, organized into four perspectives: financial, customer, internal business process, and learning and growth.

There is a logical link and hierarchy between all these perspectives. A good learning and growth performance will lead to improved internal processes, leading to better performance on customer-related performance measures, thereby improving the financial performance.

Financial Perspective

The balanced scorecard retains financial measures as they are readily measurable, and they indicate whether the company's strategy, implementation, and execution are contributing to bottom-line improvement. Most commonly used financial measures are ROCE (return on capital employed), economic value added, sales growth, and cash flow.

This helps a retailer to methodically develop an action agenda. This can include solution to critical problem and constant feedback mechanism to improve operational efficiency. As the operation grows, it is important to improve the scope of analysis leading to higher sales and better profitability.

The success of any performance measurement program requires following key factors:

1. Engaging the employees by bringing "purpose centricity" to achieve the desired performance of the store.
2. Leveraging technology for appropriate collation, analysis, and sharing of information.
3. Effective review and goal-setting mechanism.

Customer Service Perspective

The customer perspective includes customer- and market-related measures, through which an assessment of effectiveness of the organization toward its customers and market segment is done. Customer perspective would typically include measures like customer satisfaction, customer retention, customer loyalty, new customer acquisition, customer profitability, and market share.

Internal business process perspective critical internal processes are identified as they would enable the organization to achieve financial- and customer-related performance goals. Each business has a unique set of processes for creating value for customers and obtaining financial results. The generic processes that would be adapted to specific conditions are:

- Innovation
- Operational efficiency
- Post-sales services

Learning and Growth Perspective

The learning and growth perspective focuses on the infrastructure that the organization must build to create a long-term growth and improvement. Organizational growth comes from three principal sources: people, systems, and organizational procedures. An organization must invest in people, systems, and procedures in order to bridge the gap between the existing capabilities and expected performance. The people-related measures in this category would include employee satisfaction, employee retention and long-term career planning, developing the culture of collaboration among employees, training, skilling and re-skilling, reward systems, and so on. The systems-related measures would be like real-time availability of relevant information, appropriateness of IT systems, and so on. Organizational procedures are examined to check the alignment of employee incentives with overall organizational success factors and rates of improvement in critical customer-related internal processes.

Transformation and Collaboration Perspective

In today's retail business scenario, one more facet needs to be added, that is, "transformation." Transformation is nothing but the ability to change rapidly in response to global and economic changes. However, the internal transformations in the business should lead to greater transparency and quick decision-making. The perfect collaboration and consensus are needed for quick decision-making mechanism, which is driven by the enterprise solutions today. Collaboration can improve the competitiveness and productivity of an organization. With the increasing complexities of businesses, organizations have taken the cognizance of the significance of employee engagement in achieving business goals and excellence. Over the years, with the growth and the geographical expansion of multi-store retail organizations, employee engagement has become crucial as a consequence of the constraints in ensuring frequent professional and personal conversation opportunities across all the possible touch points. Technology has enabled the organizations to bring people closer to each other than ever before, irrespective of geographic distances. E-mails, enterprise solutions, mobile connects, virtual sessions, social media, blogs, and customized intranet portals are some of the ways by which managers are able to connect with their employees anytime, anywhere, and thus are able to enhance the employee engagement. While HR function continues to act as the catalyst to enhance employee engagement, immediate managers play much bigger role than ever before in building teams that are engaged and motivated.

Thus, once the effective collaboration is achieved, it is easy to have a single point of information and data generation. In the obvious sense, collaboration can synergize and energize the whole ecosystem, leading to reduction in duplication of efforts and hence increase in the efficiency. The power of collaboration is bringing about very positive changes between businesses not only at the internal level but also at the global level. Hence, the collaboration, innovation, and technology are not merely redefining businesses; they are also restating the very rules of business. Hence, the collaboration, technology, and innovation have emerged as the major pillars of modern retailing.

Benchmarking

Despite significant evolution of the retail industry in the past few years, profitability remains the sector's biggest challenge. Benchmarking is a way of identifying potential improvements in effectiveness and efficiency. Stores have to turn their inventory at a faster pace with focus on offering quality of merchandise and seamless shopping experience. The organization looks at its internal processes and then looks at the best practices in those areas in other organizations. It can also be done within the organization, between various departments. It is commonly used for more generic or common processes and functions such as merchandise management, HR, overall shopping experience, processes, inventory/warehouse/delivery management, and finance.

Today, it is rapidly becoming the need of the hour for brick-and-mortar retailers to set their benchmarks and/or to achieve set by others to flourish in the subdued macroeconomic environment and to face the stiff competition from online retailers. Many times, companies keep on moving on the growth path, without paying attention to profitability, which could be detrimental in the long run. Profitability is built when growth is sustainable, and adequate measures are taken for enhancing the customer loyalty. Hence, profitability has to be visible during the course of investments that are being made to scale up.

Most of the brick-and-mortar chains have been focusing on profitability even if it means, in some cases, going slow in revenue growth. They are increasingly taking initiatives to improve operating efficiency, including the rightsizing of stores, increasing focus on PLs, exiting unviable product categories, and undertaking cluster-based store expansion. They are also accentuating on channelizing the resources toward revamping existing stores to improve same store sales (SSS) growth.

In today's retailing scenario, gaining customer loyalty has become very difficult. Customer is very demanding, tend to go for the next big discount or the next new thing, and demand seamless shopping experience. In such a context, the omni-channel models are becoming more relevant, and many players are revisiting their strategies and business models accordingly. This includes adopting the multichannel or omni-channel model of retailing. By going multichannel way, they are striving to push both physical and online sales in an attempt to provide a coherent shopping experience, increase revenue growth profitability and focus on Tier II and Tier III cities, new geographies, and/or new micro-markets within cities for expansion.

Also there is a major focus on consolidation among these retailers. The consolidation is aimed at leveraging the scale of operations and extent of reach to take on competition. These measures have the right potential to help the retailers to improve the financial risk profiles and enable them to successfully face the changing retailing business scenario and environment.

Example: Videocon

For example, Videocon Group is consolidating its retail operation across its three formats—Next Retail, Planet M, and Digiworld—by merging their back-end operations to form a common sourcing platform with the aim to bring scale, to improve profitability, make the operations leaner, and fighting online sales by ensuring better bargaining power with the brands for margins. The group has floated a new company, Techno Kart India, which will manage the back-end operations of all the three retail formats such as sourcing, marketing, HR, IT, warehousing, and supply chain. This structure is designed in such a way that it will also free up a lot of working capital, make the operations efficient, and will offer a united front to the brands for better margins.

The combined store count of Videocon's retail operation will be more than 1,150. Next Retail, which focuses on sales of multi-brand appliances and TVs, has 150 company-owned stores and 400 franchise outlets, while the cell phone/gaming/toys format Planet M has 75 company-owned stores. Digiworld, which used to sell only Videocon Group brands, has recently started selling Samsung and Panasonic brands as well, and has more than 500 franchisee-run stores and 40 company outlets.

This makes Videocon the third largest consumer electronics and cell phone retailer in India, next only after to Tata-owned Croma (first) and Reliance Digital (second).

Caselet: Juvalia & You

Juvalia & You is an innovative online jewelry brand that showcases international styles of fashion jewelry and accessories around the globe. It is basically a private-label e-commerce portal that sells fashion jewelry and works with a team of in-house external designers, including well-known names such as Ritika Sachdeva and Pooja Bhargava. The company designs products in-house and gives manufacturing contracts to third-party units. The company started its operations in 2012 in Delhi/NCR with a small team and around 20 founding stylist, and today, it has emerged as India's largest social selling jewelry brand.

The retailer follows a unique social selling concept (direct selling) wherein the company has strategically democratized entrepreneurship. The retailer brings fashion jewelry from around the globe to the Indian market. It essentially offers a flexible but, at the same time, very promising opportunity for women to establish their own business. However, with this unique model of social selling concept, the retailer faced some challenges as well, because finding entrepreneurial spirit in people was a big challenge. Considering this challenge, they have appointed some experienced professionals to take care of the different teams like creative, product, sales, marketing, operations, accounts, CRM, and IT, according to their expertise.

In a very short span of time, the company created a benchmark by reinventing power of social selling for the digital age and has evolved as a brand to reckon with. The company currently operates in many states of India with a robust team of professionals and over 80,000 stylist across India and still counting. Juvalia has an inventory-led model and ships products to different states depending on the demand. The company has witnessed a phenomenal growth rate and business expansion. The online jewelry brand has taken up the mission to create an entrepreneurial platform for women and blend it with design, fashion, jewelry, and accessories. It has launched its mobile application to facilitate on-the-go shopping. This also enhanced the shopping experience for its customers by allowing them to buy the latest international designs online from their mobile devices.

Juvalia & You India has been extensively following unique marketing strategies since its inception, which include their successful ATL and BTL activities like mall activations through pop-up retailing, product placements across leading GE (general entertainment) shows across leading channels like Sony and Star, and hosting style shows across nooks and corners of the country to propagate the direct selling business. They also offer customers a chance to touch and feel the merchandise through the direct selling channel, before they place their orders online. Hence, the off-line medium allows prospective buyers to research extensively before making a purchase decision online. With all these marketing programs and campaigns, Juvalia & You has successfully positioned itself as young, fashionable, warm, trendy, trustworthy, and vivacious brand. The brand is all about today's woman who is conscious about style and vogue. Each and every collection of Juvalia & You is designed exclusively keeping in mind the ever-changing preferences and taste of the modern women. Juvalia & You also performs on corporate citizenship (CSR) front by forging a partnership with NGO Lakshyam. Under this initiative, it trains underprivileged girls in jewelry design and selling techniques with an objective to promote self-reliance among women.

POS Management

It is essential for any retailer to analyze and understand customers' shopping behavior. For this purpose, retail stores require valuable customer insights before deploying and integrating the retail store automation systems. The key reason for retail automation is to enable and empower the store associates to provide better buying experience to the shoppers. This has led to deployment of many technology interfaces such as e-commerce, RFID, self-checkout, and touch screen information kiosk, among others. All this enables a retailer to inspire their customers to buy more with better shopping experience.

Now POS management is a crucial component of store operations that includes both front-end cashiering and back-end cash management, including banking. The process is essentially enabled by POS and back-end automation systems. We can see, and many times experienced, the inconvenience and irritation of waiting at the POS because of long queue. Shoppers generally do not want to wait while or after shopping. The brick-and-mortar retailers are already wrestling with their online rivals and are using cutting-edge POS solutions like handheld POS machines to help customers who are impatient with long queue at billing (checkout) counters, especially on weekends, festivals, and during promotional offers. Today, when many day-to-day transactions are increasingly done online or through a smartphone app, shoppers get annoyed by long queues. It is observed that many times, customers abandoning trolleys because of longer queues, and such mobile billing devices can help retailers to capture higher sales during peak demand time.

Keeping this in mind, many retailers are coming up with the POS solutions, which include touch screen terminals and applications to increase the speed of checkout. Retailers are increasingly exploring mobile POS, mobile payments, and related biometric technologies for shortening queue and to make the buying/billing process as simple as one-click online. Retailers are leveraging such solutions not only to bring essential changes to reduce checkout time but also to monitor and enhance productivity levels of their sales associates. There are two aspects here: one is convenience for customers and the other is tracking of transactions. This eventually leads to swifter movement of shoppers through the checkout lanes and provides them better buying experience.

For example, Shoppers Stop and Reliance Retail are among the retailers experimenting with system where store associates will be provided with handheld bar-code readers and POS machines. These associates will assist customers who have done with their shopping and ready for billing. They will help the customers for making payments, and the bill invoice will be sent to them by e-mail. This will save their time for waiting at the billing counter. Reliance Digital has deployed credit card swiping instruments at various places inside the store to enable shoppers to make payments. Customers need to visit the billing counter only if they want to convert the transaction into easy monthly installments. These mobile checkout solutions or systems are more or less similar to that of Apple, in which tablets equipped with credit card readers are used.

Such kind of cutting-edge innovative POS solutions help retailers to develop an efficient and reliable POS environment, which in turn improve the operational efficiency.

Some of the key benefits are as follows:

- Enhancement of shopping experience by stepping up of checkout process.
- Efficient execution of promotional activities and initiatives such as loyalty card programs through real-time customer sales tracking.
- Increase revenue by enabling promotions and advertising at the POS.
- Reduce lost sales by integrating supply chain and inventory information across the enterprise.
- Enhancement in productivity of sales associates by providing user-friendly interfaces.
- Integration of new media technologies to have audiovisual communication with shoppers at many touch points in the store.
- Integrating the web-based technologies and optimizing hybrid "click and brick" model.

As far as the SCM is concerned, for better efficiency, the retailers need to gain efficient consumer response time. Here the demand-driven replenishment system comes into play. The replenishment is essentially based on consumer demand pattern. The demand pattern can be derived from transactional information obtained from POS terminal. Along with this pattern, retailers are also leveraging technology to improve the efficiency of in-store processes such as digital price displays and RFID recognition of merchandise stock levels. So the inputs from the integration of these systems can be used to connect all the players in the logistics chain in a better way. This results in a systematic and quick flow of information through distribution network, which enables the timely delivery of merchandise or services, hence increasing the efficient consumer response rate.

Shrinkage and Loss Prevention

In the context of loss of business to burgeoning e-tailers and today's growing movement toward omni-channel retailing, brick-and-mortar retailers face more complex challenges than ever before. In addition, their margins are under a pressure due to losses attributed to shoplifting, internal theft and online frauds, organized crime, and so on. Shoplifters are the shoppers who enter the retail store with the intention of stealing merchandise, that is, taking away the things without paying. Though retailers take utmost care to protect the merchandise, incidents of shoplifting are happening that ultimately result in the shrinkage.

In this scenario, the store management team, particularly the loss prevention stewards, is at a tipping point once again. The tools and tactics that had worked incredibly well in the past are not enough and relevant today. So for the retailers, it is the need of the hour to invest in technologies that collate data from various sources and applications across the outlets to assemble a complete picture of shrink.

$$\text{Shrinkage to net sales} = \frac{\text{Actual inventory} - \text{Book inventory}}{\text{Net sales}} \times 100$$

Retailers use this control ratio to determine the percentage of net sales lost due to shrinkage. It does not indicate the cause of the shrinkage, but it does indicate the magnitude of the problem. In retail business, it is imperative to keep a tab on shrinkages; it is also proven that a store's performance can improve significantly if it effectively manages losses. Shoplifters, employee thefts, internal errors, and poor SCM contribute to sizeable retail loss and addressing this challenge can show immediate results.

Hence, it is imperative for the retailers to develop a holistic loss prevention strategy and deploy the new technologies integrated with traditional systems to reduce the shrinkage. Retailers are aggressively implementing preventative solutions to regain their sales profits.

Leverage the Cutting-edge Technologies

Today, there is availability of many advanced technology tools to prevent theft and shrink. The use of electronic article surveillance (EAS) technology is a feasible and practical element of retailers' efforts in shrink reduction. This includes deploying antitheft tags, spider wraps and systems that detect foil-lined bags, and EAS jammers used by some "smart shoplifters" to bypass surveillance systems. Theft denial systems are also widely used by retailers. For instance, benefit denial systems comprise ink tags and various other devices such as magnetic stainless steel clips designed to protect neckwear, eyewear, and lingerie, among others.

RFID systems use tags and readers that enable retailers to keep track on items when they are moved within and outside of a store. They are being used to stop thieving from the stores if in case the tag is not removed at the POS, it will activate the radio sensors at the exit of the store. Also most of the analytics, which can help retailers from preventing the shrinkage, require accurate, clean, and consistent data. RFID solves the purpose by automatically logging all the necessary data from systems of record, which can then be mined in real time to obtain analytical insights. This effectively helps deter theft and provide information about the type of merchandise that is being lifted or taken.

An RFID technology is very effective for tracking the merchandise, but the store adoption of RFID has been resisted by feasibility factor caused due to high front-end costs. However in the near future, RFID is expected to play two major roles: first, as a replacement for EAS tags and second, as a means to secure supply chains. Today, RFID usage is limited to very high-value merchandise, and it is expected to continue. Nevertheless, this threshold of "high value" will begin to come down in terms of value, with increase in adoption of RFID tags and reduction in its manufacturing cost.

Though EAS is still the most ubiquitous theft-deterrent tag used in retail, RFID tags are all set to replace EAS tags as a more effective and also feasible (with the reduction in costs) way to protect both merchandise and the supply chain.

Though RFID will not prevent internal and external theft, it will certainly provide valuable, actionable insights regarding a store's physical inventory. Retailers can also use EPC (electronic product code) tags to recognize individual items uniquely, and by combining and integrating EAS and RFID systems, retailers can have real-time information about the missing merchandise items. Dual EAS and RFID tags provide not only security but also inventory visibility. This system, in turn, enables the retailers to track inventory effectively.

A video system such as closed-circuit television (CCTV) is another technology support that can be used to prevent theft. The CCTV camera surveillance can be strategically deployed at the POS and other vulnerable areas in stores with facial recognition systems, which can be used to capture images of offenders. The use of video analytics with overhead CCTV observation of the sales counter can be a real-time deterrent to incidents of internal shrink. Video analytics is the facility of automatically analyzing video to sense and determine if an anomaly or incongruity has taken place based on a set of instructions built into the video software. This makes video analytics very helpful for effective monitoring of the shrink-prone areas in the store. Advancements in the technology of visual analytics have enabled the retailers to automatically tag certain events, such as processing of returns when no customer is present. This intelligent technology is capable to count items, overlay the register receipt over the video, and then track things like item count compared to the register receipt, voids, returns, and even instances where the cash register drawer has been open too long. These features accelerate the detection and revealing of relevant events, which enable investigating store managers to be precisely targeted in their investigations that ultimately save time spent watching and reviewing random video footage on trial-and-error basis.

Tracking the variances of these types of irregularities and indiscretions can be an indicator and evidence that something might be amiss at the POS, and it can be followed up with an internal inquiry by loss prevention team.

Summary

The changing role of the store has far-reaching effects on both inside the store and outside the store, that is, overall retail organization. Here, fundamental transformations are needed to be exercised across the organization and across all the functions in order to support the operations of the store in the future. So the role of the store needs to be: go forward to become a crucial part of a much complex relationships between the retailer and consumer. It is expected to find a new balance between providing emotional and inspiring engagement while offering innovative ways of experiencing the breadth and depth of the range. And above all, they need to deliver in a consistent and relevant way across all the channels.

To sum up, if a performance plan is developed properly, executed appropriately, and measured accurately, it would always lead to excellent result even in economically tough times. The function of retail store operations is to ensure that the store runs smoothly and efficiently through thoroughly defined processes in every area. Retail operations must ensure that every process in the store is both customer-friendly and cost-effective. With proper planning, staffing, merchandise tracking, and salesperson training, some of these inhibitors—or at least the impact of these inhibitors—could potentially be avoided or minimized.

Retailers should consider taking some or all of the following actions: increase holiday hours (for shoppers who want to avoid crowds); provide ample coverage at checkout lanes and multiple checkout options; manage merchandise inventory to avoid obsolescence and stockouts; and train store associates to help customers find merchandise, select alternatives, and take advantage of efficient checkout options.

Review Questions

1. What are the major functions and key responsibilities of the store management in modern times?
2. Discuss briefly the store operating parameters with its importance in the operations and performance of the store.

3. Write short notes on:

   - Stock turn ratio
   - GMROI
   - GMROF
   - GMROL
   - POS management

4. Discuss in detail the essentials for designing an effective performance management system for a multi-store retailer.
5. Briefly discuss the significance of employee engagement and collaborative work culture in store management. Justify your views with appropriate examples.
6. Discuss the significance of shrinkage and loss prevention in store management and how retailers doing it by leveraging technology.

Mall Management

Introduction

Today, we can see that with increasing aspirations of the consumers toward the overall shopping experience, both consumers and retailers have limited choice in terms of mall shopping experience. Shopping malls have been the harbinger of change in the way Indians have been shopping and have been at the forefront of urbanization. A significant proportion of retailers are preferring malls over high streets as a preferred destination for their expansion, specifically in metro cities. This preference is mainly attributed to the "mall management," which has become the deciding factor for a mall's success.

However, in the current scenario of retailing, emerged after the global economic meltdown and increasing inclination of consumers toward the online retailing, the success of malls will be achieved not only by housing the biggest and the best mix of retailers (also referred as tenant mix), but also by creating right size of stores for tenants and setting up new standards and procedures in mall management that will provide a platform to differentiate its offerings from competition, in terms of products, service, and experience. Thus, a tenant mix is the particular assortment of different stores grouped together in a cluster, shopping center, or mall. A typical tenant mix comprises stand-alone brands, anchor stores, men and women fashion (lifestyle) stores, jewelry (watch) stores, exclusive boutiques, electronics (consumer) durables store, furniture (furnishing) stores, supermarkets, coffee shops, restaurants, QSR (quick service restaurant) chains, offices (in some cases) and multiplexes. The shopping/retail area is complemented with other basic amenities (like parking, washrooms, and restrooms) and recreational facilities (like amusement/entertainment/play zones). Hence, today's malls are increasingly becoming all-under-one-roof destinations wherein the consumers can get affordable as well as aspirational merchandise and brands for all categories and class of consumers with interesting and relevant shopping experience.

Phoenix, Oberoi, Palladium, Inorbit, R City Mall, Select Citywalk, Orion, Forum, Seasons, Mantri, and DLF's Emporio are among the leading malls.

Essentials of Effective Mall Management

The essentials for effective mall management are as follows:

- Positioning and branding: creating brand image of the mall
- Providing an unmatched value proposition by developing right mix of tenants
- Zoning: devising the right tenant mix and its placement in a mall
- Promotional initiatives and programs
- Facility management: infrastructure, traffic, and ambience management
- Finance management
- Leveraging solutions that improve operational efficiencies
- Leveraging technologies that improves customer experience and engagement
- Leverage new business models like online portals for customer convenience, mobile engagement, and smartphone applications, among others

With all these factors, developers of shopping mall are increasingly focusing on to position their facilities as a desired destination with exotic recreational, entertainment, dining, and exceptional shopping environment.

Positioning a Mall

Positioning a mall actually refers to defining the tenant mix (which retailer brands are present in that mall): the location, service level, amenities, overall ambience (visual cues), entertainment, and the shopping experience offered. All these factors are essentially based on demographics, psychographics, behavioral factors, income levels, competition in neighboring areas, and extensive market research of the catchment. For instance, if the market research shows that the average number of households living in a particular area belongs to the upper middle class to rich class, then a high-end retail mall will have higher chances of success in that location. The malls provide high-end luxury products catering to the elite class (socioeconomic classification A and B consumers) residing in that city (area).

For example, DLF's Emporio located in the Vasant Kunj area of Delhi and Palladium in Mumbai. These malls are aesthetically designed; they are spacious with well-furnished lobbies, offer premium merchandise (lifestyle) and luxury products (brands), great ambience, and large visual displays (eye-catching windows, wide corridors, and artistic lighting). The brands like Zara is located in Mumbai's Palladium Mall. Hence, they are designed and managed to offer the shopping experience that is glamorous and exotic as expected by the target audience.

Here the mall management needs to understand the brand very well. Whenever an interested tenant brand approaches to them, they need to undertake their own research regarding the relevance and appeal for the brand in the expected catchment area, as it is the key to their survival and success. The tenant mix with the same target audience, rather than a general mix, helps collectively attract the shoppers to the mall. Malls need to keep pace with the taste, preferences, and pockets of shoppers. The same customer who used to shop at a Lifestyle, Shoppers Stop, Westside, Pantaloon, or Central now wants to shop at H&M, Armani, Zara, Forever 21, Hamleys, Mango, and so on, and malls need to cater for these changes. From a mall owner's point of view, it makes sense to bring in power brands like Zara and H&M as it increases footfalls of targeted shoppers, and this helps not just the mall but also other tenants. Hence, exceptional locations, a good mix of labels, and active involvement of the owners help malls establish themselves as brands to reckon with.

Consider the example of Select Citywalk, one of the best performing mall in Saket, Delhi. Select Citywalk is often regarded as the benchmark for modern retailing in the region surrounding Delhi and NCR. Meticulous attention has been given while designing the mall to ensure a suitable blend of tradition and modernity in terms of shopping and other value-added services. It brings exotic and glamorous shopping and lifestyle experience with plethora of brands, served apartments, multiplexes, health clubs, bistros, cafés, and destination restaurants, among others, to the targeted affluent South Delhi audience. It is home to premium brands such as H&M, Zara, Steve Madden, Good Earth, and many others. It also has a huge outdoor landscape plaza (Sanskriti) where many events are held. This is another feather to its cap. In addition, the Select CITYWALK Reward program has also been designed to enhance the patronage loyalty.

The mall has successfully created a strong value proposition for the South Delhi women as its targeted customer and actively curates the tenant brands, even discontinuing those that do not click or appeal. The growth is attributed to the affluent catchment consisting of Saket, Greater Kailash, Panchsheel, Sainik Farms. The shoppers are well-traveled abroad, know international brands, can afford, and ready to buy luxury high-end brands. In the same neighborhood are malls such as MGF Metropolitan and DLF Courtyard.

Similarly, High Street Phoenix, which previously used to be the Phoenix Mills, is located in Lower Parel, a suburb of South Mumbai. The area has many strategic advantages: its catchment area is home to the city's most affluent residents and has very few high-end shopping destinations. The big size of the mall helped them to house brands across the pyramid. They have luxury, mass, bridge brands and department stores that are in sync with targeted shoppers' tastes and preferences. It is situated in the heart of highest per capita income locality of South Mumbai. The international brands and retailers in the luxury space always look for such properties.

Here the size of the mall also plays a significant role, as it enables the mall management to ensure optimum tenant mix, which is essential for the success of the mall. For example, the relatively smaller size of Nirmal Lifestyle and Center One in Mumbai among the major factors that led to their downfall.

Strategic Significance of Location

Location, Location, Location

Location of the mall also plays a very significant role in creating the positioning of the mall. This eventually plays a major role in attracting the targeted tenant brands and the targeted customers.

A prime (good) location is defined in terms of factors like ease of access via roads, the visibility aspect, and the catchment area, among others. All these factors are some of the prime prerequisites and critical success factors for a mall. The other factors such as tenant mix, ambience, and amenities can be revisited or redefined, the location remains fixed, making it a crucial factor for the success of a mall. The tenant brands also evaluate meticulously, that whether they can be supported in a catchment area or not, which eventually become a critical success factor of a mall. Hence, while there is the set of hygiene factors like track record of the developer, its credibility, and marketing skills, location is the most critical.

The metro cities like Mumbai, Delhi, Pune, and Hyderabad, including their satellite cities, have seen malls come up in the same neighborhood. This leaves tenant brands to decide whether to be present at any one or at both. This consideration is essential because there may be possibility of cannibalization wherein both the stores of the same parent retailer may compete with each other. In such cases, the retailers having a portfolio of several brands generally ensure the presence at all neighborhood malls but through different brands/formats under its umbrella. This approach gives wide exposure to the retailers without being trapped in cannibalization.

For example, if the Future Group has Big Bazaar in a city, let us say Nagpur, and another mall comes up in the vicinity where they would like to be in, then they may turn to other brands of their portfolio such as Food Bazaar or FBB (fashion store), as these are distinct from each other. Being different from each other, they do not cannibalize and, at the same time, ensure wide exposure for their parent company and also cater to wide audience.

Promotional Activities, Events, and Programs

Promotional activities, events, and programs constitute an integral component of mall management. Activities like various shopping promotions and events, food festivals, handicraft exhibitions, film promotions, musical concerts, and celebrity visits increase footfalls and in turn revenues. Also the innovations and the campaigns led by various tenant retailers routing through either the ATL or the BTL is a common practice at all times during the year with special focus during the festive seasons.

Organizing sociocultural celebrations and entertainment events in way that will attract the targeted audience plays a significant role in increasing walk-ins in the mall. Many times, the central mall management or developers work on drafting marketing (promotional) strategies for individual malls in their umbrella to cater the taste, preference, and needs of the local consumer base. With this approach, they can effectively counter challenges posed by local and, in some cases, regional competitors. Such kind of initiatives reinforces the desired positioning of the mall and may also act as a key differentiating factor for a mall.

Today, the mall management is increasingly focusing on experiential marketing. They are attracting the prospects to experience, enjoy, and engage in the offerings, ambience, amenities, events, celebrations, crowd, and entertainment. Also the consumer engagement through social media marketing is also another effective tool that mall management and tenant brands can leverage for achieving higher impact. Malls are using social media to promote their space and brands. The malls at their social media pages are creating a fan base by engaging them into regular conversations, interactions events, promotions, offers, and contests. The social media has emerged as a cost-effective, time-efficient, dynamic, interactive, engaging tool and gets the promoter right to the its audience. The biggest advantage that social media offers is easy reach to target audience and also brings back real-time feedback. This real-time feedback is leveraged to offer best shopping experience. Such social media campaigns are also very fruitful for the tenant brands as well. They allow these brands to promote their latest collections, new offers, and other promotional activities in the store. This eventually helps them to get better eyeballs and footfalls.

Social media buzz can be created by promoting:

- New launches: brands, stores, and latest collections
- Interlinked offers and joint initiatives between the mall and tenant brands or among the tenant stores/brands
- Upcoming launches
- Events

- Eentertainment programs, musical concerts, and so on
- Promotional activities and programs
- Loyalty programs
- Festival celebrations
- Celebrity visits and film promotions
- Seasonal and other special offers

They are striving hard to shift the eyeballs from digital screens to their physical spaces. For which they are becoming a "destination" by offering a social experience that is pleasurable and entertaining. Here the experiential marketing brings the brand personality to life by using sensory techniques to connect with people on an emotional level. It is imperative for the owners to be active in brand building and promotion to ensure the success of the mall.

Let us take the example of Infiniti Mall located at Malad area of Mumbai. The mall presents the perfect blend of shopping and entertainment. This made it popular among the target audiences like college goers, professionals (office goers), and TV and film professionals residing in Malad and neighborhood localities, having high disposable income and seeking good destination/opportunities for leisure shopping. Along with leading national and international brands, food courts, and restaurants, the mall also offers entertainment facilities like indoor roller coaster, multiplex, and indoor games, among others. The mall also offers the Astro Express, a 360-degree roller coaster, which is a center of attraction for many, specially kids and youths.

The mall also conducted several promotional activities like Mast Monsoon and Fun Mania, among others. The mall is visitor-friendly and allows easy access to senior citizens and handicaps by providing ramps at the entrance, wheelchairs, seating area, and special elevator service. In addition to all these facilities, the mall offers world-class landscaping that enhances the shopping ambience and environment.

Zoning: Devising the Right Tenant Mix and Its Strategic Placement in a Mall

Tenant mix refers to the combination of retail stores that are housed in a mall. A right tenant mix basically forms a grouping and arrangement of the right tenants in such a way that it ensures optimum footfalls, sales, rents, service to the retailers, as well as shopping experience to the visitors (shoppers) and profitability of the shopping mall venture. The strategic selection of the right anchor tenant plays a vital role in developing the right tenant mix. The anchor tenant is referred as the largest retailer in a mall in terms of space occupied. The anchor tenant is typically complemented by single-brand retailer's cluster around the anchor. This kind of arrangement generally caters to the multiple shopping needs of the customers. Here, a mall developer has to ensure that floor space planning has done in a well-researched manner instead of depending solely on tenant retailers to choose their preferred location within the mall; here, zoning plays an important role.

Today, the average size of malls is 5,00,000 sq. ft, and big malls are above a million square feet. Zoning is nothing but the division of mall space into zones for the allocation of space to various functions/operations and for the placement of various retailers. Success of a mall venture is basically dependent on the success of its tenants. Success of the tenants eventually translates into the financial feasibility of the mall as a business venture. The right tenant mix and strategic placement of retailers followed by articulate and meticulous zoning exercise can help retailers attract the targeted audience. The successful execution of the zoning exercise for a mall is carried forward through lease management on an ongoing basis. Forging into leases after a detailed evaluation process of the interested retailers on all the fronts is an essential part of ensuring the presence of the right retailers in a mall. This eventually enhances the shopping experience and increases the loyalty behavior.

Hence, formulating the right tenant mix, which is essentially based on strategic zoning, helps attract and retain shoppers by offering them multiple choices, satisfying multiple shopping needs, and provide holistic shopping experience. The layout of the mall is important as it facilitates the crowd to circulate evenly, and not get concentrated in certain pockets. The smooth flow of shoppers within the mall also ensures sufficient exposure to all the tenants by avoiding clusters and bottlenecks. This helps influence shoppers' mall preference and frequency of visits as they can enjoy the "property, amenities, and ambience" along with the shopping. It also reinforces the positioning of the mall.

Facility Management

The tenant mix, parking, accessibility, and facility management (maintenance) become more important as more malls compete for the same audience in larger cities. Facility management refers to the integration of people, place, process, technology, and technology-enabled collaboration of people in an establishment like hotel, mall, and multiplex. In the case of mall management, it typically includes the management of:

- Entire mall property and infrastructure.
- Traffic management, that is, managing customer traffic and the flow of shoppers inside the operational area of the mall and parking facilities.
- Other supporting infrastructure like lifts and elevators, central air turbo ventilators (air conditioners), backup DG set, communication, and life-safety equipments.
- Basic facilities like drinking water, tea (coffee) vending machines, washrooms (restrooms) for customers and employees.
- Ambience, amenities, and atmospherics.
- Amusement facilities.
- Parking area traffic.
- Regular and emergency (safety and security) issues.
- Customer traffic inside the operational area of the mall.
- Water (electricity) supply and Wi-Fi hotspots.
- Other legal and regulatory considerations pertaining to the local municipal controlling office/authority.

Facility management ensures the optimal utilization of available resources to meet tenant retailer's and shopper's needs. Though the size matters, because it means more categories to keep the consumer engaged with, but does not work without requisite infrastructure.

Financial Management

A mall is a kind of business venture wherein the professional financial management is a crucial factor for the success. Mall management also includes financial management, which involves monitoring and controlling of various finance-related aspects such as:

- Cash receipts and income from rentals, service charges, car park receipts, electricity, and other utility income.
- Following and maintaining accounting systems to track the ageing of debts, payment delay patterns, bad debts, and payment of all invoices and expenses.

- Following and maintaining standard financial systems so that a detailed annual property budget is prepared.
- Organizing resources to deliver an efficient and effective annual external audit, whenever required (demanded).
- Other related compliances pertaining to government and local taxes, fees, and so on.

The key here is to run a mall and treat it like a business that needs constant overview.

Managing the Feasibility

Professional mall management with best international practices is increasingly being adopted because of growing direct and indirect competition, the latter being from e-retailers and established high-street locations across all cities. Here the mall management needs to ensure ROI for investors and tenant retail brands.

One of the key performing indices that the mall management needs to focus is "sales per square foot," which is the average revenue a retail business generates for every square foot of sales space. Most of the performing malls do business of ₹1,000–₹1,500 per sq. ft. In some cases, even a prime location does not help.

For instance, the success of both Phoenix and Select is in sharp contrast to the failure of malls in their neighborhood. MGF Metropolitan is sold out but Select City Walk is fully occupied (fully leased) and achieving handsome numbers in terms of sales per square feet. Similarly, Atria, another mall in South Mumbai, could not perform in the way High Street Phoenix did. Here the difference is made by the way malls are managed, a judicious mix of brands on their properties is managed and financial feasibility is maintained.

Today, the market has become more competitive with new emerging retailing formats (models), and consumers are highly demanding and less loyal. On the other hand, market is witnessing a high degree of volatility. Mall owners typically follow either a leased model or strata-sold model, where shops are sold to brands. However, due to the increasing incidences of multiple ownerships creating legal problems, international brands prefer malls that are leased rather than sold to achieve maximum operational efficiency.

In this kind of market scenario, most malls typically have a revenue-sharing arrangement with retailers that pay both a fixed rental and a share of the revenues. Under this arrangement, the tenant brands pay a portion of their rent depending on how well the store is performing. They pay either a fixed monthly base rent as minimum guarantee and/or a "percentage of sales" rent, whichever is higher. The financial viability is a crucial factor, and many times, besides revenue share, developers also share the Capex (capital expenditure). Malls may get in financial trouble when they sign up anchor stores but fail to attract right vanilla (single-brand smaller retailer) tenants, and some of their floors remain empty.

This is beneficial for both mall owners/mall management and tenant retailers as the mall owners/mall management are encouraged to organize promotional activities that would increase retailers' revenues as they are also the stakeholders in it (in the form of a percentage share). The model works effectively for both the parties and all the other stakeholders in bullish and bearish (volatile, uncertain, complex, and ambiguity) market conditions. When the market is slow or weak, retailers are protected from rising rental costs. As more and more Indian developers are becoming corporatized, the use of the revenue share model is expected to gain momentum in the future.

Also as far as the lease period is concerned, the malls are increasingly trying to be more dynamic in terms of tenant mix by reducing the lease time. With the retailing landscape changing at a faster rate, mall management is avoiding long-term agreements with tenants. Today, shoppers want freshness, and to ensure that the mall premise attract footfalls, mall operators are leasing out shops for shorter periods. They are also constantly evaluating the performance of various tenant brands before renewing the lease because rental yield is typically a significant part of their portfolio.

The long-term agreements limit the scope for mall management to churn tenant brands regularly. It also limits a mall's capability to correct, optimize, and innovate the tenant mix. The leading malls have reduced average anchor leases to maximum nine years and smaller brands are being signed for only a maximum of six years. This is for the simple reason that the world of retailing has become very dynamic with entry of new international brands and emergence of new models. So the mall operators are increasingly finding it practical to have shorter leases.

For example, when Swedish fashion retailing giant H&M opened its shop in Delhi's Select Citywalk in October 2015, the mall's operators relocated anchor tenant Pantaloons' department stores to make way for H&M.

Many mall operators have even brought down the lease tenure to three years from the earlier 8–10 years with entry of new brands in order to bring the much-needed pull factor and freshness into their premises. For example, Virtuous Retail brought down the vanilla leases (850–2,000 sq. ft) to around three years from ten. Such kind of reshuffling is becoming necessary to bring long-term viability to their retail assets, besides continuous footfalls.

The categories and brands that are housed in the mall are a result of a meticulous study and understanding of the catchment that is being served. The mall management tracks the performance of these brands on a continuous basis and also provides them support in the form of signage, social media, and promotions. The mall management needs to focus on category modifications periodically according to the changing consumer needs and preferences. Strategically planned adding of new categories add new flavors to the overall mall offering.

Discretion of Mall Owner's Toward Tenant Retailers

- Suitability of the brands/stores to the demographic features and attributes of catchment area
- Revenue generation by the tenants
- Brand evolution
- Fitting: complementing with the other tenants
- Footfall generation
- Accuracy of payments of rentals
- Stock maintenance, frequency of launching new collection, and pricing strategies
- Quality of staff and their motivational level

Lookouts of Tenant Brands/Stores

- Catchment area of the mall
- Location and space provided within the mall in the given rentals
- Footfalls the mall generates
- Demographic features: buying behavior, taste, preferences, and pattern of the targeted audience of the mall, primarily located in the catchment area
- Basic facilities and augmented amenities provided

- Efficiency and effectiveness of mall management
- USP of the creation of the mall
- Other support in the form of promotions, events, and so on
- Rentals and other cost vis-à-vis business opportunity, in short the viability of the rentals

The New Trends in Mall Management

In India, with higher domestic demand and technology adoption, the e-commerce is growing at a phenomenal rate. One of the biggest concerns for malls is the "showrooming" behavior wherein shoppers walk into branded stores to try, touch, and feel the merchandise and check out sizes, designs, and prices. But they order the same through online portal where it is available at a cheaper price. So here, the brick-and-mortar players are increasingly looking toward click-and-mortar strategy to address these concerns as it offers a virtual showroom as well.

An online marketplace model can build brands around convenience. For example, picking a particular set of user needs, personalized experiences, and offer higher degree of browsing ability options that let users peek into various stores and options.

For instance, one of the leading mall in New Delhi is foraying into the e-commerce space to serve as a bridge between online and off-line models, where in the mall's existing clients (tenant brands) will be able to use its website to sell their merchandise with the mall will be charging a commission on actual sales. Here the existing mall tenants can sell their brands (merchandise) alongside products essentially marketed by the mall. The mall management are also becoming more cautious while allotting spaces—trimming them, if necessary.

Summary

Until recently, mall management was considered to be managing the facility and property. However, with the changing market dynamics, both mall owners/developers and retailers have taken the cognizance of the fact that mall management is a wide concept and facility management is just a component of it.

The changing market scenario especially in the space of retailing has brought many challenges that the mall owners/developers and retailers both need to overcome. Here the professional mall management practices need to be adopted, which essentially start from rigorous feasibility exercise or market research to facilities, ambience, and finance management of a mall. The leases are well researched to ensure maximum crowd pull, and laggards are often asked to vacate for newer entrants. The ambience in the mall needs to be improvised (customized) and adapted to the tastes of the consumer. The entire experience needs to be relooked periodically.

The mall developers will need to create a differentiation for their product by bringing innovation in mall operations. Here the need of the hour is to strategically combine leisure and entertainment along with the world-class shopping experience all under one roof. Consumers and retailers will be attracted to malls that are professionally managed and can successfully create a coherent shopping experience. Hence, the effective mall management a critical factor behind the success of a mall.

Review Questions

1. Briefly discuss the significance of and essentials for effective mall management.
2. Discuss in detail how a mall is positioned. What is the role of location and promotional campaigns in marketing a mall?
3. Discuss in detail the various functions of mall operator/mall management.
4. Discuss the various strategic decisions/considerations the mall management need to work upon for managing the profitability/feasibility of the mall. Quote appropriate examples.
5. Write short notes on:

   - Importance of zoning in mall management
   - New trends in mall management

Balmford, Gemma. n.d. 'Visual Merchandising in Luxury Store: Life of Luxury.' *Retail Focus*. Available at: http://www.retail-focus.co.uk/features/1032-life-of-luxury (accessed on 3 February 2015).

Becker-Olsen, Karen L., B.A. Cudmore, and Ronald P. Hill. 2006. 'The Impact of Perceived Corporate Social Responsibility on Consumer Behavior.' *Journal of Business Research*, 59(1): 46–53.

Bhattacharya, C.B., and Sankar Sen. 2004. 'Doing Better at Doing Good: When, Why, and How Consumers Respond to Corporate Social Initiatives.' *California Management Review*, 47(1): 9–24.

Bijlani, Jitesh, and Sangeeta Singh. n.d. 'Ecommerce in India.' Available at: http://www.pwc.in/assets/pdfs/publications/2015/ecommerce-in-india-accelerating-growth.pdf (accessed on 15 March 2015).

Bisen, Ankur, Pragya Singh, and Ashima Anand. May 2013. 'E-tailing in India: Unlocking the Potential.' A Whitepaper. *Technopak*.

Brandão, Euler Alves, Reynaldo Maia Muniz, Cid Gonçalves Filh, Gian Franco Rocchiccioli, Gustavo Quiroga Souki, and Renata Livramento. Jan/Apr. 2011. 'Brand Relationships on Retailing: The Impact of Image on Behavioral Intentions of Consumers.' *ReA UFSM, Santa Maria*, 4(1): 170–186.

Brodén, A., and C. Söderberg. 2011. *Impulse Buying, Reasons Why and Consumer Electronics, Oh My!* Gothenburg. Available at: https://gupea.ub.gu.se/bitstream/2077/25619/1/gupea_2077_25619_1.pdf (accessed on 3 February, 2015).

Chandon, P., J. Hutchinson, E. Bradlow, and S. Young. 2009. 'Does In-Store Marketing Work? Effects of the Number and Position Shelf Facings on Brand Attention and Evaluation at the Point of Purchase.' *Journal of Marketing*. Available at: http://www.insead.edu/facultyresearch/research/doc.cfm?did=41902 (accessed on 15 March 2015).

Charania, Barkat. 2013. 'Emerging Role of HR in Today's Retail World.' *Images Retail*, November.

Chaudhary, Prashant, and Rahul Jadhav. 2014. 'Visual Merchandising In Retailing: Influencing Consumer Buying Behavior Towards Apparels With Special Reference To Pune City In India.' *International Journals of Multidisciplinary Research Academy (IJMRA)*, 4(5): 74–94, May.

Chaudhary, Prashant, and Sagar Patil. 2015. 'Gift Card Business: A Gifted Opportunity.' *International Journal of Management, IT and Engineering*, 5(4), April.

Chaudhary, Prashant. 2015. '7-"Ps" of Private Label Brands.' *International Journal in Management & Social Science (IJMSS)*, 3(2), February.

Darden, W.R., O. Erdem, and D.K. Darden. 1983. 'A Comparison and Test of Three Casual Models of Patronage Intentions'. In *Patronge Behavior and Retail Management*. New York, NY: North Holland.

David, Prabu, Susan Kline, and Dai Yang. 2005. 'Corporate Social Responsibility Practices, Corporate Identity, and Purchase Intention: A Dual-Process Model.' *Journal of Public Relations Research*, 17(3): 291–313.

de Swaan Arons, Marc, Frank van den Driest, and Keith Weed. 2014. 'The Ultimate Marketing Machine'. *Harvard Business Review South Asia*, July–August, 53–62.

Deloitte. 2013. 'Global Powers of Retailing'. 16th edn. *Retail Beyond*.

Department of Industrial Policy and Promotion (DIPP). 2013–2014. 'Government of India-Ministry of Commerce and Industry.' Discussion Paper on E-Commerce in India.

Dunne, David, and Narasimhan Chakravarthi. 1999. 'The New Appeal of Private Labels.' *Harvard Business Review*, 77(3), May–June.

Edelman, David C., and Marc Singer. 2015. 'Competing on Customer Journeys.' *Harvard Business Review South Asia*, November.

González-Benito, Óscar, and Javier González-Benito. 2005. 'The Role of Geodemographic Segmentation in Retail Location Strategy.' *International Journal of Market Research*, 47(3): 295–316. Available at: https://www.mrs.org.uk/ijmr_article/article/80197 (accessed on 3 February 2015).

Guenzi, G., M.D. Johnson, and S. Castaldo. 2009. *A Comprehensive Model of Customer Trust in Two Retail Stores* (electronic version). Cornell University. Available at: http://scholarship.sha.cornell.edu/articles/705 (School of Hospitality Administration site).

Kasper, Gabriel, and Katherine Fulton. 2006. *The Future of Corporate Philanthropy: A Framework for Understanding your Options*. San Francisco, CA: Monitor Institute.

Kottar, John P. 2015. 'Leading Change: Why Transformation Efforts Fail.' *Harvard Business Review South Asia,* February–July, 34–41.

Shun Yin Lam. 2001. 'The Effects of Store Environment on Shopping Behaviors: a Critical Review.' In *NA: Advances in Consumer Research* Volume 28, eds. Mary C. Gilly and Joan Meyers-Levy. 190–197, Valdosta, GA : Association for Consumer Research.

Madhavi, S., and T.S. Leelavati. 2013. 'Impact of Visual Merchandising on Consumer Behavior towards Women Apparel.' *International Journal of Management Research and Business Strategy*, 2(4): 61–72.

Magids, Scott, Alan Zorfas, and Daniel Leeman. 2015. 'Digital Customer Engagement: The New Science of Customer Emotions.' *Harvard Business Review South Asia*. November.

Martinelli, Elisa, and Leigh Sparks. 2014. 'Extending The Retail Brand: The Influence of Customer Loyalty Towards the Private Label and Towards the Retailer.' Available at: http://www.marketing-trends congress.com/archives/2014/pages/PDF/273.pdf (accessed on 4 February 2015).

Morgan, Tony. 2011. *Visual Merchandising: Windows and In-store Displays for Retail*. 2nd ed. London: Laurence King.

Morrison, Michael. 2002. *The Power of In-store Music and its Influence on International Retail Brands and Shopper Behaviour: A Multi-Case Study Approach*. Australia: Department of Marketing, Monash University.

Morton, Fiona Scott, and Florian Zettelmeyer. 2004. *The Strategic Positioning of Store Brands in Retailer–Manufacturer Negotiations*, 161–94. The Netherlands: Kluwer Academic Publishers.

Oliver, Richard L. 1997. *Satisfaction: A Behavioral Perspective on the Consumer*. New York: McGraw Hill, p. 392.

Palonka, Joanna, and Teresa Porębska. n.d. *Social Recruiting—The Use of Social Networks in The Recruiting Process*. Katowice: Miąc University of Economics.

Rajasekharan, Pillai, Azmiya Iqbal, Habiba Umer, Aisha Maqbool, and Namrata Sunil. 2011. 'Design, Effectiveness and Role of Visual Merchandising in Creating Customer Appeal.' *MPRA: Munich Personal RePEc Archive*. Birla Institute of Technology, Kingdom of Bahrain. Available at: https://mpra.ub.uni-muenchen.de/30365/1/MPRA_paper_30365.pdf (accessed on 15 March, 2015).

Rangan, Kasturi, Lisa Chase, and Sohel Karim. 2015. 'The Truth about CSR.' *Harvard Business Review South Asia*, January–February, 41–50.

Rao, Bharat. 1998. 'Developing an Effective E-tailing Strategy'. *Electronic Markets*, 9. Available at: http://faculty.poly.edu/~brao/EMe-Tailing.pdf

Rugman, Alan, and Ste´phane Girod. 2003. 'Globalization: The Evidence is Regional.' *European Management Journal*, 21(1): 24–37.

Schramm-Klein, Hanna, and Joachim Zentes. n.d. 'Corporate Social Responsibility of Retail Companies: Is it relevant for Consumers' Purchasing Behaviour?' Available at: http://thil-memoirevivante.prd.fr/wp-content/uploads/sites/43/2014/11/2008-Corporate-Social-Responsibility-of-Retail-Companies.pdf (accessed on 15 March 2015).

Shankar, Venkatesh, and Ruth N. Bolton. Winter 2004. 'An Empirical Analysis of Determinants of Retailer Pricing Strategy.' *Marketing Science*, 23(1): 28–49.

Tănase, George Cosmin. n.d. 'An Overview of Retail Branding and Positioning as Marketing Management Concepts.' *Romanian Distribution Committee Magazine,* 2(1): 35–39.

Weldon, Robert, Jigar Shah, and Vinay Kumar Nayak. 2014. 'Cognizant 20–20 Insights: Strategies to Mitigate Shrink in a Boundary-less Retail World', July. Available at: http://www.cognizant.com/InsightsWhitepapers/Strategies-to-Mitigate-Shrink-in-a-Boundary-less-Retail-World-codex897

Wirtz, Jochen. 2010. 'Case 5. Giordano: Positioning for International Expansion.' *Emerald Emerging Markets Case Studies: Emerging Markets Case Studies Collection (Marketing)*, December, 1–13.